Crowell's Handbook of

CLASSICAL

LITERATURE

By Lillian Feder

CROWELL'S HANDBOOK OF CLASSICAL LITERATURE

ANCIENT MYTH IN MODERN POETRY

MADNESS IN LITERATURE

Crowell's Handbook of

CLASSICAL

LITERATURE

By LILLIAN FEDER

HARPER COLOPHON BOOKS
Harper & Row, Publishers
New York, Cambridge, Hagerstown, Philadelphia, San Francisco
London, Mexico City, São Paulo, Sydney

First HARPER COLOPHON edition published 1980.
ISBN: 0-06-090802-5
80 81 82 83 84 10 9 8 7 6 5 4 3 2 1

To my parents

Preface

THE AIM OF THIS HANDBOOK is to assist the growing number of people interested in Greek and Roman civilization—both students and readers outside the universities—to understand and enjoy classical literature. It is addressed to college students studying classics, humanities, history, and English and European literature and to general readers interested in ancient literature and society. For those who are eager to read or reread classical literature but are uncertain about how to approach its subject matter, basic themes, stylistic conventions, and historical and cultural background, it is hoped that the summaries will serve as guides to complicated works such as epics, histories, tragedies, and satires; that the definitions of genres will elucidate conventions and techniques employed in epic, lyric, tragedy, comedy, pastoral, and other forms; that the factual material on authors, characters, myths, and places will provide necessary background information; and that the critical commentaries will suggest an approach to themes and characters. This book is also intended as a reference work for those seeking factual information on classical literature or tracing classical allusions in connection with their reading in other fields.

In a book of this size it is impossible to deal adequately with all the material related to classical literature. Though major characters and deities are identified, it would take many volumes to give a detailed account of their characteristics, their history, and their religious and cultural significance. Here it seemed best to give the fullest account of them in the summaries of the works in which they appear. The most important myths are also told in the summaries of the works in which they occur, but many less important ones are covered briefly in the entries for characters. No single volume could ever convey the profound influence classical literature has had on the assumptions, ideas, and artistic expression of Western civilization; here only the most important examples of the classical influence on English and American literature and on a few Continental works can be mentioned. Limits of space also made it necessary to eliminate all but the best-known writers of the Hellenistic period and the Silver Age of Latin literature.

A handbook must necessarily consist mainly of factual information generally accepted by scholars in the field. Nonetheless, I cannot claim complete objectivity in my approach to the material of this book for, even if I regarded such an attitude as advantageous, it would be impossible to avoid suggesting an individual approach in the choice of works to be summarized, the interpretations conveyed by the summaries themselves, the allotment of space to and appraisals of the various authors, and the brief critical suggestions in the commentaries. Moreover, I cannot help believing that a reader will find guidance more pleasant and more profitable if he senses an individual response, however fallible, to a literature that has become the *publica materies* of Western civilization.

In planning and writing this book I was continually aware of how much I owed to the scholars and critics who made the experience of classical literature available to me. Though I have referred to works that have influenced my ideas and attitudes, it is impossible to acknowledge my full debt to the large group of scholars and critics in classical and English literature on whom I have relied throughout many years of study. It is, however, a great pleasure to mention those on whom I called for assistance as I worked on this book. I am grateful for the advice and encouragement of my brother Irving Leonard Feder and for the enthusiastic interest of my sister-in-law Marianne Feder, who drew the maps. It was a delight to work with members of the editorial staff of Thomas Y. Crowell Company, especially Edward Tripp, editor of Reference Books, who edited the manuscript and on whose broad knowledge and critical insight I was often dependent, and Patrick Barrett, whose advice was extremely helpful. Professor Konrad Gries, Chairman of the Department of Classics of Queens College of the City University of New York, read the manuscript and offered many valuable suggestions. Among the other friends and colleagues on whom I relied for sound advice and encouragement were Professors Robert H. Ball, Malcolm Goldstein, Yvette Louria, Myron Matlaw, and Dr. Rudolph Wittenberg.

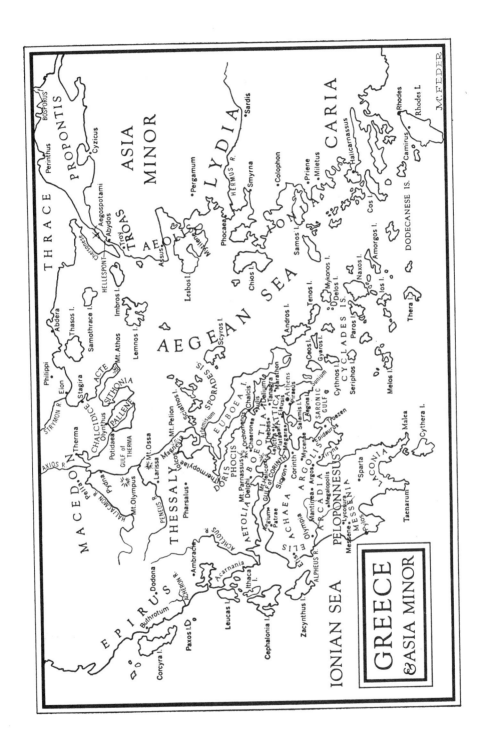

GREECE
&ASIA MINOR

The
GREEK
WORLD

SCYTHIA

BLACK SEA

COLCHIS

CASPIAN SEA

BITHYNIA

P O N T U S

•Sinope
•Amisus
•Trapezus

•Amasia

HALYS R.

CAPPADOCIA

ARMENIA

MEDIA

Rhagae•

IA

CILICIA

•Tarsus
⨯Issus

MESOPOTAMIA

Gaugamela⨯

ASSYRIA

Ecbatana•

•Antioch

EUPHRATES R.

TIGRIS R.

CYPRUS

SYRIA

•Palmyra

Sidon•

•Damascus

Seleucia•

•Ctesiphon

Susa•

SUSIANA

•Tyre

Babylon•

BABYLONIA

PALESTINE

•Gaza

PERSIAN GULF

ARABIA

•Heliopolis
•Memphis

E G Y P T

NILE R.

RED SEA

•Thebes

•Syene

MARIANNE FEDER

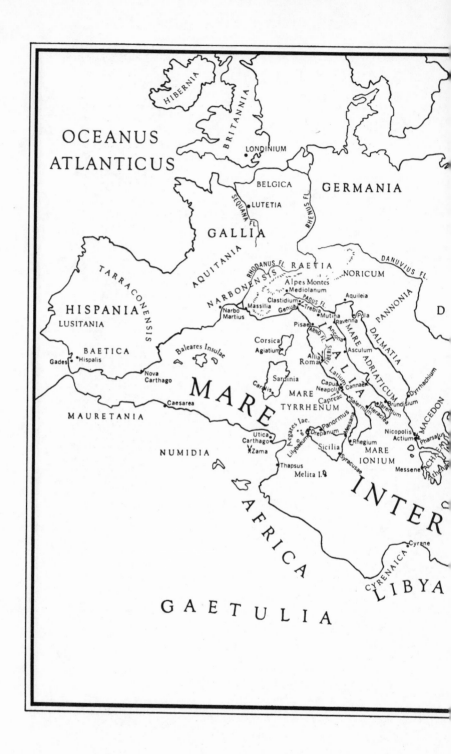

The World of

IMPERIAL ROME

ACIA

SARMATIA

MOESIA

Tomis

THRACIA

Philippi

Byzantium

BOSPORUS

PONTUS EUXINUS

Sinope

Amisus

P O N T U S

ARMENIA

MARE CASPIUM

BITHYNIA

Cyzicus

HELLESPONT

Pergamum

Magnesia

GALATIA

HALYS FL.

CAPPADOCIA

HYRCANIA

ASIA

Sardis

Ephesus

MARE AEGAEUM

LYCIA

CILICIA

Tarsus

Gaugamela

MESOPOTAMIA

Rhodus I.

Creta I.

Cyprus

Antiochia

EUPHRATES FL.

TIGRIS

NUM

SYRIA

Phoenicia

Palmyra

Sidon

Damascus

Ctesiphon

FL.

Tyrus

Palaestina

Susa

SUSIANA

Alexandria

Hierosolyma

ARABIA

SINUS PERSICUS

AEGYPTUS

NILUS FL.

SINUS ARABICUS

Thebae

MARIANNE FEDER

ALPES MONTES

Augusta Praetoria
Augusta Taurinorum
Comum
Bergomum
Mediolanum Brixia
Ticinus Ticinum
BENACUS LACUS
VENETIA
Verona
Patavium
Venetia
Aquileia
Tergeste
Emona
Dertona Placentia
Cremona
Atria
SINUS
VENETIAE
ISTRIA
LIGURIA
Genua
Parma
PADUS FL.
Mutina
Pola
GALLIA CISALPINA
Bononia
Nicaea
Ravenna
MARE
LIGURIAE
Luca
Pisae
ARNO FL.
Faventia
RUBICO FL.
Ariminum
Sarsina
MARE
ADRIATICUM
Florentia
Faesulae
Volaterrae
ETRURIA
Arretium
Sentinum
Ancona
Perusia Asisium
Salonae
ILLYRICUM
Ilva I.
Agiatium
Vetulonia
VOLSINIENSIS LACUS
Volsinii
UMBRIA
PICENUM
Spoletium
Amiternum
Aternum
CORSICA
Vulci
Tarquinii
Caere
Reate
SABINI
Allia
Arpinum
Tibur
SAMNIUM
Sulmo
SARDINIA
Roma
Alba Longa
Antium
LATIUM
Tarracina
Setia
Formiae
Capua
Beneventum
Venusia
APULIA
Canusium
Barium
Dyrrhachium
MARE
TYRRHENUM
Portus Misenum
Neapolis
Caprae I.
Atella
Puteoli
Vesuvius M.
Pompeii
Salernum
Surrentum
Paestum
Potentia
LUCANIA
Metapontum
Tarentum
CALABRIA
Brundisium
Apollonia
Hydruntum
Palaeste
SINUS
TARENTINUS
Sallentinum
Promontorium
Consentia
FRETUM MESSANA
Liparaeae Iae
BRUTTIUM
Croton
FRETUM
HYDRUNTI
Eryx
Drepanum
Lilybaeum
Panormus
Segesta
Mylae
Messana
Rhegium
FRETUM SICILIAE
SICILIA
Aetna M.
Henna
Tauromenium
Catana
MARE IONIUM
Carthago
Tunes
Agrigentum
Leontini
Syracusae
TUNISIA

Melita I.

N
W E
S

ROMAN
ITALY

M. FEDER

Crowell's Handbook of

CLASSICAL
LITERATURE

A

Abdera. An ancient Greek city in Thrace, founded, according to myth, by Heracles in memory of his attendant Abderus. Actually the city was established in the seventh century B.C. by settlers from Clazomenae, in Asia Minor. During the sixth century B.C. Abdera was overcome and destroyed by the Thracians and reestablished by Ionians from Teos who fled when the Persians occupied their own city. Though both Protagoras and Democritus were born at Abdera, the ancient Greeks accepted the superstition that the air of the city caused its inhabitants to be stupid.

Abydus (Abydos). A city in Mysia in Asia Minor, situated on the Hellespont. It was founded by Milesians at the beginning of the seventh century B.C. Abydus was the home of Leander, who swam across the Hellespont to see his beloved Hero. (See Ovid's HEROIDES XVIII, XIX.) During the Persian Wars, Xerxes had a bridge built from Abydus across the Hellespont, so that his army could cross into Greece. When this bridge was destroyed by a storm, he arranged for a second one to be made from boats.

Academica. A dialogue by CICERO on epistemology, first written in 45 B.C. The first book of this edition, entitled "Catulus," is lost; the second book, "Lucullus," is extant, except for a section at the end; it is sometimes referred to as the *Academica Priora*. Dissatisfied with this version, Cicero did a second edition of the *Academica*, in which he changed the interlocutors, making one of them Varro, who wished to be named in one of Cicero's works. Cicero also arranged the second edition in four books and made some stylistic corrections and revisions. Of this edition, sometimes referred to as the *Academica Posteriora*, only the first book remains. The theory of knowledge set forth in the *Academica* is a skeptical one, a denial of the possibility of absolute knowledge.

Academy (Akademeia). An olive grove on the Cephissus River near Athens, once owned by Academus, a hero who disclosed the place where Theseus had concealed the child Helen. Cimon, the son of Miltiades, gave the land to Athens. Here Plato and his followers taught philosophy, and as a result his school was called the Academy.

Acastus (Akastos). In Greek mythology, son of Pelias. He was one of the Argonauts, who set out under the leadership of Jason to obtain the Golden Fleece. When Medea brought about the death of Pelias, Acastus became king of Iolcus.

Accius, Lucius. A Latin tragedian, born at Pisaurum (Pesaro) in Umbria in 170 B.C., died about 86 B.C. Accius' parents were probably freedmen. A younger contemporary of Pacuvius, he became his friend and his competitor in tragedy. About forty-five titles and brief fragments of his tragedies exist, indicating that he wrote on the traditional mythological subjects. In addition to these we have the titles of two of his *fabulae praetextae: Aeneadae* or *Decius* and *Brutus,* of which very brief fragments remain. Accius also wrote on literature; his *Didascalica,* of which twenty-two lines remain, is a history of Greek and Latin poetry; *Pragmatica,* of which two lines remain, may have dealt with the language of drama. Other works were *Annales,* which probably dealt with festivals, *Parerga* and *Praxidica,* on farming, and some love poems. In antiquity Accius was greatly admired as a tragedian.

Achaeans (Achaioi). One of the first Hellenic tribes who invaded Greece. It is generally thought that they arrived during the third millennium and settled both in northern Greece in Thessaly and in the southern area of the Peloponnesus. Having overcome the Pelasgians, who had inhabited Greece before them, the Achaeans imposed their Indo-European language. Gradually the religious beliefs and social customs of the Achaeans were fused with those of the older inhabitants. Moreover, both groups were influenced by the flourishing Cretan (Minoan) civilization. Soon the Achaeans became the dominant tribe in the area of Greece. During the height of the Mycenaean period (1400–1100 B.C.), they ruled not only MYCENAE but many other areas as well. In the ILIAD Homer uses the term *Achaeans* to identify either the followers of ACHILLES and Achilles' subjects in Phthia or the entire Greek army.

Acharnae (Acharnai). A deme of Attica, located about seven miles north of Athens. Its main industry was the production of charcoal. See THE ACHARNIANS.

Acharnians, The (Acharnes). An Old Comedy (425 B.C.) by ARISTOPHANES. Translations: in verse, John Hookham Frere, 1839; in verse, Benjamin B. Rogers, 1924; in verse, Arthur S. Way, 1927; in prose and verse, Lionel Casson, 1960; in verse, Douglass Parker, 1962.

B A C K G R O U N D . Aristophanes satirically reveals the trivial concerns of the Athenian popular Assembly and its refusal to deal with the important problem of bringing an end to the Peloponnesian War with Sparta. The serious theme of this comedy is the meaningless suffering caused by war and a demand for peace, a theme which recurs in *Peace* and *Lysistrata.* Acharnae, a deme (division) of Attica, was located about seven miles north of Athens near Mt. Parnes. At the beginning of the Peloponnesian War the Spartans occupied Acharnae, and the Acharnians were forced within the walls of Athens.

S C E N E . The Pnyx (the place where the meetings of the Assembly were held) at Athens; in the background are the houses of Dicaeopolis, Euripides, and Lamachus.

S U M M A R Y . Dicaeopolis, an Athenian citizen who is deeply concerned with important affairs of state, especially with ending the war with Sparta, sits alone in the Pnyx. Everyone else is late for the Assembly, and as he waits he thinks of his problems, mostly of his determination to bring up the subject of peace at today's session. Finally the Athenians gather, and the meeting begins. Amphitheus immediately raises the question of making peace with Sparta, but he is told to be quiet. The question is ignored as the Assembly listens to an absurd report by the Ambassador to Persia. Declaring that all this trivia and corruption are enough to drive a man to suicide, Dicaeopolis sends Amphitheus to arrange a personal truce with Sparta for himself, his wife, and his children. After another ridiculous report by Theorus, an Athenian ambassador, Dicaeopolis pretends to feel a drop of rain, which he calls an omen, and the Assembly is over for the day.

Amphitheus comes in, fleeing from the Chorus of Acharnian Charcoal Burners, who want to stone him because they object to peace. Amphitheus has brought three possible truces from Sparta—for periods of five, ten, or thirty years. Dicaeopolis accepts the truce of thirty years, and, relieved of the burdens of war, decides to celebrate the rural Dionysia (festival of Dionysus). Amphitheus, still fearful of the Acharnians, runs away, as the Chorus enters, hoping to seize the person who has made an agreement for peace with Sparta.

Soon Dicaeopolis and his family come out of their house with two slaves carrying the phallus. As Dicaeopolis happily leads the phallic procession, the Chorus sees him and threatens to stone him to death. Telling the Charcoal Burners that he has hostages in his house whom he will kill, Dicaeopolis goes inside and soon returns with a basket of coals, which he calls the "fellow citizen" of the Charcoal Burners and threatens to murder. In this way he persuades the Chorus to listen to his case, but he must plead with his head on a block. He obtains permission of the Acharnians to dress in a way that will inspire pity and goes for help to the home of Euripides. From Euripides he obtains the ragged clothing worn by Telephus, one of the most beggarly and miserable of Euripides' characters, a staff, and other accouterments of a beggar. Dicaeopolis then puts his head on the block and defends his position on a truce with Sparta, saying that Pericles and Athens are actually responsible for the war. Half the Chorus condemns him, and half agrees with his point of view. The first group summons its hero, General Lamachus. Lamachus cannot defend himself against the cleverness of Dicaeopolis. Declaring that he favors a continual war with Sparta, Lamachus returns to his home. Dicaeopolis announces that all the boycotts of the war are over and enters his house.

The Chorus, now accepting Dicaeopolis' point of view, delivers the parabasis: a declaration of all the benefits Aristophanes has conferred on the Athenians. He has exposed hypocrisy and revealed the truth; he has given good advice and demanded justice. Soon Dicaeopolis reappears and sets up his market before his house. Since he has ended the boycott he will trade here with all Greeks. A Megarian enters, saluting the market. He graphically illustrates the extreme suffering that Pericles' boycott has caused Megara, by disguising his two little daughters as pigs so that he can sell them to Dicaeopolis. An Informer threatens to report the Megarian, but Dicaeopolis chases him away. Then a Boeotian comes in to trade with Dicaeopolis. He is followed by another informer, Nicarchus, whom Dicaeopolis ties, gags, and packs in hay. When the Slave of Lamachus comes in to buy food, Dicaeopolis will sell him nothing.

After a choral ode praising Dicaeopolis, the man of peace, and peace itself, a Herald announces the Anthesteria, a festival in honor of Dionysus. Dicaeopolis tells his wife and children to prepare all kinds of tempting foods. Various people, envying Dicaeopolis' pleasure, beg him to share his peace with them. As Dicaeopolis is happily preparing for the feast, a Herald summons Lamachus to battle. Full of envy for Dicaeopolis, who goes off to the festival, Lamachus reluctantly departs for the battlefield. The contrast between the man of peace and the man of war continues when Lamachus comes back from battle, limping and groaning in pain, while Dicaeopolis, singing merrily, returns with two courtesans whom he embraces. The Chorus salutes the victory of Dicaeopolis.

Achates. A warrior known as *fidus Achates* in the *Aeneid* because he is the loyal attendant and friend of Aeneas. See AENEID I.

Achelous (Acheloos). God of the river Achelous in northwest Greece. Worshiped in Greece as the god of all streams, he could take the form of either a bull or a serpent or a man with the head of a bull. In these forms he courted Deianira, who was also being wooed by Heracles and others. Heracles and Achelous engaged in a wrestling match for the hand of Deianira, and though the river-god changed into all his forms, Heracles overcame him and won Deianira as his bride. See Sophocles' WOMEN OF TRACHIS.

Achemenides (Achaemenides). A warrior who, according to AENEID III, accompanied Odysseus on his long journey home from Troy. He was left behind in Sicily, in the land of the Cyclopes, when Odysseus and his other followers escaped. Some time later, when in the course of his wanderings Aeneas arrived at the island, Achemenides told him of the monstrous deeds of the Cyclops Polyphemus and urged him to flee from the land. Aeneas fled, taking Achemenides with him.

Acheron. A river in Epirus, flowing into Lake Acherusia. After the Acheron received the flow of the tributary river Cocytus, it emptied into the Thesprotian Gulf. In mythology the Acheron is one of the five rivers of the Underworld that the dead souls must cross.

Achilleid (Achilleis). See STATIUS.

Achilles (Achilleus). Son of PELEUS, king of Phthia, and Thetis. He was educated by Phoenix, who taught him to speak eloquently and to fight bravely, and by Chiron the centaur, who instructed him in the art of healing. According to post-Homeric legends, Thetis, while attempting to make Achilles immortal, dipped him in the river Styx or in the fire at Peleus' hearth; thus he was vulnerable only in the heel by which she held him. Thetis tried to prevent his participation in the Trojan War by disguising him as a maiden at the court of

Lycomedes, king of the Dolopians on the island of Scyros. Here he lived with the daughters of Lycomedes, one of whom, Deidameia, bore his son Neoptolemus. Calchas, the prophet, revealed Achilles' hiding place, and there he was found by Odysseus and Diomedes, who exposed his true identity.

In the ILIAD Achilles is faced with the choice of a long, inglorious life or a short, heroic one. His choice of the latter is used by Homer to symbolize the heroic code by which Achilles lives. He is the handsomest and bravest of the Greeks who participate in the Trojan War. As the hero of the *Iliad*, Achilles reveals intelligence, great courage, and, perhaps most important, deep intensity of feeling. He loves deeply and hates violently. His wrath is the subject of the *Iliad*, but Homer conveys also Achilles' wisdom, his loyalty, and his final understanding of the grief of a man he has hated, Priam, the father of Hector.

Achilles was killed by Paris in the battle of the Scaean Gate. Another version of his death is that he was struck in his vulnerable heel by Paris in the temple of Athene or Apollo, where he had gone to marry Polyxena, a daughter of Priam. Later myths tell of how Thetis rescued Achilles from the funeral pyre and took his body to Leuce, an island where the souls of heroes lived on in eternal happiness. There Achilles was married to Iphigenia. He is also placed in Elysium, where he was married to Medea or Helen. Achilles was worshiped at Leuce, Thessaly, Sigeum, Mytilene, and many other places, probably as a tribal hero of the Achaeans, who continued to revere him in the many places to which they migrated (see Gilbert Murray, *The Rise of the Greek Epic*, 4th ed. [Galaxy Books, 1960], p. 207).

In Book XI of the ODYSSEY Odysseus meets Achilles in the Underworld. Here he says that he would prefer to be alive, though a poor man's serf, than king among the dead. In Book XXIV of the *Odyssey* he speaks to the shade of Agamemnon, who describes to him the arrival of Thetis and the other seanymphs after Achilles' death and the seventeen days and nights of mourning for him. Once again the image of his heroic exchange of life for glory is depicted. In Euripides' IPHIGENIA IN AULIS Achilles is no longer the heroic and tormented figure of the Homeric poems. Though willing to fight to save Iphigenia from death, he does not attempt to stop her when she decides to sacrifice herself for her country. Achilles is the subject of Statius' *Achilleid* and is mentioned by Xenophon, Plutarch, Vergil, Horace, Juvenal, and other ancient writers.

Acis (Akis). In Greek mythology, a young man loved by the sea nymph Galatea. In *Metamorphoses* XIII Ovid tells of the Cyclops Polyphemus' love for Galatea and his jealousy of the youth Acis, whom he crushed under a stone. Acis implored Galatea to save him, and she transformed him into a river which bore his name. The English poet John Gay wrote the libretto to Handel's lovely opera *Acis and Galatea* (1732), which is based on this myth.

Acontius. A young man from Ceos who fell in love with Cydippe of Athens and tried by a trick to win her as his bride. See Ovid's HEROIDES XX, XXI.

Acragas (Agrigentum; modern **Agrigento, Girgenti).** A city in southwestern

5

Sicily. It was established around 580 B.C. by settlers from Gela, a Dorian city in southern Sicily. Under the rule of Theron, a fifth-century tyrant, Acragas flourished and became one of the wealthiest and most powerful of the Greek settlements in Sicily. Theron and Acragas are praised by Pindar in his odes (see CHORAL LYRICS, *Olympian* II, III). Acragas was repeatedly attacked by the Carthaginians, and after a fierce siege in 406 B.C. the city never recovered its former power or splendor. Empedocles was born at Acragas.

Acrisius (Akrisios). In Greek mythology, a king of Argos. He learned from an oracle that his daughter Danaë would bear a son who would kill him. In an attempt to prevent the fulfillment of this prophecy Acrisius imprisoned his daughter. Nonetheless, Zeus came to Danaë in the form of a shower of gold, and from their union came Perseus. Though Acrisius tried to do away with his daughter and her offspring by placing them in a chest, which he set adrift on the sea, he was not successful. Danaë and Perseus were carried to the island of Seriphos, where they received help from Dictys, brother of King Polydectes. Perseus became a great hero, and when Acrisius heard of the fame of his grandson he fled to Larissa, hoping to avoid the fulfillment of the oracle. However, Perseus, without knowing that his grandfather was at Larissa, came there to participate in funeral games. A discus he threw accidentally killed Acrisius. See Ovid's *Metamorphoses* IV and V.

Adelphi. See THE BROTHERS.

Ad Helviam de Consolatione. See DIALOGUES.

Ad Marciam de Consolatione. See DIALOGUES.

Admetus (Admetos). King of Pherae in Thessaly. See Euripides' ALCESTIS.

Adonis. In Greek mythology, the son of Myrrha; an exceedingly handsome young man, who was loved by the goddess Aphrodite. In *Metamorphoses* x Ovid tells of how Myrrha fell in love with her own father Cinyras, king of Cyprus. Concealing her identity, she had a love affair with him. When Cinyras discovered who she was, he tried to kill her, but she escaped and was transformed by the gods into a myrtle tree. From this tree their child Adonis came forth. The goddess Aphrodite fell in love with Adonis; and, when he was killed by a boar while hunting, she created the anemone from his blood. To assuage Aphrodite's grief the gods of the Underworld allowed Adonis to spend six months of the year with her on earth. The story of Adonis' birth from a tree, his death, and rebirth for six months of every year suggest that he was originally a vegetation deity, whose death and rebirth symbolize the cyclic rebirth of natural life. (See Theocritus' *Idyl* xv and Bion's LAMENT FOR ADONIS.) The death and rebirth of Adonis were celebrated at festivals in Athens, Alexandria, and elsewhere in the ancient world.

Adrastus (Adrastos). See Aeschylus' THE SEVEN AGAINST THEBES and Euripides' THE SUPPLIANTS.

Aea (Aia). A city in Colchis, ruled by King Aeëtes. Here Jason and the other Argonauts came to obtain the Golden Fleece.

6

Aeacus (Aiakos). In Greek mythology, son of Zeus and the nymph Aegina, and father of Telamon and Peleus. A noble man, he became a judge in the Underworld, where he appears in Aristophanes' THE FROGS.

Aeaea (Aiaie). The island of Circe, where Odysseus remained for a year. See ODYSSEY X, XII.

Aeëtes (Aietes). In Greek mythology, son of Helios and Persa. King of Aea, in Colchis, he was a brother of Circe, Pasiphaë, and Perses and father of Medea. See ARGONAUTICA and Euripides' MEDEA.

Aegeus (Aigeus). In Greek mythology, a son of Pandion and king of Athens. His brother Pallas denied that Aegeus was the real son of Pandion and, with his fifty sons, attempted unsuccessfully to drive Aegeus from the throne of Athens. Though he married twice, Aegeus had no children; troubled by the possibility that he would leave no heir to his throne, he went to the oracle for help. The oracle at Delphi warned him not to untie his wineskin until he returned to Athens, or he would die of sorrow. On his way home Aegeus stopped at Troezen, where he told King Pittheus of the prophetic warning, which he did not comprehend. Perhaps sensing the prophecy of a noble birth, Pittheus sent his daughter Aethra to Aegeus. That night she also received the god Poseidon. Thus Theseus, the child Aethra conceived, was the son of the mortal Aegeus and the god Poseidon. When Aegeus left Troezen he concealed a sword and sandals under a rock, instructing Aethra to challenge Theseus to recover these when he grew to manhood and, if he could do so, to come with them to Athens. The story of Theseus' first meeting with Aegeus is told in Bacchylides' CHORAL LYRIC XVIII. When Theseus left Athens as part of the tribute of young men and women to Minos of Crete, he promised that if he returned after conquering the Minotaur, his ship would have a white sail. Theseus did return victorious but forgot to substitute a white sail for the black one on the ship. Aegeus spotted the black sail and, believing that his son had been killed, leaped from the Acropolis to his death. See Euripides' MEDEA.

Aegisthus (Aigisthos). In Greek mythology, the son of Thyestes and Pelopeia, Thyestes' daughter. Pelopeia exposed Thyestes as an infant, but he was saved by shepherds and reared by Atreus, Thyestes' brother. Atreus commanded Aegisthus to kill Thyestes, but Thyestes recognized his son and with him plotted the death of Atreus. After Atreus' death, Thyestes became king of Mycenae but was forced into exile by Agamemnon, a son of Atreus. When Agamemnon led the Greek forces against Troy, Aegisthus became the lover of his wife, Clytemnestra, and the two murdered Agamemnon on his return. Aegisthus ruled Mycenae with Clytemnestra until they were slain by her son Orestes. See Aeschylus' ORESTEIA and Seneca's AGAMEMNON. The story of his murder is also told in Euripides' ELECTRA and Sophocles' ELECTRA.

Aegyptus (Aigyptos). In Greek mythology, the brother of DANAUS.

Aeneas. In Greek and Roman mythology, the son of Aphrodite (in Roman myth, Venus) and Anchises (see HOMERIC HYMN V). He led the Trojan survivors

7

from their ruined city to their destined home in Italy, and thus is the founder of the Roman people (see ROME). For his genealogy see ILIAD XX; the story of his heroic mission is told in the AENEID. He also appears in RHESUS.

Aeneid (Aeneis). Epic poem (30–19 B.C.) in dactylic hexameters by VERGIL. Translations: in verse, John Dryden, 1697; in prose, J. W. Mackail, 1885; in verse, James Rhoades, 1907; in prose, H. Rushton Fairclough, 1916; in verse, C. Day Lewis, 1952; in prose, W. F. Jackson Knight, 1956; in verse, L. R. Lind, 1963; in verse, Frank O. Copley, 1965; in verse, Allen Mandelbaum, 1971.

BACKGROUND. In Book XX of the *Iliad* the god Poseidon urges the other gods to protect Aeneas, predicting that he will become the king of the Trojans. After the fall of Troy, impelled by a divine inspiration to establish his people in their destined home, which as yet was unknown to him, Aeneas led the surviving Trojans away from their ruined city, seeking their new land. Enduring great hardships, the Trojans wandered for seven years, mistaking various places for their destined home. Finally they learned from the Penates that the land they sought was in Italy. As the *Aeneid* begins, Aeneas and his followers have just left Sicily and are looking forward to reaching Italy and their promised land.

SUMMARY. *Book I.* The poem begins with a statement of the subject: Vergil sings of war and of a hero who, exiled by fate, at last arrived in Italy after having endured much hardship on land and sea because of the wrath of cruel Juno. Aeneas suffered a great deal in war also before he could found his city and establish his gods in the Latin land. From this origin came the Latin race, the lords of Alba, and the mighty walls of Rome. Vergil then addresses the Muse, asking for her aid as he attempts to explain why the queen of the gods caused so good and noble a man as Aeneas to endure so much danger and suffering. Can such fierce anger live in the hearts of the gods?

Vergil then gives the traditional reasons for Juno's hatred of the Trojans, one of which was that she had learned that the new race destined to spring from the Trojans would one day destroy her favorite city, Carthage, which was inhabited by settlers from Tyre. Another reason was Juno's deep resentment of the judgment of Paris, who had chosen Aphrodite as the most beautiful goddess (see *Mythical Background* under ILIAD). Furthermore, Juno hated the race that sprang from Dardanus, the son of Jupiter and Electra. Also she resented the honors given to the Trojan youth Ganymede, who was made cup-bearer to the gods. Thus Juno has caused the survivors of the Trojan nation to wander for many years far from their destined home in Latium. The Roman nation was founded only after great labor and suffering.

Juno, observing the ships of the Trojans leaving Sicily, goes to Aeolus, the king of the winds, and asks him to send forth his winds and cause a storm so that the ships of the Trojans will be overwhelmed. Aeolus obeys the goddess, and as Aeneas faces this new disaster, he cries out in despair, envying the heroes who met a glorious death fighting at Troy. After the ships of the Trojans have been hurled on rocks and scattered and one has been sunk, Neptune, the god of the seas, scolds the winds and commands them to return to their home. When the sea is calm again Aeneas leads the seven ships still with him to shelter on the coast of Africa. Then, as his men build a fire and try to save the grain they have rescued from the sea, Aeneas and Achates kill seven deer. Aeneas encourages his followers, reminding them that they have endured greater hardships in the past. He recalls their heroic destiny and suggests that one day perhaps even their difficulties will be pleasing to remember. However, even as he urges his men to be strong and to endure, his own mind is troubled and he hides the anguish of his own spirit.

Aeneas' mother, the goddess Venus, greatly distressed at the suffering of her son and the other Trojans, goes to see Jupiter on Olympus and scolds him for not fulfilling his promise that from the Trojans were to spring the mighty Roman people, who would rule a great empire. Jupiter calms her fears and reveals the destined future of Aeneas and the Trojans: Aeneas and his followers will wage war in Italy and overcome the Latins who oppose him; then he will establish the city of Lavinium. His son, Ascanius (Iulus), will found Alba Longa. Here his descendants will rule for three hundred years, until the priestess Ilia (Rhea Silvia), daughter of Numitor, bears to the god Mars the twins Romulus and Remus. Romulus will establish the city of Rome, and its people will be named after him. Jupiter goes on to prophesy the future strength and glory of Rome, which will conquer Greece and many other nations. The Romans, the "people of the toga," will one day be rulers of the world, cherished even by Juno. Finally Jupiter speaks of the career of Augustus Caesar, who will bring peace to the Romans after long years of warfare. After making this prophecy Jupiter sends Mercury to Carthage to inspire Dido, the queen, and her people with sympathy for the Trojans.

That night Aeneas cannot sleep because he is troubled about the future of his people. In the morning he and Achates explore the land. Venus comes to her son in the disguise of a huntress and tells Aeneas that he is in the land of Carthage, founded by Dido, who came there with her followers from Tyre after her cruel brother Pygmalion had slain her husband Sychaeus. When Aeneas speaks of his own hardships, Venus comforts him, telling him that his ships and comrades are safe. She urges him to go to the palace of Dido. As she departs Aeneas recognizes his mother and cries out in despair because she comes to him only in disguise, and he is denied the warmth of a human relationship with her.

As Aeneas and Achates walk on, they observe the people of Carthage eagerly building the city. Aeneas, who longs to see his own land being established, envies those who already have the opportunity to build the walls of their city. Then he and Achates come to a grove in which a great temple to Juno is located. On the walls of this temple are depicted scenes of pain and glory from the Trojan War. Aeneas, seeing the artistic representations of the struggle and sorrow of his own people, expresses his feelings to Achates.

This passage, and especially the line *Sunt lacrimae rerum et mentem mortalia tangunt,* is often quoted. The line, which has been interpreted in various ways, has been regarded by many scholars and poets as a statement of Aeneas' tragic conception of his own destiny: "Sorrow is implicit in the affairs of men and human frailty touches the heart." The terrible fate of Priam and the other Trojans depicted in the murals suggests the tragic price of heroism, yet Aeneas is reconciled to his destiny, for the passage ends with his encouraging remark to Achates: "Give up your fears; the fame of this will bring you a measure of deliverance." Aeneas is suggesting that human frailty and suffering are redeemed through devotion to a heroic ideal; the fallen heroes of Troy live in fame, and Aeneas is inspired by their heroism in his own devotion to the mighty task of establishing the Roman nation.

Soon Dido approaches the temple, accompanied by some of her people. When the Trojans Aeneas had feared lost during the storm at sea are led in, and Dido welcomes them and offers them help, Aeneas emerges from a protecting cloud in which Venus had enveloped him and expresses his gratitude to Dido and his joy in seeing his friends again. Dido offers the Trojans the hospitality of Carthage and plans a feast in their honor. When Aeneas sends for his son, Venus substitutes Cupid, disguising him as Ascanius so that the god may inspire Dido with love for Aeneas, thus assuring her support and aid. At the feast Dido embraces the boy she believes is Ascanius, and the god of love inspires her with a deep passion for Aeneas. She asks him many questions about his past and finally urges him to tell the whole story of the destruction of Troy and his long years of wandering.

Book II. Reluctantly Aeneas recalls the tragic story of Troy's last days. He tells of how during the tenth year of the Trojan War the Greeks built a great wooden horse and pretended they were offering it to Minerva to insure their safe return home. Inside the horse were armed men, the best of the Greek warriors. The rest of the Greeks then sailed to the nearby island of Tenedos, where they hid so that the Trojans would believe they had returned to Greece. The Trojans were uncertain about whether to bring the great horse into their city. Laocoön, a priest of Apollo, warned them against the treachery of the Greeks, especially Ulysses, but the Trojans, deceived by the lies of Sinon, a Greek left behind to ensnare them, soon agreed to bring in the horse. When Laocoön and his two sons were killed by two serpents that came out of the sea, the Trojans were certain that he was punished for his hostility to the offering to Minerva. The warning of the prophetess Cassandra was also ignored, and the Trojans dragged the huge horse into their city. That night the Greeks who had gone to Tenedos and those who had been concealed in the horse entered Troy, killed the sleeping Trojans, and destroyed the city. As Aeneas slept a vision of Hector came to him, urging him to save himself from the flames which were destroying Troy and to take the household gods (Penates) and the surviving Trojans to a new land, where he must establish the destined home of the Trojans. Aeneas frantically took up his arms and rushed into battle, but despite his valiant efforts to force the Greeks back, he realized that Troy must fall. He witnessed tragic slaughter: Pyrrhus, the son of Achilles, killed Polites before the eyes of Priam, his father, and then killed Priam as he slipped in the blood of his son. Reminded of his own father, his wife, and his son, Aeneas went to the house of his father. At first Anchises refused to flee, determined to die at Troy. But when he saw a flame above the head of Ascanius and other omens sent by Jupiter—a crash of thunder and a falling star—the old man agreed to accompany Aeneas. Aeneas carried his father on his back and held Ascanius by the hand. Aeneas' wife Creusa was to follow behind them, but in the course of their wanderings Aeneas realized that she was lost. Leaving his father and son in the care of servants, Aeneas returned to search for her. As he rushed wildly about, the ghost of Creusa came to him. Gently she tried to comfort her husband, telling him it was her destiny to die at Troy; he must wander in search of his destined home, where he would marry a royal wife. Mourning his beloved wife, Aeneas returned to his father and son. He was surprised to find that a number of Trojans had gathered, ready to follow him to whatever land he would lead them. Carrying his father, Aeneas led the Trojan men and women to Mount Ida.

Book III. The next summer Aeneas and his followers set sail in their quest for the destined land. Their first attempt to establish their city was at Thrace, but, when they discovered the tomb of Polydorus, a son of Priam who had been killed by the Thracian king for his gold, they decided to leave the land stained with blood and guilt. Their next stop was Delos, where they asked the oracle of Apollo for help in finding their destined home. When the oracle advised them to find their "ancient mother," Anchises interpreted this to mean that they must go to the island of Crete. Once again the Trojans began to build a city, which they called Pergamum. Suddenly, however, they were faced with disease and famine, and Aeneas was told by the Penates that the Trojans were not destined to settle in Crete: the oracle of Apollo had advised them to seek their home in Italy, not in Crete. Again the Trojans set forth, but soon a storm drove them to the Strophades, islands in the Ionian Sea. They landed there and began to eat when their food was seized by the Harpies, dreadful creatures, part woman and part bird, who swooped down upon them. The leader of the Harpies, Celaeno, cursed them, prophesying that they would not establish their city until, forced by hunger, they had devoured their own tables.

The Trojans fled from the Strophades and sailed along the coast of Greece. They stopped briefly at Actium and then went on to Buthrotum. There they found that Priam's son Helenus had married Hector's widow Andromache, and was now ruler of the city of Buthrotum. On seeing Aeneas, Andromache expressed her sorrow and love for Hector, yet she and Helenus had built a "small Troy" in the new land. Helenus, a prophet, advised Aeneas on how to reach Italy, and after a sad farewell, in which Aeneas revealed his envy of his friends whose destiny had already been fulfilled and who might now rest, the Trojans sailed on. Soon they saw the coast of Italy, but they had been warned by Helenus to avoid the southeast coast because, to reach it, they must encounter the monster Scylla and the whirlpool Charybdis. Thus the Trojans headed for the west coast. Soon they came to Sicily, where they stopped overnight. There they found Achemenides, one of Odysseus' men, who had been left behind when Odysseus and his men had escaped from the cave of the Cyclops Polyphemus. They allowed him to join them, and then, seeing Polyphemus on the mountain top, the Trojans hurried to leave the harbor. They sailed to Drepanum, on the west coast of Sicily, where Anchises died. Lamenting for his father, Aeneas ends his tale.

Book IV. Disturbed by her passionate love for Aeneas, Dido reveals her feelings to her sister Anna. Dido declares that if she had not made a sacred vow to be faithful to the memory of her husband Sychaeus, she might consider marrying Aeneas. Anna urges her to yield to her passion, and Dido gives way to her feelings, constantly seeking Aeneas and ignoring her obligations to her state. Juno, believing Aeneas can be prevented from establishing his people in Italy by his feelings for Dido, decides to aid Venus in uniting the pair. One day when Dido and Aeneas and their attendants are hunting in the mountains, Juno sends a storm. Dido and Aeneas seek shelter in the same cave, and as Juno gives the signal for their sexual union, the very heavens and earth respond to the consummation of this tragic and fateful love. The sky flashes with fire, and on the top of the mountain the nymphs howl. Dido now calls her love affair a marriage and makes no attempt to hide her love for Aeneas.

When Jupiter becomes aware that Aeneas, forgetful of his duty to his people, lingers in Carthage because of his love of Dido, the king of the gods sends his messenger Mercury to remind him of his duty. Mercury speaks to Aeneas of his obligations to his heroic mission, to his father, his son, and the gods. Swayed by the god's words, Aeneas determines to leave Carthage, but he dreads telling Dido of his decision. She learns of his plans for departure before he can inform her of them and cries out in her rage and pain, begging him to remain with her. Though Aeneas loves Dido deeply and finds it very hard to leave her, he accepts his heroic obligations and continues his preparations for departure. Still he hesitates long enough for a second message to come from the gods in the form of Mercury, urging him to leave. Mercury, the trickster of the gods, the god of eloquence and fraud, uses any method he feels will work to persuade Aeneas to give up his love for Dido. He warns Aeneas that Dido plans to harm him; then he ends his speech with the statement "A fickle and ever-changing thing is woman." The words applied to Dido are shocking in their tragic irony, for not only has she been so faithful to the memory of Sychaeus that only the gods could turn her from her vows of devotion, but, even as Mercury utters these words, she is plotting her own death because she cannot help being constant in her love for Aeneas. She has a great funeral pyre erected, pretending that she intends to destroy all her mementos of Aeneas in an effort to forget him. When from her watchtower Dido sees the Trojans setting sail, she gives way to her pain and frenzy, cursing Aeneas and praying that an avenger may rise from her ashes [Hannibal] to wage war on the race of Aeneas. Then she mounts the funeral pyre and falls on her sword. Her sister Anna rushes to her side, and finally Juno, pitying Dido's suffering, sends Iris to free her soul. Dido's death is that of a tragic heroine; she is the victim of the gods and of her own intense passions.

Book V. As the Trojans sail away from Carthage, Aeneas sees the fire from Dido's funeral pyre, and though he does not know the cause, he fears that Dido has harmed herself in her frenzy. The Trojans are forced back to Sicily by a storm and are welcomed by King Acestes. A year has passed since the death of Anchises; thus Aeneas holds a festival to honor his father. First, sacrifices are offered at Anchises' tomb, and after nine days have passed funeral games are held. In one of these contests, a foot race, Euryalus wins through the help of his loyal friend Nisus.

While the men are engaging in the games, Juno sends Iris, disguised as an old Trojan woman, to incite the Trojan matrons, discouraged after seven years of searching for the destined land, to burn the ships of the Trojans so that they will be forced to establish a home in Sicily. At first the women hesitate, torn between their desire to accomplish the heroic task and their longing for a place of rest. Finally, overcome by their own despair and the force of the goddess, they set fire to the ships. When the men hear of the disaster, they rush to the seashore. Aeneas prays for the help of Jupiter, who sends rain to put out the fire, and all but four of the ships are rescued.

Observing the violence of the women, to whom the heroic mission has become an overwhelming burden, Aeneas is greatly disturbed, for, like them, he yearns for peace and rest, *oblitus fatorum* (forgetful of his fate), and at the same time he cannot give up his painful but insistent duty. He is comforted by one of his followers, old Nautes, who declares that all fortune can be conquered by endurance, and advises him to leave those of his people who are old and weary behind in Sicily, where they will found the city of Acesta. Aeneas' father comes to him in a dream and urges him to accept this advice, warning him that he must overcome a strong people in Latium. Then Anchises tells his son that he must come to visit him in the Elysian Fields in Hades. After arranging to leave some of his people behind, Aeneas prepares to leave with the rest for Italy, where he himself will set out for Hades. When Venus asks Neptune to grant the Trojans a safe voyage, he agrees, but demands one Trojan life for many. The one life is that of Palinurus, the pilot who falls asleep and falls into the sea.

Book VI. Weeping for his dead friend, Aeneas sails on, and at last the Trojans reach Cumae in Italy. As his followers explore the land, Aeneas climbs the hill to the temple of Apollo in order to consult the Sibyl. He prays that the gods may allow the Trojans to remain in their destined land in Italy. The Sibyl then tells him of the Trojans' future: they will indeed remain in Italy, but they will conquer the land only after a dreadful war, for another Achilles (Turnus) awaits them in Latium. Despite the difficulties before him, Aeneas must not yield to misfortune but must face it with more courage than Fortune seems to permit, a statement which suggests the heroic endurance so characteristic of Aeneas in the accomplishment of his mighty task. When Aeneas asks the Sibyl to lead him to the Underworld, she warns him that, though the descent into Hades is easy, to return from that world to the light of day is difficult. However, if he wishes to go, he must first pluck a golden bough from a tree in a grove nearby, and then he must bury his friend Misenus, who was drowned by Triton. After accomplishing these tasks and making sacrifices, Aeneas is led by the Sibyl to the Underworld. Before the entrance to Hades, Aeneas encounters such frightening figures as Grief, Cares, Diseases, Age, Fear, Famine, Want, Death, and War. He sees the horrible forms of mythical beasts and monsters, such as the chimaera and the centaurs. Finally the Sibyl and he come to the River Styx, which the squalid ferryman Charon guards. He is surrounded by a huge crowd of unburied souls, who are not permitted to cross until a hundred years have passed. One of these is Palinurus, whom Aeneas promises to bury. When the Sibyl shows Charon the golden bough, he is willing to ferry Aeneas across the river.

When they land they are threatened by Cerberus, the huge dog with three heads, but the Sibyl drugs him and they enter the land of Hades. The first group of souls that Aeneas encounters consists of those who died as infants; near them is a group of those who were put to death because of false charges, and the next part is inhabited by those who took their own lives. Then Aeneas sees the souls who died of the sorrows of love: among them is Dido. Aeneas calls to her, declaring that he left her land unwillingly, but she passes by without responding to him and returns to the soul of her husband Sychaeus. Then Aeneas sees a group of heroic warriors who died in battle. He speaks to Deiphobus, a son of Priam, and learns of how he was killed by Menelaus and Helen, who had become the wife of Deiphobus after the death of Paris.

Urging Aeneas not to spend all his time in talk, the Sibyl leads him past the huge gate of Tartarus, the section of the Underworld where the evil souls are punished. The Sibyl tells Aeneas of the dreadful tortures endured in Tartarus by such evil souls as Ixion and Pirithous, by others who hated their brothers, committed adultery, or engaged in war against their own country. Indeed, she says, if she had a hundred tongues, a hundred mouths, and an iron voice, she could not tell him all the various crimes of the sinners and all the tortures they suffer in Tartarus.

Finally Aeneas and the Sibyl come to the Elysian Fields, where the virtuous souls dwell. There Aeneas finds Anchises, who weeps as he expresses his love for his son. Vainly Aeneas tries to embrace the insubstantial form of his beloved father. Then Aeneas notices a great many souls gathered at the

River Lethe. When he inquires about them, Anchises explains that these souls are drinking the waters of Lethe so that they will have no memories of the past. Anchises goes on to explain that the soul after death pays the penalties for sins committed in life. After a thousand years of expiation and preparation, the soul drinks of the River Lethe; then it is reborn in a new body. After speaking of reincarnation Anchises tells Aeneas who his descendants will be and prophesies the future of the Roman nation. [Thus, through the prophecies and warnings of Anchises, Vergil is able to survey the history of Rome, even as he describes the difficult task of establishing the Trojan people in Italy.] Anchises speaks of the son Aeneas will have by Lavinia, the Latin princess he will marry, Silvius, who will be a king and the father of kings. After mentioning other kings, Anchises tells his son of Romulus, the child of Mars, who will found the city of Rome. Then Anchises prophesies the future glory of Rome and the terrible price in bloodshed and cruelty that must be paid for her triumphs. [Even as he warns his descendants against civil war and bloodshed, he is actually giving a history of what it cost Rome to become ruler of the world.] When Anchises has inspired his son to fulfill his heroic destiny and told him of the war he must wage in Italy, Aeneas and the Sibyl leave the Underworld through the ivory gates.

Book VII. The Trojans once again set sail. Having passed the home of Circe, they finally come to the River Tiber and prepare to land at its mouth. Vergil again calls upon the Muse to inspire him, declaring that he now undertakes a greater theme, a mightier task, the story of the war between the Trojans and the Latins. King Latinus, now an old man, has ruled Latium for a long time. He has an only daughter, Lavinia, who has been promised in marriage by her mother Amata to Turnus, king of the Rutulians. However, many divine omens have suggested that this marriage must not take place, and Latinus has received a prophecy that his daughter would marry a stranger. Although Lavinia would win great fame, she would cause her people to suffer a dreadful war.

When the Trojans land they rest and prepare a meal. As they are eating their round cakes, which have served as tables and plates for their food, Iulus remarks that they are consuming their very tables. Aeneas now realizes that the prophecy that they would not reach their destined land until they had consumed their very tables has been fulfilled. He sends one hundred envoys with messages and gifts to King Latinus, asking for a peaceful reception for the Trojans. Then Aeneas starts to plan the city he will build.

King Latinus receives the Trojan envoys cordially and asks to see Aeneas. Revealing the prophecy that his daughter is destined to marry a stranger who will bring glory to Latium, Latinus declares that Aeneas shall be her husband. Meanwhile, Juno, observing the Trojans already building their city, furiously plans to involve them in a destructive war with the Latins. She calls forth from Hades Allecto, a Fury who is the spirit of strife and crime. Allecto visits Amata and, flinging a snake from her hair into Amata's breast, incites the queen to anger against the Trojans. Attempting to prevent the marriage of her daughter to Aeneas, she hides Lavinia in the mountains. Allecto then transforms herself into an old woman and goes to Turnus as he sleeps. The Fury inspires the proud and courageous young man with rage and lust for war, and he calls forth his people, urging them to protect their land against the Trojans.

As Turnus rouses his people, Allecto goes to the Trojans to create new mischief. Finding that Ascanius is hunting, she fills his dogs with frenzy, and they chase a pet stag. Then the Fury guides the hand of Ascanius as he shoots the stag and wounds it. The animal, crying piteously, returns to the house of its master, Tyrrhus, the keeper of the royal herds. The Latins gather to attack Ascanius, and the Trojans rush to his rescue. In the battle that follows, a young Latin, Almo, the son of Tyrrhus, and many others are slain. Now Turnus demands war with the Trojans, and the Latins, inspired by the frenzy of Amata, agree to rush to arms. Only King Latinus refuses to engage in warfare and, realizing that he cannot calm his furious people, retires to his palace and gives up his rule. Because Latinus will not officially proclaim that war has started by opening the gates of Janus, Juno performs this act, and preparations for war begin.

Vergil then asks the Muse to describe the great kings who led their hosts to war against the Trojans. Among these is Mezentius, the cruel Etruscan tyrant, accompanied by his son Lausus and a thousand men. Another is Aventinus, a son of Hercules. Turnus is among the foremost, glorious in his armor and followed by warriors from almost all the native tribes of Italy. Also Camilla, the warrior maiden, comes leading her forces, marvelous in her beauty and power.

Book VIII. Throughout Latium preparations for war continue. Greatly disturbed, Aeneas is comforted by a dream in which the god of the River Tiber assures him that he has reached his destined home. The god suggests that Aeneas join in a league with the Greek king Evander, who rules over the Arcadians at Pallanteum (the future site of Rome). When Aeneas goes to see Evander and asks for his aid, the king receives him warmly, telling him that Aeneas reminds him of Anchises, whom he had known. Evander agrees to join in a league with the Trojans against the people of Italy; then he explains the meaning of a yearly festival in honor of Hercules in which he is at present engaged. He points out a nearby cliff, where once a cave existed, inhabited by a giant Cacus, a cannibalistic son of Vulcan. Hercules killed this monstrous creature, and ever since has been honored by the Arcadians. Evander then leads Aeneas about his city, showing him various places which are to become famous in the Rome of the future.

While Aeneas is enjoying the hospitality of Evander, Venus goes to see her husband Vulcan and, bribing him with embraces, persuades him to forge arms for her son. Evander offers Aeneas the assistance of the men he can spare and sends his only son Pallas to lead them. He also suggests that Aeneas ask assistance from the Etruscans, for they have lately driven out the cruel tyrant

Mezentius, who ruled their city of Agylla. Because Mezentius sought and received the protection of Turnus, the Etruscans will aid Aeneas. Finally, weeping, Evander says farewell to his only son as the young man prepares to depart with Aeneas.

When Aeneas, Pallas, and the warriors who accompany them have reached Etruria, Venus brings her son the armor forged by Vulcan. Vergil describes the shield at great length [compare the shield of Achilles in ILIAD XVIII]; engraved on it are the most important scenes in Rome's future history: the offspring of Ascanius, Romulus and Remus, the rape of the Sabines, and many other wars and triumphs, ending with the great victories and accomplishments of Augustus.

Book IX. Juno sends Iris to persuade Turnus to take advantage of Aeneas' absence and attack the Trojans. When the Trojans see the army advancing against them, they follow the orders Aeneas had given before he departed, and they retreat to the safety of their camp. Turnus then decides to set fire to the Trojan fleet, but Cybele intervenes and transforms the ships into nymphs, who jump into the water. During the night Nisus and Euryalus, who are guarding the gate, decide to find their way past the enemy and warn Aeneas. They long to accomplish a great deed, either because, as Nisus says, the gods have inspired them or because a man's desire for glory becomes to him a god. When their plan is approved by the military authorities, the two young men go forth and, discovering the Rutulians asleep, manage to slay a great many. Euryalus is spotted by a group of horsemen. As he tries to escape he is hindered by the branches of trees and by the spoils he is carrying. Nisus manages to escape but, unable to see his friend, retraces his steps and discovers that Euryalus has been captured by the horsemen. From his place of hiding he manages to kill two of the horsemen. When Volcens, the leader of the troop, kills Euryalus to avenge these deaths, Nisus can no longer remain in hiding. He rushes out, crying that it is he who has killed the men. He kills Volcens and is killed himself, falling upon the body of his friend. Vergil's comment is that at last in death the two young men found peace; he calls them fortunate because his poem will give them eternal fame.

The next morning the Rutulians display the heads of Nisus and Euryalus on spears. When Euryalus' mother hears of the death of her son, she shrieks and tears her hair in her grief and the other Trojans also lament the deaths of the youths. Then the Rutulians, aided by other tribes, try to break into the Trojan camp, and many Trojans are slain while defending themselves. Ascanius kills Numanus, the husband of Turnus' sister, for scoffing at the Trojans. Apollo congratulates Ascanius, but tells him that he must now refrain from warfare. Two Trojan youths, Pandarus and Bitias, open the gates, eager to fight with the enemy. The Rutulians enter fighting savagely and kill many Trojans. When Turnus hears that the gates of the Trojan camp have been opened, he rushes inside the camp and slays many heroes of Troy. Mars inspires the Latins with strength and courage, but to the Trojans the war god gives only a desire for flight and fear. Pandarus, seeing the body of his slain brother, closes the gates of the Trojan camp, unaware that Turnus is still within. Turnus kills Pandarus; then, surrounded by Trojans, he leaps from the walls into the Tiber.

Book X. Jupiter calls a council of the gods on Olympus and orders them to end the war between the Trojans and the Latins. Venus speaks in behalf of the Trojans, and Juno attacks them, complaining of Venus' aid to them. Jupiter declares that fate will decide the outcome.

Meanwhile, the Rutulians besiege the gates of the Trojan camp. Aeneas, who has obtained the help of the Etruscans, is on his way back with thirty ships. Sailing at night, Aeneas is informed by nymphs, who formerly were his fleet, of the attack on the Trojan camp. He prepares his forces for battle, and as the Trojans see him coming they are greatly encouraged. Despite Turnus' attempts to prevent Aeneas and his men from landing, they manage to reach the shore, and a battle follows. Pallas encourages his men and fights bravely, killing many of the Latins. Lausus, the son of Mezentius, observing the valor of Pallas, urges his own men on. The two young heroes, Pallas, who fights on the side of the Trojans, and Lausus, who has allied himself with Turnus, are alike in many respects and are treated with equal sympathy by Vergil. As he describes the two leading their men to confront each other, Vergil remarks that they are practically the same age and both are unusually handsome, but fate has decreed that neither will return to his home.

Turnus comes to the aid of Lausus and engages in combat with Pallas. As Pallas is about to fight with the mighty Turnus, he prays to Hercules for help. Knowing that Pallas must die, Hercules weeps as he hears this prayer. Jupiter comforts him by reminding him of the heroic code: "For all men life is brief and death inevitable, but to extend one's fame by deeds, this is the accomplishment of valor." Turnus kills Pallas and takes his belt, enjoying the spoils of war, not knowing that one day he will regret this prize. The friends of Pallas mourn over his body. When Aeneas hears of the death of the young man, he fights fiercely, trying to reach Turnus and slaying many Latins as he proceeds. In the meantime, the other Trojans come from the camp led by Ascanius. Jupiter now allows Juno to save Turnus and put off the hour of his death. She fashions from mist a phantom of Aeneas and sends it into battle before Turnus, who pursues the phantom onto a ship moored nearby, whereupon Juno sets the ship adrift, and Turnus, though ungrateful, is borne to safety.

Cruel Mezentius has been killing many Trojans when Aeneas meets and wounds him. Lausus rushes to protect his father. As the young man rashly attempts combat with Aeneas, Aeneas tries to warn him and prevent his death, but Lausus will not listen. Aeneas wounds him; then, seeing him dying, he groans in pity, thinking of his own son. Moved by paternal sorrow and tenderness for his enemy, he reaches out to touch the young man and asks what solace he can offer him. Ironically all he can offer him is the fact that he has won glory by meeting his death at the hands of the great Aeneas. Viewing his own fame quite objectively, Aeneas offers Lausus the only comfort he knows, the solace he himself is seeking, the belief that the deed of valor redeems the brevity of life and the tragic waste and destruction of war. Overcome by remorse over his son's death, Mezentius rushes to meet Aeneas and is slain by him. Dying, he asks that he and his son may be buried properly.

Book XI. Aeneas fulfills his vows to the gods by creating a trophy to Mars with the arms of Mezentius. He then encourages his men to besiege the very walls of Laurentum. First, however, the Trojans must bury their dead and send the body of Pallas home to his father. Envoys arrive from the Latins asking for a truce of twelve days in which to bury the dead and negotiate on peace. The Latins meet in assembly, and many express their dissatisfaction with the war and their disapproval of Turnus. King Latinus again urges the Latins to make peace with the Trojans and to allow them to settle in Italy and found their destined city. He is supported by Drances, for whom Turnus expresses his contempt. Turnus then says he will meet Aeneas in single combat. As the Latins continue to debate, they learn that the Trojans and Etruscans are approaching the city. Turnus takes advantage of his people's distress and calls them to arms. After fighting heroically, Camilla, the warrior maiden, is slain. In describing her death Vergil echoes Homer's words on the deaths of Patroclus and Hector (see ILIAD XVI): "With a groan, indignant, her life fled to the Shades." After the death of Camilla, the cavalry which she had led retreats, and many of her men are slain. When Turnus hears of how badly the Latins are faring, he leaves the hills where he has been lying in ambush and returns to the city.

Book XII. When Turnus realizes how discouraged the Latins are, he announces that he will meet Aeneas in single combat, and the victor will take Lavinia as his bride. Latinus tries to dissuade him, but Turnus declares that he is willing to exchange death for glory. Aeneas gladly agrees to the contest which will put an end to the slaughter of war. When Juno hears of the agreement she goes to Turnus' sister, the nymph Juturna, and warns her that if the combat takes place, Turnus will be overcome. After Aeneas and Latinus have agreed on the combat and the terms of peace, swearing oaths and performing sacrifices to express their good faith, Juturna incites the Latins to battle. When Tolumnius, a Rutulian seer, hurls a spear and kills an ally of the Trojans, the war starts again. Aeneas is wounded by an arrow from an unseen hand and is forced to leave the battle. Turnus now has new hope and fights with great courage, slaying many Trojans. Aeneas is soon cured by Venus and returns to battle. He tries to find Turnus, but Juturna keeps her brother away from him.

Venus inspires Aeneas with the plan of besieging the walls of the city of the Latins. When Aeneas and the other Trojans attack the city, the Latins are terrified. Amata, assuming that Turnus has been killed, hangs herself in despair.

When Turnus hears of the destruction of the city, he again suggests a contest between Aeneas and himself, and finally the two heroes come together in combat. As they fight, Jupiter tells Juno that she must accept the inevitable victory of Aeneas and no longer torment the Trojans. Juno agrees, demanding only that the Latins and Trojans join in peace and that the Trojans accept the name and language of the Latins. The name of Troy must no longer exist. Jupiter grants this request.

Aeneas finally wounds Turnus, who asks him to give his body to his father for burial. As Aeneas stands over his wounded enemy, he pities him and hesitates to kill him. Then seeing on Turnus' shoulder the belt he had taken from the dead Pallas, Aeneas cries out that it is Pallas who demands atonement and plunges his sword into the breast of Turnus. Vergil repeats his comment on the death of Camilla as he says of Turnus in the last line of the *Aeneid:* "With a groan, indignant, his life fled to the Shades."

Aeolus (Aiolos) (i). In Greek mythology, the grandson of Deucalion and Pyrrha and a son of Hellen and the nymph Orseis. Aeolus' brothers were Dorus and Xuthus. Aeolus is the mythical founder of the Aeolian people. Among his many sons were Sisyphus, Athamas, and Salmoneus; among his daughters, Arne, Alcyone, Calyce, and Canace. A grandson of Aeolus, who bore his name, was the guardian of the winds.

Aeolus (Aiolos) (ii). According to Greek mythology, Aeolus, the son of Arne and Poseidon, or of Hippotes, was the guardian of the winds on the island of Aeolia. See ODYSSEY X and AENEID I.

Aeschines (Aischines). An Athenian orator, born around 390 B.C. As a leader of the pro-Macedonian party, he was DEMOSTHENES' opponent and was impeached by him in 343 B.C. The three extant speeches of Aeschines deal with his political controversies with Demosthenes and others of the anti-Macedonian party. *Against Timarchus* is a speech Aeschines delivered during his prosecution of Timarchus, who had joined with Demosthenes in charging Aeschines with betraying the Athenians in negotiating the peace treaty of 346 B.C with Philip of Macedon. Aeschines turned the prosecution on Timarchus' personal character, charging him with immorality, and Timarchus was convicted.

Aeschines' second extant speech, *On the Embassy,* is an answer to Demosthenes' charges in his oration of the same name, delivered in 343 B.C., that Aeschines had deceived the Athenians in negotiating the peace of 346 B.C. Though Aeschines' defense seems ineffective and unconvincing, he was again acquitted. In *Against Ctesiphon,* delivered in 330 B.C., he tries to prove the illegality of Ctesiphon's proposal that Demosthenes be awarded a golden crown for his services to the state. The speech is essentially an attack on Demosthenes, who in his greatest oration, *On the Crown,* answers Aeschines' charges with a long defense of his own public career. Aeschines lost his case and was fined a thousand drachmas. He did not pay the fine, but left Athens for Rhodes, where he remained for the rest of his life, teaching rhetoric.

Aeschylus (Aischylos). Greek tragic playwright, son of Euphorion, born in

525 B.C. at Eleusis, a town in Attica about fourteen miles from Athens. He came from an aristocratic family. His epitaph, which, it is thought, he himself composed, does not mention his career as a dramatist, but says that he fought at Marathon in the Persian Wars. He also fought against the Persians in the battles of Salamis and Plataea.

In 500 B.C. Aeschylus first competed for the prize for tragedy at Athens, but he did not win until 484 B.C. In 476 B.C. he visited the court of Hiero I of Syracuse, where he wrote the *Aetnaeans* in honor of the city of Aetna. Though Sophocles defeated him in a contest for tragedy in 468 B.C., Aeschylus was again victor in 467 B.C., with a trilogy, the only extant play of which is THE SEVEN AGAINST THEBES. His ORESTEIA, for which he won his last prize, was first performed in 458 B.C. In this year he once again left Athens for Gela in Sicily, where he died three years later, in 456 B.C. A well-known account of his death is that an eagle, dropping a tortoise on his head, killed him. Thus was fulfilled a prophecy that he would die as the result of a blow from heaven. Of the ninety plays he wrote, only seven remain: THE SUPPLIANTS (about 460 B.C.), THE PERSIANS (472 B.C.), *The Seven Against Thebes* (467 B.C.), PROMETHEUS BOUND (date uncertain; the variety of opinion is so great that it has been regarded as earlier than *The Persians* and later than *The Oresteia*), the three plays of the only remaining complete trilogy in Greek drama, *The Oresteia: Agamemnon, The Libation Bearers*, and *The Eumenides* (all 458 B.C.).

Aeschylus also wrote lyric poetry, but of this only brief fragments remain. Aeschylus' position as the first great tragedian is due not only to the depth and magnificence of his individual plays, but to his innovations in dramatic technique. He was the first to introduce a second actor, thus creating real dialogue and limiting the role of the chorus. He initiated the use of appropriate costumes, masks, and thick-soled boots (*cothurni*) to suggest tragic grandeur. Moreover, his later plays contain involved dramatic action and subtle characterization. Aeschylus' constant theme is the triumph of democracy over tyranny, of enlightenment and order over irrationality and violence. His language is intense and eloquent, his imagery strong; basic symbols—the eagle, the net, the snake—recur in his plays with intense emotional force. For Aristophanes' portrayal of him see THE FROGS.

Aesop (Aisopos). The supposed author of many animal fables. According to tradition Aesop was a Greek slave who lived during the sixth century B.C. Probably he was not an actual person, though he is mentioned by Herodotus, Aristophanes, and Plato. Aesop's fables were recounted in choliambic verse (see METER) by the writer Valerius Babrius, about whom nothing else is known. He probably lived in the second century A.D., and his version of the fables is extant. The fables were also told in Latin verse by Gaius Julius Phaedrus, a freedman who lived during the first century A.D. Aesop's fables became an important issue in the seventeenth-century controversy among intellectuals over whether the ancients or the moderns had superior talents. The argument came to a head in England when Sir William Temple's recommendations of the ancients Aesop and Phalaris as examples to the moderns in his "Essay on Ancient and Modern Learning" (1690) were revealed (in William Wotton's "Reflections Upon Ancient and Modern Learning" [1694] and Richard Bentley's appendix to his *Dissertation Upon the Epistles of Phalaris* [1699]) to be praises of spurious works. Jonathan Swift wittily defended Temple's incorrect position and brilliantly attacked the correct scholarship of Wotton and Bentley in *A Tale of a Tub* and *The Battle of the Books*.

Aethiopica (Aithiopika; Theagenes and Chariclea). A prose romance (third century A.D.) by HELIODORUS. The *Aethiopica* deals with the love of Theagenes and Chariclea, a priestess of Delphi, and their many adventures as they wander about Egypt. It is a sensational tale, with kidnapings, disguises, plots of all sorts, and much suspense. Finally, just as Chariclea is about to be sacrificed, she is recognized as a priestess of Ethiopia.

Aethra (Aithra). In Greek mythology, the mother of Theseus by AEGEUS or Poseidon. See Euripides' THE SUPPLIANTS.

Aetna. A poem in dactylic hexameters attributed by some to VERGIL, but probably not his. This didactic poem explains the causes of eruptions of Mt. Etna and concludes that nature is essentially moral.

Agamemnon. In Greek mythology, a son of Atreus and brother of Menelaus. As king of MYCENAE he was the leader of the Greek forces against Troy. In this role he is an important character in the ILIAD. His murder by his wife Clytemnestra is mentioned frequently in the ODYSSEY, where he appears in the Underworld (Books XI and XXIV). Aeschylus also deals with the murder of Agamemnon and its consequences in the ORESTEIA, as does Seneca in his AGAMEMNON. The *Electra* of Sophocles and that of Euripides both deal with the revenge of Orestes on Clytemnestra and her lover Aegisthus for the murder of Agamemnon. Agamemnon also has a significant role in Sophocles' AJAX, Euripides' IPHIGENIA IN AULIS and HECUBA, and Seneca's THE TROJAN WOMEN.

Agamemnon. A tragedy by Aeschylus. See under ORESTEIA.

Agamemnon. A tragedy by SENECA. The play was based on Aeschylus' *Agamemnon* as well as on other works no longer extant. Though Seneca employs the basic plot of Aeschylus' play, he makes many changes in structure and character. The prologue of Seneca's play is delivered by the ghost of Thyestes. The relationship between Clytemnestra and Aegisthus is far more important in Seneca's play, and the character of Clytemnestra is diminished by her not very convincing conflict between love and duty. Seneca also adds a Nurse of Clytemnestra, Electra, Strophius, King of Phocis, and Orestes, who escapes at the end. Cassandra describes the murder of Agamemnon; she herself is killed later. There are two choruses, one of Argive women and one of captive Trojan women.

Agathon. An Athenian tragedian, second half of the fifth century B.C. Though he made important contributions to the drama, being the first to write on a subject and characters of his own invention and to employ choral odes merely as interludes, only brief fragments of his work remain. He appears in Plato's SYMPOSIUM. Aristophanes ridicules him in the THESMOPHORIAZUSAE.

Agave (Agaue). In Greek mythology, the mother of Pentheus and an important character in Euripides' THE BACCHAE.

Agenor. In Greek mythology, the king of Tyre and father of Cadmus and Europa.

Agesilaus (Agesilaos). A king of Sparta from about 398 B.C. to 361 B.C. His victories over the Persians and the Thebans are described by XENOPHON in *Hellenica*. Xenophon also praises his character and accomplishments in his *Agesilaus*.

Agricola. A biography (A.D. 98) by TACITUS of his father-in-law, Cn. Julius Agricola. Tacitus' chief aim in this work, which appeared five years after Agricola's death, is to make known and to praise his father-in-law's virtues and accomplishments. He tells of Agricola's military successes, his various political posts, and his achievements as governor of Britain. Tacitus also summarizes the steps in Rome's conquest of Britain and relates this history to the life of Agricola by illustrating his significant role in the final stages of the conquest. In telling of how Agricola was recalled to Rome by the emperor Domitian, Tacitus writes brilliantly of the "sickness" of the state during the rule of this tyrant. The biography ends with a magnificent eulogy of Agricola.

Agrigentum. See ACRAGAS.

Aides, Aidoneus. See HADES.

Ajax (Aias) (I). In Greek mythology, a son of Telamon and one of the bravest Greek warriors in Homer's ILIAD. During the Trojan War, after Achilles' death Odysseus and Ajax both demanded his arms. When they were given to Odysseus, Ajax, mad with rage, killed a flock of sheep, imagining that they were the Greek leaders. In his play AJAX, Sophocles sympathetically depicts Ajax as he recovers his senses and is driven by agony and shame to commit suicide. In *Odyssey* XI, XXIV, Ajax appears in the Underworld.

Ajax (Aias) (II). In Greek mythology, a son of Oïleus. He was known as the "lesser Ajax" because he was inferior as a warrior to Telamonian Ajax. He led the Locrians in the Trojan War (see ILIAD XIV). Ajax forced Cassandra away from an image of Athene and raped her. Shipwrecked on his journey home from Troy, but aided by Poseidon, he managed to swim to shore. He boasted that he had saved himself despite the will of the gods, and for this arrogance Poseidon killed him by hurling the rock he stood on into the sea. See ODYSSEY III, IV.

Ajax (Aias). A tragedy (c. 447 B.C.) by SOPHOCLES. Translations: in verse, Thomas Francklin, 1759; in verse, Edward H. Plumptre, 1865; in prose R. C. Jebb, 1904; in verse, F. Storr, 1912; in verse, R. C. Trevelyan, 1919; in verse, John Moore, 1957.

MYTHICAL BACKGROUND. When Achilles died in combat, Ajax, Odysseus, and other Greek heroes competed for his arms. The leaders of the

Greek forces against Troy decided that Odysseus should have the arms. Ajax, insulted by this decision, which he thought was made by Agamemnon and Menelaus, planned to murder them at night. Because Ajax had once offended Athene by proudly refusing her aid in battle, for which he in his arrogance felt no need, Athene repaid him by afflicting him with a fit of madness. Deluded, he killed the sheep and the cattle of the Greeks, mistaking them for the Greek leaders.

SCENE. The camp of the Greeks at Troy; later, on the seashore.

SUMMARY. Athene comes to Odysseus outside the tent of Ajax, and tells him of how she afflicted Ajax with madness, which drove him to kill many sheep, mistaking them for the Greeks and to capture others and bring them to his tent to torture them. Despite Odysseus' protests, Athene summons Ajax. Still insane, he boasts of having killed Menelaus, Agamemnon, and many other Greek leaders and of having taken Odysseus captive. Athene pretends to believe him and cruelly encourages his delusion. When he leaves her and enters his tent, she turns to Odysseus and tells him to note the power of the gods over men, but Odysseus says he cannot help pitying Ajax, though he is his enemy.

When Athene and Odysseus leave, the Chorus of Seamen of Salamis enters and sings of the shame the mad deeds of Ajax have brought on them. Such madness must be the punishment of the gods. Tecmessa, the concubine of Ajax, comes out of the tent and tells the Chorus of the way in which Ajax madly slew the animals, thinking them men. The insanity has now passed, but the remembrance of the deeds he committed in his madness torments him. Ajax now comes from his tent, moaning in his despair, and calling for his son Eurysaces and his half brother Teucer. Though the Chorus tries to comfort Ajax, he cannot stop thinking about the frenzy that overcame him, and he imagines the scorn and laughter of the other Greeks. He says his name (Aias, in Greek) is suited to his wretchedness (the cry of grief is *aiai*) and speaks of his dishonor. Yet, he says, he knows that if Achilles had made the choice, he would have given his arms to him. He considers what to do: he cannot remain dishonored among the Greeks, who now hate and scorn him, nor can he return in disgrace to his father, Telamon. He must find a way to die honorably. Tecmessa pleads with Ajax not to take his own life; she says that if he dies, she and his son will become slaves of the Greeks, treated with contempt and cruelty. Ajax then asks to see his son, and the child is brought in. He says farewell to him, and despite the pleas of Tecmessa and the Chorus to remain with them, he leaves the stage.

After an ode in which the Chorus expresses sympathy for his plight, Ajax returns and pretends that Tecmessa's pleas have persuaded him not to take his own life; he says he is going to the sea to beg forgiveness of Athene and to hide his sword, a gift from Hector which has brought him only dishonor. The Chorus now sings of its joy, because Ajax is no longer tormented. A Messenger comes in to announce that Teucer has returned from battle and that the Greeks have insulted and attacked him as the kin of the mad Ajax. When the Messenger learns that Ajax has left his tent, he is disturbed, because Calchas, the prophet, has told Teucer that he must keep Ajax in his tent for this one day. Only on this day will Ajax be threatened with Athene's anger at his pride; if he is able to live through this day, he will escape her wrath. When Tecmessa hears this news, she is frightened and asks some of the seamen to find Teucer and urge him to come quickly and others to seek Ajax near the sea.

The scene shifts to the seashore, where Ajax, alone, plants his sword in the ground and prays to Zeus to send a messenger to Teucer who will tell him where he may find the body of Ajax, so that Teucer may bury it. He asks Hermes to bring him swiftly to the Underworld and the Furies to punish Agamemnon and Menelaus. He says farewell to life—to light, to his country, to Salamis, to Athens and Troy—and then falls on his sword. Tecmessa finds the dead Ajax and is joined by the Chorus of Seamen, who lament with her. Teucer then enters and learns the tragic story. He tells Tecmessa to bring her son to him before he is taken away by their enemies. Teucer then expresses his love for his half brother and his anguish over his suicide.

Menelaus comes in as Teucer and the Seamen are planning the funeral of Ajax. Regarding Ajax as a traitor, Menelaus says he must not be buried, but must be left on the beach to be consumed by the birds and thus never find peace in the world of the dead. Courageously Teucer defies Menelaus and insists that he will bury Ajax. He speaks of Ajax's courage and loyalty and the ingratitude of Menelaus. After Menelaus leaves, Agamemnon approaches, and he too tries to prevent the burial of Ajax. At the height of the argument with Teucer, Odysseus enters. He admits that, after Achilles, Ajax was the greatest of the Greek warriors, and though he was his enemy, he respected him. He persuades Agamemnon to allow the burial. Teucer and the Chorus then begin to prepare the grave of Ajax.

Alcaeus (Alkaios). A lyric poet, born about 620 B.C. in Mytilene, on the island of Lesbos. An aristocrat, he fought against a series of tyrants who had seized control of Lesbos. When the tyrant Pittacus gained absolute power, Alcaeus, like his friend Sappho, was forced to go into exile. During this period he traveled in Thrace and Egypt. Around 580 B.C. he returned to Lesbos. The date of his death is unknown.

Alcaeus wrote mostly monody in the Aeolic dialect. Only fragments of his poems remain. He was much admired by Horace, who imitated his style and meter, and by the Latin rhetorician Quintilian, who praised Alcaeus' themes and style. For his work see LYRICS.

Alcestis (Alkestis). Wife of King Admetus. See Euripides' ALCESTIS.

Alcestis (Alkestis). A tragedy (438 B.C.) by EURIPIDES. Translations: in verse, Arthur S. Way, 1912; in prose and verse, Richard Aldington, 1930; in prose, Augustus T. Murray, 1931; in verse, Richmond Lattimore, 1955.

SCENE. Pherae, outside the palace of King Admetus of Thessaly.

SUMMARY. Apollo comes out of the palace of Admetus, carrying an unstrung bow. He provides the background of the play, saying that when Zeus killed Apollo's son, Asclepius, Apollo, in a violent rage slew the Cyclops. Zeus punished Apollo by forcing him to take the role of a mortal laborer and work for King Admetus of Thessaly. To repay Admetus' kindness to him, Apollo obtained the pledge of the Fates that Admetus could escape death if someone would take his place in Hades. All his friends and relatives refused to do so except his wife, Alcestis. This is the day on which she will give her life for her husband's, and already she grows weak. Apollo sees Death with a sword in his hand approaching the palace. When Death observes Apollo he stops and scolds the god for influencing the Fates and saving Admetus. Apollo tries to persuade Death to allow Alcestis to live to old age, but Death, true to his nature, refuses. Apollo prophesies that Heracles will snatch Alcestis from Death. As Apollo leaves, Death enters the palace to seize Alcestis.

The Chorus of Elders of Pherae enters, praising Alcestis and mourning her imminent death. A Woman Servant of Alcestis, who has come from the palace, sadly describes Alcestis' preparations for death and praises her loyalty to her husband. The Servant also speaks of the agony of Admetus, who weeps as he holds his dying wife in his arms. As the Chorus mourns the inevitable death of Alcestis, Admetus enters, holding his wife, while their two children cling to their mother. Alcestis, on the verge of death, is frightened as she imagines herself entering the world of the dead. She asks Admetus not to marry again, because she fears a stepmother will treat her children badly. Admetus promises to love and mourn for Alcestis for the rest of his life. Saying a last farewell to her husband and children, Alcestis dies. Her son Eumelus cries out in grief. Admetus gives orders for the funeral and mourning period. The body of Alcestis is carried into the palace. Admetus follows with his children. The Chorus praises the goodness of Alcestis, who willingly gave her life to save her husband from death.

Heracles, wearing a lion skin and carrying a huge club, enters and asks the Chorus if Admetus is at home. He explains that he is seeking the horses of Diomedes, which he must obtain to accomplish one of the twelve labors imposed on him by King Eurystheus. Admetus, dressed in mourning, comes out of the palace, but tries to hide his grief because he feels obliged by the laws of hospitality to offer his guest a warm welcome and spare him pain. Though Heracles realizes that a member of Admetus' family has died, Admetus avoids speaking directly of Alcestis' death and insists that Heracles remain as his guest. Admetus instructs his servants to close the doors of the guest room so that Heracles will be spared the sounds of mourning.

The funeral procession of Alcestis comes from the palace. Admetus and his children walk behind the body. Pheres, the father of Admetus, comes to comfort his son, but Admetus angrily refuses his father's burial gifts, saying it would have been proper for Pheres, an old man, to offer his life for his son rather than allowing the young Alcestis to die. Admetus rejects his father and mother, declaring that only Alcestis cared for him. Pheres defends himself, saying he reared his son and gave him land and power, but it is surely not his duty to die for him. It is Admetus who is a coward, says Pheres, for he chose to avoid death by accepting the sacrifice of a woman. It is Admetus who is selfish and cruel; he is responsible for the death of Alcestis. Father and son part bitterly, and the funeral procession goes on its way.

A Man Servant enters and says that Heracles has been drinking and singing wildly. Then Heracles staggers in, carrying wine. When the Servant reveals to him that Alcestis has died, Heracles goes out, determined to bring her back from Hades.

Meanwhile, Admetus and the Chorus mourn for Alcestis. Admetus realizes he has been selfish and cowardly. He feels that in some ways Alcestis' fate is more tolerable than his own. Soon Heracles returns, leading a veiled woman whom, he says, he won in a contest. He asks Admetus to care for the woman until he returns from accomplishing his labor. Admetus is reluctant to keep the woman under his roof, especially since she seems to resemble Alcestis, but finally he agrees to do so. Heracles takes off the woman's veil and reveals Alcestis alive. Heracles has restored her from death, but she may not speak for the three days necessary for her purification after the rites for the dead. Heracles then goes off to accomplish his task, leaving Admetus rejoicing in his good fortune.

Alcibiades (Alkibiades). A Greek general, born into a noble family of Athens about 450 B.C. Because his father died when Alcibiades was only about three years old, he became a ward of his relative Pericles. A handsome and brilliant man, Alcibiades was popular with both men and women, but he was unethical in his dealings with people and unscrupulous in political and military affairs. He was a friend of Socrates, and the two men fought together in the campaign against Potidaea (432–431 B.C.). Alcibiades' military skill there and at Delium helped to bring about his election as *strategus* (general) in 420 B.C. He helped to renew hostilities with Sparta after the Peace of Nicias in 421 B.C. and was one of the three generals chosen by the Athenians to lead the expedition against Sicily. For his involvement in the destruction of the herms throughout Athens, see THE PELOPONNESIAN WARS VI. Despite Alcibiades' desertion to Sparta, he was called back to Athens in 407 B.C., and once again became a popular figure there and the leading general in the struggle with Sparta. After Athens' defeat in the Peloponnesian War, Alcibiades attempted to ally himself with the Persian king, Artaxerxes, but a Spartan command was issued for his death, and he was slain in 404 B.C. Alcibiades' career is treated by Thucydides, he appears in some of Plato's dialogues, and Persius criticizes him in SATIRE IV. The modern novelist Mary Renault presents an interesting interpretation of Alcibiades in *The Last of the Wine*.

Alcibiades (Alkibiades). A dialogue by PLATO named after the brilliant and unscrupulous political leader and warrior who was a friend of Socrates. The dialogue, the authorship of which is questioned by some scholars, deals with questions of ethics and the knowledge needed by a political leader.

Alcinous (Alkinoos). The king of the Phaeacians in the ODYSSEY (VI–IX) and the *Argonautica* of Apollonius Rhodius.

Alcmaeon (Alkmaion). The son of the seer AMPHIARAUS. He participated in the expedition against Thebes of the Epigoni (the descendants of the Seven Against Thebes). For murdering his mother Eriphyle he was, like Orestes, hounded by the Furies, and wandered from place to place, seeking release from his guilt. At Psophis, Alcmaeon married Arsinoë, the daughter of Phegeus, and presented her with the necklace of Harmonia, made by Hephaestus, which, though a beautiful piece of work, always brought bad fortune. The necklace had belonged to Eriphyle, who had obtained it from Polyneices when he bribed her to persuade Amphiaraus to fight against Thebes. When a blight fell on the land of Psophis, Alcmaeon left to seek once more for purification. Alcmaeon then married Callirhoe, a daughter of Oeneus, king of Calydon. When she desired the necklace of Harmonia, Alcmaeon deceived Phegeus in order to obtain it, but Phegeus, realizing that he had been tricked, ordered his sons to kill Alcmaeon. Alcmaeon's murder was avenged by his sons, Acarnan and Amphoteros, who slew Phegeus and his sons.

Alcman (Alkman). A Greek lyric poet, probably born at Sardis. He came to Sparta during the second half of the seventh century B.C. At Sparta Alcman was known for his choral odes written for the festivals, especially for his *partheneia*, or maiden songs. An extended fragment of one of these is our earliest example of Greek choral poetry (see PARTHENEION). Alcman wrote other types of choral poetry and also monody—love songs, drinking songs, and others—but only brief fragments of these remain.

Alcmena (Alkmene). In Greek mythology, the wife of Amphitryon, and, by Zeus, the mother of Heracles. She appears in Plautus' AMPHITRYON and Euripides' THE CHILDREN OF HERACLES.

Alcyone (Alkyone). In Greek mythology, wife of Ceyx. When Ceyx was drowned Alcyone was overcome with grief. The gods pitied her and transformed both her husband and her into birds. (See Ovid's *Metamorphoses* XI.) Another explanation for their metamorphosis is that they were impious.

Alexander (Alexandros) the Great. The son of Philip of Macedon and Olympias, born at Pella (Macedonia) in 356 B.C. His teacher was Aristotle. When Philip was killed in 336 B.C., Alexander, then twenty years old, became king of Macedon. As soon as he ascended the throne, Alexander put down rebellions in Greece and Macedon. He then invaded Persia and was victorious at the battle at the River Granicus in 334 B.C. He conquered Sardis, Halicarnassus, Lycia, and the next year he again defeated the Persians in the battle of Issus

(333 B.C.). Alexander now conquered Syria and turned to Egypt, where he found no opposition. In 331 B.C. he established the city of Alexandria at the mouth of the Nile. At the temple of Jupiter Ammon in Libya he was declared a god, the son of Jupiter Ammon.

While Alexander remained in Egypt, Darius, the king of Persia, had gathered another army. Alexander invaded Persia again in 331 B.C. and completed his conquest of that nation. Now ruler of Asia, he set out in 327 B.C. to conquer India. After four years of attempting to penetrate that land he reached the River Hyphasis, where his fatigued and discouraged army demanded that he return home. After a long and difficult march the army reached Susa in 324 B.C. In the summer of 323 B.C. Alexander died of fever in Babylon at the age of thirty-two.

Alexander was a great military leader who almost accomplished his aim: to create and rule a world empire. His influence on the culture of ancient Greece was twofold: he ended forever the autonomy of Greek city-states, which became part of his huge empire, and he spread Greek civilization and culture throughout the East. See Plutarch's life of Alexander.

Alexandria (Alexandreia). Egyptian city on the western mouth of the Nile, founded by Alexander the Great in 331 B.C. It was one of the main centers of culture during the Hellenistic period, and was especially known for its Museum (actually an Academy where scholars sponsored by the state engaged in study and research) and its great Library founded by Ptolemy I.

Allecto. One of the FURIES. She plays an important role in Vergil's AENEID (VII).

Amata. The wife of King Latinus and the mother of Aeneas' destined bride Lavinia. See AENEID VII, XII.

Amazons, The (Amazones). A mythical tribe of female warriors, who lived in Asia Minor. Their name means "breastless"; so that they might better be able to use the bow, they cut off their right breasts. They fought on the side of the Trojans in the Trojan War, in which their queen Penthesilea was slain by Achilles. Theseus engaged in battle with the Amazons and fell in love with their queen Hippolyte, who bore his son Hippolytus. In some versions of the myth it is Antiope whom Theseus loved.

amoebean verses. Verses used mainly in pastoral poetry, sung alternately by poets engaging in a contest.

Amores (Love Poems). Elegies by OVID (before A.D. 8). Translations: in prose, Grant Showerman, 1921; in verse, Rolfe Humphries, 1957.

S U M M A R Y. The *Amores* consists of forty-nine elegies, mainly on the subject of love. In the "Epigram of the Poet Himself," which introduces the work, OVID explains that in the original edition there were five books of elegies, but now there are only three. Many of the love poems are addressed to Corinna, who is probably not an actual woman but a composite of a number of women

Ovid knew or imagined. Ovid's love poems are mainly light in spirit, witty, and charming; he writes of the great pleasures of love, but even its disappointments are amusing in his verses. Though the experiences he relates are not necessarily his own and he is not always sincere in his expressions of love for a particular woman, what is genuine is his delight in woman herself: fair or dark, short or tall, responsive or shy, young or mature, all women enchant him (II, 4). He declares himself the servant of Cupid (I, 1) and Venus (I, 3), and no one was ever more willingly enslaved. There is little of the conflict of love in Ovid and much of the sensual pleasure and amusement.

Many of the elegies are concerned with the subject of poetry—Ovid's own or that of others. In fact, Ovid's only real conflict in the *Amores* seems to be whether to devote himself to his favorite subject of love or to seek fame through the more traditional themes and techniques of the tragic poet (II, 18; III, 1, 15). In I, 15 Ovid deals with a theme common in classical poetry: like Sappho, Horace, Martial, and others, he writes of the immortality of verse. After speaking of the certainty of the everlasting fame of Homer, Hesiod, Callimachus, Sophocles, Aratus, Menander, Ennius, Accius, Varro, Lucretius, Vergil, Tibullus, and Gallus, Ovid declares that he too will live on in his poetry after his death. The best part of him will survive. In his lament on the death of Tibullus (III, 9) Ovid again says that "only song can avoid the greedy funeral pyre." Though he mourns over the death of Tibullus, he knows the poet will live forever in his work. Even though Ovid rejects serious subjects of poetry—the wars of the gods and other traditional themes—and says he will write only of love in light elegiacs, he speaks with ardor about the fabulous powers of song (II, 1).

Amphiaraus (Amphiaraos). In Greek mythology, a seer who participated in the Calydonian boar hunt (see MELEAGER) and in the expedition of the Argonauts. His wife Eriphyle persuaded him to fight with the Seven Against Thebes. Amphiaraus foresaw his own death in this expedition and made his children promise to avenge him by murdering their mother. At Thebes the earth swallowed him.

Amphion. See ANTIOPE (1).

Amphitryon. In Greek mythology, the son of Alcaeus and grandson of Perseus. He was married to Alcmena, to whom Zeus came disguised as Amphitryon. The child of this union was Heracles. See Euripides' THE MADNESS OF HERACLES, Plautus' AMPHITRYON, and Seneca's HERCULES FURENS.

Amphitryon (Amphitruo). A comedy by PLAUTUS. Translations: in verse, Lionel Casson, 1963; in prose and verse, E. F. Watling, 1964.

BACKGROUND. *Amphitryon* is the only extant Roman burlesque of a mythological subject. It is based on the popular myth of Jupiter's love for Alcmena, the wife of Amphitryon, and the god's assumption of Amphitryon's form in order to deceive her. When Amphitryon went off to war against the Teloboians, he left his wife Alcmena pregnant. Just before Amphitryon's return Jupiter took his form and spent a night with Alcmena, during which she conceived Hercules. Thus the twins to which she later gave birth were Iphicles, son of Amphitryon, and Hercules, son of Jupiter.

In Plautus' *Amphitryon* the god Mercury takes the form of Sosia, the slave of Amphitryon, and the double disguises add to the confusion and humor resulting from the deception.

SCENE. Thebes, before the house of Amphitryon.

SUMMARY. In the Prologue, Mercury (in the form of Sosia) reveals that Jupiter (as Amphitryon) is now inside with Alcmena. When the real Sosia enters to inform Alcmena that the victorious Amphitryon has just landed and will soon be home, Mercury mistreats him in an effort to prevent his entering the house. Sosia is utterly mystified at discovering someone who looks just like him and who knows all the details of his life. Jupiter, who has prolonged the night in order to enjoy greater pleasure with Alcmena, finally leaves with Mercury, allowing the day to dawn.

The confusion really begins when Sosia reenters with Amphitryon, who refuses to believe his slave's account of the events of the night before. Moreover, Alcmena cannot understand why her husband, who, she thinks, has just left for battle, has returned so soon. Amphitryon, who has not been home recently, concludes that his wife is insane. Resolved to learn what has really happened, he goes off to find a relative who can prove he was on board ship during the night.

Disguised as Amphitryon, Jupiter pays another visit to Alcmena. Meanwhile, Amphitryon returns and is mocked by Mercury in the form of Sosia. There is a gap in the manuscript at this point. From the few lines that remain it is assumed that Alcmena comes out of the house and again quarrels with Amphitryon. Jupiter and Amphitryon meet and argue fiercely. Then Jupiter reenters the house, for Alcmena is about to give birth. Puzzled and angry, Amphitryon decides to murder everyone in the house, when suddenly he hears a peal of thunder. He falls to the ground. Bromia, the servant of Alcmena, comes out of the house and describes the lightning and thunder that accompanied the birth of Alcmena's twins, one of whom (Hercules) is already large and powerful. Then the voice of Jupiter spoke to Alcmena and revealed that he was her lover and the father of Hercules. Amphitryon is the father of the other. Jupiter then speaks to Amphitryon, who rejoices in the god's prophecy of the future glory of Hercules.

Amycus (Amykos). In Greek mythology, the king of the Bebryces. A son of Poseidon, he was a great boxer. Apollonius Rhodius describes his boxing match wth Pollux, one of the Argonauts, who defeated and killed him. When the Bebryces tried to avenge this insult to Amycus, the Argonauts drove them off. See also Theocritus' IDYL XXII.

Anabasis. See XENOPHON.

Anacreon (Anakreon). Lyric poet, born about 570 B.C. at Teos in Ionia. He left Teos for Abdera in Thrace, but spent little time there. He stayed for a while at the court of Polycrates, tyrant of Samos, and then went to the court of the tyrant Hipparchus at Athens. He may have died in Thessaly, but neither the place nor the date of his death is certain.

Anacreon wrote many monodic lyrics in a variety of meters, but most of these poems have been lost. He also wrote iambics and elegiacs that have not survived. His chief dialect was Ionic. Poets of the Hellenistic and Byzantine periods imitated Anacreon and produced sixty poems called the *Anacreontics,* which were often mistaken for Anacreon's work by later periods. Anacreon's style and tone have been emulated by many other poets, but none has equaled the skill of the seventeenth-century English poet Robert Herrick, who revitalizes the spirit of Anacreon as he imitates his poems. For his work see LYRICS.

Anaxagoras. A Greek philosopher, born in Clazomenae in Ionia around 500 B.C. Anaxagoras lived in Athens for about thirty years and was a good friend of Pericles. Only fragments remain of his *On Nature.* Anaxagoras believed in a "supreme intelligence" (*Nous*), of which he said: "Other things all contain a part of everything, but Mind is infinite and self-ruling, and is mixed with no Thing, but is alone by itself" (Kathleen Freeman, *Ancilla to the Pre-Socratic Philosophers,* Harvard University Press, 1957, p. 84). This Mind or supreme intelligence directs the unlimited and changing elements of the universe. Anaxagoras was accused of impiety by the Athenians, and only the intervention of Pericles saved his life, but he was banished from Athens.

Anaximander (Anaximandros). A Greek philosopher and scientist of Miletus, early sixth century B.C. He believed that life originated in the sea, that the essence of living things is an unlimited material (the infinite), and that the "unlimited" cannot be destroyed. He is thought to be the first Greek writer of prose. The titles of his works are unknown, and only the briefest fragments of them remain.

Anaximenes. A Greek philosopher of Miletus, middle of the sixth century B.C. Only one complete sentence of his work survives. He was the teacher of the philosopher Anaxagoras. He believed that air was the essence of all things and that the soul was made of air.

Anchises. In Greek mythology, the son of Capys and Themiste, was loved by Aphrodite. The child of Anchises and the goddess was Aeneas, the leader of the Trojans. The love of Aphrodite for Anchises is narrated in HOMERIC HYMN V. He has a significant role in Vergil's AENEID.

Ancus Marcius. One of Rome's legendary kings. Lucretius refers to him in a brilliant passage on death in *De Rerum Natura,* III, 1025 (see ON THE NATURE OF THINGS).

Andocides (Andokides). An early Athenian orator, second half of the fifth century B.C. He was accused of two major crimes against the state, mutilation of the herms in 415 B.C. (see THE PELOPONNESIAN WAR VI) and desecration of the Eleusinian mysteries in 399 B.C. When he admitted his involvement in the destruction of the herms and named his associates, he received a sentence of *atimia* (disgrace), which meant banishment from Athens. In one of his extant speeches, *On His Return* (410 B.C.), he asked that the sentence be repealed, but his plea was unsuccessful. In 403 B.C., however, Andocides was permitted to return to Athens. He defended himself against the charge of violating the Eleusinian mysteries in another extant speech, *On the Mysteries.* A third oration attributed to him by most authorities is *On the Peace,* in which he pleads for peace with Sparta during the Corinthian War (390 B.C.). These orations are his only remaining works.

Andria. See THE WOMAN OF ANDROS.

Andromache. In Greek mythology, the daughter of Eëtion and the wife of Hector, the great Trojan hero. She appears in the ILIAD and Euripides' THE TROJAN WOMEN, and is the heroine of Euripides' ANDROMACHE. Aeneas encounters her and her second husband, Helenus, in AENEID III.

Andromache. A tragedy (c. 426 B.C.) by Euripides. Translations: in prose, E. P. Coleridge, 1891; in verse, Arthur S. Way, 1912; in verse, Hugh O. Meredith, 1937; in prose, Van L. Johnson, 1955; in verse, John Frederick Nims, 1958.

S C E N E . Thessaly, before the palace of Neoptolemus. Nearby is a temple of Thetis with an altar before it.

S U M M A R Y . Andromache clings to the altar before the temple of Thetis, and in a long speech dealing with her fall from a noble position to her present degradation, provides the background of the play. Andromache speaks of the time when, as the wife of Hector, the great Trojan hero, she enjoyed an enviable position, living in the palace of Priam, the ruler of Troy. After Hector was killed in the Trojan War, the Greeks destroyed Troy. She was taken captive, and her son Astyanax was hurled to his death from the walls of the city by the Greeks. Andromache was taken to Greece as the slave and concubine of Neoptolemus, the son of the dead Achilles. She has been living with Neoptolemus and has borne him a son, Molossus. When Neoptolemus married Hermione, the daughter of Helen and Menelaus, Andromache's troubles increased. Hermione, who bore no children, accused Andromache of casting some evil spell on her and of trying to break up her marriage. Hermione wants to kill her, and now Menelaus has come from Sparta to help his daughter plan the murder. Andromache has come to the temple of Thetis in the hope that the goddess will protect her and has sent her son away because she fears for his life. Neoptolemus has left for Delphi to atone for his earlier impudence in demanding that Apollo explain why Achilles died.

A Servant enters and warns Andromache that Menelaus and Hermione plan to kill her son Molossus. Andromache persuades the Servant to go to King Peleus, the grandfather of Neoptolemus, and ask for help. After the Servant goes out Andromache returns to her sorrowful thoughts on the loss of her beloved husband and her own captivity. The Chorus of Thessalian Women enters and expresses its compassion for Andromache.

Hermione enters and reveals her hostility toward and contempt for

Andromache. She blames Andromache for her husband's lack of interest in her and her inability to bear a child and declares that Andromache will die. Andromache points out to Hermione that her own pride and selfishness drive her husband away. She advises her not to imitate her mother, Helen, whose passion was so destructive. The women continue to quarrel until Hermione leaves. After a choral ode dealing with the judgment of Paris and the Trojan War, from which the present suffering derives, Menelaus enters, bringing with him Andromache's son Molossus, whom he threatens to kill if Andromache continues to refuse to leave the altar. Andromache expresses her contempt for Menelaus, calling him unworthy of the conquest of Troy. When Menelaus offers her the choice of giving her life for her son's, Andromache rushes from the altar and embraces her child, glad to have an opportunity to save his life. She has been tricked by Menelaus, however, who has her seized and informs her that Hermione will now decide the fate of Molossus. When Andromache realizes she has been deceived, she inveighs against Spartan dishonesty, greed, cruelty, and evil.

Andromache and Molossus go out briefly, while the Chorus laments their fate, and then return with their hands bound. They are followed by Menelaus, who coldly tells them they must die. Soon King Peleus enters, and after a long quarrel with Menelaus, he frees Andromache and Molossus. Menelaus gives in for the present, saying he must return to Sparta to wage war on a neighboring city. He says he will come back and persuade Neoptolemus to punish Andromache. Peleus comforts Andromache, promising to shelter her, and the Chorus praises him.

The Nurse enters and reveals to the Chorus that Hermione, afraid of Neoptolemus' wrath when he hears of her plot against Andromache, is contemplating suicide. Carrying a sword, Hermione comes in and talks wildly of her fear of her husband and her desire to kill herself. As the Nurse tries to calm her, Orestes, the nephew of Menelaus, enters, seeking Hermione. She welcomes him enthusiastically and immediately asks his help. Orestes, who was betrothed to Hermione before her marriage to Neoptolemus, reveals that he has come to take her away and that he has arranged for the assassination of Neoptolemus at Delphi. Hermione and Orestes go off together. Soon Peleus returns, saying he has been told that Hermione has deserted her home. The Chorus replies that this report is true and that Orestes plans to murder Neoptolemus. Soon a Messenger reports that Neoptolemus, while praying to Apollo, was murdered by Orestes and his comrades. As the Messenger leaves, the body of Neoptolemus is carried in. Peleus and the Chorus mourn the death of the young man and Peleus curses the marriage to Hermione that destroyed his grandson. At this moment of intense grief, Thetis appears as the *deus ex machina*. The sea-goddess announces that Neoptolemus is to be buried at Delphi, where his tomb will be a reproach for the violent death inflicted on him; Andromache will marry Helenus, the brother of Hector, and will settle in Molossia, where her son and his descendants will be kings; Peleus will become immortal and live with Thetis forever in the house of Nereus, her father. Thetis releases Peleus from the suffering he endures over the death of Neoptolemus; he leaves for Delphi to bury his grandson before joining the goddess to take on immortality.

Andromeda (Andromede). See PERSEUS.

Anna. The sister of Dido, queen of Carthage, in AENEID IV.

Annals (1). (**Annales, Ab Excessu Divi Augusti,** From the Death of the Deified Augustus). A history by TACITUS, probably written around A.D. 115–117. Translations: John Jackson, 1925; Michael Grant, 1959.

S U M M A R Y . The *Annals,* only part of which remain, originally consisted of eighteen books dealing with the period in Roman history from the death of Augustus in A.D. 14 to the death of Nero in A.D. 68. The text that remains consists of Books I–IV, part of Book V, most of Book VI, most of Book XI, Books XII–XV, and the beginning of Book XVI.

Book I (A.D. 14–15) begins with a criticism of the existing histories of the reigns of Tiberius, Caligula, Claudius, and Nero, declaring that these are untrustworthy because their authors were restrained by fear while these emperors were alive and influenced by the general hatred for them after their deaths. Tacitus himself intends to deal with the last part of Augustus' reign, the return of Tiberius, and the emperors who followed him without wrath or partiality (*sine ira et studio*). After briefly summarizing the reign of Augustus, Tacitus goes on to that of Tiberius. Soon after he came to power the legions in Pannonia, hoping that a change in monarchs would help to bring about civil war, mutinied. Tiberius sent his son Drusus to Pannonia to suppress this uprising and his adopted son Germanicus to crush a rebellion in Germany. Two campaigns of Germanicus against the Germans are described.

Book II (A.D. 16–19) deals with Germanicus' third campaign in Germany and his victory over the German leader Arminius. When trouble arose in the Eastern provinces, Germanicus was sent there with Cn. Piso, governor of Syria. Germanicus grew sick and died, and it was thought that Piso had poisoned him.

Book III (A.D. 20–22) begins with the return to Italy of Agrippina, the widow of Germanicus, with her two children. Her grief and the sympathy of the Roman people for her are described. Then Tacitus deals with Piso's trial, the hostility the Romans felt toward him, and his death either by murder or suicide. The rest of the book is concerned with the growing corruption in private and political life in Rome.

Book IV (A.D. 23–28) deals with Aelius Sejanus, the favorite of the Emperor Tiberius, who seduced Livia, the wife of Tiberius' son Drusus Caesar, and then with her aid had Drusus poisoned in A.D. 23. Sejanus is described as a fearless, arrogant, overly ambitious, hypocritical man. Sejanus also tried to get rid of the three children of Germanicus. When he asked permission to marry Livia, Tiberius neither forbade the marriage nor consented, suggesting that the Roman people would object. Tacitus then discusses Tiberius' decision to leave

35

Rome and take up residence at Capri. The Emperor, says Tacitus, may have been persuaded to do so by the scheming Sejanus, as most historians suggest, but Tacitus suspects there were also other reasons: Tiberius' desire to commit his acts of lust and cruelty in secret and his self-consciousness about his hideous appearance, his completely bald head, and his ulcerous face.

Book V (A.D. 29), which is fragmentary, deals with the death of Tiberius' mother Livia (later called Julia Augusta). Unfortunately the parts of the book describing the fall of Sejanus in A.D. 31 are not extant. (Juvenal mentions Sejanus in Satire X and Ben Jonson wrote a play Sejanus.)

Book VI (A.D. 31–37) describes the brutal murder of the two surviving children of Sejanus and the lust and violence of Tiberius. Tacitus tells of Drusus, the son of Germanicus, who was starved to death in prison, of the death of his mother Agrippina by suicide or murder, and of the countless political intrigues at Rome which resulted in murder and suicide. Cocceius Nerva, a close friend of Tiberius, observing the corruption at Rome, decided to starve himself to death so that he could at least die honorably. The book ends with a description of the death of Tiberius and a brief summary of his life.

Book XI (A.D. 47–49) begins with the seventh year of the reign of Claudius, whose wife was the notorious Messalina. Though still married to Claudius in A.D. 48, Messalina went through a marriage ceremony with a senator, Silius. Both she and Silius were killed.

Book XII (A.D. 49–54) describes the marriage of Claudius to his niece Agrippina and Claudius' adoption of her son Domitius, who was to become the Emperor Nero. Agrippina persuaded Claudius to recall Annaeus Seneca from exile, and he became the tutor of her son. Domitius was married to Claudius' daughter Octavia. In Britain the Roman army under P. Ostorius Scapula defeated the Silurians of South Wales. Caratacus, the king of the Silurians, was captured and taken to Rome. Claudius allowed him to go free, but he had to remain in Rome. The book ends with a description of the poisoning of Claudius by Agrippina. Nero then became emperor (A.D. 54).

Book XIII (A.D. 55–58) deals with the first three years of Nero's reign. Learning that the Parthian king Vologeses had appointed his brother Tiridates king of Armenia, Nero sent Cn. Domitius Corbulo to lead an attack against Tiridates. The Senate applauded Nero's choice of Corbulo. When Agrippina found that she could no longer control her son, she supported Claudius' son Britannicus. Nero had him poisoned and expelled Agrippina from the palace. Nero, who detested his wife Octavia, fell in love with a freedwoman, Acte, and later with Poppaea Sabina, a beautiful woman whom Tacitus describes as having everything but a soul.

Book XIV (A.D. 59–62) Spurred on by Poppaea, Nero had his mother murdered. An uprising in Britain led by Boudicca was put down, and Corbulo was victorious in Armenia. Nero sent Octavia into exile in Pandataria, where she was killed, and he married Poppaea.

Book XV (A.D. 62–65) begins with an account of Corbulo's request that Nero send a commander to defend the Roman forces in Armenia. Nero selected the consul L. Caesennius Paetus, but, without the help of the troops of Corbulo, Paetus and his men were forced to surrender to the Parthians. Paetus was called back, and Corbulo was given complete charge of the Roman army in the East. His conquest of Armenia reduced the country to a dependency of Rome. A long description is given of the great fire of Rome, which lasted for six days in A.D. 64 and destroyed most of Rome. The reconstruction of the city is described. A long section is devoted to the conspiracy led by C. Calpurnius Piso to murder Nero, which resulted in the death of many Romans, among them Lucan and Seneca.

Book XVI (A.D. 65–66) describes the excesses of Nero and his extravagant indulgence in every whim. He insisted on competing in a song contest. At the end of the festival, coming upon the pregnant Poppaea, Nero, in a fit of rage, kicked her. Tacitus attributes her death to this blow, though some writers believe that poison was also used. Tacitus analyzes the character of Petronius, once a favorite of Nero, but now suspected by Nero of intrigue, as a result of the lies of the jealous schemer Tigellinus. When ordered by Nero to remain at Cumae, Petronius committed suicide. The rest of the book describes other acts of cruelty and violence by Nero and contains Tacitus' mournful comment on Rome's history of blood and terror.

Annals (Annales) (II). See ENNIUS.

Antaeus (Antaios). A giant, son of Poseidon and Ge, who was always victorious in wrestling matches, because, when he was thrown to the ground, the Earth, his mother, renewed his strength. Heracles, aware of Antaeus' relationship with Earth, held the giant up in the air and throttled him.

Antenor. An elder of Troy who appears in ILIAD III, VII.

Anticlea (Antikleia). The wife of Laertes and mother of Odysseus, whom he visits in the Underworld in ODYSSEY XI.

Antigone. A daughter of Oedipus and Jocasta. For her story see Sophocles' OEDIPUS AT COLONUS and ANTIGONE, Aeschylus' SEVEN AGAINST THEBES, and Euripides' THE PHOENICIAN WOMEN.

Antigone. A tragedy (c. 442 B.C.) by Sophocles. Translations: in verse, G. H. Palmer, 1899; in prose, R. C. Jebb, 1904; in verse, F. Storr, 1912; in prose, Shaemas O'Sheel, 1931; in verse, Dudley Fitts and Robert Fitzgerald, 1938; in verse, Theodore Howard Banks, 1950; in verse, Elizabeth Wyckoff, 1954; in verse, Paul Roche, 1958; in verse, H. D. F. Kitto, 1962.

MYTHICAL BACKGROUND. Just before Oedipus died he cursed his sons Polyneices and Eteocles, prophesying that they would kill each other. The two brothers quarreled over the throne of Thebes, and Eteocles, the younger, sent Polyneices into exile. Eteocles became king of Thebes. Polyneices went to Argos, where he married Argeia, the daughter of Adrastus. Polyneices persuaded his father-in-law to wage war on Thebes. Adrastus led the expedition,

and Polyneices and six other warriors joined forces with him to make up the
Seven against Thebes. During the war Eteocles and Polyneices met in single
combat and slew each other. Creon, their mother's brother, who then became
king of Thebes, ordered that Eteocles, the defender of the city, be buried with
full honors, but he refused burial to Polyneices, thus denying him peace in the
Underworld.

SCENE. Thebes, before the palace of Oedipus.

SUMMARY. The daughters of Oedipus, Antigone and Ismene, discuss
Creon's edict that Eteocles will be buried with honor but that Polyneices must
lie unburied to be consumed by the birds and dogs. Whoever disobeys this
edict will be put to death by stoning. Antigone declares that she will not obey
Creon's decree. A noble and courageous young woman, she is devoted not
only to the memory of her brother and her responsibilities to her family but to
her own unswerving principles, to the laws of the gods as opposed to the
ephemeral laws of man. Ismene, a gentle and passive girl, accepts the rule of
Creon; she cannot defy the law of the state. Antigone rather harshly tells her
sister that she alone will place earth upon their brother, a symbol of the rites
of burial, and the sisters leave the stage. The Chorus of Theban Elders enters
and sings an ode that deals with the attack of the Seven against Thebes and
their defeat by the Theban army.

Creon enters with two attendants. He speaks of his decree, which evokes
only a lukewarm response from the Leader of the Chorus. A guard enters and
reports that someone has placed earth on the body of Polyneices. The Leader of
the Chorus suggests that this may be the work of the gods, but this idea only
makes Creon angry. He threatens the Guard with torture and death if he does
not find the person who disobeyed his decree.

When Creon and the Guard leave the stage, the Chorus sings a beautiful
ode on man, the greatest marvel of all the marvels on earth. Man conquers the
sea and the earth. He catches the birds of the air and the fish of the sea; he
tames wild beasts. He has the powers of thought and speech, yet despite all his
conquests, he is the victim of death. Man, the artful creature, can achieve good
or evil. When he honors the gods and upholds the laws of the land and
cherishes justice, his state flourishes, but the corrupt man has no nation.

The Guard then comes in leading Antigone. He calls out for Creon, declaring he has found Antigone burying her brother. Creon is shocked by the
news. Antigone defends her disobedience of Creon's edict, saying that in burying
her brother she was obeying the laws of the gods. Ismene enters and offers to
share Antigone's punishment, but Antigone refuses, saying that Ismene chose
life, she death. Ismene asks Creon if he really intends to carry out his threat and
kill Antigone, who is the betrothed of his own son, Haemon. Creon's reply is
that Antigone must die. Ismene and Antigone leave the stage, guarded by
attendants.

The Chorus sings an ode in which it relates the present suffering of Antigone to the history of sorrow of the family of Labdacus, father of Laius. The theme of conflict and suffering continuing through the generations from parent to child is a familiar one in Greek myth and tragedy. The chorus then deals with another theme characteristic of Greek tragedy: when mortals exceed the mean in love or hate, when they go beyond the norm in experience or feeling, they inevitably suffer.

Haemon enters and tries to persuade his father to change his mind about Antigone's punishment, declaring that her deed was glorious. When he realizes that Creon cannot be moved, Haemon calls him unjust, and as he goes out the young man tells his father that he will never see him again. Creon informs the Chorus that he intends to imprison Antigone in a rocky vault, where she can pray to Hades for release.

Antigone comes out of the palace, to be led to her death by Creon's attendants. In a lyrical dialogue with the Chorus Antigone says sadly that she will never see the sunlight again, she will never participate in the traditional marriage rites, but instead will be married to Hades. Creon enters and coldly urges the attendants on; they must imprison Antigone in the vault and leave her. This is Creon's way of avoiding a direct murder of Antigone; as he says, his hands are clean, yet he knows she will die in the vault.

After Antigone has been led away, the blind prophet Tiresias is led in by a boy. Tiresias rebukes Creon for allowing the body of Polyneices to lie unburied and for sending Antigone to her death. He predicts that Creon will regret his tyrannical acts. Influenced by the prophet's words, Creon is deeply troubled. Finally he accepts the advice of the Leader of the Chorus that he free Antigone from her tomb, and he and his servants rush off to the vault.

A Messenger comes in and begins to tell a dreadful tale about the deaths of Antigone and Haemon. Then Eurydice, the wife of Creon, enters and asks the Messenger to tell her the whole story. He tells of how Creon and his servants entered the tomb to find that Antigone had hanged herself. Haemon, embracing her dead body, wept over his bride and his father's evil deeds. When the young man saw Creon he spat in his father's face, then drew his sword and, as Creon fled, killed himself. Dying, Haemon embraced the corpse of Antigone. After hearing this terrible report Eurydice enters the palace. The Messenger follows shortly after. Then Creon enters with attendants carrying the body of Haemon. Soon the Messenger appears again to announce that Eurydice has killed herself. The doors of the palace are opened and her corpse is revealed. Creon accepts his guilt for the death of his loved ones. As he laments over the bodies of his wife and his son, he calls himself their slayer.

Antinous (Antinoos). The chief suitor of Penelope in the ODYSSEY.

Antiope (1). According to Homer, the daughter of the river-god Asopus. She was loved by Zeus and bore him the twins Amphion and Zethus. In later myth she was the daughter of Nycteus, king of Thebes, from whom she fled because of his wrath over her love affair with Zeus. She went to Sicyon and asked its king Epopeus for protection, but he was killed by Antiope's uncle Lycus, who conquered Sicyon and imprisoned Antiope. When she gave birth to her twin sons Amphion and Zethus, Lycus exposed them on Mount Cithaeron, but they were rescued and reared by a shepherd. After many years of imprisonment, during which she was cruelly treated by Lycus' wife Dirce, Antiope managed to escape to Mount Cithaeron and find her sons, who were by then grown men. They avenged the suffering of their mother by tying Dirce to the horns of a bull, which dragged her along until she died. Amphion and Zethus also deposed Lycus, became kings of Thebes, and constructed the walls of the city. Amphion was so great a harper that his music had the power to draw the stones into place. Zethus married the nymph Thebe, from whom the city derives its name. Driven insane by Dionysus for asking her sons to avenge her sufferings in so harsh a manner, Antiope wandered about Greece until Phocus, the king of Phocis, cured and married her.

Antiope (II). In Greek mythology, a sister of Hippolyte, queen of the AMAZONS. In some myths she is the mother of Hippolytus by Theseus.

Antiphon. The earliest Athenian writer of surviving orations, about 480 B.C. to about 411 B.C. He was a *logopoios*, a professional author of speeches delivered by litigants, and a teacher of rhetoric. According to Thucydides in *The Peloponnesian War*, Antiphon organized the conspiracy of 411 B.C. that brought about the rule of the Four Hundred. When the conspirators were deposed, Antiphon was put to death for treason. Thucydides praised his speech in self-defense as the best of its type he had ever heard. Antiphon is said to have written sixty speeches, of which fifteen remain, all of them dealing with homicide. His language is highly stylized and poetic, and he makes frequent use of periodic sentence structure.

Antisthenes. See CYNICS.

Antoninus Pius. Emperor of Rome from A.D. 138 to 161. His name was originally Titus Aurelius Fulvius Boionius Arrius Antoninus. After he was adopted by Hadrian, whom he succeeded, he assumed the name Titus Aelius Hadrianus Antoninus.

Antony, Mark (Marcus Antonius). A Roman general, born around 82 B.C. He was a member of Caesar's forces in Gaul and fought on his side in the Civil War of 49 B.C. In 44 B.C. Antony was consul, and after the assassination of Caesar, when the Republicans were unprepared to take over the government of Rome, Antony, a shrewd and eloquent man, was able to win the Roman people to his side. His aim was to replace Caesar as dictator. In his *Philippics* CICERO warned the Senate against the tyranny of Antony and was influential in arousing the Republicans to unite against him. In 43 B.C. the forces of Antony were overcome at Mutina, but he then allied himself with Caesar's grandnephew and heir, the young Octavian. With Lepidus, the *pontifex maximus* (chief pontiff), they formed the second triumvirate, a committee of dictators legally assigned to exact punishment for the assassination of Caesar and to reform the Roman government.

Octavian and Antony defeated the army of Brutus and Cassius at Philippi in 42 B.C. and became supreme commanders of the Roman Empire; Octavian ruled Italy and the Western provinces, Antony the East. Conflict arose between them, but their differences were temporarily settled by the treaty of Brundisium in 40 B.C. and by Antony's marriage to Octavia, the sister of Octavian. Antony now sought to strengthen his hold on the Eastern provinces of Rome. He allied himself with Cleopatra, the queen of Egypt, whom he loved, and to whom he surrendered Roman territories. They had three children. After Antony divorced Octavia (32 B.C.), Octavian persuaded the Senate to divest him of his rights as a triumvir and to wage war on Egypt. Antony and Cleopatra were defeated by the forces of Octavian at Actium in Epirus in 31 B.C. They returned to Egypt and, when Octavian invaded the country in 30 B.C., they committed suicide. Shakespeare idealizes Antony and Cleopatra and depicts them as magnificent tragic figures in his play *Antony and Cleopatra,* based on Plutarch's life of Antony.

Aphrodite. The Greek goddess of love. She was originally not a Hellenic but an Asiatic goddess, related to the Asian mother goddesses Ishtar and Astarte. According to Homer, Aphrodite is the daughter of Zeus and Dione. Hesiod describes her as rising from the sea foam (*aphros*) that collected about the severed male organ of Uranus, who had been castrated by his son Cronus. Aphrodite went first either to the island of Cythera (from which came her name Cytherea) or to Paphos in Cyprus (from which she was called Cypris); both regions claimed her as theirs.

Aphrodite was married to Hephaestus, the lame craftsman of the gods. In ODYSSEY VIII Homer tells a delightful tale about her love affair with the handsome "butcher," Ares. Aphrodite is associated with beauty and pleasure, but she can be a cruel goddess who enslaves and destroys those in her power or those who deny her significance. In later Greek literature she has a son Eros. For her love of Anchises see HOMERIC HYMN V. For her significant role in the Trojan War see the ILIAD. See also ADONIS.

Apollo (Apollon). A Greek god of varied attributes. One of the most appealing and significant of the Greek gods, Apollo was not Hellenic in origin, though the area in which he did originate is unknown. Scholars believe that he came either from a non-Hellenic nation of Asia Minor or was brought by migrating Greeks from some area in the North. Among the Greeks, Apollo was regarded as the son of Zeus and Leto and the brother of Artemis. As Phoebus (bright) he was the god of light; he was also the god of prophecy, healing, music, and archery and protector of the herds. His epithet Lyceius may refer to Lycia in Asia Minor, thus meaning Lycian, or it may refer to Apollo as a "wolf-god," with the power to harm or protect the shepherd. According to Greek mythology, after

Apollo destroyed the huge Python that guarded the oracular shrine at Delphi, he was worshiped at Delphi, and the oracle became his. (See HOMERIC HYMN III.) He was also worshiped at his birthplace, Delos. For Apollo's relationship with Hermes see HOMERIC HYMN IV and Sophocles' ICHNEUTAI.

Apollodorus (Apollodoros). Athenian grammarian who flourished about 140 B.C. Although he was once regarded as the author of BIBLIOTHECA, there is good evidence refuting his authorship of this work. Fragments remain of Apollodorus' prose treatise *On the Gods,* a naturalistic explanation of divine beings, and of *Chronicle,* a Greek history in verse.

Apollonius Rhodius (Apollonius of Rhodes). A Greek poet, born at Alexandria around 295 B.C. A student of CALLIMACHUS, Apollonius began to write his Greek epic poem ARGONAUTICA (1) early in life and recited portions of it in public. Either because the poem was badly received or because he quarreled with Callimachus, first over literary matters and then over personal ones, Apollonius left Alexandria for Rhodes, where a revised version of the *Argonautica* was highly praised. From this time Apollonius regarded himself as a Rhodian. Either before leaving Alexandria or on his eventual return there he was head of the great Library at Alexandria. He died around 215 B.C. See VALERIUS FLACCUS.

Apology (Apologia). Plato's account of the defense of Socrates to charges of impiety.

BACKGROUND. In 399 B.C. Socrates was brought to trial on the charges that he had corrupted the youth of Athens and had brought in new gods. Actually he had aroused suspicion by constantly probing into and questioning accepted values. More important, however, was the fact that some of his disciples, Alcibiades, Critias, the leader of the Thirty (see PLATO), and Xenophon were in favor of oligarchy; thus Socrates was regarded as a harmful influence by the extreme democratic faction. His accusers were Meletus, Anytus, and Lycon. In the *Apology* (Defense) Socrates answers their charges and defends his own position. Plato apparently was present at Socrates' trial and recorded his words; however, we do not know whether the *Apology* consists of Socrates' actual speech or a version of it as interpreted by Plato.

SUMMARY. Socrates begins with a reference to his accusers' warning to the jury to beware of his eloquence. His only eloquence, he declares, is his truthfulness. He then turns to the old accusations that he inquired about heaven and earth, that he is an atheist and a sophist. Except for Aristophanes (see THE CLOUDS), he does not even know the names of those who spread these false accusations. Having denied that he is either a scientist or a sophist, Socrates declares that he does possess a certain wisdom, which results from his understanding that he knows nothing. He then tells of how his friend Chaerephon reported to him that the oracle of Delphi had told him no one was wiser than Socrates. Socrates did not take the statement literally but considered its meaning for a long time and sought among many men to find one wiser than he.

Finally, after a great deal of thought and trouble, he arrived at a solution to the riddle of the meaning of the oracular statement: that man is wisest who, like Socrates, knows that he actually knows nothing. When he questioned so-called wise men and revealed their ignorance, they grew angry and accused him of impiety. Although Socrates knew he was making enemies by exposing the ignorance of these men, he felt it was his mission to continue.

Socrates then turns from the old accusations against him to the more recent ones: that he corrupts the youth and worships his own gods. Because his accusers are led by Meletus, Socrates cross-examines him. Then Socrates speaks to the judges, insisting that he is innocent of the charges and that he will continue to obey the command of the god that he seek the truth about himself and other men. If the Athenians decide to kill him, it will be hard for them to find his successor, for he is a kind of "gadfly" whom the gods sent to rouse the noble but slow steed which is the state.

The jurors then decide by a vote of 280–221 that Socrates is guilty and propose a penalty of death. Socrates now has the legal right to suggest an alternate penalty. He declares that his only surprise at the verdict is that it received so small a majority of the votes. He is now expected to propose his punishment, but he cannot suggest a penalty; instead he suggests that for his services to Athens the Athenians reward him with a pension. Because he knows that a prison sentence, a fine, or exile are penalties that he does not deserve, he feels it is irrational to propose one of these, but he does not know whether death is a good or an evil. He cannot promise to be silent, for he believes that the search for virtue is the supreme good and that "for man the unexamined life is not worth living." Finally he does suggest a fine of thirty minae, which his friends will guarantee.

The jury votes the death penalty; the vote is now 360–141. Socrates calmly accepts his sentence and predicts that his judges will be condemned by men in the future. Socrates then addresses his friends, telling them that death is either a state of unconsciousness or a journey to another world where he will find true judges and other great beings, such as Orpheus, Musaeus, Hesiod, and Homer. There he can continue his search for truth. Neither in life nor in death can evil happen to a good man. Socrates declares he is not angry with his accusers, for they have not harmed him; he blames them only a little because they did not intend to do him any good.

Apology (Apologia Sokratous). A discussion by XENOPHON of Socrates' trial and his defense.

Apuleius, Lucius. A Roman author. Apuleius was born about A.D. 125 at Madaura, an African colony of Rome in Numidia. He came from a wealthy and prominent family, and was educated at Carthage and later at Athens. In Greece he was initiated into the mysteries of the goddess Isis. After completing his studies he traveled for a period, visiting many lands. In Rome he became a prominent figure in the cult of Isis and Osiris and well-known as a rhetorician and advocate. When still a young man Apuleius married the mother of a friend, a wealthy widow much older than he, Pudentilla of Oea (Tripoli). Soon after the marriage Pudentilla's son died. Her relatives accused Apuleius of using magic to win her and of killing her son in order to take possession of his wealth. The latter charge was soon dropped, but Apuleius was brought to trial for using magic. To defend himself he wrote a learned and witty speech, the *Apology* (also known as *De Magia*), that no doubt helped to win his acquittal before the governor, Claudius Maximus. His life with Pudentilla was apparently a happy one. Probably Apuleius spent the rest of his life at Carthage, honored as a writer. The date of his death is unknown.

A great many of Apuleius' writings have been lost. In addition to the *Apology* his extant works are *Florida*, a collection of passages from his speeches; *De Platone*, a commentary on the philosophy of Plato; *De Deo Socratis*, a treatise on Socrates' conception of God and the daemons; a translation of a Greek treatise *On the Universe* (*De Mundo*), erroneously attributed to Aristotle; and his most famous work, the romance THE GOLDEN ASS, or *Metamorphoses*, the plot of which was taken from an earlier Greek story, *Lucius or the Ass*, that some have attributed to Lucian. Apuleius' adaptation of the plot, his addition of delightful stories that interrupt the main narrative, and the final redemption of Lucius by the goddess Isis create an entirely new work. In *The Golden Ass*, Apuleius brilliantly combines wit with deep moral seriousness, a fascination with magic and fantasy with sincere and even mystical religious feeling.

Arachne. In Greek mythology, a young girl from Maeonia, who considered herself superior to Athene in weaving. In *Metamorphoses* VI Ovid tells the story of how Arachne in her pride declared that she would not hesitate to compete with the goddess herself. Athene appeared, and she and Arachne set up two looms. Arachne wove many beautiful scenes depicting the love affairs of the gods. Furious at the excellent workmanship of Arachne, the jealous Athene destroyed her web and struck Arachne. In her shame the young girl hanged herself, but Athene would not allow her the peace of death. Declaring that Arachne must "hang forever," she transformed her into a spider, who would weave eternally.

Aratus (Aratos). A Greek poet from Soli in Cicilia, born at the end of the fourth century B.C. Aratus' extant poem *Phaenomena*, which consists of 1154 hexameter lines, deals with astronomy and weather. Cicero translated *Phaenomena* into Latin, and it is thought that Lucretius was influenced by this version.

Arbitration, The (Epitrepontes). A New Comedy (perhaps c. 300 B.C.) by MENANDER. Translations: in prose, L. A. Post, 1929; in prose and verse, Francis G. Allinson, 1930; in verse, Gilbert Murray, 1945; in prose, Lionel Casson, 1960.

BACKGROUND. The extant fragments of *The Arbitration* contain more than half the play. Most of the first act is missing. It probably supplied the background, which can be deduced from the remainder of the play. Some months before the events of the play, at the festival of the Tauropolia, Pamphila, a young girl, was assaulted by Charisius, a wealthy young man. Though Pamphila could not recognize the face of her attacker, she secured his ring. A few months later she met and was married to Charisius, unaware that he was the man who had assaulted her. Five months after their marriage, at a time when Charisius was away from home, Pamphila bore a son. Pamphila's nurse helped her to expose the child, with whom Pamphila left some jewelry, among which was the ring of the man who had violated her. When Charisius' slave, Onesimus, disclosed these events to his master, Charisius was deeply disturbed. He loved Pamphila and therefore would not divorce her. Instead he tried to overcome his despair by spending all his time away from home, indulging in drink and pleasure with a harp girl, Habrotonon.

S C E N E . In the country near Athens; in the background are two houses; one belongs to Chaerestratus and is now inhabited by Charisius; the other is the house of Charisius, where his abandoned wife, Pamphila, lives.

S U M M A R Y . When Pamphila's father, Smicrines, hears of Charisius' unfaithfulness and his life of revelry, which is consuming the dowry of Pamphila, he urges his daughter to leave her husband, but she remains loyal to him. Smicrines is returning to Athens after seeing his daughter when he comes upon two slaves, Syriscus, a charcoal burner, and Davus, a shepherd. They are quarreling and looking for an arbiter to settle their dispute. Smicrines agrees to arbitrate and requests that Davus present his case first. Davus explains that about a month ago, while tending his flocks, he found a baby exposed. With the child were a necklace and other pieces of jewelry. Davus took the baby home with him and at first thought he would keep him, but later, having decided it was too expensive to rear a child, gave him to Syriscus, whose own baby had recently died. Now Syriscus is demanding the jewelry Davus found with the baby, but Davus will not give it to him. Syriscus defends his position, and finally Smicrines decides in favor of Syriscus.

After Davus angrily departs Syriscus hands the trinkets to his wife. Onesimus enters and recognizes a ring as one his master had lost some time ago. Syriscus allows Onesimus to take the ring to Charisius, who is now in the house of Chaerestratus, so that he may find out if the ring really belongs to his master. Onesimus, however, is hesitant to show the ring to his master, who is already angry with him for causing him so much pain by telling him Pamphila's secret. Onesimus fears Charisius' reaction to further problems.

Habrotonon comes out of Chaerestratus' house, unhappy because Charisius is uninterested in her. At this point, Syriscus enters and demands that Onesimus either return the ring to him or show it to his master. Onesimus then reveals his suspicion that his master had assaulted a young woman at the Tauropolia and that she bore the child whom Davus gave to Syriscus. Habrotonon, who was present at the festival, decides to find out whether Charisius is really the father of the baby by pretending she is the girl he assaulted. She hopes that Charisius will buy her freedom when she convinces him she is the mother of his child. She takes the ring and goes into the house.

A good deal of the play is missing at this point in the story. In the next part Habrotonon appears, carrying the baby she pretends is hers. Pamphila also appears, disheartened because she believes that Charisius will be even more fond of his mistress now that she has borne him a child. Habrotonon soon recognizes Pamphila as the young woman whom Charisius assaulted at the Tauropolia. At that moment Pamphila recognizes the baby as her own by the trinkets the child is wearing. Meanwhile, Charisius, who has overheard Smicrines' renewed attempt to persuade Pamphila to leave her husband and her refusal to break her marriage vows, realizes that he has hurt a loving and faithful wife and regrets his cruelty to her. Then Habrotonon reveals that Charisius is the father of the baby Pamphila exposed. He and Pamphila are reconciled, and the play ends happily.

Arcadia (Arkadia). An area in the central Peloponnesus. The Arcadians claimed to be the oldest inhabitants of Greece.

Archilochus (Archilochos). A Greek poet who lived during the seventh century B.C. Archilochus was born at Paros, the son of an aristocrat and a slave woman. It is thought that he was forced to leave Paros because of poverty. When Lycambes, the father of Neobule, the young woman Archilochus loved, refused to allow him to marry her, he retaliated with such a violent satirical attack that both Lycambes and his daughter committed suicide.

Archilochus is regarded as the inventor of iambics (see IAMBIC POETRY), in which he wrote wittily and frankly about his personal feelings of anger, sorrow, or love. Horace in *The Art of Poetry* describes Archilochus as "armed with his own iambics." He also wrote elegies. Only fragments of his poetry remain. Perhaps his best-known fragment is a poem on his shield, which he justifies having thrown away in battle because in doing so he saved his life. This approach is exactly the opposite of the heroic ideal, which demands that a warrior sacrifice his life for his honor. Archilochus' open mockery of the heroic code is one of the refreshing and novel qualities of his poetry. Another is his ability to express the pain of unfulfilled love, in some fragments with a bitterness that seems to spring from his suffering, in others with tenderness. In one fragment he prays that he may touch Neobule's hand; in another he speaks of a girl so beautiful that even an old man must love her.

Areopagiticus. See ISOCRATES.

Ares. In Greek mythology, a son of Zeus and Hera and the god of war. He was identified by the Romans with Mars. For his love affair with Aphrodite see ODYSSEY VIII.

arete. An extremely important word in Greek literature, *arete* can be translated as courage, manliness, a sense of one's own dignity or honor, glory.

For an excellent discussion of the term see Werner Jaeger, *Paideia*, trans. Gilbert Highet (New York: Oxford University Press, 1945), I, *passim.*

Arete was the name of the wife of King Alcinous of the Phaeacians. A woman of great influence, she induced her husband to aid the shipwrecked Odysseus (see ODYSSEY VI, VII) and saved Medea from the pursuing Colchians by marrying her to Jason.

Argonautica (I). A Greek epic in four books by APOLLONIUS RHODIUS. The poem tells the story of Jason and the Argonauts, who sailed in the ship Argo, built by the great craftsman Argus with the help of Athene, from Pagasae, the harbor of Iolcos, to Colchis to obtain the Golden Fleece. In Book I, Apollonius lists the Argonauts who sailed with Jason, among whom were Orpheus, Admetus, Peleus, Telamon, Heracles, and Heracles' squire Hylas. He describes Jason's farewell to his mother and tells of how Heracles was left behind in Mysia, seeking Hylas, whom he loved.

The second book deals with the adventurous voyage of the Argonauts. The most effective book is the third, which tells of Medea's love for Jason and her suffering when she learns the conditions under which her father, King Aeëtes, will surrender the fleece: Jason must yoke fire-breathing oxen, plow a field with them, sow dragon's teeth, and kill the armed men that will spring up. Having helped Jason to accomplish these tasks and to obtain the Golden Fleece, Medea flees from Colchis with him. The *Argonautica* presents a most sympathetic portrayal of Medea. Though she has magic powers, Apollonius' Medea is not primarily the sorceress she is in Seneca's tragedy or the violent creature who dominates Euripides' tragedy, but a woman torn by love for Jason and fear of her father.

The fourth book tells how Medea helps to kill her own brother, Absyrtus, who has pursued her and Jason, and of the long journey and the many adventures of Jason and Medea on their way to Iolcos. Married in the land of the Phaeacians, they finally reach Pagasae.

Although the *Argonautica* is not a great epic, its beautiful passages on Medea's love for Jason influenced Ovid and Vergil, and the poem was the model for the *Argonautica* of Valerius Flaccus.

There is a good translation of Apollonius' *Argonautica* in prose by E. V. Rieu (1959).

Argonautica (II). An unfinished Latin epic in eight books by VALERIUS FLACCUS. The poem was influenced by Apollonius' ARGONAUTICA and by Vergil's *Aeneid*. The events of the first four books are similar to those of Apollonius' epic. Valerius Flaccus then adds the story of the war between King Aeëtes of Colchis and his exiled brother Perses, who unsuccessfully attempts to seize the throne of Colchis. Jason aids Aeëtes in his defense of his land, but despite his bravery in battle, Jason is a weak and uninteresting figure. As in Book IV of the *Aeneid*, Juno is instrumental in bringing about a painful and finally disastrous love affair; she inspires Medea with love for Jason. After an agonizing conflict between her feelings for Jason and her loyalty to her father, Medea helps Jason to accomplish the tasks Aeëtes has set for him and to obtain the Golden Fleece. The lovers flee from Colchis and are later married. They are pursued by Medea's brother, and as the poem ends, the Argonauts are considering giving up Medea so that they may keep the Golden Fleece.

Argonauts. See ARGONAUTICA (I, II) and JASON.

Argos. See MYCENAE.

Argus (Argos) (I). A herdsman with one hundred eyes whom Hera sent to guard the cow Io (see Aeschylus' PROMETHEUS BOUND). After Hermes killed Argus, Hera put his eyes in the tail of the peacock.

Argus (Argos) (II). The brilliant craftsman who built the Argo (see ARGONAUTICA I).

Argus (Argos) (III). Odysseus' dog (see ODYSSEY XVII).

Ariadne. See THESEUS and Ovid's HEROIDES X.

Arion. A Greek lyric poet, probably of the seventh century B.C., whose fame is both historical and legendary. He was born at Lesbos and supposedly spent much of his time at the court of Periander, tyrant of Corinth. According to the legend told by Herodotus, Arion was returning from a trip to Italy when some sailors who desired his wealth threw him overboard. He was permitted to sing one song before he died. This was so beautiful that it moved a dolphin to rescue him. Arion is the legendary inventor of the dithyramb, the ode in honor of Dionysus; but actually he merely transformed an ancient ritual song into a literary composition to be sung by a chorus around an altar of Dionysus (see TRAGEDY). None of Arion's work survives.

Aristaeus (Aristaios). In Greek mythology, the son of the nymph Cyrene, a god of husbandry and of beekeeping. For the story of his love for Eurydice see GEORGIC IV by Vergil.

Aristophanes. A Greek comic playwright, born around 445 B.C. in Athens. Little is known about his life. He produced his first comedy in 427 B.C., a lost play called *Daitaleis* (the Banqueters), which won a second prize. The next year his *The Babylonians,* also lost, was produced. The play attacked the demagogue Cleon, who retaliated by charging Aristophanes with treason. The next year, 425 B.C., in THE ACHARNIANS, his earliest surviving play, Aristophanes again ridiculed the war party, of which Cleon was a leader. A brilliant comedy that urges the Athenians to end the war with Sparta, it won first prize. THE KNIGHTS, Aristophanes' next play, produced in 424 B.C., ridicules Cleon openly. This play also won first prize. THE CLOUDS was produced in 423 B.C., THE WASPS in 422 B.C., and PEACE in 421 B.C. None of the plays of the six years following are extant. Aristophanes produced THE BIRDS in 414 B.C., LYSISTRATA and THESMOPHORIAZUSAE in 411 B.C., THE FROGS in 405 B.C., ECCLESIAZUSAE in 392 B.C., and PLUTUS, his last extant comedy, in 388 B.C. He wrote two comedies after this, but they have not survived. Aristophanes died in 380 B.C.

48

Aristophanes is the only writer of Old Comedy (see under COMEDY) whose work survives. Like his predecessors in the field, whose comedies are lost, Aristophanes used drama as a vehicle for social and political satire. He is an outspoken and brilliant critic of the political leaders of his day and of the Peloponnesian War, which was destroying Athens. As a critic of his age, Aristophanes attacks not only politicians; he ridicules whatever he considers pretentious: Socrates, in his eyes, is a pretender to learning; Euripides a pretentious playwright.

The plays of Aristophanes reflect his intense emotional and intellectual involvement in the political and cultural affairs of his day, yet they are farcical, witty, lyrical, and fantastic as well. His comedy is brilliant; one wild fantasy leads to another. He can be satirical, didactic, ribald, and witty at the same time that he expresses his most sincere thoughts on war or political corruption. Though ribald, Aristophanes is never offensive; the bodily references that occur constantly in his plays are always amusing, and more important, they recall the ritual obscenities of the phallic fertility rites from which Greek comedy was derived. Often Aristophanes contrasts sexual pleasure and its suggestion of productivity with the wastefulness and destruction of war. Though Aristophanes' plays are topical and his characters mainly types, they are not dated. His commentaries on war and on political corruption, his exposure of demagogues, braggart soldiers, and pretenders to learning, seem all too pertinent today. Writers of English comedy learned a great deal from Aristophanes. The work of Ben Jonson, Thomas Middleton, Henry Fielding, and, in our time, T. S. Eliot all reflect his influence. Aristophanes appears in Plato's SYMPOSIUM.

Aristotle (Aristoteles). A Greek philosopher, born at Stagira in Macedonia in 384 B.C. His father Nicomachus was the physician of Amyntas II, king of Macedon. At seventeen Aristotle went to Athens, where he became Plato's pupil at the Academy, remaining there until Plato's death in 347 B.C. Aristotle then went to Assos in Asia Minor, where he stayed for three years, and from there to Mytilene in Lesbos, where he remained until 342 B.C., when Philip of Macedon appointed him tutor of his son Alexander. Aristotle held this position for three years before returning to Athens in 335, where he founded the Lyceum, a school of philosophy named Peripatetic because of the lovely walks on its grounds. Here Aristotle remained for about twelve years, teaching and writing most of his many works on science, literature, and philosophy. He also established a museum and a fine library. When Alexander the Great died suddenly in 323 B.C., the anti-Macedonian party at Athens accused Aristotle of impiety. He left Athens and lived for a year in the Macedonian Chalcis in Euboea, where he died in 322 B.C.

Four hundred works were attributed to Aristotle, of which two hundred titles are known. His writings were of two kinds. The first consisted of fairly popular works called *exoteric* (*exoterikoi logoi*) on philosophy, some in the form of dialogues, which were published in his time. Unfortunately, only brief fragments of these are extant. The second were treatises of a scientific nature, in which he or his students recorded his lectures; these were later called *esoteric* (*esoterikoi logoi*). They were organized rather haphazardly by editors and were unknown from the time of Aristotle's death until their discovery, possibly in a cave or a cellar in Asia Minor, in the first century B.C. The current editions of Aristotle's works are based on those made at the order of the Roman leader Sulla, who obtained Aristotle's remaining treatises in Athens in 78 B.C.

Aristotle's extant treatises cover a wide range of subjects. The six grouped under the title *Organon* (Instrument) deal with methods of reasoning and establishing proof. The titles of these are *Categories, Concerning Interpretation, Prior Analytics, Posterior Analytics, Topics,* and *Concerning Sophistical Refutation.* In the field of natural philosophy or science, four works remain, the most significant being *Physics,* which deals with the laws of nature, especially movement and change. All motion, Aristotle says, goes back to an "unmoved" or "prime mover." He also treats matter, form, time, void, and infinity. *On the Heavens* deals with the movement of heavenly and sublunary bodies. In *On Generation and Corruption* Aristotle analyzes changes resulting from causes other than motion. His *Meteorology* is concerned with the causes of such natural phenomena as rain, snow, winds, rainbows, comets, earthquakes, thunder, and lightning.

An early editor of Aristotle's writings gave the title *Metaphysics* to a series of treatises that he placed "after the *Physics.*" Aristotle called the problems analyzed in these treatises "First Philosophy," "Theology," or "Wisdom" because they represented his thought on ultimate science or wisdom, which went beyond the limited truth revealed by particular sciences. In the *Metaphysics* he discusses his objections to the Theory of Ideas of PLATO. Aristotle's view is that only in material reality can one discover the nature of the universal or essential. The most important philosophical problem is the explanation of the nature of motion and change. The four "causes" that explain the relationship between form and matter are the material, the formal, the efficient, and the final.

Aristotle's nine psychological works are *On the Soul, On Sensation, On Memory, On Sleep, On Dreams, On Prophesying Through Dreams, On Length and Brevity of Life, On Life and Death, On Respiration.* His treatises on biology include *The History of Animals, On the Parts of Animals, On the Motion of Animals, On the Progression of Animals,* and *On the Generation of Animals.*

The practical sciences are discussed in NICOMACHEAN ETHICS named for his son Nicomachus (Nikomachos), who may have edited them; the *Eudemian Ethics,* which may have been edited by Aristotle's student Eudemus; and the *Politics.* The *Nicomachean Ethics* is considered superior to the *Eudemian Ethics;* there is no agreement on the relationship between these two works. In the *Nicomachean Ethics* Aristotle considers the *ethos* or character of man in relation to the kind of life he requires to achieve happiness. The *Politics,* a sequel to the *Ethics*, discusses the kind of society and government that will provide the best way of life for man. According to Aristotle the city-state is the highest type of community; it fulfills man's social needs and prepares him for the good life. Aristotle envisions the ideal state and considers the best existing states. His *Constitution of Athens* describes the development of the Athenian constitution from its beginnings to the end of the rule of the Thirty Tyrants.

The RHETORIC and the POETICS, treatises on literary theory, are among Aristotle's best-known writings. He discusses rhetoric from a philosophical point of view, and his ideas on poetry and tragedy are directly related to his theory that the ideal or essential quality of experience can be apprehended only through material reality. In the *Poetics*, Aristotle suggests that through *mimesis* (which is translated as "imitation," but actually means "capturing the essential quality") of action, character, and emotion the artist completes nature. When the artist "imitates nature," he is seeking the universal laws of human life and experience. Thus through the temporal and the material, the poet or other artist creates the universal, the ideal.

Coleridge's observation that all men are either Platonists or Aristotelians suggests the great differences in the approaches of the two philosophers to material reality. Plato scorns the physical universe as a world of shadows; Aristotle, though he sometimes draws on the idealism of his teacher, consistently conveys his inspired curiosity about external reality and his total acceptance of and delight in natural phenomena. Even his scientific works, written in the terse prose of notes, reveal a love for physical reality. Nature to Aristotle is marvelous; its meanest product contains beauty for the man of scientific training and insight; it provides an endless field for study, contemplation, and, best of all, discovery.

The influence of Aristotle on science, theology, literature, and philosophy has been so pervasive that any but the most superficial discussion of it would require many volumes. Aristotle was reinterpreted by every age that approached his work. He was equally revered by the Medieval Schoolmen, notably Aquinas, and by Sir Francis Bacon, who objected to their methods and sought new scientific and experimental techniques. Even Charles Darwin admired Aristotle. The *Poetics* served as a guide to Renaissance and neoclassical poets and critics. It has been translated and interpreted hundreds of times, and its cryptic remarks still produce fruitful speculation and commentary.

Arpinum. The city in Latium where Cicero was born.

Ars Amatoria. See ART OF LOVE.

Ars Poetica. See ART OF POETRY.

Artemis. A Greek goddess of varied attributes. Originally an Asian mother goddess, she also had this role in early Greek religion. In Arcadia, for example, she was closely related to Demeter and Persephone; sometimes she was associated with Hecate. In her great temple at Ephesus she was represented as having many breasts, a sign of her function as a fertility goddess. In Greek mythology

Artemis was the daughter of Zeus and Leto and the sister of Apollo, a virgin goddess who protected the young of all species. She was the goddess of the hunt, of childbirth, and of the moon. See Bacchylides' CHORAL LYRIC XI.

Art of Love, The (Ars Amatoria). Mock-didactic elegiac poem (before A.D. 8) in three books, by OVID. Translations: in verse, F. A. Wright, 1920; in prose, Lewis May, 1926; in prose, J. H. Mozley, 1929; in prose, Ronald Seth, 1953; in verse, Rolfe Humphries, 1957.

SUMMARY. *Book I*. Ovid declares that the first task is to find a beloved, the next to win her love, the third to make certain that love will last. These steps are the subjects of his poem. The first book is mainly concerned with where to find a beloved and how to obtain her interest. After recommending various places, especially the theaters, as "hunting-grounds" for the prospective lover, Ovid suggests ways to approach the lady and gain her attention. No woman who is properly wooed, he insists, will resist. Woman's lust is greater than man's and has more of the fury of madness in it.

One should get to know the servant of the desired lady, for she can help in the courtship. It may seem advisable to seduce the servant, but it is better to abstain. Letters, entreaties, promises, and other techniques are recommended.

Book II. The book begins with a triumphant cry, for the lady has been won. Now the lover is advised on how to retain her love. He must educate himself so that he can charm her by his eloquence, as Odysseus did Calypso, when his youthful beauty is gone. Also he must indulge his lady and refrain from quarreling; he must agree with her opinions and respond to her moods. He must wait upon her and serve her. Most important, the lady must be made to feel that her lover is overwhelmed by her beauty. He must care for her when she is sick. Brief absences inspire love, but long ones justify adultery. Ovid uses the example of Helen, whom he refuses to blame for taking Paris as a lover, because her husband Menelaus had left her alone. The lover may have more than one mistress, but he must carefully conceal his adventures. In a passage that recalls Lucretius' *De Rerum Natura* IV, 1149–1169, Ovid suggests that the lover regard the flaws of his lady as virtues. The book ends with advice on the act of love, as Ovid imagines a pair of lovers embracing.

Book III. Ovid now gives advice to women on how to win a lover and keep his affection, for women must also be "armed for battle." Medea, Ariadne, and Dido all lacked skill in love and, as a result, they were deserted. Venus has inspired Ovid to teach women the arts of love.

He first warns women that years pass quickly, so they must take advantage of their youth and enjoy the lovers who are available. Women must care for themselves and make themselves look as beautiful as possible, arranging their hair in the most becoming fashion, wearing colors that suit them, and using make-up ("art") to cover the imperfections of nature. They must not allow their lovers to observe these efforts to improve their appearance, but must try to make them believe that their beauty is natural. Various methods of concealing flaws are then described.

Women must learn to laugh and to weep becomingly, to walk gracefully and sing sweetly, to play the lyre and to read a poem by Propertius, Gallus, Tibullus, or perhaps Ovid, to dance, and to play games. Various places where lovers may be sought are mentioned; even at one's husband's funeral another husband may be found.

Ovid then warns women against various types of deceitful men. Next he gives advice on proper behavior at the beginning of the love affair. Women should be neither too submissive nor too cold. They are told how to reply to a love letter and are warned against excessive anger, haughtiness, and melancholy. Instruction is given on how to deceive a husband or a guardian and how to make men feel loved. The book ends with advice on the act of love.

Art of Poetry, The (**Ars Poetica**; Epistle to the Pisos). Poem (date uncertain) by HORACE. Translations: in verse, Ben Jonson, 1640; in verse, Francis Howes, 1845; in verse, Theodore Martin, 1888; in verse, J. Conington, 1905; in prose, H. Rushton Fairclough, 1926; in verse, Palmer Bovie, 1959; in prose, Norman J. DeWitt, in *Drama Survey*, Fall, 1961.

S U M M A R Y . Drawing on Hellenistic manuals on style, Horace wrote his longest poem, the *Ars Poetica*, on literary matters, particularly the drama. It is addressed to the Pisos, a father and two sons, whose identity is not certain. They may have been Cn. Calpurnius Piso, who was consul in 23 B.C., and his two sons, Gnaeus and Lucius, both of whom became consuls.

The *Ars Poetica* begins with a description of a bizarre painting of a human head joined to the neck of a horse; feathers are spread over the limbs of the creature depicted and it ends in a black fish. Would not the Pisos laugh at the painter of so mad a picture? Poets, says Horace, who do not observe propriety are equally mad. A poem must be simple and unified. The poet must avoid obscurity and turgidity; however, in attempting to write correctly he must not "creep along the ground," desiring only to be safe or free from error. Before undertaking a subject a writer should carefully consider whether he is capable of dealing with it adequately. If he writes on a theme he truly comprehends, his poem will succeed in saying exactly what should be said. Furthermore, the poet should be able to give a well-known word fresh appeal through skillful use. Newly coined words must be used sparingly, but they should be permitted.

The meter suited to heroic subjects is dactylic hexameter. The elegiac couplet, first used to express lamentation, later was employed for prayer. The rage of Archilochus inspired him to write iambics; this meter was later used for dialogue in comedy and tragedy. Lyric poetry was written about the gods and their offspring, victors in athletic contests, love, and wine. Each type of poetry has an appropriate meter, tone, and language. He who refuses to learn these distinctions is no poet. A comic theme cannot be expressed in the poetry appropriate to tragedy, nor can a story such as that about the feast of Thyestes be told in the naturalistic style of comedy. Yet there are times when each form needs to borrow techniques from the other, for comedy has its intense moments, tragedy its prosaic ones.

Poetry must have beauty and power to rouse the emotions of the audience. Only appropriate language will make a character effective. A dramatist must either use traditional material or create a consistent plot of his own. When well-known figures of myth are used, they should have their traditional characteristics; when new characters are invented they must be consistent.

It is difficult to transmit universal qualities in an original way. Employing *publica materies* ("traditional material"), the poet must assert his own rights. Without originality "a mountain labors and produces a ridiculous mouse." Like Homer, a poet should begin *in medias res* ("in the middle of things"), omitting what is not essential.

To know how to please an audience a dramatist must observe the chief traits of human beings in each stage of life and must characterize children and mature and old people as they actually are. The two methods of developing a plot are narration and action. Action is the more effective. Violence and bloodshed, however, should not be shown on stage.

A play must have five acts. The DEUS EX MACHINA should not be employed unless it is absolutely necessary. Only three actors who have speaking parts should be on stage at the same time. The chorus should have an intrinsic role in the play, as if it were an actor. The music of the flute, which accompanies a play, should be simple, as it was in the past, not loud and harsh as it is at present. Satyr plays, while gay and charming, must avoid vulgarity.

Meter is then discussed, and the poet is advised constantly to study the ancient Greek writers as models. The metrical ability and wit of Plautus have been overvalued in the past.

Tragedy was discovered by Thespis and developed into a noble form by Aeschylus. The excesses of Old Comedy were responsible for its being outlawed.

When the poets of Rome dared to cease emulating the Greeks, they produced original tragedy and comedy. The chief reason that Roman poets have not produced greater literature is that they have not had the discipline to revise and polish their work sufficiently.

The source of effective writing is wisdom. A writer must know life not only by reading, but by observing reality, on which he must model his work. A poet desires to teach or delight or to do both at once. Instruction should be brief. The work that both teaches and pleases will be popular and will assure its author's fame in the future.

In a work essentially beautiful a few faults may be excused. The reader laughs in amazement when a poor poet writes a few good lines, but he is upset "when good Homer occasionally nods." A mediocre poem fails entirely. A poet should keep his work nine years before allowing it to be published.

Through his songs, Orpheus, the sacred prophet of the gods, taught men to give up their primitive and violent ways; thus the myth arose that he tamed wild beasts. Another myth tells of how Amphion built the walls of Thebes by the power of his lyre. The noble history of poetry is then traced: Homer, Solon, Tyrtaeus, Hesiod, Pindar, Simonides, and Bacchylides all benefited man through their songs.

Both natural ability and careful training and discipline are required to produce a good poem. An honest critic will reveal a poet's errors to him.

The *Ars Poetica* ends humorously with a portrait of a mad poet, who, if he manages to seize hold of a listener, recites his poems until the poor victim dies.

Ascanius (Iulus). Son of Aeneas. See AENEID and ROME.

Asclepius (Asklepios). In Greek mythology, the son of Apollo and god of medicine. See Euripides' ALCESTIS.

Asinaria. See THE COMEDY OF ASSES.

Astyanax (also called Skamandrios). The son of Hector and Andromache. See ILIAD VI, Euripides' THE TROJAN WOMEN and ANDROMACHE, and Seneca's THE TROJAN WOMEN.

Atalanta (Atalante). In Greek mythology, a famous huntress (see MELE-AGER). In *Metamorphoses* X, Ovid tells of her refusal to marry any suitor who could not win a foot race against her. All defeated suitors were doomed to death. Hippomenes, who fell in love with Atalanta, was helped by Aphrodite, who gave him three golden apples of the Hesperides. These he dropped as he ran against Atalanta, who paused to pick up the beautiful apples. Thus Hippomenes won the race and a bride.

Ate. In Greek mythology, the goddess of moral blindness and fury. See ILIAD IX.

Athamas. See INO.

Athene or Athena. In Greek mythology, daughter of Zeus and Metis; generally regarded as a pre-Hellenic goddess. According to one legend Athene was born by Lake Tritonis in Libya; her epithet *Tritogeneia* probably means "water-born." The more widely known account of her birth suggests an attempt to relate her to the Hellenic god Zeus. According to this version Zeus feared that Metis, pregnant with Athene, would bear children more powerful than he; he swallowed her, and Athene sprang from his head, which Hephaestus or Prometheus had split open.

At first Athene was probably a household goddess; later, as protector of the city of Athens, she became a goddess both of war and of crafts such as spinning (see ARACHNE). Still later she is regarded as the goddess of wisdom. One of Athene's apparently Minoan attributes is her sacred snake. As a war goddess she wears armor and a helmet and carries the aegis, a goatskin shield bearing the head of Medusa. Other attributes are the olive branch and the owl, from which comes her epithet *Glaukopis* ("owl-eyed," usually translated "bright-eyed"). In Boeotia, Athene was thought to have invented the flute. She is regarded as responsible for the establishment of the Areopagus at Athens, as is implied in *The Eumenides,* and as an intellectual and ethical influence on Athenian life.

Athens (Athenai). Administrative center of Attica. According to Thucydides, Attica, a peninsula of southeastern Greece, originally consisted of many independent states ruled by kings who sometimes were friendly and sometimes hostile to Athens, its principal city. Around the eighth century B.C. Theseus did away with these separate governments and unified Attica under the domination of the king of Athens. The traditional view is that Athens was ruled by kings, whose reign was hereditary from Cecrops (Kekrops) I to Hippomenes; all of these but Cecrops I belonged to one of two dynasties, the first of fourteen kings and the second of nineteen. Many of these kings are unquestionably mythical, but there is evidence that some were historical figures.

Gradually the Athenian nobles created the positions of archons (magistrates, three at first and later, during the seventh century B.C., nine), elected at first every ten years and later annually, to replace the king in power. However, even after Athens became a republic, one of these archons was the "king." This "king" of the republic had no regal powers; his role was a judicial one in cases of homicide. By allowing the king to become one of the archons the Athenians deprived him of his rule without any great upheaval, and the aristocracy replaced the king as the governing body of the state. In the classical period the government was headed by three elected magistrates—the archon, highest judge in civil suits; the king-archon; and the polemarch, highest commander of the army, who also had judicial powers—and by a council or senate, the *Boule.*

Around the middle of the seventh century B.C. the ruling nobles of the aristocratic republic of Athens were threatened with rebellion by members of the merchant class, who had acquired some wealth and demanded more power. Also, the peasants and workers, suffering economic hardship and greatly in debt, demanded laws less harsh than those administered by the nobles, who enslaved them if they could not pay their debts and exacted the death penalty for minor offenses. In 621 B.C. Draco (Drakon) was appointed to codify the laws of Athens, so that the common man would be protected by law rather than subject to the harsh penalties based on custom. The laws of Draco, however, were so harsh that it was said they were "written in blood, not ink," and his name came to symbolize extreme severity. As economic conditions worsened and citizens lost their land, rebellion again threatened, and in 594 B.C. SOLON was given dictatorial powers to reform the laws of Athens once again.

Despite the efforts of Solon to prevent the seizure of the Athenian government by a tyrant, there was a period when Athens, like most of the Greek city-states during the sixth century B.C., fell under the rule of autocrats. The first of the tyrants was Pisistratus, who seized power in 561 B.C. Though twice expelled, Pisistratus managed to regain power and to rule Athens until his death in 527 B.C. Pisistratus was a temperate ruler who enforced the laws of Solon and did much to improve the economic condition of small farmers. He also encouraged poets and artists, welcoming them to his court. During his reign many magnificent temples were built in Athens, and it is thought that he ordered that the first edited texts of the *Iliad* and the *Odyssey* be made.

After the death of Pisistratus his sons Hippias and Hipparchus became tyrants of Athens. When Hipparchus was murdered, Hippias, fearful for his own life, became a suspicious and harsh ruler. Soon exiled nobles formed an alliance to depose him and, with the aid of Sparta, succeeded in driving him out in 510 B.C.

Under Cleisthenes, the leader of the democratic party, the government of Athens was reorganized, and the city-state became a democracy. Cleisthenes reorganized the *Boule* and, by organizing the state on the basis of territories, did away with the system of voting by clans. The Areopagus (*Areios pagos,* hill of Ares), the old aristocratic ruling body, now became only a court of appeal in cases of homicide. Cleisthenes also introduced ostracism, an annual practice by which Athenians could write on potsherds the name of any person they wished to banish from the state. If a person was named by more than six thousand Athenians, he was banished for ten years.

Athens now grew in strength and prestige, but was threatened by the powerful Persian Empire, which invaded Greece and was defeated at Marathon in 490 B.C. (See THE PERSIAN WARS and THEMISTOCLES.) To defend herself from renewed attacks by Persia, Athens joined with other Greek states in 478 B.C. to form the Delian Confederacy, the seat of which was Delos. After the defeat of Persia, Athens began to dominate her allies, who became subjects of the growing Athenian Empire. She demanded high tributes, and the treasury of the Confederacy was moved to Athens. The formation of the Delian Confederacy was an important step in the development of the Athenian Empire. PERICLES (Perikles), who came to power around 461 B.C., supported the imperialist policy and no doubt was partially responsible for Athens' wars with Sparta, Corinth, Aegina, and Boeotia between 459 and 446 B.C., and for her later involvement in the Peloponnesian War against Sparta and her allies (431–404 B.C.). See Thucydides' THE PELOPONNESIAN WAR.

Defeated in this war in 404 B.C., Athens was practically destroyed and was subject to the Spartan commander Lysander (Lysandros), who established the rule of the Thirty Tyrants in Athens. A council of five hundred supported the tyrants, but after a brief period of internal dissension and bloodshed, during which the democratic party was headed by Thrasybulus (Thrasyboulos), the tyrants were deposed. Athens then united with Thebes, Argos, and Corinth in another fruitless attempt to overcome Sparta (the Corinthian War, 395–387

B.C.). In 378 B.C. Athens again formed an alliance with Thebes against Sparta, and again an Athenian Confederacy was formed, through which Athens managed once more to build up a naval empire. In 371 B.C. Thebes defeated Sparta at the battle of Leuctra. Athens, fearful of the growing power of Thebes, was soon engaged in war again, this time as an ally of her old enemy Sparta against Thebes. In 357 B.C. the islands of Chios, Cos, and Rhodes, which had been dependencies of Athens, rebelled against her, and she was not only forced to give them their freedom in 355 B.C. but to give up her efforts to rebuild her empire.

Athens now became involved in a long and destructive series of wars with Macedon. The events of this period are extremely complicated, and only the briefest outline of them can be given here. Philip II, who became king of Macedon in 359 B.C., was determined to transform his backward nation into a leading power in the Greek world. In 357 B.C. he deceived Athens; having promised to exchange the city of Amphipolis, on the Strymon, for Pydna, Philip conquered Amphipolis and kept it as part of his empire. He also seized Pydna, Potidaea, and Methone.

Without either the islands that had achieved their independence in 355 B.C. or the allies conquered by Philip, Athens was in a poor position to resist the further advances of Philip, who conquered Thessaly and Thrace. Soon after these victories Philip became ill, and, during this brief pause in his violent career, the great Athenian orator DEMOSTHENES, who belonged to the war party, urged the Athenians in his *First Philippic* to take aggressive action against Philip. The Athenians, he declared, must no longer rely on mercenary forces, but must form an army of citizens. Demosthenes was opposed by the statesman Eubulus (Euboulos), the orator Aeschines, and other members of the peace party.

When Philip recovered, he conquered the Chalcidian League and its chief city, Olynthus. In 346 B.C. Athens, debilitated by constant war, was willing to sign a treaty with Macedon, the Peace of Philocrates, the terms of which were that each side would keep the territory it possessed at that time.

Demosthenes and the anti-Macedonian faction attempted during the following years to build up the strength of Athens and to form a Panhellenic alliance against Philip. However, in the final struggle with Philip in 339–338 B.C. Athens and her many allies, including Thebes, whose allegiance Demosthenes had succeeded in wresting from Philip, were defeated at Chaeronea. The city-states lost their autonomy, and all but Sparta became part of a Hellenic Confederacy controlled by Macedon.

Assassinated in 336 B.C., Philip was succeeded by his son Alexander the Great. After Alexander's death in 323 B.C. Athens was able to join with the states of northern Greece in a rebellion against Macedon, but Athens was defeated in this Lamian War in the battle of Crannon in 322 B.C. Demosthenes committed suicide to avoid being taken prisoner.

Athens fought against Macedon in the Chremonidean War (266–262 B.C.), but was again defeated. However, Athens did achieve a brief period of freedom from 229 to 146 B.C., when the city became a protectorate of Rome. During the Mithridatic War (88–86 B.C.) Athens, which supported Mithridates, was attacked and ravaged by the Roman leader Sulla. In 27 B.C. Greece became a province of Rome.

Despite the decline of Athens after the Peloponnesian War, the reputation it had achieved during the fifth and fourth centuries as a center of intellectual and artistic productivity remained. Romans regarded Athens as a cultural center and sent their youth there to be educated. Athenian literature, philosophy, and art provided models for the Romans throughout their history. For Western civilization Athens of the fifth century has remained an ideal of democracy and cultural and artistic achievement.

Atlas. In Greek mythology, the son of Iapetus and Clymene, who was punished for taking part in the rebellion of the Titans by being forced to hold up the heavens with his head and hands. PERSEUS transformed Atlas into a mountain.

Atossa. The widow of Darius, king of Persia, and mother of Xerxes, who succeeded Darius as king. She appears in Aeschylus' THE PERSIANS.

Atreus. In Greek mythology, a son of Pelops and king of MYCENAE. For his terrible vengeance on his brother Thyestes see Seneca's THYESTES. The sons of Atreus were Agamemnon and Menelaus.

Augustus. See OCTAVIAN.

Aurora. The Roman goddess of the dawn, identified with the Greek goddess Eos.

Autolycus (Autolykos). In Greek mythology, a son of Hermes, who inherited his father's bent for tricks and deceit. Hermes gave Autolycus the ability to make himself and whatever he had stolen invisible. Autolycus was the father of Anticlea and thus the grandfather of Odysseus.

Avernus. A lake near Cumae. Near Avernus was the cave through which Aeneas descended into Hades (see AENEID VI). Avernus was also used as a name for the Underworld.

B

Bacchae, The (Bakchai). A tragedy (c. 405 B.C.) by EURIPIDES. Translations: in verse, Henry Hart Milman, 1865; in verse, Gilbert Murray, 1911; in verse, Arthur S. Way, 1912; in prose, D. W. Lucas, 1930; in prose and verse, Philip Vellacott, 1954; in verse, Henry Birkhead, 1957; in verse, William Arrowsmith, 1958; in prose and verse, Geoffrey Kirk, 1970.

MYTHICAL BACKGROUND. Zeus fell in love with the mortal maiden Semele, daughter of Cadmus. When she conceived the god's child, the jealous Hera persuaded her to ask Zeus to come to her in the glorious form in which he appeared to Hera. Reluctantly Zeus agreed and appeared to Semele in the form of lightning and thunder, which consumed her. Zeus managed to save their child, born prematurely, by sewing him into his own thigh, where he remained until he was ready for birth. The child was Dionysus, god of wine, of intoxication or ecstasy, of productivity, and of tragedy. In *The Bacchae* he comes to Thebes, the home of his mother. Cadmus, the old king, has given the kingdom to his grandson, Pentheus, son of Agave, a sister of Semele.

SCENE. Before the palace of Pentheus at Thebes.

SUMMARY. In the form of a man Dionysus enters and speaks of his birth from Zeus and Semele. He then tells of how he has established rites in his honor in many distant lands. Thebes, the home of his mother, Semele, is the first Greek city where he has worshipers. Because the sisters of Semele refused to worship Dionysus, claiming he was no god, Dionysus aroused them to a wild religious frenzy that compels them to perform continuous rites in his honor. Pentheus, the son of Agave and present ruler of Thebes, who also opposes the worship of Dionysus, must learn to accept his divinity. After proving himself to Pentheus, Dionysus will leave Thebes and establish his worship in still another land. After making this declaration Dionysus goes out, and the Chorus of Bacchantes enters, waving thyrsus wands (reeds entwined with ivy, with pine cones at their heads) and carrying timbrels and pipes. They sing a hymn to Dionysus, telling of how they have followed him from Asia, celebrating the Dionysiac mysteries. They urge the city of Thebes, home of the god's mother, to join in celebrating Dionysus with the sacred rites of killing a goat and drinking its blood, with dancing and singing in ecstatic release.

Tiresias, who is a follower of Dionysus, enters and calls for Cadmus, who has also accepted the god. Soon Cadmus joins the prophet, and the two old men speak of their renewed youthfulness and their desire to dance as they worship Dionysus. Then Pentheus comes in. While away on a journey, he has heard how the women of Thebes have left their homes to join in the Bacchic rites and festivities. He strongly disapproves of the cult of Dionysus and the sexual and emotional freedom he believes it encourages. Refusing to believe that Dionysus is a god, he insists he is merely pretending to immortality. Morally outraged by what he considers the excesses of the Bacchantes, he has had some of them imprisoned and intends to capture the others who are now participating in the Bacchic rites. He says if he can capture Dionysus, he will have him killed. When Pentheus sees Cadmus and Tiresias dressed in fawn skins and carrying the thyrsus, he begs them to give up their foolish allegiance to Dionysus. Tiresias explains to Pentheus that the two chief deities are Demeter, the earth goddess, who provides food for men, and Dionysus, who nourishes the vine. Tiresias speaks eloquently of the prophetic powers of Dionysus and the beauty of his rites. Cadmus also tries to persuade his grandson to accept Dionysus, but Pentheus scorns the old men and orders his attendants to destroy Dionysus' shrine and to capture and chain Dionysus. Pentheus enters the palace, and Tiresias and Cadmus go off to join the worshipers. The Chorus comments on the remarks of Pentheus, calling them blasphemous. The Bacchantes praise the emotional release and the physical pleasures that Dionysus encourages, saying the god takes delight in the exultation and joy of his followers.

As the song ends a group of Pentheus' attendants enters, leading Dionysus bound. Pentheus comes out of the palace, and the chief guard tells him that Dionysus has gently submitted to capture. The Bacchantes who were imprisoned, however, have mysteriously escaped and fled to the hills, where they dance and celebrate Dionysus. The guard himself seems amazed by the strange powers of Dionysus, but Pentheus, refusing to admit the necessity of intense emotion and pleasure, is unimpressed. He speaks contemptuously to Dionysus and orders him bound and imprisoned.

After a choral ode celebrating the birth of Dionysus and the beauty of his worship, the voice of Dionysus is heard within, speaking to his Bacchantes. He is heard calling for an earthquake, which causes Pentheus' palace to crash to the ground. Then Dionysus orders fire to spread and completely destroy the palace. [This puzzling passage has been variously interpreted, by some as a metaphorical destruction, because no character in the play comments on it.] Dionysus comes out of the palace and tells the Chorus how he has deceived Pentheus and freed himself. Soon Pentheus enters, angrily exclaiming that his prisoner has escaped. Seeing Dionysus before him, he demands to know how he escaped, but Dionysus only asks mysteriously if gods cannot go over walls. The First Messenger, a herdsman, enters and reports that he has seen Bacchantes from Thebes dancing in the hills. Among them was Pentheus' mother, Agave, leading a band of Bacchantes. He describes their wild revelries and their miraculous feats, and tells Pentheus that, if he had been there, he too would worship Dionysus. The herdsman begs Pentheus to welcome Dionysus to Thebes, but Pentheus wishes only to destroy Dionysus and eliminate his influence. He calls his army and plans an attack. Dionysus warns him not to take arms against a god and offers to bring the women back without force, but Pentheus does not trust him. Dionysus then cruelly tricks Pentheus. He hypnotizes him and slowly Pentheus' repressed sexual desires and curiosity emerge. When Dionysus offers him the opportunity to spy on the Bacchantes drunk with wine, he seizes on it. Because no man is allowed to observe the women participating in these ecstatic rites, Pentheus agrees to dress as a woman. Dionysus informs the Chorus that Pentheus will be discovered by the women and killed.

The Chorus sings of the ecstatic joys of Dionysian revelry, and warns men against skepticism of the gods, for the godless are always punished. Pentheus returns, dressed as a woman. He is now under the spell of Dionysus and is eager to spy on the Bacchantes. The Chorus prophesies the terrible events to come, the discovery and murder of Pentheus, for justice demands his death. Dionysus can be a harsh lord. The Second Messenger comes from the hills and tells the Chorus of the discovery and murder of Pentheus. Having helped Pentheus to hide in a tree top, Dionysus then revealed his hiding place to the Bacchantes. The women, led by Agave and her sisters, mistaking Pentheus for an animal, uprooted the tree. When Pentheus fell to the ground, the intoxicated and shrieking women tore his body to pieces. He cried out to his mother, begging for mercy, but she did not recognize her son. Madly she and the other women tore his limbs from his body. Now his body lies scattered over the rocks and woods, while his head is fastened to the point of Agave's thyrsus, which she carries triumphantly.

As the Messenger concludes his tale, the Chorus sees Agave approaching, carrying the head of Pentheus, which she still believes is that of a lion's whelp. Agave wishes to show her prize to her son. Then Cadmus comes in with attendants, who carry a bier with the remains of Pentheus' body. When Agave proudly shows her prize to her father and offers to give it to him, Cadmus cries out in anguish. Slowly Agave regains her reason and realizes what she has done. She looks at the head on her thyrsus and awakens to a reality of horror. Then she and Cadmus lament for the young Pentheus, who, in denying the power of Dionysus, the spirit of intoxication, irrationality, and all the dark, unknown impulses of man, brought upon himself only destruction.

Dionysus appears and announces that Agave, Cadmus, and Harmonia, his wife, are also to be punished, because they delayed too long in acknowledging the power of the god. All will be exiled from Thebes, and Cadmus and Harmonia, transformed into serpents, will lead many battles and destroy many cities. Finally Zeus will grant them peace in Elysium. Agave complains about the cruel punishment Dionysus demands; then she and her father bid each other a sad farewell.

C O M M E N T A R Y . *The Bacchae,* the greatest extant work centered around Dionysus, evokes and clarifies the primordial qualities of the god, especially the frenzy that characterizes him and his worshipers. *The Bacchae* has presented many difficulties in the way of interpretation, none more frequently alluded to than the ambiguity of the character of Dionysus, the benevolent and destructive god who, like nature itself, releases the productive and joyous spirit of human beings and punishes those who deny his powers.

It is striking that *The Bacchae,* a tragedy in which frenzied violence is the central action, should develop the concept of self-control (a word used repeatedly in the play), the capacity of the human mind for judgment, temperance, and self-knowledge. The rites the "new" god would institute enact a unification of his ambiguous qualities as hunter and nourisher, his various animal forms and his role in fostering the civilizing skills of agriculture, and his powers to bind with frenzy as Bacchus and to free the spirit from that affliction as *Lusios.* The ultimate purpose of his rite in Euripides' tragedy lies not in the expression of frenzy but in the enactment of human beings' achievement of a new apprehension of themselves: a recognition of their own potential creativity and violence and of their capacity to control the demands of their own nature, as they finally accept the power of the god.

For the modern world, Euripides' drama has itself become a source of Dionysiac power—in Friedrich Nietzsche's view, in *The Birth of Tragedy,* straining against Euripides' very intention to set limits upon it. The god of *The Bacchae* was identified with Christ by Friedrich Hölderlin and W. B. Yeats, and, more recently, the play has served as a model for W. H. Auden's and Chester Kallman's *The Bassarids,* the Performance Group's *Dionysus in 69,* and Wole Soyinka's *Bacchae,* which attempt to revitalize Dionysiac frenzy as a psychological, social, and political force.

Bacchus (Bakchos). See DIONYSUS.

Bacchylides (Bakchylides). A Greek poet, born about 505 B.C. on Ceos. Little is known of his life. He probably learned some of his lyric techniques from the poet SIMONIDES, his uncle. Bacchylides visited the court of Hiero, tyrant of Syracuse, whom he addresses in three odes. He died around 450 B.C.

Of Bacchylides' work (see CHORAL LYRICS) fourteen *epinicia* and six poems called dithyrambs remain, though portions of some are missing. These were discovered in an Egyptian papyrus in 1896. Bacchylides was a competitor of Pindar, but since ancient times has been regarded as his inferior. "Longinus," in expressing his preference for the intensity and passion of Pindar to the cold perfection of Bacchylides, sums up the major differences between the two poets. Bacchylides' style is elegant and his knowledge of myth impressive, but he lacks the fervor and the brilliance of Pindar. The *epinicia* of Bacchylides are artful tributes to a hero, but they do not convey the glory of victory as do Pindar's. Although Bacchylides' dithyrambs are poems in honor of Dionysus, the god is seldom mentioned, and the poems express none of the powerful feelings traditionally associated with both Dionysus and the dithyramb. See EPINICION.

Batrachoi. See THE FROGS.

Batrachomyomachia (The Battle of the Frogs and the Mice). Mock-epic (probably the latter half of the sixth century B.C.) in dactylic hexameter, by an unknown author; in ancient times, attributed to HOMER. Translations: in verse, George Chapman, 1625; in verse, Thomas Parnell, 1717; in verse, J. Barlow, 1894; in prose, H. G. Evelyn-White, 1915.

SUMMARY. In the epic manner the poet calls upon the Muses to inspire his song; then he announces his subject—the battle of the frogs and the mice. The war results from a small incident. A mouse, Psicharpax (stealer of crumbs) accepts the offer of a frog, Physignathos (swollen cheeks), to carry him across a stream and visit his home. On the way they encounter a water snake; forgetting the mouse on his back, the frog dives, and the mouse is drowned. Lychopinax (he who licks dishes), another mouse, observes the death of his friend and informs the kingdom of mice. As in the Homeric poems, a council is called, and preparations for war begin. The frogs too call a council and after Physignathos justifies himself in a lofty speech, they prepare to defend themselves. The gods also meet, but Athene persuades them not to take sides. The war is described in epic language and simile, and the deaths of the frogs and the mice are depicted as the fall of heroic warriors. Finally, as the mice seem to be victorious, Zeus sends an army of crabs to drive them back, and the war ends.

Bellerophon. In the sixth book of the *Iliad* Bellerophon's story is told by his grandson Glaucus to Diomedes, whom he encounters in battle. Bellerophon, the son of an earlier Glaucus, the son of Sisyphus, went to the court of Proteus, king of Argos. Proteus' wife Anteia became infatuated with Bellerophon, and when the young man spurned her advances, lied to her husband, telling him that Bellerophon had tried to seduce her. Proteus, unwilling to commit murder himself, sent Bellerophon to Iobates of Lycia, his father-in-law, with a message asking him to put Bellerophon to death. Iobates demanded that Bellerophon slay the Chimaera, a monster with the front of a lion, the middle part of a goat, and the hind part of a serpent. With the help of the winged horse Pegasus, Bellerophon killed the Chimaera; then he conquered the Solymi, a mighty tribe of warriors, and the Amazons. He also managed to slay the bravest warriors of Lycia, who lay in ambush waiting for his return. When Iobates realized that he could not kill Bellerophon, he gave him his daughter as his wife and half of his kingly power. The children of this marriage were Isander, Laodameia, who bore Sarpedon, the child of Zeus, and Hippolochus, the father of the Glaucus of the *Iliad*. Bellerophon's last years were unhappy, for the gods hated him; his son Isander was killed in war, and his daughter was killed by Artemis. Bellerophon wandered about alone, shunning all men. In some legends he tried to ascend to heaven on Pegasus, but was thrown when Zeus sent a gadfly to sting the horse.

Bellona. The Roman goddess of war.

Bellum Punicum. See NAEVIUS.

Bibliotheca (Bibliotheke; The Library). A summary of the Greek myths and legends employed in literature. Nothing is known of the author of the *Bibliotheca*. The work was once attributed to APOLLODORUS, but there is good evidence refuting his authorship. There is some evidence to indicate that the author of the *Bibliotheca* lived no earlier than the middle of the first century B.C. He does not mention Rome at all, and he was not mentioned by his contemporaries or by subsequent writers until the ninth century A.D. The quality of his Greek style seems to suggest an early period of the first century A.D. The author relied on excellent sources; he is accurate, clear, and objective. He traces the history of creation from a mythological point of view, and then tells the stories of mythical, semihistorical, and historical figures. An excellent translation of the *Bibliotheca* was done by Sir James Frazer in 1921.

Bion. A Greek poet, born in Smyrna, who probably lived during the second century B.C. Very little is known about his life. He imitated the style of Theocritus. Only a few of Bion's poems remain, the most famous being THE LAMENT FOR ADONIS, a hymn for Adonis like the one in Theocritus' *Idyl* xv. Bion's other extant poems deal with love. See also LAMENT FOR BION.

Birds, The (Ornithes). An Old Comedy (414 B.C.) by ARISTOPHANES. Translations: in verse, John Hookham Frere, 1839; in verse, Benjamin B. Rogers, 1924; in verse, Arthur S. Way, 1934; in prose and verse, Dudley Fitts, 1957; in verse, William Arrowsmith, 1962.

S C E N E . A desolate wilderness; later, Cloudcuckooland.

S U M M A R Y . Euelpides, holding a jay, and Pisthetaerus, holding a crow, enter, speaking to their birds. The two old men, tired of paying taxes to Athens and of the endless litigation in which Athenians are engaged, have decided to leave the city and seek a home in a more peaceful spot. Now they hope their birds will direct them to Epops, the hoopoe, who originally was a man, Tereus, in order to ask him if, while flying about, he has observed a quiet place where they might settle down. Finally the birds lead Euelpides and Pisthetaerus to a rock near the home of Epops, who soon emerges from a thicket. When the two Athenians tell him they are looking for a pleasant city that offers simple pastimes and is free of corruption, Epops names a few places, to which they object. Pisthetaerus then conceives of a wonderful plan: the birds must create a city of their own, located between the earth and heaven. Thus they will be able to control both the gods and men. Epops, who heartily approves of the plan, sings sweetly to call forth his wife, Procne, and the other birds to discuss the idea with them. The Chorus of Birds appears, but, suspicious of Euelpides and Pisthetaerus, it begins to attack them. Epops establishes peace, and the two Athenians explain their utopian project. Pisthetaerus points out that the birds ruled men before the gods did; if they now build their city between earth and heaven they can force both men and gods to worship them. The Chorus gladly accepts the plan and then speaks to the audience, which, it says, is unfortunately limited and mortal, about the origin, nature, and glory of birds and of their great value to man. If the members of the audience are weary of their restricted lives as men, they may join the birds and live freely and happily.

Pisthetaerus and Euelpides, who now have wings, examine and laugh at each other's appearance. They agree on the name Nephelococcygia (Cloud-cuckooland) for their utopia; then Pisthetaerus sends Euelpides to help build the walls and other parts of the city. Pisthetaerus prays to various bird gods and interviews a poet, an oraclemonger, an astronomer, and others who wish to do work for the new city, but rejects all of them.

In a choral ode the Birds declare that they are gods and must be worshiped by mortals. They promise the judges rewards more precious than those that Paris received if they will award first prize to this play. A Messenger enters, seeking Pisthetaerus, to whom he describes the beautiful city built by the birds. Then a Second Messenger arrives in despair because an unknown god has penetrated the city. This god turns out to be Iris, the messenger of the gods, who is dismissed contemptuously by Pisthetaerus and warned not to annoy the birds. The Chorus declares that the gods may not enter the city, nor may the smoke from the sacrifices of mortals pass through it.

A Herald from earth comes in and announces that many mortals now have the "bird madness" and wish to live in the new city. Then a parricide, a dithyrambic poet, and an informer all ask for wings to help them perform their work more effectively. These are driven away. The next visitor is Prometheus, who comes in masked; as usual he is rebelling against the gods, and he offers his services as an informer. He tells Pisthetaerus that because the gods have been deprived of the offerings of men, they are starving; furthermore the barbarian gods (the Triballi) are threatening to wage war on the Olympians. Zeus and the Triballi are therefore planning to send ambassadors to make peace with the birds. Prometheus suggests that Pisthetaerus refuse to come to an agreement with the gods unless Zeus gives him Basileia (Sovereignty) as his wife and surrenders his scepter to the birds.

After Prometheus leaves, Poseidon, Heracles, and Triballus, one of the barbarous Thracian gods, arrive to seek peace. Having discussed the matter for a while, they agree to Pisthetearus' terms, and the three gods depart. Pisthetaerus and Basileia enter, dressed for their wedding. Pisthetaerus now possesses the thunder and lightning of Zeus. As the Birds sing a marriage song Pisthetaerus invites them to follow him and his bride to the palace of Zeus.

Boreas. In Greek mythology, the north wind. In Latin literature the north wind is Aquilo.

Braggart Warrior, The (Miles Gloriosus). A comedy (c. 205 B.C.) by

PLAUTUS. Translations: in verse, R. Allison, 1914; in prose, Paul Nixon, 1924; in prose, George E. Duckworth, 1942.

SCENE. Ephesus, before the adjoining homes of Pyrgopolynices and Periplectomenus.

SUMMARY. *The Braggart Warrior*, one of Plautus' best-known plays, is based on a Greek comedy *Braggart*, the author of which is unknown. Most authorities believe that Plautus actually used two Greek comedies that he adapted and combined (*contaminatio*). The braggart warrior is a common figure in ancient comedy, and Plautus' delightful version of this stock character established the prototype for later writers, especially the Elizabethan playwrights.

Pyrgopolynices, whose name suggests his fantasies of his many conquests in war, also regards himself as a conqueror in love. His conceit is boundless and his lechery ridiculous; he is the perfect dupe. Pyrgopolynices took the courtesan Philocomasium from Athens to Ephesus while her lover Pleusicles was away. Palaestrio, the faithful slave of Pleusicles, set out to inform his master of what happened, but on his journey his ship was seized by pirates, and Palaestrio was handed over to Pyrgopolynices at Ephesus. Palaestrio wrote to his master, who came to Ephesus, and is now staying at the home of Periplectomenus, his father's friend, who lives next door to Pyrgopolynices.

The ingenious Palaestrio digs a hole through the wall that separates the houses of Pyrgopolynices and Periplectomenus and Philocomasium is able to go to her lover. When Sceledrus, another slave of Pyrgopolynices, observes the two lovers embracing, Palaestrio and Philocomasium manage to convince him that he saw not Philocomasium but her twin sister Dicea. In a delightful scene Philocomasium pretends to be her own twin who just arrived in Ephesus the evening before.

Now Palaestrio conceives a complicated plan for Pleusicles and Philocomasium to escape from Ephesus to Athens. The bachelor Periplectomenus is to pretend to be married to the courtesan Acroteleutium, and she will pretend to be in love with Pyrgopolynices. Palaestrio will act as Acroteleutium's messenger and deliver her ring to Pyrgopolynices, as a token of her desire for him. Thus the braggart warrior will be tricked into apparent adultery.

Flattered by Palaestrio's story of the passion of Acroteleutium, Pyrgopolynices is all too willing to take his advice that he order Philocomasium to leave his house. Meanwhile Pleusicles, disguised as the captain of a ship, announces to Pyrgopolynices that Philocomasium's mother demands that her daughter return to her. The braggart warrior allows her to go and gives her many presents, among them Palaestrio. Soon Pleusicles, Philocomasium, and the clever Palaestrio are sailing for Athens.

Pyrgopolynices, eager to enjoy his new love Acroteleutium, goes into the house of Periplectomenus, where he is caught by the master and his slaves,

67

accused of adultery, and beaten. He confesses his guilt and pathetically begs them to spare his manhood.

Briseis. See ILIAD I, IX, XIX, and Ovid's HEROIDES III.

Brothers, The (Adelphoi). A comedy (160 B.C.) by TERENCE. Translations: in prose, John Sargeaunt, 1912; in verse, W. Ritchie, 1927; in prose, anonymous translation in George Duckworth, ed. *The Complete Roman Drama*, 1942; in prose, Samuel Lieberman, 1964.

SCENE. Athens, before the houses of Micio and Sostrata.

SUMMARY. *The Brothers* is based on a comedy of the same name by Menander. In his Prologue, Terence says that he also uses a scene from Diphilus' play *Comrades in Death*. In *The Brothers*, Terence combines the amusing with the serious, the trivial with the significant. The play deals lightly with the serious problem of rearing children, and Terence seems to suggest that any system man attempts will fail to produce the perfect product he expects.

Demea has two sons, Aeschinus and Ctesipho. Because his brother Micio is a bachelor, Demea allowed him to rear Aeschinus as his own son. Thus Ctesipho has been raised by his father in the country, Aeschinus by his uncle in Athens. The two men believe in and practice entirely different methods of child rearing. Demea is strict and harsh with his son, Micio gentle and indulgent with his nephew. Though neither Ctesipho nor Aeschinus, now grown men, is a model of propriety, it is clear that Terence prefers Micio's point of view to Demea's, for Micio and Aeschinus are far more subtle and sympathetic characters than Demea and Ctesipho.

Demea is disturbed by the news that Aeschinus has kidnaped a courtesan from her procurer. Micio excuses Aeschinus, but Demea, horrified at such an attitude, speaks smugly of Ctesipho, the good son he himself has reared. It turns out that Aeschinus has actually kidnaped the girl for Ctesipho, who loves her. Aeschinus is in love with Pamphila, who bears his child. Sostrata, the widowed mother of Pamphila, is greatly disturbed when she hears that Aeschinus has abducted a courtesan, and Demea, learning of Aeschinus' seduction of Pamphila, is all the more convinced that Micio has reared his son badly.

After further complications Aeschinus reassures Pamphila and Sostrata and confesses his involvement with Pamphila to the sympathetic Micio, who forgives the young man and permits him to marry Pamphila. Demea then learns that it is Ctesipho who loves the courtesan. First he berates Micio, blaming him for his sons' licentious and foolish ways. However, he is soon convinced that his own rigid code of conduct is old-fashioned, and his leniency is now as exaggerated as was his earlier strictness. In his sudden expansiveness he urges Micio to marry Sostrata, and Micio reluctantly agrees. Demea is generous to his slaves and even allows Ctesipho to keep his courtesan.

Brutus, Marcus Junius. A Roman Republican leader, born around 78 B.C. He is known mainly for his important role in the Republican resistance to Caesar and his followers. Though Caesar pardoned Brutus for his support of

Pompey in the Civil War of 49 B.C., and appointed him governor of Cisalpine Gaul in 46 B.C. and praetor in 44 B.C., Brutus was one of the Republicans who planned and executed his assassination in 44 B.C. Brutus and Cassius then joined in resisting the forces of Antony, Octavian, and Lepidus, the second triumvirate. Defeated at Philippi in 42 B.C., Brutus and Cassius committed suicide. Brutus is depicted as a heroic and tragic figure in Shakespeare's *Julius Caesar*.

Brutus. A treatise (46 B.C.) on rhetoric by CICERO. The work takes the form of a dialogue between M. Junius Brutus, T. Pomponius Atticus, and Cicero himself. After suggesting that the death of the famous orator Hortensius has come at a time when liberty is dying in Rome, Cicero begins the dialogue with a brief summary of the origins of oratory in Greece. Then he traces the history of Roman oratory, dealing with the great speakers of the past and present. When he comes to Gaius Licinius Calvus, Cicero takes the opportunity to criticize the Attic movement in oratory, led by Calvus and Brutus. The Atticists were a group of young Roman orators who, influenced by the Attic prose writers of the fifth and fourth centuries B.C., rejected the copiousness and the linguistic and rhythmical artfulness of Ciceronian oratory, preferring an unadorned style, the chief virtue of which was lucidity. The Attic style is restrained, unemotional, and plain to the point of severity. Atticism was regarded as the opposite of the Asianic style, which Cicero describes as being of two types: the first extremely artful, characterized by balance and symmetry; the second both swift and ornate. Both types of Asianic style, says Cicero, are suitable for the young orator, but do not have the dignity appropriate to a mature speaker.

Cicero also describes his own early training and his career as an orator. He speaks of his association with Hortensius and praises his oratorical ability. Now that Hortensius is dead, Cicero and Brutus must guard the dignity of eloquence. Cicero expresses his regret that civic strife and the loss of liberty at Rome prevent Brutus from realizing his great powers as an orator. The end of *Brutus* is fragmentary.

Bucolics. See ECLOGUES.

C

Cacus. In Roman mythology, Cacus, a son of Vulcan, was a giant who lived in a cave on Mount Aventine. When Hercules was bringing home the cattle of Geryon, which he had taken in Spain, he passed through Italy briefly. Cacus stole some of the cattle, but Hercules discovered the theft and killed him. See *Aeneid* VIII.

Cadmus (Kadmos). In Greek myth, son of Agenor and founder of the Greek city of THEBES. Cadmus married Harmonia, the daughter of either Ares and Aphrodite or Zeus and Electra, and she bore him four daughters, Autonoë, Agave, Ino, and Semele, and a son Polydorus, who became the father of Labdacus and grandfather of Laius, the father of Oedipus. For Cadmus' involvement with Dionysus and the god's punishment of Cadmus and Harmonia, see Euripides' THE BACCHAE.

Caesar, Gaius Julius. A Roman military and political leader, born at Rome in 102 B.C. (according to some authorities 100 B.C.). He received a good education, and by 77 B.C. was practicing law. Caesar was regarded an outstanding orator, almost the equal of CICERO. Marius, the leader of the popular party, was Caesar's uncle by marriage, and Caesar married Cornelia, the daughter of Cinna, a follower of Marius. When Sulla, the leader of the aristocratic party, ordered Caesar to divorce his wife, he left Rome for Bithynia. After a brief return to Rome he left again to study rhetoric at Rhodes. On the voyage he was captured by pirates, whom he confidently threatened to crucify. Released after the payment of a ransom, Caesar did manage to capture them and carry out his threat.

Caesar took part in the second Mithridatic War and established a reputation as a brave warrior. In 68 B.C. he was quaestor (financial officer) in Spain; in 65 B.C., as curule aedile (a plebeian magistrate in charge of public buildings and games), he spent great sums of money in an effort to win public support. In 63 B.C. Caesar urged the Senate to be lenient to the followers of Catiline. That year he was elected *pontifex maximus* (chief pontiff) of Rome, and in 62 B.C. he became praetor (judge). Next he was governor of Spain. Returning to Rome in 60 B.C. Caesar formed the first triumvirate with Pompey and Crassus. They agreed to support him for consul in 59 B.C.; in return he would help to further their political ambitions. A marriage was arranged between Pompey and Caesar's daughter Julia. After his consulship Caesar became governor of Gaul.

For nine years he waged war against the tribes of Gaul, finally conquering them and extending the rule of Rome to the English Channel. To show the Germans the strength of Rome, he crossed the Rhine twice. He also crossed the English Channel in 55 B.C. and in 54 B.C., fearing that a free Britain would threaten Roman dominion in Gaul. Caesar describes his conquest of Gaul in his *Commentaries on the Gallic War* (*Commentarii de Bello Gallico*), dealing in seven books, one for each year, with his campaigns from 58 B.C. to 52 B.C. One of Caesar's officers, Hirtius, added an eighth book.

After the death of his wife Julia in 54 B.C., Pompey openly supported the Senate in its opposition to Caesar. With the death of Crassus in 53 B.C. the first triumvirate was entirely dissolved. Caesar wished to return to Rome as consul in 49 B.C., but was opposed by Pompey and the Senate. In an act of open rebellion against the Republic Caesar led his thirteenth legion across the Rubicon, a stream on the southern boundary of his province, and thus marked the beginning of civil war at Rome. Caesar's army found Pompey unprepared and forced him to flee from Italy to the East, where he hoped to build up an army. Caesar, now dictator of Rome, pursued Pompey and his followers until 48 B.C., when he defeated him at Pharsalus (see Lucan's ON THE CIVIL WAR). Caesar followed him to Egypt and discovered that Pompey had been murdered by the Egyptians. After remaining in Egypt with the young queen Cleopatra for eight months Caesar went to the Near East, where Pharnaces, the son of Mithridates, was stirring up an insurrection. In 47 B.C., when Caesar conquered Pharnaces at Zela, he sent his famous message *"Veni, vidi, vici."*

After returning to Rome for only a short time, Caesar left for North Africa, where, under the leadership of Scipio and Cato, the Republican forces had built up an army to oppose him. On April 6, 46 B.C., Caesar conquered Scipio's army at Thapsus. After Caesar's victory Cato fled to Utica and took his own life. The survivors of the Republican army managed to get to Spain, but Caesar defeated them at Munda on March 17, 45 B.C.

Caesar returned to Rome victorious and, as dictator, began to reform the administration of the government. He confiscated the property of his enemies and controlled all "elected" magistrates. On the Ides of March, 44 B.C., he was assassinated by a group of Republicans led by Brutus and Cassius.

Despite the enormous demands of his military and political affairs, Caesar managed to write a great deal besides the *Commentaries on the Gallic War* mentioned above, but the only other remaining works are three books of his unfinished *Commentaries on the Civil War* (*Commentarii de Bello Civili*), which describe his battles with the Republican forces from the time he crossed the Rubicon to Pompey's death in Egypt. Among his lost writings are *De Analogia*, on grammar; *Anticatones*, a reply to a treatise by Cicero; *De Astris*, on astronomy; a play on Oedipus; and some poetry.

Caesar's *Commentaries on the Gallic War* has been much admired by literary critics and historians. In *Brutus*, Cicero praises the purity and elegance of Caesar's language, and most modern readers would agree with his evaluation. Caesar's style is unadorned, but it is forceful in its precision and its compression. Though Caesar's purpose in the *Commentaries* is to establish his own glory as a leader and general, his approach to his material is detached and factual. See Plutarch's life of Caesar.

Calchas (Kalchas). A seer on the side of the Greeks at Troy. He appears in Homer's ILIAD (1) and Vergil's *Aeneid*. See also IPHIGENIA IN AULIS.

Caligula (nickname of **Gaius Caesar**). Emperor of Rome from A.D. 37 to 41. The major contemporary sources for his life are Tacitus' *Annals* and Suetonius' *Lives of the Caesars*.

Callimachus (Kallimachos). A Greek poet, scholar, and critic, born late in the fourth century B.C. at Cyrene, on the North African coast. Little is known about his life. After studying at Athens he went to Alexandria, where he taught school for a while and then was appointed to an important position in the great Library of Alexandria, though he was not made director, as was once thought. Callimachus was assigned to prepare a catalogue of the books in the library and became known as a bibliographer and literary historian. He was also a prolific writer, thought to have produced more than eight hundred works. The famous literary quarrel between Callimachus and Apollonius Rhodius began with their disagreement over whether the short, polished poem or the traditional epic was the superior work of art, a controversy that had existed in earlier literary circles. Probably one of the reasons the quarrel became a personal one is that Callimachus objected to Apollonius' adaptation to his own purposes of passages from Callimachus' poems. Most scholars believe that this quarrel was the cause of Apollonius' departure from Alexandria. Callimachus' famous epigram "Large book, large evil" sums up his attitude toward the conventional long epic; his more specific attacks on Apollonius were made in his *Ibis*, a poem that has not survived, and at the end of his *Hymn to Apollo*. The date of Callimachus' death is unknown.

Callimachus' extant works consist of six hymns—to Zeus, Apollo, Artemis, Delos, the Bath of Pallas, and Demeter, all written in hexameter verse, except for one in elegiacs; sixty-four epigrams, mainly in the GREEK ANTHOLOGY; and various fragments from *Aetia*, an elegiac poem in four books dealing with the "causes" of myths, rites, and customs; *Iambi*, a book of thirteen iambic poems; *Hecale*, an epic poem on Theseus; and minor epic and elegiac poems.

Callimachus was one of the best-known poets of the Alexandrian period. Catullus translated his *The Lock of Berenice*, and Ovid imitated Callimachus in his *Fasti* and his *Ibis*. Today Callimachus is best known for his brilliant epigrams, which suggest the essence of an experience with remarkable grace and economy. The most famous of these is one Callimachus wrote on the death of Heraclitus of Halicarnassus, known to most readers in the version of William Cory, beginning, "They told me, Heraclitus, they told me you were dead."

Others less well known are equally effective in their expression of bitterness, sorrow, or love in epigrammatic form.

Callinus (Kallinos). Born in Ephesus during the seventh century B.C., Callinus is the earliest poet known to have employed elegiacs. Very few fragments of his work remain. The only one of any length is a poem calling the Ephesians to arms to defend their state against an attack by the Cimmerians. Because all men must die, says Callinus, a courageous man goes boldly into battle, seeking heroic fame.

Callisto (Kallisto). In Greek mythology, a nymph who followed Artemis. By Zeus she became the mother of Arcas, the legendary founder of the Arcadians. Hera, jealous of Callisto, transformed her into a bear. Zeus prevented her son, who encountered her while hunting, from killing her and transformed mother and son into the constellations Ursa Major (Great Bear) and Arctophylax, sometimes known as Arcturus, who is a character in Plautus' ROPE.

Calypso (Kalypso). In Greek mythology, a daughter of Atlas. See ODYSSEY I, V.

Camilla. A maiden warrior, ally of Turnus in Vergil's AENEID VII, XI.

Captives, The (Captivi). A comedy by PLAUTUS adapted from an unknown Greek play. In tone and mood *The Captives* is more serious than most of Plautus' other plays; the comedy is often ironic and never farcical. Hegio, an old man, has lost both his sons. One was kidnaped by a slave when four years old; the other, Philopolemus, has been taken as a prisoner of war by the Eleans. In an effort to recover the captive son, Hegio has bought two Elean prisoners of war, Philocrates and his slave Tyndarus, and he plans to send Tyndarus to Elis to arrange for the exchange of Philopolemus.

The Prologue explains that Tyndarus is actually Hegio's son, who was kidnaped when he was a child and sold to the father of Philocrates, but Hegio, of course, does not recognize him. The audience is also informed that Philocrates and his loyal slave Tyndarus have thought up a plan by which the young master may return to his home. They have decided to exchange clothing and roles; thus Hegio will send the master Philocrates rather than the slave Tyndarus back to Elis. Moreover, Tyndarus, in freeing his master, will unwittingly aid in the recovery of his captive brother.

Hegio, believing that Philocrates is the slave of Tyndarus, sends him off to Elis to make arrangements for the exchange of his son. Later, however, Aristophantes, another Elean prisoner bought by Hegio, turns out to be a friend of Philocrates. He reveals that Tyndarus is actually Philocrates' slave. Unaware that he is tormenting his own son, Hegio has the unrepentant Tyndarus chained and orders him to work in the quarries.

Soon Philocrates returns with Hegio's son Philopolemus and with the slave Stalagmus who had kidnaped his other son many years before. Thankful for the return of Philopolemus, Hegio offers to return Tyndarus to Philocrates, but after questioning Stalagmus and Philocrates, Hegio learns that Tyndarus is his lost son.

Carmen Saeculare (Secular Song). A poem (17 B.C.) by HORACE. It was written at the request of Augustus for ceremonies connected with the *Ludi Saeculares* (games held at intervals of 110 years to celebrate the foundation of Rome). The poem consists of nineteen Sapphic strophes (see METER). Twenty-seven girls sang the first nine, twenty-seven boys the second nine, and the two groups together sang the last strophe. A formal hymn, the *Carmen Saeculare*, calls on the most important Roman gods to protect and nourish the state. A surviving inscription describes the ceremony and the singing of the *Carmen Saeculare* and names the poet as its author.

Carmina. See ODES (Horace).

Carneades (Karneades). A Greek philosopher of the New Academy, lived from about 214 to about 129 B.C. Carneades held the philosophical position that absolute knowledge was unattainable. Carneades was known for his eloquence and powers of persuasion. He left no works, but his students spread his philosophical ideas. Carneades was mainly opposed to the Stoics, whose dogmatism repelled him.

Carthage (Carthago). A Phoenician colony situated on a peninsula on the northern coast of Africa, near the modern Tunis; founded by settlers from Tyre around the ninth century B.C. In Latin literature the Carthaginians are often referred to as *Poeni* (the Phoenicians) because of their Phoenician origin. For the legendary account of the establishment of Carthage see DIDO. As Carthage flourished in agriculture and in commerce, it became a competitor of Rome, and the three Punic (from *Poenicus* and later *Punicus*, Latin for Carthaginian) Wars between Rome and Carthage resulted. The First Punic War was fought from 264 B.C. to 241 B.C. In 247 B.C. Hamilcar Barca, the great general and the father of Hannibal, was placed in command of the Carthaginian troops in Sicily, where he managed to hold off the Roman forces for years. Nonetheless, the Romans defeated the Carthaginians in 241 B.C. The Second Punic War started in 218 B.C., when Hannibal, whose father had pledged him to lifelong hatred of Rome, was commander of the Carthaginian army in Spain. He managed to cross the Alps into Italy with his army and, in alliance with the Gauls, defeated the Romans in many important battles. Though Hannibal conquered the Roman army at Cannae and allied himself with Philip V of Macedon, the Romans, led by P. Cornelius Scipio, finally conquered large parts of Spain, which became Roman provinces, and won the war at the battle of Zama in 202 B.C. With this Roman victory Carthage lost her important position in the Mediterranean. The Third Punic War began in 149 B.C., and under the command of the Roman general Scipio Aemilianus, Carthage was destroyed in 146 B.C.

Carthaginian, The (Poenulus). A comedy by PLAUTUS, based on an unknown Greek play. One of Plautus' least interesting plays, *The Carthaginian* is poorly constructed and unnecessarily long. The complications of the plot have little humòr and no intrinsic relation to the theme. The two daughters of Hanno, a Carthaginian, were kidnaped as children and later bought by a procurer and taken to Calydon. There a young man, Agorastocles, who had also been kidnaped as a child, falls in love with Adelphasium, the older sister. Agorastocles, actually the son of a cousin of Hanno, does not know that they are relatives. Hanno arrives in time to prevent his daughters from being forced into prostitution. He recognizes Agorastocles and approves of his marriage to Adelphasium. At the end the procurer is ruined. *The Carthaginian* contains the only extant examples of passages in the Carthaginian language.

Casina. A farce (possibly 185 B.C.) by PLAUTUS. The play is based on *Lot-Drawers*, a lost Greek play by Diphilus. Though the play was popular, it is not one of Plautus' most interesting comedies. Casina, the heroine, is a sixteen-year-old slave girl, brought up in the household of Lysidamus, an Athenian. Both he and his son Euthynicus are infatuated with Casina, and each tries to arrange a marriage for her that will make her available to him. Thus Lysidamus wishes to marry her to Olympio, his bailiff; Euthynicus tries to marry her to Chalinus, his slave and armor-bearer. Lysidamus' wife, Cleustrata, aware of her husband's infatuation with Casina, objects to his plan for her marriage. When he arranges for Chalinus and Olympio to draw lots for the girl, Olympio wins. However, Cleustrata and the others arrange for the "bride" to be Chalinus, disguised as Casina. Both Olympio and Lysidamus discover to their horror that the "bride" they attempt to embrace is Chalinus. The shamefaced Lysidamus is forgiven by Cleustrata. The Epilogue reveals that Casina will discover she is a freeborn Athenian and will marry Euthynicus.

Casket, The (Cistellaria). A comedy (no later than 202 B.C.) by Plautus. It is based on the lost Greek play *Women at Luncheon* by Menander. The text of the play is in bad condition; sections are lost, and many lines are fragmentary. *The Casket* is concerned with the discovery of the true parentage of a young courtesan Selenium, the mistress of Alcesimarchus, whose father disapproves of her. Finally a casket of trinkets reveals Selenium's true identity as the daughter of Demipho, a citizen. Selenium and Alcesimarchus may now marry.

Cassandra (Kassandra). In Greek mythology, a daughter of Priam, king of Troy, and Hecuba. Apollo fell in love with her, and because she seemed to return his love the god gave her the gift of prophecy. When Cassandra spurned Apollo, however, he turned her gift into a source of torment, for he decreed that no one would ever believe Cassandra's prophecies. For her tragic story see Aeschylus' *Agamemnon* (under ORESTEIA) and Euripides' THE TROJAN WOMEN. Cassandra also appears in the *Iliad,* the *Aeneid,* and Seneca's *Agamemnon.* Pausanias writes of her, especially in I, V, and X.

Cassius Longinus, Gaius. A Roman Republican leader. He is known mainly for his role in the assassination of Caesar and for his resistance to the second triumvirate. Though he was on the side of Pompey in the Civil War of 49 B.C., Caesar pardoned him and appointed him praetor. Cassius helped to plan and execute the assassination of Caesar, then joined with Brutus against the forces of Antony, Octavian, and Lepidus. Defeated at Philippi in 42 B.C., he committed suicide.

Castor. See DIOSCURI.

Catalepton (Trifles). A group of short poems in various meters, some thought to be by VERGIL. Most of them are in elegiac couplets and some in iambics. They have various subjects, such as love, language, friendship, and Siro's villa, which Vergil visited for a time.

Catiline (real name **Lucius Sergius Catilina**). A Roman nobleman, born around 108 B.C., is well known in Roman history mainly because CICERO, in several orations, denounced his plots against the Republic. Catiline came from an impoverished aristocratic family. In his youth he acquired a reputation for licentious and irresponsible behavior and for his association with degenerate aristocrats like himself. Catiline held the position of quaestor, and in 68 B.C. was elected praetor. After serving as propraetor of Africa in 67 B.C. he returned to Rome and in 66 B.C. became a candidate for a consulship. When he was accused of extortion by the African people he had governed, the Senate would not allow him to run for the consulship. Catiline then conspired to murder the consuls of 65 B.C., but this first conspiracy failed. In 64 B.C. Catiline and Cicero were among the seven candidates for the consulships. Catiline was defeated, and Cicero and Gaius Antonius Hybrida, who had joined with Catiline against Cicero, were elected. When Catiline was again defeated in 63 B.C. in his attempt to win the consulship for 62 B.C., Cicero prevented his plot to seize the government of Rome by force. Cicero had five of the conspirators arrested and put to death; Catiline met his death in a battle against the Republican army near Pistoria (Pistoia, north of Florence) in 62 B.C. See SALLUST (*Bellum Catilinae*) and Ben Jonson's play *Catiline*.

Cato (the Censor), **Marcus Porcius.** A Roman statesman, born at Tusculum (near modern Frascati, fifteen miles southeast of Rome) in 234 B.C. He was a soldier in the Second Punic War and held many public offices before becoming consul in 195 B.C. He earned his greatest fame as censor, when, attempting to reestablish the values of early Rome, he openly attacked the immorality of the Roman nobility. He attempted to reform Roman moral standards and to check the strong influence of Greek literature and philosophy on Roman cultural life. Nonetheless, Cato pursued Greek studies as an old man. He was also known for his preoccupation with the threat of Carthage to Rome and for his famous warning to the Roman Senate: *Carthago delenda est* (Carthage must be destroyed). He died in 149 B.C.

Cato was a famous orator of his time; actually it can be said that Roman oratory starts with him. Cicero knew and admired his speeches, of which only fragments remain. Cato also wrote a lost work called *Origines*, dealing with the beginnings of Italian civilization and the early history of Rome. His *De Agri*

Cultura, also known as *De Re Rustica,* most of which is extant, is a handbook on agriculture. Cato is the chief character in Cicero's *De Senectute.*

Cato, Marcus Porcius (of Utica). The great-grandson of Cato the Censor, born in 95 B.C. Like his great-grandfather, Cato was known for his integrity and his strict, even rigid, morality. He was Cicero's chief supporter against Catiline and voted for the death penalty for the Catilinarian conspirators. Cato, who was called by the historian Livy "the conscience of Rome," was an ardent Republican who strongly opposed Caesar. When Caesar crossed the Rubicon, Cato advised the Senate to allow Pompey to lead the Republican forces against him. After the death of Pompey, Cato joined the army of Scipio. When Scipio was also defeated, Cato, realizing that Caesar would conquer Rome, fled to Utica and took his own life in 46 B.C. Lucan idealizes Cato in *On the Civil War (De Bello Civili),* and he is the hero of Joseph Addison's play *Cato.*

Catullus, Gaius Valerius. A Roman poet, born at Verona around 84 B.C. He came from a wealthy family and received a good education. When Catullus was about twenty-two, he went to Rome, where he entered a circle of political and social leaders. Julius Caesar was a friend of Catullus' father, and this friendship continued despite Catullus' bitter attacks on Caesar in some of his poems. When Catullus apologized, Caesar was willing to forgive the young poet.

It is commonly thought that among the people Catullus met at Rome was Clodia, the wife of Q. Caecilius Metellus and sister of Publius Clodius, a corrupt and violent man, known for his hatred of Cicero, that Catullus fell deeply in love with Clodia, who was some years older than he, and that she became the object of his most moving love poems, in which he calls her Lesbia. Though Apuleius says in his *Apologia* that Catullus' Lesbia was actually named Clodia, it is by no means certain that she was the Clodia referred to above. Catullus' love poems suggest that after a brief period of happiness during which Lesbia responded to his love, he endured the anguish of her unfaithfulness and rejection. From this time on his poems convey the feeling that his love for her has become an obsession, and they record his fruitless efforts to free himself from his infatuation, his bitterness and pain.

Catullus returned to Verona for a brief time, and came back to Rome still desperately in love with Clodia, who had already taken a new lover. In 57 B.C. Catullus went on a journey to Bithynia as a member of the staff of the governor Gaius Memmius. During this journey Catullus paid a visit to the grave of his brother, who was buried near Troy. His visit is recorded in a beautiful elegy (No. 101). After his return to Rome, Catullus had not long to live; he died in about 54 B.C., when he was around thirty years old.

Unlike most ancient writers, Catullus is a deeply personal poet; his poems (see LYRICS) suggest a great deal about his brief, intense life. Though the series of Lesbia poems may not record the exact details of his experience, they convey personal delight, conflict, and despair. Moreover, his poems to friends, to his brother, and to his beloved home at Sirmio reveal Catullus' sensitive nature and his immense capacity for love and pain. Like Sappho, whose meters and style he imitated, Catullus expresses deep and powerful feelings with apparent spontaneity. Yet he is a highly conscious artist. Although the Lesbia poems probably do reveal Catullus' own emotional experience, they should not be read merely as a record of personal feeling. In a fine essay K. F. Quinn discusses Catullus' use of conventional learned allusions in a love poem to Lesbia and shows how Catullus "exploits this learning" to intensify personal expression. Quinn also develops the thesis that Catullus transforms *versiculi*, or *vers de société*, conventional Hellenistic and Roman literary exercises, into "genuine poetry" ("Docte Catulle," in *Critical Essays on Roman Literature*, J. P. Sullivan, ed. [Harvard University Press, 1962]). Most of Catullus' poems are short; in a few concise lines he is able to create an experience of love, friendship, or sometimes bitterness and anger either at Lesbia or at some person he despised, such as Caesar or the poet Suffenus or a contemptible father and son whom Catullus mocks in his thirty-third poem. However, he also wrote some longer poems: two magnificent marriage songs, a moving poem on the story of Attis, an epyllion on the marriage of Peleus and Thetis, and a poem on the lock of Berenice, a translation of a poem by Callimachus.

Catullus, whose love poetry was never surpassed in ancient times, has influenced a great many poets both ancient and modern. Tibullus, Propertius, Horace, and Ovid imitated his techniques. During the Elizabethan period and the seventeenth century, English poets such as Ben Jonson and Robert Herrick attempted to capture the quality of Catullus in English, but they could never convey either his passionate intensity or his brilliant spontaneity.

Cecrops (Kekrops). Regarded in legend as the first king of Attica and the founder of Athens. He was part man, part serpent.

Centaurs (Kentauroi). A mythical race of creatures with the heads and upper bodies of men and the lower bodies of horses, who were descended from Ixion and Nephele. During the wedding feast of Pirithous, king of the Lapiths, and Hippodamia, the Centaurs attempted to kidnap the bride, but they were defeated by the Lapiths and driven away from their homes on Mount Pelion.

Cephalus (Kephalos). In Greek mythology, the husband of Procris, whom he accidentally killed. In Ovid's *Metamorphoses* VII Cephalus tells the story of how Eos, who had fallen in love with him, warned him that one day he would wish he had never set eyes on Procris, whom he loved so much. When Cephalus expressed doubts of his wife's loyalty, Procris left him and followed the goddess Diana. However, Cephalus persuaded Procris to return to him, and she presented him with two gifts that Diana had given her, a dog that always caught whatever it chased and a spear that never missed its target. Suspicious of her husband, Procris hid in the bushes one day to observe him while he hunted. Hearing a rustle of leaves, Cephalus thought an animal was hiding, and throwing the spear, killed Procris.

Cerberus (Kerberos). In Greek mythology, a monstrous dog depicted as having fifty or one hundred or, in later writers, three heads. He guarded the entrance to Hades. See Euripides' THE MADNESS OF HERACLES.

Ceres. An Italian goddess of fertility who became identified with DEMETER.

Ceyx (Keyx). See ALCYONE.

Characters (Characteres). Prose sketches (fourth century B.C.) by THEOPHRASTUS. Translations: J. Healy, 1899; R. C. Jebb, 1909; J. M. Edmond, 1929.

SUMMARY. In thirty brief sketches of "distinguishing characteristics" of mankind Theophrastus reveals his capacity to observe and delineate human weakness. Though he describes types, his use of detail and brief incidents gives his characters a concrete reality. For example, in his second sketch, "Flattery," he depicts the flatterer picking a piece of chaff out of the beard of the recipient of his attentions and, as he does so, declaring that the man is getting gray because he has not seen the flatterer for a day, then complimenting him on his dark beard, for it is a sign of youthfulness. Theophrastus' representations are dramatic: his flatterer runs all over town, praising one man's children and the shape of another's foot; his boor (IV) stands and watches an ox, an ass, or a goat with deep absorption, makes love to the servant, and goes to a neighbor's house in the middle of the night to retrieve something he has lent him. One character is obsessed by his superstitions (XVI), another by a need to grumble (XVII). Pride, stinginess, stupidity, and other weaknesses are exposed and analyzed.

By accumulating examples that illustrate and dramatize the characteristic he describes, Theophrastus suggests a person controlled by the weakness that dominates his character and his way of life. Yet Theophrastus' criticism is not harsh; he gently exposes folly, poking fun at the absurdity of the types he depicts, who are extreme examples of weaknesses found in all men.

Charmides. A dialogue by PLATO, named after his uncle, who was one of the leaders of the Thirty Tyrants. The subject of the dialogue is temperance (*sophrosyne*).

Charon. Son of Erebus, Charon was an old man, dirty and poorly dressed, who ferried the souls of the dead across the rivers of Hades. The cost of this service was an *obolus*, a coin which was placed in the mouth of a dead person before his burial. Charon appears in Aristophanes' THE FROGS, Vergil's AENEID VI, and Lucian's *Dialogues of the Dead*.

Charybdis. In Greek legend, a whirlpool near Sicily. See ODYSSEY XII.

Children of Heracles, The (Herakleidai). A tragedy (probably 427 B.C.) by EURIPIDES. Translations: in prose, E. P. Coleridge, 1891; in verse, Arthur S. Way, 1912; in verse, Ralph Gladstone, 1955.

MYTHICAL BACKGROUND. Eurystheus, king of Argos, at whose

command Heracles had performed the Twelve Labors, persecuted Heracles' family after the death of Heracles. Iolaus, an old friend of Heracles, protected his children against the hatred of Eurystheus, who attempted to kill them. Iolaus and Heracles' children fled from place to place, always pursued by the wrath of Eurystheus. Finally they came to Marathon, which belonged to Athens.

SUMMARY. Iolaus and the sons of Heracles sit on the steps of the altar of Zeus at Marathon, where they have come, driven by the wrath of Eurystheus, king of Argos. Iolaus speaks of the years of flight during which he has protected the children of Heracles, whom Eurystheus has tried to murder. As Iolaus sits at the altar with Heracles' sons, Alcmena guards his daughters within the temple of Zeus. Iolaus grows fearful as he sees Eurystheus' herald, Copreus, approaching. Copreus curses Iolaus and tries to seize Heracles' sons. When Iolaus resists him, Copreus throws the old man to the ground. At this point the Chorus of Aged Men of Marathon enters and expresses its sympathy for Iolaus, the suppliant. Soon Demophon, king of Athens, enters, accompanied by his brother, Acamas. Copreus identifies himself to the King as an Argive who is merely doing his duty by attempting to force Argives who have been condemned to death to return to their land. If Demophon cooperates with Copreus and allows him to seize Iolaus and the children, the powerful Eurystheus will befriend Athens, but if he refuses, he faces war with Argos. Iolaus pleads for asylum in Athens, known as a place of refuge for the oppressed. Moreover, the descendants of Heracles and the king of Athens have common ancestors and the friendship of Heracles and Theseus to bind them. If Athens did not protect holy suppliants, says Iolaus, the city would be shamed. Demophon agrees to protect Iolaus and the sons of Heracles. Speaking of his obligations to Zeus, to kinship, and to old ties of friendship, he refuses to surrender those whom he believes Athens should protect. When Copreus once more tries to seize the children, Demophon threatens him with his staff. Copreus leaves, promising to return with an Argive army.

The Chorus and Demophon decide it is time to prepare for the attack of the Argives. Demophon leaves Iolaus and the children at the altar and goes off to send out scouts, consult the seers, and prepare for sacrifices. After a choral ode praising Athens' courage and love of freedom, her justice and kindness to the oppressed, Demophon returns to announce that the Argive army, led by Eurystheus, has arrived. The Athenians are prepared for battle, he says, but the city is troubled by a prophecy that declares that a maiden born of a noble father must be sacrificed to Persephone. Iolaus is willing to give himself up to Eurystheus to avoid such a sacrifice, but Macaria, the daughter of Heracles, comes out of the temple to declare that she is ready to sacrifice herself for her brothers. She says farewell and courageously goes to her sacrificial death. The Chorus comments on Macaria's nobility, saying she has won fame through death.

The Servant of Hyllus, Heracles' oldest son, comes to tell Iolaus and Alcmena, who has come out of the temple, that Hyllus has brought an army to aid Demophon. Iolaus decides to leave the children in the care of Alcmena and to fight beside the Athenians. After a choral ode in praise of Athens and Athene, a servant enters and reports victory for the Athenian forces. He tells of how the gods gave Iolaus renewed youth for one day so that he could fight gloriously. Soon a Messenger enters, accompanied by guards who lead Eurystheus in chains. Alcmena cries out that justice has seized Eurystheus, who is now a slave, and she demands that he be killed. The Chorus protests, explaining that it is unjust to kill someone taken in war. Eurystheus, however, asks no mercy. He reveals an old prophecy of Apollo that if the Athenians bury him properly, his spirit will protect the city against the unworthy descendants of Heracles (the Spartans) who will attack the city. The Chorus now agrees with Alcmena that Eurystheus should be killed, and the guards lead him to his death.

COMMENTARY. Written during the Peloponnesian War, the *Heracleidae* glorifies Athens as the home of freedom and as a great military power. Euripides suggests that in his own time Athens, the traditional defender of the oppressed, is being attacked by the descendants of those whom his city once aided. The implication is that the Spartans, descendants of Heracles, are desecrating the memory of the friendship of Theseus and Heracles.

Chimaera (Chimaira). See BELLEROPHON.

Chios. An Ionian island off the coast of Asia Minor, thought by many ancients to be the birthplace of Homer.

Chiron (Cheiron). In Greek mythology, one of the CENTAURS and a learned and wise teacher of many great heroes of Greece, including Asclepius, Achilles, and Jason.

Choephoroi. See under ORESTEIA.

Choerilus (Choirilos). One of the earliest Greek tragedians. His first play is said to have been performed in 523 B.C. and his career as a dramatist to have lasted until 468 B.C. Though it is thought that he wrote 160 plays, only the name of one of them, *Alope*, and two very brief fragments of his work remain.

choral lyric. See LYRIC POETRY.

Choral Lyrics (BACCHYLIDES). Epinicia and Dithyrambs (first half of fifth century B.C.). Translations: in prose, E. Poste, 1898; in prose, R. C. Jebb, 1905; in verse, Arthur S. Way, 1929; in verse, Robert Fagles, 1961.

SUMMARY. I. Epinician. *Isthmian Ode for Argeius of Ceos*, victor in a boxing match. The first lines are fragmentary. The poem begins with a myth about the founding of Ceos by Euxantius, the son of Dexithea (she who receives a god) and Minos, king of Crete. Then it tells of the strength and courage of Argeius, who fought valiantly in the boxing match. Pantheides, the father of Argeius, who is a wealthy physician, is praised for his generosity and hospitality. Pantheides' reward is his five sons. One of these, Argeius, has achieved excellence and glory. Valor is the noblest goal, greater than wealth.

II. Epinician. *Isthmian Ode for Argeius of Ceos*, victor in a boxing match.

The subject of this brief poem is the same as that of I. The poet asks Fame to carry the glory of Argeius to Ceos, where his praises will be sung to the music of flutes.

III. Epinician. *Olympian Ode for Hiero of Syracuse,* for victory in a chariot race which he sponsored (468 B.C.). The poet asks the Muse Clio to sing the praises of the mighty horses of Hiero (Hieron), who won great honor for him. Great numbers of men celebrate this victory of Hiero, tyrant of Syracuse. The gold of the tripods that Hiero presented to the temple of Apollo at Delphi suggests the glow of fire. Hiero's generosity brings to mind the precious gifts that Croesus, king of Lydia, also gave to the temple of Apollo. In return for his generosity Croesus was saved by Apollo from death by fire. However, not even the wealthy Croesus gave more lavishly to Apollo than Hiero, who is loved by gods and men. Hiero, once a warrior, is now very ill, and he understands only too well the brevity of mortal life. Bacchylides reminds him of Apollo's sound advice to Admetus, that man must think in double terms: on the one hand, that tomorrow he will die, and on the other, that he will live to be fifty and that each of his years will be a prosperous one. Though man dies, virtue and fame continue. Hiero's splendor will survive.

IV. Epinician. *Pythian Ode for Hiero of Syracuse,* for victory in a chariot race (470 B.C.). In a short poem Bacchylides salutes Hiero, son of Deinomenes, and the city of Syracuse, which Apollo loves.

Pindar's *Pythian* I celebrates the same victory of Hiero.

V. Epinician. *Olympian Ode for Hiero of Syracuse,* for victory in a horse race (476 B.C.). The poem begins with praise of Hiero's power and his generosity. He is blessed by the gods. Yet no man is fortunate in all things, as is indicated by the story of Heracles' encounter with Meleager during Heracles' descent into Hades. Meleager's life had depended on the preservation of a brand that his mother, Althaea, possessed. When the young hero Meleager killed Althaea's brothers, in her pain and grief she hurled the brand into the fire. As it was consumed in the flames, Meleager at the height of his manhood died, and now he is a soul in Hades. Heracles, driven by the enmity of Hera, is always ready for battle, and now he prepares to defend himself against the warrior Meleager, who, recognizing him, sadly tells him not to contest with a soul whose manhood is dead. Weeping, Meleager speaks of how the gods involved his father, Oeneus, and his whole family in sorrow and of how his mother, impelled by uncontrollable anguish, took the brand that determined his life span from its chest and destroyed her own son when she hurled it into the fire. Meleager describes his feelings as his strength and his life departed. At these words Heracles weeps and considers the pain that man endures. The poet then turns to the great horse Pherenicus, who won the contest for Hiero. In spite of man's suffering and his limitations, he may achieve excellence and glory. The figure of Meleager suggests both the potentialities and the limitations of man.

Pindar's *Olympian* I celebrates the same victory.

VI. Epinician. *Olympian Ode for Lachon of Ceos*, victor in a foot race. Lachon is compared with the wind in his swiftness. He brings fame and honor to Ceos.

VII. Epinician. *Olympian Ode for Lachon of Ceos*, victor in a foot race. The subject is the same as that of VI.

VIII. Epinician. *Olympian Ode for Liparion of Ceos*. A good deal of this poem is missing. Zeus has answered the prayers of the victor.

IX. Epinician. *Nemean Ode for Automedes of Phlius*, victor in the pentathlon. Nemea is famous as the place where Heracles accomplished the first of his labors, the slaying of the mighty lion. There also the great games take place; these were established by the Seven against Thebes in memory of Archemorus, a son of one of the kings of Nemea. Archemorus, while asleep, was killed by a serpent that the Seven later slew. Even so tragic a fate as that of Archemorus can provide an opportunity for immortal glory. The achievement of Automedes will live.

X. Epinician. *Isthmian Ode for Aglaus of Athens*, victor in a foot race. Fame makes virtue immortal. The brother-in-law of Aglaus has assured the immortality of his triumph by commissioning this poem. Men seek various ways of fulfillment, through art, gold, the tending of flocks and the cultivation of the soil, and, best of all, through skill.

XI. Epinician. *Pythian Ode for Alexidamus of Metapontion*, victor in a wrestling match. Alexidamus is favored by Apollo, who approves of his victory. Actually Alexidamus would have won an earlier contest at Olympia had the judges been fair. The young man must not be bitter, however; mortal judges err, and now Apollo and his sister Artemis, a goddess honored by Metapontion, have brought him victory at Delphi. Artemis has settled grievances before this: when the mythical heroes Proetus and Acrisius, sons of King Abas of Argos, quarreled, Artemis helped to divide the land, allotting Tiryns to Proetus. Proetus' daughters in their pride declared that the palace of their father was finer than the temple of Hera. The goddess punished them by inspiring them with a frenzy that made them run shrieking from Tiryns to the hills of Arcadia. Proetus sought help from Artemis at her sacred spring. She persuaded Hera to release Proetus' daughters, and from then on Artemis was worshiped as a healer. Metapontion, home of Alexidamus, honors Artemis, goddess of productivity and of healing.

XII. Epinician. *Nemean Ode for Teisias of Aegina*, victor in a wrestling match. More than half this poem is missing. The poet asks the Muse Clio to inspire him with a song for Teisias, who lives on the famous island of Aegina, home of Aeacu. Teisias and relatives of his have won thirty victories in all the great games.

XIII. Epinician. *Nemean Ode for Pytheas of Aegina*, victor in the pancratium. The beginning of the poem is missing. When Heracles slew the Nemean lion, his victory signified a condemnation of pride and heralded future triumphs of the Greeks. Pytheas' victory is associated with this noble tradition, and he returns triumphant to Aegina. There a girl dances and sings of Endeis, the wife of Aeacus, king of Aegina. The sons of Endeis and Aeacus were Peleus, father of Achilles, and Telamon, father of Ajax. Bacchylides then sings of the glory of Achilles and Ajax in the Trojan War. Though these heroes are dead, song keeps their *arete* alive. The island of Aegina has also won fame for the *arete* of its heroes, among them Pytheas.

xiv. A. Epinician. *Petraean Ode for Cleoptolemus of Thessaly,* for victory in a horse race (a local contest at Petra [the Rock], in Thessaly, to honor Poseidon). Only the first half of the ode remains. Discretion is man's most potent weapon against the unknown elements and forces of life. Now is the time to sing of the glory of Cleoptolemus.

xiv. B. Epinician. *Pythian Ode for Aristoteles of Larisa,* for victory in a horse race. Hestia, goddess of the hearth, is told of the triumph of Aristoteles, which brings fame to Larisa.

xv. Dithyramb. *The Return of Helen Demanded.* After Paris abducted Helen, Menelaus, her husband, and Odysseus, in an attempt to avoid war, went to Troy to ask that the Trojans return her (see *Iliad* iii, 205–224). They were welcomed by Theano, the wife of Antenor. Menelaus spoke briefly and eloquently, reminding the Trojans that man brings grief upon himself, and he must not blame Zeus for the violence that unjust men commit.

xvi. Dithyramb. *Heracles.* Heracles fell in love with Iole and destroyed the town of Oechalia to obtain the girl. Heracles' wife, Deianeira, hoping to regain the love of her husband, smeared a robe with the blood of the centaur Nessus, which she believed was a love potion, and sent the robe as a gift to Heracles. When he put on the robe, the blood, which was actually poisonous, entered his body and killed Heracles.

xvii. Dithyramb. *Theseus.* Minos, king of Crete, annually demanded seven Athenian girls and seven boys to sacrifice to the Minotaur. Theseus brought an end to this sacrifice by going to Crete with the young victims and killing the Minotaur. This dithyramb tells of how, during his journey to Crete, Theseus proved to Minos his descent from Poseidon.

xviii. Dithyramb. *Theseus.* Theseus' mortal father, Aegeus, king of Athens, left the boy to grow up with his mother, Aethra, in Troezen. When Theseus was a young man he moved a rock hiding the sword and sandals of his father, and with these tokens he set out for Athens. On his way he killed several monsters. Though Theseus' reputation as a bold and noble warrior preceded him to Athens, Aegeus did not know it was his son who approached. In the first strophe the Chorus of Athenians asks Aegeus why the horns are playing a song of war, and in the first antistrophe Aegeus replies that a mighty hero who has vanquished many monsters approaches. In the second strophe the chorus asks his name and his land, and Aegeus in the second antistrophe describes Theseus' costume and his youthful appearance, but he still is unaware that his son is coming.

xix. Dithyramb. *Io.* Hera, jealous of Zeus' love for the maiden Io, transformed her into a cow and sent Argus, who had a hundred eyes, to watch her and prevent Zeus from coming to her. Argus, however, either weary from his heavy task or lulled by the music of Hermes, finally fell asleep. Hera then sent a gadfly to torment Io, who wandered from place to place until she came to Egypt, where, restored to her original form, she bore the son of Zeus, Epaphus, who was to become king of Egypt. Other descendants of Io were Cadmus, who founded Thebes, and the god Dionysus, son of Zeus and Semele.

xx. Dithyramb. *Idas.* Only the beginning remains. Idas, who came from Messenia, went to Pleuron in Aetolia, where he won Marpessa, daughter of the king, Evenus, by defeating her father in a chariot race.

xxi. Dithyramb. *Cassandra's Vision.* A brief fragment dealing with a vision of Cassandra.

Choral Lyrics (PINDAR). Epinicia (498–466 B.C.). Translations: in verse, (actually paraphrase) Abraham Cowley, 1656; in verse, Abraham Moore, 1822; in prose, Ernest Myers, 1874; in prose, Sir John Sandys, 1915; in verse, Arthur S. Way, 1922; in verse, C. J. Billson, 1929; in verse, Richmond Lattimore, 1947.

S U M M A R Y . Olympian I. *For Hiero of Syracuse,* victor in a horse race (476 B.C.). The poet praises Hiero (Hieron), the tyrant of Syracuse, in rich and fruitful Sicily. He then speaks of the glory of the great horse Pherenicus, who triumphed in the contest. Hiero is now famous in Elis, the land of Pelops, whom the god Poseidon loved. Pindar rejects the well-known myth that Tantalus served his own son Pelops to the gods at a feast. All the gods except Demeter refused to eat. Because she ate Pelops' shoulder, the gods replaced it with one of ivory and restored Pelops to life. Pindar objects to the myth because it suggests that the gods can act as cannibals. His view of the gods is too lofty to allow for such a possibility, and he says that those who were jealous of Poseidon's love for Pelops invented this lie. Poseidon took his beloved Pelops to Olympus. After his return to earth he went to Pisa, the capital of Elis. There King Oenomaus demanded that all who sought the hand of his daughter Hippodameia compete with him in a chariot race at the risk of death if they were defeated. Pelops won in his competition with Oenomaus, thus becoming the model for all Olympic winners. He was married to Hippodameia, who bore him six valiant sons. Pelops' fame lived after him in Elis, and the Olympic games were conducted near his tomb.

Pindar then returns to the subject of Hiero's glory, hoping that in the future Hiero will win an even greater honor at the Olympics, the four-horse chariot race. Moreover, Pindar hopes that he may have the honor of singing the praises of Hiero on that occasion. Each man has his own powers and ambitions. Pindar's aim is to write in praise of the victorious.

Bacchylides' fifth ode celebrates the same victory. Despite Pindar's expressed hope that he would be called upon to write the ode in honor of Hiero's victory in a chariot race, it was Bacchylides and not Pindar who was asked to celebrate Hiero's victory in the four-horse chariot race of 468 B.C. (see Bacchylides' CHORAL LYRIC III).

Olympian II. *For Theron of Acragas,* for victory in a chariot race (476 B.C.). Pindar begins by asking what god, what great hero of the past, and what man he should praise. The god will be Zeus, the hero Heracles, who first established the Olympic games, and the man Theron, the present victor, whose ancestors ruled over Sicily. Pindar prays that Zeus may grant good fortune to the family of Theron. Theron can trace his ancestry back to Cadmus, whose daughters suffered a great deal but achieved high honor that compensated for their pain: Semele, though killed by a thunderbolt, bore the god Dionysus. Other descendants of Cadmus are recalled: Laius, who was slain by his son Oedipus; Polyneices, the son of Oedipus, who, though slain by his brother Eteocles, left a noble son Thersander. Noble ancestors of Theron have won Olympic contests; thus he continues the tradition of glory.

Honor comes from wealth combined with virtue. After death the virtuous join Peleus, Achilles, and Cadmus in the Islands of the Blessed.

Pindar then speaks of himself, proudly asserting that he has many an "arrow" to shoot forth that the wise will understand. A real poet has been instructed by nature; he himself is an eagle, while his competitors are like crows. Pindar's praises of Theron will triumph over envy.

Olympian III. *For Theron of Acragas,* for victory in a chariot race (476 B.C.). This ode, written for the same occasion as the second, was sung in the temple of the Dioscuri at Acragas during the festival of Theoxenia, when the Dioscuri were hosts to the other gods. Thus the ode begins with a request for the goodwill of Castor and Pollux and their sister Helen as the poet sings of the glory of Theron. Pindar has been inspired by the Muse to create a new type of poem in the Dorian measure that is to be sung to the music of the lyre and the flute. Pisa has also commanded him to sing, for Pisa is the city from which songs are sent to all parts of the world in honor of those who have won the contests and have received the olive spray as a prize. It was Heracles who first obtained the olive from the Hyperboreans and brought it to Olympia. Now Heracles has come to the festival of the Theoxenia with Castor and Pollux, whom he put in charge of the Olympic Games. Theron has been rewarded with glory for his devotion to the Dioscuri.

Olympian IV. *For Psaumis of Camarina,* for victory in a chariot race (452 B.C.). Pindar thanks Zeus, who is responsible for his presence at the Olympic games, and he asks Zeus to welcome the victor and the chorus that sings of his glory. Psaumis is a kind and generous man, peace-loving and devoted to the state. Mortals can prove themselves only through a test, as is illustrated by the story of Erginus, the Argonaut, who when mocked by the women of Lemnos, won a foot race while wearing armor.

Olympian v. *For Psaumis of Camarina,* for victory in the mule chariot race (perhaps 448 B.C.). Pindar addresses the Nymph of Camarina, asking her to receive the great tribute that Psaumis pays her, for his victories have brought her glory. Victory comes only as a result of great expense and labor, but even his fellow citizens hail a successful man. Zeus is asked to grant Camarina noble citizens and Psaumis health and long life, as with his sons at his side he enjoys his victorious horses.

Olympian vi. *For Hagesias of Syracuse,* for victory in the mule chariot race (perhaps 472 B.C.). This poem must have a glorious opening, for Hagesias deserves great praise. Without risk and danger no noble deed can be done. Hagesias reminds Pindar of the prophet Amphiaraus, who fought with the Seven against Thebes. Because Hagesias is a descendant of Iamus, son of Apollo, Pindar tells the story of how Evadne bore Iamus to Apollo and how Apollo gave the power of prophecy to Iamus and his offspring. The Iamids are a noble and prosperous family.

Both Zeus and Hermes have brought victory to Hagesias. Pindar, writing at Thebes, asks Aeneas, the man who trained the chorus, to bring a message to Hiero at Syracuse, requesting that he offer the chorus his hospitality when it comes from Stymphalus, in Arcadia, where one of the homes of Hagesias was located, to his other home in Syracuse. May Zeus grant good fortune to the people of Syracuse and Stymphalus.

Olympian vii. *For Diagoras of Rhodes,* victor in a boxing match (464 B.C.). Pindar compares his poem to a golden bowl that a father gives to the bridegroom of his daughter as a token of love, for his poem is a gift of fame. Pindar has come to Rhodes to honor the great skill of Diagoras and to praise his noble father, Damagetus.

Pindar then tells the myth of Tlepolemus, a son of Heracles, who was king of Argos but, after killing his uncle Licymnius, left Argos and settled in Rhodes. He also tells the story of how Rhodes was given as a present to the sun-god. Athletic contests still honor Tlepolemus at Rhodes, and Diagoras has been victorious in these games as he has been in many others. The poet asks Zeus to grant honor to his ode and to the heroic boxer, Diagoras.

Olympian viii. *For Alcimedon of Aegina,* victor in a wrestling match (460 B.C.). The poet salutes Olympia as the "queen of truth." He speaks of the victories of Alcimedon and his brother, which bring fame to Aegina, known for its respect for law since the time of Aeacus, who was called by Zeus to help Apollo and Poseidon build the walls of Troy. The poet salutes Alcimedon's trainer, Melesias, and declares that the victory will please Alcimedon's grandfather. His father and his uncle, who are dead, will hear of his glory in the Underworld.

Olympian IX. *For Epharmostus of Opus,* victor in a wrestling match (468 B.C.). The fame of Epharmostus and this song will glorify his great city, Opus, already famous as the area where Pyrrha and Deucalion cast behind them the bones of their mother, Earth (stones), and caused men to spring forth. Pindar recalls the founding of the city by the eponymous hero, Opus, son of Locrus and Protogeneia. Pindar prays to the Muses for inspiration so that he may sing of other victories won by Epharmostus and his friends.

Olympian X. *For Hagesidamus of Locri Epizephyrii,* victor in a boxing match (476 B.C.). The poet praises the victor's home and his trainer. Then he tells of how Heracles established the Olympic Games. Great deeds live through song. Pindar, inspired by the Muses, will assure the lasting glory of Hagesidamus.

Olympian XI. *For Hagesidamus of Locri Epizephyrii,* victor in a boxing match (476 B.C.). This poem celebrates the same victory as does X; whereas X was sung at the victor's home, XI was performed at Olympia following Hagesidamus' victory. The poet assures the lasting fame of noble accomplishments, but both he and the victor must rely on Zeus for power and vitality.

Olympian XII. *For Ergoteles of Himera,* victor in a long foot race (472 B.C.). Compelled to leave his home in Crete as a political exile, Ergoteles has brought honor to his new home in Sicily, where he enjoys a prosperous life.

Olympian XIII. *For Xenophon of Corinth,* victor in the short foot race and the pentathlon (464 B.C.). The poet salutes the victor's home and his family, famous for victories in the Great Games.

Olympian XIV. *For Asopichus of Orchomenus,* victor in a short foot race (possibly 488 B.C.). Pindar calls on the Graces, the queens of Orchomenus, to hear his song of triumph.

Pythian I. *For Hiero of Aetna,* for victory in a chariot race (470 B.C.). After a tribute to the power of music, Pindar speaks of the monster, Typhon, who is held under Mount Etna, from which he sends forth dreadful fire. (This probably refers to an eruption of Etna in 475 B.C.) The poet then salutes Hiero, founder of the city of Aetna in 476 B.C. Hiero's victory prophesies glory for his city. Because all of men's accomplishments are inspired by the gods, may Hiero, like Philoctetes, have a god to guide him. Then Pindar speaks of Hiero's vast power; his son Deinomenes is king of Aetna, and Hiero defeated the Etruscans who attacked Cumae (474 B.C.). Hiero must continue to be just and honest, and his fame will live after him in poetry.

Bacchylides' fourth ode celebrates the same victory.

Pythian II. *For Hiero of Syracuse,* for victory in a chariot race at the Theban Iolaia (perhaps 475 B.C.). Pindar has come from Thebes with this song to the mighty conqueror, Hiero, who is aided by the gods Artemis, Hermes, and Poseidon. The myth of Ixion is told as a warning that men must be grateful to those who help them. Hiero is praised for his riches and honor, his accomplishments in war and in government. Then there is a long moral discourse on honesty to one's self and to others. The poem ends with a declaration that Pindar's only aim is to enjoy the presence of the noble and to please them.

Pythian III. *For Hiero of Syracuse,* for victory in horse races (482, 478 B.C.; the ode was probably written in 474 B.C.). Because Hiero is ill, Pindar wishes that Chiron, who taught the physician Asclepius, Apollo's son, were alive, for then Chiron could teach another physician whom Pindar would bring to Sicily to cure Hiero. Because he cannot do so, Pindar will remain at Thebes and pray that the health of Hiero may be restored. The gods give man ill fortune as well as good, and Hiero endures his suffering with courage. Poetry is the means to immortality. Great heroes like Nestor and Sarpedon live because the poets have sung their fame.

Pythian IV. *For Arcesilas of Cyrene,* for victory in a chariot race (462 B.C.). Damophilus, an aristocrat who had been sent into exile by Battus IV, king of Cyrene, tried to regain the king's friendship by asking Pindar to write this ode in honor of Arcesilas, Battus' son. Pindar relates the victory of Arcesilas at Delphi to an old prophecy of Medea to his ancestor Battus that he must establish the city of Cyrene. After a summary of the voyage of the Argonauts and their return, Pindar turns to the subject of the exiled Damophilus. Pindar flatters Battus IV, implying that he can be like Zeus, who forgave the Titans, if he allows Damophilus to return to his home.

Pythian V. *For Arcesilas of Cyrene,* for victory in a chariot race (462 B.C.). This ode celebrates the same victory as Pythian IV. Arcesilas is praised for his wealth and honor, but is urged to give due credit to the gods and to the charioteer, who drove his chariot. Arcesilas' glory is related to that of his noble ancestors.

Pythian VI. *For Xenocrates of Acragas,* for victory in a chariot race (490 B.C.). Pindar praises the filial loyalty of Thrasybulus, son of Xenocrates, who drove his father's chariot to victory.

Pythian VII. *For Megacles of Athens,* for victory in the chariot race (486 B.C.). Pindar praises the victor, his ancestors (the Alcmaeonidae), and his city, Athens.

Pythian VIII. *For Aristomenes of Aegina,* victor in a wrestling match (446 B.C.). Pindar praises the goddess of Peace and the city of Aegina, known for its justice, its courageous men, and its victors in war and in games. Aristomenes has emulated his noble uncles in his courage. It is to Apollo that he owes his many victories.

Pythian IX. *For Telesicrates of Cyrene,* victor in the foot race in armor (474 B.C.). Pindar tells the myth of Cyrene, the nymph whom Apollo loved and carried away to the city that bears her name and is the home of the victor. Telesicrates has brought glory to Cyrene. The poet thanks Heracles and his half brother Iphicles for granting his prayer for victory.

Pythian X. *For Hippocleas of Thessaly,* victor in the double stadium foot race (498 B.C.). Both Lacedaemon and Thessaly are ruled by men descended from Heracles. Pindar has been asked by the sons of Aleuas, the Thessalian descendants of Heracles, to sing of the victory of Hippocleas, who imitates the courage of his father. Even Hippocleas' father, who has achieved as much happiness as is possible for man, could not go to the Hyperboreans (people who lived in eternal happiness in the far north, where the sun rose and set only once during the year). However, the gods could send Perseus to the Hyperboreans, for the immortals may do as they wish. Pindar looks forward to writing more victory odes for Hippocleas.

Pythian XI. *For Thrasydaeus of Thebes,* victor in the short foot race (474 B.C.). Pindar asks the legendary heroines of Thebes to sing in honor of Thrasydaeus in the Temple of the Ismenian Apollo. After a digression on Orestes, Pindar says that the Muse is obliged to sing in honor of the victor and his father, who also was a winner in the Great Games. A life without excess is better than that of a tyrant. A great athlete who leads a good life wins fame.

Pythian XII. *For Midas of Acragas,* victor in the contest of flute playing (490 B.C.). Acragas must honor Midas, for his success in the skill invented by Athene, who through music re-created the dirge of the Gorgons when Perseus slew Medusa. After telling the myth of Perseus, Pindar speaks of labor, which only a god can end.

Nemean I. *For Chromius of Aetna,* for victory in a chariot race (possibly 476 B.C.). Because Chromius was the governor of the city of Aetna in Sicily, the poet speaks of the productivity and fame of Sicily. Then Chromius is praised for his generosity, courage, and wisdom. Pindar next turns to the myth of Heracles, for it is appropriate to his theme of strength and courage. He tells of the infant Heracles killing the serpents sent by Hera and of the prophet Tiresias' predictions of the labors Heracles would accomplish and his final peace.

Nemean II. *For Timodemus of Acharnae,* victor in the pancratium (possibly 485 B.C.). Timodemus by this first victory indicates that he will live up to the reputation of his noble family, known for triumphs in the Great Games. It is probable that Timodemus grew up in Salamis and therefore Pindar refers to Ajax, the great hero of that city.

Nemean III. *For Aristocleides of Aegina,* victor in the pancratium (the victory was won some years before the composition of the ode, which was probably written in 475 B.C.). Pindar asks the Muse to come to Aegina and sing of Nemean Zeus and of Aegina, glorified by Aristocleides. Because Aegina is the land of the Myrmidons, the followers of Achilles, Pindar speaks of Aeacus, Peleus, and Achilles. Then he continues to praise Zeus, Aegina, and the victor.

Nemean IV. *For Timasarchus of Aegina,* victor in a wrestling match (possibly 473 B.C.). If the father of Timasarchus were alive, he would sing of his son's triumph, for he was a fine musician. Past heroes of Aegina are evoked in relation to the present victory.

Nemean V. *For Pytheas of Aegina,* victor in the pancratium (possibly 485

B.C.). The victory of Pytheas honors the memory of Aegina's great heroes, Aeacus and his offspring Telamon, Peleus, and Phocus. Pindar speaks of Pytheas' great trainer, Menander of Athens, and of victories won by relatives of Pytheas.

Nemean VI. *For Alcimidas of Aegina,* victor in a wrestling match (possibly 463 B.C.). The nobility of Alcimidas' family suggests that in some respects man resembles the gods. Alcimidas' relatives have distinguished themselves in many games, and the Muse has kept their glory alive. The island of Aegina is famous for the family of Aeacus and especially for the great hero, Achilles, the subject of ancient bards. Pindar follows the path of the great poets of the past and hails both the victor and his clan.

Nemean VII. *For Sogenes of Aegina,* victor in the pentathlon (possibly 485 B.C.). The goddess of birth, who determines men's lives, has given Sogenes the capacity to win this contest. Poets love to celebrate triumphs. Homer's genius exaggerated the valor of Odysseus, who should not have won the arms of Achilles; nor should Aias, who was denied this prize, have taken his own life. Heroism is a means of defeating mortality. It was fated that Neoptolemus, the son of Achilles, be killed at Delphi; thus a descendant of Aeacus will always preside at the rites there. Pindar then praises the victor, Sogenes, and offers a prayer for him and his father to Heracles.

Nemean VIII. *For Deinias of Aegina,* victor in a double foot race (possibly 459 B.C.). Pindar dedicates his ode to Zeus and the nymph Aegina, telling of their union and of their offspring Aeacus. Great heroes are often the victims of envy, as was Ajax, who was denied the arms of Achilles. Declaring that he himself is honest and direct, Pindar hopes to be honored for these qualities. Though the poet cannot bring back Deinias' father from the dead, he can keep his fame alive through song, man's oldest source of relief from pain.

Nemean IX. *For Chromius of Aetna,* for victory in a chariot race (possibly 474 B.C.). This chariot race was won not at Nemea but at Sicyon, but the ode was listed as the ninth Nemean by the Alexandrian scholars. Pindar asks the Muses to come from Sicyon to Aetna to sing of Chromius' triumph, which must live in fame. After telling the story of the Seven against Thebes, Pindar offers a prayer to Zeus for the city of Aetna and praises the victorious Chromius.

Nemean X. *For Theaeus of Argos,* victor in a wrestling match (possibly 463 B.C.). This wrestling match was won not at Nemea but at Argos, but the ode was listed as the tenth Nemean by the Alexandrian scholars. Pindar calls on the Graces to sing of the glory of Argos, the land of Hera. He then tells of former triumphs of the victor at the Pythian, Isthmian, and Nemean Games and prays that Zeus may give him victory at Olympia. Theaeus has been aided by Castor and Polydeuces. The poem ends with the story of Polydeuces' love for and loyalty to his brother.

Nemean XI. *For Aristagoras of Tenedos,* on his election as president of the Council (possibly 446 B.C.). This ode has no relation to the Nemean Contests, but was listed as the eleventh Nemean by the Alexandrian scholars. The poem celebrates the election of Aristagoras as President of the Council of Tenedos. Aristagoras is praised for his riches and the beauty and grace of his body, but he is reminded of his mortality. Pindar speaks of Aristagoras' athletic ability and the achievements of his noble family.

Isthmian I. *For Herodotus of Thebes,* for victory in a chariot race (possibly 458 B.C.). Pindar apologizes to Delos for interrupting his work on an ode for Apollo in order to write his ode for a fellow Theban. Herodotus' triumph is related to the athletic victories of Castor and Iolaus. Pindar expresses the hope that Herodotus may win more games in the future.

Isthmian II. *For Xenocrates of Acragas,* for victory in a chariot race (the date of the contest is probably 477 B.C., that of the ode possibly 472 B.C.). The victor, Xenocrates, has died, but he is famous for his triumphs in the Pythian (see *Pythian* VI) and the Isthmian Games. Xenocrates is praised for his skill and his generosity. Then Pindar tells Nicasippus, who is to carry the ode to Thrasybulus, the son of Xenocrates, to advise him to ignore the envy of those who would like him to be silent about his father's accomplishments.

Isthmian III. *For Melissus of Thebes,* for victory in a chariot race at Nemea (possibly 477 B.C.). This ode may have been composed as a prelude to *Isthmian* IV, which was written shortly before it; thus Melissus' Nemean victory is celebrated in an Isthmian ode along with his Isthmian victory. Melissus is praised for his strength and skill, which bring fame to Thebes.

Isthmian IV. *For Melissus of Thebes,* victor in the pancratium (probably 478 B.C.). Pindar praises Melissus and his glorious family, who have achieved fame in athletics and in battle. Melissus is compared with Heracles, who overcame the giant Antaeus, who far surpassed Heracles in size.

Isthmian V. *For Phylacidas of Aegina,* victor in the pancratium (possibly 476 B.C.). This is the second victory of Phylacidas in the Isthmian pancratium (see *Isthmian* VI, which is earlier than V); his brother Pytheas is also praised for his Nemean triumph (see *Nemean* V). Because the victor's home is the island of Aegina, Pindar speaks of the glory of the family of Aeacus and of the heroes from Aegina who fought in the battle of Salamis (in the Persian War, 480 B.C.).

Isthmian VI. *For Phylacidas of Aegina,* victor in the pancratium (possibly 480 B.C.). The two sons of Lampon, Phylacidas, the victor, and his brother Pytheas, are praised. Pindar cannot speak of Aegina without mentioning the glory of the descendants of Aeacus. He then returns to Phylacidas, Pytheas, their uncle, and their father, who is praised for his generosity, honesty, temperance, and for the encouragement he gives to athletes.

Isthmian VII. *For Strepsiades of Thebes,* victor in the pancratium (possibly 456 B.C.). Because only song keeps great deeds alive, Pindar must celebrate the triumph of Strepsiades. The victor's uncle, who had the same name, died heroically in battle. Poseidon has granted this victory after the sad death of the victor's uncle. Pindar then speaks of himself, praying that the gods will not begrudge him happiness as he grows old.

Isthmian VIII. *For Cleandros of Aegina,* victor in the pancratium (possibly 478 B.C.). Pindar expresses conflicting feelings about the Greeks' defeat of the Persians in the Persian War, for as a loyal Theban he accepts and yet laments Thebes' collaboration with the Persians, while as a Greek he rejoices in the liberation of his people. He then celebrates the island of Aegina, for the nymph Aegina was the sister of Thebe, both of whom were loved by Zeus. He tells of the family of Aeacus and of the glory of Achilles. As song keeps the heroic fame of Achilles alive, so will it immortalize the cousin of Cleandros, Nicocles, who won an Isthmian victory in a boxing match. Then Cleandros is praised for his victory in the pancratium and in other contests.

Chryseis. See ILIAD I.

Chrysippus (Chrysippos). See STOICS.

Chrysothemis. Daughter of Agamemnon and the sister of Electra. See Sophocles' ELECTRA.

Cicero, Marcus Tullius. A Roman statesman, born at Arpinum (Arpino) in Latium in 106 B.C. His family was a prosperous one of the equestrian rank. Cicero and his younger brother Quintus were taken to Rome to be educated. There Cicero became acquainted with the Greek poet Archias and studied rhetoric, philosophy, and law. Among his teachers were Philo, the Academic philosopher; Diodotus, the Stoic; Quintus Mucius Scaevola, the orator; and his relative Quintus Mucius Scaevola, the augur and jurist. Cicero also heard the famous orators Marcus Antonius (the grandfather of Mark Antony) and Lucius Licinius Crassus.

Cicero's earliest extant speech was delivered in 81 B.C., when he was practicing law at Rome: *Pro Quinctio* is a defense of Publius Quinctius against Servius Naevius. Though the dispute over some land in Gaul was unimportant, the occasion was significant because the young Cicero argued against the famous orator Hortensius. In 80 B.C. Cicero delivered a more important early oration, *Pro Sexto Roscio Amerino,* a defense of Sextus Roscius, who had been accused of murdering his father. In proving the innocence of his client, Cicero was obliged to reveal the guilt of Chrysogonus, a favorite of Sulla, the leader of the aristocratic party then in power at Rome.

In 79 B.C. Cicero left Rome to travel abroad for two years. He spent time at Athens and Rhodes, studying rhetoric and philosophy. On returning to Rome he established himself as one of the leading pleaders in the Roman courts. Around 76 B.C. he married Terentia, whom he later divorced after more than thirty years of marriage. They had two children, a daughter Tullia and a son Marcus, twelve years younger. In 75 B.C. Cicero began his political career as quaestor (financial officer) in Sicily, thus gaining admission to the Senate. As prosecutor for the Sicilians against their former governor Verres in 70 B.C., he succeeded in forcing Verres into exile. Cicero now became the leading advocate of Rome. He held the position of curule aedile (a plebeian magistrate in charge of public buildings and games) in 69 B.C. and praetor (judge) in 66 B.C., the year in which he made his first political speech, *De Lege Manilia* (also called *De Imperio Cn. Pompeii*), in support of the tribune Manilius' proposal that Pompey be put in command of the war against King Mithridates of Pontus.

In 64 B.C., as a candidate for consul (the two consuls, who were elected annually, were the chief magistrates of Rome), Cicero denounced the revolutionary program of Catiline, one of the other contestants for the office. As consul in 63 B.C. he exposed in a series of brilliant orations Catiline's plot to seize the government and cancel all debts. The first of these speeches, *In Catilinam* I, perhaps Cicero's best-known oration, was delivered on November 8, 63 B.C. and was effective enough to force Catiline to leave Rome for Faesulae. In Cicero's next oration, *In Catilinam* II, delivered on the following day, he described the preparations that had been made for protecting the city against Catiline and his followers. This speech persuaded the Senate to name Catiline a public enemy. Cicero then managed to have the five leading followers of Catiline who had remained in Rome arrested. In *In Catilinam* III, delivered in the Forum on December 3, 63 B.C., Cicero explained how he had obtained his evidence against these conspirators. On December 5 the Senate met to decide on the conspirators' sentence. After Caesar had made a persuasive speech in favor of life imprisonment rather than the death penalty, Cicero delivered *In Catilinam* IV, urging that the conspirators be executed. Cato supported this position, and the Senate voted for the death penalty. That very evening Cicero had the five conspirators strangled in their prison.

Cicero's defeat of the conspirators won him the praise of Cato, who called him the "father of his country," but in his pride in this achievement Cicero could not foresee the difficulties it would later bring him. As consul Cicero attempted to hold a position midway between the popular party of Caesar and the conservative group (the *optimates*). When, however, Caesar used the name of Rullus, a Tribune of the People, to introduce a bill proposing confiscation of lands for the purpose of distributing them to the lower classes, Cicero felt obliged to ally himself with the *optimates*. After the execution of Catiline's fellow conspirators, the popular party, incensed at Cicero's allegiance with the landed aristocracy, protested that the consul had condemned Romans to death without the approval of the people. Furthermore, Cicero apparently refused to accept Caesar's invitation to join the triumvirate that he, Pompey, and Crassus had formed in 60 B.C. Cicero was thus without protection when, in 58 B.C., the tribune Publius Clodius, supported by Caesar, introduced a bill demanding death or exile for anyone who had executed a Roman before allowing him to appeal to the people. Thus Cicero was forced into exile. In August of 57 B.C., however, another law was passed that allowed him to return to Rome.

During 51–50 B.C. Cicero was proconsul (governor) of Cilicia. When he returned to Rome, Crassus was dead, and the hostility between Caesar and

Pompey had brought Rome to the brink of civil war. Although Cicero left Rome to join the forces of Pompey, after the latter's defeat, Caesar allowed Cicero to return to Rome in 47 B.C. In 46 B.C. Cicero was divorced from Terentia and shortly afterward married his young ward Publilia. On the death of his daughter Tullia in 45 B.C. Cicero, shattered by grief, could not forgive his young wife's lack of compassion and soon divorced her.

During Caesar's supremacy Cicero took no part in politics, but after the death of Caesar in 44 B.C. his vigorous leadership of the opposition to Mark Antony brought about his execution in December of 43 B.C.

Cicero achieved a vast reputation as an orator, politician, rhetorician, and philosopher. Fifty-eight of his orations are extant, though some are fragmentary. It is known that he wrote at least forty-eight others that no longer exist. Around 77 B.C. (though possibly later) he defended his friend the actor Roscius in *Pro Roscio Comoedo,* and in 72 B.C., in *Pro Tullio,* he argued for the property rights of M. Tullius. In Cicero's prosecution of Verres in 70 B.C. he argued once more against the famous Hortensius. Cicero delivered only two of the seven brilliant speeches he wrote for this trial.

In 69 B.C. Cicero delivered *Pro Fonteio,* which is fragmentary, and *Pro Caecina.* In 66 B.C. he delivered *Pro Cluentio,* in defense of Aulus Cluentius Habitus, who was accused of poisoning an enemy. Cicero was proud of the speech, which was much praised in his time. In 63 B.C., during his consulship, Cicero delivered three orations, *Contra Rullum,* attacking the proposal of Rullus, who spoke for Caesar, to confiscate and redistribute land. He also defended an old senator accused by the popular party of having murdered a man thirty-seven years before (*Pro C. Rabirio*). Cicero's most famous orations of this year were his attacks on Catiline, discussed above. During the period of the Catilinarian conspiracy Cicero defended the consul-elect for 62 B.C., L. Murena, who had been accused by Cato of bribery. In *Pro Murena,* Cicero argues with eloquence and wit, answering Cato's charge that he should not have undertaken the defense of Murena by asking rhetorically, "Who is more fit to defend a consul than a consul?"

In 62 B.C. Cicero delivered *Pro Sulla,* a defense against the accusation that a certain Sulla had been involved in the Catilinarian conspiracy. During this year Cicero also defended the poet Archias, whose claim to Roman citizenship had been contested. *Pro Archia* contains a beautiful and famous tribute to the powers of literature, which, says Cicero, serves man in every condition and period of life. *Pro Flacco,* given in 59 B.C., is a defense of Flaccus, one of the praetors involved in the apprehension of the followers of Catiline.

After Cicero returned from exile in 57 B.C. he gave four orations on the subject of his exile. In *Post Reditum in Senatu* and *Post Reditum ad Quirites* he expresses his gratitude for his recall to the senate and the people. *De Domo Sua* and *De Haruspicum Responso* are concerned with his recovery of his home, which had been confiscated during his exile. In 56 B.C. Cicero defended P.

Sestius, a tribune, against the charges of the notorious Clodius. *Pro Sestio* attempts to unite the aristocratic party in an effort to defeat the first triumvirate. *In Vatinium,* given the same year, is an attack on a witness against Sestius. Another oration of this year is *Pro Caelio,* a defense of M. Caelius Rufus against the accusation of attempted poisoning made by Clodius' sister Clodia (see CATULLUS). In 56 B.C. Cicero also delivered *De Provinciis Consularibus,* a speech of submission to Caesar in which Cicero approves of Caesar's continued command of Gaul. *Pro Balbo,* also of 56 B.C., another speech indicating Cicero's submission, defends the citizenship rights of a friend of the triumvirate. In *De Provinciis Consularibus* Cicero had attacked L. Calpurnius Piso and demanded that he be recalled from Macedonia, where he was governor. When Piso replied angrily, Cicero delivered *In Pisonem* in 56 B.C., again attacking Piso.

In 54 B.C. Cicero delivered *Pro Plancio,* in defense of his friend Plancius, and *Pro C. Rabirio Postumo,* in defense of a friend of Caesar, who was obviously guilty of the extortion of which he was accused. Only fragments remain of Cicero's defense of M. Aemilius Scaurus, also charged with extortion at about the same time. Cicero's speech *Pro Milone,* written in 52 B.C. to defend Titus Annius Milo Papinianus against the accusation that he had murdered Clodius, was not delivered because, it is said, Cicero feared the friends of Clodius present at the trial. The extant version is one revised by Cicero for publication.

After Cicero's return to Rome in 47 B.C. he gave three orations that reveal his attempts to conciliate Caesar. *Pro Marcello,* delivered in 46 B.C., contains much flattery of Caesar. In *Pro Ligario* (45 B.C.) Cicero defends Q. Ligarius, accused of hostility to Caesar, and in *Pro Rege Deiotaro* (45 B.C.) he defends the king of Galatia against the accusation that he had tried to murder Caesar.

Cicero's last orations are the fourteen *Philippics,* written after the death of Caesar in 44 and 43 B.C. Taking his title from Demosthenes' three orations against Philip of Macedon, Cicero attacks the tyranny of Antony and urges the Roman people to demand their liberty. In the last *Philippic,* Cicero suggests a public celebration over the defeat of Antony at Mutina. Cicero did not foresee Antony's reconciliation with Octavian and the formation of the second triumvirate in 43 B.C. As Juvenal points out (*Satire* x), Cicero's eloquence brought about his execution at the command of Antony.

In his early twenties Cicero wrote his first treatise on rhetoric, *De Inventione,* actually a handbook defining terms and analyzing types of speeches. Cicero's most impressive oratorical work is his *De Oratore* (ON ORATORY), a dialogue in three books, written in 55 B.C. In order to teach his son rhetoric Cicero wrote *Partitiones Oratoriae* (the rhetorical divisions of oratory) in the form of a dialogue between father and son. The date of this work is probably 55 B.C., though some authorities place it earlier. In BRUTUS, written in 46 B.C., Cicero traces the history of ancient oratory and the background of its development. He also criticizes the so-called Attic school of oratory, which demanded an unadorned, bare style close to that of the mere logician. Brutus replied to this criticism, and Cicero took up the subject of Atticism again in ORATOR, also written in 46 B.C. The basic subject of the *Orator* is the ideal orator. *De Optimo Genere Oratorum* (*On the Best Type of Orators*), which Cicero also wrote around 46 B.C., is intended, he says, as a preface to his translations of Aeschines' *Against Ctesiphon* and the reply by Demosthenes, *On the Crown;* these translations, however, are apparently lost. The *Topica*, composed in 44 B.C. for C. Trebatius, is Cicero's last rhetorical treatise. He conceived it as an adaptation of Aristotle's *Topica*, but it seems unrelated to that work.

Perhaps the best-known of Cicero's political and philosophical writings is his fragmentary DE RE PUBLICA, which was begun in 54 B.C. and appeared around 51 B.C. Before its publication Cicero began *De Legibus* as a sequel, but never finished the treatise, which deals with the laws of the state envisioned in *De Re Publica*. Only three books of *De Legibus* are extant. In 46 B.C. Cicero began work on the *Paradoxa Stoicorum* (*Stoic Paradoxes*), but probably finished it somewhat later. The next year Cicero sought relief from his sorrow over the death of his daughter Tullia in writing *De Consolatione*, which is not extant. ACADEMICA, a dialogue on epistemology, was also composed around 45 B.C. Around this period Cicero also wrote the lost *Hortensius;* in his *Confessions*, St. Augustine describes its powerful influence on him. During 45 B.C. Cicero also wrote the five books of *De Finibus Bonorum et Malorum* (*On the Greatest Good and the Greatest Evil*). His *Tusculanae Disputationes* (*Tusculan Disputations*), a work in five books begun in 45 B.C. and published in 44 B.C., deals with the subject of happiness. In 44 B.C. Cicero finished his *De Natura Deorum*, in which he gives the Epicurean, Stoic, and Academic conceptions of the gods, and wrote *De Divinatione* as a sequel to it. A second sequel to *De Natura Deorum* is *De Fato*, also written in 44 B.C., a fragmentary work in which Cicero considers the role of fate in human behavior. During 44 B.C. Cicero also wrote his dialogue *De Senectute* (*On Old Age*), also called *Cato Major; De Amicitia* (*On Friendship*), also called *Laelius;* and his last philosophical work *De Officiis* (*On Duties*), a treatise in three books addressed to his son, dealing with the four essential virtues and their role in achieving success.

Cicero's extensive correspondence has been organized into four groups: sixteen books of letters to his friend Atticus (*Ad Atticum*), sixteen to other friends (*Ad Familiares*), three to his brother Quintus (*Ad Quintum Fratrem*), and two to Brutus (*Ad Brutum*). These four collections contain 864 letters, 774 of which were written by Cicero. It is known that he wrote many other letters that have not survived.

Though Cicero's reputation as a poet declined after his death (see Juvenal's SATIRE X), his poetry was respected in his own time. Only brief quotations from it survive, though long passages of his verse translations can be found in his essays.

Cicero's career as a statesman, lawyer, orator, and writer suggests the richness of his own personality, but it cannot be separated from the period in which he flourished and was destroyed. Actually in his enormous productivity, the dignity of his ideals, his unwillingness to compromise, his respect for political freedom, his final need to express what he felt was truth in the face of death, as in his shortcomings—his pride and vanity, his lapses into expediency and opportunism, his submission to the dictatorial authority of the triumvirate—Cicero symbolizes essential qualities of the Republic he defended and loved.

As lawyer and politician Cicero was primarily an orator. In order to understand the speeches and rhetorical writings of Cicero, one must hold two concepts of him at once: that of the orator in courtroom or Forum, using his wits to defeat an adversary, and that of an artist who regarded his role as a calling and whose work on rhetoric is intended as a means to guide others toward the exalted image he held of the orator. It is this complex attitude toward his work that makes Cicero a forceful and realistic theorist and an orator whose speeches transcend the requirements of the moment. Though political arguments usually have only a brief and immediate interest, many of Cicero's speeches can still absorb and move the reader, for they reflect his broad knowledge of history and literature, his insight into important events, and his understanding of the relationship between past and present. Furthermore, Cicero's eloquence and control, his ability to combine the copiousness of the Asianic style with the stark clarity of the Attic give his language perennial vitality. Cicero's legacy to the ancient and modern worlds was pure and expressive prose, exact, subtle, rhythmic, and forceful. In his rhetorical writings he establishes an idealized conception of the orator as a man who possesses all moral and intellectual virtues and he gives sound, practical instruction on writing and speaking.

Cicero's philosophical writings have neither the originality nor the profundity of his rhetorical work; they are essentially interpretations and adaptations of the writings of Greek Stoics, Epicureans, and Academics of the Hellenistic period. His basic philosophical position was Academic; as a disciple of Carneades of the New Academy, he held a skeptical position, objecting to all dogma and asserting that absolute knowledge could not be attained. Nonetheless, Cicero did believe in the existence of deities, and he accepted many of the Stoic views on ethics. His interpretations of the Greek philosophers, like everything else he wrote, convey his own spirit, his intellectual curiosity, and his practical wisdom.

The influence of Cicero's theory and practice was profound in ancient and modern society; it is reflected in political oratory, education, and literature. For the most part ancient critics admired Cicero's rhetorical works and regarded him as the ideal orator; only during the age of Hadrian was there a reaction against the Ciceronian model. Though only minor works of Cicero were generally known during the Middle Ages, St. Jerome, St. Ambrose, and St. Augustine all acknowledge their indebtedness to him. In England he was admired by Roger Bacon and John of Salisbury. The humanists of the Renaissance rediscovered Cicero's great rhetorical works and regarded him as a model

and guide. Despite the satirical attack of Erasmus (*Dialogus Ciceronianus,*
1528) on the excessive influence of Cicero, he remained for most of the humanists the example of the stylist, rhetorician, orator, and letter writer. Renaissance handbooks on rhetoric, such as Thomas Wilson's *Arte of Rhetorique,* are
based on Cicero's rhetorical writings, and in English schools during the
Renaissance and the seventeenth and eighteenth centuries, education was
largely training in Ciceronian rhetoric and declamation. Political speeches in
the English Parliament of the seventeenth and eighteenth centuries are modeled
on Ciceronian orations. Even the "anti-Ciceronianism" of the seventeenth century, a movement that reflects a desire for a new simplicity in prose style, is
actually not a reaction against Cicero himself but against those who merely
aped his technique without understanding his spirit. Cicero's rhetorical theory
influenced the literary criticism of such great English writers as Sir Philip
Sidney, John Dryden, and Samuel Johnson; the cadences of Ciceronian prose
and his methods of argumentation can be recognized even in the poetry of
Milton and Dryden. Plutarch wrote a life of Cicero.

Cinyras (Kinyras). See ADONIS.

Circe (Kirke). In Greek myth, daughter of Helios. For her love affair with
Odysseus see ODYSSEY X. According to later writers Circe bore Odysseus a son
Telegonus, who unwittingly killed his father.

Ciris. An epyllion of unknown authorship, sometimes attributed to VERGIL.
Written in dactylic hexameter, *Ciris* tells the story of how SCYLLA, the daughter
of Nisus, king of Megara, is transformed into a *ciris* or seabird. In a long introduction the author speaks first of himself, then of Messalla, to whom the poem
is dedicated, and finally of the other version of the Scylla myth (in which she
is a monster who inhabits a rock and vexes seamen—see ODYSSEY XII). When
the actual story begins Megara is being attacked by Minos, but neither the
citizens of Megara nor their king fear him, because they have full confidence
in the miraculous power of the lock of red hair that grows on Nisus' head.
As long as this *roseus crinis,* a symbol of the goodwill of the Parcae, is safe,
both Nisus and his country will be secure.

However, neither the citizens of Megara nor Nisus is aware of the danger
from Scylla, who has fallen in love with Minos. Scylla is the victim not only
of Minos but of Juno, whom she has offended by exposing herself in the temple
of the goddess and then, out of fear, denying her act. Scylla's infatuation with
Minos is described as a type of madness; there is a fire in her veins and she
raves like a priestess of Cybele. Finally she feels that the fates drive her to
commit the gravest act of treachery against her father and her country. The
author implies that Minos will not accept her unless she cuts the lock from her
father's head, and, after a period of great conflict and an unsuccessful attempt
to obtain her father's permission to marry Minos, she cuts off the magic red lock
of hair.

The poet quickly sums up the consequences of her act. As the oracles had prophesied, Megara is seized. Scylla is suspended from Minos' ship and dragged over the sea. Many nymphs marvel at her and along with them the gods Neptune, Leucothea, and Palaemon. Anticipating death, Scylla tells her story to the winds of the sea. She cries out against the treachery of love and speaks of all she has lost. The author describes her journey and the cities and towns she passes. Amphritrite, pitying her, transforms her first into a fish and then into a bird, the unidentified *ciris*, more beautiful than Leda's swan. There is a long, detailed description of the transformation of first her face, then her head, and finally her body. At last she flies to the sky and is described as living a wild life among rocks and cliffs and deserted shores. Nisus, too, is changed into a bird: the sea eagle, that perpetually pursues the *ciris*, for the two birds, mindful of their origins, are enemies for all time. (Compare Ovid's version of the Scylla legend in the METAMORPHOSES.)

Cistellaria. See THE CASKET.

Claudian (Claudius Claudianus). Regarded as the last of the classical Roman writers, Claudian lived from about A.D. 370 to about A.D. 405. He was born in Alexandria and went to live in Rome, where his patron was the powerful general Stilicho. Claudian wrote eulogies of his patron and of the emperor Honorius in Latin hexameters, poems criticizing the opponents of the emperor, epics on the wars against the Goths, an epithalamium on the occasion of Honorius' marriage, an unfinished poem called *The Rape of Proserpine* (*De Raptu Proserpinae*), and many idyls and epigrams. Some authorities believe that Claudian was a Christian.

Claudius (Tiberius Claudius Drusus Nero Germanicus). Emperor of ROME from A.D. 41 to 54. Claudius wrote an autobiography and several historical works, but none of these has survived. In Robert Graves' novel *I, Claudius*, Claudius tells of his life and the events of his time up to the period when he became emperor. See Tacitus' ANNALS XI, XII.

Cleanthes (Kleanthes). Greek poet and philosopher, born at Assos in the Troad, who lived from about 330 B.C. to about 231 B.C. He succeeded Zeno as leader of the STOIC school. Cleanthes' extant *Hymn to Zeus* treats Zeus not as an anthropomorphic deity but as a spirit that exists throughout the universe.

Cleisthenes (Kleisthenes). See ATHENS.

Cleon (Kleon). An Athenian leather merchant and statesman of the fifth century B.C. He actively supported an imperialist policy and insisted that the Athenians continue to fight against Sparta in the Peloponnesian War until they achieved victory. When the inhabitants of Mytilene rebelled against Athens in 427 B.C., Cleon demanded that they be killed or made slaves (see THE PELO-PONNESIAN WAR III, V). After leading a successful attack against the island of Sphacteria, Cleon became the most important political and military leader of Athens. He was killed in battle in 422 B.C. ARISTOPHANES, who regarded him as a dangerous demagogue, ridiculed him in THE KNIGHTS and THE WASPS.

Clouds, The (Nephelai). An Old Comedy by ARISTOPHANES. The extant play, which probably was never produced, is a revised version of a play produced in 423 B.C. Translations: in verse, Arthur S. Way, 1934; in verse, Benjamin B. Rogers, 1924; in verse, Robert Henning Webb, 1960; in prose and verse, William Arrowsmith, 1962.

BACKGROUND. Aristophanes' use of Socrates as the prototype of the Sophist raises many questions, because Socrates constantly criticized the Sophists. Moreover, Socrates differed from the character Aristophanes draws in the following important respects: he did not accept money for teaching; he refused to found a school; his extraordinary modesty was manifested in his claim that he knew nothing; he did not accept the theories about natural science popular in his time. Furthermore, Socrates, whose life was devoted to a search for truth, can hardly be associated with the Sophists' interest in the effective argument rather than in the true nature of a problem. Aristophanes' image of Socrates is clearly a distorted one; whether this distortion results from personal animosity or artistic necessity is impossible to determine.

SCENE. Two houses, in the background; one is the home of Strepsiades, and the other the "Thinkery" of Socrates.

SUMMARY. Strepsiades, an old man, is lying in bed unable to sleep because he is troubled by the debts of his son, who has spent a great deal of money on chariot racing, his chief interest. In another bed Strepsiades' son, Phidippides, talks in his sleep about the chariot races. Strepsiades thinks back on the happy days of his youth before his marriage when he lived an untroubled, simple life in the country. After his marriage to a haughty woman of the city all his troubles began. His wife was extravagant and affected. Even in choosing a name for their son she revealed her social aspirations: she insisted that the name contain the word *hippos* (meaning "horse" and commonly found in aristocratic names because in early times owning a horse was possible only for those in high military and social positions). After much discussion the child was given the name Phidippides which combines *pheido* (thrift) with the aristocratic ending, connoting wealth.

Suddenly Strepsiades thinks of a way to solve the problem of his son's debts. He gets out of bed, awakens Phidippides, and suggests that the young man enroll in the "Thinkery," Socrates' school, where for a fee he can learn to lie so well that he can win the lawsuits which will result from his debts. The young man is unwilling to enroll because attendance at school will spoil his suntan, so old Strepsiades decides to take the course himself. He rushes off to the "Thinkery" and knocks at the door. A Disciple of Socrates scolds him because he has disturbed an idea and caused it to "miscarry." The old man is then told about the strange and complicated problems that Socrates' students are involved in. He observes some of these students, and finally he sees Socrates in a basket suspended from the ceiling. Socrates explains that he must let his mind associate with the upper air in order to have lofty thoughts.

Strepsiades tells the master of his intention to learn to speak effectively so he can reason with his creditors and thus avoid payment of his debts. Socrates then prays to the Air and the Clouds, the goddesses he adores, and soon the Chorus of Clouds enters. Socrates explains to Strepsiades that these are the goddesses who come to the indolent; they are responsible for discourse and all the arts of persuasion. The Clouds, who support sophists, quacks, fops, and bad poets, are the only real deities; the others are mythical. Since Zeus does not exist, it is the Clouds that create rain, thunder, and lightning. Socrates then goes on to tell Strepsiades that he must follow the example of the master and honor no gods but Chaos, the Clouds, and the Tongue. Strepsiades agrees. The Leader of the Chorus asks Strepsiades what he wants, and he replies that he wishes to surpass all other Greeks in the gift of speech, but when the Leader grants him eloquence that will assure him political power, he refuses it, for he wants only the ability to deceive his creditors and win lawsuits, i.e., courtroom eloquence. The leader then tells Strepsiades that he must entrust himself to the Sophists, and Strepsiades agrees to do so in the hope that he will then appear to be arrogant, boastful, shameless, deceitful, cunning, and entirely corrupt. The Chorus is delighted with its new pupil.

After Socrates and Strepsiades enter the "Thinkery" the Chorus speaks to the audience, expressing the view that *The Clouds* is Aristophanes' best play and urging the audience to worship the Clouds. Socrates enters, annoyed by the vulgarity and stupidity of Strepsiades, who comes out of the "Thinkery" carrying a bed. He lies on the bed while Socrates teaches him. Strepsiades' only interest is in learning the art of false reasoning so he can overcome his creditors. Socrates finally loses patience with the old man and sends him away, advising him to send his son to the "Thinkery."

Although Phidippides regards what his father has learned at the "Thinkery" as sheer madness, he reluctantly obeys him and enters the school. There his teachers are to be Just Discourse and Unjust Discourse. These two come out engaged in a quarrel as to who is superior. Just Discourse is on the side of truth and justice, and pleads for the old system of education, which required obedience, modesty, discipline, and physical training, and which taught the traditional values and respect for elders. Unjust Discourse argues for the new Sophistic theory of education, which approves of physical pleasure, including hot baths and sexual indulgence; it teaches rhetorical tricks for winning an argument or a lawsuit, even when in the wrong, and general dishonesty and knavery. Unjust Discourse wins the argument by a trick and becomes the teacher of Phidippides.

After Unjust Discourse and Phidippides enter the "Thinkery" the Chorus turns to the audience and tells the judges of the contest for comedy, in which Aristophanes is competing, that if they award the prize to this play, the Clouds will reward them by caring for their crops. Later Strepsiades goes back to the "Thinkery" to find out what his son has been learning. Socrates praises Phidippides, saying now Strepsiades will win all his lawsuits. Phidippides soon appears and shows how well he has learned the tricks of the Sophists. Then Strepsiades gets rid of two creditors, Pasias and Amynias, by using Sophistic tricks.

A little later Strepsiades rushes out of his house, followed by Phidippides. They have been quarreling. Arguing with Sophistic trickery, Phidippides insists it is right to beat his father. When Strepsiades cannot refute Phidippides' arguments, the young man claims it is also right to beat his mother. Strepsiades is now convinced that Socrates and the Clouds have caused all his trouble. The Clouds, however, tell him that his own corruption has brought him to his present disgrace. Strepsiades admits he should not have cheated his creditors. His faith in the old gods is now restored, and he and his slaves set fire to the "Thinkery" of Socrates.

Clytemnestra (Klytaimnestra). In Greek mythology, a daughter of Leda and Tyndareus, king of Sparta. For Clytemnestra's sorrow over the sacrifice of her daughter Iphigenia see Euripides' IPHIGENIA IN AULIS. For the story of Clytemnestra's murder of her husband Agamemnon and the vengeance of her children Orestes and Electra see Aeschylus' ORESTEIA, Sophocles' ELECTRA, Euripides' ELECTRA, and Seneca's AGAMEMNON.

Cocytus (Kokytos). A river in Hades.

Comedy. The word comedy is derived from *komos* ("revel"), the term used to describe celebrations in honor of the god Dionysus.

OLD COMEDY. Gilbert Murray's thesis that ancient tragedy grew out of a *Sacer Ludus,* a sacred play in honor of Dionysus (see TRAGEDY), suggested to Francis Macdonald Cornford that Old Comedy also originated in this ancient ritual. Tragedy acted out the death of the traditional year-daemon or vegetation god, comedy his marriage festivities or revel. Cornford shows that the plot structure of Old Comedy "preserves the stereotyped action of ritual or folk drama, older than literary Comedy" (*The Origins of Attic Comedy,* Longmans, 1914, p. 5). This ritual or revel is, as Aristotle points out in POETICS, phallic in character and is related to a worship of the principles of fertility and productivity in nature. Though some of Cornford's conclusions have been challenged (see especially A. W. Pickard-Cambridge, *Dithyramb, Tragedy, and Comedy,* rev. T. B. Webster, Oxford University Press, 1962), they have been generally accepted by contemporary scholars.

The structure of Old Comedy takes the following pattern: (1) a prologue, which explains the essential elements of the plot; (2) a *parodos,* the entrance song and dance of the chorus; (3) an *agon,* a contest or dispute, which is the essential conflict of the play; (4) a *parabasis,* an address to the audience by the chorus, speaking for the author; the *parabasis* consists of (a) the *anapests,* a passage named after its meter, in which the chorus often discusses a political or literary subject; (b) a *pnigos* ("choker"), one long sentence recited at a high pitch of excitement in one breath; (c) an ode addressed to a god; (d) an *epirrhema,* a speech on contemporary matters; (e) an *antode,* similar to the ode; and finally (f) an *antepirrhema,* which returns to the comic mood; (5)

several episodes separated by choral odes; and (6) the *exodos*, the conclusion, in which all rejoice in a revel (*komos*) or a marriage (*gamos*) or both.

From the evidence of ARISTOPHANES' plays the plots of Old Comedy were fantastic and the characters essentially caricatures. The characters wore everyday clothing and highly stylized masks. The twenty-four members of the chorus were sometimes divided into two groups. Only brief fragments remain of the works of the writers of Old Comedy who were contemporaries and rivals of Aristophanes: Cratinus (c. 520–423 B.C.), whom Aristophanes ridicules in *The Knights,* and Eupolis (c. 446–411 B.C.). Thus the plays of Aristophanes are the sole surviving examples of this brilliant form. Aristophanes' fantastic plots and his extravagant, grotesque, and licentious wit reveal both the comic and the deeply serious aspects of the political, social, and literary conflicts of his time.

At Athens comedies were presented at the festivals in honor of Dionysus, the great Dionysia (during March and April) and the Lenaea (during January and February).

MIDDLE COMEDY. Old Comedy could no longer exist when freedom of speech was repressed in Athens after that city's defeat in the Peloponnesian War, for an essential feature of the form is its freedom to satirize political leaders and state policy. Middle Comedy, which flourished from about 400 B.C. to about 338 B.C., is milder drama, which criticizes types rather than individuals, general evils of mankind rather than specific corruption in the state. In Middle Comedy one finds mockery of myths, literature, and philosophy. The *Plutus* and *Ecclesiazusai* of Aristophanes can be regarded as Middle Comedies, but apart from these no complete representatives of the form exist, though there are many fragments.

NEW COMEDY. New Comedy, which grew out of Middle Comedy, began to appear around 336 B.C. In this drama the chorus was transformed into a group of singers and dancers who performed in interludes rather than taking a significant part in the play. Probably there were four such interludes (these were eliminated in Roman comedy), and thus five scenes were suggested. The characters and situations of New Comedy are drawn from contemporary life, and the plots are mainly built around domestic problems and conflicts, such as love, marriage, lost and rediscovered offspring. The characters are mostly types—the wealthy young man, the difficult father, the wronged young woman —all of whom were easily identifiable to the Greeks by their masks (the Romans did not use masks during the third and second century B.C., when Plautus and Terence wrote their comedies, but probably did use them during the first century B.C.). The endings are always happy.

Though a great many Greek New Comedies were written, only one whole play by MENANDER survives; however, whole plays can be reconstructed from a few of his larger fragments. The plays of his contemporaries are lost, but we have some knowledge of them from the work of PLAUTUS, who imitated them as well as Menander. TERENCE also imitated the plays of Menander. In fact, all the Latin comedies that remain—twenty plays of Plautus and six of Terence—are adaptations of Greek New Comedies.

Comedy of Asses, The (Asinaria). An adaptation by PLAUTUS of a Greek play by Demophilus. The plot is concerned with the efforts of Demaenetus, an old Athenian, to secure the money required by his son Argyrippus to obtain his beloved Philaenium, who lives next door with her mother, a procuress. Demaenetus is intimidated by his stingy wife Artemona. With the help of his slave, Demaenetus finally manages to obtain the money owed for some asses sold by his steward. Delighted at this good fortune, Demaenetus, Argyrippus, and Philaenium celebrate at a banquet. The old man kisses and embraces Philaenium, but his pleasure is spoiled when Artemona, informed by the parasite of Diabolus, a rival suitor, appears and demands that Demaenetus go home.

Consolatio ad Polybium. See DIALOGUES.

Copa (The Hostess). An elegiac poem attributed by some to VERGIL, though the subject matter and tone indicate that the poem is not his. It tells of a hostess of an inn or tavern who dances to castanets and invites all to pleasure, to enjoy life while they can.

Corinna (Korinna). Lyric poet born in either Tanagra or Thebes in Boeotia during the sixth century B.C. The few surviving fragments of her poems indicate that she wrote on mythological subjects. According to tradition she was the teacher of Pindar, and first urged him to employ more myths in his poems. When, in his attempt to follow her advice, he weighed down his lines with mythological allusions, she taught him with the proverb "Sow with handfuls, not with the sack."

Corinth (Korinthos). A city on the isthmus of Corinth. It was described in Homer (who calls it Ephyre) as a "rich" city, and archeological evidence suggests that it flourished as a center of commerce in ancient times. In Greek mythology Corinth is the city where Oedipus was raised by King Polybus and his wife Merope. Sisyphus was a legendary king of Corinth. During the Peloponnesian War Corinth was an opponent of Athens. However, in the Corinthian War (394–387 B.C.) Corinth was an ally of Athens, Thebes, and Argos in the struggle against the domination of Sparta. Corinth was conquered by Philip of Macedon, and in 146 B.C. it was entirely destroyed by the forces of the Roman consul L. Mummius.

Corybantes (Korybantes). Mythical followers of the goddess Cybele, who performed orgiastic dances in her honor. In historical times the name was applied to the eunuch priests of Cybele. By the fifth century B.C. the mythical Corybantes had been identified with the Curetes.

Crassus, Marcus Licinius. Roman leader. He was consul with POMPEY in 70 B.C. He allied himself with CAESAR and the popular party and became a member of the first triumvirate. Crassus was killed by the Parthians at Carrhae in 53 B.C.

Crates (Krates). See CYNICS.

Cratylus (Kratylos). A dialogue by PLATO named for the philosopher who was Plato's friend. Cratylus and Socrates discuss the origin and nature of language.

Creon (Kreon) (I). In Greek mythology, the brother of Jocasta, who became king of Thebes. See Sophocles' OEDIPUS THE KING, OEDIPUS AT COLONUS, ANTIGONE; Euripides' THE PHOENICIAN WOMEN; Seneca's OEDIPUS.

Creon (Kreon) (II). A legendary king of Corinth. See Euripides' MEDEA.

Crete (Krete). Cretan, or Minoan, civilization flourished long before the Greeks migrated to the area of the Aegean. Little is known about the origins of the Cretans, but evidence suggests that they were not an Indo-European people. In the years 1700–1400 B.C. Minoan civilization was at its height: the Cretans achieved great wealth through extensive trade, and the magnificent paintings and sculpture that have been excavated provide evidence that they were a highly cultivated and artistically sensitive people. The constant recurrence of the name MINOS in Greek myths about Crete indicates either that many kings called Minos ruled Crete or that Minos was a title meaning king. Around 1400 B.C. the palace at Cnossus was destroyed, possibly by a Greek invasion, and after this period Cretan civilization declined.

At the beginning of the twentieth century, Sir Arthur Evans led the excavations at Cnossus, the most important city of ancient Crete. At the site of the palace of Minos, Evans (who coined the term "Minoan") found clay tablets with curious hieroglyphic inscriptions. Many scholars worked on the decipherment of these scripts, one of which, Linear B, has been deciphered by Michael Ventris (see John Chadwick, *The Decipherment of Linear B* [Cambridge University Press, 1958], and Leonard R. Palmer, *Mycenaeans and Minoans: Aegean Prehistory in the Light of Linear B Tablets* [Alfred A. Knopf, 1963]). Ventris discovered that Linear B was a script employed to write an archaic form of Greek. As Chadwick says, "We can now see that Linear B is the result of adapting the Minoan script for the writing of Greek," and he concludes, "the masters of Knossos [Cnossus] spoke Greek," a clear indication that Minoan civilization was conquered by the Greeks from the mainland.

Creusa (Kreousa) (I). The first wife of Aeneas. See Vergil's AENEID II.

Creusa (Kreousa) (II). See Euripides' ION.

Critias (Kritias). A dialogue by PLATO, named for his uncle, who was leader of the Thirty Tyrants. The dialogue, which was left unfinished, is a sequel to *Timaeus* and deals with the imaginary island of Atlantis, which has sunk in the Atlantic.

Crito (Kriton). A dialogue by PLATO. Crito goes to visit his friend Socrates in prison. The hour when Socrates must take the poison is near. Crito attempts to persuade Socrates to escape, but Socrates refuses to break the law of Athens and to commit an unjust act. By remaining in Athens, Socrates accepted her law; he cannot justly break it to save his life.

Croesus (Kroisos). See THE PERSIAN WARS I and Bacchylides' CHORAL LYRIC III.

Cronus (Kronos). In Greek mythology, a Titan imprisoned in Tartarus along with his brothers and sisters by their father Uranus (the Heavens). With the help of his mother Ge (the Earth), Cronus castrated Uranus and became the ruler of the Titans. Cronus was married to Rhea, who bore him Zeus, Demeter, Hestia, Hera, Hades, and Poseidon. Rhea aided Zeus in overcoming his father. See Hesiod's THEOGONY.

Culex (the Gnat). A poem in dactylic hexameter, attributed by some to VERGIL. It tells the story of an old shepherd who is threatened by a serpent when he falls asleep. The sting of a gnat awakens the shepherd, who kills the gnat, then becomes aware of the serpent and kills it too. That night the ghost of the gnat comes to the shepherd as he sleeps and describes the Underworld to him. The insect reproaches the shepherd for his cruelty to the creature who saved his life. In gratitude the shepherd builds a tomb and writes an epitaph for the gnat.

Cupid (Cupido). In Roman mythology, the son of Venus. The god of love. He is identified with the Greek Eros. See PSYCHE.

Curculio (The Weevil). A comedy by PLAUTUS, based on an unknown Greek play. The comedy deals with the love of Phaedromus, a young man of Epidaurus, for Planaesium, a slave girl whom he cannot afford to buy. Phaedromus sends the parasite Curculio to Caria to obtain the money. Though Curculio cannot get the money, he does return with valuable information: a soldier named Therapontigonus has arranged to buy Planaesium and has left the necessary money with a banker of Epidaurus named Lyco, who will give the money to anyone who brings him a letter sealed with the ring of Therapontigonus. Because Curculio has stolen the ring, it is easy enough for Phaedromus to write the letter, seal it, and send Curculio for the money. Curculio then buys Planaesium, and the young lovers are reunited. When Therapontigonus, one of Plautus' braggart warriors, discovers that he has been cheated by Curculio, he is furious. However, Planaesium soon recognizes Therapontigonus' ring and realizes that she is his sister. Because she is now able to establish her identity as a freeborn citizen, she and Phaedromus may marry. The characters, plot, and structure of the play are rather obvious; it is one of Plautus' least successful plays.

Curetes (Kouretes). A group of young men (Kouroi), originating in Crete, who engaged in a wild war dance as a form of worship of the boy-god Zeus. In the *Theogony*, Hesiod tells the myth of how the Curetes, demigods armed with brass weapons, protected the infant Zeus, whom Rhea hid in a cave to prevent Cronus from devouring him. Fearing that Cronus might hear the child crying, the Curetes struck their spears against their shields and shouted war cries so that their noise would drown out the sounds of the infant god. The Curetes were traditionally followers of Rhea, and by the fifth century B.C. they were identified with the Corybantes.

Cybele (Kybele). A nature deity, originally the great mother goddess of Asia. In her native Phrygia the seat of her worship was Pessinus, where a block of stone represented the goddess; she was also called Dindymene, from the mountain Dindymon in Phrygia, where a shrine to her was located. Cybele, identified with Rhea by the Greeks and Romans, was first worshiped in Athens in 430 B.C. and in Rome in 204 B.C. Her worship was conducted by a group of eunuch priests called Corybantes or Galli (see Catullus' LYRIC on Attis).

Cyclops (Kyklops). One of a race of giants having but one eye, in the center of their foreheads. Hesiod's *Theogony* tells of their birth from the union of Heaven and Earth; Pausanias says that Perseus had them build the walls of the acropolis at Mycenae. They are described by Homer in the ODYSSEY IX. See also POLYPHEMUS.

Cyclops, The (Kyklops). A satyr play by EURIPIDES (probably about 423 B.C.). Translations: in verse, Percy B. Shelley, 1819; in prose, E. P. Coleridge, 1891; in verse, A. S. Way, 1912; in verse, J. T. Sheppard, 1923; in verse, Roger Lancelyn Green, 1957.

MYTHICAL BACKGROUND. When the Satyrs, led by their leader Silenus, sought their god, Dionysus, they were taken prisoner by the Cyclops Polyphemus in Sicily.

SCENE. Before the cave of the Cyclops Polyphemus at the foot of Mount Etna in Sicily.

SUMMARY. Silenus comes in carrying a rake. He addresses Dionysus and begs the god not to forget him, for he is suffering as a slave of the Cyclops Polyphemus. He tells of how hard he must work cleaning the Cyclops' cave and tending his flocks. He feels debased by this toil, he who followed Dionysus. Soon the Chorus of Satyrs enters, driving the Cyclops' sheep. The Satyrs also complain to Dionysus of their unhappiness as slaves of Polyphemus and ask the god to hear their prayers for help.

Silenus tells his followers he has seen a Greek ship near the coast. He pities the poor men who no doubt have landed to ask for help. They cannot guess that Polyphemus will eat them as he usually does strangers. Odysseus and his followers enter and ask the Satyrs for food and water. Odysseus believes he has come to the home of Dionysus, but Silenus soon informs him that he is in the land of the man-eating Cyclopes. Odysseus gives Silenus wine and in exchange receives cheese and goat's meat.

When Polyphemus appears Silenus pretends that Odysseus and his men beat and robbed him. Polyphemus decides he will eat Odysseus and his men because he is bored with his usual diet. Despite Odysseus' pleas that the Cyclops spare him and his men, Polyphemus forces them to enter the cave. The Chorus tells in humorous and gruesome detail of how the Cyclops cooks and eats men. Meanwhile cries are heard from within the cave. Odysseus comes out of the cave, horrified at having seen two of his men cooked and eaten. He gives a grotesquely humorous description of the feast, emphasizing the disgusting details. Then he tells of how some god inspired him with the idea of giving the Cyclops a great deal of wine to make him drunk. Odysseus' plan is to destroy Polyphemus' one eye with an olive stake sharpened and heated in the fire. When the Cyclops is blinded they can all escape. The Chorus greets this plan with wild enthusiasm.

The Cyclops appears in his drunken state, singing of the pleasure he has had in feasting on Odysseus' men. When Polyphemus asks Odysseus what his name is, Odysseus replies, "Nobody." Polyphemus promises to show his "friendship" for Odysseus by eating him last of all. Odysseus gives Polyphemus more wine, and exceedingly drunk, the Cyclops retreats to his cave, dragging with him Silenus, whom he calls Ganymedes, mistaking him for the Trojan boy with whom Zeus was infatuated.

Odysseus decides that this is the time to blind the Cyclops. With the help of the Satyrs he prepares the stake. Because the Satyrs are afraid to help with the actual blinding, Odysseus goes alone into the cave. Soon the blinded Polyphemus, crying out in pain and rage, appears at the entrance to the cave. He remains in this place to prevent Odysseus and his men from escaping. As the Satyrs tease and trip the Cyclops to distract him, Odysseus and his men emerge from the cave. Odysseus then reveals to the Cyclops who he is, and Polyphemus predicts that Odysseus will wander for a long time before he reaches his home. Though the Cyclops threatens to throw stones at Odysseus' ship in order to sink it, Odysseus, his men, and the Satyrs go off happily to the ship.

Cynics. A school of philosophy established in Athens by Antisthenes (c. 445–365 B.C.), a pupil of Gorgias and later of Socrates. None of Antisthenes' philosophical works survive. The name Cynic is derived either from the gymnasium Cynosarges (*Kynosarges*) where Antisthenes founded his school or from the word "doggish" (Gr. *kyon*, dog) used to describe DIOGENES, a disciple of Antisthenes and the most famous member of the school. The Cynics scorned the material and social values of most men and regarded society and civilization itself as false and corrupt. They were contemptuous of the arts and sciences. Happiness, the Cynics preached, could be found only in virtue, which they defined as freedom from false desires and possession of true values. Many of the Cynics traveled about preaching, living as beggars. Crates of Thebes, a pupil of Diogenes, was a wealthy man who gave up his entire fortune to live the life of a mendicant, preach the Cynic doctrine, and write plays and poems, the best known of which is the fragmentary *Beggar's Wallet,* a mock-heroic poem. Only fragments of his work survive.

Cyprus (Kypros). A large island in the Mediterranean. Cyprus was settled by the Phoenicians and the Greeks and was dominated at various times by the Egyptians, the Persians, and the Romans. The island was one of the main centers for the worship of Aphrodite, who is sometimes called Cypris or Cypria. She is also referred to as the Paphian, after Paphos, one of the major cities of Cyprus.

Cyropaedia (Kyrou Paideia). See XENOPHON.

Cyrus (Kyros). See THE PERSIAN WARS I and XENOPHON.

Cythera (Kythera). An island south of Laconia. According to one tradition, Cythera was the place to which Aphrodite first went after her birth in the sea; thus she is sometimes called Cytherea.

D

Daedalus (Daidalos). A legendary Athenian inventor and architect, the son of Metion and a descendant of Hephaestus. In *Metamorphoses* VIII, Ovid tells the story of how Daedalus, jealous of the skill of his nephew Talus (Talos), whom Daedalus' sister had sent to study with the great inventor, pushed the boy off the Acropolis and then pretended that Talus had slipped. Athene saved Talus and transformed him into a partridge (*Perdix*). Daedalus was found guilty of his crime and fled to Crete. There he built the Labyrinth for MINOS. Tired of exile and longing for Athens, Daedalus decided to construct wings made of wax and feathers for himself and his son Icarus so that they could escape from Crete. Daedalus warned Icarus not to fly too near the sun, but when Icarus did not heed this warning his wings melted and he fell into the sea named for him, the Icarian Sea. James Joyce's character Stephen Dedalus of *A Portrait of the Artist as a Young Man* and *Ulysses* is based on the great legendary artist of antiquity.

Danaë. See ACRISIUS.

Danaus (Danaos). According to Greek mythology, a descendant of Io and a son of Belus, king of Egypt. Danaus' brother Aegyptus wished Danaus' fifty daughters (the Danaidae) to marry his fifty sons, but Danaus refused and fled with his fifty daughters to Argos. The sons of Aegyptus followed the Danaidae to Argos and forced them into marriage. On the wedding night all the Danaidae except Hypermnestra slew their husbands. Danaus became king of Argos; *Danaoi*, which the people of Argos were called, may derive from his name. For the story of the Danaidae see Aeschylus' THE SUPPLIANTS. The story of Hypermnestra's loyalty to her husband Lynceus is told in Ovid's HEROIDES XI.

Daphne. In Greek mythology, a nymph, the daughter of the river Peneus. In *Metamorphoses* I, Ovid tells of how the god Apollo fell in love with Daphne and pursued her until she was transformed into a laurel, a tree sacred to Apollo.

Dardania. See TROY.

Dardanus (Dardanos). See TROY.

Dares Phrygius. The priest of Hephaestus in Troy in the *Iliad*. A Latin work of the fifth century A.D. called *Daretis Phrygii de Excidio Troiae Historia* (*The History of Dares the Phrygian of the Destruction of Troy*) was supposed to be a translation of Dares' Greek poem on the Trojan War. The author of this rather poor fraud wrote a preface signed with the name of the historian Cornelius Nepos and addressed to the historian Sallust. In this preface "Nepos" declares that he has found the original manuscript of Dares Phrygius and has translated it into Latin. He suggests that Dares is a better authority on the Trojan War than Homer, who did not witness the events he describes and was foolish enough to depict gods at war with men. Despite the obvious forgery and the poor quality of the work, Dares was regarded as a greater authority than Homer during the Middle Ages, and his work was much admired. In fact, during this period the Trojan myths became known chiefly through this work and through another equally fraudulent work attributed to Dictys Cretensis.

Darius (Dareios). See THE PERSIAN WARS III, IV, VI and Aeschylus' THE PERSIANS.

De Agri Cultura. See CATO THE CENSOR.

De Amicitia. See CICERO.

De Bello Civili. See CAESAR.

De Bello Civili (Lucan). See ON THE CIVIL WAR.

De Bello Gallico. See CAESAR.

De Beneficiis. See SENECA THE PHILOSOPHER.

De Brevitate Vitae. See DIALOGUES.

De Clementia. See SENECA THE PHILOSOPHER.

De Constantia Sapientis. See DIALOGUES.

De Divinatione. See CICERO.

De Domo Sua. See CICERO.

De Fato. See CICERO.

De Finibus Bonorum et Malorum. See CICERO.

De Haruspicum Responso. See CICERO.

Deianira (Deianeira). Wife of Heracles. See Sophocles' WOMEN OF TRACHIS, Bacchylides' CHORAL LYRIC XVI, Ovid's HEROIDES IX, and Seneca's HERCULES OETAEUS. Her story is also told in Ovid's *Metamorphoses* IX.

De Inventione. See CICERO.

Deiphobus (Deiphobos). In the *Iliad,* a son of Priam and Hecuba, a Trojan warrior. Aeneas speaks to him in Hades in the AENEID VI.

De Ira. See DIALOGUES.

De Legibus. See CICERO.

De Lingua Latina. See VARRO.

Delos. An island in the Aegean. Delos was regarded the birthplace of Apollo and Artemis (see HOMERIC HYMN III). Apollo was worshiped at Delos, and one of his oracles was located there. For the Delian Confederacy see ATHENS.

Delphi (Delphoi). A town in Phocis in central Greece, on the southern slope of Mount Parnassus. Delphi was known for the oracle of Apollo located there. For Apollo's establishment of his oracle at Delphi see HOMERIC HYMN III. In ancient times Delphi was regarded as the "navel" or center of the earth. The

Delphic oracle was extremely important in ancient Greek history and literature. An excellent study of the subject is H. W. Parke and D. E. W. Wormell, *The Delphic Oracle* (Blackwell, 1956).

Demeter. A Greek earth goddess. According to Hesiod, she was a daughter of Cronus and Rhea and a sister of Zeus. The worship of Demeter, a goddess of corn and of agriculture in general, probably originated in early Mediterranean culture long before the coming of the Achaeans. She was no doubt worshiped as a mother goddess and a principle of life. For her loss of her daughter PERSEPHONE see HOMERIC HYMN II, which also tells of how Demeter founded the ELEUSINIAN MYSTERIES, in which she, her daughter, and Iacchos (identified with Dionysus) were worshiped. The Romans identified her with Ceres.

Demetrius (Demetrios). See ON STYLE.

Democritus (Demokritos). A Greek philosopher, born at Abdera (Thrace) (c. 460 B.C.). Known as the "laughing philosopher" because he found amusement in the foolishness of man (Juvenal refers to him in *Satire* x), Democritus accepted and added to the atomic theory of Leucippus, believing that all of matter, including the soul of man, was composed of atoms. Democritus' ethical writings emphasized moderation as the means to happiness. Only brief fragments of his work remain.

Demodocus (Demodokos). The blind minstrel at the court of Alcinous in the ODYSSEY (VIII).

Demosthenes. A Greek orator, born at Athens in 383 B.C. His father, a rich manufacturer of swords and other arms, died when Demosthenes was seven. The guardians of his father's estate handled it dishonestly, and at eighteen Demosthenes demanded his inheritance. After studying with Isaeus, an orator and specialist in law, Demosthenes brought charges against his guardians and finally won his case, but actually received little of his rightful share of the estate.

To earn a living Demosthenes became a professional writer of speeches. According to tradition, his failure as an orator when speaking before the Assembly for the first time only stimulated him to intense study and practice, which included speaking with pebbles in his mouth and other extremely difficult exercises. Demosthenes' great talent and extraordinary self-discipline made him the greatest and most famous Athenian orator.

Though sixty-one orations, six letters, and fifty-four proems are listed as works of Demosthenes, most scholars believe that only thirty-five or forty speeches are actually his. Some of the extant speeches deal with typical legal questions, but the most interesting, and certainly the best-known are the political orations. Demosthenes became known as a political leader when Philip of Macedon first threatened Athens in the middle of the fourth century B.C. The *First Philippic,* delivered in 351 B.C., is a passionate plea to the Athenians to face the danger that threatened them from Macedon. He asks them not to rely on mercenaries to defend their state, but to build up an army of citizens, and begs them to prepare for war with the concern and diligence with which they arrange festivals.

Demosthenes did not succeed in arousing the Athenians. In 349 B.C. Philip attacked the city of Olynthus, which asked for the aid of Athens. Demosthenes supported Olynthus' plea in his three *Olynthiacs*, but Athens' help came too late. The city of Olynthus and the others of the Chalcidian League were conquered. In 346 B.C. Athens signed the Peace of Philocrates with Macedon, a treaty unfavorable to Athens and unpopular with her citizens. Demosthenes' *On the Peace*, delivered in 346 B.C., attempted to quiet popular disapproval, because any attempt to violate the treaty would bring disastrous effects. He did suggest, however, that the orator AESCHINES, one of the Athenian representatives who had negotiated the treaty, had betrayed his country. In his *Second Philippic*, delivered in 344 B.C., Demosthenes again warned the Athenians against the threat of Philip, pointing out that Philip intended to ally himself with Thebes, Messene, and Argos against Athens.

In 343 B.C. Hyperides, an orator who, with Demosthenes and the orator Lycurgus, led the anti-Macedonian party, brought about the impeachment of Philocrates, for whom the peace treaty of 346 B.C. was named. Demosthenes impeached Aeschines and, in *On the Embassy*, delivered in 343 B.C., declared that Aeschines had intentionally misrepresented Philip's position to the Athenian Assembly and thus persuaded the Athenians to accept the unfavorable terms of the peace treaty. Aeschines' reply helped to win him an acquittal by thirty votes. In his *Third Philippic*, delivered in 341 B.C., Demosthenes tried to persuade the Athenians to continue to support the Chersonese (the peninsula of Gallipoli on the western Hellespont) against the advances of Philip, who, Demosthenes said, "threatens all of Greece."

In August, 330 B.C., Demosthenes delivered *On the Crown*, also called *In Defense of Ctesiphon*, perhaps his best-known oration, to persuade an Athenian jury of more than five hundred members of the constitutionality of Ctesiphon's proposal six years earlier that Demosthenes be awarded a golden crown for service to the state. Ctesiphon had been indicted by Aeschines (who charged that Ctesiphon's praises of Demosthenes were false), and therefore his proposal could not be put before the Assembly for a vote.

In *On the Crown*, Demosthenes answers the charges of Aeschines that he was responsible for the poor terms of the peace treaty of 346 B.C., justifies his attempts to persuade the Athenians to take action against Macedonian aggression, and defends his entire career in public life. He begins the oration with a prayer to the gods for kind treatment by the Athenians and a prayer for their honorable conduct in judging the case impartially. He objects to charges of Aeschines that he regards as irrelevant and to Aeschines' attacks on his private life. Demosthenes then takes up Aeschines' accusation that he has committed crimes against the state of Athens. He defends his role in the conflict with

Macedon and denies his responsibility for the unfavorable terms of the peace treaty of 346 B.C. He sharply attacks Aeschines, calling him bombastic, uneducated, and corrupt and criticizes his public career. He defends his own position on resistance to Macedon, then recalls all the evidence of Athens' respect for him, and continues to attack the character and policies of Aeschines. Demosthenes' final defense is that his policies and acts are like those of the heroes of antiquity. His loyalty to Athens and his love for the state, he declares, prove him a good citizen.

Demosthenes won his case and his crown, clearing Ctesiphon and defeating Aeschines. The last years of Demosthenes' life, however, were troubled ones. He was accused of having misappropriated a large sum of money brought to Athens by Harpalus, the treasurer of Alexander the Great. Harpalus had tried to persuade the Athenians to rebel against Alexander, but was arrested and the money he had brought with him was placed in the Acropolis for safekeeping. Because half of it disappeared, Demosthenes, one of the commissioners in charge of the funds, was suspected of misappropriation. He was imprisoned but escaped and went into exile. He returned to Athens after the death of Alexander the Great in 323 B.C. When Athens was defeated in the Lamian War against Macedon in 322 B.C., Demosthenes committed suicide to avoid being taken prisoner.

Cicero and Quintilian regarded Demosthenes as the greatest of Greek orators, and his work had a profound influence on Roman rhetorical theory and practice. The modern world has also regarded Demosthenes as a great political figure and prose stylist. His language is powerful and intensely emotional; his rhythms suggest a voice raised in anger or pleading with deep conviction. His precise language and his brilliant, sometimes shocking, metaphors communicate Demosthenes' total commitment to the cause of Athenian freedom.

De Natura Deorum. See CICERO.

De Officiis. See CICERO.

De Optimo Genere Oratorum. See CICERO.

De Oratore. See ON ORATORY.

De Otio. See DIALOGUES.

De Providentia. See DIALOGUES.

De Re Publica. A dialogue by CICERO in six books on political philosophy, begun in 54 B.C. and published around 51 B.C. Before 1820 only a portion of the sixth book was known: *Somnium Scipionis* (The Dream of Scipio), with a commentary by Macrobius. In 1820 the first three books and fragments of the others were discovered in a Vatican palimpsest. Like Plato's *Republic*, on which it is modeled, *De Re Publica* deals with the ideal state.

Cicero says that the dialogue was reported to him. The chief speakers are Scipio Aemilianus, the famous consul, general, and orator (c. 185–129 B.C.), in whose garden it takes place, and his friend Gaius Laelius, a consul, warrior, and orator. Scipio describes the three types of government: monarchy, aristocracy, and democracy. The Roman Republic, which combined elements of all three, is the best form of government. He traces the development of Rome from its beginnings and discusses justice and law.

De Rerum Natura. See ON THE NATURE OF THINGS.

De Re Rustica. See CATO THE CENSOR.

De Senectute. See CICERO.

De Tranquillitate Animi. See DIALOGUES.

Deucalion (Deukalion). In Greek mythology, the son of Prometheus. His story is told in Ovid's METAMORPHOSES.

deus ex machina. The "machine" was a mechanical device, perhaps a crane or a derrick, used by the Greek dramatists, especially Euripides, to bring in an actor who represented a god. Because the deity thus introduced sometimes appeared just in time to resolve the main conflict of the plot, the term *deus ex machina* ("the god from the machine") has come to mean any mechanical or superficial method of resolving a dramatic conflict.

De Viris Illustribus. See SUETONIUS.

De Vita Beata. See DIALOGUES.

De Vita Caesarum. See LIVES OF THE CAESARS.

Dialogue on Orators (Dialogus de Oratoribus). A dialogue usually attributed to TACITUS, but of uncertain authorship and date. The discussion, at which the author says he was present when he was young (about A.D. 75), is concerned with the decline of oratory since the days of Cicero because of the lowering of educational standards, poor teaching, and the loss of political freedom in Rome. The speakers are Curiatius Maternus, a poet at whose home the discussion is held; Marcus Aper, an advocate; Julius Secundus, a historian; and Vipstanus Messalla.

Marcus Aper, whom the author calls a man imbued with all learning, places the orator far beyond the poet and says that a great orator is capable of mastering provinces. The profession of oratory, he says, gives more practical rewards and a deeper sense of personal satisfaction, brings more honors in Rome and throughout the Empire than does any other profession imaginable. He speaks of the power to move men as a sacred function. Messalla, however, says that oratory has declined in his day because education is poor and virtue itself is considered old-fashioned. In the past it was considered necessary for an orator to have all the accomplishments and all the virtues, but at the present time he gets but a narrow training and that chiefly in declamation, the training of the tongue and the voice in imaginary controversies in no way connected with reality. Messalla continues to contrast the oratory of the past, its training and practice closely related to experience and the vital needs of the state, with contemporary oratory, which has lost its dignity as an art.

The author regards the decline of oratory as the result of its disassociation from the affairs of state and the lives of men. No longer a vital part of the state, oratory has become a plaything of the schools. The author looks back to the orators of the past not only as great speakers but as representatives of a dignified way of life.

Dialogues (Dialogi). Ten treatises by SENECA THE PHILOSOPHER. They are arranged in twelve books:

1. *De Providentia* (*On Providence*) deals with the question of why good men must endure misfortune when there is a Providence. Seneca's answer is that apparent evils actually are tests of a man's virtue and powers of endurance. 2. *De Constantia Sapientis* (*On the Constancy of the Sage*) discusses the Stoic's tranquility of spirit. The Stoic sage cannot be wronged or harmed because he cannot be made evil. Since he is above insult, no insulting person can affect him. 3–5. *De Ira* (*On Wrath*) is in three books. In the first, Seneca discusses wrath itself, indicating that it serves no useful purpose; in the second, he shows that one need not be affected by wrath; in the third, he indicates and illustrates ways of controlling this emotion. 6. *Ad Marciam de Consolatione* (*To Marcia, on Consolation*) attempts to console the daughter of the Stoic Cremutius Cordus, who had lost her son three years before. 7. *De Vita Beata* (*On the Happy Life*), which is fragmentary, recommends the STOIC ideal of a "life according to nature." 8. *De Otio* (*On Leisure*), which is fragmentary, recommends retirement from public life and deals with the satisfactions of a life of contemplation. 9. *De Tranquillitate Animi* (*On Tranquility of Spirit*) deals mainly with the many fears to which men who lead idle and worthless lives are subject. A man must know himself, choose a career for which he is suited, and find worthy friends; he must not value property or wealth and must not fear death. 10. *De Brevitate Vitae* (*On the Brevity of Life*) suggests that if men did not waste much of their time, life would be sufficiently long. 11. *Consolatio ad Polybium* (*Consolation to Polybius*) was written during Seneca's exile in Corsica. It is addressed to Polybius, a freedman with influence at the court of Claudius. In consoling Polybius on the recent death of his brother, Seneca flatters Polybius and Claudius outrageously in an obvious attempt to obtain a recall from exile. 12. *Ad Helviam Matrem de Consolatione* (*A Consolation to His Mother, Helvia*), also written from Corsica, comforts his mother, assuring her that banishment is not as painful or as difficult as is commonly thought.

Diana. An Italian goddess, early identified with the Greek goddess Artemis. Diana was the goddess of the moon, of the country and forest, of the hunt, of springs and brooks, of chastity, and of childbirth. She was worshiped mainly by women. Her most important shrine was in a grove in the Alban hills in Aricia, where she was worshiped as *Diana Nemorensis* (Diana of the Grove), along with a god of the forest and the hunt, Virbius, who was later associated with Hippolytus.

Dictys Cretensis. A mythical Cretan author, Dictys of Crete, who supposedly accompanied his friend Idomeneus to the Trojan War and wrote a journal recounting the entire story. During the fourth century A.D. Quintus Septimius published his *Ephemeris Belli Troiani* (*A Journal of the Trojan War*), pretending that it was a Latin translation of Dictys' journal, written originally in Phoenician and transliterated into Greek during the first century A.D., during the thirteenth year of Nero's reign. The style of the *Ephemeris Belli Troiani* resembles that of Sallust, whom its author obviously imitated. During the Middle Ages the story of Troy was known chiefly through the *Ephemeris Belli Troiani* and the *Daretis Phrygii de Excidio Troiae Historia* (see DARES PHRYGIUS).

Dido (also called **Elissa**). The daughter of King Belus of Tyre. When her brother Pygmalion killed Dido's wealthy husband Sychaeus, Dido left her homeland and went to Africa. There King Iarbas said she might have as much land as could be enclosed by the hide of a bull. Dido wisely commanded that the hide be cut into extremely thin strips and thus obtained land enough to build a fortress, Byrsa, which became the center of her kingdom, Carthage. For her tragic love affair with Aeneas see Vergil's AENEID IV and Ovid's HEROIDES VII.

Dinarchus (**Deinarchos**). A Greek orator, born at Corinth around 360 B.C. He practiced at Athens as a professional speech writer. Three of his speeches survive, all of them related to the charge against DEMOSTHENES that he had misappropriated the money of Harpalus.

Dio Chrysostom (**Dion Chrysostomos** [Gr. "Golden-Mouthed"]). A Greek philosopher and orator (A.D. 40–120). Dio came from Bithynia to Rome, where he had lived until his banishment in A.D. 82. His extant work, written in Greek, includes discourses on political subjects, philosophy, and literature. His remarks on myth and literature are valuable both for his interpretations and for the information they provide on works no longer extant.

Diodorus Siculus. A Greek historian, born at Agyrium in Sicily in the first century B.C. He wrote a Greek history of the world, the *Bibliotheke Historike* (*Historical Library*) in forty books, of which fifteen remain. The chief interest of the work lies in the myths that Diodorus records.

Diogenes. A Greek philosopher, born in Sinope (fourth century B.C.). Diogenes was the principal proponent of the Cynic school of philosophy and is often called Diogenes the Cynic. The position of this school was that happiness could result only from virtue and could be found only when men renounced the conventional requirements and desires. To exemplify his freedom from conventional needs, Diogenes, it is said, lived in a tub in the sanctuary of the Mother of the Gods (Cybele) in Athens.

Diogenes Laertius (**Laertios**). Author of the Greek biography *Lives of Eminent Philosophers*. He lived during the third century A.D. Nothing is known of his life. In ten books Diogenes summarizes the lives and ideas of eighty-two Greek thinkers. He describes their appearance, tells anecdotes, and quotes from some of their writings. Diogenes also wrote *Epigrams in Various Meters*.

Diogenes the Babylonian. See STOICS.

Diomedes. One of the greatest of the Greek warriors in the ILIAD. He also appears in RHESUS.

Dionysius (Dionysios) of Halicarnassus. A Greek literary critic and historian who lived in Rome during the Augustan period. Some of his extant critical works, which were written in Greek, are *On the Arrangement of Words*, which discusses prose style and in which are preserved Sappho's *Aphrodite* and Simonides' *Danaë*, *On Imitation*, a fragmentary work, three of six essays *On the Ancient Orators*, *On the Style of Demosthenes*, *On Dinarchus*, and *On Thucydides*. Dionysius' *Romaike Archaiologia* (*Roman Antiquities*) deals with the history of Rome from its beginnings to the First Punic War. Only the first ten books and fragments of others remain.

Dionysus (Dionysos) (also called Bacchus). The Greek god of wine and a fertility and year spirit. The obscure deity Iacchos, who was honored in the Eleusinian Mysteries, along with Demeter, was later identified with Dionysus. In Euripides' *The Bacchae* the god Dionysus comes to Thebes from Asia Minor; elsewhere in Greek literature his original home is said to be Thrace. As W. K. C. Guthrie points out, "This is no contradiction, for Thracians and Phrygians [of Asia Minor] were of the same race, since some time in the second millennium B.C. there was a movement of tribes from Thrace across the Hellespont to settle in Asia Minor. Thus, the religions of Dionysos and of Kybele [Cybele], the Asiatic mother-goddess with her young attendant Attis, were of the same orgiastic type, and by historical times had become inextricably mingled. . . ." (W. K. C. Guthrie, *The Greeks and Their Gods* [Beacon Press, 1955], p. 154.) In ancient Greece, Dionysus was the god of wine, fertility, intoxication, and even frenzy, music, and drama, and he was worshiped in cults that flourished in various parts of Greece. In Homer, Dionysus is one of the less significant deities, but there is an extended reference to him in *Iliad* VI. He is also the subject of HOMERIC HYMNS I, VII, XXVI, and in Aristophanes' THE FROGS he visits Hades. For the myth of his birth, his role as a god of productivity and destruction, and his relation to the origins of Greek tragedy see THE BACCHAE and TRAGEDY. *The Bacchae* treats his punishment of Pentheus, who opposed the worship of Dionysus in Thebes. See also COMEDY, LYCURGUS I, and the ELEUSINIAN MYSTERIES. Dionysus, one of the most complicated of the ancient Greek gods, has been investigated by many scholars of Greek literature, history, and religion. Perhaps the best brief study of Dionysus for the student of literature is E. R. Dodds, "Introduction" to his *Euripides' Bacchae* (Oxford University Press, 1944). See also E. R. Dodds, "Maenadism," Appendix I of *The Greeks and the Irrational* (Beacon Press, 1957), and R. P. Winnington-Ingram, *Euripides and Dionysus* (Macmillan, 1948).

Dioscuri (Dios Kouroi [Gr. "sons of Zeus"]). In Greek mythology, Castor and Polydeuces (Latin Pollux), the twin sons either of Zeus and LEDA or of Leda and her husband Tyndareus. In a third version, Castor is the son of Leda and

Tyndareus, Polydeuces the son of Leda and Zeus. In literature the Dioscuri are regarded both as courageous mortals and gods who protect sailors. In the *Iliad* they are mentioned as the brothers of Helen, who have died in battle. When the Dioscuri sailed with the Argonauts, Pollux, a great boxer, killed Amycus, king of the Bebryces, and the twins established the city of Dioscurias in Colchis. The story of their death varies. In one version, when the immortal Polydeuces saw his mortal brother Castor slain in battle, he prayed for death also, and Zeus granted the twins the right to share alternate days in Heaven and in the Underworld. In Rome, Castor was worshiped before Pollux and was more highly regarded. The Romans sometimes referred to the twins as *Castores*. The Dioscuri were later identified with the constellation Gemini. Theocritus writes of the Dioscuri in *Idyl* xxii, Pindar addresses them in *Olympian* iii, and they appear in Euripides' *Helen*.

Dirae. See FURIES.

Dirae (Curses). A poem in dactylic hexameter attributed by some to VERGIL. The speaker's lands have been confiscated (see Vergil's ECLOGUE I), and he curses those who took away his farm. Then he says farewell to his beloved land as he leaves.

Dis. The Roman god of the Underworld. See HADES.

dithyramb. A Greek choral lyric. In its earliest forms, the dithyramb was probably sung by a chorus of fifty men dressed as satyrs, to honor the god Dionysus. Arion probably developed the dithyramb into an artistic composition to be sung by a chorus around an altar of Dionysus. Dithyrambs were also written by Lasus, Simonides, Bacchylides, and Pindar. At Athens, late in the sixth century B.C., contests were held for the best dithyrambs. By the time Bacchylides and Pindar wrote in this form it was customary for poets to write dithyrambs in honor of Apollo and other gods as well as Dionysus. Many modern scholars believe with Aristotle that TRAGEDY grew out of the early dithyramb.

Dolon. A Trojan spy, killed by Odysseus and Diomedes (see the ILIAD X and RHESUS).

Domitian (Titus Flavius Domitianus). Emperor of ROME from A.D. 81 to 96. A contemporary source for his life is Suetonius' *Lives of the Caesars*. See the SATIRES (IV) of JUVENAL.

Dorians. Generally regarded as a band of Greeks who, forced to leave the region of Epirus, came from the North—according to Thucydides, eighty years after the fall of Troy—and destroyed Mycenae and the other great kingdoms of the Achaeans. The Dorian invasion, which conquered practically all of Greece and Crete, marked the end of the great Mycenaean period. Most scholars believe that one of the important results of the Dorian invasion was the migration of many Greeks to the Aegean islands and the western coast of Asia Minor.

Dorus (Doros). See Euripides' ION.

Draco (Drakon). See ATHENS.

Dyskolos (The Bad-Tempered Man; The Misanthrope; The Grouch). A New Comedy (317 B.C.) by MENANDER. Translations: in prose and verse, Philip Vellacott, 1960; in prose, W. G. Arnott, 1960; in prose, Lionel Casson, 1960.

S C E N E . Phyle in Attica; in the center, a shrine with a statue of Pan; on the right, Cnemon's house; on the left, Gorgias' house.

S U M M A R Y . Pan enters from his shrine and explains that the farm on the right belongs to Cnemon, a misanthrope, who speaks only to Pan and then only because he is obliged to acknowledge a god. Years ago Cnemon married a widow who had one son, Gorgias. She bore Cnemon a daughter, but life with him became unbearable, and she finally left him and went to live with her grown son, Gorgias, in the farm on the left. Gorgias is an intelligent and able man, mature beyond his years. Old Cnemon lives with his daughter, Myrrhine, a gentle and kind girl, whom Pan has decided to help. He has caused Sostratus, a rich young man, to fall in love with the girl.

As Pan goes out, Sostratus and Chaereas enter, speaking of Cnemon's daughter. Sostratus is in love with her and asks Chaereas to help him win her. All of Sostratus' efforts to court the girl have been frustrated by her father, who chases all strangers from his door, threatening them with violence. Cnemon ran two miles after Sostratus' slave boy Pyrrhias, whom Sostratus had sent with a message. Finding Sostratus at the door of his house, Cnemon screams with rage, and the young man withdraws. Sostratus does manage to speak to Myrrhine for a moment and to draw water from the well for her; then, moaning with love, he goes out.

Sostratus convinces Gorgias that he wishes to marry Myrrhine, and Gorgias promises to help him. In the meantime Cnemon's slave Simice has dropped his bucket down the well and then dropped the hoe down while trying to rescue the bucket. When Cnemon discovers what she has done, he is furious. Rather than ask for help he decides to recover his bucket and hoe by himself. Soon Simice screams for help, declaring that Cnemon has fallen into the well. When Gorgias and Sostratus rescue him, Cnemon admits that a man sometimes does need help from others. Therefore, he adopts Gorgias as his son and allows him to choose a husband for Myrrhine. Gorgias at once chooses Sostratus. Sostratus persuades his father, Callippides, to allow his daughter to marry Gorgias. As the play ends even Cnemon is made to take part in the joyous marriage festivities.

E

Ecclesiazusae (Ekklesiazousai; Women in the Assembly). A Middle Comedy (392 B.C.) by ARISTOPHANES. Translations: in verse, Benjamin B. Rogers, 1924; in verse, Arthur S. Way, 1934.

S C E N E . Athens, a public square; the house of Praxagora is in the background, separated by an alley from another house. Later the two houses are those of prostitutes.

S U M M A R Y . Praxagora enters, signaling with a lantern to women she is expecting. They plan to dress in men's clothing and attend the Assembly, where they will pass a law that the government of Athens be taken over by the women. Soon the women enter, bringing staffs and men's clothing. They put on false beards and dress as men and, after outlining their arguments concerning the dishonesty and ineffectuality of the present leaders and the poor condition of Athens, which the women will correct, they depart for the Assembly. The Chorus of Women sings of how mercenary the citizens have become, and then they too march off to the Assembly.

Blepyrus, the husband of Praxagora, is seen in the doorway of his house, wearing his wife's robe and sandals. Having awakened and unable to find his own clothing so he could go outside, he put on his wife's mantle and sandals. The Man in the next house cannot find his wife or clothing either.

Soon Chremes comes from the Assembly, which has already ended for the day. He describes the huge crowd attending, who looked pale and thin, like shoemakers. A handsome young "man" proposed that the women be allowed to run the government and was wildly applauded by the "shoemakers," who outnumbered the others present. Blepyrus is pleased to hear that this motion was carried because now he will not have to work.

The Chorus returns, making sure no man is following. Then the women quickly remove their disguises so that their deception will not be discovered by the men. Praxagora and her companions enter, proud of their success. As Praxagora is about to enter her house, her husband sees her and informs her that the government of Athens has been handed over to the women. Pretending to be surprised, she expresses her joy as Chremes reappears. Praxagora describes to the two men the ideal society the women will create. All property in this society will be shared by rich and poor alike. Everything, including women, will be held in common. The law will require that men make love to the least attractive women and that women accept the unattractive men before they may approach the desirable ones, so that nobody will be cheated. There will be neither rich nor poor, debtor nor creditor, and all will live happily in this Utopia run by women. Praxagora announces that she must be off to the market-place to take care of the affairs of state.

Chremes brings forth all his property to contribute it to the state. A citizen calls him a fool and a madman, saying he intends to wait to contribute his property until the majority does so. However, the citizen happily obeys the summons to a public feast. His real aim is to keep his possessions and yet enjoy the common feast.

The two houses in the background now represent those of prostitutes, one young and beautiful and the other old and ugly. A young man enters, longing to make love to the young girl but aware of his legal obligation to first satisfy the old woman. As the young girl manages to get him away from the first old woman, a second old woman enters, followed soon after by a third old woman, and together the two force him to go with them, as he cries out in protest, begging the gods to pity him.

As the play ends, Blepyrus announces that all are invited to the feast; then he leads the Chorus in dancing and singing.

eccyclema (ekkyklema). Platform on wheels used by Greek playwrights. It was rolled out to reveal a scene which had taken place within a palace, a temple, or other interior.

Eclogues (Bucolics; Eclogae, Bucolica). Pastoral poems (37 B.C.) in dactylic hexameter by VERGIL. Translations: in verse, John Dryden, 1697; in prose, H. R. Fairclough, 1916; in prose, E. V. Rieu, 1949; in verse, C. Day Lewis, 1963.

SUMMARY. *I.* Though the scene of the first *Eclogue* is the stylized pastoral realm, the poem alludes to important contemporary events, particularly the eviction of farmers in Cremona and Mantua from their lands, which were then given to the veterans of the Civil War who had fought on the side of Octavian (Augustus). Vergil's own farm in Mantua was seized; however, he was introduced either by Maecenas or by his friend Pollio, governor of Cisalpine Gaul (see *Eclogue* IV), to Octavian, who arranged either to have Vergil's land restored to him or to give him a farm in Campania. In the pastoral dialogue of the first *Eclogue*, Tityrus is usually taken to represent Vergil, though some scholars offer significant evidence to contradict this view. In any case, Vergil is certainly expressing his sympathy for the husbandman driven from his land by conquering soldiers. The *Eclogue* begins with Meliboeus' comment that Tityrus lies under his beech tree, enjoying his ease as he watches his sheep, while the other shepherds, including Meliboeus, must leave the country they love. Tityrus explains that a god gave him this peaceful way of life, a statement usually interpreted as a reference to the restoration of Vergil's farm by Augustus. Again in lines 42–45 Tityrus refers to the "youth" who restored his land and flocks to him. In contrast the lamentations of Meliboeus for his lost land and his dying flock tell of the misery of the farmer and the shepherd deprived of the land which they have loved and toiled over for many years. This, says Meliboeus, is the result of war.

II. The shepherd Corydon, in love with his master's beloved Alexis, expresses his longing for the boy and the pain of unrequited love. This *Eclogue* clearly shows the influence of Theocritus, especially of his *Idyl* xi.

III. Two shepherds, Menalcas and Damoetas, engage in a singing match, a surprisingly hostile contest judged by Palaemon. The poem is influenced by Theocritus' *Idyls* iv, v.

IV. Often referred to as the Messianic *Eclogue,* this is the best known of the ten. Vergil asks the Muses to inspire him with a loftier song as he foresees a golden age. Vergil also prophesies the birth of a child and relates the new life that is expected to the new and glorious age that he envisions. The question of who the child was has been widely discussed. Most commentators agree that it was either the son of Gaius Asinius Pollio, consul in 40 B.C. when the poem was written, or a child expected by Octavian and Scribonia, who, as it turned out, was a girl, the notorious Julia. Because the tone and language of the poem are exalted and the birth of a child is connected with the coming of a glorious age, Christian commentators considered the *Eclogue* a prophecy of the coming of the Messiah. When the golden age returns, says Vergil, Astraea (Justice), the last of the gods to leave the earth, will come back again, the earth and the animals will be fruitful, and great heroes will once more arise.

V. Two shepherds, Menalcas and Mopsus, engage in a singing match. Mopsus begins by singing of the death of the ideal shepherd, Daphnis, and Menalcas then takes up the theme and sings of Daphnis' deification. Vergil no doubt imitates Theocritus' *Idyl* i in his lament for Daphnis; however, the deification of the shepherd is Vergil's own idea; some scholars believe this is a veiled reference to Julius Caesar.

VI. This *Eclogue* is dedicated to a Varus, thought by some scholars to be Publius Quinctilius Varus, who helped Vergil to recover his land. Vergil seems to be replying to Varus' request that he write an epic by declaring that he intends to devote himself to pastoral poetry at this time. Two shepherds, Chromis and Mnasyllos, finding Silenus asleep, bind him and compel him to sing for them. His song, which tells of the creation of the world, is based on both the Lucretian atomic conception and traditional myths.

VII. Again imitating Theocritus, Vergil describes another singing match between two shepherds. Corydon and Thyrsis compete in alternate (AMOEBEAN) verse, and Corydon wins the contest.

VIII. Vergil again imitates Theocritus in the eighth *Eclogue.* The verse is amoebean, and the song of Alphesiboeus about the maiden who used charms to bring her lover back is clearly based on the second idyl of Theocritus.

IX. Like the first *Eclogue* the ninth deals with Vergil's loss of his land.

The shepherd Menalcas is usually thought to be Vergil, and the poem, addressed to Varus, has been interpreted as Vergil's request for help in recovering his land. Two shepherds, Lycidas and Moeris, speak of Menalcas' attempts to "save all by means of his songs," though they wonder how effective songs can be among the harsh weapons of warfare.

X. Vergil declares that his last task is to tell of the unrequited love of his friend Gaius Cornelius Gallus, an elegiac poet, for Lycoris. The laurels and tamarisks weep for the unhappy Gallus, and all nature seems to respond to his sorrowful mood. Vergil quotes lines from the poetry of Gallus in this eclogue.

For commentary on the *Eclogues* see PASTORAL POETRY.

Education of Cyrus (Cyropaedia, Kyropaideia). See XENOPHON.

Egeria. A Roman goddess of fountains and childbirth. According to legend, Numa, who succeeded Romulus as king of Rome, used to visit Egeria at night at her sacred spring near the Porta Capena in order to seek her advice.

Eileithyia. The Greek goddess of childbirth.

Eirene. See PEACE.

Electra (Elektra). In Greek mythology, a daughter of Agamemnon and Clytemnestra. For her story see Aeschylus' ORESTEIA, Sophocles' ELECTRA, Euripides' ELECTRA and ORESTES, and Seneca's AGAMEMNON.

Electra (Elektra). A tragedy (413 B.C.) by EURIPIDES. Translations: in prose, E. P. Coleridge, 1891; in verse, Gilbert Murray, 1911; in verse, A. S. Way, 1912; in verse, Emily Townsend Vermeule, 1958.

MYTHICAL BACKGROUND. After the murder of Agamemnon by Clytemnestra and Aegisthus, a faithful servant of Agamemnon sent Orestes to Phocis, where he could grow up safely. Electra, who remained at home, was forced by Aegisthus to marry a peasant so that her offspring would be of humble origin and thus no threat to Aegisthus' rule. Electra's husband, loyal to the memory of Agamemnon and feeling unworthy of so noble a wife, has never wished to consummate the marriage. Electra lives in poverty and despair, hoping only for the return of her brother Orestes.

SCENE. Before a peasant's hut in the country near the borders of Argos.

SUMMARY. The Peasant, the husband of Electra, stands before his hut and speaks of the bloody past of his wife's mother Clytemnestra, who slew her husband Agamemnon. The peasant recalls how a faithful servant of Agamemnon took Orestes to King Strophius of Phocis to protect him from Aegisthus, who would have killed him. Electra, who remained at home, was kept a prisoner and was not wedded to a suitable youth, but given to the peasant. He loves and respects her, but will not consummate his marriage with her because she is of noble blood. Electra comes out of the hut and bitterly curses her mother, blaming Clytemnestra for her own lowly condition. Though the peasant urges her not to work at menial tasks, she insists on doing so, using her humiliation to feed her resentment and hatred of her mother.

After Electra and the peasant go out Orestes and Pylades enter. Orestes says that the oracle of Apollo has ordered him to kill his father's murderers, Clytemnestra and Aegisthus. He soon sees Electra, but does not recognize her. Electra laments her sad past and the humiliations of her daily existence and prays for Orestes' return. The Chorus of Argive women enters and tells Electra of a festival that will be held in honor of Hera, but Electra, pointing to her unkempt hair and her ragged clothing, says she is too miserable to attend.

Orestes and Pylades come forth, and Orestes tells Electra he has news of her brother. She tells him of her wretched life and says she would willingly assist her brother in killing her mother and Aegisthus. Orestes replies that he wishes Orestes could hear her. The peasant then enters and offers Orestes and his friend the hospitality of his hut. Touched by the peasant's inner nobility, Orestes says he prefers this man's generosity to richer offerings. Electra, however, is embarrassed to entertain such noble men in so poor a hut. She sends the peasant to the Old Servant of her father to ask him to bring food for the strangers. The peasant goes off and Electra enters the hut. The Chorus sings of the Trojan War and how Agamemnon met his death when he returned from battle. The old servant enters, calling affectionately for Electra. He tells her that when he went to make offerings at Agamemnon's grave, he saw a lock of hair that resembled hers on the tomb. He suggests that this might be an offering of Orestes, but Electra says that a lock of hair like hers proves nothing. She takes a similar attitude toward the old man's suggestion that footprints near the grave resemble hers and even when he imagines that Orestes might arrive bearing a piece of clothing Electra once made for him, she rationally explains that he would long have outgrown such a garment. When Orestes and Pylades come from the hut, the old man recognizes Orestes, whom he had saved from Aegisthus, by a scar on his brow. Electra and Orestes joyfully embrace, and the Chorus welcomes Orestes and wishes him well. With the help of the old servant, the brother and sister plan the murders of Clytemnestra and Aegisthus. Aegisthus is to be killed by Orestes at a feast to the wood nymphs that he is attending. Clytemnestra will be trapped by Electra, who will announce that she has given birth to a son and thus entice her mother to her hut.

The Chorus once again relates the bloody history of the House of Atreus to the present struggle for justice and vengeance. The Messenger then brings the news that Orestes has killed Aegisthus. Soon Orestes and Pylades enter, followed by attendants, bearing the body of Aegisthus. Electra expresses her hatred and contempt for Aegisthus as she stands over his body; then the corpse is taken into the hut.

When Orestes sees Clytemnestra approaching, he asks how he can kill the mother who bore and nursed him. Electra urges him on, reminding him that Clytemnestra slew his father. Orestes questions the authenticity of the oracle, saying that it might have been a fiend disguised as Apollo, but Electra persuades her brother to commit the murder, and he and Pylades enter the house.

Clytemnestra, arriving with her Trojan slave women, guiltily tries to justify her murder of her husband and to gain Electra's sympathy. As she enters the hut, believing she will make offerings for Electra's newborn son, she seems a pathetic victim of her own weakness and her children's obsessive rage. The Argive Women weep as they hear her death cry. After the murder Electra and Orestes are tormented by regret and guilt. Blaming Apollo's prophecy and their own folly, they relive the details of the murder, horrified at their own cruelty.

Finally a vision of Castor and Polydeuces appears. Castor declares that Clytemnestra received her just punishment, but the act of Orestes was wrong. Castor blames Apollo, saying the god of light taught Orestes darkness. Electra also is guilty. Castor tells Orestes to marry Electra to Pylades. She will now have a proper husband and a home, but she is to be punished by exile from Argos. Orestes, after enduring the tortures of the Furies, the hideous goddesses of vengeance, must go to Athens, where he will be tried and acquitted. A tomb for Clytemnestra will be provided by Menelaus, the husband of Helen and the brother of Agamemnon. Menelaus has just returned from Egypt, bringing with him Helen, who was there throughout the Trojan War. Only a wraith of Helen was in Troy, sent by Zeus to bring about the Trojan War. After Orestes and Electra hear these instructions, they embrace and sorrowfully part.

COMMENTARY. It has been pointed out that Electra's criticism of the old servant's evidence that Orestes has appeared, i.e., the hair, the footprints, and possibly a piece of clothing, is actually Euripides' criticism of Aeschylus' recognition scene in *The Libation Bearers.*

The appearance of Castor and Polydeuces is an example of Euripides' use of the DEUS EX MACHINA. The Dioscuri, no doubt representing Euripides' point of view, approach the tragic situation with a reasonableness and an objectivity of which the protagonists are incapable. They thus reveal the complexity of the conflict within Orestes and Electra and within all human beings dealing with a crime. Clytemnestra, Castor says, was guilty, but vengeance is clearly not the solution, for it brings with it only fresh guilt. Euripides' development of this theme is very similar to that of Aeschylus in the *Oresteia.* Sophocles, on the other hand, in his *Electra* seems to justify the slaying of Clytemnestra. His approach to Orestes is similar to that of Homer in the *Odyssey:* Orestes has performed the duty of a loyal son, who slays the murderers of his father. In Sophocles' play the character of Electra overshadows all the others; moreover, her intense suffering and her obsessive concentration on vengeance are the most important elements of the play. Both Aeschylus and Euripides are more interested in the problem of justice and the agonizing price man pays for even a limited understanding of its nature. Torn by ambivalent feelings of love and hate, obsessed by a need for vengeance and tortured by guilt over the vengeful act, the characters of Aeschylus and Euripides learn that the old code of blood vengeance can no longer serve.

In his treatment of Electra's character, on the other hand, Euripides differs markedly from the other two playwrights. The Electras of Aeschylus and Sophocles are noble and dignified in their debased condition; Euripides' Electra is pathetic in her self-pity and in her constant absorption in her wretchedness.

Electra (Elektra). A tragedy (c. 418–414 B.C.) by SOPHOCLES. Translations: in verse, Lewis Campbell, 1883; in prose, R. C. Jebb, 1904; in verse, F. Storr, 1912; in verse, Francis Fergusson, 1938; in verse, David Grene, 1957; in verse, H. D. F. Kitto, 1962.

MYTHICAL BACKGROUND. According to Sophocles' version of the myth of the House of Atreus, when Agamemnon was murdered by his wife, Clytemnestra, and her lover, Aegisthus, Electra, the daughter of Agamemnon and Clytemnestra, sent her brother Orestes to Phocis in order to protect him from harm. With him she sent the one servant who was loyal to Agamemnon. Clytemnestra and the usurper Aegisthus, who became her husband, ruled tyrannically, mistreating the rebellious Electra, who was faithful to the memory of her murdered father. In despair, Electra prayed that Orestes would return to avenge the murder of his father, but she had little hope that he would come. Orestes has been ordered by the Delphic oracle to avenge his father's death, and he now arrives in Mycenae with the old servant who took him to Phocis and with his friend Pylades.

SCENE. Before the palace of Clytemnestra at Mycenae.

SUMMARY. Orestes, his friend Pylades, and the Paedogogus, Orestes' old servant, come to Mycenae. The old servant points out Argos before them and then speaks of the palace of Clytemnestra, to which they have come, a place stained with the hatred and bloodshed of the past. Orestes tells his servant to enter the palace and pretend that he has come from Phocis to report the death of Orestes. In the meantime Orestes and Pylades will make offerings at the grave of Agamemnon. Then they will bring forth an urn which, they will claim, contains the ashes of Orestes. In this way they will be able to discover the best opportunity for avenging the death of Agamemnon by murdering Aegisthus and Clytemnestra.

As the three go out Electra enters, expressing intense sorrow over her dead father and her wretched life. The Chorus of Mycenaean Women comes in and joins in her lamentations. Electra says she merely endures life, awaiting the return of Orestes, but she fears he will not come. The Chorus advises her to try to be more moderate in her grief; her reckless defiance of her mother and Aegisthus only increases her suffering. Electra, however, cannot be temperate; her grief for her dead father is extreme; her hatred of her mother and Aegisthus is violent. She bitterly tells the Chorus how her mother mocks and mistreats her.

Electra's sister, Chrysothemis, approaches, carrying gifts for the tomb of Agamemnon. In a scene that resembles the one in which Antigone and Ismene discuss the burial of Polyneices in the *Antigone,* Electra and Chrysothemis argue about Electra's behavior. Chrysothemis, a passive girl, says that she too dislikes the deeds of Clytemnestra and Aegisthus, but because they are the rulers, it is best to obey them. When Electra scolds her sister for her timidity and her willingness to compromise, Chrysothemis reveals that Aegisthus plans to imprison Electra in a dungeon if she does not stop complaining, but Electra is unmoved. She asks her sister where she is going, and Chrysothemis replies that she has been sent by Clytemnestra to pour libations on the grave of Agamemnon. Clytemnestra has had a dream in which she saw Agamemnon's spirit return to earth and plant his old scepter on the hearth, where it bloomed and a bough sprang from it, which spread its shadow over all of Mycenae. The dream, clearly prophetic, terrified Clytemnestra, and she has sent Chryso-themis forth to appease the spirit of Agamemnon with libations. Electra persuades her sister not to bring her mother's gifts of guilt, but rather to place locks of hair from their own heads upon the tomb of their father.

After Chrysothemis goes out the Chorus interprets Clytemnestra's dream as a sign that the spirit of Agamemnon desires vengeance. Justice will yet exist in the House of Atreus. Clytemnestra enters and immediately rebukes Electra for censuring her and Aegisthus. She attempts to justify her murder of Agamemnon, saying that he had sacrificed her child, Iphigenia. Electra replies that Clytemnestra committed murder not out of love for the dead Iphigenia but out of desire for Aegisthus. She says that Artemis, angry at Agamemnon, who once shot a stag of hers, demanded the life of Iphigenia, if the fleet were to leave Aulis at all. Sophocles' interpretation of the myth is here clearly sympathetic to Agamemnon, and quite different from Aeschylus' view in the *Agamemnon* (see under ORESTEIA). Electra continues to rail against her mother, who threatens her with punishment when Aegisthus returns.

The old servant of Orestes enters and tells Clytemnestra that Orestes is dead. Electra cries out in agony, but Clytemnestra merely asks about the circumstances and details of his death. She is relieved to hear this news, though she feigns sorrow. However, she finally admits that the news leaves her free of fear of Orestes' vengeance, and she gloats over Electra. She then enters the palace with the old servant.

Chrysothemis comes in happily exclaiming that when she arrived at the tomb of Agamemnon, she found a lock of hair on it that must belong to Orestes. She is certain that her brother has returned. Electra sorrowfully tells her the news of Orestes' death and declares that now that their brother cannot avenge their father's murder, it is their duty to kill his slayer, Aegisthus. When Chrysothemis calls Electra reckless and rash, Electra says she alone will kill Aegisthus.

After an ode in which the Chorus expresses sympathy for Electra, Orestes and Pylades enter carrying an urn that supposedly contains the ashes of Orestes. Electra laments and weeps over the urn. Finally Orestes, pitying his beloved sister, reveals his true identity, and shows Electra a signet ring that once belonged to Agamemnon. They plan the murder of Aegisthus and Clytemnestra. The brother and sister express their joy at being together so wildly that the old servant comes out of the palace to warn them not to reveal themselves to their enemies. He says Orestes and Pylades must act now while Clytemnestra is alone. Orestes, Pylades, and the servant enter the palace. After praying to Apollo for help, Electra also goes in.

When Electra returns she informs the Chorus that Orestes and Pylades are about to kill Clytemnestra. Electra has come out to watch for the arrival of Aegisthus. Clytemnestra is heard within, begging her son for mercy and shrieking as she is murdered. Orestes and Pylades come out of the palace to tell of Clytemnestra's death, but Electra quickly sends them back as she sees Aegisthus approaching. Aegisthus has heard that Orestes is dead, and he orders that the gates be opened so that his corpse may be revealed. The body of Clytemnestra is shown beneath a veil. Mistaking it for the corpse of Orestes, Aegisthus lifts the veil, and sees the dead body of his wife. Orestes then orders Aegisthus to enter the palace: he will be killed in the place where he helped to murder Agamemnon. The leader of the Chorus exclaims with joy over the triumph of Orestes.

Elegiac Poetry. Elegiac poetry is written in couplets, a line of dactylic hexameter alternating with a line of dactylic pentameter, in which the third and sixth feet consist of a single long syllable, which may be considered as making up one foot. Sometimes the second line of the couplet is described as dactylic hexameter with half of the third and sixth feet silent (see METER). Though the word *elegos* originally referred to a sad song sung to the music of the flute, the elegiac form was actually used for the expression of personal thoughts or feelings or reflection of any kind. Early elegies were written to the music of the flute, but soon this type of poetry ceased to be written for any musical accompaniment.

The poets Callinus and Mimnermus employ the elegiac form for subjects as different as love and war; Tyrtaeus uses elegiacs to inspire men to fight heroically, Solon for political persuasion, Simonides for concise and moving epigrams, Theognis for a statement of the aristocratic code of conduct. The form was very popular among the Romans and was employed by Catullus, Propertius, Tibullus, and Ovid.

Elegies. Poems (between c. 28 and 16 B.C.) by PROPERTIUS. Translations: in prose, J. S. Phillimore, 1906; in prose, H. E. Butler, 1912; in verse, S. G. Tremenheere, 1931; in verse, E. H. W. Meyerstein, 1935; in verse, A. E. Watts, 1961; in verse, Constance Carrier, 1963.

SUMMARY. The *Elegies* of Propertius appeared in four books: Book I around 28 B.C., Book II around 25 B.C., Book III around 22 B.C., and Book IV around 16 B.C. The poems are mainly concerned with Propertius' love for Cynthia, his brief pleasure in this relationship, and more often, his passionate attachment to her despite the suffering he endures. In the first elegy of the first book Propertius tells of how his love for Cynthia has enslaved and humiliated him. Like Catullus, he describes his love as madness, as a disease. He prays for help for his "sick heart" and warns all lovers against such pain as he endures. Yet in 1, 4 Propertius asks his friend Bassus why he attempts to persuade him to leave Cynthia. His heart, says Propertius, grows accustomed to its chains. Praises of the beauty of other women will have no effect on him. Cynthia's beauty is unsurpassed, yet her beauty is the least of her attractions for him. 1, 5 tells of the great intensity of Propertius' love for Cynthia and of his suffering, and 1, 6 of his inability to leave Cynthia to accompany his friend Tullus on a journey. "Fate," says Propertius, "has assigned to me the warfare of love." In 1, 7 Propertius says that his friend Pontius may sing of Thebes and the warfare between brothers; Propertius' only theme is love. His fame will come only from his poems, which reveal the pain of love and will tell lovers of the future of the sorrows he endured. Young men who see his tomb will cry out, "You lie here, great poet of our passion."

A few of the elegies tell of Propertius' happiness in this turbulent relationship. 1, 8b expresses his relief that Cynthia has not gone away on a journey as she said she would. In 1, 11 Propertius declares, "You alone are my home, Cynthia, you my parents, you every moment of my happiness," and in 1, 12 he says, "Cynthia was the first, Cynthia will be the end." However, neither Propertius' happiness nor his resignation lasted very long. In 1, 16, imagining Cynthia in the arms of another lover, Propertius laments and weeps over her licentious way of life. The second book records the increasing unhappiness of Propertius in this relationship, and the third book, though it contains some deep expressions of love, also contains some of his bitterest poems and his final rejection of Cynthia. In III, 11 Propertius asks, "Why do you wonder that a woman controls my life and drags me, a conquered man, under her rule?" III, 24 and 25 record the end of the love affair. In III, 24 Propertius says he is ashamed of his exaggerations of Cynthia's beauty in his poems; blinded by love, he was incapable of reason. In 25, the last elegy of Book III, Propertius says that for five years he served Cynthia faithfully and now she will miss his loyalty and devotion. However, he will not be moved by her tears, which in the past enslaved him. She weeps only to deceive him. He weeps also, but now his sense of being wronged is more intense than his sorrow. He curses Cynthia, praying that old age may destroy her beauty and, scorned by others, she may regret her cruelty to him.

Book IV contains only two poems about Cynthia. IV, 7 tells of how after her death she comes to Propertius in a dream, scolds him for forgetting her so soon, but then declares that she does not really blame him because her "reign in his books was long." She asks him to write on her tomb: "Here in the land of Tibur lies golden Cynthia. Praise has come to your bank, Anio." IV, 8 is a humorous poem in which Propertius describes Cynthia interrupting his revelry with two young women.

Though most of Propertius' elegies deal with his love for Cynthia, he has written some interesting ones on other subjects. In III, 12 Propertius asks his friend Postumus how he was able to leave his wife Galla to go to war with Augustus. Postumus is fortunate in having so chaste a wife. He can go without fear, for she will surpass Penelope in fidelity. III, 7 is about the death of Paetus, who was drowned, and III, 17 deals with the death of the young Marcellus whom Vergil mourns in the sixth book of the *Aeneid.* In III, 20 Propertius asks Tullus to come home from the East and speaks of the great virtues of Italy and Rome.

Book IV contains a number of poems on Roman themes. In IV, 1 Propertius imagines that he is the guide of Horus, an astrologer who has come to Rome, and informs Horus of the historical background of various important places he visits. Propertius declares that his aim as a poet is to celebrate ancient religious rites and historical events and places. Other poems of the book reflect this antiquarian interest. The last poem of IV, number 11, is regarded by many as Propertius' greatest elegy. It honors the memory of Cornelia, the daughter of Augustus' wife Scribonia. Cornelia speaks from the world of the dead, urging her husband not to grieve for her. She speaks with pride of her family and her "blameless life" and finds consolation in the good reputation and the fine children she leaves behind. Her concern for her husband, her attempt to console her children and teach them how to accept a stepmother if they must, and her pleas that they take care of their father are at once touching and noble.

Elegies. Poems by TIBULLUS. Book I appeared in 26 B.C.; Book II in 19 B.C.; Book III, after his death. Translations: in verse, James Grainger, 1759; in verse, J. Cranstoun, 1872; in verse, Theodore C. Williams, 1905; in prose, J. P. Postgate, 1912.

SUMMARY. In the first poem of his first book, which celebrates a girl named Delia, Tibullus declares that he has no need for gold or property; he prefers the simple rustic life. For Messalla it is right to strive for glory in battle, but Tibullus cares only for Delia. He then addresses Delia, reminding her of the brevity of life and urging her to enjoy their love before old age and death overwhelm them. In many of the poems of Book I, Tibullus writes of Delia; he describes her beauty, tells of how she observes the rites of Isis, and prays that she may remain virtuous; but mainly he writes of his love for her.

Book II celebrates another girl, Nemesis. Tibullus again speaks of his enslavement to love and of the cruelty of his mistress, whom he cannot help adoring. When Nemesis goes to the country, says Tibullus, he must be made of iron who can remain in town.

Other poems are addressed to Priapus, a fertility god (1, 4); to Messalla, on his victory in battle (1, 7); to Pholoe, a young girl, warning her not to disdain the love of Marathus (I, 8); to Marathus, on Tibullus' love for him (I, 9); to Cornutus, on his birthday (II, 2); and to Macer, bound for war (II, 6). In II, 1 Tibullus writes of the Ambarvalia, a country festival. He praises the gods of the country and the country itself and describes the traditional rituals of purification of the land and the crops.

Eleusinian Mysteries. Secret religious rites conducted at Eleusis, a city in Attica. The mysteries honored the earth goddess Demeter and her daughter Persephone. Later Iacchos, widely identified with Dionysus, was honored as a son of Zeus and Demeter or Persephone (for Dionysus as the son of Zeus and Semele see THE BACCHAE). The myth of Demeter's establishment of the Eleusinian Mysteries is told in HOMERIC HYMN II. The rites at Eleusis probably originated in primitive agricultural ceremonies of purification, the purpose of which was to promote the fertility of the soil and the growth of crops. Apparently the process of planting seeds in the earth that nourished them and from which sprang the living crops suggested that man, whose body was placed in the earth when he died, could also take on renewed life in the Underworld. Thus participation in the ceremonies at Eleusis became a means of seeking immortality for the initiated (see THE FROGS). An excellent study of the mysteries is George E. Mylonas, *Eleusis and the Eleusinian Mysteries* (Princeton University Press, 1961).

Eleusis. A city fourteen miles northwest of Athens. A great temple of Demeter which was located there was the center of the Eleusinian mysteries in honor of Demeter and her daughter Persephone. Eleusis was the birthplace of Aeschylus.

Elissa. See DIDO.

Elysium (Elysion, the Elysian Fields, the Islands of the Blessed). In Homer, an ideal land to the west of the earth to which heroes pass at their death. In Latin literature Elysium is the part of the Underworld to which the souls of the good and the noble go after death.

Empedocles (Empedokles). A Greek scientist and philosopher (c. 495–435 B.C.). Empedocles was born into a distinguished family of Acragas (Agrigento) and participated in public affairs. It is thought that he was offered a king's crown in Acragas, but refused it. Toward the end of his life he was banished from his native city and died in the Peloponnesus. The legend arose that Empedocles threw himself into the crater of Mount Etna.

It is known that Empedocles wrote two poems in hexameter verse, *On Nature* and *Katharmoi* (*Purifications*), fragments of which survive. Empedocles has been compared with Faust in his intense desire for scientific knowledge and his attempt to go beyond the limits of nature itself (see Eduard Zeller, *Outlines of the History of Greek Philosophy*, 13th ed., trans. L. P. Palmer [Humanities Press, 1955], p. 71). He sought the laws that governed the universe in a "compromise between Heraclitus and Parmenides, between eternal change and eternal invariability" (Zeller, p. 72). According to Empedocles there are four unchanging elements: earth, air, fire, and water, which combine to produce the changing material of objective reality. These elements come together as a result of the two forces, love and hate, which cause creation, destruction, and re-creation. Lucretius admired and was influenced by the work of Empedocles.

encomium (enkomion). A Greek choral lyric that praises a fellow human being. Since the name means "at a revel," the song probably originated in a toast to the host of some feast. The EPINICION and the THRENOS can be regarded as types of *encomia*. The term is later applied to any type of literary eulogy.

Endymion. In Greek mythology, a youth known for his great physical beauty. The moon (Selene) fell in love with him, and either because of her power or his own desire, Endymion slept eternally. Each night Selene came to embrace him.

Ennius, Quintus. A Roman playwright and poet, born at Rudiae (Rugge) in Calabria in 239 B.C. Ennius, one of the Latin writers most revered in antiquity, said of himself that he had "three hearts" because he knew Oscan, Greek, and Latin. After serving in the Roman army he was brought to Rome by M. Porcius Cato and granted Roman citizenship. He devoted himself to teaching and writing tragedies, comedies, the *Annals* (*Annales*), satires, narrative and didactic poems, and epigrams. Ennius' interest in Roman myth and history, his exalted conception of Rome's past, and his belief in her heroic destiny had a profound influence on his own age and on writers of succeeding generations, such as Lucretius, Cicero, Vergil, and Ovid. Ennius died in 169 B.C.

It is known that Ennius wrote at least twenty tragedies, but of these only four hundred lines remain. Their titles suggest that they dealt with traditional mythological subjects: *Andromache, Andromeda, Erectheus, Hecuba, Iphigenia, Medea, Achilles, Ajax,* and others reflect the influence of Greek tragedy. Ennius also composed a *fabula praetexta* on the rape of the Sabines and at least two comedies, *palliatae,* called the *Cupuncula* and the *Pancratiastes,* but these are lost. The *Annals,* Ennius' most important work, was an epic poem of eighteen books in hexameter verse dealing with the history of Rome from the destruction of Troy to Ennius' own time. Only about six hundred lines of the poem remain. In this Latin epic Ennius was the first writer to adapt Greek hexameter verse to the Latin language and to imitate the Homeric manner in his tone and diction. His aim in the *Annals* is obviously not only to record the great events of the Roman past, but to suggest that Rome is a nation destined for glory. Among Ennius' other poems were *Epicharmus,* on the physical universe; *Euhemerus,* which echoes EUHEMERUS' explanation of the origin of the gods; *Scipio; Sota;* a mock epic, *Hedyphagetica;* four books of satire; and epigrams. Only brief fragments of these remain.

Eos. In Greek mythology, the daughter of Hyperion and goddess of the dawn. She is identified with the Roman goddess Aurora. See TITHONUS.

Ephialtes. See OTUS.

epic. The songs of Demodocus and Phemius in the *Odyssey* are probably typical of the short heroic lays from which the epic springs. The earliest extant epics, the *Iliad* and the *Odyssey*, which minstrels chanted to the music of the lyre, represent the culmination of a long tradition of heroic poetry composed for oral presentation.

Ancient epic is narrative poetry employing traditional and legendary material about gods and heroes. Its repetitions of poetic formulas, as well as of lines, whole passages, and incidents, suggest its beginnings in improvisation and its oral nature. The various lists of ships, warriors, gods and goddesses, and those slain in battle in the *Iliad* recall a time when historical records were transmitted by recitation. The genealogies which appear in all ancient epics served the same function.

Even when they no longer serve to transmit history, these traditional elements continue to appear in the epic, e.g., the *Aeneid*, for their poetic effect is powerful. They help to create the majestic and ceremonial tone of the epic and to establish the heroic grandeur of its chief figures. The meter of most ancient epics, dactylic hexameter, has a heroic quality, and the language is a literary one; Homer's language is a combination of many dialects, not the spoken Greek of his period, Vergil's a highly polished literary Latin.

The traditional material concerning gods and heroes, stock lines and phrases, ceremonial language and heroic meter, the long formal speeches, all suggest that the epic deals with important events that have universal implications. Personal and general experience, the individual and the universal, are unified in the great epics through a particular poet's view of a traditional hero and through his adaptation of well-known formulas to his own artistic conception. For Aristotle's comparison of epic and tragedy see POETICS, especially XXIII, XXIV.

Extant Greek epics are the *Iliad*, the *Odyssey*, and the *Argonautica*, though brief fragments of other epics belonging to the *Epic Cycle* do exist. Of significant Latin epics the following remain: fragments of Naevius' *Bellum Punicum*, written in Saturnian verse, and fragments of Ennius' *Annals*, both of which are as much chronicles as epics; Vergil's *Aeneid*, the greatest Latin epic; Lucan's *On the Civil War;* Silius Italicus' *Punica;* Valerius Flaccus' *Argonautica;* and Statius' *Thebaid* and one book and part of a second of his *Achilleid*.

Epicharmus (Epicharmos). A Greek writer of comedy, probably born at Cos (c. 560 B.C.). He spent much of his life in Sicily. Only very brief fragments of his comedies remain. Epicharmus was also regarded a philosopher.

Epictetus (Epiktetos). A Stoic philosopher of Hierapolis in Phrygia (c. A.D. 60–c. 140). Epictetus was a slave of Epaphroditus, a freedman of Nero, but obtained his freedom. Banished from Rome by Domitian, he lived in Nicopolis, where he taught philosophy. Though he left no written works, his ideas are known through the notes of his pupil Arrian, who recorded his *Discourses*, four of which remain, and wrote a *Manual* (*Encheiridion*) that summarizes Epictetus' theories. The philosophy he advocates is essentially one of acceptance and endurance.

Epicurus (**Epikouros**). Greek philosopher, born at Samos in 341 B.C. Most of what we know about Epicurus comes from the *Lives of Eminent Philosophers* of Diogenes Laertius, which was probably written in the third century A.D. His parents were Athenian, and Epicurus settled in Athens in 306 B.C. Near the city walls he founded his school in a garden, from which it received the name "The Garden." Here Epicurus taught his philosophy of materialism until his death in 270 B.C. Epicurus wrote about three hundred volumes, but very little of his work remains. Diogenes Laertius preserved three letters to Herodotus, Pythocles, and Menoeceus, which contain a great many of Epicurus' scientific and philosophical ideas, and his *Principal Doctrines*, forty maxims stating his views. Some fragments of Epicurus' *On Nature* and a few from sources that are uncertain also remain.

Epicurus' philosophical materialism is based on the atomic theory of matter, first invented by Leucippus (fifth century B.C.) and developed by Democritus (fifth century B.C.). According to Epicurus, all matter, including the mind and soul of man, is composed of atoms. The gods have nothing to do with the lives of men and should be neither feared nor entreated. Because death means merely a dispersal of atoms, there is no afterlife. Man should be afraid neither of the gods, with whom he has no relationship, nor of death, which is outside his experience. He should seek pleasure by attempting to achieve peace and tranquility of spirit through a simple life. The best summary of the philosophical and scientific ideas of Epicurus is the *De Rerum Natura* (ON THE NATURE OF THINGS) of Lucretius.

Epidicus. A comedy by PLAUTUS, adapted from an unknown Greek play. The plot is concerned with the slave Epidicus' schemes for aiding his master Stratippocles, an amorous and fickle young Athenian. The youth, who was in love with a music girl, Acropolistis, had to leave for battle, and asked Epidicus to buy her for him. Epidicus persuaded Periphanes, the father of Stratippocles, to give him the money for Acropolistis by telling him that she was actually Telestis, a daughter Periphanes had lost many years before. Now Acropolistis is living in Periphanes' home, but Stratippocles returns from war so infatuated with a captive girl that he has taken a loan from a moneylender in order to buy her. Once more Epidicus must help him: he must obtain the money due the moneylender, and he must arrange for Acropolistis to leave the home of Periphanes. The complications increase when Epidicus must again deceive Periphanes and when Philippa, the mother of Telestis, appears and denies that Acropolistis is her daughter. Periphanes soon discovers he has been tricked by his slave, but Epidicus is forgiven when the captive girl turns out to be the real Telestis, the lost daughter of Periphanes.

epigram. A very brief poem. Originally the epigram was an inscription on a monument, a temple, a tombstone, or on various other objects. Epigrams were often written in verse, mainly elegiac. The best-known writer of these early epigrams was Simonides of Ceos. Later the word was applied to a brief poem that, in its precision, economy of language, and polish, suggests the qualities of an inscription. The form was popular during the Hellenistic period and among the Romans. The *Greek Anthology* contains thousands of epigrams produced from the period of Simonides (c. 556–468 B.C.) to the tenth century A.D. In Rome epigrams were written from the time of Ennius. The greatest epigrams were written by the Latin poet Martial, who used the form brilliantly for satire.

Epigrams (Epigrammata). Short poems in 14 books (A.D. 80–102) by MARTIAL, mainly in elegiacs; also hendecasyllabics, choliambics, and hexameters. Translations: in prose and verse, by various translators, H. G. Bohn, ed. Bohn's Classical Library, 1877; in prose, W. C. Ker, 1919–20; selections in verse, A. L. Francis and H. F. Tatum, 1923; in verse, J. A. Pott and F. A. Wright, 1923.

SUMMARY. Martial's *Epigrams* deal with a great variety of subjects. Despite their brevity, a number of them reveal fascinating material about the society of ancient Rome in the first century A.D. Like Juvenal (see SATIRE I), Martial refuses to employ the traditional material of myth; instead, he declares, he writes of actual men: *"Hominem pagina nostra sapit"* ("My page contains the flavor of man"; x, 4). He writes of himself and the humiliations he suffers as a poor poet who must depend on the support of unreliable patrons (III, 4, 7, 60 [compare Juvenal, SATIRE V]; IV, 40; VI, 30, 88); of the corruption of Rome (III, 38; IV, 5) and the luxurious life of inferior men (III, 62); of the behavior of homosexuals (I, 23, 40, 96; XII, 38, 39); and the vanity and folly of women (VI, 12; VII, 13; VIII, 79).

Though Martial's epigrams are mainly satirical and often his attack is sharp, he is true to his word that he "spares the persons but exposes the vices" (x, 33). Thus in warning Maximina not to take Ovid's advice (see THE ART OF LOVE III) that she laugh to attract a beau because poor Maximina has only three teeth, Martial actually pokes fun at women who do not see their own shortcomings. Also he gently implies a criticism of Ovid's romantic conception of the female. Maximina, says Martial, will be most attractive lamenting and weeping (II, 41). Martial's poems on the humiliations of the dependent, though based on his own experience, are general, not personal. Even his attacks on those who copied his work are criticism of plagiarism without personal bitterness (I, 52, 53, 66, 72). Martial's remarks on poor critics are more amusing than angry, even when he defends his own work. He tells Vacerra, who likes only the work of the ancients, that "death is too much to pay" for his praise (VIII, 69), and he urges Laelius to stop criticizing his work if Laelius refuses to publish his own (I, 91).

Sometimes Martial takes up themes treated by the Greek lyric poets and by Horace and Catullus; with his unique sharpness and wit he adapts them to the epigrammatic form. In I, 15 he urges his friend Julius to embrace the joy of the present: "Do not say I shall live;/ the life of tomorrow is too late: live today" (see also v, 58; vIII, 46.). Martial expresses his faith in himself as a poet through the traditional theme of the *monumentum aere perennius:* "Theft cannot harm these pages and time is advantageous to them./ They are the only monument which will never be destroyed" (x, 2). Martial's brevity and economy in speaking of his work intensify a serious idea. He can also employ the epigrammatic style to express warmth and friendship, as in a poem to Julius Martialis (xII, 34), whom he has known for thirty-four years and has addressed in several other charming epigrams (Iv, 64; v, 50; x, 47). In writing of Erotion, a little slave girl who died at the age of six, Martial uses the conciseness of the epigram to convey pain, sorrow, and love: the poem ends with an entreaty to the earth to "lie gently on the child who walked so lightly on the earth" (v, 34).

Epimetheus. See PANDORA.

epinicion (epinikion; victory ode). A Greek choral ode that celebrates the victor (one who sponsored or entered a horse or a team of horses or mules or who actually competed in and won an athletic contest) in one of the four national games. The Olympian games were held in honor of Zeus at Pisa in Elis; the Nemean, in honor of Zeus at Nemea in Argolis; the Pythian, in honor of Apollo at Delphi (Pytho); the Isthmian, in honor of Poseidon at Corinth. The contests were many and varied, consisting of the four-horse chariot, mule chariot, and horse races, in all of which the victor celebrated was the sponsor; boxing and wrestling matches, the *pancratium* (which combined boxing and wrestling), long and short foot races, and the *pentathlon* (made up of five contests: racing, jumping, hurling of the discus and the javelin, and wrestling), in all of which the victor was a participant.

Victory odes, which were commissioned either by the winner of a contest, his friends, or his relatives, were sung to music by a chorus of his friends, usually at a celebration on the return of the victor to his homeland; sometimes, however, the performance was given to celebrate an anniversary of his triumph. Because the ode was commissioned, the poet was often obliged to include facts about the victor's ancestors or relatives only remotely connected with his subject.

No actual description of the athletic contest is given in a victory ode. Instead the victor's *arete*, his dignity, and the quality of his performance are suggested through the poet's association of the present triumph with great mythical victories of the past. The poet praises the victor's city, evokes its deity, and alludes to its mythical past. This identification of the triumphant moment of the present with the glorious past gives the epinicion its exalted and heroic tone. The present victory takes its place in a continuous line of heroic achievement.

Most epinicia contain praise of the victor, an invocation to a deity, references to a myth related to the victor's homeland or to his achievement, moral or didactic statements about temperance, courage, *arete*, and, in Pindar's odes, some assertion on the part of the poet about his art and his role in assuring immortality for the triumphant athlete. Most epinicia are triadic in structure: their stanzas are arranged in three parts, strophe, antistrophe, and epode, the strophe and the antistrophe having the same structure and the epode a different one. A few epinicia are antistrophic, having only strophes and antistrophes, and a few are monostrophic, that is, having stanzas that are all alike.

The best-known writers of epinicia were Simonides, Bacchylides, and Pindar. Though most of Pindar's and a good many of Bacchylides' victory odes remain, we have only brief fragments of those of Simonides. Bacchylides and Pindar use the same basic pattern for their victory odes, but their poems are very different in tone and quality. The preference of "Longinus" for Pindar's extravagance and swiftness to Bacchylides' polished grace is well known and certainly justifiable. Bacchylides is simpler and more direct than Pindar, but he lacks Pindar's fire, his enthusiasm, and his grand imaginative sweep. In Pindar's poems image seems to give birth to image, fact to myth, and myth to theme. The reader is always aware of the presence of Pindar in his poems as the exalted bard, asserting that only he, the poet, can give the ephemeral lives of men eternal meaning through the fame his songs will bring them. This theme, which is implicit in some of the songs of Sappho and is later expressed directly by Horace, who declares that he has "built a monument more lasting than bronze," is basic to Pindar's conception of the events and the people he writes of. It is the poet's voice that transforms the games into historic contests for *arete* and the participants into heroes who emulate Heracles and Achilles.

The Pindaric ode was much admired in seventeenth- and eighteenth-century England and was widely imitated. During the Restoration, Abraham Cowley's *Pindarics* were highly praised, though later critics have found his efforts to emulate Pindar's extravagant imagery and exalted tone somewhat strained. Both John Dryden and Thomas Gray were more successful in adapting the Pindaric structure and language to their own time and their own themes.

Epistle to the Pisos. See ART OF POETRY.

Epistles (Epistulae). Verse letters in dactylic hexameter by HORACE (Book I, 20 B.C.; Book II, uncertain, possibly 18 B.C.). Translations: in verse, J. Conington, 1870; in verse, Sir Theodore Martin, 1888; in prose, H. Rushton Fairclough, 1926; in verse, Palmer Bovie, 1959.

SUMMARY. Horace's *Epistles* are letters in verse addressed to various friends. The epistles of Book I are mainly didactic and are concerned with such subjects as the value of virtue, the simple life, and the Stoic ideal of the "wise man." One of the most famous is I, 6, which begins with the words *Nil admirari* ("Be astonished at nothing"), a well-known philosophical idea, and recommends that man neither "marvel at" nor overly value any possession. There is a limit even to the pursuit of virtue. Pope's translation of this passage is brilliant: "For Virtue's self may too much zeal be had/ The worst of madmen is a saint run mad." Some of the epistles of Book I reveal Horace in a more casual mood, inviting friends to dinner or speaking of his own discontent and lethargy.

The second book contains three long epistles. The third, *The Art of Poetry*, is discussed separately. All the epistles of the second book are interesting for the literary criticism they contain. In the first, addressed to Augustus (who, according to Suetonius, had remarked that none of the *Satires* were addressed to him), Horace discusses poets of the past and present. He speaks of the work of Ennius, Naevius, Pacuvius, Accius, Afranius, Plautus, Caecilius, and Terence, all of whom are much admired by the Romans. Horace believes, however, that their work is imperfect and should be viewed more critically. In discussing the mania to write that is current at Rome, Horace speaks of the poet's "madness" tenderly. The poet, he says, never cheats anyone or covets wealth; all he cares about is creation. Moreover, he teaches virtue through noble examples. "Songs are pleasing to the gods above, to the gods below." Horace then discusses the influence of Greek literature on the Romans. Greece, the conquered, says Horace, made her victor captive. The epistle ends with praise of the poetry of Vergil and Varius and some modest comments about Horace's own work.

Epistle II, 2, is addressed to Florus, to whom Horace speaks of the difficulty of writing poetry at Rome, where there are so many distractions. One laughs at poor poets, but they take great satisfaction in their work. The true poet works hard at his art and is very critical of his own work. He will give the riches of his language to his land. At his age, says Horace, it is time to give up poetry and turn to philosophy. He then deals with the disease of avarice and the uselessness of seeking wealth. True wisdom lies in moderation. The poem ends with an allusion to Lucretius (III, 938): "You have enjoyed enough; you have eaten and drunk sufficiently. It is time to withdraw from the banquet. . . ."

Epistulae ex Ponto (Epistles from Pontus). Four books of letters (A.D. 12–16) written by OVID in exile. The epistles, like those of *Tristia*, are in elegiacs. All the recipients of the *Epistulae ex Ponto*, except one friend (III, 6) and two enemies (IV, 3, 16), are named. In I, 1 Ovid says that these epistles are as sorrowful as those of *Tristia*. Throughout the *Epistulae ex Ponto* Ovid writes of the bitterness of exile, his hatred of the cold, bare winters of Tomis, his fear of attack by its inhabitants or their barbaric neighbors, his longing for intellectual companionship, his sorrow, and his frequent prayers for death. He speaks sadly of the past when he had a great name and was "numbered among the living." Though most of the poems alternate between expression of despair and hope that he may be released from exile, there are some on other subjects, such as I, 9, to his friend Maximus on the death of Celsus; III, 8, on a gift to Maximus; and IV, 11, a consolation to Gallio on the death of his wife.

Epitrepontes. See THE ARBITRATION.

Epodes. The earliest poems of HORACE, composed between 41 and 31 B.C.

They are written in iambic meters, especially the iambic couplet, and Horace called them *Iambi*. An editor gave them the title *Epodes*, from the name of the second, short line of the couplet, *epodos* ("aftersong").

The seventeen *Epodes* deal with many subjects: friendship and loyalty to Maecenas, whom Horace says he will accompany to war (I); praise of country life (II); a description of the vicious witch Canidia (V) and a mock *palinode* (recantation) to her (XVII); an attack on a *nouveau riche*, formerly a slave (IV), and on a blackmailer (VI); a prayer that civil war may not begin again (VII); and a celebration of the victory of Actium (IX). Though the *Epodes* have neither the brilliance nor the grace of the *Odes*, even in these early poems one can perceive Horace's wit and recognize his unique skill in handling language and meter.

epyllion. A brief epic poem. Examples are the *Ciris* and the poem on the marriage of Peleus and Thetis by Catullus.

Erebus (Erebos). According to Hesiod's *Theogony*, the son of Chaos. He is primeval darkness. From the union of Erebus and his sister Night (Nyx) came Aether and Day (Hemera).

Erechtheus. The guardian of the Acropolis of Athens. In form partly a serpent, Erechtheus was originally a chthonian god, probably connected with the fruitfulness of the earth. In Greek legend he was either the same as ERICHTHONIUS or his son. Erechtheus was a king of Athens. When Athens was at war with Eleusis, he followed the advice of the Delphic oracle that he sacrifice one of his daughters. Erechtheus won the war, but he and his family were killed by Poseidon.

Erga kai Hemerai. See WORKS AND DAYS.

Erichthonius (Erichthonios). In Greek mythology, the son of Hephaestus and Earth. Erichthonius is often identified with Erechtheus, and is also represented as part man, part serpent. When Erichthonius was an infant, Athene put him in a chest, which she entrusted to the three daughters of Cecrops, warning them not to open it. The command of the goddess was disobeyed, and the three daughters of Cecrops, driven mad by Athene, committed suicide by throwing themselves from the Acropolis. Erichthonius, like Erechtheus, is regarded as a legendary king of Athens.

Erinyes. See FURIES.

Eros. A Greek god of love. In later Greek literature he accompanies his mother Aphrodite. He was identified by the Romans with Cupid.

Eteocles (Eteokles). See POLYNEICES.

Etruscans or Tyrrhenians. A people who inhabited northwestern Italy in ancient times. Modern scholars disagree on their origins: some authorities believe that the Etruscans were indigenous to Italy; others have found evidence to support the claim of Herodotus that the Etruscans came from the Near East. Until recently little was known about this people who had a thriving civilization by the eighth century B.C. and ruled a large area of Italy until they were defeated by the Romans, whose civilization they influenced (see ROME). In 1956 a team of archeologists from the Swedish Institute in Rome began excavations on an Etruscan site in San Giovenale, a narrow area north of Rome. Their findings were published in Axel Boëthius *et al., Etruscan Culture: Land and People* (Columbia University Press, 1963), a valuable study that reveals much about ancient Etruria and elucidates Etruscan history and culture.

Euhemerus (Euemeros). A Greek writer, born in Sicily, who lived from about 330 B.C. to about 260 B.C. In his book *The Sacred Record (Hiera Anagraphe)* he tells of his journey to Panchaea, an island in the Indian Ocean off the coast of Arabia, where Zeus himself had built a temple when he was a man and king of the inhabited earth. According to Euhemerus, Zeus was born in Crete, and after many voyages, returned there to die; his tomb still exists in Crete. Euhemerus believed that the gods were originally great men, kings or philosophers, who were deified after their deaths. Thus myth is merely an imaginative distortion of history. Euhemerism, as his theory is called, was attacked by Plutarch as atheistic.

Eumaeus (Eumaios). The loyal swineherd of Odysseus in the ODYSSEY (XIII *ff.*).

Eumenides. See FURIES.

Eumenides. A tragedy by Aeschylus. See under ORESTEIA.

Eunuch, The (Eunuchus). A comedy (produced in 161 B.C.) by TERENCE and based on Menander's *The Eunuch* and *The Flatterers*. Phaedria, a young Athenian, is in love with Thais, a courtesan. His rival for her love is Thraso, a braggart soldier. Thraso had promised to give Thais a slave girl Pamphila, whom he had brought from Rhodes. Thais has found out that this girl is actually an Athenian who had been kidnapped, given to Thais' mother in Rhodes, brought up with Thais, and, after her mother's death, sold as a slave. Thus, in the hope of protecting Pamphila, Thais encourages Thraso, but when he discovers that Thais is involved in a love affair with Phaedria, he refuses to give her the girl. Thais begs Phaedria to go away for two days so that she can convince Thraso of her affection and in this way obtain Pamphila.

Pamphila is brought to Thais by Thraso's parasite. Chaerea, Phaedria's younger brother, who has fallen in love with Pamphila, decides to take the role of a eunuch, whom Phaedria has given as a present to Thais, in order to have access to Pamphila. His impersonation is successful, and later he reveals to a friend that he has raped Pamphila. Soon Phaedria returns to the city and learns of his brother's impersonation of the eunuch. In the meantime, Thais has discovered that Pamphila is a sister of the Athenian Chremes, who declares that the girl is freeborn and no longer the property of Thraso. Chaerea admits that he has ravished Pamphila and agrees to marry her. Phaedria, who needs money to support Thais, consents to share her with Thraso, who will provide her with a large income.

Euripides. Greek tragedian (480–405 B.C.). Euripides was born in Salamis, possibly on the very day on which the Greeks won a great victory against Xerxes, who led the Persian fleet. Though Aristophanes and other writers of comedy insisted that Euripides' mother sold vegetables, actually the tragedian came from a family of high social position and was given the conventional education in music, dancing, and gymnastics. He prepared for and entered public athletic contests in his youth. When Euripides was twenty-five he competed for the first time for the prize for tragedy, but he did not win until 441 B.C., when he was thirty-nine. In 409 B.C. Euripides left Athens for Magnesia in Thessaly. From there he went to the court of Archelaus, king of Macedonia, where he remained until his death in 405 B.C. Euripides wrote between eighty and ninety plays, of which eighteen tragedies (including RHESUS, which may not be his) and one satyr play remain. Fragments of about fifty-five other plays exist. His extant tragedies are ALCESTIS (438 B.C.), MEDEA (431 B.C.), HIPPOLYTUS (428 B.C.), THE CHILDREN OF HERACLES (c. 427 B.C.), ANDROMACHE (c. 426 B.C.), HECUBA (c. 425 B.C.), THE MADNESS OF HERACLES (c. 422 B.C.), THE SUPPLIANTS (420 B.C.), ION (c. 417 B.C.), THE TROJAN WOMEN (415 B.C.), IPHIGENIA IN TAURIS (c. 414–412 B.C.), ELECTRA (413 B.C.), HELEN (412 B.C.), THE PHOENICIAN WOMEN (409 B.C.), ORESTES (408 B.C.), IPHIGENIA IN AULIS (c. 405 B.C.), THE BACCHAE (c. 405 B.C.), and RHESUS (date unknown). Euripides' satyr play is THE CYCLOPS (c. 423 B.C.).

A fragmentary life of Euripides written by Satyrus, a philosopher and historian of the third century B.C., and discovered in 1911, tells of Euripides' friendship with the philosopher Anaxagoras and the musician Timotheus, who introduced many innovations in musical technique. Euripides was deeply interested in the political, social, artistic, and philosophical ideas of his time, and this involvement is reflected in his plays. He is said to have been a "realist," and certainly he depicts traditional heroes in more naturalistic attitudes than do Aeschylus or Sophocles. However, the realism of Euripides is psychological rather than literal or technical. Whereas the dialogue of his plays is sometimes closer to ordinary speech than is that of Aeschylus or Sophocles, it is hardly colloquial. Moreover, his use of the prologue, his elaborate choral odes, and his reliance on the *deus ex machina* all give his plays a stylized and formal quality. If some of the scenes in the *Medea* or *The Trojan Women* seem realistic, *The Bacchae* is closer to a stylized ritual than any other extant Greek tragedy.

Euripides' subtle psychological insight, especially into human beings in pain or conflict, and his ability to suggest a contemporary problem or injustice through a traditional myth are the unique qualities of his art. For Aristophanes' portrayal of him see THE FROGS and THESMOPHORIAZUSAE.

Europa (Europe). In Greek mythology, the daughter of Agenor, king of Tyre. In *Metamorphoses* II and VI, Ovid tells of how Zeus fell in love with her and, taking the form of a bull, was so endearing that Europa climbed on his back. He carried her off to Crete, where she bore Minos and Rhadamanthus. Moschus also wrote about Europa's love affair with Zeus in his epyllion *Europa*.

Euryalus. See AENEID IX.

Eurycleia (Eurykleia). See ODYSSEY IV, XIX, XXII.

Eurydice (Eurydike) (i). See ORPHEUS.

Eurydice (Eurydike) (ii). Wife of Creon. See Sophocles' ANTIGONE.

Eurystheus. See THE CHILDREN OF HERACLES and THE MADNESS OF HERACLES.

Euthydemus (Euthydemos). A dialogue by PLATO which satirizes the Sophists.

Euthyphro (Euthyphron). A dialogue by PLATO. Socrates, who is waiting outside the courtroom to face an indictment of impiety, encounters the soothsayer Euthyphro, who has brought charges of murder against his own father. The old man had unintentionally caused the death of a dependent of Euthyphro, and now Euthyphro defends his prosecution of his father as a pious act. In the discussion of piety between Euthyphro and Socrates, Socrates exposes the superficial and conventional views of Euthyphro and suggests a deeper, more spiritual conception of piety.

Evander. See AENEID VIII.

Ex Ponto, Epistulae. See EPISTULAE EX PONTO.

F

Fabius Pictor (Quintus). The first known Roman historian (second half of the third century B.C.). He wrote, in Greek, a history of Rome from its legendary origin to his own period. Only brief fragments of this work remain.

fabula palliata. A Latin comedy adapted from a Greek original; e.g., the comedies of Plautus and Terence.

fabula praetexta. A drama, the plot of which was based on a Roman subject. The name derives from the garment bordered (*praetexta*) with purple worn by the main characters. See OCTAVIA.

fabula togata. A Latin comedy that had the form of a Greek comedy but was Roman in its characters and setting. The genre was popular only during the second century B.C. There are only fragments extant.

Fasti. A poem by OVID in six books of elegiacs. The subject is the Roman calendar; originally the *Fasti* were lists of days on which praetors were permitted to conduct legal transactions. Ovid's *Fasti* was probably begun before he was sent into exile, and may have been completed in Tomis, but only the first six books of the poem remain. It was first dedicated to Augustus, later to Germanicus, the nephew of Tiberius, whom the emperor adopted as his son.

Ovid devotes a book to each month and writes of the historical, astronomical, and religious significance of the days of the year. The *Fasti* contains a wealth of information on history and legend and on religious customs, rites, and festivals. Though Ovid does not name his sources, he obviously had read widely in the ancient historians and poets. In the *Fasti*, as in the *Metamorphoses*, the poet's narrative skill transforms traditional material. For example, in telling of the rape of Lucretia by Sextus, son of Tarquinius Superbus, and Brutus' defeat of the tyrant, Ovid creates a moving and dramatic episode (II, 685–852). In recording religious customs Ovid suggests the atmosphere of a sacrifice or a festival. The antiquarian material is most interesting, and Ovid's method of presenting it is imaginative and lively. An excellent prose translation of the *Fasti* was done by Sir James George Frazer (1929).

Fates (Moirai). In Greek mythology, daughters either of Night or of Zeus and Themis. As spirits of birth, the Fates allot a person his "portion" of life. They were often represented as three old women, Clotho, Lachesis, and Atropos, carrying staffs, a sign of their power. Sometimes they were depicted as spinning, and they broke the thread when a life was over. The Roman Fates (Parcae or

Fata) were named Nona, Decuma, and Morta. In Homer, *Moira* sometimes seems to be subject to the will of Zeus and at other times more powerful than Zeus himself: e.g., Sarpedon, the son of Zeus, is doomed to death by fate in the *Iliad*, and in the *Odyssey*, the gods apparently cannot save a man from his fate of death. Similarly, in the *Aeneid*, *fatum* often seems a force beyond the control of Jupiter, to which he is subject.

Faunus. A Roman god of the woods who protected the herds. Faunus was also a prophetic deity and an agricultural god. When the Greek god Pan was introduced into Italy, Faunus became associated with him and was sometimes depicted with horns and the feet of a goat. Fauni were also identified with SATYRS. In Roman legend, Faunus was the father of Latinus, king of Latium.

Frogs, The (Batrachoi). An Old Comedy (405 B.C.) by ARISTOPHANES. Translations: in verse, Benjamin B. Rogers, 1924; in verse, Arthur S. Way, 1934; in verse, Richmond Lattimore, 1962; in prose and verse, David Barrett, 1964.

B A C K G R O U N D . Written near the end of the Peloponnesian War when Athens was exhausted by military defeats and torn by political upheaval, *The Frogs* suggests the need for an ethical and inspired poet, who believes in the traditional values, to guide the state. Thus the literary and political satire become one.

S C E N E . Before the house of Heracles; later, the Underworld.

S U M M A R Y . Dionysus enters wearing his traditional yellow tunic and the buskins associated with tragedy and at the same time imitating the dress of Heracles by wearing a lion's skin and carrying a club. His slave Xanthias follows him on a donkey, carrying their luggage on a pole. They come to the house of Heracles and knock at the door. Heracles cannot help laughing at the combination of a lion's skin and a silk tunic. Dionysus tells Heracles that he longs for the dramatist Euripides, who has recently died, and plans to go down to Hades in the hope of restoring a real poet to Athens. Because Heracles once descended into Hades, Dionysus has come to ask his advice about the fastest way to get there, places to rest, lodgings, and other matters. Heracles, after teasing Dionysus for a while with the suggestion that he commit suicide if he wishes to go to Hades, finally describes the difficult and terrifying experience of the descent. Dionysus refuses to be frightened and goes on his way.

When he and Xanthias arrive at the River Styx [the chief river of Hades, which the souls of the dead must cross], the ferryman Charon refuses to transport Xanthias because he is a slave and has not redeemed himself by fighting at sea. Xanthias is told to go around the river on foot. Despite his protests Dionysus is forced to row, and soon he hears an unseen chorus of frogs singing their famous refrain: Brekekekex, ko-ax, ko-ax; Brekekekex, ko-ax, ko-ax. His hands sore from rowing, Dionysus wearily asks the frogs to stop singing, but they only sing more loudly, and finally Dionysus joins in the refrain. The boat reaches the other bank of the Styx, and Dionysus pays Charon two obols and finds Xanthias on the shore.

Terrified by the sights and sounds of Hades, Dionysus asks his priest to protect him. [A priest of Dionysus sat in a place of honor at all dramatic performances.] Soon Dionysus and Xanthias hear the music of a flute. They hide as the Chorus of Men initiated in the Eleusinian Mysteries enters, led by a priest. The men, wearing white robes and carrying lighted torches, praise Dionysus and pray that he will come to them and join in their ceremonies. They then ask the profane to leave them; those unworthy of the Mysteries include Aristophanes' customary targets: the politician who accepts bribes or who betrays his embattled city and the Athenians who try to censor the writers of comedy. Soon Dionysus and Xanthias leave their hiding place and join in the dance. As he sings Dionysus asks the Chorus to direct him to the dwelling of Hades. When he and Xanthias arrive there, they are greeted by Aeacus, a judge of the dead. Because Dionysus is pretending to be Heracles, Aeacus upbraids him for having taken the dog Cerberus from the Underworld and threatens to call forth the monsters of Hades to punish him. Terrified, Dionysus asks Xanthias to change clothing with him, but he regrets this ruse when the maid of Persephone, mistaking Xanthias for Heracles, greets the slave warmly and tells him that her mistress invites him to an excellent dinner at which dancing girls will be present. After the maid leaves, Dionysus has some difficulty persuading Xanthias to give him back his clothes, but finally he succeeds. However, when a landlady, mistaking Dionysus for Heracles, violently upbraids him for having left an unpaid bill, he again changes clothes with Xanthias.

At this point Aeacus appears with some slaves to arrest Dionysus. When they seize and disarm Xanthias, he points to his "slave" Dionysus and suggests that they examine him by torture, a legal procedure customary in Athens, where a slave could be forced to testify about the conduct of his master. Dionysus now reveals that he is a god, Dionysus, the child of Zeus. Aeacus refuses to believe him, and in order to discover who actually is the god, decides to whip both Xanthias and Dionysus, believing that an immortal will not cry out. When Aeacus beats them, both Dionysus and Xanthias wail, so Aeacus concludes it would be best to take them to Hades, who will be able to recognize a god.

After they all go out the Chorus sings the parabasis, in which it attacks the demagogue Cleophon, who objected to making peace with Sparta during the last painful years of the Peloponnesian War. It pleads that the oligarchs, who, misguided by Phrynichus, had seized power in 411 B.C. and had since been overthrown and sent into exile, be restored to citizenship. Athens, the Chorus declares, does not sufficiently value its old and respected families, but turns instead to leaders unknown and untried.

Soon Aeacus and Xanthias return. Aeacus now knows who the real Dionysus is. Soon shouts and sounds of quarreling are heard. Aeacus explains that the dead dramatists Aeschylus and Euripides are arguing over the right to eat at the table of Hades. Aeschylus held this honored seat until Euripides arrived in Hades. Admired by the thieves and other criminals of the Underworld,

Euripides grew bold enough to seize the chair of Aeschylus. Hades has decided to hold a contest between the two playwrights to test their abilities by weighing their poetry line by line, and Dionysus is to decide on the victor.

Euripides, Aeschylus, and Dionysus enter. Before the contest each of the dramatists prays; Aeschylus addresses Demeter in a conventional prayer, but Euripides calls on his unique gods: Ether, his own vocal cords, reason, and the capacity to smell and sneer. Euripides then expresses contempt for Aeschylus' silent characters, his turgid, stilted, high-sounding diction, and his preoccupation with war. Euripides boasts of his own simplicity, his rationality, his use of the prologue to clarify his action, and his adaptation of the material of daily life. These are the very qualities of Euripides' drama which Aeschylus attacks, calling the prologues boring, the realism shamefully immoral, the style dull, and the so-called rationality sophistic. The mutual criticism continues until finally the scales are brought in, and the dramatists compete three times in weighing a line from their plays. Aeschylus' heavy lines, his references to rivers, chariots, and dead bodies outweigh Euripides' "winged" lines, but Dionysus still cannot reach a decision. Both poets are his friends, and each pleases him in his way. He then decides to take back to earth with him the dramatist who can help save Athens from destruction in the Peloponnesian War. Aeschylus' sound counsel wins the contest for him. When Euripides points out to Dionysus that the whole point of his descent into the Underworld was to bring him back, Dionysus replies that it was only his tongue that swore, but his choice is Aeschylus. Hades then asks Dionysus and Aeschylus to dine with him before they sail.

After the feast Hades says farewell to Aeschylus, telling him to save Athens with good advice. He sends presents of a sword, ropes, and poisons for those who are ruining Athens and the message that they must come to visit Hades soon. Aeschylus asks Hades to allow Sophocles to occupy his honored place but never Euripides. The Chorus wishes Aeschylus peace and joy as he goes forth to the world of light to aid his country.

Fronto, Marcus Cornelius. The tutor of the emperor Marcus Aurelius and an advocate and orator in Rome during the second century A.D. Some of his correspondence with Marcus Aurelius is extant. The letters contain comments on literature and on writers such as Plautus, Seneca, and Sallust. In an effort to reform the language of his period Fronto urged his contemporaries to emulate the style of preclassical Latin authors.

Furies (Erinyes). Avenging goddesses who sprang from the blood of the castrated Uranus. Winged, with bloody eyes and snakes in their hair, they pursued the guilty. The Furies have an important role in Aeschylus' ORESTEIA, in which they are transformed into the Eumenides (the Kindly Ones)—actually a euphemism used to propitiate the Furies. The Roman name for these goddesses was Dirae.

G

Gaius Caesar. See CALIGULA.

Galatea (Galateia). A nymph whom the Cyclops Polyphemus loved. See Theocritus' IDYLS VI, XI and ACIS.

Galba, Servius Sulpicius. An emperor of ROME for about six months in A.D. 68–69. See Tacitus' HISTORIES and Plutarch's life of Galba.

Gallus, Gaius Cornelius. A Roman poet, born at Forum Iulii (modern Fréjus) in southern France in 69 B.C. It is thought that he came from a poor family, but he achieved success both as a public official and as an elegiac poet. He was one of those in charge of the distribution of land after the victory of the forces of Octavian and Antony at Philippi, and he aided Vergil when his property was seized. During the reign of Augustus, Gallus was made first prefect of Egypt, but he lost favor with Augustus and committed suicide in 26 B.C. Gallus wrote four books of elegies on love and was important in establishing the elegy as a significant form of Latin poetry. Ovid praises him in Tristia IV, 10. Unfortunately, except for one line of poetry, all of Gallus' work has been lost. Vergil quotes him in Eclogue X.

Ganymede (Ganymedes). In Greek mythology, a son of Tros. Because of his extraordinary beauty, he was taken to Olympus by the gods or by Zeus to be their cupbearer.

Ge (Gaea, Gaia). In Greek mythology, the Earth. Brought forth by Chaos, Ge produced Uranus (the Heavens) and by him brought forth Cronus and the other Titans, the Cyclopes, and the giants with a hundred arms and fifty heads. See Hesiod's THEOGONY.

Georgics (Georgica). Didactic poem in dactylic hexameter (29 B.C.) by Vergil. Translations: in verse, John Dryden, 1697; in verse, James Rhoades, 1907; in prose, H. R. Fairclough, 1916; in verse, C. Day Lewis, 1940; in verse, S. Palmer Bovie, 1956.

BACKGROUND. The Georgics, suggested by Vergil's patron Maecenas, who was helping to promote Octavian's program of restoring the population of the cities to the farmland, is, on one level, a manual on farming. Influenced by Hesiod and Alexandrian didactic poets, such as Aratus and Nicander, Vergil gives precise directions to farmers and shepherds and information about weather and beekeeping. The Georgics, however, are closer in spirit to the work of Lucretius, for, if Vergil conscientiously set down directions and technical information for husbandmen, he was perhaps more concerned with writing a manual for those who sought a fruitful way of life, release from the *everso saeclo*, the "torn world," of the Roman citizen. In the second *Georgic*, Vergil suggests a comparison between his own poems and the *De Rerum Natura*: "Fortunate is he who knows the causes of things, and who no longer fears inexorable fate and the groans of Acheron." Lucretius has offered one answer to a world torn by war and bitterness; Vergil goes on to give his own view: "And he too is fortunate who understands the rural gods." Thus the *Georgics* also deal with "the nature of things." They are psalms in praise of the earth's beauty and fertility. Exulting in the plenitude of the rural gods' creation, Vergil is always aware of the contrast between the fruitful sphere of husbandry and the destructive and barren life that man creates for himself. He reminds the reader that when the plow is not properly honored, the scythes will be turned into swords.

SUMMARY. *Book I.* Addressing his poem to Maecenas, Vergil tells the subjects of the four *Georgics*: the first deals with caring for soil and crops and with weather; the second with trees, especially the olive and the vine; the third with cattle; and the fourth with beekeeping. After invoking many gods and the presence of Caesar, Vergil gives instructions for plowing. The farmer must know his soil and the climate that produces the various crops. He then speaks of alternating crops and other means of nourishing the earth. Directions are given for irrigation and for the control of insects. As he gives these directions, Vergil emphasizes the dignity of labor, which "conquers all." He then tells which are the best seasons for various tasks and signs that predict weather.

Book II. The second *Georgic* opens with an invocation to Bacchus, for Vergil will sing of the vine. He speaks of the various ways in which trees are made to grow, some only after great effort and some apparently of their own will. He then describes trees typical of various countries, praising those of Italy. The next subject is soils, what they can bear and their value as pasture land. After the discussion of soils, Vergil turns to grapevines and the supporting trees. The rich olive, pleasing to Peace, needs little care, says Vergil. He then discusses fruit trees and other trees. The *Georgic* ends with a description of the blessed life of the fortunate husbandman. He enjoys the sweetness and beauty of country life and avoids the dishonesty and danger of the city. He who knows the gods of the country lives a productive and peaceful life. His work is rewarding and his leisure joyous. This was the way of life of the great heroes of the past and of all those who established Rome as the greatest of cities.

Book III. Animals are the subject of the third *Georgic*, first large animals, such as the cow and the horse, and then smaller ones. Vergil gives a detailed description of the best types of cow and the distinguishing marks of a noble horse. Mingled with his realistic descriptions are references to great horses of myth and literature: the steeds of Mars and of Achilles. Warning the reader against the danger of the gadfly, Vergil refers to the tortures of Io. There is a long and beautiful digression on the desires and passions of animals. Every creature—man and animal, fish, cattle, birds—experiences the same love. The next subject is the care of sheep and goats. Vergil describes their pasture lands and the deep pools in which they drink, the shady places where at midday they seek shelter from the sun, and the cool air of afternoon when they graze. The various diseases that threaten cattle are discussed, and the book ends with a description of a pestilence that once killed all the animals of the land. Imitating Lucretius, Vergil recounts in great detail the symptoms of the disease and its dreadful effects.

Book IV. In treating the subject of bees in the fourth *Georgic* Vergil declares that he is dealing with a microcosm. He first gives advice about the location of hives and their construction. Then he describes the bees' habits, their production of honey, their battles, their manner of living in a city, their laws, and their conscientious labor. He illustrates their way of dividing the work, and speaks of their respect for their king. With great sympathy Vergil also tells of the diseases that afflict bees and suggests remedies for them. The rest of the fourth *Georgic* is devoted to an account of Aristaeus, a god of husbandry and beekeeping. Aristaeus loved Eurydice, but one day, fleeing his advances, she stepped on a serpent and was killed. To avenge her death Orpheus and the Dryads killed all the bees of Aristaeus. Aristaeus' mother, the nymph Cyrene, advised him to ask the seer Proteus to help him, but first he had to capture Proteus, who could change his shape at will. When Proteus could find no way of escaping Aristaeus, he told him the story of the death of Eurydice and the mourning of the Dryads and Orpheus, of Orpheus' visit to Erebus to find his beloved, and of how he had almost brought her back to earth, but, just as they approached the light of day, he looked back at Eurydice and so lost her forever. Orpheus continually lamented his beloved until finally the Ciconian women in a Bacchic frenzy tore his limbs from his body and scattered them over the fields. As his head floated down the Hebrus, he continued to cry out the name of Eurydice. Cyrene now advised her son to sacrifice four oxen to Orpheus and Eurydice. When he had done as she suggested, he discovered in the carcasses of these oxen a generation of bees. This is a mythological explanation for the ancient theory that bees could be generated from the body of an ox.

Germania. A treatise (c. A.D. 98) by Tacitus. It deals with the geography, political and social life, and customs of the German people. Tacitus' approach to his subject is essentially didactic; he contrasts the virtuous Germans (like the Romans of the Republic) with the corrupt Romans of the Empire. Yet he is objective enough to observe and describe the flaws of the Germans: their laziness, gluttony, drunkenness, and love of warfare. For the most part, however, Tacitus emphasizes German morality, particularly in family relations.

Girl From Persia, The (Persa). A farce by PLAUTUS, based on an unknown

Greek play. The farce, more correctly known as *The Persian,* is concerned with the adventures of Toxilus, a slave, and his love for the courtesan Lemniselenis, who belongs to the procurer Dordalus. With the help of his parasite Saturio, Toxilus manages to dupe Dordalus and to free his sweetheart.

Girl From Samos, The (Samia). A New Comedy (c. 300 B.C.) by MENANDER. Translations: in prose, L. A. Post, 1929; in prose and verse, Francis G. Allinson 1930; in prose, Lionel Casson, 1960.

BACKGROUND. The extant fragments of *The Girl From Samos* contain less than half the play. The following events precede the material contained in the fragments. Demeas, a wealthy Athenian, is living with Chrysis, who was forced to leave Samos in 322 B.C., when Macedonia conquered Athens. Because she cannot prove Athenian citizenship, Demeas is not able to marry her, but keeps her as his mistress. Demeas has an adopted son, Moschion, who believes Demeas is his real father. Moschion is having a love affair with Plangon, the daughter of Demeas' neighbor, Niceratus, a poor man who cannot provide a dowry for his daughter. At a time when both Demeas and Niceratus were away from Athens, Plangon gave birth to Moschion's child. During this period Chrysis bore a child that died; therefore, she decided to help the young couple by taking Plangon's baby and claiming it as her child by Demeas. When Demeas returns he is disturbed to learn that he has an illegitimate child, but he reluctantly agrees to rear it. Demeas has decided to marry Moschion to Plangon despite her poverty, but the problems that result from Chrysis' claim that Plangon's baby is hers interfere with the plans for the wedding.

SCENE. Athens; in the background are the houses of Demeas and Niceratus.

SUMMARY. The beginning of the extant fragment consists of Demeas' account of his suspicions that his mistress Chrysis has had a child by Moschion. Recalling how Chrysis begged to be allowed to keep the baby, he is extremely angry. When his slave Parmeno comes from the market with a cook and slaves bringing food for the wedding, Demeas tries to find out from Parmeno if his suspicions about Chrysis and Moschion have any foundation, but Parmeno avoids answering his master's questions. Demeas is now convinced that Chrysis has corrupted Moschion, who had always behaved honorably in the past, and he determines to send her away despite his affection for her. When Demeas angrily expels Chrysis and her child from his house, she exclaims in amazement that she does not know why he treats her so cruelly. Soon Niceratus enters and finds Chrysis in tears. She tells him of the strange conduct of Demeas.

Here a large portion of the play is missing. It can be assumed that the complications in this "comedy of errors" increase. In the next fragment Demeas has discovered that the baby is Plangon's and regrets his cruel treatment of Chrysis. Niceratus, having also learned the truth of the child's parentage, is violently angry, and when Chrysis refuses to give up the child, he tries to beat her. Demeas, protecting Chrysis, fights with Niceratus. When Demeas assures

Niceratus that Moschion will marry Plangon and pleads with Niceratus to hasten preparations for the wedding, the two men are reconciled.

Meanwhile Moschion, angry with his father for suspecting him of seducing Chrysis, plans to punish Demeas by pretending to be so offended that he will leave Athens. When Parmeno enters, Moschion orders him to bring him a cloak and a sword. Parmeno reappears and tries to persuade Moschion to change his plans and go on with his wedding, for which all are preparing. Moschion, however, is determined to frighten his father with the pretense that he is leaving the city. The fragment ends here.

No doubt at the end of the play Moschion and his father are reconciled, and Moschion is married to Plangon. Possibly Moschion discovers he is the adopted son of Demeas and that Chrysis is his sister. Because she is related to an Athenian citizen the girl from Samos has Athenian citizenship and can legally marry Demeas.

Glaucus (Glaukos). See ILIAD, especially VI, and BELLEROPHON.

Golden Ass, The (Metamorphoses). A Latin romance (second century A.D.) by APULEIUS. In the Introduction to his excellent translation of *The Golden Ass* (1951) Robert Graves remarks, "The original title of this book, *The Transformation of Lucius Apuleius of Madaura*, was early shortened to *The Golden Ass* because Apuleius had written it in the style of the professional storytellers who, as Pliny mentions in one of his letters, used to preface their street-corner entertainments with: 'Give me a copper and I'll tell you a golden story.'" The tale is told in the first person by Lucius, a Greek, who, during a visit to Thessaly, a region famous for magic, is transformed into an ass. In this form he is seized by robbers, who beat and humiliate him. In their cave he hears some of the excellent stories that constantly interrupt the narrative of Lucius' adventures and add to the great charm of *The Golden Ass*. One of these is the story of how the robbers were forced to cut off the arm of their chief, Lamachus, in order to free him when the owner of a house they intended to rob managed to nail Lamachus' arm to the door. Another is the most famous and most beautiful tale in the book, the love of Cupid and PSYCHE.

After much suffering and many reflections on the blindness and injustice of Fortune, Lucius, still in the form of an ass, manages to escape from the robbers. He has many strange experiences; among them are his association with a group of eunuch priests and his adventures as a performing ass, whose talents are so admired that a noble woman falls in love with him. Finally, through the aid of the goddess Isis, Lucius is restored to his human form. The priest of Isis tells him that it was his own foolish curiosity and blind Fortune that caused him so much distress, from which neither his high position nor his learning could save him. However, Fortune has also given him the opportunity to embrace the religion of Isis. Once he accepts this religion Fortune will have no power over him. After a period of preparation Lucius is initated into the sacred mysteries of Isis.

Gorgias. A Sicilian rhetorician and orator, about 485 B.C. to 375 B.C. He came to Athens in 427 B.C. and achieved great fame through his epideictic orations. Gorgias was also known as a leading Sophist. His style was ornate, the rhythm of his speeches close to that of poetry. Fragments of a funeral address and of two *encomia* are his only remaining works. Both his speeches and his rhetorical writings influenced Attic prose and the work of later orators, especially Isocrates.

Gorgias. A dialogue by PLATO, named for the famous Sicilian Sophist and rhetorician. Socrates discusses rhetoric as a means of flattery. Rhetoric is also criticized because the orator, in his desire to be successful, must hurt others. Socrates declares that doing evil is worse than enduring it.

Gorgons (Gorgones). According to Hesiod, the daughters of Phorcys and Ceto. Their names were Sthenno, Euryale, and Medusa. Only Medusa was mortal. They were often depicted as monstrous creatures with serpents in their hair, claws, and huge teeth. Anyone who met the gaze of Medusa was turned into stone. For the slaying of Medusa see PERSEUS.

Greek (Palatine) Anthology, The. A collection of about four thousand epigrams, mainly in elegiac verse, written between the seventh century B.C. and the tenth century A.D. The poems were organized in fifteen books by the Byzantine scholar Constantinus Cephalas, who lived during the tenth century A.D. At the beginning of the fourteenth century Maximus Planudes, a monk, made an abridgement of the anthology of Cephalas and added some poems to the collection, which was then called the *Anthologia Planudea*. The original anthology compiled by Cephalas was unknown from the fourteenth to the seventeenth century, when it was discovered in the Palatine Library of Heidelberg by the French scholar Saumaise (then a young man of nineteen, later known as John Milton's adversary Salmasius). The *Greek Anthology* now consists of the original collection of Cephalas with the addition of a sixteenth book containing the poems supplied by Maximus Planudes in the *Anthologia Planudea*.

The poems in the *Greek Anthology* vary a great deal in subject matter and tone. Epitaphs by Simonides convey the heroic and tragic experiences of the Persian Wars; epigrams by Callimachus tell of the bitterness of death and the pleasures of love. A great many of the epigrams by Asclepiades and others deal with love, the brevity of life, and the necessity of seizing what pleasures are available. There are also humorous and satirical poems, riddles, puzzles, and oracles.

H

Hades (Haides, Aides, Aidoneus). The Greek god of the Underworld, son of Cronus and Rhea and brother of Zeus. Hades was also called Pluto, a name suggesting wealth (Plouton, "rich") and indicating Hades' possible origin as a god of agriculture, of the richness or fertility of the earth. For Hades' abduction of PERSEPHONE see HOMERIC HYMN II. With her as his queen Hades ruled the world of the dead. The Romans called Hades Pluto or Dis. Hades is also the name for the world of the dead. See ODYSSEY XI, AENEID VI, and Aristophanes' THE FROGS.

Hadrian (Publius Aelius Hadrianus). The emperor of ROME from A.D. 117 to 138. In Marguerite Yourcenar's novel *Hadrian's Memoirs* the emperor writes of himself and his era to his grandson Marcus Aurelius. The book re-creates both the character of one of the so-called good Roman emperors and the history of his period.

Haemon (Haimon). See Sophocles' ANTIGONE.

Halicarnassus (Halikarnassos). A city on the southwest coast of Asia Minor. Halicarnassus was first established by the Dorians. It was the birthplace of Herodotus and Dionysius, the historian and literary critic, and site of the famous tomb of King Mausolus.

Halieutica. A fragmentary poem by OVID on fishing in the Black Sea. In the 132 lines that remain Ovid deals mainly with various types of fish.

Hamilcar Barca. See CARTHAGE.

Hannibal. See CARTHAGE.

Harmonia. See CADMUS.

Harpies (Harpyiai; "Robbers"). In Greek mythology, the daughters of Thaumas and Electra (daughter of Oceanus). According to Homer, the Harpies snatch people away like a wind; Hesiod depicts them as winged maidens; but in later literature they are hideous birds with the heads of women. For Vergil's depiction of them see AENEID III.

Haunted House, The (Mostellaria). A comedy by PLAUTUS probably based on a Greek play *The Ghost* by Philemon. While his father Theopropides is abroad, Philolaches, a young Athenian, borrows money from a usurer and buys Philematium, a slave girl he loves, and sets her free. She now lives with him in his father's house, and Philolaches is having a fine time spending his father's money on a life of pleasure. Tranio, his father's slave, encourages Philolaches' extravagance and self-indulgence. Soon, however, Tranio hears that Theopropides has returned to Athens. Certain that his father will be very angry when he learns how his son has been living, Philolaches is terrified, but the ingenious Tranio devises a plan for preventing the old man from discovering what has been going on in his house during his absence. He locks Philolaches and his drunken friends in the house, instructing them not to respond when Theopropides knocks. When the old man arrives Tranio tells him that his house is haunted by the ghost of someone who was murdered by the former owner. The ghost came to Philolaches while he slept, and seven months ago Philolaches, Tranio, and the other members of the household all moved out of the haunted house. When the usurer appears to collect the money due him, Tranio pretends that Philolaches borrowed it in order to buy the house next door, which belongs to Simo. Though Simo agrees not to expose Philolaches and Tranio, the slave finds it increasingly difficult to carry on the deception. Finally Theopropides learns the truth. When he is convinced that his son is repentant, he forgives him and even pardons the delightful rogue Tranio.

Heauton Timorumenos. See THE SELF-TORMENTOR.

Hebe. In Greek mythology, the daughter of Zeus and Hera. As handmaiden of the gods, she served them nectar. After Heracles achieved divinity he married Hebe. Hebe was called Juventas by the Romans.

Hecate (Hekate). A Greek goddess of the Underworld. No doubt originally an earth goddess, Hecate was regarded as the only Titan who remained in power after Zeus had dethroned Cronus. Hecate was later associated with the moon and identified with the goddess Selene. Because she also came to be identified with Artemis and with Persephone, Hecate was considered a goddess of triple form. As a goddess of the Underworld, Hecate was thought to send ghosts and demons up to earth and to accompany the souls of the dead. She was capable of witchcraft, and protected those involved in sorcery. Hecate lived at places where roads met.

Hector (Hektor). The son of Priam and Hecuba and one of the greatest of the Trojan warriors in the ILIAD. See also Vergil's AENEID II and RHESUS.

Hecuba (Hekabe). The wife of Priam, king of Troy. Hecuba was the mother of Hector, PARIS, and many other warriors who fell at Troy. Her daughters too—Cassandra, Polyxena, and others—met tragic ends. For Hecuba's story see the ILIAD, Euripides' THE TROJAN WOMEN and HECUBA, Vergil's *Aeneid*, and Seneca's *The Trojan Women*. In Ovid's *Metamorphoses* XIII Hecuba is transformed into a dog.

Hecuba (Hekabe). A tragedy (c. 425 B.C.) by Euripides. Translations: in prose, E. P. Coleridge, 1891; in verse, Arthur S. Way, 1912; in verse, J. T. Sheppard, 1927; in verse, Hugh O. Meredith, 1937; in verse, William Arrowsmith, 1958; in verse, Philip Vellacott, 1963.

MYTHICAL BACKGROUND. When Troy fell and most of its heroes lay dead, its women became the slaves of the Greek army. Hecuba, the wife of Priam, the dead king of Troy, and her daughters endured not only the anguish of war and the deaths of loved ones, but the humiliation of slavery. Hecuba now belongs to Agamemnon, and she is forced to accompany him back to Greece. The army has paused briefly at the Thracian Chersonese, the scene of the play.

SCENE. Before Agamemnon's tent on the shore of the Thracian Chersonese.

SUMMARY. The Ghost of Polydorus appears and recalls the time when Priam, his father, sent him and a great deal of gold to his friend, Polymestor, king of Thrace, in order to save the boy and to provide for his surviving children if Troy should fall. After the Trojans were defeated, says the Ghost, the treacherous Polymestor, desiring Priam's gold, killed Polydorus. Unburied, he hovers about his mother Hecuba, now a slave of Agamemnon. The Ghost then declares that Achilles' spirit is withholding the winds from the Greeks until Polyxena, Polydorus' sister, is sacrificed at Achilles tomb. On this day, the Ghost prophesies, Hecuba must face the deaths of two of her children, his own, of which she is as yet ignorant, and that of Polyxena.

As the Ghost disappears Hecuba and her attendants, other captive women, come from the tent of Agamemnon. Hecuba speaks of frightening dreams she has had, which suggest suffering for Polyxena and Polydorus. As she prays to the gods to prevent the sacrifice of her daughter, the Chorus of Captive Women enters and informs her that Polyxena has been chosen by the Greeks as a sacrifice to Achilles. Hecuba cries out in her helplessness and sorrow. When she reveals the Greeks' decision to Polyxena, however, the young girl feels more sorrow for her mother than for herself, for she welcomes death as an escape from slavery.

Odysseus arrives to take Polyxena. Hecuba reminds Odysseus of the time when she saved his life and begs him to spare Polyxena in return, but Odysseus refuses, explaining with cruel detachment the necessity for a noble victim to honor the great Achilles. Polyxena proudly declares that the daughter of Priam and the sister of Hector gladly exchanges death for slavery. She bids farewell to her mother and accompanies Odysseus. Hecuba faints in her grief and the Chorus intensifies the mood of despair by singing of the anguish of captivity. The women wonder where their captors will take them and what kind of life they will lead as slaves. The herald Talthybius comes to find Hecuba, who must now bury the dead Polyxena. He describes the girl's dignified acceptance of her role as sacrificial victim.

The Captive Women sing of the beginnings of their sorrow, when Paris first took Helen from Menelaus and caused the Trojan War. A Maid enters, accompanied by attendants who carry a corpse. When Hecuba comes out of the tent, the Maid reveals to her the body of Polydorus, which has been washed up on the seashore. Again Hecuba weeps and groans, guessing that her son was slain by her supposed friend Polymestor. Then Agamemnon enters, asking why Hecuba does not come to prepare Polyxena's body for burial. He sees the corpse of Polydorus and learns from Hecuba how the young man was murdered by Polymestor. Hecuba asks the aid of her enemy Agamemnon in avenging the death of Polydorus. Although Agamemnon feels sympathy for Hecuba, he is afraid to help her kill the king of Thrace because the Greek army regards Polymestor as a friend; however, he agrees not to reveal her plot and to check any effort the Greeks may make to rescue Polymestor.

Hecuba sends a servant to Polymestor with the message that she wishes to see him and his children. After a choral ode recalling the tragic fall of Troy, Polymestor enters with his children. Polymestor pretends to feel pity for the captive Hecuba and assures her that Polydorus is still alive. Hecuba tricks him and his children into entering the tent by telling him that she has gold hidden within. Then from the tent come Polymestor's cries of fear and pain. Hecuba comes out and announces that Polymestor has been blinded and his children slain. Polymestor emerges from the tent screaming in agony. At this point Agamemnon returns and learns how Hecuba, aided by the other captive Trojan women, performed the bloody acts. Polymestor tries to justify his murder of Polydorus, saying he killed him because he feared the young man would try to avenge the destruction of Troy. Hecuba discloses Polymestor's true nature, his hypocrisy and greed, which led him to violate the sacred laws of hospitality. Realizing that Polymestor is guilty, Agamemnon refuses to help him. Polymestor then prophesies that Hecuba will be changed into a dog and will fall into the sea and that Clytemnestra, Agamemnon's wife, will kill Cassandra and Agamemnon. Agamemnon angrily orders his guards to take Polymestor to a desert island and leave him there. Turning to Hecuba, Agamemnon gently urges her to bury her two children. Then she and the other captive women must get ready to leave Thrace.

Hecyra. See THE MOTHER-IN-LAW.

Helen (Helene). Daughter of Zeus and LEDA, for whom the Trojan War was fought. Helen was regarded in Greek myth as the most beautiful woman in the world. She was worshiped as a goddess of marriage in Sparta. In Greek and Latin literature her character is depicted with a great deal of variety. In some works she is an extremely sympathetic character, apparently the victim of Aphrodite and her own great beauty; in others she is a cold and selfish woman, concerned only with her own appetites. See the ILIAD and the ODYSSEY (IV). Though Helen does not appear in the ORESTEIA, the many references to her are significant. See also Euripides' HELEN, THE TROJAN WOMEN, and ORESTES, and Ovid's HEROIDES XVI and XVII.

Helen (Helene). A tragedy (412 B.C.) by EURIPIDES. Translations: in prose, E. P. Coleridge, 1891; in verse, Arthur S. Way, 1912; in prose and verse, Philip Vellacott, 1954; in verse, Richmond Lattimore, 1956.

MYTHICAL BACKGROUND. According to the *Palinodia* (Recantation) of Stesichorus, a lyric poet (c. 640–555 B.C.), Helen did not go with Paris to Troy. Only a phantom of Helen accompanied her lover, whereas the real Helen was taken to Egypt by King Proteus and held there until her husband Menelaus should come to her. Herodotus' version of the abduction of Helen is similar to this one. In the *Persian Wars* (II, 113–116) he tells of being informed by an Egyptian priest that on the way home from Sparta a gale drove Paris' ship to Egypt. Here King Proteus scolded him for his violation of Menelaus' hospitality, kept Helen and the stolen treasures in Egypt awaiting Menelaus, and ordered Paris to leave Egypt. Euripides employs this version of the legend of Helen and adapts it to suit his own theme, the tragic folly of warfare. As the modern poet H.D. says in the introduction to her *Helen in Egypt,* "The Greeks and the Trojans alike fought for an illusion."

SCENE. Egypt, before the palace of Theoclymenus; nearby is the tomb of Proteus, father of Theoclymenus.

SUMMARY. Helen speaks of her parents, her mother Leda, her mortal father Tyndareus, and her immortal father Zeus, who had come to Leda in the form of a swan. Then Helen tells of the suffering she has endured because Paris chose Aphrodite over Hera and Athene as the most beautiful goddess. Aphrodite had promised Paris the loveliest woman in the world as his wife, but Hera, furious at Paris' insult to her, created a phantom of Helen, which Paris abducted and took to Troy. Helen herself was brought to Egypt by Hermes, who left her in the palace of King Proteus. Here she remained throughout the Trojan War, waiting to be reunited with Menelaus, as Hermes had promised. When Proteus died, his son Theoclymenus became king. Now Theoclymenus wishes to marry Helen. Thus she prays at the tomb of Proteus for protection of her honor as the wife of Menelaus.

Teucer, a Greek warrior forced into exile by his father Telamon, enters and is shocked to discover a woman who resembles Helen, whom all Hellas hates. Having seen the phantom Helen at Troy, he is unaware that the real Helen is before him. He tells her that it took the Greeks ten years to destroy Troy, and seven years have passed since the war ended. No one knows what has happened to Menelaus, whose ships were lost on his way home. Helen's mother Leda and her brothers Castor and Polydeuces killed themselves because they were ashamed of Helen's disloyalty to Menelaus. After she hears of these sad events Helen advises Teucer to leave Egypt before his presence is known to Theoclymenus, who kills every stranger from Greece. Teucer thanks her and leaves, declaring that she may look like Helen, but her soul is different from that of the evil woman.

As Helen weeps over her sad fate, the Chorus of Captive Greek Women enters and echoes her lament. Helen bitterly cries out against her own beauty, which has caused so much destruction. Believing that Menelaus is dead, she contemplates suicide. The Leader of the Chorus suggests that Helen seek out

Theoclymenus' sister Theonoe, who has powers of prophecy, to discover if Menelaus is actually dead.

When Helen and the Chorus have entered the palace, Menelaus appears, alone and in ragged clothing. He speaks of his ancestors and of his past glory, when he and his brother Agamemnon fought at Troy. Then he tells of his long years of wandering and his fruitless efforts to return to Sparta. Now his ship has been wrecked, and he has left the phantom Helen (whom he regards as the true one) and his men in a cave, while he has gone forth seeking help. A Portress answers his call at the gate of the palace and tells him to leave at once. The Egyptians will have nothing to do with the Greeks. Menelaus persists in trying to speak to the king and is surprised to hear that Helen lives in the palace. He decides to wait outside for the king's return.

Helen and the Chorus come out of the palace, having learned from Theonoe that Menelaus is still alive. As Helen returns to the tomb of Proteus, she and Menelaus recognize each other. A Messenger then arrives to tell Menelaus that the woman he thought was his wife revealed she was a phantom and vanished into the air. He joyfully accepts the real Helen as his wife. She informs him that Hera ordered Hermes to bring her to Egypt. As Helen and Menelaus speak of the Trojan War and their separation, the Messenger enters the conversation. Menelaus bitterly says that the Greeks fought for a phantom, and the Messenger inveighs against the seers, Calchas and Helenus, who never realized that all the slaughter was in vain. Menelaus sends the Messenger to instruct his other comrades to await his return.

Helen then reveals that Theoclymenus wishes to marry her and that he will slay Menelaus if he tries to interfere. They decide to ask Theonoe to help them, and after some persuasion, she agrees to do so. Helen suggests a way of escape. She will pretend to Theoclymenus that Menelaus has died and will beg him to lend her a ship so that she may conduct funeral services for Menelaus at sea. Thus they will have a ship in which to escape from Egypt. As Helen enters the palace, the Chorus sings of the senseless sorrow and the meaningless destruction caused by the Trojan War. Theoclymenus enters, followed soon after by Helen, who persuades him to lend her the ship. She promises to marry Theoclymenus after she has performed the proper rites for her dead husband. Menelaus pretends to be one of the Greeks who sailed with Menelaus and aids Helen in convincing Theoclymenus that her story is authentic.

Soon Helen, Menelaus, and attendants of Theoclymenus, bearing offerings for the funeral ceremonies, go off to the ship. Then a Messenger rushes in to inform Theoclymenus that he has been deceived by Menelaus and Helen. Menelaus has killed the attendants of Theoclymenus, and only the Messenger has escaped. With Menelaus' comrades, Helen and Menelaus set sail for Greece. Theoclymenus realizes his sister has befriended them and is determined to kill her. However, the Dioscuri appear in the sky as the *deus ex machina*. They inform Theoclymenus that he was not destined to marry Helen, nor has his sister wronged him. She merely accepted the word of the gods. Castor and Polydeuces prophesy the safe homecoming of Menelaus and Helen. Moreover, they declare that Helen will become a goddess after her death, and Menelaus will live in the Isles of the Blest. Theoclymenus agrees to spare his sister and to accept the decrees of the gods. He praises the noble and chaste Helen.

Helenus (Helenos). A son of Priam and Hecuba, a seer and a warrior. See the ILIAD VI, XIII and the AENEID III.

Heliodorus (Heliodoros). A Greek writer of prose romances of the third century A.D. Heliodorus' only extant work is the AETHIOPICA, or *Theagenes and Chariclea.*

Helios. In Greek mythology, the child of the Titans Hyperion and Thea and god of the sun. His sisters were Selene, the moon, and Eos, the dawn. Helios daily drove a chariot across the heavens, returning to the west in the evening. For the story of the eating of his cattle on the island of Thrinacia (Sicily), which was sacred to him, see ODYSSEY XII.

Hellenica (Hellenika). See XENOPHON.

Hephaestus (Hephaistos). In Greek mythology, the son of Zeus and Hera and god of fire, possibly replacing Prometheus. Hephaestus, who excelled as an artist and a craftsman, forged the shield of Achilles, described in the ILIAD XVIII, and created Pandora out of clay. The only lame and unattractive god, Hephaestus, was married to the beautiful Aphrodite. An amusing story of her unfaithfulness and Hephaestus' revenge is told in the ODYSSEY VIII. See also PROMETHEUS BOUND.

Hepta epi Thebas. See SEVEN AGAINST THEBES.

Hera. In Greek mythology, the daughter of Cronus and Rhea and the sister and wife of Zeus. She was the protector of women and marriage. Many of the myths about Hera have to do with her punishment of her rivals for Zeus' love and the offspring of Zeus' love affairs with mortals. For her hatred of Heracles see Euripides' THE MADNESS OF HERACLES.

Heracleidae (Herakleidai). See THE CHILDREN OF HERACLES.

Heracles (Herakles; Latin Hercules). A Greek hero noted for his strength. Heracles was sometimes regarded as a god, but more often considered one of the greatest of the Greek heroes. W. K. C. Guthrie says of Heracles: "It is a unique case of a mortal who by his own superhuman efforts was raised to the plane of the upper gods" (W. K. C. Guthrie, *The Greeks and Their Gods* [Beacon, 1955], pp. 237–238). Heracles is best known for his courage and his amazing physical strength. Perhaps his most impressive quality, however, is his power to endure the burden of great toil and danger and agonizing personal sorrow.

Heracles was the son of Zeus and Alcmena. For the story of his conception and birth see Plautus' AMPHITRYON. In *Metamorphoses* IX Ovid depicts Alcmena as an old woman describing her difficulties in giving birth to Heracles. Theocritus' IDYL XXIV tells of Hera's hatred for Heracles, the child of her mortal rival, of Heracles' great feats as an infant (see also Pindar's *Nemean Ode* I) and of his education as he grew older. Heracles received training in the bow from Eurytus, a grandson of Apollo; Autolycus taught him wrestling, and Polydeuces taught him how to use arms. When Heracles' music teacher Linus scolded him, Heracles killed him with his lyre. In IDYL XXV, which appears with the poems of Theocritus but was probably not written by him, the poet tells of how Heracles killed the great Nemean lion.

For Heracles' accomplishment of the twelve labors and his murder of his wife Megara and their children see Euripides' THE MADNESS OF HERACLES. In other versions of the story Heracles must perform the twelve labors as penance after the murder of Megara and the children or for various other reasons. Seneca's HERCULES FURENS also deals with Heracles' madness and his murder of his wife and children.

One of Heracles' many great feats, related in Euripides' ALCESTIS, was the restoration of Alcestis from Hades. Heracles also overcame the river-god Achelous, a suitor of Deianira. For Heracles' victory over the river-god, his marriage to Deianira, which ended tragically, and his death see Sophocles' THE WOMEN OF TRACHIS, Ovid's *Metamorphoses* IX and HEROIDES IX, and Seneca's HERCULES OETAEUS. Bacchylides also describes his death, as well as his meeting with Meleager in Hades (see CHORAL LYRICS V, XVI). In Sophocles' PHILOCTETES, Heracles appears as a god. Heracles is mentioned in the *Iliad;* in the *Odyssey,* Odysseus encounters him in Hades. Heracles also appears in Aristophanes' *The Birds* and THE FROGS. An interesting study, *The Herculean Hero* as he appears in the writings of Marlowe, Chapman, Shakespeare, and Dryden, was written by Eugene M. Waith (Columbia University Press, 1962). See also HYLAS.

Heraclitus (Herakleitos). A Greek philosopher of Ephesus (fl. c. 500 B.C.). Heraclitus wrote one book, which dealt with metaphysical, scientific, and political ideas; only fragments of it survive. One of the first Greek prose writers, he wrote in oracular prose and was regarded by the ancients as obscure. Heraclitus' most important idea was that in the universe all matter is constantly changing. His best-known statement, "It is not possible to step twice into the same river" (Frag. 91, Kathleen Freeman, *Ancilla to the Pre-Socratic Philosophers* [Harvard University Press, 1957], p. 31), illustrates his conception of eternal mutability. Heraclitus also believed that fire is the essence of all matter.

Herakles Mainomenos. See THE MADNESS OF HERACLES.

Hercules. See HERACLES.

Hercules Furens (Mad Hercules). A tragedy by SENECA, modeled on Euripides' MADNESS OF HERACLES. Seneca makes several changes in the plot. Juno delivers the prologue; Lycus does not threaten to kill Hercules' children, but decides to marry his wife, Megara, in order to strengthen his own hold on the throne. Megara, of course, despises Lycus and rejects his offer. Only then does Lycus say he will murder Megara and her children. In Seneca's play Hercules' murder of his wife and children, though it takes place off stage, is observed and described in sensational detail by Amphitryon, and Megara can be heard pleading with her husband for mercy. The deluded Hercules believes he is killing Juno and the sons of Lycus. Seneca's most effective change occurs in the scene in which Hercules, recovering from his delusion and seeing his dead family and blood on his own arrows, realizes, without being told, that he himself has slain his wife and children.

Hercules Oetaeus (Hercules on Oeta). The longest tragedy attributed to SENECA, probably modeled on Sophocles' THE WOMEN OF TRACHIS. The play may have been influenced by the episode of Hercules and Deianira in Ovid's *Metamorphoses*. Many scholars believe that *Hercules Oetaeus* was written not by Seneca but by an imitator of his work. In this play Deianira is a rather shallow character, merely a jealous wife, and Hercules is a suffering and enduring Stoic. The play ends with the deification of Hercules on Mount Oeta.

Hermes. A Greek god. His name has been translated "he of the stone heap" (see M. P. Nilsson, *History of Greek Religion* [2nd ed.; Oxford University Press, 1949], p. 109), and it is thought that his personality emerged from the worship of boundary stones used as fetishes. From these, no doubt, emerged both the anthropomorphic Hermes and the herms that, in classical times, consisted of busts of Hermes on four-cornered pillars with phalli to suggest the principle of fertility.

The anthropomorphic Hermes was said to be the son of Zeus and Maia, born on Mount Cyllene in Arcadia. For the story of his birth and his invention of the lyre see HOMERIC HYMN IV and Sophocles' ICHNEUTAI. Hermes was the messenger of the gods, and could provide good luck and riches for men. He was the god of secrets, cunning, and tricks, of arts, markets, roads, merchants, and thieves. He dealt in dreams and led souls to Hades. The Romans identified him with Mercury.

Hermione. The daughter of Helen and Menelaus and wife of Neoptolemus. See ANDROMACHE, ORESTES, and HEROIDES VIII.

Hero. A priestess of Aphrodite in Sestos, loved by the youth Leander. At night Hero would hold a lighted torch to guide Leander, who lived at Abydus, as he swam across the Hellespont to visit her. When Leander was drowned in a storm, Hero took her own life by throwing herself into the sea. See Ovid's HEROIDES XVIII and XIX.

Herodas or **Herondas.** A Greek writer of mimes (first half of the third century B.C.). Eight of the mimes (dramatic sketches of ordinary life) of Herodas were discovered in Egypt in 1891. They depict such scenes as a conversation between a lady and a matchmaker (I), the owner of a brothel addressing a jury (II), and two poor women offering a cock at the temple of Asclepius at Cos (IV).

Herodotus (Herodotos). Historian (c. 480 B.C.–c. 425 B.C.), born at Halicarnassus, on the southwest coast of Asia Minor. He came from an aristocratic family, and his uncle was the poet Panyasis. In 460 B.C. Herodotus was forced into exile by the tyrant Lygdamis, who ruled Halicarnassus. After leaving his home Herodotus went to the island of Samos. Then he traveled through Asia Minor and into the interior of Asia; he also visited Egypt and many parts of the Greek world. About 450 B.C. Herodotus and Panyasis returned to Halicarnassus and helped to expel Lygdamis, but again because of political troubles Herodotus was forced into exile. In 445 B.C. Herodotus was at Athens. He helped to colonize Thurii, in southern Italy, and later settled there as a citizen. It is thought that Herodotus gave public readings from his history at Athens and that these were so well received that he was awarded a prize of ten talents. Herodotus visited Athens many times and knew Pericles and Sophocles, who wrote a poem honoring him. Herodotus probably died at Thurii in 425 B.C. The only work of his that remains is his great history, THE PERSIAN WARS, which may be unfinished.

Herodotus was named by Cicero "the father of history," and certainly he was the first to approach the past with the point of view of an historian. Despite the many inaccuracies of Herodotus' history and his inclusion of folk tales, oracular pronouncements, irrelevant stories, and incorrect statistics, he approached his material as a writer of history doing serious research and attempting to present past events with a certain degree of objectivity and authenticity. He tried to find the best authorities and sources, and he reveals a sympathy and understanding for customs and attitudes alien to his own that mark the true historian. Also, in writing about the conflict between Asia and Greece from the time of Croesus to that of Xerxes, he actually writes a study of civilization: customs, religion, geography, human nature, all these interest Herodotus. His approach is broad and humane, sometimes closer to that of the poet or the dramatist than to that of the historian. He was concerned with human destiny and saw historical figures as the victims of their own *hybris* as well as of divine retribution; he assumed that historical events fit into the design of tragic drama. Thus he suggests the feelings and motivations of historical persons as he writes of the events in which they were involved. Herodotus is regarded as the first writer who used prose artfully, and his history, with its many digressions that give breadth and depth to his main subject, its commentaries on human weakness and dignity, its charm and clarity of style, can certainly be regarded as a work of art. Each of the nine books of the history was named after one of the Muses, not by Herodotus but, it is said, by the Greeks who heard Herodotus read from them. Whether or not this story is true, it indicates the response of Herodotus' contemporaries to his work. This praise continued: he was admired by the great ancient critics, by "Longinus" for his ability to involve the reader's feelings and by Quintilian for his lucid style, and today scholars are impressed by the authenticity of his comments on religious and social customs, as well as by his historical and literary genius.

heroic hymn. A choral lyric sung to the music of the lyre. The hymn dealt with the adventures of the great heroes of the epics, and was probably performed at festivals. Stesichorus, who is said to have invented the heroic hymn, embellished the tales connected with Agamemnon, Orestes, Aeneas, and other figures of the epics.

Heroides (Heroidum Epistulae; Letters of Heroines). Imaginary letters in elegiacs (before A.D. 8) by OVID. Translation: in prose, Grant Showerman, 1921; in verse, Harold C. Cannon, 1972.

S U M M A R Y . The *Heroides* consists of eighteen imaginary letters written by mythical heroines to their lovers and three letters by lovers to which the recipients reply. Some scholars have questioned the authorship of the last three pairs of letters between Paris and Helen, Leander and Hero, and Acontius and Cydippe, but they are usually accepted as Ovid's.

I. Penelope writes the first letter to Ulysses shortly after the fall of Troy. The faithful wife expresses her longing for her husband and her despair because, though other Greek heroes have already returned, Ulysses is still absent. "For others," she says, "Troy has been destroyed, but for me only it remains standing." She expresses her great devotion to her husband and begs him to return.

II. The second letter is from Phyllis, queen of Thrace, to Demophoon, a son of Theseus. On his way home from Troy, Demophoon had stopped at Thrace, where Phyllis fell in love with him. When he left, he promised to come back to her in a month and to marry her, but he has not returned. Phyllis reproaches her faithless lover, threatening to commit suicide and to have the tale of his betrayal inscribed on her tomb.

III. Briseis tearfully tells Achilles that she has heard he intends to sail for Greece, leaving her behind. Since Agamemnon now regrets his anger and will make amends to Achilles, she begs Achilles to return to battle. Because Agamemnon has unjustly taken Briseis from Achilles, she feels she was the cause of Achilles' wrath; now she begs him to allow her to soothe his anger.

IV. Phaedra expresses her passion for her stepson Hippolytus, an unlawful love, which she accepts as her destiny. Her ancestor Europa was loved by Jupiter, who came to her in the form of a bull. Pasiphae, Phaedra's mother, loved a bull; her sister Ariadne helped Theseus, whom she loved, to find his way in the Labyrinth, and then was deserted by him. Phaedra tells Hippolytus that Theseus, his father and her husband, now prefers his friend Pirithous to both of them, and she tries to convince the young man that he owes his father no loyalty. Her final argument in this attempt to persuade Hippolytus to respond to her love is that the only real virtue is pleasure. Euripides tells their story in *Hippolytus.*

V. The nymph Oenone writes to Paris, who was her husband before he deserted her for Helen. Scornfully she asks him if his new wife will permit him to read the letter. She reminds him of their pleasures of the past and prays that Helen may suffer as she has. Despite Paris' cruelty, Oenone remains faithful to him.

VI. On his way to Colchis to obtain the Golden Fleece, Jason, the leader of the Argonauts, stopped at Lemnos, where he stayed for two years and became the lover of Queen Hypsipyle, promising to return and marry her. Now she has heard that he has captured the fleece and gone off with Medea. Hypsipyle writes of her anger and her love. She is certain that Medea has won Jason by her magic powers and wonders how he can love such a woman. Hypsipyle tells Jason that she has borne him twin sons, then prays that Medea may endure desertion and exile.

VII. Dido writes to Aeneas as he leaves Carthage. Despite the fact that Ovid is obviously influenced by Book IV of the *Aeneid*, his Dido is very different from Vergil's. Whereas the Dido of the *Aeneid* is a tragic and noble woman, the Dido of the *Heroides*, like the Scylla of the *Metamorphoses*, is a pathetic and lost woman. She accuses Aeneas of deceitfulness, yet pleads with him to remain with her. She will accept him on any terms; if he is ashamed to call her his wife, she will be his "hostess." Aeneas' sword is in her lap as she writes, and she plans her suicide. On her tomb will be inscribed: "Aeneas furnished the cause of her death and the sword;/ Dido died by her own hand."

VIII. Hermione, the daughter of Menelaus and Helen, writes to her beloved Orestes, begging him to claim her as his bride and take her away from Pyrrhus (Neoptolemus), the son of Achilles, whom Agamemnon has forced her to marry. Her grandfather Tyndareus had given her to Orestes, so his is a legal right. Her story is told in Euripides' ANDROMACHE.

IX. Deianira writes to her husband Hercules, who has just conquered Oechalia. She is grateful for her husband's victory, but is saddened by rumors that he has fallen in love with the princess Iole. As she expresses her anger at Hercules' past and present infidelities, she learns that Hercules is dying on Mount Oeta, poisoned by a cloak containing the blood of the Centaur Nessus, which Deianira has sent him in the belief that it would work as a love charm to bring him back to her. Sophocles' *The Women of Trachis* also treats this story.

X. Ariadne, left behind by Theseus on the island of Naxos, writes of her sorrow, her longing for him, and her hope that he will return. She reminds him of how she helped him to find his way within the Labyrinth and to slay her brother, the Minotaur. Now, alone on Naxos, she cannot return to her home and thinks only of death.

XI. Canace writes to her brother Macareus, with whom she has had an incestuous relationship. When their father Aeolus discovered this relationship and the baby Canace had borne, he had the child exposed and sent Canace a sword, a suggestion that she take her own life. Canace begs her brother to bury their child with her and to remember her.

XII. Medea writes to Jason, who has deserted her and their two sons to marry Creusa, daughter of the king of Corinth. Like the Nurse at the opening of Euripides' *Medea,* Ovid's Medea wishes Jason and the Argonauts had never come to Colchis to seek the Golden Fleece. Medea tells of her passionate love for Jason, which drove her to deceive her father and murder her brother in order to help Jason accomplish his mission. Her letter reveals Medea's violent anger at Jason and the intense love she still feels for him as she pleads with him to return to her. Ovid is influenced not only by Euripides but by Apollonius Rhodius' *Argonautica.* The figure of Medea obviously fascinated Ovid; his portrait of her in the *Metamorphoses* is a moving one, and he wrote a play *Medea,* of which only two lines remain. Seneca's *Medea* is clearly influenced by Ovid's characterization of her in the *Heroides.*

XIII. Laodamia writes to her husband Protesilaus, who is detained with the Greek fleet at Aulis, to warn him that there has been a prophecy that the first Greek to land on the soil of Troy will die. She expresses her love and begs her husband to take care of himself for her sake. See *Iliad* ii, 698–702.

XIV. Hypermnestra was the only one of Danaus' fifty daughters who would not obey her father and kill her husband, one of the fifty sons of Aegyptus, Danaus' brother. For this disobedience her father imprisoned her, and now she writes from her cell to her husband Lynceus that, despite her chains, she does not regret her disobedience. Aeschylus tells the story of the Danaidae in *The Suppliant.*

XV. A legend existed that Sappho had fallen in love with a boatman of Mytilene, Phaon, and, when he rejected her, she leaped from the rock of Leucas, off the coast of Epirus. Sappho weeps as she writes of her passionate, unrequited love and says that a naiad came to her and revealed that she could rid herself of her passion by leaping from the Leucadian rock.

XVI. Paris writes to Helen, declaring his love. He tells her of his past as a shepherd on Mount Ida and of his choice of Venus as the most beautiful of the three goddesses. His reward for this decision is the opportunity to love Helen, the most beautiful of women. Paris begs Helen to allow him to visit her at night. Surely her husband Menelaus, who has left Sparta for Crete, would not object to their love, because by his absence he has given his consent.

XVII. Helen responds angrily to the above letter, calling Paris shameless. She admits that she does love him, but fears the destruction this love may bring about.

XVIII. Leander writes from Abydus to his beloved Hero, a priestess of Aphrodite at Sestos. Usually Leander swims across the Hellespont to see Hero at night, but because of the stormy seas he has been unable to go to her for seven nights. He writes of his despair and his longing for his beloved, telling her he must come to her soon and asking her to hold up the lighted torch which guides him.

XIX. Hero responds to the above letter, telling Leander how impatient she is to see him. Though she urges him to come to her, she fears for his safety.

XX. Acontius, a young man from Ceos, writes to Cydippe of Athens, whose pledge to marry him he obtained by a trick. When Cydippe was in the temple of Diana at Delos, Acontius threw before her an apple on which was inscribed a pledge to marry Acontius. Cydippe read the words aloud and thus vowed to marry him. Since Cydippe has been ill, Acontius fears that Diana is punishing her for her delays in fulfilling this vow.

XXI. Cydippe replies to the above letter, telling Acontius of how ill she is and expressing the fear that Diana has caused her illness.

Hesiod (Hesiodos). Greek poet (eighth century B.C.). His father was born in Cyme in Aeolis, but since, as a trader and possibly a farmer, he found it impossible to support himself and his family, he left Cyme and went to Ascra, near Thespiae in Boeotia. Hesiod and his brother Perses were born in Cyme or in Ascra. After the death of their father the brothers were each to inherit half of his farm. By bribing the rulers of Thespiae, Perses managed to obtain the larger share. An impractical, lazy man, Perses finally lost his inheritance and was reduced to poverty, whereas Hesiod worked conscientiously as a farmer. According to the *Theogony* ll. 22–23, it was while he was taking care of his sheep on Mount Helicon that the Muses came to him and inspired him to write *Works and Days.* Though there is no certainty about any of the details of his life or his death, most scholars accept the traditional account that Hesiod was murdered and buried at Oenoe.

The dates of Hesiod's life and work are unknown, but it is generally accepted that he flourished during the eighth century B.C. Most ancient authorities assumed that Hesiod was the author of WORKS AND DAYS, the THEOGONY, the *Catalogue of Women,* and the *Eoeae,* which may have been part of the *Catalogue;* however, modern scholars are doubtful about the authorship of the *Theogony,* which some think was written a century after *Works and Days,* and about that of the fragmentary *Catalogue* and the *Eoeae.* Other poems attributed to Hesiod may have been interpolations into the *Catalogue;* this is certainly true of the *Shield of Heracles,* which was written by an imitator of Hesiod. Others which probably were interpolations into the *Catalogue* are the *Epithalamium of Peleus and Thetis,* the *Descent of Theseus into Hades,* the *Suitors of Helen,* the *Daughters of Leucippus,* and the *Marriage of Ceyx.* Poems similar to *Works and Days* and attributed to Hesiod survive in brief fragments: *Precepts of Chiron, Great Works, Idaean Dactyls,* and *Astronomy.*

Hestia. In Greek mythology, the daughter of Cronos and Rhea and the guardian of the hearth.

Hiero (Hieron). See SYRACUSE; XENOPHON.

Hiketides. See THE SUPPLIANTS.

Hipparchus (Hipparchos). See ATHENS.

Hippeis. See THE KNIGHTS.

Hippias. See ATHENS.

Hippias Major. A dialogue by PLATO named for Hippias, a learned sophist of Elis. Socrates reveals the superficiality of Hippias' knowledge. The dialogue deals with the nature of the beautiful.

Hippias Minor. A dialogue by PLATO named for Hippias, a learned sophist of Elis. The dialogue deals with the relationship between knowledge and virtue.

Hippolyta (Hippolyte). The queen of the AMAZONS, who bore Hippolytus to Theseus.

Hippolytus (Hippolytos). In Greek mythology, the son of Theseus by Hippolyta or Antiope. For his story see Euripides' HIPPOLYTUS, Ovid's HEROIDES IV, and Seneca's PHAEDRA. In some myths Hippolytus is brought back to life through the intervention of Artemis, which suggests to many scholars that he was originally a year god, like Adonis and Dionysus, whose death and rebirth represent the seasonal cycle of the earth.

Hippolytus (Hippolytos). A tragedy (428 B.C.) by EURIPIDES. Translations: in prose, E. P. Coleridge, 1891; in verse, Arthur S. Way, 1912; in verse, Gilbert Murray, 1911; in prose, Augustus T. Murray, 1931; in verse, David Grene, 1942; in verse, Philip Vellacott, 1953.

MYTHICAL BACKGROUND. Theseus was the son of Aegeus, king of Athens (or, according to another account, of the god Poseidon), and of Aethra, daughter of Pittheus, king of Troezen. Theseus lived an adventurous and heroic life and became king of Athens and of Troezen. One of his mistresses was Hippolyta, queen of the Amazons (in other versions of the myth it is Antiope, the sister of Hippolyta), who bore him a son, Hippolytus. Theseus married Phaedra, daughter of King Minos of Crete, and brought her to live in Troezen. With them lives Hippolytus, who despises women and love, and is entirely devoted to hunting. Phaedra has fallen in love with Hippolytus and, in spite of all her efforts to restrain her feelings, has become sick with passion and despair.

SCENE. Before the royal palace at Troezen; on one side is a statue of Aphrodite and on the other a statue of Artemis.

SUMMARY. The goddess Aphrodite enters and proudly speaks of her vast power and her capacity to destroy those who do not worship her. Among these is Hippolytus, who scorns Aphrodite's sphere—love and marriage. Artemis, the goddess of chastity and of hunting, is his favorite. Aphrodite declares she will make Hippolytus pay for his disrespect this very day. She made her initial preparations long ago when she afflicted Phaedra, the wife of Theseus, with love for the boy even before she came to Troezen. Since she has been in this land, Phaedra has suffered the pains of unexpressed love. No one knows what troubles her. Today Aphrodite will reveal Phaedra's love for Hippolytus to Theseus, and the goddess will bring about the deaths of Phaedra and Hippolytus.

As Aphrodite disappears, Hippolytus enters with his Attendants. They approach the altar of Artemis, where they place a wreath. Ignoring Aphrodite's altar, Hippolytus praises Artemis, declaring he will worship her all his life. The Leader of his Attendants advises Hippolytus not to neglect so important a deity as Aphrodite, but Hippolytus pays no attention to his warning.

After Hippolytus and his Attendants enter the palace, the Chorus of Troezenian Women enters, singing of Phaedra's sick despair and wondering whether it results from possession by a god, jealousy over some secret love of Theseus, bad news from her home in Crete, or the pains of pregnancy. Soon Phaedra is led out to a couch by the Nurse and other attendants. The Nurse exclaims over Phaedra's strange illness, for which she can find no cure, while Phaedra talks wildly, wishing she were at a spring in the woods or in the mountains. When she realizes she is speaking of the places in which Hippolytus hunts, she becomes fearful of revealing her feelings. The Nurse questions Phaedra as to the cause of her illness until Phaedra's need to express her conflicting feelings becomes stronger than her sense of honor and her family pride, and she reveals her love for Hippolytus. The Nurse and the Chorus are shocked by the revelation, and Phaedra herself is deeply ashamed. She despises women who have been faithless to their husbands, and she prefers death to being driven to dishonor by her love for Hippolytus. The Nurse, frightened by Phaedra's apparent decision to kill herself, calls her own earlier criticism foolish and now urges Phaedra to give up her high standards of conduct, which suggest pride, and to accept her feelings. Phaedra still tries to cling to her sense of honor and her conception of herself as a dignified and faithful wife, and she is horrified by the Nurse's proposal that they reveal her feelings to Hippolytus. In conflict between her passionate love and her sense of honor, Phaedra begs the Nurse to say no more, for she fears she will be influenced by the very plan she despises. The Nurse promises to cure Phaedra's illness with charms that she possesses, and she goes into the palace.

The Chorus sings of the power of love over man and the gods. Phaedra asks the women to be silent, for she hears loud voices within the palace and, frightened that the Nurse has revealed her secret, she tries to overhear what is being said. Finally Hippolytus comes out, followed by the Nurse. It is obvious that she has revealed Phaedra's love, for Hippolytus exclaims angrily that he has heard words unsuited to human lips. Cold and entirely unsympathetic to human feelings, Hippolytus recoils from the Nurse and Phaedra. The Nurse reminds him of his oath not to disclose the secret, but he scorns a promise made to those he considers wicked. He makes a prudish speech against women, blaming them for all the troubles of life, and then angrily goes off.

Phaedra reproaches the Nurse for having revealed her secret. Fearing that Hippolytus will tell Theseus about her shameful desires, Phaedra decides she can salvage her honor and that of her children only by killing herself and ruining Hippolytus, who, she imagines, will delight in her wretchedness. As Phaedra enters the palace, the Chorus sings of her unhappy plight, pitying the woman afflicted with the disease of love. The Nurse rushes out and announces that Phaedra has hanged herself. As the Chorus expresses its compassion, Theseus returns from a journey and demands to know the meaning of all the sounds of grief that are coming from the palace. The Leader of the Chorus tells him about Phaedra's suicide, but will not disclose her motive. The doors of the palace are opened, revealing Phaedra's body. As Theseus weeps and groans over the corpse of his wife, crying that she slew him when she slew herself, he notices a letter in her hand. When Theseus reads Phaedra's last words, which say that Hippolytus has violated her, he curses his son and asks his father, Poseidon, to grant one of the three prayers the god had allotted him: he prays that Poseidon kill Hippolytus that day. The Leader of the Chorus begs Theseus to cancel this prayer, but Theseus goes even further in expressing his hatred for the son he thinks has wronged him; he banishes Hippolytus from Troezen. Thus if Poseidon does not kill him, he must live wretchedly in exile.

At this point Hippolytus enters, greets his father, and asks the reason for his sorrow. Seeing Phaedra's body, Hippolytus questions Theseus about the cause of her death. Theseus angrily denounces the hypocrisy and corruption of man and finally accuses his son of having violated Phaedra. He sneers at Hippolytus' claims of chastity and, calling him a hypocritical villain, banishes him from all the lands under his dominion. Hippolytus' attempts to defend himself, his insistence that he has had no relations with women, and his oath that he is innocent do not convince Theseus. Hippolytus, tormented by his father's hatred, for a moment considers revealing the truth about Phaedra's love for him, but he is bound by his honor to keep his oath of secrecy. In despair he attributes his unhappy lot to his illegitimate birth; he partakes of the unhappy fate of his unfortunate mother, Hippolyta. When Theseus orders the servants to drag Hippolytus away, Hippolytus says he will leave only if his father expels him. Theseus replies that he will do so if Hippolytus does not leave, and goes into the palace. Sadly Hippolytus says good-bye to Troezen and leaves with his attendants.

After the Chorus sings of the unhappy fate of Hippolytus, the Messenger enters, asking for Theseus. He tells Theseus that his prayer has been answered: as Hippolytus and his friends rode by the seashore, his horses were terrified by a tremendous wave and a huge bull that came forth from it, bellowing loudly. Hippolytus could not control the frightened animals; his chariot was wrecked, and as he was dragged along, he was dashed against the rocks. He now lies dying.

Theseus consents to see his son, and the Messenger departs. Artemis now appears and reveals to Theseus the true story of Phaedra's love and Hippolytus' innocence. The goddess upbraids Theseus, who rashly misused one of the prayers Poseidon granted him. Hippolytus comes in, helped by his attendants. He cries out that he has been destroyed by his father, and moans in pain. Artemis comforts him, and then Theseus expresses his anguish in the wish that he could die for his son. Father and son are reconciled, and Hippolytus frees Theseus of the guilt of murder. As Hippolytus dies he bids a tender farewell to Theseus, who speaks of the dignity and nobility of his dead child.

COMMENTARY. Both Phaedra and Hippolytus are clearly the victims of excess, she of passion so intense that it overcomes her reason and honor, he of chastity carried to the point of prudery and inhuman coldness. Neither is capable of *sophrosyne*, one of the key words in the play: self-restraint, temperance, a sense of balance. Exclusive worship of either Aphrodite or Artemis, Euripides suggests, is self-defeating and destructive because it is inhuman.

Hipponax. Greek poet born at Ephesus, flourished during the middle of the sixth century B.C. Though very few fragments of his work remain, he was clearly a satirical poet, who wrote in iambics. His name is associated with the invention of the *choliamb* (scazon), or halting iambic, a regular iambic line with the exception of the last foot, which is a trochee or a spondee.

Histories (Historiae). Histories by TACITUS (between A.D. 104 and 109). Translations: Arthur Murphy, 1793; W. Hamilton Fyfe, 1912; G. G. Ramsay, 1915; Clifford H. Moore, 1925; Kenneth Wellesley, 1964.

SUMMARY. Originally the *Histories* consisted of twelve books and dealt with the period from January 1, A.D. 69 to the year A.D. 96, when Domitian died; however, only Books I–IV and part of Book V have survived. What remains of the *Histories* covers only the period up to August of A.D. 70. Book I deals with the reign of Galba, his proclamation that Piso was to be his successor, the defeat of Galba by the followers of Otho, and the murder of Galba and Piso. When Otho became emperor, the Romans, horrified by his past reputation and his outrageous treatment of Galba and his followers, feared the rule of a man notorious for homosexuality, extravagance, and cruelty. In Germany, moreover, the Roman legions had rebelled and were approaching Italy, led by Vitellius, whom they acknowledged as emperor. As Otho prepared to defend himself against them, the Roman people wondered how they could pray for the victory of either Otho or Vitellius, because the two men were equally shameless, cruel, and irresponsible. The only certainty was that the more corrupt of the two would win.

The first part of Book II deals with Vespasian, governor of Judea, and his son Titus, who, hearing of the civil war at home, united with Mucianus, governor of Syria, and awaited their own opportunity to seize power. In Italy the war between the followers of Otho and Vitellius concluded with the defeat of Otho, who took his own life. Vitellius, a cruel and arrogant man of extravagant tastes and insatiable appetites, now became emperor. Soon, however, he was forced into war by Vespasian, who had been declared emperor in Egypt and Syria.

In Book III the combat between the forces of Vespasian and Vitellius is described in some detail. One of the most remarkable passages in this book is the description of the cruelty and barbarism of the soldiers of Vespasian, who tortured the citizens and destroyed the city of Cremona. Vitellius was finally defeated and murdered on December 20, A.D. 69.

In Book IV Tacitus says that though the war ended with the death of Vitellius, peace was not yet restored. The victorious armies plundered Rome, unrestrained in their savagery. Vespasian, though now ruler, still remained in the East. Meanwhile the Batavians were being prepared for rebellion against Rome by their leader Julius Civilis. The revolt of the Batavians is described.

In Book V, after giving a brief history of the Jews, which contains many errors, and a description of their customs, Tacitus discusses Titus' campaign against Jerusalem. Then he continues his account of the revolt of the Batavians.

Homer (Homeros). Greek epic poet. Most ancient critics believed Homer was the author of the ILIAD and the ODYSSEY, though a few Alexandrian "separatists" suggested that two different poets had written the two epics. Alexandrian scholars also pointed out many interpolated lines and passages. In antiquity Homer was regarded with great reverence, not only as a poet but as a teacher and sage. Eight ancient lives of him remain, but these are of uncertain date and origin. Thomas W. Allen, who edited them (Oxford, 1912), concludes that "most of the information they contain does not reach the level of historical fact" (Thomas W. Allen, *Homer: the Origins and the Transmissions* [Oxford University Press, 1924], p. 14).

According to ancient tradition Homer was the son of Meles or Maion. Herodotus claimed that Homer lived four hundred years before his own lifetime, or about the middle of the ninth century. Seven cities that claimed fame as his birthplace were Smyrna, Chios, Colophon, Salamis, Rhodes, Argos, and Athens. It was thought that, as an old man, Homer, like Demodocus in the *Odyssey*, was blind. He was reputed to have written, in addition to the *Iliad* and the *Odyssey*, a satire called MARGITES, of which only six lines remain; BATRACHOMYOMACHIA (*The Battle of the Frogs and the Mice*), an extant mock epic; the *Thebais*, the *Epigoni*, the *Cypria*, and the *Nosti* of the *Epic Cycle*, only fragments of which are extant; and the HOMERIC HYMNS. His authorship of some of these poems was disputed by Herodotus and other ancient writers, and today none of these poems are regarded as his.

Actually nothing is known about Homer, and since the seventeenth century scholars have questioned his very existence. It has been suggested that his name—variously translated as "hostage," "comrade," "one who does not see," and "orderer"—merely represents the ideal poet and that the "attribution of both *Iliad* and *Odyssey* (and, incidentally, a number of other Epic poems) to Homer may, for all we know, mean no more than that a poet of this name was preeminent among those through whose hands the traditional poems passed towards the end of a long period of development" (Denys Page, *The Homeric Odyssey* [Oxford University Press, 1955], p. 137).

The "Homeric question"—the problem of whether the poet existed, whether he wrote either the *Iliad* or the *Odyssey* or both poems and whether the epics are merely edited collections of several separate lays or the result of centuries of creation by many minstrels who added to an original nucleus— has occupied scholars for the last two hundred years. Although the question of Homer's existence was first raised in seventeenth-century France, the problem did not assume significance until 1795, when F. A. Wolf, a German scholar, published his famous essay "Prolegomena ad Homerum," in which he suggested that the *Iliad* and the *Odyssey* were originally short lays that Pisistratus, the sixth-century tyrant of Athens, had ordered to be collected and arranged by editors. Wolf's essay, the first important document of the "analytic" school, inspired a great deal of speculation that drew on his evidence. Wolf himself has been justly called "the founder, not merely of the school which disintegrated Homer into the work of many hands, but of all modern Homeric scholarship" (Cedric Whitman, *Homer and the Heroic Tradition* [Harvard University Press, 1958], p. 3). In 1832 Gottfried Hermann proposed that the original *Iliad* dealt merely with the wrath of Achilles and that gradually poets added to this nucleus until the poem grew in size and scope. This theory was accepted and developed by George Grote in his *History of Greece* (1846–1856). According to E. R. Dodds, who summarizes the Homeric question in three brief and excellent essays (Maurice Platnauer, ed., *Fifty Years of Classical Scholarship* [B. H. Blackwell, 1954], pp. 1–16, 31–35), Grote's viewpoint "held the field at the turn of the century, and is still today the most widely accepted alternative to unitarianism." A significant variation on this theory was developed by U. von Wilamowitz-Moellendorff in *Die Ilias und Homer* (Weidmann, 1916). His position is that Homer took up the work of earlier poets, added to it, and adapted it to his own purposes; then his poem was similarly treated by his successors.

Most members of the analytic school agree that the *Odyssey* results from the combination of various versions of Odysseus' return and vengeance and that the story of Telemachus was not included in the original version. However, Dodds says, "it has often been remarked, even by analysts, that the *Odyssey* for all its discrepancies bears, much more than the *Iliad*, the impress of a single mind" (p. 8).

Early in the twentieth century the analytic school was severely criticized by scholars who returned to the view that a single poet had written the *Iliad* and the *Odyssey*. Among the earliest of the twentieth-century unitarians were J. A. Scott, whose book *The Unity of Homer* (University of California Press, 1921) emphasizes Homer's originality rather than the traditional elements discovered by the analysts, and J. T. Sheppard, who based his argument in

The Pattern of the Iliad (Methuen, 1922) on the structural unity of the poem. Most contemporary unitarians, however, concede that the poet who wrote the *Iliad* and the *Odyssey* used traditional stories, folk tales, historical material, traditional language, epic formulas, and conventional meter. They also agree that Homer's poems are based on earlier lays, going back even to Mycenaean times, and that interpolations written earlier and later than the *Iliad* and the *Odyssey* are contained within them, but they insist that the internal unity of structure, theme, and character suggests a principal single author of each poem. Though they hold a great variety of opinions, most modern unitarians believe that one poet was the principal author of each poem but that two different poets are the authors of the *Iliad* and the *Odyssey*.

The best-known unitarians are T. W. Allen (*op. cit.*), C. M. Bowra (*Tradition and Design in the Iliad* [Oxford University Press, 1930]), Cedric Whitman (*op. cit.*), H. T. Wade-Gery (*The Poet of the Iliad* [Cambridge University Press, 1952]), W. J. Woodhouse (*The Composition of Homer's Odyssey* [Oxford University Press, 1930]), Rhys Carpenter (*Folk Tale, Fiction, and Saga in the Homeric Epics* [University of California Press, 1946]), and Denys Page (*op. cit.*). Whitman, who regards the idea that Pisistratus is responsible for the first collection of the "scattered remains of Homer's poetry" as pure "legend" (pp. 66–67), says that the *Iliad* is a "profoundly personal creation" (p. 9). C. M. Bowra also bases his conclusion that the *Iliad* is primarily the work of one poet on the poem's "unity of character and style, its dramatic impetus and high imaginative life" (p. 270). "As a man [Homer] may elude us, but as a poet we know him and catch his individual utterance" (p. 9).

Commentators on the *Odyssey* who belong to the unitarian group, yet emphasize Homer's dependence on earlier sources and the inclusion of later material in the poems, are Woodhouse, Carpenter, and Page. Woodhouse showed how deep-sea yarns, folk tale motifs, and the saga of Odysseus are unified in the Odyssey by a single poet. Page also discusses the complexity of the composition of the *Odyssey*, indicating that the central plot of the poem, "the folk-tale of the Returning Hero," has been "transferred to a person believed to be historical, Odysseus. . . . Into the framework of the main theme, the folk-tale of the Returning Hero, are fitted certain other folk-tales which, before their inclusion in the story of Odysseus, had nothing whatever to do with that theme" (pp. 1–2). Moreover, he convincingly develops a thesis suggested by earlier scholars that the story of Odysseus is interwoven with that of Jason and the Argonauts. Further complications arise because the poet of the *Odyssey* combines different versions of one folk tale and adds features of other unrelated tales to create a new story. Page, along with other contemporary scholars, believes that the poet of the *Odyssey* lived in a later time and in a different place from the poet of the *Iliad*.

The study of sources and interpolations has thus led most scholars back to acceptance of a single poet who shaped and revitalized traditional material.

Either as author of the *Iliad* or the *Odyssey* or of both poems, Homer is regarded by most classicists today as the creator of the ancient epic. It is probable that he lived some time during the eighth or ninth century B.C., the ninth century being the more commonly accepted. It is almost certain that he was an Asiatic Greek, but there is no agreement on his birthplace. The texts of the *Iliad* and the *Odyssey* were derived originally from Athenian versions, probably of the sixth century. These in turn were edited during the second century B.C. by the Alexandrian scholars Aristophanes of Byzantium and Aristarchus of Samothrace. The texts of the poems existing today are based on the editions of Aristarchus. (See *A Companion to Homer*, ed. Alan J. B. Wace and Frank H. Stubbings [Macmillan, 1962].)

Homeric Hymns. Invocations in dactylic hexameter to various gods. The hymns are mainly *prooemia*, or preludes to the recitations of rhapsodists (minstrels). The five longer hymns, though technically regarded as preludes, probably were performed as independent works. The Hymns were written by members of the Homeric school, most of them during the seventh and sixth centuries B.C. Translations: in verse, George Chapman, 1624; in verse, Percy B. Shelley, 1821; in prose, John Edgar, 1891; in prose, Andrew Lang, 1899; in prose, Hugh G. Evelyn-White, 1914.

S U M M A R Y . I. *Hymn to Dionysus.* Only two brief fragments remain, which refer to the double birth of the god Dionysus, who came forth prematurely from his mother, Semele. His father, Zeus, sewed him in his thigh and kept him there until he was ready for his second birth.

II. *Hymn to Demeter.* This hymn tells of Hades' abduction of Persephone, the daughter of Demeter, the sorrow of Demeter at the loss of her child, and her search for information about her. Demeter learns from Helios that Hades abducted Persephone. In anger, Demeter leaves Olympus and, taking the form of an old woman, comes to Eleusis, where the daughters of King Celeus ask her to nurse Demophoön, their brother. Before she leaves Eleusis, Demeter reveals her identity to the people, instructing them to honor her by building a temple. In vengeance for the loss of her child, for whom she yearns, Demeter causes the earth to be barren. Zeus prevents her from destroying all mankind with famine by ordering Hermes to lead Persephone back to her mother. Hades, however, has tricked Persephone into eating pomegranate seeds, so she is forced to return to him for one third of every year. Grateful that she may have her daughter for two thirds of the year, Demeter makes the earth fruitful again. Moreover, she establishes the Eleusinian Mysteries to commemorate her suffering. If man wishes peace in the world of the dead, he must know the rites of Eleusis.

III. *Hymn to Apollo.* There are two parts, originally separate and probably written at different times: (1) a hymn to Delian Apollo and (2) a hymn to Pythian Apollo. The Delian Hymn tells of the birth of Apollo. His mother, Leto, after traveling to many cities seeking a place to bear her son, is joyously received by the island of Delos. After nine days of labor, Leto bears Apollo. As soon as the god tastes nectar and ambrosia, he says that the lyre and the bow will be his, and he will make known to men the will of Zeus through prophecy. Apollo is loved and honored in Delos, where he is constantly praised in songs and festivals.

The Pythian Hymn tells of how Delphi became the home of the oracle of Apollo. After leaving Olympus, Apollo wanders all over the earth, looking for a place for his oracle. When he comes to the spring of Telphusa, he wishes to establish his oracle there, but the nymph of the spring tells him to go to Pytho. In Pytho, Apollo must first kill a dragon. After accomplishing this feat, he is called Pythius, and builds his temple. However, he returns to Telphusa and stops the spring's waters for not revealing the presence of the dragon at Pytho. Apollo then takes the form of a dolphin and guides the ship of some Cretans from Cnossos to Crisa. There he identifies himself as the god Apollo. After building an altar in his honor, the Cretans accompany him to Pytho, where Apollo establishes them as priests in his temple.

iv. *The Hymn to Hermes.* This is the most widely known of the Homeric Hymns. The poet asks the muse to sing of Hermes, the son of Zeus and Maia, the nymph who lived in a cave. There Hermes was born at dawn. On the very day of his birth, Hermes creates the first lyre from a tortoise shell, ox-hide, and sheepgut. Then he plays and sings of the love of Zeus for Maia and of his own birth. Later in the day Hermes steals the cattle of the god Apollo (the plot of Sophocles' *Ichneutai*). When Maia scolds him for the theft, Hermes defiantly says he will steal more of Apollo's possessions. Apollo soon discovers that the infant Hermes has stolen his cattle and threatens to thrust him into Tartarus. Hermes, of course, denies the theft, arguing that surely a newborn child could not accomplish such a deed. Apollo laughs at the cleverness of the newborn god of deceit and tricks. Finally Apollo and Hermes go to Olympus to ask their father, Zeus, to settle their dispute. Apollo tells Zeus how Hermes stole his cattle and then pretended to be innocent. Hermes declares that he is incapable of deceit and too young and frail to steal from Apollo. Zeus knows the nature of Hermes too well to be taken in by him, so he orders Hermes to guide Apollo to the cattle he has hidden. At first Apollo is very angry at his young brother, but when Hermes plays the lyre and sings for him, Apollo declares that the song is as valuable as fifty cows. He expresses his great love for the lyre, and Hermes presents it to him as a gift. In return Apollo gives Hermes a shining whip that signifies that he has power over herds and also offers him some knowledge of divination. Zeus, approving of the friendship of the two gods, also appoints Hermes messenger to Hades.

v. *Hymn to Aphrodite.* Though Aphrodite has no power over Athene, Artemis, or Hestia, who are not concerned with love, she has conquered all the other gods and all men, animals, fish, and birds through her ability to inspire passion. Even Zeus is subject to Aphrodite's spell and falls in love with mortal women. To prevent Aphrodite's feeling superior to the other gods, Zeus decides that she must endure the experience of a mortal love, and he causes her to desire Anchises, a handsome young shepherd, whom she finds tending his flocks on Ida. Aphrodite goes to him in the form of a maiden, and only after they have made love does she reveal that she is the immortal Aphrodite. She promises Anchises that they will have a glorious son, Aeneas, who will rule the Trojans. Ashamed of her love for the mortal Anchises and warning him not to boast of his conquest, she goes off to Olympus.

VI. *Hymn to Aphrodite.* This hymn celebrates her beauty and her birth in Cyprus.

VII. *Hymn to Dionysus.* This hymn tells of how the god is seized by pirates and forced to board their ship. When the pirates cannot bind him, the helmsman realizes he is a god, but the others do not heed his warning. Dionysus causes wine to stream all through the ship and a vine to grow from the sail. Dionysus then takes the form of a lion and seizes the leader. The frightened sailors jump overboard and are transformed into dolphins. Only the helmsman is saved by Dionysus.

VIII. *Hymn to Ares.* The hymn praises the strength and courage of Ares and asks for his help in avoiding both cowardice and cruelty.

IX. *Hymn to Artemis.* The hymn salutes the goddess of the hunt.

X. *Hymn to Aphrodite.* This hymn salutes Aphrodite and her gifts.

XI. *Hymn to Athene.* The hymn salutes the goddess of war.

XII. *Hymn to Hera.* The hymn salutes the beautiful queen of the gods, wife and sister of Zeus.

XIII. *Hymn to Demeter and her daughter Persephone.*

XIV. *Hymn to the Mother of all gods and men.*

XV. *Hymn to Heracles.* The hymn salutes the son of Zeus and Alcmena, the strongest man on earth, who once performed many difficult labors and now lives peacefully in Olympus, married to Hebe.

XVI. *Hymn to Asclepius.* The hymn salutes the son of Apollo, Asclepius, as a healer who comforts men.

XVII. *Hymn to the Dioscuri.* This hymn salutes Castor and Polydeuces, children of Leda and Zeus.

XVIII. *Hymn to Hermes.* This hymn salutes the son of Zeus and Maia.

XIX. *Hymn to Pan,* the son of Hermes. Pan, who has goat's feet and horns, dances with the nymphs in the woods and mountains. In the evenings he plays lovely songs on his pipes made of reed.

XX. *Hymn to Hephaestus.* This hymn salutes the god of crafts and skills.

XXI. *Hymn to Apollo.* This hymn salutes all that sing, even the swan.

XXII. *Hymn to Poseidon,* the god of the sea and the Earthshaker. He is asked to help those who travel by sea.

XXIII. *Hymn to Zeus.* This hymn salutes the lord of the gods.

XXIV. *Hymn to Hestia.* She cares for the house of Apollo.

xxv. *Hymn to the Muses, Apollo, and Zeus.* All music comes from Apollo and the Muses, and all kings descend from Zeus.

xxvi. *Hymn to Dionysus,* son of Zeus and Semele. This hymn tells how the nymphs cared for the god and reared him in a cave in Nysa. When he was grown, Dionysus became the leader of the nymphs.

xxvii. *Hymn to Artemis,* goddess of the hunt. This hymn tells of how, after hunting, Artemis goes to the home of her brother Apollo at Delphi, where she leads the dances.

xxviii. *Hymn to Athene,* the strong virgin goddess, who protects cities. Athene came forth armed from the head of Zeus, and her presence frightened the Olympians.

xxix. *Hymn to Hestia and Hermes.* The hymn asks for their aid.

xxx. *Hymn to Earth.* This hymn says that earth brings forth all things and nourishes all.

xxxi. *Hymn to Helios,* son of Hyperion and Euryphaëssa, who were brother and sister. Helios rides in a chariot and shines on all. He is all brightness.

xxxii. *Hymn to Selene,* the moon. The hymn salutes the beauty of her light.

xxxiii. *Hymn to the Dioscuri,* Castor and Polydeuces. They aid ships, delivering them from storms at sea.

Homeridae. "Sons or followers of Homer," a clan of rhapsodists or minstrels in ancient Greece who regarded themselves as descendants of Homer and emulated the Homeric style.

Horace (Quintus Horatius Flaccus). A Roman poet, born at Venusia (Venosa) in Apulia in 65 B.C. His father, a freedman, gave his son an excellent education at Rome and at Athens. In his poetry Horace refers to his humble origins (*Odes* II, xx; III, xxx) and his gratitude to his father, who, though a poor man, gave his son the care and education ordinarily received only by the aristocracy (*Satires* I, vi). Horace left Athens to join the army of Brutus and fought in the battle at Philippi (42 B.C.), where the forces of Brutus and Cassius were defeated and the two leaders died. Returning to Rome, Horace discovered that his father had died and his land had been confiscated. He managed to obtain a position as one of the *scribae quaestorii,* clerks of the quaestors (financial officers), and at this time he began to write poetry. He soon met VERGIL, who became a lifelong friend and who, in about 38 B.C., introduced him to Maecenas, the wealthy and influential patron of the arts. The patronage of Maecenas provided Horace with freedom from economic stress and acceptance as a member of the group of artists encouraged by Octavian. In about 33 B.C. Maecenas gave Horace his Sabine Farm, near Tibur, which has become a symbol of a peaceful way of life and the satisfactions of simplicity and moderation. In 35 B.C. the first book of Horace's SATIRES was published; in 30 B.C. the second book of *Satires* and the EPODES, his earliest poems, appeared. Three books of ODES written between 33 B.C. and 23 B.C. appeared in 23 B.C.

They were followed by the first book of EPISTLES in 20 B.C. In 17 B.C. Horace's CARMEN SAECULARE was published, and in 15 B.C., the fourth book of the *Odes*. Book II of the *Epistles* and the *Epistle to the Pisos* (ART OF POETRY) were probably written toward the end of Horace's life, though there is no certainty about their dates. Horace died in 8 B.C.

In speaking of the various pleasures of men Horace says that for him it is a delight "to enclose words in feet" (*Satire* II, i), and this is perhaps the best description of him as a poet. Though Horace does not achieve the grandeur or the depth of Vergil or the passion of Catullus, so brilliant is his artistry that he is regarded as one of the greatest of the Latin poets and his influence has been vast. Horace's most moving poems are those in which he speaks of his image of himself as a poet who has "built a monument more durable than bronze" and therefore "shall never entirely die" (*Ode* III, xxx). The odes in general contain his finest poetry. The precision of his language, the grace of his phrases and sentences, the subtlety of his word order, and the exquisite harmony of his rhythms result in poems untranslatable in their lyric perfection. In the *Satires*, Horace says, his language is closer to prose than to poetry (I, iv), but even in this informal style his wit and urbanity suggest the highly conscious artist.

Critics have often remarked that Horace's skill lies in expressing the commonplace well, but this judgment is actually a bit superficial. Horace's accomplishment lies in stating with a rare precision a general truth about man, life, or art. The accuracy and subtlety with which he demonstrates the values of a simple existence or comments on the brevity of life reveal new facets of an old truth. Horace appeals not because he expresses what is common but because he discloses the significance, value, or pain of the ordinary that is at the same time universal. He does not probe deeply into human conflict or into individual experience of any kind; ever the man in society, he observes the world around him with wit and wisdom. His commentary on life has more insight than its smooth and elegant surface seems to suggest.

The influence of Horace was vast during the English Renaissance and neoclassical period. He was imitated by poets as different as Sir Thomas Wyatt, Robert Herrick, John Dryden, and Alexander Pope. In Dryden's preface to his *Religio Laici* he tells his readers that he has imitated the "style of [Horace's] *Epistles*", and Pope wrote a series of *Imitations of Horace*, poems in which, through a Horatian image, Pope realizes some of his greatest poetic gifts. Actually Horace's influence as a lyric poet, a satirist, and a critic is so pervasive that it is part of the very texture of European culture. See also SATIRE.

Hyacinthus (Hyakinthos). The son of Amyclas, a handsome young man whom both Apollo and Zephyrus (the west wind) loved. In *Metamorphoses* x, Ovid describes the accidental death of Hyacinthus by a discus hurled by Apollo. According to another version of the myth the jealous Zephyrus blew the discus, causing it to strike Hyacinthus. From his blood a flower bloomed, with petals bearing the letters *ai* (alas!), the lament of Apollo for the death of the young man he loved.

Hyades. Daughters of Atlas, nymphs who provided the earth with rain.

hybris (hubris). In ancient Greek literature, probably the violation of a law or the failure to recognize the limitations of mortality by regarding oneself as equal to the gods. The word occurs first in the *Iliad,* and is found in Sophocles, Euripides, Pindar, Aristotle, and other Greek writers. Usually translated as "insolence" or "pride," it is often regarded as a characteristic of the tragic hero. An interesting book on the subject is *Hubris, A Study of Pride* by Robert Payne (Peter Smith, 1960).

Hyginus, Gaius Julius. Roman scholar born in Spain. He was originally a slave, but was freed by the emperor Augustus, who appointed him head of a library he had recently established. An extremely learned man, Hyginus wrote on a variety of subjects—agriculture, bees, Vergil, geography, and history. None of his writings have survived; scholars agree that two extant works attributed to him are not his: *Fabulae,* sometimes called *Genealogiae,* which consists mainly of a collection of myths, and *De Astronomia,* parts of which also deal with myth.

Hylas. In Greek mythology, the page whom Heracles loved. When Heracles and Hylas accompanied the Argonauts, they stopped at Cios. Hylas went to obtain water and was drowned by the nymphs, who were infatuated with his beauty. Heracles refused to continue the journey with the Argonauts and stayed behind to search for Hylas. The story is told in Apollonius Rhodius' *Argonautica* and in Theocritus' IDYL XIII.

Hyllus (Hyllos). A son of Heracles. See THE WOMEN OF TRACHIS.

Hyperides (Hypereides). An Athenian orator; a contemporary of DEMOSTHENES and his associate in the anti-Macedonian party. Five of his speeches are extant. He was sentenced to death in 322 B.C. after the defeat of Athens in the Lamian War.

Hyperion. In Greek mythology, a Titan and the father of Helios, the sun. Hyperion himself was sometimes regarded as the sun.

Hypsipyle. In Greek mythology, the daughter of Thoas, king of Lemnos. When the women of Lemnos agreed to murder all the men on the island, Hypsipyle helped Thoas to escape. For her love affair with Jason see Ovid's HEROIDES VI, and Apollonius Rhodius' *Argonautica.*

I

Iacchos. See DIONYSUS and ELEUSINIAN MYSTERIES.

iambic poetry. Iambic poetry is written primarily in iambs, feet consisting of a short syllable followed by a long one; but it is usually varied with trochees, feet of a long syllable followed by a short one (see METER). Archilochus, the reputed inventor of iambic poetry, and his followers, Semonides of Amorgus and Hipponax of Ephesus, used iambics for the expression of personal feelings of anger, for satire, irony, and argument. The simple language of most early iambic poetry suggests that it derives from popular verse in this meter which was recited at rustic festivals in honor of the goddess Demeter. According to legend, the word *iambus* (*iambos*) comes from the name of the young girl Iambe, who amused Demeter with her jests, when in despair over the loss of her daughter Persephone, the goddess came to the home of Celeus in Eleusis. Iambics were used by Solon for political poetry, and became the meter of dialogue in drama. Iambics also became popular among the Romans of the first century B.C., and were used by both Catullus and Horace.

Iapetus (Iapetos). In Greek mythology, a Titan, a son of Uranus and Ge and father of Prometheus, Epimetheus, and Atlas.

Ibis. An elegiac poem by OVID. This poem, named for a bird regarded as sacred by the Egyptians, is an imitation of a lost poem by CALLIMACHUS. Ovid's *Ibis* is an attack on a former friend who has injured him and his wife.

Ibycus (Ibykos). Greek lyric poet (fl. mid-sixth century B.C.). Ibycus was born at Rhegium (Reggio di Calabria) in southern Italy. He spent some time at the court of Polycrates, tyrant of Samos, and wrote a hymn in triadic form (the earliest in existence) praising him. A papyrus containing a large fragment of this poem was found not long ago. Other fragments of Ibycus' work indicate that he wrote mainly choral lyrics like those of Stesichorus and love poems, but little of his work remains. A well-known legend about the death of Ibycus became the basis of a poem by Schiller. According to this story, on his way to Corinth Ibycus met his death at the hands of robbers. As he was dying he observed a flock of cranes flying above and declared that they would be his avengers. Later, in a theater at Corinth, one of the robbers noticed a flock of cranes and remarked on the "avengers of Ibycus"—thus revealing the murder, for which he and his companions were soon punished.

Icarus (Ikaros). See DAEDALUS.

Ichneutai (The Searching Satyrs, or The Trackers). Satyr play (c. 440 B.C.) by SOPHOCLES. Translations: in verse, R. J. Walker, 1919; in prose, Denys Page, 1942; in verse, Roger Lancelyn Green, 1957.

MYTHICAL BACKGROUND. The god Apollo has lost his cows, one of his best-known possessions, no doubt associated with his traditional identification with the flocks and pastures.

SCENE. Before the cave of the nymph Cyllene on the mountain Cyllene in Arcadia.

SUMMARY. Apollo, deeply disturbed because his cows have been stolen, offers a valuable reward to anyone who finds them. He tells of how he has been searching for them among many men and nations. Silenus, the leader of the Satyrs, offers to help in the search if he is rewarded. Apollo offers him gold and release from labor for him and his sons, the Chorus of Satyrs. Delighted with the offer, Silenus calls to his sons, who eagerly join in the quest.

Soon the Satyrs see the hoofmarks of cows on the ground, but as they listen for the sound of the animals, they hear a lyre and observe that the hoofprints are reversed. First they grow fearful, but then they respond to the music and begin to dance wildly. Silenus, unaware of the music, scolds them for giving up the quest, but soon he too hears the music of the lyre and becomes frightened. He wants to leave, but the other Satyrs insist that he stay.

The nymph Cyllene comes out of her cave and scolds the Satyrs for the noise they have been making. When they ask her what is the source of the beautiful music, she tells them a secret. Because Hera is very jealous of Zeus' other loves, Zeus hid with his beloved Maia in this cave. She bore the god a child, Hermes, who, now six days old, is being cared for by Cyllene in her cave. Hermes has grown miraculously in this time; already he is almost a youth. Today the young god invented the lyre, creating it from the shell of a tortoise, some ox-hide, and a piece of gut. The Satyrs praise the sweetness of the sound of the lyre; nevertheless, they suspect that Hermes is the one who stole Apollo's cattle, for they see newly tanned ox-hide in his lyre. Cyllene strongly objects to this idea, calling it ridiculous because Hermes is only six days old. She warns them against accusing a god, the child of Zeus, but the Chorus insists that it was Hermes who stole the cows, and Silenus demands that Cyllene bring forth the child.

The remainder of the play is missing. Roger Lancelyn Green has reconstructed it in his translation, using the Homeric *Hymn to Hermes* as the chief source of his ending (*Two Satyr Plays*, Penguin Books, 1957). According to Green's version Hermes, already a young man, comes in and denies that he is the thief. Soon Apollo appears and recognizes his half brother, Hermes. When Hermes begins to play the lyre, Apollo is overwhelmed with joy at the sound. Finally Hermes promises never again to play tricks on Apollo or to steal from him. He gives Apollo his lyre, praying that beautiful music may always issue from the god's hand. Apollo frees Silenus and his followers, and they go off dancing to the music of Apollo's lyre.

Ida (Ide). Mountain in Phrygia, where the judgment of Paris took place.

Idomeneus. In Greek mythology, the son of Deucalion and the grandson of Minos. Idomeneus led the Cretan forces against Troy. When, on the way home, a terrible storm arose, Idomeneus promised Poseidon that if he returned safely to his homeland, he would sacrifice to the god the first thing he encountered. It turned out that Idomeneus' son came to greet his father when he landed, and Idomeneus felt obliged to carry out his vow. Crete was punished for this sacrifice with a dreadful plague, and Idomeneus was banished from his land.

Idyls (Little Poems). Pastorals, love poems, poems of everyday life, eulogies, little epics, lyrics, and hymns, mainly in hexameters, by THEOCRITUS and others whose identity is unknown (the first half of the third century B.C.). Translations: in verse, M. J. Chapman, 1836; in verse, C. S. Calverley, 1868; in verse, Sir Edwin Arnold, 1869; in verse, J. H. Hallard, 1894; in prose, Andrew Lang, 1889; in prose and verse, J. M. Edmonds, 1912; in verse, J. A. Symonds, 1920.

S U M M A R Y . I. *Thyrsis.* Thyrsis, a shepherd, meets a goatherd as they are tending their flocks at noon in the pastures of Cos. Thyrsis praises the melodies that the goatherd plays on his pipe, and the goatherd replies that Thyrsis' songs are as lovely as the sound of water falling over a rock. He offers Thyrsis a reward if he will sing "The Affliction of Daphnis," a ballad of the country. Thyrsis agrees and sings this song about the perfect shepherd Daphnis, who loved all the wild creatures and was loved by them. Though he cherished the nymphs and the Muses, Daphnis was the victim of Aphrodite and died of love.

II. *The Spell.* Simaetha, a young girl, is neglected by her lover, Delphis. She decides to put a fire spell upon him, and, with the help of her maid Thestylis, she burns barley meal, bay leaves, a wax image, bran, an herb, and a fringe from Delphis' cloak on an altar to Hecate. As Simaetha carries out this strange rite to regain her beloved, she complains of the pain he is causing her. Then she sends Thestylis to smear the ashes, which represent the bones of Delphis, on his doorpost. When Simaetha is alone, she tells the Moon of how she fell in love with Delphis, who first wooed her and then deserted her.

III. *Serenade.* The poet, taking the form of a goatherd, asks his friend Tityrus to care for his goats while he goes off to court his sweetheart, Amaryllis. The rest of the poem consists of a song to the beautiful Amaryllis, expressing the lover's pain and longing.

IV. *The Herdsmen.* The shepherd Battus meets Corydon, who is tending the flock of Aegon. Milon, son of Lampriades, has arranged for Aegon to enter a boxing match at Olympia. Battus teases Corydon, who is rather dull and does not recognize the banter. Corydon then sings a song about Amaryllis, who now prefers Milon to Battus.

v. *The Goatherd and the Shepherd.* A goatherd, Comatas, and a shepherd, Lacon, meet as they are tending their flocks. They speak harshly to each other, and then Lacon, the younger of the two, challenges Comatas to a singing match. The woodcutter, Morson, agrees to act as judge, and Lacon stakes a lamb and Comatas a goat. The match begins: Comatas sings a couplet on a subject he chooses, and then Lacon tries to sing a superior couplet on the same theme. Mainly they sing of love. Comatas wins and receives Lacon's lamb.

vi. *A Singing Match.* Daphnis, a cowherd, has challenged Damoetas to a singing match. Daphnis sings first; addressing the Cyclops Polyphemus, he asks him why he does not respond to the love of the nymph, Galatea. Damoetas, pretending to be Polyphemus, replies that he is aware of her love, but he pretends not to care for her in order to make her jealous and thus make sure that she will agree to marry him.

vii. *The Harvest Home.* The poet and two of his friends, Eucritus and Amyntas, leave Cos to attend a harvest festival. On their way they meet Lycidas, a goatherd from Crete. Lycidas and the poet, who is called Simichidas, engage in a singing match. Lycidas sings first, beginning with hopes for a good journey for his friend Ageanax, who has gone to Mitylene, and then describing the celebration upon his arrival. Finally he evokes Comatas, a famous goatherd-poet, who while imprisoned was fed by the bees. Simichidas' song calls on Pan to bring Philinus to Aratus, who loves him. After the singing Lycidas gives his crook to Simichidas and goes on his way. Simichidas, Eucritus, and Amyntas enter the farm of Phrasidamus and participate in the harvest festival. This poem may be autobiographical: many scholars believe that Simichidas actually represents Theocritus and that several of the other figures in the poem can be identified as contemporaries of Theocritus. See PASTORAL POETRY.

viii. *A Singing Match.* (Not by Theocritus.) The cowherd Daphnis and the shepherd Menalcas engage in a singing match, which a goatherd judges. Most of the songs deal with love.

ix. *A Singing Match.* The poet asks two cowherds, Daphnis and Menalcas, to engage in a singing match, which the poet will judge. Daphnis begins with a song about the life of the cowherd, and Menalcas takes up the pastoral theme. The poet gives each a prize, and then he too sings a song.

x. *The Reapers.* Two reapers, Milon and his younger friend Bucaeus, speak as they work. Bucaeus is concerned only about his beloved, and Milon asks him to sing of his love to lighten his toil. After Bucaeus sings a love song, Milon sings a reaping song, calling on Demeter to bless their fields and make them prosper. Then he addresses the binders, threshers, reapers, and finally the steward.

xi. *The Cyclops.* The poet, in attempting to console his friend the physician Nicias of Miletus, who is unhappy in love, repeats for him the song that the Cyclops Polyphemus sang to his beloved, the nymph Galatea. The Cyclops, a grotesque and touching creature, tells of how he fell in love with Galatea and how she has continually shunned him. He knows he is ugly, but he tries to lure her by describing his wealth and the comforts and delights of his cave. Then Polyphemus chides himself for his complete absorption in the nymph who does not return his love. Without much conviction he urges himself to find another beloved.

XII. *The Beloved.* Grateful that his beloved has returned, the poet sings him a song that tells of their noble friendship.

XIII. *Hylas.* The poet tells his friend Nicias the story of Heracles' love for Hylas, the young page who accompanied him when he joined the Argonauts on their voyage to Colchis. On the way the ship stopped at Cios, and Hylas went to fetch water. The water nymphs fell in love with the boy and pulled him into the spring. The Argonauts left without Heracles as he searched frantically for Hylas. Heracles ordered that Hylas be worshiped at the spring.

XIV. *The Love of Cynisca.* Aeschinas meets his friend Thyonichus and tells him that he has quarreled with his beloved, Cynisca. The best cure for love, he says, would be to go overseas as a soldier. Thyonichus advises him to join the army of Ptolemy II.

XV. *The Women at the Festival of Adonis.* Gorgo visits her friend Praxinoë and invites her to go to the Festival of Adonis, which is held at the palace of Ptolemy II. They walk through the streets of Alexandria with two maids and then go into the palace. There the *Dirge* for Adonis is sung.

XVI. *The Graces.* The poet asks who will welcome the Graces in a material-istic age when men value only money. A wise man honors the poets. Theocritus is seeking someone who will welcome him as he comes accompanied by the Muses, and he asks that Hiero, general (and later king) of Syracuse, become his patron, promising to sing his glory. The poem ends with a prayer that the Graces will always be with him.

XVII. *An Encomium to Ptolemy* II. Theocritus praises Ptolemy II, Philadel-phus, by speaking of the deification of his father, Ptolemy I, Soter, son of Lagus, and by tracing the ancestry of the Ptolemies back to Heracles. He also speaks of the virtues of the mother of Ptolemy II, Berenice, who, like her husband, was deified. He speaks of the greatness and fertility of Egypt, the land the Ptolemies rule, and the industry and bravery of its people.

XVII. *The Epithalamion of Helen.* This is a song sung by twelve maidens in honor of the marriage of Menelaus and Helen.

XIX. *The Stealer of Honey.* (Not by Theocritus.) Eros complains to Aphro-dite that a bee stung his finger when he tried to steal a honeycomb. Aphrodite replies that since Eros causes such great hurts, surely he can defeat a little bee.

XX. *The Cowherd.* (Probably not by Theocritus.) A young cowherd angrily tells of how Eunica, a girl from the city, spurned him. He prays to Aphrodite that Eunica be forever alone.

XXI. *The Fishermen.* (Probably not by Theocritus.) As two poor old fisher-men lie in their cabin at night, one tells the other that he has had a dream in which he caught a golden fish. He promised to fish no more, but now he is worried about this oath. His friend interprets the dream to mean that fisherman's gold is to be found in the sea. Thus his oath is no more literal than is the golden fish.

xxii. *The Hymn to the Dioscuri.* The poet begins with praise of Castor and Polydeuces, the Spartan brothers of Helen, who became gods. Then he divides his song into two sections, the first about Polydeuces' heroic defeat of the great boxer Amycus and the second about Castor's glorious contest with Lynceus.

xxiii. *The Lover.* (Not by Theocritus.) The poem tells the story of an unhappy lover who committed suicide. His beloved, untouched by this suicide of his friend, was killed when a statue of the god of love fell upon him.

xxiv. *Little Heracles.* The poem tells of the great feats of the infant Heracles. Hera, who hated Heracles, sent two great serpents to kill him, as he slept. Heracles, who was only ten months old, awoke in time to destroy the serpents. The prophet Tiresias predicts to Alcmena, the mother of Heracles, the future heroism and glory of her son and suggests that she perform certain rites to avoid the enmity of Hera. Then the poet tells of how Heracles was taught to read, to use the bow, and to sing and play the lyre. He learned to box, to drive a chariot, and all the skills of warfare.

xxv. *Lion-killing Heracles.* (Probably not by Theocritus.) *Part I.* An old plowman describes to Heracles the vast farmlands of Augeas, king of the Epeians of Elis. He guides Heracles to the estate. Though he wonders about the lion skin in which Heracles is clad and the club he carries, the old man does not dare ask about them or even where Heracles has come from. On their way they encounter some dogs that the old man drives back with stones.

Part II. The poet describes the great herd of cattle that the Sun gave to his child Augeas. Augeas and his son Phyleus show Heracles the estate, and Heracles subdues the strongest bull they own.

Part III. Phyleus and Heracles set off for town. As they walk together Heracles tells Phyleus how he killed the Nemean lion.

xxvi. *The Bacchanals.* (Probably not by Theocritus.) A father whose son is to be initiated into the mystery religion of Dionysus tells the story of how Agave, inspired by Dionysus, killed her son, Pentheus. Euripides' *The Bacchae* also tells this story.

xxvii. *Familiar Conversation.* (Not by Theocritus.) This fragment tells of a singing match, but only part of one shepherd's song and the awarding of the prize remains. The song is in the form of a dialogue between Daphnis and his beloved, Acrotime.

xxviii. *The Distaff.* Theocritus addresses the distaff that he will give to the wife of his friend Nicias. The poem, which says that great love comes with this little gift, is to accompany the present of the distaff.

xxix. *Love Poem.* As two men drink together the older one expresses his love for the younger, urging him to enjoy life while he can and to form a love relationship with him like that of Achilles and Patroclus.

xxx. *Love Poem*. The poet, who is growing old, expresses the pain of love and urges himself to be temperate because he is no longer young.

Iliad, The (Ilias). Epic by HOMER, in twenty-four books of dactylic hexameters. Most authorities agree that the *Iliad* was written in the ninth century B.C. Translations: in verse, George Chapman, 1611; in verse, Alexander Pope, 1715–20; in prose, Samuel Butler, 1898; in verse, W. Marris, 1934; in prose, E. V. Rieu, 1950; in prose, Alston Hurd Chase and William G. Perry, 1950; in verse, Richmond Lattimore, 1951; in verse, Ennis Rees, 1963.

HISTORICAL BACKGROUND. Homer, an Asiatic Greek who lived around 850 B.C., reconstructs the glorious legendary and historical past of his people in the *Iliad* and the *Odyssey*. He sings of great events that had taken place in the twelfth century B.C., when the Achaeans, the most powerful tribe on the mainland of Greece, were the lords of the Mycenaean world. Homer tells of the Achaeans' exploits in war and of their relationship with their gods and their fellow men. It is not really possible to distinguish history from legend in the Homeric poems, but it is certainly probable that the Trojan War, the most significant event that the two epics record, did take place.

The ancient historians Herodotus, Thucydides, and Eratosthenes raised questions about the events, date, and causes of the Trojan War, but they did believe there was a war between the Greeks and the Trojans. According to Herodotus, Troy fell in 1250 B.C.; Eratosthenes thought the date was 1183 B.C., which has become the "traditional" date for the fall of Troy. During the nineteenth century many scholars attempted to show that the war was merely mythical, and some still hold this position today. The majority of contemporary scholars, however, agree that the Trojan War was a real event that brought about the destruction of one of the cities unearthed at the legendary site of Troy, and they provide both historical and archeological evidence for this conclusion.

Thomas W. Allen believes the war was a real event and that it was fought to remove "the last power which dominated the Asiatic coast and prevented settlement" by the Greeks. He suggests as evidence the fact that very soon after the fall of Troy large numbers of Greeks migrated to the islands and coasts of Asia Minor (*The Homeric Catalogue of the Ships* [Oxford University Press, 1921], pp. 173–177). Walter Leaf also believes in the "historical reality" of the Trojan War. Leaf says that some of the heroes of the Homeric poems were real people who actually fought in the war and that even the Trojan horse has a basis in reality. It may have been a "mechanical device" similar to the "wheeled towers familiar to the Assyrians, drawn up close to the walls and disgorging upon them their hidden freight of warriors." The Trojan War, according to Leaf, resulted from the Achaean desire for expansion, for colonization, and for trade routes through the Euxine or Black Sea (*Homer and History*

[Macmillan, 1915], pp. 4–31). Other scholars who hold much the same position are J. B. Bury in his *History of Greece* (3rd ed., rev. by Russell Meiggs, Macmillan, 1951) and Denys L. Page, who also believes that some of the Greek and Trojan leaders described by Homer were historical figures (*History and the Homeric Iliad* [University of California Press, 1959]). Alan J. B. Wace in "The Early Age of Greece," *A Companion to Homer* (ed. Alan J. B. Wace and Frank H. Stubbings, Macmillan, 1962), says, "In the light of archeological evidence there is nothing improbable in the picture of Agamemnon, king of Mycenae, heading a pan-Achaean host against Troy and a number of Asiatic allies." However, he goes on to say, "Though Troy fell, the success led to no Greek expansion" (p. 356). The report of the University of Cincinnati team that excavated Troy in the nineteen thirties substantiates some of these conclusions through archeological evidence, which indicates that the city archeologists label Troy VIIa endured war and destruction during the period generally accepted as that of the Trojan War (*Troy: Excavations Conducted by the University of Cincinnati 1932–1938* [ed. Carl W. Blegen with the collaboration of John L. Caskey and Marion Rawson, Princeton University Press, 1950]). See also Carl W. Blegen, *Troy and the Trojans* (Praeger, 1963). See also MYCENAE and TROY.

RELIGIOUS BACKGROUND. The Homeric gods possess the powers of natural forces; some of them, especially Zeus, enjoy the wealth and kingly position of a Mycenaean overlord. However, it is not this remote authority that makes them continually vital; it is rather their intense emotions and conflicts which reflect their essentially human characteristics and their suggestion of earlier, more primitive qualities beneath their smooth Olympian surface.

Zeus, the weather god who controls thunder, lightning, and clouds, and who rules the other gods, lives, like a Mycenaean king, in a great palace, while the lesser gods inhabit neighboring palaces, as did the Mycenaean nobles. Zeus' magnificence, his great authority, and his prophetic powers help to create the heroic tone of the *Iliad*, but his compassion for mortals, his huge capacity for sensual pleasure, his anger and even violence, his gentleness and his wisdom are far more important in the development of the complicated theme of the poem. There has been some question as to Zeus' omnipotence. For the most part he seems to have complete power over the affairs of gods and men. Yet there are times when he seems to be only the chief instrument of fate. In the *Iliad*, Zeus weighs the fates of the Greeks and the Trojans on his golden scales (VIII, 68–74), apparently to discover that the Trojans will at present be victorious, and later he again uses his scales to weigh the fates of Achilles and Hector and finds that Hector will be slain (XXII, 210–213). Though it has been said that this is merely a conventional means of suggesting his omniscience, the passages do seem to indicate Zeus' search for a knowledge of what must be, of fate itself.

That fate represents the inevitable, beyond even Zeus' control, is indicated also by Zeus' reluctant acceptance of the fact that his son Sarpedon must die.

When Zeus expresses his despair on foreseeing this event, Hera asks incredulously if he intends to prevent the death of a man doomed by fate. Zeus makes no such attempt; instead he weeps for the doom of his son (XVI, 431–461). In the *Odyssey*, Athene says that even the gods cannot shield someone they love from death, which is the common fate of all men (III, 236–238). Zeus is sometimes deceived by Hera, and Homer tells us (*Iliad*, XIX, 95) that Ate (moral blindness), a daughter of Zeus, once blinded Zeus himself. The other gods respect Zeus' power, but they do not always obey him.

Except for Hephaestus, who is lame, the gods are beautiful, and except for Ares, hated by Zeus for his savage and warlike nature, they are attractive and often humorous in their intense loves and hates. Although the gods are interesting in themselves, they are more so for their involvement in human affairs. Here they have an ambivalent role, for the gods are used by Homer both as literal presences and at the same time as externalizations of inner experiences. This use of the gods is perhaps clarified by an analogy with contemporary externalizations reflected in colloquial language. When we say, "I don't know what got into me," or "Something hit me," we literally mean, "I do not understand the strange thought or feeling which came forth from me." We externalize such thoughts or feelings because they seem alien to our usual selves—yet they are our own. When a Homeric god visits or "enters into" a hero we must assume the god *is* literally there, but he is also a representation of the hero's exceptional courage or wisdom or, in the case of Helen visited by Aphrodite, her desire for a man she both loves and despises. When in *Iliad*, IX, 702–703, Diomedes says that Achilles will once again fight when his heart bids him and a god urges him, he explicitly expresses this double quality. When Ares "enters into" a warrior he also represents the warrior's own feelings of courage and strength. When Athene comes to Telemachus in the first book of the *Odyssey*, she leaves him feeling more manly and bold. He has begun to feel the manhood inherent in him. Gods tend to come to those who deserve them. Thus Aphrodite is the goddess of Helen and Paris; Athene has a close and loving relationship with Odysseus. Athene and Odysseus understand and appreciate each other's wit and wisdom; they respect each other's capacity to deal with difficulties by means of a stratagem or a tall tale.

In the *Iliad* the gods intensify the magnificence of the heroes and add to the heroic quality of their exploits. Moreover, Zeus' compassionate commentaries on the struggles of mortals are one expression of the tragic theme of the poem. In the *Odyssey* the gods reflect the moral tone of the poem. They condemn the false Aegisthus; they support the good host, the suppliant, the honorable man. In both the *Iliad* and the *Odyssey* the gods are deeply involved in human affairs, but it is man who ultimately determines his own destiny. As Zeus says at the beginning of the *Odyssey*: "What a sad thing it is that men should blame the gods for their troubles when it is their own flaws which bring them suffering."

SOCIAL BACKGROUND. The society which Homer describes in the *Iliad* and the *Odyssey* is the Mycenaean one in the last period of its glory. Though the scene of the *Iliad* is mainly the battlefield of Troy, the poem does reveal certain features of the social structure of the Mycenaean world. In the opinion of Thucydides, the Greek princes did not follow Agamemnon to war because of their promise to Tyndareus (see *Mythical Background* of the *Iliad*), but because of his superior strength. Thucydides goes on to say that Agamemnon had a far stronger navy than the other princes, and fear was as much the motivation for their allegiance to him as was love (*The Peloponnesian War*, I, i, 9). There is no question that Agamemnon was the most powerful king in the whole Peloponnesus and that he ruled over the Achaeans, the dominant tribe of Greece during the thirteenth and twelfth centuries B.C. In the *Iliad* we are told that Agamemnon had one hundred ships, the largest fleet, that he was king of many isles and of all Argos, and that he ruled many lands besides Mycenae, among them Corinth, Cleonae, Orneiae, Araethyrea, Sicyon, and others.

Because Homer is concerned almost exclusively with the aristocracy, the accepted relationship between the king and the nobles who follow him is an important element in the *Iliad* and the *Odyssey*. The king or overlord in the Homeric world ruled over a society which was organized according to clans. Kinship was the unifying factor in this society. Villages were inhabited and run by clans, with a patriarch at the head, who had a great deal of power over the members of his family. Many of these clans formed a tribe, which constituted a kingdom; this in turn was part of a larger kingdom run by a powerful king or overlord like Agamemnon, who, in time of war, relied upon the allegiance of the noble heads of clans. The king (*basileus*), who lived in a palace on an acropolis, was regarded as descended from the gods, and his rule came from Zeus—yet he did not have exclusive power. Among the other nobles he was *primus inter pares*, first among equals. Any noble (for example, Achilles in Book I of the *Iliad*) could call an assembly, at which an important issue could be discussed. The king was not forced to accept the view of the majority of the nobles, but if he ignored it, as Agamemnon does in the *Iliad*, he did so at the risk of strong disapproval. Certainly Achilles' resentment of Agamemnon's tyranny indicates that the nobles did not regard the king's power as unlimited. Moreover, Agamemnon pays heavily in the *Iliad* for his stubborn resistance to reason.

The king's role as war lord was a significant one in a society in which wars were fought for booty, such as cattle, iron, gold, and other treasures, and for slaves. The booty or prizes taken in war were a sign of power and honor. Thus when Agamemnon demands that Achilles return the girl Briseis, who has been given to him as booty, he is depriving Achilles of his honor.

Because wealth and power in this society were often obtained through victory in battle, war in the *Iliad* is described as both the "bane of men" and "where men win glory." This ambivalence toward warfare, one of the most important features of the poem, is also reflected in the heroic code of the noble warriors in the *Iliad*. According to the heroic code the performance of a heroic deed offers man a chance to exceed the limitation of mortality, a chance to snatch from life a glory that defines it. This opportunity comes in a heroic contest in war, in which the hero often dies. Achilles' choice of a short, glorious life in battle over a long, peaceful, but inglorious one represents his acceptance of the heroic code.

Warfare in Homer, though destructive and hideous, is also personal, ceremonial, and aristocratic. Warriors are dressed in magnificent armor; before they fight they identify themselves and their backgrounds, often in long speeches; they exchanged gifts and vows of friendship when a contest is interrupted.

Ceremony involving gifts was important in many other phases of life in the Homeric world. When Agamemnon and Achilles are reconciled, Achilles is given many gifts of atonement (*Iliad*, XIX, 243–248). A bridegroom was expected to bring gifts of courtship. A guest, to whom one owed hospitality as a religious obligation, was always given a gift at parting. "Guest-friendship" involved more than gifts; it involved the protection of a stranger by the host and sometimes even a military allegiance between host and guest. It is one of the many relationships in Homeric society for which there are established rules and customs.

Though the *Iliad* reveals mainly the relationships and occupations of a society at war, suggestions of a more peaceful way of life also come through in the poem. For example, the shield of Achilles (XVIII, 480–608) depicts the pursuits of two cities, one at war and one at peace. In the peaceful city the people partake of a marriage feast, and a bride is led through the streets by the light of flaming torches. A traditional bridal song is sung. Dancing and the music of the lyre and the flute are described. We see land ploughed three times, laborers working on a king's estate, a vineyard, and a boy singing a harvest song.

The *Odyssey* reveals many more details of daily life and customs among the Mycenaean Greeks than does the *Iliad*. The palaces of Odysseus and Menelaus are well furnished with golden jugs and cups, silver basins, and handsome carved furniture. The palace of Menelaus is a magnificent one, gleaming with copper, gold, amber, silver, and ivory. To Telemachus it seems that the court of Zeus on Olympus must resemble this palace. Actually treasures found in the royal graves at Mycenae suggest the authenticity of Homer's description.

At these palaces guests were treated with ceremonious courtesy. Each guest was served at his own table; he was entertained by the minstrel and by groups of dancers and, at parting, was presented with valuable gifts. Even Eumaeus, the swineherd, knows how to treat a guest.

Women of the noble classes managed the household and themselves participated in the work. They spun and even took care of washing the clothes and linen of the household. The more tedious tasks were done by slaves. The noble princes took care of their estates, hunted, and participated in the assemblies and law courts.

MYTHICAL BACKGROUND. According to Homer the Trojan War was caused by Paris' abduction of Helen from her husband Menelaus, king of Sparta. He and his brother, Agamemnon, king of Mycenae and many other lands, then persuaded the other Greek leaders to join in an expedition against Troy. Accounts later than Homer explain that these leaders, who had been suitors of Helen before her marriage to Menelaus, were bound by an oath to Tyndareus, the husband of her mother, Leda (Helen herself was the child of Zeus and Leda), to come to the aid of Helen's husband if he should encounter any trouble through the marriage. Later versions of the story also trace the crime of Paris back to the marriage ceremony of Peleus and Thetis, to which all the gods and goddesses except Eris (Strife) were invited. To avenge this slight the goddess threw a golden apple inscribed "To the Fairest" among those present. When Hera, Athene, and Aphrodite each claimed the apple, Hermes, commanded by Zeus, led the goddesses to Mount Ida, where the shepherd Paris was asked to choose among the three the one who most deserved the apple. Hera offered to make him ruler of Asia, Athene promised him great fame in battle—but it was Aphrodite who won the apple, for she offered Paris the most beautiful woman as his wife. Insulted by Paris, Hera and Athene from this time on hated the whole Trojan race. Aphrodite sent Paris to Sparta, where he violated the religious laws of hospitality by stealing many treasures and taking Helen, the wife of his host, Menelaus. The Greek chieftains then united in their attack upon Troy. Homer shows how the Trojans, though despising Paris for his preoccupation with his lyre, his own handsome face, and love, nonetheless felt obliged to wage war on his behalf because he was the son of their king, Priam.

According to the *Palinodia* (recantation) of Stesichorus, a lyric poet (c. 640 B.C.–555 B.C.), Helen did not go with Paris to Troy. Only a phantom of Helen accompanied her lover, but the real Helen was taken to Egypt by the gods and kept there by King Proteus until Menelaus should come for her. This version of the story is developed by Euripides in his *Helen* and referred to in his *Electra*. Herodotus' version of the abduction is similar. In the *Persian Wars* (II, 113–116) he tells of being informed by an Egyptian priest that on the way home from Sparta a gale drove Paris' ship to Egypt. Here King Proteus scolded him for his violation of Menelaus' hospitality, kept Helen and the stolen treasures in Egypt awaiting Menelaus, and ordered Paris to leave Egypt alone. Herodotus believes that Homer knew this version of the story but discarded it because he considered it less suitable to epic poetry than the one he used. As evidence Herodotus offers Homer's reference in the *Iliad* to Paris' journeys to Egypt and Syria. Herodotus goes on (II, 118) to say that he questioned Egyptian priests as to the authenticity of the story of the Trojan War. According to their account, when the embassy of Greeks arrived at Troy to demand Helen and the treasures of Menelaus that Paris had stolen, the Trojans replied truthfully that both Helen and the treasures were held by King Proteus of Egypt. Though the Trojans were telling the truth, the Greeks did not believe them; they attacked Troy and conquered the city. However, even then they did not find Helen, and finally they sent Menelaus to the court of Proteus, where he found his wife. Herodotus accepts this version of the story as authentic.

In the *Iliad* and the *Odyssey*, Helen remains at Troy throughout the Trojan War. In the *Odyssey*, Nestor tells Telemachus of how, on Menelaus' journey home after the Trojan War, much of his fleet was destroyed and he was driven by a storm to Egypt. Menelaus himself informs Telemachus that he was detained in Egypt because he had not made proper offerings to the gods. His voyage to Egypt as reported by Homer is not involved with a search for Helen.

SUMMARY. *Book I.* Prior to the events of the poem, the Greeks have taken as captives two young women, Chryseis and Briseis. Chryseis has been given to Agamemnon and Briseis to Achilles. After the announcement of the subject—the wrath of Achilles, which brought innumerable disasters upon the Greeks—and the invocation to the Muse, Homer tells of how Chryses, father of Chryseis and a priest of Apollo, comes to ransom his daughter. Agamemnon refuses to return her, and to punish the Greeks for this refusal, Apollo sends a pestilence on them. At a council of the Greek leaders, called by Achilles, the prophet Calchas says that he will reveal the cause of the pestilence if Achilles will protect him against the wrath of Agamemnon, which the prophet fears his disclosure will evoke. Achilles promises to protect Calchas, who then reveals that the cause of the pestilence is Agamemnon's refusal to return Chryseis. Agamemnon's response to this revelation is anger at the prophet and a threat to take away the "prize" of another warrior because he is to be deprived of his own. When Achilles says that it is unjust to take back prizes already distributed, Agamemnon, concerned most for his own gratification and glory, says that he will take Briseis from Achilles. Greatly angered, Achilles is in conflict as to whether to draw his sword and kill Agamemnon or to restrain his wrath. Athene, catching hold of Achilles' hair, makes her presence known to him, though none of the other Greeks sees her, and persuades him to express his wrath only in words. Nestor attempts to make peace between Agamemnon and Achilles, but he is unsuccessful. Unfairly deprived of his prize, Achilles withdraws himself and his men from battle.

Talthybius and Eurybates, Agamemnon's heralds, come to Achilles' hut to take Briseis. The two young men are frightened of the great Achilles, but despite his anger at Agamemnon, Achilles is aware of the feelings of the heralds and comforts them, assuring them gently that he knows they are guilt-less. When they leave with the girl, Achilles sits down on the shore of the sea, weeping, and prays to his mother, the sea-goddess Thetis. He mentions the brief span of life allotted to him and says that Agamemnon has dishonored him. Thetis, coming from the sea like a mist, listens to her son's sorrows. Achilles asks Thetis to go to Olympus and beg Zeus to help restore his honor. Zeus, he says, will surely aid Thetis, because, with the help of the hundred-armed giant Briareus, she once rescued Zeus when Hera, Poseidon, and Athene were about to bind him. Achilles wishes Zeus to help the Trojans, so that the Greeks will be aware of the injustice to him. Thetis leaves him, promising to do as he asks.

Meanwhile, Odysseus takes Chryseis back to her home in Chryse and returns her to her father. After making an offering to Apollo, feasting, and singing beautiful hymns to the god, Odysseus and his men return to the camp.

When Thetis asks Zeus to give the Trojans strength so that her son can regain his honor, Zeus agrees to do so despite his fear of conflict with Hera, who supports the Greeks. After Thetis leaves, Hera approaches her husband, for she has guessed what Thetis has requested. Zeus and Hera begin to quarrel, but they are calmed by Hephaestus, the great craftsman of the gods, whose skill and artistry created the beautiful palaces of the gods, though his lameness is the object of their laughter.

Book II. In order to aid the Trojans, Zeus sends a misleading dream to Agamemnon, which urges him to lead the Greeks to battle. Encouraged by this dream, but fearing that his men are disheartened by ten long years of war, Agamemnon assembles them to put them to a test. He says that he is in favor of a return to Greece—and, to his dismay, his men agree unanimously. Through this reaction of the Greeks, Homer suggests their years of suffering. As the Greeks prepare to go home, Hera sends Athene down from Olympus to urge Odysseus to persuade the Greeks to remain at Troy. Odysseus helps to rally the troops, speaking gently to the nobles and angrily to the commoners. When Thersites, an ugly, lame man with a vicious tongue, attacks Agamemnon, Odysseus beats him.

When the assembly is recalled, Nestor advises that the troops be divided into their separate tribes, so that the warriors will be inspired to fight bravely for the glory of their tribes or clans. Then the chief warriors of the Greeks and Trojans are listed in two catalogues. [It is generally agreed that this passage was not written by Homer but by unknown authors and incorporated into the *Iliad*. Thomas W. Allen points out that the Catalogue "is in no sense an order of fighting or a scheme of encampment. It is a survey of a people, consisting of many nations or tribes, inhabiting a wide area, from the Ionian Sea to Rhodes, arranged in a geographical zone" (*The Homeric Catalogue of Ships* [Oxford University Press, 1921], p. 34). Allen considers the Catalogue the oldest Greek poem in existence (see EPIC). Most scholars agree that the Catalogue was regarded as an authoritative source of information about history, ancestry, and territorial rights, not only by Homer's contemporaries, but by post-Homeric Greeks, and it still has great historical interest as a source of information about significant figures and places.]

Book III. As the Greek and Trojan armies advance against each other,

Menelaus approaches Paris, who withdraws in fear. Hector scolds his brother, reminding Paris that he had had courage enough to steal the wife of Menelaus and implying that Paris' concern with the lyre, his handsome appearance, and love is contemptible. Hector denounces the Trojans for defending Paris and speaks of all the destruction Paris has caused. Paris admits his fault and agrees to engage in a contest with Menelaus. Whoever wins the contest will possess Helen and her treasures. Hector, delighted at Paris' agreement to fight, interrupts the battle and announces Paris' decision. He declares that the two armies are to cease fighting while these leaders contest. Menelaus agrees to the truce and the single combat.

Iris, a messenger of the gods, leads Helen to the walls of Troy to observe the duel. There Helen finds Priam, Antenor, and other Trojan elders. Homer suggests Helen's remarkable beauty by the reaction of these old men to her. Though they hate and fear the war resulting from Paris' abduction of Helen, a war which is destroying their land and people, they are so overwhelmed by the beauty of Helen that they declare it is no wonder the Greeks and Trojans are willing to fight for such a woman. Nonetheless, they wish she would return to her home in Sparta and prevent further slaughter. Helen points out various leaders to Priam.

Meanwhile, the contest between Menelaus and Paris begins. When Menelaus' sword breaks, he jumps upon Paris and seizes him by the helmet. At this point Aphrodite covers Paris with a mist and removes him from the battle. She takes him to his room and goes to summon Helen, who tries to resist the power of Aphrodite by refusing to go to Paris. The scene depicts Helen's conflicting emotions: her shame before the Trojan women because of her destructive affair with Paris and her bondage to him, symbolized by her obedience to Aphrodite. She does follow Aphrodite to Paris' room, and though she chides him for his cowardice and says angrily that she wishes he had died in battle, she does not resist his embraces.

Book IV. The gods hold a council on the Trojan War and decide that the Trojans will break the truce that was declared before the contest of Paris and Menelaus. Zeus sends Athene in the disguise of Laodocus, a Trojan, to urge Pandarus to shoot an arrow at Menelaus. Pandarus takes up his bow and wounds Menelaus, who is cured by Machaon, the physician. Agamemnon and Nestor rouse the Greeks to battle. The war begins again. Homer emphasizes its sounds: cries of triumph and groans of death, the clang of armor and the thud of bodies. The men are compared with wolves leaping upon one another and with trees falling in full bloom. When Apollo comes to encourage the Trojans, he reminds them that Achilles is not fighting. The book ends with the comment that that day many Trojans and Greeks lay in the dust by each other's side.

Book V. Athene inspires Diomedes to fight with great courage and skill. She also leads Ares, who supports the Trojans, away from the battle; his departure at this time signifies the temporary success of the Greeks. Many warriors are killed in battle, among them Phereclus, a Trojan who was a skilled craftsman and had built the ships that took Paris to Sparta. Diomedes fights savagely, like "a winter storm at its height," and kills many Trojans. Aeneas urges Pandarus to fight with Diomedes. In the contest between them Athene guides the spear of Diomedes, and he kills Pandarus. Aeneas defends the body of Pandarus, and he is wounded in the hip by Diomedes. Aphrodite, the mother of Aeneas, rescues her son from battle, but she herself is wounded by Diomedes. Led away from the battle by Iris, Aphrodite obtains the horses and chariot of Ares and returns to Olympus. There her mother, Dione, comforts her, and Zeus reminds her that her true work lies not in war but in love. Apollo takes Aeneas back to Troy, where he is healed by Leto and Artemis. Ares now returns to battle among the Trojan ranks; he urges the Trojans on and inspires them with courage. Apollo sends Aeneas back to the battlefield, where he is welcomed by his comrades. Aeneas, fighting bravely, kills many Greeks. Hera and Athene enter the war to contest the power of Ares. Athene urges Diomedes to fight with Ares, and Diomedes succeeds in wounding the god. Ares' cry of pain is as loud as the cry of nine or ten thousand warriors in battle. When Ares returns to Olympus to complain to Zeus, Zeus gives him no sympathy; he tells Ares that he is the most hateful of all the gods, for he cares only for strife and warfare.

Book VI. The gods leave the battlefield, and the Greeks, led by Ajax, son of Telamon, and Diomedes, are again in the lead. Helenus, a Trojan seer, suggests that Hector return to Troy to ask Hecuba and the other Trojan matrons to pray that Athene may prevent Diomedes from entering Troy. As Hector leaves for Troy, Glaucus, a Trojan warrior, and Diomedes meet on the battlefield. Diomedes asks Glaucus who he is, adding that if he is one of the gods he will not contend with him. Instead of simply giving his name and listing his ancestors, as would be expected, Glaucus replies by questioning the very meaning of man's life. First he asks why Diomedes should want to know his lineage, and then he compares man's life to that of a leaf, which flourishes briefly and dies as another comes to birth. The simile suggests the tragic implications of man's heroic struggle against his mortality; unlike a leaf, man struggles to accomplish heroic deeds, yet like a leaf he dies after a short span of life. After this brief commentary on man's fate, Glaucus goes on to tell his lineage, and when he has finished, Diomedes joyously remarks on the friendship of their ancestors: Glaucus' grandfather, Bellerophon, was a friend of his own grandfather, Oeneus. Thus, he says, they in turn must be friends, and instead of fighting, they agree to exchange armor. The passage ends on a humorous note; Homer remarks that at this point Zeus must have deprived Glaucus of his wits, for he gives golden armor to Diomedes but receives only armor of bronze in exchange.

After recounting this episode, Homer returns to Hector, who comes to the palace of his father, Priam. Hector asks his mother to sacrifice and pray to

Athene that the goddess may keep Diomedes away from Troy. He then finds Paris and Helen and rebukes his brother, urging him once more to fight. Paris promises to follow Hector to battle, and Helen speaks of the guilt she feels for causing so much destruction; she calls herself a "dog" and says she is hated by all. She also condemns Paris for his folly, and she sadly comments that Zeus has brought this doom on her and her lover so that they may be the subject of a song for men of the future.

After leaving Paris and Helen, Hector finds his wife, Andromache. With her is a nurse, carrying their child Astyanax. Andromache weeps and begs her husband to remain with her. She recalls the sorrow she has endured, the death of her father, Eëtion, and of her seven brothers, all of whom Achilles slew. She fears that she will be left a widow and her child an orphan. Hector replies that he too fears that Troy will be destroyed. Yet not even the suffering of his father or mother or brothers moves him so much as the thought that she, his wife, will be led away, a captive of the Greeks. Despite these forebodings, he bids his wife farewell, accepts his destiny, and goes forth to battle. As he is leaving, Paris joins him, splendid in his armor.

Book VII. Paris returns to the battlefield with Hector, and the war continues. Athene, concerned about the Greeks, comes back to Troy and is met by Apollo. They agree to rouse Hector to challenge one of the Greeks to single combat. When Hector first makes his challenge, the Greeks are fearful, and no one rises to accept it. Finally, when nine heroes rise, they cast lots, and Telamonian Ajax is chosen. After a long contest, the two part for the night, exchanging gifts of friendship. The Trojans hold a council at which Antenor suggests that they return Helen to the Greeks, but Paris refuses to do so, offering to return only the treasure that he took from Greece. The Greeks refuse this offer, but agree to a truce, so that the dead may be burned. Agamemnon says that no man should deprive the dead of burning. [He thus refers to the Homeric assumption that the soul of the dead cannot be accepted among the inhabitants of the Underworld until his body has been burned and buried according to the proper rites. The recovery of the body of a comrade is thus necessary in order to be certain that he receives proper burning and burial, and time is taken from battle to perform the ceremonies for the dead.] After burning their dead, the Greeks build a rampart and dig a ditch to protect their camp. Both armies feast all night, but they are disturbed by thunder, which Zeus sends as a sign of his displeasure.

Book VIII. Zeus calls a council of the gods and threatens them with punishment if they aid either side. Athene insists that she will give advice to the Greeks, and Zeus agrees. The battle begins. Zeus weighs the fates of the two armies on his golden scales, which indicate that the Trojans will presently be victorious. Now Zeus again sends lightning, and the Greeks grow frightened at this sign of the god's wrath. When Nestor is left alone on the battlefield, Diomedes comes to help him. Nestor advises Diomedes to flee, for Zeus is now giving glory to Hector and the Trojans. As Diomedes turns his horses to flee, Hector, approaching with other Trojans, insults Diomedes, calling him a coward. Diomedes hesitates three times, in conflict as to whether to flee or to face Hector in combat; three times he hears the thunder of Zeus, a sign that the Trojans will win in battle. Hector, also hearing the thunder, proudly rallies the Trojans and speaks to his horses, urging them on to pursue Nestor for his famous shield and Diomedes for his breastplate, made by Hephaestus. When Hera hears these proud words of Hector, she grows angry and urges Poseidon to aid the Greeks, but he refuses out of fear of Zeus. Hera then rouses Agamemnon to urge the Greeks to fight. Teucer kills many Trojans, but finally Hector wounds him. The Trojans drive the Greeks toward their ditch. When Hera sees the power of the Trojans, she pities the Greeks and suggests to Athene that they aid them in their distress. Athene agrees, but Zeus sends Iris to stop them. When night comes the fighting ends. Hector gathers the Trojans and tells them to keep watch, lest the Greeks depart for home during the night.

Book IX. When panic overwhelms the Greeks as a result of their many defeats, Agamemnon summons the leaders and, weeping, decides that they must flee to their homeland. Diomedes angrily tells Agamemnon to leave if he wishes, but the other Greeks will remain and fight till they destroy Troy. Nestor suggests that Agamemnon send an embassy to Achilles to persuade him to return to battle. Moreover, he says, Agamemnon must admit his earlier folly and make amends for his unjust treatment of Achilles. Agamemnon offers to restore Briseis to Achilles and to give him many gifts, among them one of his daughters as a wife. Phoenix, Achilles' old tutor, Telamonian Ajax, and Odysseus, attended by heralds, go to the hut of Achilles. They find him playing the lyre and singing a heroic song about warriors. With him is his beloved friend Patroclus. Achilles welcomes his friends and asks Patroclus to give them wine. After they eat and drink, Odysseus eloquently urges Achilles to rejoin his comrades, whose need of him is now desperate. He speaks of the Trojans' recent victories and the Greeks' disasters. He warns Achilles that, if he does not help the Greeks now, he will be sorry later on. Reminding him of his father Peleus' advice that he control his proud nature, Odysseus urges Achilles to give up his wrath against Agamemnon, who offers him such rich gifts of atonement. Achilles, however, still very angry, is unmoved by Odysseus' words. He says that the gifts of Agamemnon are hateful to him and that he intends to leave for home on the next day. Phoenix then attempts to persuade Achilles, reminding him tenderly of how he cared for him when Achilles was a child, for he has loved Achilles as he might have loved his own son. He then reminds Achilles that even the gods listen to the supplications of men. Prayers, he says, are sent by Zeus to heal the hurt caused by Ate, the goddess of moral blindness and fury, who brings men to destruction. If a man respects Prayers (Litai), the daughters of Zeus, his own prayers will be heard, but if a man refuses to hear them, he himself will be pursued by Ate. Still

199

Achilles cannot be moved. When Ajax pleads with him, Achilles does not deny the reasonableness of Ajax's arguments; in his mind he agrees with his comrades, but his heart is still filled with wrath. Phoenix remains with Achilles, and the others return to the camp. When Odysseus reports Achilles' refusal to Agamemnon and the other chiefs, Diomedes says he wishes the Greeks had never gone to ask Achilles to return, for now he will be more proud than ever. Achilles will return, says Diomedes, when his heart shall urge him and a god inspire him. In the meantime, the Greeks must fight bravely without him.

Book X. Agamemnon, disturbed by Achilles' refusal to return, is unable to sleep. He groans and tears his hair and finally awakens the other Greek leaders in order to make plans for defeating the Trojans. A council is called, at which it is decided to send scouts into the Trojan camp to kill anyone they may encounter and to find out the Trojans' plans. Diomedes volunteers to go and chooses Odysseus as his companion. In the Trojan camp Hector has also called a council in order to propose sending a spy among the Greeks to see whether their ships are still guarded. Dolon, eager for the chariot and horses that Hector offers as a reward, volunteers to go. Odysseus and Diomedes discover Dolon and seize him. They persuade him to tell them the Trojans' plans and resources. He also reports that the Thracians, with their king Rhesus, have recently arrived to help the Trojans and that Rhesus has with him beautiful, swift horses. Though Dolon pleads for mercy, Diomedes and Odysseus kill him and then proceed to kill Rhesus and several of his men. They also capture the famous horses of Rhesus and with them return to their camp, where they are welcomed warmly by the Greeks.

Book XI. As morning comes, Zeus sends Strife (Eris) to the Greeks. The goddess utters a war cry and inspires the Greeks to battle. Agamemnon leads his men as Hector and the other Trojan leaders prepare for the attack. Agamemnon kills many Trojans, and Zeus sends Iris to warn Hector not to fight until Agamemnon is wounded. Soon Agamemnon is wounded by Coön, who is then killed by Agamemnon. Despite his wound Agamemnon remains in battle, but withdraws when it becomes too painful. When Hector sees him depart, he rallies his men, enters the battle, and fights valiantly, killing many Greeks. Odysseus and Diomedes oppose him for a time, but Diomedes is wounded by Paris and retires from the battle. Odysseus, left alone, is in conflict as to whether to flee from his dangerous position, alone among the Trojans, or to continue fighting. Just as he decides that it would be cowardly to leave the battle, he is surrounded by Trojans and wounded by Socus, whom Odysseus then kills. Menelaus and Telamonian Ajax come to rescue Odysseus, and Menelaus leads him out of the battle while Ajax attacks and slays many Trojans. Meanwhile, Idomeneus, observing that Machaon, the physician, has been wounded by Paris, asks Nestor to rescue him, for a physician is worth many men, since he can heal wounds. Nestor takes Machaon back to the Greek ships. Though surrounded by Trojans, Telamonian Ajax is roused by

Zeus to defend himself and the other Greeks bravely. When Achilles observes Nestor removing Machaon from the battle, he sends Patroclus to find out if it is truly Machaon who has been wounded. Nestor welcomes Patroclus to his hut and asks him to persuade Achilles to pity the Greeks and return to battle or at least to lend Patroclus his armor and allow him to fight, so that the Trojans will mistake him for Achilles. Leaving Nestor's hut, Patroclus meets Eurypylus, who is wounded. Patroclus pities him and leads him to his hut, where he tends his wound.

Book XII. Hector urges his men to cross the trench of the Greeks, but the horses are afraid to leap over. Polydamas says it is impossible to cross the trench on horseback, but it would be possible on foot. The Trojans take his advice, and, led by Hector and other heroes, five companies begin the attack near the wall of the Greeks. As they fight they see an eagle carrying in its talons a snake, still alive and writhing. The snake strikes the eagle on its breast, and the eagle, in pain, drops it to the ground amid the Trojans and flies away. Upset by this omen, Polydamas urges Hector to withdraw the Trojans from the battle. He says that they, like the eagle, though they seem to be conquering, never will achieve their purpose. Hector refuses to listen and entreats the Trojans to break the Greek wall. Zeus gives his son Sarpedon great strength. Thus inspired, Sarpedon asks Glaucus to join him in battle, saying that as mortals they must die eventually in any case; therefore they should seek glory in war. The two go forth, and Sarpedon makes the first breach in the wall, opening a path for the others. Ajax and Teucer attack him, but he is protected by Zeus. Then Hector lifts up a huge stone, strikes the double gates with it, and tears apart the doors. He enters the gates and urges the Trojans to climb over the walls. The Greeks are driven to their ships.

Book XIII. Poseidon, watching the battle, pities the Greeks. Taking the form of Calchas, he persuades the two Ajaxes to oppose Hector. He also rouses the other Greeks who are in despair beside their ships to join the Ajaxes in attacking Hector and his followers. Among those slain is Othryoneus, who, desiring Cassandra as his wife, had brought no wedding gifts but instead promised to perform a heroic deed. When Polydamas sees that the Trojans are being overcome, he advises Hector to call a council to decide whether to press on to the ships or to withdraw. Hector agrees, but first goes forth to encourage his men. He scolds Paris, but Paris replies that this time he is blameless, since he has been fighting bravely. He tells Hector that Adamas, Asius, and Othryoneus have been slain and that Deiphobus and Helenus are wounded. He then assures Hector that he will follow him into battle and fight courageously, and the two brothers join the other warriors engaged in a fierce battle. Hector meets Ajax, who tells him that the day will come when the Trojans will flee and Troy will be ruined. Hector in turn calls Ajax a braggart and declares that Ajax will be killed. Hector then leads the Trojans back to battle.

Book XIV. Nestor, disturbed by the sounds of war, leaves Machaon in order to see what is taking place. He finds the Greeks driven back by the Trojans and decides to go to Agamemnon, whom he encounters with Diomedes and Odysseus, all of them wounded. Agamemnon expresses his despair and again suggests that the Greeks escape by night. Odysseus is angered by his words. Diomedes suggests that, despite their wounds, they return to the battle, not to fight but to spur on the other Greeks. The others agree and follow Agamemnon back to the field. Meanwhile, Hera, knowing that Zeus is aiding the Trojans, decides to overwhelm him with her beauty and put him to sleep. First she adorns herself; then she borrows Aphrodite's magic belt, which inspires love. Finally, she obtains a promise from the god of Sleep that after she and Zeus have made love, he will lull Zeus to sleep. Hera returns to Mount Ida, and Zeus responds so enthusiastically to her beauty that he tells her never before has a woman so moved him. He then proceeds to list in a delightful catalogue many of the women he wooed in the past. As they embrace, Zeus covers them in a cloud of gold, and from the earth grass and flowers spring forth. With Zeus asleep, Poseidon is able to lead the Greeks to battle. Both forces fight savagely. Telamonian Ajax hurls a stone at Hector, who is wounded and removed from the battle by his comrades. The wounding of Hector encourages the Greeks, who slay many Trojans. The book concludes with a list of victors and slain, and with special praise for Ajax, son of Oileus, who killed the greatest number.

Book XV. When Zeus awakens he sees the Trojans driven back from the trenches in terror and Hector gasping and vomiting blood. Zeus threatens Hera with punishment, but she calms him by saying that she has not told Poseidon to help the Greeks, and will advise him to obey Zeus. Hera summons Iris and Apollo to Zeus, so that Iris may carry a message to Poseidon to stop helping the Greeks and Apollo may give Hector renewed strength to drive back the Greeks. Zeus then speaks of future events: of how Achilles will send Patroclus forth to battle and how he will be slain by Hector after he has killed many Trojans, among them Zeus' own son Sarpedon. From then on, says Zeus, the Greeks will continue to defeat the Trojans until they finally seize Troy. But until then he will not permit the gods to help the Greeks, as he promised Thetis when she came to ask his support for Achilles. Hera, overhearing these words, goes swiftly to Olympus and, finding the other gods there, attempts to evoke their anger against Zeus. She succeeds in enraging Ares by telling him that his son Ascalaphus has been killed. As Ares is about to enter the battle to avenge the death of his son, he is stopped by Athene. Iris and Apollo carry out the orders of Zeus. Apollo restores Hector's strength and takes him back to the battle. Carrying his aegis, Apollo leads the Trojans and helps them to drive back the Greeks. He breaks a portion of the Greek wall, and the Trojans rush through in their chariots, while the Greeks flee to their ships. When Patroclus sees the feats of the Trojans, he leaves Eurypylus and returns to Achilles to try to persuade him to return to battle. Though many of their men are slain, the Greeks continue to defend their ships. Telamonian Ajax is especially brave in preventing the Trojans from burning the ships.

Book XVI. Patroclus persuades Achilles to allow him to enter the war. Achilles gives him his own armor, but tells him he may only drive the Trojans back from the ships. Beyond that he must not aid the Greeks, lest he diminish the honor of Achilles. When Patroclus has put on the armor of Achilles and the Myrmidons have prepared themselves for battle, Achilles prays to Zeus for Patroclus' success and his safe return. On seeing Patroclus, the Trojans mistake him for Achilles and become frightened. Patroclus kills many Trojans and drives the rest away from the ships. Zeus, observing Patroclus fighting with Sarpedon, weeps for the fate of his son just before Sarpedon is killed. Many Greeks and Trojans are slain as the battle continues. Patroclus, disobeying the command of Achilles, drives the Trojans to the wall of Troy. He is described as blind in heart, for had he obeyed Achilles, he would have escaped death. After Patroclus has killed Cebriones, Hector and he fight over the corpse. Around them other Trojans and Greeks join in the contest. Apollo strikes Patroclus on his back and shoulders and knocks off his helmet. Patroclus' spear breaks and his shield falls to the ground. As he stands dazed, Euphorbus wounds him with his spear. When Hector sees Patroclus wounded, he thrusts his spear at him, and Patroclus falls. Hector stands over him, exulting in Patroclus' downfall. As he dies Patroclus prophesies the death of Hector at the hands of Achilles. The two lines describing the death of Patroclus here are repeated in Book xxii when Hector dies: "his soul, fleeing from his limbs, went down to the house of Hades, groaning at his fate, leaving behind manliness and youth."

Book XVII. Menelaus defends the body of Patroclus and prevents the Trojans from seizing it. Euphorbus, who fights with Menelaus for the corpse, is killed. Then Apollo, in the form of Mentes, leader of the Cicones, inspires Hector, who leads the Trojans against Menelaus. Menelaus retreats, leaving the corpse, and asks the help of Telamonian Ajax. After Hector has removed the armor from the body of Patroclus, he attempts to carry off the corpse so that he may cut off the head and give the body to the dogs of Troy. When Ajax appears, Hector leaps into his chariot, carrying the armor but leaving the corpse behind, and Ajax remains to guard it. Glaucus chides Hector for withdrawing. Zeus sees Hector putting on the armor of Achilles, which Patroclus had worn, and observes pityingly that in his present triumph Hector overlooks the possibility of his own death. Ares enters the body of Hector, who rallies his men to fight over the body of Patroclus. When the Trojans charge, Ajax asks Menelaus to call the other Greek chieftains, and a violent battle takes place over the corpse of Patroclus. Apollo arouses Aeneas, who joins the Trojan forces. As the battle rages the immortal horses of Achilles weep for Patroclus. Zeus, looking down on them, pities them for their association with mortal man, the most wretched creature on earth. Hector and Aeneas attempt to seize the horses, but are thrust back by Automedon. Zeus sends a rainbow, a portent of bad luck, to the Greeks. Athene attempts to encourage the Greeks; Apollo rouses Hector. Aware that Zeus is helping the Trojans, Telamonian Ajax suggests that Achilles be told of the death of Patroclus. When Ajax weeps and begs Zeus to remove the darkness he has cast over the battle, Zeus in pity drives away the mist. Menelaus asks Antilochus to inform Achilles of his friend's death. As Menelaus and Meriones raise the corpse of Patroclus to take it from the battle, the Trojans charge and the conflict continues.

 Book XVIII. Antilochus tells Achilles of the death of Patroclus. Overwhelmed by grief, Achilles covers his face and head with dust. He lies on the ground and tears his hair. The maidens taken by Achilles and Patroclus as booty add their moans to those of Achilles and beat their breasts. Weeping, Antilochus holds Achilles' hands, fearing that in the intensity of his grief Achilles may cut his own throat. This violent expression of suffering is both continued and relieved by a description of Thetis and the other Nereids, whose names are listed as they weep for Achilles' suffering. They go to Achilles, and Thetis, attempting to comfort him, reminds him that his wish has been fulfilled: the Greeks are in desperate need of him. Achilles recognizes the irony implicit in his mother's words, for the fulfillment of his prayers has brought him only suffering. Achilles' grief grows more intense, and he determines to return to battle to avenge his friend's death and to win fame for himself. Thetis then leaves him in order to go to Hephaestus and ask him to forge armor for Achilles. Iris comes to Achilles and advises him to appear on the battlefield even without his armor, because the very sight of him will frighten the Trojans who are fighting over the body of Patroclus. When Achilles does appear, the Trojans retreat, terrified, and the Greeks place Patroclus on a bier. Achilles weeps for his friend. The Trojans, meanwhile, hold a council and decide to follow Hector's advice that they remain in their camp and resume battle in the morning, rather than retreat behind their walls, as Polydamas has suggested. Achilles, groaning and weeping for his friend, is compared with a lion whose cubs have been stolen. He vows that he will not bury Patroclus until he has gained possession of the armor and head of Hector; he determines to cut the throats of twelve Trojans before the pyre of Patroclus.

 As Achilles mourns, Hephaestus forges the famous shield of Achilles with its threefold silver rim. The shield has five layers; on it Hephaestus depicts the earth, the sky, the sea, the sun, the moon, and the constellations. He also creates two cities, one at peace and one at war. In the peaceful city he depicts marriage ceremonies and feasts, young men dancing and playing the lyre, and an argument over the "blood price," payment to the relatives, of a man who has been murdered. In the city at war he creates two armies, women and children guarding the wall, and Ares and Athene leading the warriors. He also depicts farmland and men tilling the soil and tending cattle, a vineyard rich in grapes, a boy singing a harvest song, and a dancing floor on which young men and women, dressed in fresh linen, dance as a large group of people watch with delight. Around the outermost rim of the shield Hephaestus forges the ocean. [Thus, the shield of Achilles contains a picture of the whole universe. Its sweeping depiction of earth, sky, ocean, and the various aspects of the life of man provide a broad framework for the narrow world of war and the intense self-absorption of Achilles in his own wrath and grief. The shield provides perspective; it reminds us that the wrath of Achilles and the Trojan War are only part of the universe, disorder within essential order. As Werner Jaeger suggests, "That deep sense of harmony between man and nature, which inspires the description of Achilles' shield, is dominant in Homer's conception of the world" (*Paideia* [Oxford University Press, 1945], i, 50).]

Book XIX. Thetis gives the armor that Hephaestus has made to Achilles, whom she finds weeping over the body of Patroclus. She promises to prevent the body of Patroclus from decaying. Achilles then summons the Greek warriors and announces that he no longer nurses his wrath against Agamemnon. Agamemnon admits his own wrong in taking Briseis, blaming his arrogance on Ate, the goddess of moral blindness, who, although a daughter of Zeus, once blinded Zeus himself. Agamemnon goes on to offer Achilles the gifts he offered him when he sought a reconciliation before. Achilles replies that Agamemnon may give or withhold the gifts; all he wants is to rush into battle immediately. His wrath against Agamemnon is gone, but he is consumed with a violent hatred for Hector and the Trojans. Odysseus realistically urges Achilles to allow the men to eat and drink before battle.

Agamemnon sends Briseis, along with many gifts, to the tent of Achilles. On seeing the body of Patroclus and remembering his kindness, the girl shrieks and tears her face and breast. She recalls that he would never allow her to weep and that he promised to arrange for her marriage to Achilles. Continuing to mourn for Patroclus, Achilles refuses food and the comfort of friends. Athene then inspires him, and he puts on his armor. Addressing his immortal horses, Xanthus and Balius, he bitterly tells them not to leave him dead on the battlefield, as they left Patroclus. The horse Xanthus replies that though Achilles will be safe in the coming battle, his fate is to die soon. Unafraid, Achilles tells the horse that he already knows his fate and rushes into battle.

Book XX. Zeus orders Themis to summon the gods to a council and tells them that they may enter the war. Hera, Athene, Poseidon, Hermes, and Hephaestus go to aid the Greeks, while Ares, Apollo, Artemis, Leto, the god of the Xanthus River, and Aphrodite aid the Trojans. When the Trojans see Achilles, they are terrified. The gods battle, while Zeus thunders in heaven and the earth quakes. Even Hades is frightened by the battle on earth. Apollo, coming to Aeneas in the form of Lycaon, inspires him with great strength and urges him to fight with Achilles. When Aeneas and Achilles meet, Achilles asks Aeneas why he wishes to fight with him. He tells him not to hope to inherit the throne of Priam even if he is victorious in this contest, for Priam will leave his throne to his sons. He then reminds Aeneas of the time Aeneas fled from him. Aeneas replies bravely that Achilles should not attempt to frighten him. He goes on to speak proudly of his lineage, tracing it back to Dardanus, son of Zeus. The son of Dardanus was Erichthonius, who was the father of Tros, king of the Trojans. One of Tros' sons was Ilus, grandfather of Priam, and another was Assaracus, grandfather of Anchises, the father of Aeneas. Having indicated that his ancestry is as noble as Priam's, Aeneas says that he is tired of angry words and eager for a contest with Achilles. The two fight furiously until Poseidon, seeing that Aeneas is in great danger, urges the other gods to save him, because he is a descendant of Dardanus, whom Zeus loved more than all his other offspring from mortal women. He fears that if Aeneas should be killed, the race of Dardanus would forever die, because Zeus now hates Priam and his children. He predicts that one day Aeneas will be king of the Trojans and his descendants will inherit his throne. Hera tells Poseidon to do as he likes about saving Aeneas; she and Athene have sworn never to help the Trojans. Poseidon goes down to the battlefield and sheds a mist over Achilles' eyes. He then removes Aeneas from the battlefield and warns him not to contest with Achilles. Once Achilles is dead, Aeneas may fight with any of the Greeks, for none but Achilles can slay him. When Achilles sees that Aeneas is gone, he realizes that Aeneas did not merely brag about his lineage; he is indeed loved by the gods.

Achilles then slays many Trojans, among them Polydorus, a son of Priam. Achilles and Hector meet and begin to fight, but Apollo shrouds Hector in a mist and carries him away. Vowing to kill Hector when he next meets him, Achilles pursues other Trojans and kills many.

Book XXI. The Trojans flee from Achilles in two groups, one to the plain near the city and the other to the river Scamander. Achilles pursues those in the river and slays so many that the waters of the Scamander grow red with their blood. He takes twelve young Trojans alive, planning to sacrifice them to Patroclus. He then meets Lycaon, a son of Priam, fleeing from the river. Lycaon had been captured before by Achilles, who at that time had sold him as a captive. Now, unarmed, Lycaon begs Achilles for mercy again, but Achilles cannot be persuaded. He says that until Patroclus was killed, he was willing to spare the Trojans and sell them as prisoners, but now not one will escape death. His irrational involvement in grief is expressed in his wonder that Lycaon should even lament at his own impending death when Patroclus has died. Then, in his loneliness, Achilles seems to reveal the tragedy of his own life to a man he is about to kill; he asks Lycaon to look at him, Achilles, the son of a goddess, a man tall and handsome, yet doomed to death. After these words he kills Lycaon and then kills Asteropaeus and many others who had fled to the river. The god of the Xanthus River chides Achilles for filling his beautiful streams with dead bodies. The river then rushes upon Achilles and attacks him. Poseidon and Athene come to help him, and Hera obtains the assistance of Hephaestus, who burns those slain by Achilles on the plain and then turns his fire against the river. He has almost dried up the river itself when Hera stops him. The other gods enter the battle. Ares strikes Athene and is wounded by her. Achilles continues to kill many Trojans, and Priam, observing him from the Trojan wall, calls to the gatekeepers to open the gates and allow the Trojans to flee to safety. Agenor refuses to flee and attempts to fight with Achilles. Apollo snatches Agenor away and, in the form of Agenor, takes his place against Achilles. As Achilles pursues Apollo the Trojans retreat safely behind their walls.

Book XXII. All the Trojans except Hector remain within the walls. Priam and Hecuba plead with Hector to retreat to safety. As Hector tries to decide what to do, Achilles approaches him, and he flees. As Achilles chases Hector three times about Troy, Hector is compared with a dove pursued by a falcon, with a deer pursued by a hound. The chase, says Homer, is like one in a dream, apparently endless. The gods observe the pursuit, and Zeus expresses his pity for Hector. Athene comes to the aid of Achilles. Taking the form of Hector's brother Deiphobus, Athene persuades Hector to engage in combat with Achilles. Hector asks Achilles to agree that the victor in the contest between them will return the body of the other to his own people, but Achilles angrily refuses. While fighting, Hector loses his spear; he turns to Deiphobus to ask for another and, finding him gone, realizes that Athene has deceived him. Ironically, however, the goddess has also helped Hector to fulfill his heroic obligations. Recognizing that death is near, he nonetheless determines to fight gloriously. When Achilles wounds him fatally with his spear and he lies dying in the dust, he once again begs Achilles to return his body to his people so that he may receive the rites of burning and burial. Achilles replies with savage rage that he would like to devour Hector raw; he vows that he will never return the body, but will leave it to be consumed by the dogs and birds. Hector prophesies that Achilles will be killed by Paris and Apollo. When Hector dies, Achilles ties his body to his chariot by the feet, the head trailing in the dust. Achilles then drives his chariot beneath the Trojan walls. Priam and Hecuba, seeing Hector dragged in the dust, groan and weep for their son, and Andromache, hearing of the death of her husband, faints in her grief. When she is revived she expresses her sorrow and her fears for the future of her child.

Book XXIII. Achilles and the Myrmidons mourn over Patroclus, driving their horses three times around his body to honor him. Then, after they hold a funeral feast, the Myrmidons retire to their huts. Achilles lies down to sleep on the beach and dreams of Patroclus, who urges his friend to bury him quickly, so that he may enter the gates of Hades. In the morning the soldiers gather wood for the funeral pyre. Achilles cuts off a lock of his hair and puts it in the hands of Patroclus. The funeral pyre is made, and Achilles sacrifices horses and dogs. He then slays twelve Trojan captives to be burned as sacrifices. He pours libations to the north wind and the west wind, imploring them to come and raise the fire. The next morning the Greeks quench the flames with wine, gather the bones of Patroclus, and place them in a golden urn, which they cover with a linen cloth and put in his hut. They then pile up the earth to build his barrow. The funeral games in honor of Patroclus begin. These consist of a chariot race, a boxing match, a wrestling match, a foot race, and contests in spear-thrusting, hurling of the discus, and archery.

Book XXIV. When the games are over, the Greeks return to their ships for food and sleep, but Achilles, unable to sleep, longs for Patroclus. He drives his chariot, with Hector trailing in the dust, three times around the barrow of Patroclus. Despite this cruel treatment, the body of Hector is not mutilated, for Apollo protects it from destruction. Apollo and the other gods pity Hector and urge Hermes to steal his body from Achilles, but Hera, Poseidon, and Athene object to this idea. After twelve days of observing this cruel treatment of Hector, Apollo again speaks to the other gods of his disapproval of Achilles and his pity for Hector. Finally, Zeus asks Iris to summon Thetis, and he instructs her to order Achilles to return Hector's body to the Trojans. When Thetis asks Achilles to accept ransom for the body, he agrees immediately.

Meanwhile, Zeus sends Iris to urge Priam to ransom his son's body. As Priam prepares to go to the ships of the Greeks, Hecuba attempts to persuade him to remain at home, for she fears that Achilles will harm him. But Priam is determined to recover his son's body. Hermes, sent by Zeus, arrives in the form of a young prince and guides Priam on his journey. When they arrive at the hut of Achilles, Hermes identifies himself and leaves for Olympus.

Entering the hut of Achilles, Priam sees him sitting at his table. Priam kneels at Achilles' feet, clasps his knees, and kisses the hands that have slain his sons. The old king attempts to evoke Achilles' pity by reminding him of his own father, Peleus, who, like him, is an old man. Priam speaks of his sorrows, the loss of his children, and begs Achilles to have mercy. He is more piteous than Peleus, Priam says, for he has experienced what no other man has, touching the face of the man who has killed his sons. Achilles' violent rage is spent, and he is moved by the sorrow of Priam. They weep together, Priam for Hector and Achilles for his father and for Patroclus. Then Achilles speaks to Priam with compassion, asking him how he had the heart to come alone to the man who has killed his many sons. He agrees to return Hector's body.

After they have eaten together, Priam and Achilles look at each other as if for the first time, Priam marveling at the tall and godlike figure of Achilles, Achilles at the noble appearance and words of Priam. This concern of Achilles for the suffering of his enemy redeems him; his rage has caused death and brought anguish to himself and others, but he has emerged from its blindness with a deeper insight into himself and other men. Rachel Bespaloff says of him, "The killer is a man again, burdened with childhood and death" (*On the Iliad* [trans. Mary McCarthy, Pantheon Books, 1947], p. 98).

When Achilles and Priam have gone to sleep, Hermes appears to Priam and takes him back to the Trojan camp with the body of Hector. Cassandra first sees them approaching and cries out, summoning the other Trojans, who rush forth to meet Priam. Andromache flings herself on the wagon, wailing and tearing her hair, Hecuba weeps for her favorite son, and Helen laments, remembering Hector's kindness to her. For nine days the Trojans gather wood for the pyre; on the tenth day they burn the body of Hector. The next morning they quench the flames with wine, gather the bones, and build Hector's barrow.

COMMENTARY. The principal theme of the *Iliad* is the anger of Achilles. This violent, tortured hero reflects the agony of warfare on the plains of Troy and deep inner conflict within the human heart. In his suffering and his grandeur Achilles exemplifies the tragic implications of heroic events. In his blind absorption in his own wounded soul and his final insight into the sufferings of his enemy Priam, he symbolizes the extremes of human limitations and capacities.

Achilles' very choice of a short, heroic life over a long, inglorious one suggests the tragic conditions of the heroic code, by which a man barters life for honor. Achilles is not the only one who lives by this code; it is accepted by all the Greek and Trojan heroes. In the *Iliad* man tragically achieves glory, for which he pays with life. A heroic deed in battle is his means of achieving immortality, yet it is the very act that may destroy him. It is the conflict between man's unwilling acceptance of his mortality and his yearning for immortality that commits him to the heroic code, to the ironic dilemma of attempting to achieve immortality through destructive and violent deeds. His heroic contest in warfare is also his ironic contest with his fate.

Another important theme in the *Iliad* that is most intensely expressed through the experience of Achilles is the potential friendship and sympathy among enemies. The idea is implicit in the very ceremonies of heroic warfare: when Hector and Telamonian Ajax stop fighting because night has come, Hector suggests that they exchange gifts so that men may say, "The two fought in soul-consuming strife, but they were united in friendship before parting" (VII, 301–302). The theme is even more explicit in the episode in which Glaucus, a Trojan, and Diomedes, a Greek, come together on the battlefield, but discover that they have more reason for friendship than for enmity (VI, 119–236).

The most striking and moving expression of this theme is the scene between Achilles and Priam, when Priam comes to ransom the body of his son Hector. When Achilles kills Priam's sons, he seems to the old king a murderous force, hardly human. To Achilles the father of Hector, the man who has killed his beloved Patroclus, is the hated begetter of an enemy he continues to detest even after killing him in a violent rage. Yet when the two men finally come face to face, they look at each other and discover only that they are united in suffering. The sight of Priam brings to Achilles' mind the image of his own father, and Priam admires the handsome and dignified form of the young

Achilles, who might be his own son (xxiv, 477–676). This lucidity has come at a tragic price and is itself a painful awakening to human limitation, but it is a richer reward than heroic fame.

Homer's sympathetic depiction of the Trojans also suggests that there are no simple enemies in the *Iliad*, but only men trapped by forces beyond their control, which can be regarded as directed by fate or the will of the gods—death, human weakness, violence, and all the other incomprehensible and continuous dangers of man's external and inner worlds.

The structure of the *Iliad* is simple and dramatic. The story is divided into four main sections. Books i–viii tell of the cause and early consequences of Achilles' wrath, which at this time to a large extent seems justified. Books ix–xvii begin with Achilles' irrational refusal to accept Agamemnon's apologies and efforts to make amends for his injustice to Achilles and end with the death of Patroclus in xvi and the fighting over his body in xvii. In Books xviii–xxii Achilles expresses intense and almost insane wrath, mercilessly killing many Trojans and finally Hector. Books xxiii–xxiv describe the funeral games for Patroclus, which mark the end of Achilles' utter involvement in mourning, and the meeting of Priam and Achilles, in which tragic insight replaces blind wrath.

Achilles is absent from a great deal of the action of the *Iliad*. He retires to his tent in Book i, and except for Book ix, in which he is entreated to return and refuses, and Books xi and xvi, in which he sends Patroclus forth, first to see what is taking place among the Greek warriors and then to fight, he is not actually involved in the action again until Book xviii. Yet the reader is constantly aware of him. Homer mentions him often, briefly remarking that Achilles does not fight or Achilles remains in his tent. Moreover, his dignity, courage, and grace, his great emotional capacity are so strongly delineated in Book i that we are concerned for him even in his absence. We are also aware, because of the strength of his character and the conviction behind his decision not to fight, that all the action we perceive is the consequence of his wrath, and we know he must return. Thus Achilles' very absence helps to create the dramatic suspense of the poem.

The *Iliad* has been imitated and alluded to constantly since Homer's time. Vergil's Turnus in the *Aeneid* is referred to as "another Achilles," and Vergil clearly models his battle scenes and many other episodes in the *Aeneid* on the *Iliad*. Milton too relies heavily on the *Iliad* in his descriptions of the battle in heaven and in his use of epic conventions. The *Iliad* was used constantly for ironic comparison by the great satirists Alexander Pope and Jonathan Swift; Pope's "Rape of the Lock" and his "Dunciad" and Swift's "Battle of the Books" are almost incomprehensible without a knowledge of the *Iliad*. It is interesting to compare Pope's rather lighthearted reference to the shield of Achilles in his description of Belinda's petticoat in the "Rape of the Lock" with W. H. Auden's ironic use of it in his poem "The Shield of Achilles." Belinda's petticoat, "silver bound," like Achilles' shield, is a sign that she is a warrior, prepared for the battle of the sexes, a war which, to her, is as grand and significant as the Trojan War. Auden uses the shield of Achilles, which depicts the whole world, as an instrument for ironic comparison; the world depicted on the shield of his Achilles has neither vineyard nor dancing floor; the heroic code no longer exists, and his Achilles is the "iron-hearted, man-slaying," anonymous warrior of our time.

Ilium (Ilion). See TROY.

Ino. In Greek mythology, a daughter of Cadmus and Harmonia. She married Athamas, a son of Aeolus and king of Thebes. When the god Dionysus was born from the thigh of Zeus, Ino cared for the infant. Hera, who hated the offspring of her rivals, afflicted Ino and Athamas with madness. Athamas killed one of their sons, Learchus, and Ino jumped into the sea with the other son, Melicertes. Ovid tells their story in *Metamorphoses* IV, and depicts Venus (Aphrodite) pleading with Neptune (Poseidon) to help the unfortunate mother and son. Neptune then transformed Ino into the sea-goddess Leucothea, who aids the shipwrecked Odysseus (see ODYSSEY V), and Melicertes into the sea-god Palaemon.

Institutio Oratoria (The Education of an Orator). An educational treatise in twelve books (c. A.D. 95) by QUINTILIAN. Translations: J. S. Watson, 1856; H. E. Butler, 1921.

S U M M A R Y . In the *Institutio Oratoria*, Quintilian's purpose is to describe the education of the perfect orator. He begins by saying that the most important qualification is that he be a "good man," for without integrity one can never attain greatness as an orator. No amount of training, he goes on to say, can produce an orator if he does not have talent. Book I deals primarily with the elementary education of an orator. Quintilian's assumption that it is essential for the child to enjoy learning and his warning against corporal punishment suggest the reasonableness of his approach to education. He stresses the importance of proficiency in language. In connection with usage, Quintilian agrees with Cicero that the language of the present time is to be preferred to the language of the past. Correct usage is the agreed manner of speaking of educated men. Both writers and speakers must observe certain rules. Language is based upon reason, antiquity, authority, and custom.

Book II deals with the nature of rhetorical training and the characteristics of a competent teacher. Books III to IX are mainly technical, dealing with the three main types of speeches, their various parts, kinds of arguments, style, language, simile, metaphor, and rhythm. Some of Quintilian's remarks are important not only for the orator but for the literary artist working in any form. For example, in one sentence he sums up what he believes is the intrinsic relationship between language and subject matter: "I would therefore wish that one be careful in his choice of words because of his concern for his subject" (VIII, proem, 20). Quintilian's discussion of propriety is thorough and technical. One of his main points is that language is mean when it is below the dignity or rank of the speaker. Obscurity and ambiguity are to be avoided. He approves of the simile as an "ornament," but similes should be neither obscure nor unfamiliar. They should serve to illuminate by creating a mental picture.

A metaphor, says Quintilian, is the most beautiful of tropes. Its effect must never be commonplace, low, or unpleasant. He calls the metaphor a short form of simile, differing from it in that the object is not compared to, but substituted for, the thing described. Metaphor is to be used sparingly. He discusses several other tropes, the most important of which is the hyperbole, which he calls an elegant exaggeration of the truth. Hyperbole must employ the incredible, but it must be used with restraint. He attributes the effectiveness of the hyperbole to man's innate desire to exaggerate.

The best-known book of the *Institutio Oratoria* is the tenth, in which Quintilian discusses the value of reading for the future orator. The student must follow certain models, both writers and speakers. He must read not only the best orators, but the best poets, philosophers, and historians as well. Quintilian's remarks about the poets as models are very interesting. Homer, who has provided both an example and an inspiration to every department of eloquence, is excellent for his oratorical as well as his poetic powers. Homer displays an understanding of all the rules of forensic or deliberative oratory. His similes, amplifications, illustrations, digressions, and all his methods of proof are admirable. Quintilian discusses Hesiod as an example of the intermediate style, Euripides as a finer orator than Sophocles, Menander as a writer of speeches. Among the Romans, Vergil ranks first. Indeed, the uniformity of his excellence is perhaps equal to Homer's superiority in single passages. Macer and Lucretius are worth reading, but not as examples for the orator; the one is *humilis* (uninspiring), the other *difficilis* (too involved). Quintilian's literary criticism in this survey is determined almost entirely by standards of oratory.

Book xi is concerned with memory and delivery, and Book xii with the ethical standards of the orator. In describing the orator, Quintilian quotes Cato's definition: *vir bonus dicendi peritus* ("a good man skilled in speech"). In the twelfth book Quintilian sums up the elements of good oratorical style as follows: "An oration should be noble but not extravagant, exalted but not bombastic, daring but not rash, severe but not gloomy, grave but not slow, copious but not immoderate, pleasing but not careless, grand but not pompous." He goes on to say, "The principle is the same in all things; the safest way is the mean, for the worst vice is to be found at either extreme." It is significant that Quintilian defines the "mean" as "exalted," "copious," and "grand." The "mean" sets no limits on the feelings or ideas of the artist. Like Cicero and Horace, Quintilian suggests that the careful stylist achieves the mean only when, through artistry, he molds his deepest feelings and thoughts into restrained and harmonious expression.

Io. In Greek mythology, the daughter of Inachus, king of Argos. For her story see Bacchylides' CHORAL LYRIC XIX and Aeschylus' PROMETHEUS BOUND. See also Aeschylus' THE SUPPLIANTS.

Iolaus (Iolaos). See THE CHILDREN OF HERACLES.

Iole. See THE WOMEN OF TRACHIS.

Ion. In Greek mythology, the son of Apollo and Creusa. For his story see Euripides' ION. (He is not to be confused with the rhapsode who is the subject of Plato's *Ion*.)

Ion. A dialogue by PLATO that mocks the affectations of the rhapsode Ion. The dialogue deals with the inspiration and art of the poet.

Ion. A tragedy (date disputed; perhaps c. 417 B.C.) by EURIPIDES. Translations: in verse, Robert Potter, 1781–83; in verse, Arthur S. Way, 1912; in verse, H.D. [Hilda Doolittle], 1937; in verse, Ronald Frederick Willets, 1958.

S C E N E . Delphi, before the temple of Apollo.

S U M M A R Y . The god Hermes enters and in a long speech gives the background of the play. King Erechtheus of Athens had a daughter Creusa, whom Apollo loved. When she gave birth to Apollo's son, Creusa in her shame placed the baby in a cradle and exposed him in a cave, leaving some identifying ornaments with him. Apollo sent Hermes to rescue the child and bring him to Apollo's temple at Delphi. There the child was discovered by the priestess, who cared for the boy until he grew to manhood, when he began to serve in the temple. Creusa was married to Xuthus, who became king of Athens. When after some years they had had no children, they decided to go for advice to the oracle at Delphi. Hermes predicts that Apollo will now decree that Ion is the son of Xuthus, so that the boy may claim the lands he is entitled to by birth.

Ion comes out of the temple, chanting of the great power of Apollo and of his own devotion to the god and his temple. The Chorus of Handmaidens of Creusa enters and with Ion chants in praise of the temple and its beautiful sculptures. Soon Creusa enters and informs Ion of her desire to consult the oracle. Creusa also pretends that she wants to do a favor for a friend who has born a child by Apollo and wishes her to ask the god if the child is still alive. Ion is disturbed by Creusa's remarks about Apollo. Surely the gods should not be as intemperate and irresponsible as the mortals whom they condemn for such behavior.

The Chorus asks Athene and Artemis to implore Apollo to give offspring to Creusa and Xuthus. Then Xuthus comes out of the temple and eagerly addresses Ion as his son. When Ion expresses bewilderment, Xuthus explains that the oracle has told him that the first man he encountered on leaving the temple would be his son. Xuthus and Ion assume that Ion is an illegitimate son of Xuthus. Though Ion is willing to call Xuthus his father, he fears the Athenians will not welcome him because both his father and he are aliens. Xuthus persuades him to accompany him to Athens, but not to reveal to Creusa that he is Xuthus' son. The Chorus, pledged by Xuthus to secrecy, dislikes the deception.

When Creusa enters with her old Tutor, the Leader of the Chorus reveals that Xuthus has a grown son. Creusa is disturbed because she believes that she will have no child of her own. Moreover, the Tutor tells her they have been tricked by Xuthus into believing that Ion, his son by a slave girl, has been assigned to him by Apollo. He urges Creusa to kill Xuthus and Ion. In desperation Creusa cries out that she has been twice betrayed, once by Apollo, her lover who left her and her child and then by her husband. She decides that the Tutor must poison Ion, and leaves. Creusa's handmaidens approve of the plan, for they wish to prevent Ion from inheriting the throne of Athens.

An Attendant of Creusa's comes in to announce that her plot to murder Ion has been discovered, and the people of Delphi are seeking Creusa to punish her with death. Creusa then takes refuge at the altar. When Ion and the citizens of Delphi come upon her, she tries to justify herself by accusing Ion of planning to seize the throne of Athens. As Ion and his men are about to remove Creusa from the altar, the Priestess of the temple comes in and reveals that Ion is the child whom Creusa exposed. When Creusa informs Ion that Apollo was his father, he finds it hard to believe her. As he is about to go into the temple to ask the oracle who his father is, Athene, the *deus ex machina*, appears from above, announcing that she was sent by Apollo, who is indeed the father of Ion. The Goddess says that Creusa must now take Ion to Athens, where he will become king and founder of the Ionian people. Xuthus and Creusa are destined to have two sons, Dorus, the future founder of the Dorians, and Aeolus, who will be the ancestor of the Aeolians. Creusa now is grateful to Apollo, and the Chorus echoes her praises of the god.

Iphigenia (Iphigeneia). In Greek mythology, a daughter of Agamemnon and Clytemnestra. For her story see Aeschylus' ORESTEIA, Euripides' IPHIGENIA IN AULIS and IPHIGENIA IN TAURIS, and Seneca's *Agamemnon*.

Iphigenia in Aulis (Iphigeneia he en Aulidi). A tragedy (c. 405 B.C.) by EURIPIDES. Translations: in verse, Robert Potter, 1781–83; in verse, Arthur S. Way, 1912; in verse, Florence M. Stawell, 1929; in verse, Charles R. Walker, 1958.

MYTHICAL BACKGROUND. When the Trojan Paris, son of Priam, took Helen away from her husband, Menelaus, the Greeks gathered to attack Troy. Their ships were delayed at Aulis by unfavorable weather. Finally the prophet Calchas declared that the goddess Artemis demanded the sacrifice of Iphigenia, the daughter of Agamemnon, in order that favorable winds might allow the army to set out for Troy. Despite his natural reluctance to kill his own child, Agamemnon, motivated by his desire for glory in war and persuaded by the arguments of Menelaus, sent for Iphigenia, pretending that he wanted her to marry Achilles before the Greeks left for Troy.

SCENE. Aulis, before Agamemnon's tent.

SUMMARY. Agamemnon tells his Servant that Calchas has declared he must sacrifice Iphigenia and expresses his conflicting feelings about the sacrifice.

He has written to Clytemnestra telling her to send the girl to Aulis so that she can marry Achilles before he sets sail for Troy. Now Agamemnon regrets his deception and has written a new letter bidding Clytemnestra not to send Iphigenia and using the excuse that the wedding must be postponed. He asks the Servant to take the letter to Clytemnestra at Argos immediately. As the Servant rushes out, the Chorus of women of Chalcis enters, singing of their town (on the island of Euboea opposite Aulis). They have come to see the great Greek warriors.

Menelaus and the Servant enter, struggling over Agamemnon's letter, which Menelaus has read. Menelaus accuses Agamemnon of being irresolute and contemptible. Agamemnon in turn says Menelaus could not even manage to keep his wife. He refuses to kill his child for a faithless woman. As the brothers quarrel a Messenger announces the arrival of Iphigenia, Clytemnestra, and Orestes. Agamemnon weeps at the thought of sacrificing Iphigenia. Regretting his hostile words and his demand that Iphigenia be slain for the false Helen, Menelaus urges his brother to disband the army. Agamemnon, however, feels compelled to go on with the sacrifice. He says the Greek army will force him to slay his child because Odysseus will reveal the prophecy of Calchas and asks Menelaus to make sure that Clytemnestra does not discover their plans for the sacrifice.

The Chorus sings of Paris' immoderate love for Helen, which brought about war and hatred. Soon the leader of the Chorus sees Clytemnestra, Iphigenia, and Orestes approaching. As Iphigenia greets Agamemnon, she expresses her love for him. Filled with guilt and remorse, he cannot help weeping; vainly he attempts to persuade Clytemnestra to go back to Argos. As she enters the tent, he goes to find Calchas in order to make plans for the sacrifice.

After a choral ode prophesying the fall of Troy, Achilles enters; restless and impatient, he is seeking Agamemnon to demand that he act at once to launch the ships on their way to Troy. When Clytemnestra sees Achilles, she mentions his forthcoming marriage to Iphigenia. Achilles, who knows nothing about Agamemnon's plot, declares that he is not a suitor of Iphigenia. Finally the old Servant discloses Agamemnon's plan to sacrifice Iphigenia. Achilles and Clytemnestra are horrified at the news, and when she begs him to help save her daughter, he agrees. He suggests that Clytemnestra try to persuade Agamemnon to give up his cruel plan and, if she does not succeed, to return to him for aid. The Chorus sings of the marriage of Achilles' parents, Peleus and Thetis, and the birth of their noble son; then its tone changes to a sad one, as it sings of Iphigenia, who is to be sacrificed.

Clytemnestra pleads with great feeling for the life of her child; she accuses Agamemnon of having no judgment, no heart, and begs him not to commit murder. Iphigenia, who now knows why she has been summoned to Aulis, also pleads, reminding her father of the tender and happy moments of their past; but Agamemnon, determined to fight against Troy, insists that his obligations to Greece must supersede his personal feelings. When he leaves, Clytemnestra and Iphigenia weep and moan until Achilles enters and offers to save the girl, despite the opposition of the whole Greek army. Courageously Iphigenia refuses his offer, saying she has decided to give her life for the sake of Hellas. The conquest of Troy by the Greeks will make up to her for the loss of her life, marriage, and children. Bidding her mother not to mourn and the Chorus to sing to Artemis, Iphigenia goes to her death.

COMMENTARY. *Iphigenia in Aulis* was written near the end of Euripides' life and was incomplete when he died. His son, Euripides the Younger, finished the play and produced it in 406 B.C. The text of the play is complicated by sections that scholars believe do not belong to the original version. Most scholars do not accept as genuine the conclusion in which Iphigenia is replaced by a deer at her sacrifice (see *Iphigenia in Tauris*). The passage has not been included in the present summary.

Iphigenia in Tauris (Iphigeneia he en Taurois). A tragedy (c. 414–412 B.C.) by EURIPIDES. Translations: in verse, Robert Potter, 1781–83; in verse, Arthur S. Way, 1912; in prose, Augustus T. Murray, 1931; in verse, Witter Bynner, 1956.

MYTHICAL BACKGROUND. When Agamemnon led the Greek forces against Troy, his ships were delayed at Aulis by unfavorable weather. The prophet Calchas declared that the goddess Artemis required the sacrifice of Agamemnon's daughter Iphigenia. Reluctantly Agamemnon agreed to kill his child, but (according to the version of the myth which Euripides employs) Artemis secretly replaced the girl with a hind, which was sacrificed in her stead, and took Iphigenia to Tauris, a savage land beyond the Symplegades (located in what now is the Crimea). There Artemis made Iphigenia her priestess, whose duty it was to consecrate strangers to the land; they were then sacrificed to the goddess. While Iphigenia has been in Tauris, the Trojan War has ended, and Agamemnon has been slain by his wife, Clytemnestra. Their son Orestes has avenged his father's death by slaying his mother and has endured agonizing guilt. (See Aeschylus' *Oresteia,* Sophocles' *Electra,* and Euripides' *Electra* and *Orestes.*) He has now been commanded by Apollo to go to Tauris in order to obtain the sacred image of Artemis that is there and that Orestes must bring to Attica.

SCENE. Tauris, before the temple of Artemis.

SUMMARY. Iphigenia, dressed as a priestess of Artemis, comes out of the temple and speaks of the events of the past—the prophecy of Calchas, the preparations for her sacrifice, and her rescue by Artemis—which have led up to her present position as a priestess who consecrates human victims before they are sacrificed. Iphigenia is troubled by a dream she had the night before, which suggests that her brother Orestes has died. As she goes into the temple to offer sacrifices for her brother, Orestes and his friend Pylades appear. Frightened by the sight of the bloodstained altar before the temple, Orestes addresses

Apollo, asking him what new ordeal he faces. After Orestes had wandered through many lands seeking release from his guilt, Apollo told him that if he brought the image of Artemis from Tauris to Attica, his suffering would end. Now Orestes fears he will be unable to accomplish his mission, and he considers fleeing Tauris. Encouraged by Pylades, however, he is determined to seize the image. The two men go off to a cave to wait until evening, when it will be safer to take the image from its shrine.

The Chorus of Captive Greek Women enters, soon followed by Iphigenia and her attendants. Iphigenia and the women of the Chorus mourn for Orestes, who they think is dead.

A Herdsman comes in, seeking Iphigenia. He informs her that two strangers have been seized, who will make good sacrifices to Artemis. When he tells Iphigenia that the captives are Greeks, she remarks that in all the time she has been a priestess no Greek has been sacrificed. The Herdsman goes on to describe the capture of the two young men, saying that one of them, in a fit of madness, believed himself to be pursued by the Furies and began to attack the herds. Finally he and his friend were captured. When the Herdsman goes out Iphigenia considers how hardened she has become to human suffering. At first she dreaded the day when she must consecrate a Greek for sacrifice, but now that she thinks Orestes is dead, she feels no pity for the two victims. Recalling the past, when she was lured by her father to be sacrificed for the sake of Helen, the false wife, Iphigenia feels bitterness toward the Greeks. Then she thinks of the strange sacrificial ceremonies in which she now takes part and declares they cannot be true religious rites: the savage people of Tauris merely justify their own cruelty by calling them that. She goes into the temple, and the Chorus sings of the two Greek men who have come to Tauris.

As Iphigenia comes out of the temple, Orestes and Pylades are brought in bound. Iphigenia orders the guards to untie their arms because they are to be consecrated by her. She begins to question them, and as she asks about their homes and families, she reveals the pity she cannot help feeling. Though Orestes will not tell Iphigenia his name, he does say that he comes from Argos. He then goes on to tell her about the fall of Troy and the fates of many of the heroes, including Agamemnon, who was slain by Clytemnestra. Iphigenia pities both her father and her mother. She then learns that Orestes slew Clytemnestra and that he is still alive. Realizing that the dream she feared was false, Iphigenia suddenly decides to free this unknown young man if he will deliver a letter for her when he returns to Argos. Orestes says he would prefer to save Pylades, who will deliver the letter. Touched by the youth's noble character, Iphigenia agrees to sacrifice Orestes instead. While she is away for a few moments, Pylades urges Orestes to let him die beside him, but Orestes insists that Pylades must live and marry Electra.

Iphigenia returns and asks Pylades to take an oath that he will deliver the letter she has brought from the temple. When Pylades fears that he may lose the letter and thus unwillingly be false to his oath, Iphigenia says she will tell him what the letter contains. It is a message to Orestes, informing him that Iphigenia is alive and asking him to take her back to Argos. Pylades takes the letter and hands it to Orestes, who stands beside him. At first Iphigenia cannot believe that it is really Orestes, but he soon convinces her. When he asks her to help him take the image of Artemis back to Argos, Iphigenia decides that her first duty is to her family and to Argos, and she consents. She will not agree to kill King Thoas of Tauris, who befriended her, but offers a plan by which Orestes, Pylades, and she may escape with the image of Artemis. She will tell the king that Orestes, who is polluted with the blood of the mother he murdered, has defiled the image with his touch. Therefore Orestes, his companion, and the image must be washed in the sea. Iphigenia must carry the image, because no man may touch it. Once at the shore they will sail away in Orestes' ship, which is anchored there. The Chorus vows to keep the secret and then sings of the beauty of its home in Greece in a song full of longing.

Soon King Thoas enters with his soldiers. He accepts the story Iphigenia tells him about the pollution of the Greeks and agrees to the ritual cleansing. Moreover, he consents to her request that he and his people cover their eyes supposedly to avoid seeing the pollution of Orestes. In this way Iphigenia, Pylades, and Orestes go off to their ship with the image.

After a choral ode dealing with the birth of Apollo and Artemis, a Messenger comes in to announce that Thoas and his people have been deceived by the Greeks, who are now escaping with the image of Artemis. But their ship has been driven back by a storm, and it is possible to seize them. As Thoas and his men set out for the shore, the goddess Athene, the *deus ex machina,* is seen above them. Athene informs Thoas that Orestes is merely fulfilling the command of Apollo. He must take the image of Artemis to Halae, on the boundaries of Attica. There the Greeks must build a temple to Artemis and must place the image within it. The old ritual of human sacrifice is to be preserved only symbolically in the shedding of one drop of blood when the festival celebrating Artemis' release from Tauris is held. The captive Greek women are also to return to their homes. King Thoas agrees to obey the commands of the goddess, and the Chorus joyously gives thanks to Athene.

Iphitus (Iphitos). See THE WOMEN OF TRACHIS.

Iris. In Greek mythology, the daughter of Thaumas and Electra (the daughter of Oceanus), the goddess of the rainbow and the messenger of the gods. Iris is mainly the servant of Hera.

Isis. The most important female goddess worshiped by the ancient Egyptians. Isis was the sister and wife of Osiris, the chief male god. A goddess of fertility, her symbol was the cow, and she is often represented with a cow's horns. She also ruled over the Underworld. When Osiris, a god of fertility, was dismembered by his brother Set (later identified by the Greeks with Typhon), Isis gathered the pieces of his body and buried them. Then she and her son

Horus (god of the Sun) avenged his murder. When the worship of Isis and Osiris was introduced into Greece, Isis was sometimes associated with Demeter and Osiris with Dionysus. Despite the objections of the state, the religion of Isis also became popular in Rome (see Apuleius' THE GOLDEN ASS).

Ismene. A daughter of Oedipus and Jocasta. See Sophocles' OEDIPUS AT COLONUS and ANTIGONE. Ismene also appears in Aeschylus' *Seven Against Thebes.*

Isocrates (Isokrates). A Greek oratorical writer, born in 436 B.C. to a wealthy Athenian family. Plato, in his *Phaedrus,* describes Isocrates as a "companion" of Socrates, who, Socrates predicts, will have a brilliant future. Isocrates studied with Gorgias, whose approach to oratory as an art strongly influenced his pupil. Forced to flee from Athens during the reign of the Thirty Tyrants, he stayed in Chios for a short time and there taught rhetoric. Returning to Athens, he wrote speeches to be delivered by litigants and in 392 B.C. established a school of rhetoric that brought him fame and wealth. He became a leading teacher of his time, and many of his pupils later became famous men.

Because of physical and temperamental limitations, Isocrates was unfit for a public career and never delivered the speeches he wrote. His best works are his political speeches or discourses, the main subject of which is his passionate belief that the Greek states must be unified to survive. Twenty-one of his speeches and nine letters are extant. Isocrates died in 338 B.C. at the age of ninety-eight.

In *Panegyricus,* his best-known discourse, a work on which he spent ten years and which was published in 380 B.C., Isocrates urges the Greek states to form a Panhellenic union led by Sparta and Athens in order to wage war on their common enemy Persia. Isocrates also believed that a great leader could unify the Greek states; in 346 B.C. he published a discourse urging Philip of Macedon to lead the Greek states against Persia. In *On the Peace*— another famous speech, written in 355 B.C., just before the end of the Social War in which Athens' dependencies, the islands of Chios, Cos, and Rhodes, revolted against her domination—Isocrates attempts to persuade Athens to end the war and condemns her imperialist policy. Athens, he says, can survive only by surrendering her naval empire. By her imperialism Athens is bringing about her own destruction. In *Areopagiticus,* written later in 355 B.C., after Athens had made peace by recognizing the independence of Chios, Cos, Rhodes, and the city of Byzantium, Isocrates contrasts the present democracy of Athens, with all its shortcomings, with the aristocratic democracy headed by Solon and Cleisthenes. He suggests that the Areopagus, the council of nobles, be granted the great power it once had. (John Milton's *Areopagitica* of 1644, written in the form of a classical oration, is obviously named for this work.) Six of Isocrates' extant orations are forensic, written for litigants at a trial.

Isocrates' prose indicates how strongly he was influenced by the teachings of

Gorgias; it is copious, ornate, and rhythmical. Isocrates himself had a great influence on both Greek and Latin prose stylists, among them Cicero, who adapted the techniques of Isocrates to his own language and his own great gifts.

Ithaca (Ithake). An island in the Ionian Sea, near Epirus. Ithaca was the home of Odysseus. See ODYSSEY.

Ixion. In Greek mythology, the husband of Dia. When her father Deioneus came for the promised bridal gifts, Ixion murdered him, but Zeus purged Ixion of his guilt. Ixion then tried to seduce Hera. To punish him Zeus created an image of Hera from the cloud Nephele, which bore Ixion the Centaurs Ixion was further punished by being bound to a wheel that turned continuously in the Underworld. Only the beautiful music of Orpheus (see *Metamorphoses* x) could stop that wheel, and the relief was only temporary.

J

Janus. An ancient Italian god with two faces looking in different directions. He was the god of beginnings; thus January was the month sacred to him. Janus also guarded gates and doors; in ancient Rome the doors of the temple of Janus were open during war and closed during peace. In early Rome Janus was one of the most important gods, always first in prayer and sacrifice.

Jason (Iason). In Greek myth, son of Aeson. Aeson was the rightful king of Iolcos in Thessaly, but his half brother Pelias had seized his throne. Jason was sent away to be reared by the centaur Chiron. Pelias, warned by an oracular prophecy to protect himself against a young man who should come wearing only one sandal, feared Jason when he returned to Iolcos after losing a sandal in the River Anaurus. When Jason claimed the throne of Iolcos, Pelias set what he thought would be a hopeless task for the young man: he must first obtain from Aeëtes, king of Colchis, the Golden Fleece, which had magic powers and was guarded by a gigantic serpent. Jason's adventures in obtaining the fleece are told by Apollonius Rhodius in his ARGONAUTICA and by Valerius Flaccus in his ARGONAUTICA; his later life with Medea is dramatized by Euripides in his MEDEA and by Seneca in his MEDEA. Jason also appears in connection with Medea in Ovid's METAMORPHOSES and in his HEROIDES VI and XII.

Jocasta (Iocaste). The wife of King Laius of Thebes and the mother and wife of Oedipus. See Sophocles' OEDIPUS THE KING, Euripides' THE PHOENICIAN WOMEN, and Seneca's OEDIPUS. Jocasta also appears in Statius' *Thebaid*.

Juno. The chief goddess of the Romans, the wife of Jupiter. Juno became identified with the Greek goddess Hera. As the goddess of childbirth, Juno was known as Lucina; as the goddess of good counsel, she was called Moneta. She was also known as a moon goddess. For her hatred of the Trojans see Vergil's AENEID.

Jupiter. The chief god of the Romans. His name is derived from *Diovis-pater* or *Jovis-pater* (father of the bright heavens). Originally a sky god, he became the Roman lord of the gods and later the equivalent of the Greek Zeus. His many epithets such as *Pluvius, Tonans, Fulgator,* and *Fulminator* tell of his role as the god of rain, thunder, and lightning. Because the temple of Jupiter at Rome was on the Capitoline Hill, he was also called Capitolinus and Tarpeius (the Tarpeian Rock was a peak of the Capitoline Hill). Jupiter was also called *Imperator, Victor, Invictus, Stator, Feretrius, Triumphator,* and other names indicating his association with victory and conquest in war. Like Zeus, Jupiter could foretell the future and indicate its course to man through signs and prophecies. He represented law and morality. The oak is the sacred tree of Jupiter; the eagle is his bird.

Juturna (Iuturna). A Roman goddess of fountains. In the AENEID (XII), Juturna is the sister of the warrior Turnus.

Juvenal (Decimus Junius Juvenalis). Roman satirist. Juvenal was born about A.D. 60 at Aquinum (Aquino), about eighty miles southeast of Rome. Little is known about his youth except that his family was fairly wealthy and he received a good education. His satires provide evidence that he lived in Rome for some time during the reign of the emperor Domitian (A.D. 81–96). Juvenal does not merely allude to the extreme cruelty of Domitian and the fear he inspired; in Juvenal's satires Domitian becomes a symbol of the insane pride of the tyrant whose excesses can debase a whole era. Juvenal was a friend of the poet Martial, who refers to him in his work. It is thought that Juvenal offended Domitian by a reference to the actor Paris (*Satire* VII, 87–90), once a favorite of the emperor's, but later executed at his command (A.D. 83) under suspicion of having had a love affair with the emperor's wife. Juvenal's punishment was banishment to Egypt, where he remained until Domitian was killed (A.D. 96). Since Juvenal's allusion to Paris could not have been made until A.D. 91 or 92, eight or nine years after the actor's execution, some scholars do not accept the theory that the poet's reference to him was the cause of his exile. Gilbert Highet offers the most convincing explanation: that Juvenal's apparently innocuous allusion to the dead actor Paris probably referred to some specific present corruption in Domitian's court; the emperor knew that Juvenal was using an event of the past to satirize the present power of his obsequious favorites and, outraged, Domitian sent the poet into exile (Gilbert Highet, *Juvenal the Satirist* [New York: Oxford University Press, 1954], pp. 24–25). When Juvenal returned to Rome from exile in A.D. 96, poor and embittered, he was forced to accept the patronage of men he despised, as he composed his great SATIRES on Roman life of the past and present. These satires appeared in five books: Book I, *Satires* 1–5; Book II, *Satire* 6; Book III, *Satires* 7–9; Book IV, *Satires* 10–12; and Book V, *Satires* 13–16. Finally, after some years, through the generosity of a patron—possibly the Emperor Hadrian—Juvenal achieved financial security and obtained a farm at Tibur. He died around A.D. 130.

In Juvenal's first satire, which is the best critical introduction to his work, he says that when he observes the corruption around him "it is difficult not to write satire." Indeed, "indignation creates [his] verses." In contrast to Horace, the gentle, paternal reformer who chides man for his follies, Juvenal is the outraged moralist, laying bare the ugly vice of a corrupt society. His rage is both controlled and intensified by sorrow at man's inexplicable compulsion to self-destruction. This union of violent anger and tragic irony creates the greatest satire of the ancient and modern world.

Juvenal is rarely humorous. His wit is bitter, ironic, bizarre, and painful. He is always aware of the tragic implications of evil, and he seems compelled to expose it through denunciation. His satires are impersonal, and we know far less about the man who wrote them than we do about Horace. Yet we do know the intensity of Juvenal's feelings, how his "heart burns with wrath" (1, 45) as he looks at the corruption of the world he lives in.

Though Juvenal is obviously speaking about the vices he sees around him, he constantly exposes them not by reference to contemporary persons and events but to those of the recent past. Juvenal himself tells us at the end of the first satire that it is not safe for him openly to criticize his contemporaries in power. He must refer only to those whose ashes lie beneath the monuments to the dead along the great roads that lead to Rome. This no doubt justifiable fear accounts in part for Juvenal's frequent references to the reigns of the dead Nero, Domitian, and Otho. Yet Juvenal's preoccupation with the past is not so simply explained. He is not concerned only with the recent past but with a far distant past, the idealized Rome of the Republic, which is his standard or norm. Sometimes he addresses himself to or evokes the memory of the great heroes of the past, who ruled Rome when it was a noble and virtuous nation. Juvenal wonders how the great leaders of the past could bear to look at their degenerate offspring. One of Juvenal's most effective satirical techniques is his contrast between the idealized image of Rome exemplified by the Republic with the Rome of the recent past and present, the empire, growing in power and corruption. His own period is thus only a part of the recent history of Rome, fallen, like a proud tragic hero, from a high and noble place to error and evil.

Taking the *persona* or role of the outraged orator, Juvenal addresses his audience in the language of impassioned speech, apparently attempting to shock the Romans out of their apathy. Often he adapts the techniques of oratory—argumentation, a series of rhetorical questions, accumulation of evidence—to poetry. If, in Juvenal's hands, satire lost the ease and casual grace of the Horatian *Sermones*, it gained in depth and intensity, which, it may be said, Juvenal first gave to the form. Juvenal used the same meter as Horace and Lucilius, but the hexameters that produce in Horace's lines an easy, conversational tone, in Juvenal's create the effect of powerful and sometimes violent speech. His tragic recognition of the self-destructive drives of man, his ironic and angry arguments, and his impassioned oratorical manner established satire as one of the most significant poetic forms.

Allusions to Juvenal can be found in Chaucer, John Skelton, John Marston, Joseph Hall, and John Donne, but his influence is most powerfully felt in the neoclassical writers, John Dryden, Jonathan Swift, Alexander Pope, and Samuel Johnson. In his essay on satire (1693) Dryden says that "Juvenal excels in the tragical satire, as Horace does in the comical." Dryden was drawn to Juvenal's argumentative manner; Juvenal, he says, "could not rally, but he could declaim;

and as his provocations were great, he revenged them tragically." In his own satire Dryden emulated Juvenal's oratorical manner, his scornful and sorrowful declamations, and, in so doing, Dryden achieved his own best effects. Jonathan Swift, in the epitaph that he wrote for himself, declared that only death could prevent "*saeva indignatio*" (violent indignation) from tearing at his heart—an explicit statement of his own role as a Juvenalian satirist. Pope, whose chief model was Horace, also emulated the fierce and dark portraiture of Juvenal. Samuel Johnson imitates Juvenal's third satire in his poem "London"; his "The Vanity of Human Wishes" suggests that the tragic self-delusion of man which Juvenal records in his tenth satire is still and perennially a condition of human life. See also SATIRE.

K

Knights, The (Hippeis). An Old Comedy (424 B.C.) by ARISTOPHANES. Translations: in verse, John Hookham Frere, 1839; in verse, Benjamin B. Rogers, 1924; in verse, Arthur S. Way, 1934.

BACKGROUND. In *The Knights* Aristophanes again deals with political events related to the Peloponnesian War between Athens and Sparta. He denounces Cleon, a leather merchant who has recently led a successful attack against the island of Sphacteria and thus has "stolen" the victory of Pylos from Demosthenes, the great Athenian general who was in command of the expedition. As a result Cleon has become the most important political and military leader in Athens. Aristophanes regards him a demagogue and attacks his rather showy rhetorical techniques and his appeals to the stock response of the populace.

SCENE. Before the house of Demos.

SUMMARY. Demosthenes and Nicias, generals of the Athenian army, are depicted as slaves of Demos (the people). They enter complaining of the beating they have received for which a new slave, a Paphlagonian tanner (Cleon), is responsible. He flatters and deceives their master, and has made life unbearable for the other slaves. Demosthenes decides that the way to overcome the Paphlagonian is to steal his oracle book. Since he is now lying in a drunken sleep, Nicias easily takes the book, which contains a prophecy that the tanner is to be replaced by a Sausage Seller. When a Sausage Seller appears, Demosthenes and Nicias tell him he is destined to become the greatest of men, the ruler of Athens. The Sausage Seller cannot understand how he, a man of no education or background, whose parents were rogues, can assume so much power. Demosthenes replies that these are exactly the qualifications for a great leader of Athens. The Sausage Seller is still reluctant to accept such a position, and, when Cleon comes out of the house and threatens the conspirators, the Sausage Seller starts to run. Demosthenes begs him to have courage and calls the Knights to help them.

The Chorus of Knights enters hurriedly, crying out that Cleon is a villain and accusing him of hypocrisy, fraud, and cruelty. Cleon calls the popular Assembly to rescue him. Then Cleon and the Sausage Seller denounce each other, each trying to outdo the other in vulgarity and dishonesty. The Chorus accuses Cleon of cheating and destroying Athens, and Cleon brags about his ability to fool and control the Athenian people, about his impudence and his dishonesty. He says he will hurry to the Senate, where he will bring charges of treason against the Sausage Seller. Demos urges the Sausage Seller to prepare well for the attack.

The Knights deliver the parabasis, praising Aristophanes for his honesty and singing of the glory of their ancestors, who fought nobly for Athens and not for personal gain. They then welcome the Sausage Seller, who returns to announce the victory he achieved in the Senate by imitating the audacity and hypocrisy of Cleon. Cleon rushes in, and once again he and the Sausage Seller quarrel savagely. When Demos comes out of his house to find out what is going on, both Cleon and the Sausage Seller flatter him and try to win his favor—Cleon, by recounting all he has done for Athens and the Sausage Seller by promising peace and prosperity. The Sausage Seller wins this contest and also the next two, in which he and Cleon compete in presenting their oracles and in plying Demos with food and drink. During this last contest the Sausage Seller steals a hare that Cleon has brought as an offering and presents it as his own gift to Demos (one of several references in the play to the Athenian victory at Pylos, which actually was won by Demosthenes but was claimed or "stolen" by Cleon).

Finally Cleon admits defeat and hands his chaplet to the Sausage Seller, who becomes the leader of Athens. Now the Sausage Seller reveals that his name is Agoracritus and then follows Demos into his house. The Chorus then denounces various Athenian leaders. Elaborately dressed, Agoracritus returns, announcing that he has restored Demos to his ancient vigor. Demos then speaks of the traditional Athenian values: peace, honesty, and civic devotion. Agoracritus gives Demos Truce, a beautiful young girl, whom Cleon had locked up. It is decided that Cleon's punishment will be to sell sausages to the allies of Athens, whom he has long mistreated.

L

Lacedaemon (Lakedaimon). See SPARTA.

Laches. A dialogue by PLATO on courage.

Laertes. The father of Odysseus. See the ODYSSEY, especially Book XXIV.

Laestrygones. (Laistrygones). See ODYSSEY X.

Laius (Laios). A king of Thebes, the son of Labdacus, and father of Oedipus. See Sophocles' OEDIPUS THE KING and Seneca's OEDIPUS.

Lamachus (Lamachos). A leading Athenian general in the Peloponnesian War, who was killed in battle in 414 B.C. See Thucydides' THE PELOPONNESIAN WAR VI and Aristophanes' THE ACHARNIANS.

Lament for Adonis. A pastoral elegy (possibly from the late second century B.C.) by Bion. Translations: in verse, M. J. Chapman, 1836; in prose, Andrew Lang, 1889; in verse, J. H. Hallard, 1894; in prose, J. M. Edmonds, 1912; in verse, Arthur S. Way, 1913.

S U M M A R Y . Like the dirge for Adonis sung in Theocritus' *Idyl* XV, this poem is modeled after actual dirges sung at the festivals for Adonis. The poet cries out in grief for the death of the beautiful Adonis and calls upon Cypris (Aphrodite) to awaken and mourn for her beloved. The poet describes the wound Adonis received from a boar while he was hunting and the wailing of his hounds and the lamentations of the nymphs. Aphrodite meanwhile runs wildly through the woods calling the name of her beloved. A long passage follows, describing Aphrodite's discovery of the dying Adonis and her dreadful grief. The Graces and the Fates mourn also.

Since the poem is related to the yearly ritual grief for the dead god, it ends with advice to Aphrodite to weep no more; her grief is over until the next year.

Lament for Bion. A pastoral elegy (possibly late second century B.C.) by an unknown pupil of Bion; erroneously thought to be Moschus. Translations: in verse, M. J. Chapman, 1836; in prose, Andrew Lang, 1889; in verse, J. H. Hallard, 1894; in prose, J. M. Edmonds, 1912; in verse, Arthur S. Way, 1913.

S U M M A R Y . Probably influenced by Bion's *Lament for Adonis*, the poet asks the glades, the rivers, the groves, and other parts of the natural world to join in his lamentations for the dead Bion. Bion is depicted as a conventional pastoral cowherd-poet, and in the refrain the poet asks the Muses for a song of woe. Because Bion's sweet voice can no longer be heard, all nature weeps. Apollo, the satyrs, the nymphs, indeed the whole of the pastoral world lament the dead Bion. Even the towns and cities express their grief.

The poet then refers to Bion's death by poisoning, asking how poison could touch lips like his and not be transformed into sweetness. He wishes that, like Orpheus, he could charm hell and restore Bion to life with his music. Perhaps Bion will win his own release from death through song.

Laocoön (Laokoon). See AENEID II.

Laomedon. In Greek mythology, the father of Priam and king of Troy. When Laomedon refused to pay Apollo and Poseidon for constructing the walls of Troy, Poseidon sent a sea monster to destroy the city. Only the sacrifice of Laomedon's daughter Hesione to the monster could stop him. When Heracles offered to kill the sea monster, Laomedon promised to reward him with his fabulous horses, but again he failed to keep his promise. Heracles conquered the city of Troy, slew Laomedon, and gave Hesione to Telamon, one of his friends.

Lasus (Lasos). Greek poet, born at Hermione in Argolis, who flourished during the second half of the sixth century B.C. He wrote choral poetry, mainly hymns and dithyrambs (none of them extant), and probably contributed to the development of the structure and music of the dithyramb. He is also known as a teacher of Pindar.

Latinus. In Roman legend, the son of Faunus by a nymph Marica. For his story as king of Latium and father of Lavinia see the AENEID.

Latona. The Latin name of LETO.

Lausus. See AENEID VII, X.

Lavinia. See AENEID.

Laws (Nomoi). The last dialogue by PLATO; probably left unfinished. An unnamed Athenian speaks with a Spartan, Megillus, and a Cretan, Cleinias, about the laws of Lycurgus and Minos. The Athenian objects to these laws because their chief concern is with war rather than with peace, the most important problem of the statesman. When Cleinias reveals that he intends to establish a new colony, the Athenian speaks of the organization of the state and its laws.

Leander (Leandros). See HERO.

Leda. In Greek mythology, the daughter of Thestios, king of Aetolia, and wife of Tyndareus, king of Sparta. Zeus fell in love with her and came to her in the form of a swan. In most myths Clytemnestra is Leda's child by Tyndareus, and Helen, Castor, and Polydeuces her children by Zeus. Castor is sometimes regarded as Leda's child by Tyndareus. William Butler Yeats describes the union of Zeus and Leda in one of the most beautiful poems in the English language, "Leda and the Swan."

Lemnos. An island in the Aegean Sea. Lemnos was considered sacred to Hephaestus, who was supposed to have landed there when Zeus threw him out of Olympus. The Argonauts stopped at Lemnos for a time, and the Lemnian women bore their children (see Ovid's HEROIDES VI). They and their mothers were murdered by the Pelasgians. In Sophocles PHILOCTETES, Lemnos is a deserted island on which the Greeks have abandoned the wounded hero Philoctetes. See HYPSIPYLE.

Lesbia. See CATULLUS and LYRICS.

Lesbos. An island in the Aegean, off the coast of Mysia in Asia Minor. Lesbos was the home of Terpander, Arion, ALCAEUS, SAPPHO, and Theophrastus.

Lethe. In Greek and Latin literature the plain or river of oblivion in Hades. In Aristophanes (*The Frogs*, l. 186) Lethe is a plain; in Plato (*Republic* x) it is both a plain and a river; in Vergil (AENEID VI) it is a river. Dead souls drink of the river that flows through Lethe, or of the River Lethe, before reincarnation, so that they will forget their past lives.

Leto. The mother of Apollo and Artemis. The daughter of the Titans, Coeus and Phoebe, Leto was beloved of Zeus. When she was about to give birth to his children, Apollo and Artemis, she could find no place that would welcome her, because all dreaded the wrath of Hera. Finally Leto was received at Delos, where she bore the twin gods (see HOMERIC HYMN III). In Latin, her name is Latona.

Leucippus (Leukippos). An early Greek philosopher (c. fifth century B.C.) of whom very little is known. His place of birth is uncertain. Two works are attributed to him: *The Great World Order,* of which a short fragment remains, and *On Mind,* which is lost. Leucippus is regarded the founder of the atomic theory of matter.

Leucothea. See INO.

Libation Bearers, The. See under ORESTEIA.

Liber. Originally an Italian god of fertility, who later became identified with Dionysus.

Library, The. See BIBLIOTHECA.

Lives of the Caesars (Vitae Duodecim Caesarum). Biographies (early 2nd century A.D.) by Suetonius, including lives of Julius Caesar and the emperors Augustus, Tiberius, Caligula, Claudius, Nero, Galba, Otho, Vitellius, Vespasian, Titus, and Domitian. Suetonius was able to study official documents, and the Imperial archives were available to him; moreover, a good deal of his information about the emperors from Tiberius through Nero came from persons who had lived during their reigns. Though the *Lives of the Caesars* does contain some valuable information about Roman history, this aspect of the work has been overshadowed by its more sensational sections on the personal lives and habits of the Roman emperors. Because so many of them were men of violence with bizarre tastes, which they indulged without restraint, a mere recording of facts about their lives is necessarily sensational.

Some of the most interesting passages in the *Lives of the Caesars* are those dealing with the assassination of Julius Caesar; dinner parties given by Augustus; the spectacles sponsored by Caligula and his appearances as gladiator, singer, and dancer; the tormented youth of Claudius; and Nero's reaction to the fire of Rome, for which, according to Suetonius, he was responsible. Suetonius' descriptions of the physical characteristics of the emperors are detailed and vivid; he also writes of their attitudes toward food, drink, and clothing. Probably much of Suetonius' *Lives* is based on fact, but his concentration on the almost incredible cruelty and barbarity of most of the emperors results in portraits of monstrous figures, which can hardly be imagined as human. An excellent translation of the *Lives of the Caesars* by Philemon Holland appeared in 1606. There is a fine recent translation by Robert Graves (1957).

Livius Andronicus, Lucius. Roman poet, born about 284 B.C. at Tarentum. Livius Andronicus, who is regarded as the founder of Latin literature, was probably a Greek. He was taken to Rome as a prisoner when his city was captured by the Romans in 272 B.C. When freed he assumed the name of his former master, Livius Salinator, and remained in Rome, teaching and writing. He translated the *Odyssey* into Latin Saturnian verse (see METER) and wrote the first tragedies and comedies in the Latin language, all of them adaptations of Greek dramas. In 207 B.C., during the Second Punic War, he was asked to write a hymn to be sung by a chorus of maidens in order to counteract bad omens for the state. Livius died around 204 B.C. Only fragments of his work remain, about forty-six lines of his translation of the *Odyssey* and about forty lines and eight titles of his tragedies. Though Cicero speaks contemptuously in the *Brutus* of Livius' work, his contribution to Latin literature should not be underestimated. He introduced Greek themes and forms into Rome and, through his adaptations of Greek works in the Latin language, created the foundation of a new literature.

Livy (Titus Livius). A Roman historian, born at Patavium (Padua) in 59 B.C., but spent his adult years at Rome. Little is known about his life. Despite Livy's open admiration for Republican principles, his exalted view of Roman history could only have pleased Augustus, and the two men formed a lasting friendship. Livy had no career apart from his literary one. He began work on his history of Rome *Ab Urbe Condita* (*From the Founding of the City*) about 29 B.C., and the work, which consisted of 142 books, appeared in installments. Livy died in A.D. 17. His history was admired and praised during his lifetime and long after his death.

Much of Livy's history is lost. The work was arranged in "pentads" and "decads" (groups of five and ten books). An epitome (summary) of it was written perhaps as early as Livy's own time. Also *Periochae* (abstracts) of each book were written. The extant history consists of Books I–X, XXI–XL, part of XLI, XLII, part of XLIII, XLIV, and XLV of Livy's original work. Except for Books CXXXVI and CXXXVIII, *Periochae* for the entire history still exist. There are also epitomes of Books XXXVII–XL and XLVIII–LV.

The plan of Livy's history was as follows: Books I–V, the founding of Rome, the rule of kings, the establishment of the Republic, and its history up to 390 B.C., when the Gauls conquered Rome; Books VI–XV, the period when Rome conquered Italy; Books XVI–XX, the First Punic War; Books XXI–XXX, the Second Punic War; Books XXXI–XLV, the wars with Macedon and other wars in the East; Books XLVI–XC, the period before and during the Social Wars, up to Sulla's death; Books XCI–CXVI, the period prior to the Gallic War, the Gallic War and the Civil War; Books CXVII–CXXXIII, the period following Caesar's death to Antony's death; Books CXXXIV–CXLII, the period of Augustus' reign up to 9 B.C.

In his "Preface" to his history Livy says that he wishes to record the great achievements of the Romans, the sovereigns of the world, and to teach by example noble conduct and virtue. In the history of no other nation does one observe so long a period of integrity and honor, though in recent times self-indulgence and corruption have debased the noble image of Rome. Livy begins his history with the traditional myths of the founding of Rome, not necessarily because he believes them, but because divine intervention in the establishment of so noble a state seems appropriate. The bravery of the Romans in warfare, he says, justifies their claiming Mars as their father. This declaration in his "Preface" sets the tone of the entire history. Livy is didactic, stately, and grave; he regards Roman achievement as heroic, and he is one of the Augustans who helped to establish the myth of Roman grandeur.

Though Livy has been regarded as a reliable source of Roman history, his work is sometimes inaccurate. He invents speeches for historical figures, and he is not always sound on factual matters, ignoring important materials available to him and accepting others without proper investigation of their authenticity. The sources he used for early Roman history were mainly the poet Ennius and annalists such as Fabius Pictor and Licinius Macer. Livy's gifts were not scholarly or scientific, but literary. He re-creates historical figures and episodes vividly. His Hannibal, the enemy of Rome, is fierce and heroic. His description of the Roman women rushing hysterically to the shrines of the gods as they fear Hannibal's approach is like a scene in a tragedy. Livy's depiction of the dignity of the Senate, the courage of Roman heroes, and the eloquence with which they speak convinces the reader that he is indeed dealing with heroic times.

Livy's work was admired by Tacitus, Seneca, Quintilian, and Plutarch. Philemon Holland's English translation of Livy in 1600 increased his reputation and his influence during the Renaissance.

"Longinus." The author of the critical essay LONGINUS ON THE SUBLIME is known as "Longinus" because the manuscript refers to the author as Dionysius Longinus, Dionysius, or Longinus. Nothing is known about the author of *Longinus on the Sublime.* Most authorities regard the essay as a product of the first century A.D.

Longinus, Cassius. A philosopher and rhetorician who lived from about A.D. 220 to about 273, mistakenly regarded as the author of *Longinus on the Sublime.* A neo-Platonist, Longinus is known for his friendship and loyalty to

Queen Zenobia of Palmyra, for which he was punished by death at the hands of Aurelian. His *Art of Rhetoric,* a prose treatise, survives.

Longinus on the Sublime (Peri Hupsous). A prose treatise, literary criticism (date unknown, probably first half of the first century A.D.) by "LONGINUS" or Dionysius or Dionysius Longinus. Translations: H. S. Havell, 1890; W. Rhys Roberts, 1899; A. O. Prickard, 1906; W. Hamilton Fyfe, 1932; Benedict Einarson, 1945.

SUMMARY. Addressing his essay to Postumius Terentianus, "Longinus" begins with a criticism of a treatise on the subject of the sublime by Caecilius, a Sicilian rhetorician of the first century B.C. "Longinus" finds Caecilius' work superficial mainly because Caecilius does not teach the reader how to train himself to perceive the sublime (grand or noble) elements in a work of art. Nonetheless, "Longinus" is grateful for Caecilius' very interest in the subject, to which "Longinus" now turns, beginning with a definition: the sublime consists of excellence and loftiness of language, which affects the reader not by rational argument but by an emotional appeal that transports him, "takes him out of himself." Sublimity, like lightning, works swiftly; with one stroke it conveys the great power of the artist. The sublime is an art that can be learned. Though it is true that genius is inborn, not acquired but bestowed by nature, nature itself does not exist haphazardly, but works according to law; moreover, one must learn what artistic effects can come only from natural genius.

After a gap of two pages of manuscript the discussion turns to the pitfalls that the great artist must beware of: turgidity, affectation, puerility, and frigidity. These often result from a misguided passion for novelty for its own sake. Man's best and worst qualities are closely allied and spring from the same source. Thus a distortion of the sublime becomes the puerile, the ridiculous. To avoid the faults listed above one must understand the intrinsic nature of the sublime.

One must distinguish the truly sublime from mere external show. The truly sublime is exalting; it produces pleasure and pride in the audience and identification with the creator and his work. Our satisfaction in it increases with repeated experience. The work of beauty and sublimity has universal appeal.

There are five authentic sources of the sublime in literature: the first is significant thoughts or ideas; the second, intense emotion; the third, powerful figures of thought and speech; the fourth, excellence in choice of words and imagery; and the fifth, the effective organization or arrangement of words, which ties together all the other qualities and is responsible for the total effect. The first two qualifications are inherent in the artist; the others are learned. Each of these requirements except emotion is analyzed and illustrated in some detail. Illustrating his thesis that the sublime expresses the "authentic ring" of a noble mind, "Longinus" discusses the sublimity of silence, for example, the silence of Ajax in *Odyssey* XI, 543–567. After a gap of six pages of manuscript there is more illustration of the sublimity of Homer. Having digressed in a passage on the *Odyssey*, "Longinus" next turns to Sappho's sublime power to select and depict essential and passionate feelings of the lover. Homer, Archilochus, and Demosthenes have the same ability to employ essential detail.

In the next section "Longinus" discusses amplification, development of thought by accumulation, which cannot be effective if it is merely a mechanical process. There is another gap of two pages of manuscript. Then Plato and Demosthenes are compared, and Plato's emulation of Homer is discussed. This leads to a brilliant description of the process of emulation. "Longinus" suggests that the writer imagine Homer standing over his shoulder. The writer should ask himself how Homer, Plato, or Demosthenes would have expressed his thoughts with sublimity. This process of emulation will lead not to servile copying but rather to standards of excellence (or perhaps more specifically to the writer's own idea or noblest conception of himself as a creator).

The next section deals with images and imagination and their proper employment in poetry and oratory. Illustrations are given from Euripides, Aeschylus, Sophocles, Demosthenes, and Hyperides. Then "Longinus" analyzes figures, which, without sublimity, are mere tricks. The best figures, he says, are those which are least obvious. Various figures are defined and analyzed, and after a gap of two pages of manuscript the discussion is continued. "Longinus" deals with asyndeton, hyperbaton, polyptote, periphrasis, and others.

After a gap of four pages of manuscript certain conclusions of Caecilius on so-called "vulgarity" of language are questioned, for "Longinus" finds such diction strong and effective at times. He also objects to Caecilius' decision that the number of metaphors a writer uses must be limited to two or three. Intense feeling can justify the bold sweep of a number of metaphors in succession. Also, "Longinus" cannot approve of Caecilius' preference of Lysias to Plato. This subject is developed in a discussion of the "noble errors" made by genius. A work of genius with flaws is preferable to a work which is without error but also without inspiration or grandeur. The writer who makes no errors tends to be a trivial mediocrity, for great genius refuses to be merely safe and, taking risks, naturally errs on occasion. Such errors are unimportant in relation to the whole work. Would a writer not prefer to be Homer to Apollonius, Pindar to Bacchylides, Sophocles to Ion? "Longinus" then compares Hyperides and Demosthenes, Lysias and Plato.

Sublimity, not freedom from error, causes men to approach the gods. The immortals—Homer, Demosthenes, Plato—had faults, but these are trivial compared to their genius. Their grandeur redeems their flaws.

After a gap of two pages of manuscript there is some discussion of the use of hyperbole. Then "Longinus" turns to the problem of arrangement of words, discussing the sentence, words, and phrases. He also considers the causes of low style, the opposite of sublimity.

The last section deals with the question of why there seem to be so many able men but no great men in contemporary society. The conclusion is that men always regard their own period as the worst. Poor values degrade man; he is the victim not of his society but of his own desires and needs.

COMMENTARY. The critical ideas of *Longinus on the Sublime* have been admired since its publication by Robortello in Basle in 1554. After Boileau translated it in 1674 it became one of the most celebrated critical documents, especially in seventeenth- and eighteenth-century England. Dryden, Addison, Pope, Goldsmith, Reynolds, Hurd, Fielding, and Gibbon were influenced by *Longinus on the Sublime,* and the idea of the "noble error" and the "grace beyond the reach of art" are critical clichés of the period. Pope's admiration for "fire" or the "sublimity" of genius is related to his admiration for "Longinus," which he expresses in the *Essay on Criticism* and elsewhere. A fine study of the great importance of "Longinus" in eighteenth-century thought and literature is Samuel H. Monk's *The Sublime: A Study of Critical Theories in Eighteenth-Century England* (Modern Language Association of America, 1935).

Longus. The author (c. third century A.D.) of the Greek novel *Daphnis and Chloe* (see the excellent translation by Moses Hadas, 1953). Practically nothing is known about Longus, who probably lived in Lesbos. *Daphnis and Chloe* is a pastoral love story that depicts the innocence and charm of two young lovers in their idealized natural setting.

Lotus-eaters (Lotophagoi). See ODYSSEY IX.

Lucan (Marcus Annaeus Lucanus). A Roman epic poet, born at Corduba (Cordova) in Spain in A.D. 39. A nephew of Seneca, he was taken to Rome as an infant by his wealthy family and there received an excellent education, mainly in rhetoric and philosophy. One of his teachers was the Stoic Cornutus. Lucan was a brilliant student; his early training in rhetoric and philosophy obviously influenced his poetry, which he began to write as a young man. Nero was drawn to the talented Lucan and honored him by appointing him quaestor. Soon, however, Lucan fell victim to Nero's insane jealousy. The emperor forbade Lucan to recite or publish his work. In retaliation Lucan joined the conspiracy of Piso to depose and murder Nero. Nero had him arrested and finally forced him to commit suicide on April 30, A.D. 65, at the age of twenty-six. Lucan's tragic ruin involved his father and his uncles Seneca and Gallio, who were also ordered to take their own lives.

Lucan's only extant work is his unfinished ON THE CIVIL WAR (often erroneously called *Pharsalia*), an epic poem in ten books dealing with Julius Caesar's struggle against the Senatorial party of Rome. Actually *On the Civil War* is more historical than epic, not only because Lucan deviates from epic tradition by omitting all divine intervention, but because his approach is essentially factual and descriptive. Though Lucan's epic is marred by inappropriate rhetorical flourishes, unnecessary learned allusions, and sensational details about battle and death, there are admirable passages that suggest a Roman's attitudes toward the history of his own nation. Pompey, Cato, and the Senatorial party are Lucan's heroes, and he is most effective when he reveals his feelings about these men and the principles for which they fought. As Quintilian points out, Lucan seems more the orator than the poet.

Lucian (Lucianus, Loukianos). A Greek writer, born around A.D. 120 at Samosata in Syria. Early in life he was apprenticed to a sculptor, but soon left this profession. Until he was forty, he traveled about Greece and Italy earning his livelihood as a rhetorician. Then he gave up rhetoric and settled down in Athens, studying philosophy with the Stoic Demonax and composing dialogues, especially satirical ones, a form he created. When Lucian was an old man, the Emperor Commodus appointed him to a position in Egypt, and there he probably remained until his death around A.D. 200.

Eighty-two works and some epigrams in the *Greek Anthology* are attributed to Lucian, but it is not certain that all these works are authentic. He wrote rhetorical, literary, and philosophical works, but is best-known for his satirical dialogues. His works are usually arranged in the following groups: (1) *Rhetorical writings.* The best-known of these are *Tyrannicide, The Disinherited Son,* two speeches named *Phalaris* (the tyrant of Acragas), and *An Apology for an Incorrect Greeting.* (2) *Literary Works. Lexiphanes* and *Trial Before the Vowels* mock excessive Atticists; *How to Write History* gives good advice on historiography, and *The True History* is an amusing account of an imaginary voyage to fantastic places, such as the moon and the belly of a whale. (3) *Mock-philosophical Works.* Lucian wrote a great many satires on philosophy in dialogue form. Perhaps the best-known of these is the *Dialogues of the Dead,* a collection of brief, ironic dialogues that take place in the Underworld and reveal, through the statements of such figures as Diogenes, Heracles, Menippus, and Achilles, the false values and pettiness of the living. *Charon* expresses his view of man's foibles, and *Descent into Hades* tells of the entrance of a group of people into the world of the dead. Other works in this group are *Menippus, Cock, Demonax, Hermotimus* (a satire on all types of philosophy), *The Confutation of Zeus,* and *Sale of Lives.* (4) *Satires on Various Subjects.* The best-known of these is the *Dialogues of the Gods,* in which Lucian presents the gods as rather ludicrous figures and mocks the traditional myths. Others in this group are *Dialogues of the Sea Gods, Dialogues of Courtesans, The Illiterate Bookbuyer,* and *Concerning Dependent Scholars.* (5) *Miscellaneous Writings.* Among these are *Tragic Gout,* a parody of Oedipus called *Swiftfoot,* and a novel, *Lucius, or The Ass,* which some authorities believe is based on a work by Lucius of Patrae that was also the model for Apuleius' *The Golden Ass.*

Lucilius, Gaius. A Roman satirist (180–102 B.C.). Lucilius was born at Suessa Aurunca in Campania. Important in the development of Roman SATIRE, he had an influence on the *Satires* of Horace and those of Juvenal and Persius. Of Lucilius' poems, which were written in various meters, only fragments remain.

Lucretius Carus, Titus. Roman poet. Little is known about his life, and most of the information we do have, which comes from St. Jerome's translation into Latin of Eusebius' Greek *Chronicles,* is open to question. Lucretius probably was born at Rome in 99 B.C. and died around 55 B.C He was an aristocrat and an acquaintance of Gaius Memmius, governor of Bithynia in 57 B.C., to whom *De Rerum Natura* (ON THE NATURE OF THINGS) is addressed. According to Jerome, Lucretius took a love potion, which made him insane; in his lucid times he wrote *On the Nature of Things,* which was edited by Cicero, and he committed suicide when he was forty-four years old. There is no evidence to support any of these statements.

Lucretius' admiration for the Greek philosopher Epicurus and his commitment to the Epicurean scientific and philosophical position are reflected in his only extant work, the didactic poem *On the Nature of Things,* which he left unfinished. Lucretius was mentioned by Cicero and admired by Vergil, who imitates him several times in his own poetry, by Statius, and by Ovid. However, his philosophical materialism was unattractive to the mentality of the Roman Empire and the Middle Ages, during which time he was ignored. During the Renaissance and the seventeenth century interest in *On the Nature of Things* revived, and the poem was translated and imitated. Milton echoes Lucretius in *Paradise Lost,* and Dryden, though he could not accept Lucretius' philosophical position, was drawn to his "fiery temper," his "masculine" thoughts, and the "torrent of his verse," parts of which he translated. Tennyson's poem "Lucretius" is based on the material in the account of Jerome. In recent times Allen Tate and other poets have referred to *On the Nature of Things* in image and symbol.

Lycurgus (Lykourgos) (I). In Greek legend, a king of the Edones in Thrace who was punished for his persecution of Dionysus. According to Homer (*Iliad,* VI), Lycurgus was blinded by Cronus. Another version of the legend is that the gods drove Lycurgus mad and he murdered his own son Dryas. In Sophocles' *Antigone* the chorus speaks of Lycurgus as imprisoned by Dionysus in a rocky dungeon. Lycurgus was the subject of a lost trilogy by Aeschylus.

Lycurgus (Lykourgos) (II). A legendary Spartan legislator. According to Herodotus (I, 65, 66), the oracle of Delphi hailed Lycurgus as "dear to Zeus" and "possibly a god." The oracle, according to some reports, says Herodotus, gave Lycurgus the whole legal system by which the Spartans were ruled. In antiquity Lycurgus was revered as the lawgiver of Sparta, who rewrote and reformed the constitution of the city-state. There is no evidence that he actually existed. Lycurgus was praised by Xenophon, and Plutarch wrote a life of him.

Lycurgus (Lykourgos) (III). An Attic orator of the fourth century B.C. and an ally of Demosthenes. For twelve years Lycurgus was in charge of Athenian finances. He was also responsible for significant construction in Athens. He had the harbor repaired and the fleet enlarged, the gymnasium of the Lyceum restored and the theatre of Dionysus rebuilt in marble. *Against Leocrates* is the only one of his fifteen speeches that is extant.

Lycus (Lykos). See Euripides' THE MADNESS OF HERACLES and Seneca's HERCULES FURENS.

Lydia. A poem in dactylic hexameter, attributed by some to VERGIL because Lydia is also referred to in the *Dirae*. In *Lydia* the speaker expresses his grief over the loss of his beloved.

lyric poetry. The term *lyric* originally applied only to poems meant to be sung to the music of the lyre, which expressed personal feelings about subjects such as love, old age, or poetry itself. Later, especially among Latin poets, there was no musical accompaniment.

MONODY, OR MELIC POETRY. Monodic lyrics (Gr. *monoidia*, a solo) or melic poems (Gr. *melos*, song) were composed according to a single line pattern or a monostrophic (single stanza repeated) pattern, in a variety of meters (see METER). The earliest extant lyric poetry was written during the seventh century B.C., but clearly the form is far older. There is evidence in the Homeric poems that both monodic and choral lyric existed before and during Homer's time. Though there are many mythical lyric poets of ancient Greece— Orpheus, Linus, Musaeus, Thamyris, and others—the first actual composers of lyrics that we know of are Terpander, Sappho, and Alcaeus. (Elegiac and iambic poetry, though sometimes loosely grouped with lyric, are here considered separately.) All three of these poets were natives of Lesbos. Terpander, who went to live in Sparta, established the lyric there, and in Sparta it developed into the more complicated and more formal choral lyric (see below).

Unfortunately, very little Greek lyric poetry has survived, but even the brief fragments that remain suggest the exquisite and at the same time apparently spontaneous quality of melic poetry. The words themselves are musical, and the emotions they express are intense and personal. The body of extant Roman lyrics is much larger than the Greek. Catullus, Horace, Tibullus, and Propertius imitate the themes, meters, and language of Sappho, Alcaeus, Anacreon, and the Alexandrians. Though in Roman times the lyric is no longer associated with the music of the lyre, it nonetheless retains a musical quality in its language and rhythm. The Roman lyric is descended from the Greek, but through the genius of Catullus, Horace, Propertius, and Tibullus, it develops into an independent and brilliant form.

CHORAL. The choral lyric is Dorian in origin, and was first established in Sparta by the poets Terpander and Alcman. Written for choral performance, the choral lyric was composed to be sung to music and dancing. Originally these performances were probably part of a religious ceremony, but later the choral ode, as developed by Stesichorus, Simonides, Bacchylides, and Pindar, was composed for other occasions, such as victories in the great athletic contests.

Although Stesichorus was a Sicilian, Simonides and Bacchylides were Ionians, and Pindar was a Boeotian, they wrote their choral odes in the Dorian dialect of its origin. (In the Dorian dialect the long *a* is dominant, as contrasted with the Ionian dialect in which long *e* is dominant.) Most choral odes are triadic in structure (composed of groups of three stanzas), with the first two, the strophe and the antistrophe, having the same metrical pattern and the third, the epode, a different one. Some, however, are antistrophic (having only a series of strophes and antistrophes). Stesichorus is reputed to have introduced the triadic structure, which was then taken up by Simonides and Pindar. The chief types of choral lyrics are the PAEAN, the PARTHENEION, the HEROIC HYMN, the ENCOMIUM, the EPINICION, the THRENOS, and the DITHYRAMB.

Lyrics, monodic, by ALCAEUS (first half of the sixth century B.C.). Translations: in verse, J. S. Easby-Smith, 1901; in prose, J. M. Edmonds, 1922; in verse, T. F. Higham, C. M. Bowra, and Gilbert Highet in T. F. Higham and C. M. Bowra, eds., *The Oxford Book of Greek Verse in Translation*, 1938; in verse, Willis Barnstone, 1962.

SUMMARY. The subjects of Alcaeus' poems, all of which are fragmentary, are varied; he writes of the gods in hymns, of the state of his native Lesbos besieged by tyrants, of heroic conduct in war, of wine, and of love. He scolds the citizens of Lesbos for their apathetic acceptance of a tyrant, and he sneers at the tyrant Pittacus for his low birth, urging the people to rebel against him. Alcaeus' ideal is the aristocratic heroic code. In a poem about a storm threatening the "ship of state" he demands manliness and courage. Some of Alcaeus' best lyrics are drinking songs, which, despite the elegance and lightness of the language, express the poet's sad awareness of the brevity of human life. In one poem Alcaeus explicitly urges the reader to "seize the moment," a theme which becomes extremely important in the work of Horace and later poets. Though Alcaeus neither suggests the intense experience nor conveys the intimate feelings that Sappho does, he writes more than mere graceful lyrics. His polished and elegant love and drinking songs reveal a serious poet, reflecting on the limitations of human life even as he recommends total involvement in pleasure.

Lyrics, monodic, by ANACREON (sixth century B.C.). Translations: in verse, Thomas Stanley, 1651; in verse, Thomas Moore, 1800; in prose, J. M. Edmonds, 1920; T. F. Higham and C. M. Bowra, eds., *The Oxford Book of Greek Verse in Translation*, 1938; in verse, Willis Barnstone, 1962.

SUMMARY. Anacreon writes with wit and grace about wine, love, and the brevity of life. He treats all subjects, even an address to a deity, with sophistication and charm. Unlike Sappho, he is detached from rather than totally involved in the experiences he writes of. When he recommends the golden mean, it is in connection with drinking; when he speaks of love, he is only half serious. The one thought that really seems to cause Anacreon pain is the prospect of old age when pleasure will be gone. Anacreon's wit and charm were extremely attractive to poets of the Hellenistic and Byzantine periods who imitated him in poems called *The Anacreontics*.

Lyrics, by CATULLUS (first half of the first century B.C.). His meters are dactylic hexameter, elegiac, iambic trimeter, choliambic, iambic tetrameter catalectic, phalaecean, greater asclepiadic, sapphic, and galliambic. Translations: in verse, Hugh Macnaghten, 1899; in prose, F. W. Cornish, 1912; F. A. Wright, ed., Broadway Translations, by various authors, 1926; in verse, Horace Gregory, 1956; in verse, Roy Arthur Swanson, 1959.

SUMMARY. Catullus writes on a variety of themes. His Lesbia poems deal with his love for Lesbia and his despair over his inability to renounce this love, his anger at the faithlessness of his mistress, and his determination to salvage his health and sanity despite his unhappiness. Though these are his best-known poems, they do not reveal the full range of his genius. Other brief poems deal with his experiences with his friends, his anger at Caesar, his sorrow over the death of his brother, his contempt for a poor poet or a pretentious orator, his love for his home at Sirmio. Catullus' longer poems reveal his ability in more formal, less personal expression. Whatever the subject, however, the poems are characterized by intense feeling, deep sincerity, and a quality of immediacy to be found with equal force only in the work of Sappho.

The Lesbia poems record Catullus' feelings about his beloved from his first responses of joy and delight to his last despair and agonized efforts at renunciation. One of the earliest poems addressed to Lesbia (51) is an adaptation of a poem by Sappho in which the lover describes in vivid detail the physiological effects of the presence of his beloved upon him. Catullus' capacity to express his own personal feelings in this Sapphic form and his addition of a last stanza with a warning against his own inclination to idle indulgence in his love make his adaptation an original poem. Other poems to Lesbia include the charming lyrics on the death of her sparrow (2, 3) and the passionate lines urging that they "live and love," paying no heed to the criticisms of others (5). All too soon, however, Catullus' tone changes. In a poem in which he addresses himself as though recording the conflict between the rational and passionate sides of his nature, he begs himself to cease being a fool, to give up what he sees is already lost (8). In another poem he prays that he may be rid of the "disease" of love; he does not ask what he knows is impossible, that Lesbia be faithful, only that he may find some peace (76). One of the most bitter and at the same time most beautiful of the Lesbia poems consists of only two lines, in which Catullus cries out in anguish: "I hate and I love" (85). An equally moving poem is addressed to Catullus' friend Caelius. Catullus seems to be pouring out his pain and bitterness to his friend. "That Lesbia," he says and repeats with growing intensity, "whom Catullus loved more than himself and all his other loves now in the roads and alleys strips the descendants of the magnanimous Remus" (58).

The poems of friendship, though lighter in spirit, disclose the warmth and sensitivity of spirit that made Catullus so vulnerable in his disastrous relationship with Lesbia. In a poem to Fabullus, inviting him to dinner, Catullus with wit and charm asks his friend to bring his own meal and in return promises to give him true love and a perfume given to his girl by Venus and Cupid. When Fabullus smells this perfume, he will ask the gods to make him all nose (13). Another poem addressed to C. Licinius Calvus tells of an evening during which Catullus and Calvus engaged in a contest of improvising verse. Catullus has been so inspired by the genius of Calvus that he has written a poem that he begs his friend to read at once (50). Calvus appears in another poem in which, with delicacy and tenderness, Catullus comforts his friend on the death of his wife (96). Like the poems of love and friendship, Catullus' elegy to his dead brother (101) expresses his deepest personal feelings. The reader sees the poet performing the simple ritual of bidding farewell to his brother, which seems to symbolize Catullus' mournful acceptance of the inevitability of death.

Catullus could express intense hate as well as love. His bitter attacks on Caesar (29, 57) and on his former friends Aurelius and Furius (16, 21, 23, 26) reveal the violence of his hatred. His poems on the lawyer Arrius (84), the poet Suffenus (22), and the works of Volusius (36) seem to sneer with contempt.

Among the longer poems of Catullus are two epithalamia (61, 62). The first was written for the marriage of Manlius Torquatus and Junia Aurunculeia, but was not composed to be sung by a chorus as is the traditional epithalamium. Instead the speaker hails Hymen, the god of marriage, and praises the beauty of the bride and the joys of marriage. The second epithalamium is arranged for two choruses, one of young men and the other of young women. The young men celebrate Hesperus (the evening star) and marriage itself; the young women sing of their fear and their reluctance to give up maidenhood. In another long poem (63) Catullus tells the tragic story of Attis, a young man who emasculated himself in the frenzy of his devotion to Cybele, and then, his reason restored, regretted his violent self-mutilation. With compassion and delicacy Catullus describes the thoughts and feelings of the tortured Attis, who contemptuously calls himself a girl. Catullus' epyllion in dactylic hexameter (64) deals with the marriage of Peleus and Thetis. In describing the embroidered covering of the couch of Thetis, Catullus also tells the story of Theseus and Ariadne.

As a poet of love and friendship Catullus is unique in Latin literature. With simple and direct language he depicts violent conflict, self-torture, and passionate love. In a few lines he conveys a dramatic and moving experience that seems to be taking place as he relates it. The economy and exactness of his language and the deep sincerity of his feelings make his self-revelations significant experiences and great poems.

Lyrics, monodic, by SAPPHO (first half of the sixth century B.C.), written in various meters, the best-known being the Sapphic. Translations: various translators, ed. H. T. Wharton, 1885; in verse, A. S. Way, 1920; in prose,

J. M. Edmonds, 1922; in prose and verse, E. M. Cox, 1924; in verse, P. Maurice Hill, 1954; in verse, Mary Barnard, 1958.

SUMMARY. The songs of Sappho express deep personal emotion with unique simplicity. She writes of her love for the young girls of her school and for her art, the Muses' gift, of her anger at her brother, and of her disapproval of insensitive women who cannot respond to poetry and music.

Unfortunately most of Sappho's poetry is fragmentary. Only one of her extant poems (1, 1) is known to be complete, a beautiful prayer to Aphrodite, imploring Sappho's favorite goddess to come to her aid once again, as she has in the past. Here Sappho candidly expresses her ambivalent feelings of love and hate for the unwilling beloved and suggests the presence of an indulgent and gentle Aphrodite. In some of her fragments a few lines convey the despair of unfulfilled love, the experience of loneliness and longing. In one of her poems (1, 2), possibly written to a young girl about to leave Sappho's school to get married, Sappho tells of her pain through a series of exact details describing the physical manifestations of her feelings: she cannot speak, her tongue is stopped, fire seems to run through her body, the sweat runs down her limbs as she trembles.

Though Sappho's love poems are her best-known works, she has written with equal intensity and conviction about her art; Sappho declares that her poems assure her immortality (1, 11). Moreover, she speaks with contempt of the uneducated woman, uninspired by the Muses, who will have no fame after death (III, 71). Sappho can express intense feelings of anger and hatred as well as of love. She speaks to her brother Charaxus in an angry letter, which tells of a quarrel they have had (1, 35), and then in a letter of reconciliation to Charaxus she tells of her hatred for his mistress Doricha, a well-known courtesan, calling her a dog and advising her to look for new prey (1, 36).

The conciseness of Sappho's style and her choice of exact details convey the quality of an intense personal experience. Though her artistry is exquisite, her poetry has a spontaneity and an immediacy which suggest that the poet is experiencing the emotional drama she both records and creates. Most of Sappho's poetry is written in short, simple sentences without subordination; exactness and simplicity of language, economy, and directness are her chief instruments for expressing intense and passionate feeling.

Lysias. An Athenian orator, born around 458 B.C. His brothers, Polemarchus and Euthydemus, appear in Plato's *Republic;* in Plato's *Phaedrus,* Lysias' discourse on love is discussed. When Lysias was a young man his brothers and he went to Thurii, a colony of Athens. They were expelled in 412 B.C., after the Athenian army had been defeated in Sicily, and returned to Athens. In 404 B.C., when the Thirty Tyrants controlled Athens, they confiscated the property of Lysias' family and killed his brother Polemarchus. Lysias fled from Athens, but returned the next year, when the Thirty had been deposed. To support himself he became a professional speech writer. In antiquity over four hundred speeches were attributed to him, but only 233 were regarded by Dionysius of Halicarnassus as definitely the work of Lysias. Only thirty-four orations and some fragments remain of his work. Lysias died in 380 B.C.

Of Lysias' surviving orations the best known is *Against Eratosthenes,* an attack on one of the Thirty Tyrants, the man whom Lysias blamed for the murder of his brother. Other orations by Lysias also expose the crimes of the Thirty Tyrants. Lysias' simple, direct, and lucid language and style became the model for Attic prose.

Lysis. A dialogue by PLATO on the subject of friendship.

Lysistrata (Lysistrate). An Old Comedy (411 B.C.) by ARISTOPHANES. Translations: in verse, Benjamin B. Rogers, 1924; in verse, Arthur S. Way, 1934; in prose and verse, Charles T. Murphy, 1944; in prose and verse, Dudley Fitts, 1954; in verse, Douglass Parker, 1963.

BACKGROUND. By 411 B.C. Athens had endured serious defeats in the Peloponnesian War with Sparta, and at this time was incapable of achieving peace with honor. Many Athenians had been killed in the Sicilian Expedition of 413 B.C., and the morale of the people was low. Some of Athens' strongest allies had turned against her. Whereas in *The Acharnians* and *Peace* Aristophanes argued for a peaceful settlement with Sparta, which then was possible, in *Lysistrata,* by means of a sensuous and witty fantasy, he expresses his yearning for the end of Athens' suffering and despair and for a fruitful union of the Greek states.

SCENE. Athens; on one side, the house of Lysistrata, on the other the entrance to the Acropolis. Between the two is the opening of the Cave of Pan.

SUMMARY. Lysistrata ("She Who Disbands Armies"), an Athenian woman, walks up and down before her house, annoyed because women she is expecting have not arrived. When Calonice, another Athenian woman, arrives, Lysistrata tells her she has asked the women to meet because of an extremely important matter involving the future of Greece. Finally others arrive —a third Athenian Myrrhine, Lampito, who has come from Sparta, two women from Boeotia, and one from Corinth. Lysistrata informs them she has summoned this council of females to propose a plan for ending the Peloponnesian War. They must refuse to make love to their husbands until the men agree to make peace. The women are shocked and upset by this proposal and many object to such a deprivation; however, when Lysistrata convinces them of how well the plan will work, they give in. She has arranged for the older women to seize the Acropolis, while they, the younger ones, make themselves attractive to their husbands but refuse to be touched. The women take an oath to dress beautifully and entice their husbands and then remain cold and withdrawn. Lampito returns to Sparta to organize the women there, while the others go to join the older women who have seized the Acropolis.

The Chorus of Old Men carrying faggots and fire pots comes slowly to the entrance of the Acropolis, intending to smoke out the women and drive them from the citadel. As the Old Men begin to build their fire, a Chorus of Old Women enters carrying pots of water to extinguish the fire. The two groups insult and threaten each other, and finally the women throw the water at the men. Then a Magistrate enters with some Policemen. He scolds the women and tries to force his way into the treasury to obtain money to pay rowers he has hired. Lysistrata comes out and asks him what he wants. When he orders the Policemen to seize her, the women attack them, and they retire in terror.

Lysistrata then speaks proudly of the women who are going to save Greece despite the folly of the men. When the Magistrate remarks on the insolence of women, Lysistrata replies that women have common sense, which men would do well to imitate. Finally the women throw water at him, and he goes off. Then the Chorus of Old Men criticizes women for interfering in matters of state and warfare; they are answered by the Chorus of Old Women, who speak of all that women have done for Athens, contributing their sons to the state, while the men merely waste its treasures.

Lysistrata emerges from the Acropolis, disheartened by the frailty of her colleagues. Desiring their husbands, the women are breaking their vows and trying to desert her. They pretend they must attend to their households, and one even hides a helmet under her clothes in order to pretend she is about to bear a child. Lysistrata scolds and encourages them, and at last they return to the Acropolis. Seeing Cinesias, the husband of Myrrhine, approaching, Lysistrata orders Myrrhine to flirt with and provoke him and then to turn away when he is enflamed with desire.

A Herald from Sparta enters, hoping to make peace with Athens. He tells an Athenian Magistrate that Lampito has persuaded all the Spartan women to deny themselves to their husbands, and the men are desperate. The Magistrate goes to tell the Athenian Council of the conspiracy in which all Greek women are involved. The Choruses of Old Men and Old Women agree to quarrel no more, and together they sing of their hopes for peace. Soon ambassadors from Sparta enter, announcing that they have come to arrange for peace with Athens. Lysistrata comes out of the Acropolis, and the goddess Peace is brought in by the Machine. Lysistrata inveighs against war, pointing out the responsibility of both Athenians and Spartans. She invites the men to enter the Acropolis where they will feast with the women and vow to make peace and then to take their wives home. Soon a Spartan Chorus and an Athenian Chorus enter, dancing to the music of flutes. Lysistrata and the women follow, and all sing and dance.

M

Macaria (Makaria). See THE CHILDREN OF HERACLES.

Macedon (Makedonia). See PHILIP OF MACEDON, ALEXANDER THE GREAT, and ATHENS.

Machaon. See ILIAD IV, XI, XIV.

Madness of Heracles, The (Herakles Mainomenos; Heracles; Mad Heracles). A tragedy (possibly c. 422 B.C.) by EURIPIDES. Translations: in prose, E. P. Coleridge, 1891; in verse, Arthur S. Way, 1912; in verse, Hugh Owen Meredith, 1937; in verse, William Arrowsmith, 1956.

MYTHICAL BACKGROUND. The myths connected with Heracles are extremely rich and varied. Euripides employs a different version of the Heracles legend from Sophocles in *The Women of Trachis*. Euripides is concerned with the hatred of Hera for Heracles and the terrible effects of her malice. Hera hated Heracles even before he was born, because he was the offspring of Zeus's beloved, Alcmena. As a result of Hera's connivance, Heracles became the slave of King Eurystheus of Argos and was forced to perform the Twelve Labors (recounted in the play). Before leaving to perform the last of these Labors, a descent into the Underworld to bring back Cerberus, the three-headed hound of Hades, Heracles left his father, Amphitryon, and his wife and sons in the care of Creon, his father-in-law and king of Thebes. Heracles was gone for a long time, and people began to believe he would never return from the land of the dead. While he was away, Lycus of Euboea plotted against the throne of Creon; he murdered Creon and seized the kingship of Thebes. Lycus then decided to kill all the remaining members of the family of Heracles, so that no one should be left to avenge the murder of Creon.

SUMMARY. As the play begins, Amphitryon, the mortal father of Heracles, Megara, Heracles' wife, and her three sons, in deep despair, sit on the steps of the altar of Zeus, near the royal palace of Thebes. Amphitryon speaks of how Heracles went down to Hades to bring back the three-headed dog Cerberus and how, during his absence, the usurper Lycus killed Creon. He now rules Thebes and has threatened to kill the whole family of Heracles. Amphitryon sadly says that they sit at the altar of Zeus the Savior in the hope of avoiding death. Megara says that her children continually ask for their father and that she tries to reassure them despite her own fear. When she weeps, Amphitryon tries to cheer her, telling her there is hope that Heracles may return to save them.

The Theban Elders enter and declare that if the Greeks allow the sons of Heracles to be slain, the land will lose great heroes. They then observe Lycus approaching. He immediately reveals his cruelty and coldness, demanding that Amphitryon, Megara, and the sons of Heracles prepare to die, for Heracles, already dead, will never come back to Thebes. Lycus refuses to believe that Zeus is the father of Heracles; he insists that Heracles' great labors prove him not a hero but a coward. Amphitryon angrily declares that Lycus slanders the brave Heracles and it is Lycus who is cowardly; fearing the offspring of Heracles, he has decided to kill the hero's sons. He pleads with Lycus to allow Heracles' family to leave Thebes and go into exile. Lycus' response is a command to his attendant to bring wood so that the family of Heracles may be burnt to death at the altar of Zeus. When the Chorus cries out against the tyranny of Lycus, Megara thanks the Elders for their kindness, but then goes on to tell them that she has accepted her fate and will die courageously. She urges Amphitryon to follow her example in emulating the courage and dignity of Heracles. Amphitryon says he is ready for death. He begs Lycus to kill Megara and him first, so that they will not be forced to see the children dying. Lycus assents to Megara's plea that she may dress her sons in proper funeral clothing, and Amphitryon, Megara, and her children enter the palace.

At this tragic moment the Chorus sings of the great Labors of Heracles: his victories over the Nemean lion, the centaurs, the hind with the golden horns, the horses of Diomedes, the cruel robber Cycnus, the dragon who guarded the golden apples of the Hesperides, and the pirates; his feats of holding up the heavens with his arms, of seizing the belt of the Amazon queen, of killing the many-headed Hydra, and the giant Geryon, who had three bodies. All these Labors are behind him, but now he faces the last one in Hades, from which he may never return.

Amphitryon, Megara, and the children enter, ready, Megara declares, for death. She thinks sadly of the time when Heracles made glorious plans for the future of his sons. As she is lamenting, Heracles appears. Shocked by the terrible condition in which he finds his family, Heracles inveighs against the evil of Lycus, whom he plans to kill, and the cruelty of the Thebans who did nothing to aid his helpless family. Heracles then tells of how he brought Cerberus out of Hades, but was delayed after accomplishing this last Labor because he wished to rescue Theseus, king of Athens, from Hades.

After Heracles takes his family to their home, the Chorus sings of its own sadness, that of old age. Nonetheless it can still sing of the glories of life, among them, the career of the great Heracles. Soon Lycus comes in, and, seeing only Amphitryon, goes into the palace to find Megara and the children. As the Chorus chants, welcoming justice, the cries of Lycus are heard from within as he is murdered. The Chorus celebrates the victory of Heracles by dancing and singing. The true king has been restored, the tyrant defeated.

At this triumphant moment Iris and Madness are seen above the palace. Iris explains that Hera, who cannot bear to see Heracles at peace after he has accomplished the Twelve Labors, has now sent Madness to torment him and drive him to kill his wife and children. Madness, the offspring of Uranus and Night, begs Iris not to further torment the great Heracles, but Iris insists on following the command of Hera. As Madness enters the palace, the Chorus sings of how fortune has swiftly destroyed the victorious hero. While they sing, cries and other horrible sounds are heard from within the palace. A servant comes out and describes Heracles' strange appearance and violent deeds as he was afflicted with madness. Mistaking his sons for those of King Eurystheus, for whom he performed the Twelve Labors, he has murdered his own children. When Megara tried to prevent him from killing them, he slew her also. Finally Athene threw a rock at Heracles' breast; he fell back in a deep sleep, and was bound by the servants.

The doors of the palace are opened, and the terrible scene of the murders is revealed. Heracles wakens, his sanity restored, and realizes what he has done. He feels tainted by his crime; the curse of his children's blood is on him, and it would be best for him to commit suicide. When he sees Theseus approaching, he fears the very sight of himself will taint his friend. Theseus has come to help the Thebans overcome the tyrant Lycus. When Amphitryon tells him of the dreadful murder of the children, Theseus pities Heracles, the victim of Hera. Grateful to Heracles for bringing him back from Hades, Theseus offers to help the tortured hero. He persuades Heracles to give up his thoughts of suicide, which are inappropriate to one who has endured so much with great dignity and nobility, and urges him to accompany him to Athens, where he will be cleansed of blood pollution. There he will have a home, land, and wealth. Heracles, determined to face life despite all its pain, agrees to go with Theseus. As he asks Amphitryon to bury his wife and children and bids him farewell, he symbolizes courage and endurance despite tragic affliction.

Maenads (Mainades; "frenzied women"). Female followers of Dionysus, who participated in the orgiastic rites in his honor.

Maia (I). In Greek mythology, the daughter of Atlas and the mother by Zeus of Hermes. See HOMERIC HYMN IV and Sophocles' ICHNEUTAI.

Maia (II). An Italian fertility, or earth, goddess.

Mantua. A town on the River Mincius in Cisalpine Gaul, usually regarded as the birthplace of Vergil. Actually Vergil was born in the nearby village of Andes.

Marathon. A town on the east coast of Attica, the site of the great Athenian victory over the Persians in 490 B.C.

Marcus Aurelius Antoninus. The emperor of Rome from A.D. 161 to 180. Marcus Aurelius' *Meditations,* which he wrote in Greek, are a series of moral reflections expressing a Stoic attitude toward the limitations of life and the inevitability of death. Some of his correspondence with his tutor Fronto is also extant.

Margites. A lost mock-epic, mentioned by Aristotle as a comic poem by HOMER. The date and authorship of *Margites* are unknown.

Marius, Gaius. A Roman statesman and general (157–86 B.C.). Marius was consul of Rome seven times and won great fame as a military commander and as leader of the popular party at Rome. SALLUST created a vivid characterization of Marius in the *Bellum Jugurthinum,* and Plutarch wrote a life of him. See SULLA.

Marpessa. In Greek mythology, a daughter of the river-god Euenos and the beloved of Idas, one of the Argonauts. Apollo also loved Marpessa, but, when Zeus allowed her to choose between her two admirers, she chose Idas.

Mars. Originally a Roman vegetation deity, but later the god of war. Mars was identified with the Greek god Ares. His sacred animal was the wolf.

Marsyas. In Greek mythology, a satyr who learned to play the flute so well that he entered a contest with Apollo, with the agreement that the winner could do whatever he pleased to the loser. The Muses awarded the victory to Apollo, who flayed Marsyas alive.

Martial (Marcus Valerius Martialis). Roman poet. Martial was born at Bilbilis in Spain between A.D. 38 and 41. He received a good education and went to Rome in A.D. 63. There he became a friend of Quintilian and two of his countrymen, Lucan and the younger Seneca, both of whom died in A.D. 65 as a result of their involvement in the conspiracy of L. Calpurnius Piso. For many years in Rome, Martial endured the poor and humiliating existence of a poet dependent on the bounty of wealthy patrons, a subject he deals with in his epigrams. He writes of his poor lodgings "up three flights of stairs" (I, 117) and of waiting desperately for help from a patron (IV, 40; VI, 30). Later, however, he did have a cottage at Nomentum, about fifteen miles northeast of Rome. Martial lived and wrote in Rome for thirty-five years. Among his friends were the poet Juvenal, Pliny the Younger, and Silius Italicus. Martial was awarded the rank of tribune and the *ius trium liberorum* (the tax exemptions and other privileges normally granted a father of three children, but given sometimes, as in the case of Martial, to persons who did not have those qualifications). In A.D. 100 Martial returned to Spain, where he lived until his death in about A.D. 104.

In A.D. 80 Martial's first works, his *Liber Spectaculorum* (*Book on the Public Shows*) appeared in honor of Titus' opening of the Colosseum. The thirty-three brief poems that survive are mainly praises of the Emperor. *Xenia* (now Book XIII of the EPIGRAMS; the word meant gifts to friends during the Saturnalia) and *Apophoreta* (now Book XIV of the *Epigrams;* gifts received at celebrations of the Saturnalia) appeared in A.D. 84. As their titles imply, these consist of inscriptions for gifts in elegiac couplets. The first of Martial's twelve books of actual epigrams appeared in A.D. 86, and eleven more books were published by A.D. 102.

The best-known writer of epigrams, Martial displays great skill in adapting the form to a variety of uses. Many of his poems, which vary in length, have the precision and economy of inscriptions on monuments and tombstones, the earliest examples of the form. Sometimes in a couplet Martial manages to suggest a mood or even a scene or to expose a pretentious or foolish person. Most of his epigrams are somewhat longer, building to an epigrammatic climax. When criticized for the length of his epigrams, Martial answers in a couplet: "Velox, you protest that my epigrams are too long;/ You yourself write nothing, so yours are shorter" (I, 110). He ends a longer epigram addressed to another detractor, Tucca, as follows: "Let's agree, you are allowed to skip long epigrams, I to write them" (VI, 65).

The range of Martial's subjects is wide: he writes of the hardships of the dependent and the cruelty of the patron, of vice, affectation, and folly in his society, of the immortality of poetry, of the pretentiousness of the female, the inadequacy of the physician. Perhaps the only subject on which Martial himself seems affected and hypocritical is the Emperor Domitian, whom he flatters, clearly out of necessity, but nonetheless with an obsequiousness embarrassing to the reader who knows Juvenal and Tacitus. For the most part Martial's epigrams are witty and satirical, but he is capable of expressing affection and tenderness in epigrammatic form. He tells of his love for Spain and greets friends affectionately. Perhaps his most moving poem is written for a slave girl who died six days before her sixth birthday (v, 34).

Martial's epigrams suggest that the writer was an urbane and witty man who observed the society in which he lived with detachment and amusement. Yet, for all his sophistication, he is neither pessimistic nor cynical. Both in explicit statement and in the subtlety of his workmanship he reveals that his deepest faith lay in the power of a beautifully constructed and meaningful poem.

Medea (Medeia). In Greek myth, daughter of King Aeëtes of Colchis and the niece of Circe. Like Circe, Medea was a sorceress. Her love for Jason and the other experiences of her violent and tragic life are related in Greek and Latin poetry and drama. See Euripides' MEDEA, Seneca's MEDEA, Apollonius Rhodius' ARGONAUTICA, Valerius Flaccus' ARGONAUTICA, and Ovid's METAMORPHOSES and HEROIDES VI, XII.

Medea (Medeia). A tragedy (431 B.C.) by EURIPIDES. Translations: in prose, E. P. Coleridge, 1891; in verse, Arthur S. Way, 1912; in prose, Augustus T. Murray, 1931; in verse, R. C. Trevelyan, 1939; in verse, Rex Warner, 1944.

MYTHICAL BACKGROUND. The hero Jason was commanded by his evil uncle Pelias, who had seized the throne of Iolcos, to obtain the Golden Fleece, which was owned by Aeëtes, king of Colchis. Jason, with his heroic companions, the Argonauts, built the first ship, the *Argo*, and set sail for

Colchis. There the daughter of Aeëtes, Medea, a sorceress, fell in love with Jason and aided him by deceiving her father and killing her brother. After succeeding in obtaining the Golden Fleece, Jason set sail with Medea for Iolcos, where he claimed the throne that Pelias had usurped from Jason's father Aeson. Medea tricked the daughters of Pelias into killing their father, and as a result Jason and she were forced into exile. They found a home in Corinth, where they lived for ten years. However, because Jason was not married to Medea, he was free to desert her and their two sons when Creon, king of Corinth, offered him his daughter as a wife.

SCENE. Before Medea's house in Corinth; nearby is the palace of Creon.

SUMMARY. Medea's Nurse comes out of the house and speaks of the events of the past which led to the present crisis. She wishes that Jason had never come to Colchis in the *Argo*, for then Medea could not have fallen in love with him. This love led her to kill his enemies and flee in fear. Now the love of Jason and Medea has become sick and turned to hatred. Jason has deserted Medea and his children for a royal wife and has married the daughter of King Creon. Medea fasts and weeps, regretting all she did and all she gave up for a man who now despises her. The Nurse fears she may commit a violent deed—even murder—in her desperation.

Medea's two Sons enter, accompanied by their Attendant, who informs the Nurse that Creon intends to banish Medea and her sons from Corinth. The Nurse finds it hard to believe that Jason will not protect his sons. She is fearful of Medea's violent reaction to this news and advises the Attendant not to let the children approach her. The Nurse has observed Medea looking at her children with cruel intent in her eyes.

Medea is heard within, describing her anguish, praying that she may die. The Nurse urges the children to go into the house, but to avoid their mother in her violent mood. After the Attendant leads the children into the house, the Chorus of Corinthian Women enters and asks the Nurse what is causing Medea to cry out in such pain. The Nurse explains that Jason has deserted her, and Medea's voice continues to be heard, crying for death. The women suggest that the Nurse bring Medea out so that they may comfort her and help her to restrain her intense and violent nature.

Soon Medea comes out of the house and speaks of her troubles, associating her own dilemma with the usual lot of woman, who is dependent on a man for her happiness. Medea is bitter about marriage and the role of the wife. She is destitute, without a husband, a home, or a land, yet she already plots her revenge on Jason. Creon enters with his retinue. He immediately commands her to leave Corinth with her sons. Creon is afraid Medea will use sorcery to harm his daughter, Jason, and him. Medea implores Creon to allow her to remain in Corinth for one day so that she may plan for her life of exile, and, despite his forebodings of danger, Creon grants her request.

After Creon goes out Medea informs the Chorus that she was humble to him in order to gain one day in which to kill Creon, his daughter, and Jason. She speaks of various ways of murdering them, but she is still undecided as to what form her vengeance will take. The Chorus sings of how the role of woman is changing and how women are gaining more honor and respect. Then Jason enters and justifies his own behavior by blaming Medea's violent temper for her banishment. Had she restrained herself she might have remained in Corinth. Self-righteously he declares that even now he has her interest at heart and will provide means for her survival in exile. In a fury Medea replies that he has deserted her after she saved his life. She gave up her family and home for him, and now no land will welcome her. He has cast out her and his children as beggars. Jason and Medea continue to quarrel violently, Jason defending his new marriage, declaring it will give his sons a secure position of rank and wealth, and Medea calling his arguments specious and him a villain. Finally Medea refuses the aid he offers her, and Jason leaves.

The Chorus comments on the dangers of excessive love and on the pains of exile. Then Aegeus, king of Athens, enters with his Attendants. Medea tells him how Jason has wronged her and asks him if she may come to Athens. When she promises to use sorcery to cause Aegeus, who is childless, to produce offspring, he swears he will give her a home and protection in Athens. After Aegeus leaves, Medea decides on the form her vengeance will take. She will send her sons with a present to Jason's wife—a robe and a golden chaplet smeared with poison which will kill her. Then Medea will murder her own sons so that Jason will not have offspring from either Medea or his new bride. Proudly she says no one can call her a pathetic, weak woman. The Leader of the Chorus tries to dissuade Medea from committing the cruel murders, and the Chorus asks how the blessed land of Athens can accept a polluted woman who has killed her own children. The women beg Medea to spare her sons. When Jason enters, Medea pretends to recant her angry words. She begs his pardon and says she accepts his decision to take a royal bride. She calls their children from the house to be reconciled with their father and asks Jason to persuade Creon to allow them to stay in Corinth. Then she tells Jason that she will send the children with a gift for his bride—a robe and a golden chaplet. The servant brings out the presents, and Jason, the Attendants, and the Children, bearing the poisoned gifts, go off.

Soon the Attendant returns with Medea's children and reports that they may remain in Corinth. When the Attendant has gone into the house, Medea turns to her sons. Her love for them makes her feel that she cannot kill them; however, her pride and her hatred for Jason make it impossible for her to give her sons to her enemies in Corinth. Torn between love and hate, tenderness and violent anger, she cannot bear to look at her children. She takes them into the house and returns alone. A Messenger enters hurriedly and advises Medea to flee at once. He describes the gruesome death of Jason's bride and of her father Creon, who, clasping his dying child in his arms, was held by the poisoned robe until he died with his daughter. Medea, deriving great satisfaction from the details of the horrible deaths of Creon and his daughter, and now determined to complete her vengeance, goes into the house. As the children's cries are heard, the Chorus expresses its horror at Medea's deeds.

Jason comes in and learns of the murder of his sons. At this point Medea appears above the house in a chariot drawn by dragons that has been sent to her by her grandfather Helios; with her are the bodies of her sons. Jason looks back upon his past folly in having loved so barbarous a woman. He begs Medea to let him have the corpses of his sons, so he may bury them, but she refuses. Triumphantly Medea leaves the wretched Jason, who has lost all he valued and loved. Medea is carried in her magic chariot to Athens.

Medea. A tragedy by SENECA based on Euripides' MEDEA. In Seneca's version only Medea is to be banished from Corinth; her children are to remain with their father Jason. Realizing that Jason really loves his sons, Medea exacts vengeance by killing them. In Seneca's play Jason gains the sympathy of the audience. Seneca places greater emphasis on Medea's powers as a sorceress than does Euripides, and in Seneca's tragedy she is far less human and thus less sympathetic a character. Yet she is a powerful figure. As she speaks of herself as "Medea," she seems not a woman but a symbolic representation of outraged pride and passionate love turned to hatred and violence.

Medicina Faciei (Medicamina faciei femineae, Face Lotions for Women). An elegiac poem by OVID. Only about one hundred lines remain of this mock-didactic poem, which gives advice on caring for the complexion.

Medon. The herald of the suitors in the ODYSSEY (IV, XXII). He is, however, loyal to Odysseus and is spared by him.

Medusa (Medousa). See GORGONS.

Megara. Heracles' first wife. See Euripides' THE MADNESS OF HERACLES and Seneca's HERCULES FURENS.

Melampus (Melampous). In Greek mythology, a physician who cared for some serpents whose parents had been killed. In return for his kindness, the serpents licked his ears, thus giving him the power to understand the language of the birds and to prophesy future events.

Melanthius (Melanthios). In the ODYSSEY (XVII, XX, XXII), a goatherd.

Meleager (Meleagros). In Greek mythology, the son of Oeneus, king of Calydon, and Althaea, and killer of the Calydonian boar. In *Iliad* IX Homer says that Artemis sent a huge boar to destroy Calydon because Oeneus had not offered a sacrifice to her. A slightly different and better-known version of Meleager's story is told by Ovid in *Metamorphoses* VIII. Ovid tells of how the Fates came to Althaea when Meleager was born and, tossing a brand into the fire, declared that Meleager would live only so long as the wood lasted. Althaea snatched the brand from the fire and carefully concealed it. Meleager grew to manhood and, with the help of the great huntress Atalanta, killed the boar that threatened Calydon. When Meleager gave the head of the boar to

Atalanta, whom he loved, the two brothers of Althaea angrily protested, demanding it for themselves. In a fit of rage, Meleager killed them both. Ovid describes Althaea's suffering when she learned what her son had done and her conflicting loyalties as mother and sister. After much hesitation she threw the brand into the fire; as it was consumed, Meleager's life slipped away. See also Bacchylides' CHORAL LYRIC, V.

Meleager (Meleagros) of Gadara. A Greek poet of the first century B.C. Meleager wrote mainly brief elegiacs dealing with love or death. A number of his epigrams can be found in the *Greek Anthology.*

melic poetry. See LYRIC POETRY.

Memnon. In Greek mythology, the son of Tithonus and Eos. Memnon led the Ethiopians, who were allies of the Trojans in the Trojan War.

Memorabilia (Apomnemoneumata). See XENOPHON.

Menaechmi. See THE TWIN MENAECHMI.

Menander (Menandros). A Greek writer of New Comedy, born at Athens in 342 B.C. He studied philosophy with Theophrastus. Menander's uncle Alexis was a well-known comic poet, from whom he probably learned a good deal about playwriting. Menander's first play was produced in 321 B.C.; he wrote over one hundred more. It is thought that he was drowned in the harbor of Piraeus in 292 B.C.

Until 1905 practically nothing was known of Menander's work. In that year a papyrus was discovered in Egypt that contained large fragments of THE ARBITRATION (*Epitrepontes*), PERIKEIROMENE (*The Shearing of Glycera*), THE GIRL FROM SAMOS (*Samia*), and the beginning of *Heros* (*The Family God*). DYSKOLOS (*The Bad-Tempered Man*), a complete play by Menander, was discovered in Egypt in 1957 and first published in 1958.

Menander employs type characters—the wronged young woman, the difficult father, the clever slave, the gentle courtesan—and stereotyped plots involving many complications and coincidences—discovery of unknown identity, and reconciliation of husband and wife, child and parent, or sweethearts. He deals with the problems of everyday life in his society with sympathy and sometimes pathos. Yet Menander is a sophisticated writer, often epigrammatic and witty. Menander served as a model to the Roman writers of comedy, Plautus and Terence, many of whose plays are adaptations of his. Quintilian recommended that students of rhetoric read and study the plays of Menander, whom he ranked first among the writers of New Comedy.

Menelaus (Menelaos). A king of Sparta, the son of Atreus and the brother of Agamemnon. For the story of the abduction of his wife Helen, see the ILIAD and the ODYSSEY, Aeschylus' ORESTEIA, and Euripides' HELEN and IPHIGENIA IN AULIS. Menelaus also appears in Sophocles' AJAX and Euripides' ANDROMACHE, THE TROJAN WOMEN, and ORESTES.

Menexenus (Menexenos). A dialogue by PLATO in which Socrates recites a funeral address supposedly written by Aspasia, the mistress of Pericles, for those who died in the Corinthian War. Since both Aspasia and Socrates died before the beginning of the Corinthian War (395 B.C.), the authorship of *Menexenus* has been questioned, but Aristotle attributes it to Plato.

Menippus (Menippos). A Greek Cynic philosopher (third century B.C.). Menippus was born a slave in Gadara (in Syria). Though all his written works are lost, he is known to have written satires in Greek, combining prose and verse. Menippus was imitated by many writers, among them Varro and Lucian.

Meno (Menon). A dialogue by PLATO named for a general of the Ten Thousand who fought for Cyrus, and whom Xenophon discusses in *Anabasis*. The dialogue deals with the question of whether virtue can be learned. Learning is actually recalling what was known by the soul in a former state.

Mentor. In the ODYSSEY, an old friend of Odysseus.

Merchant, The (Mercator). A comedy by PLAUTUS based on a Greek play by Philemon. Generally regarded as an early work, *The Merchant* has a fairly simple plot and dramatic structure. It deals with the adventures of an Athenian father and son in love with the same girl. The young man Charinus, sent to Rhodes on business by his father Demipho, fell in love with Pasicompsa, a courtesan, and has brought her with him back to Athens. When Demipho sees Pasicompsa, he too desires her. The efforts of father and son to outwit each other are amusing. However, when Demipho has arranged for Pasicompsa to stay at his friend's house, and Charinus is told that Pasicompsa has been sold and is gone, there is real pathos in the young man's expression of his despair. Finally, discovering that his son loves Pasicompsa, Demipho withdraws from the contest, hoping that Charinus is not angry at him. Pasicompsa is restored to her young lover at the end.

Mercury (Mercurius). Originally a Roman god of trade, he was soon associated with the Greek god Hermes, whose attributes he acquired.

Metamorphoses (Apuleius). See THE GOLDEN ASS.

Metamorphoses. A poem (c. A.D. 8) in dactylic hexameter, by OVID. Translations: in verse, Arthur Golding, 1565–67; in prose, H. T. Riley, 1869; in prose, F. J. Miller, 1926; in prose, Mary Innes, 1955; in verse, Horace Gregory, 1958; in verse, Rolfe Humphries, 1958.

SUMMARY. The *Metamorphoses*, a poem in fifteen books, is at once a collection of the most important myths of the ancient world and a commentary on the passions that rule human beings. The myths deal mainly with transformations from the human state to that of an animal, a bird, a tree, a rock, a body of water, or a star. Beginning with the first great transformation—from chaos to order—Ovid has collected and retold about two hundred fifty myths from before the time of Homer to his own time, ending with the deification of Julius Caesar. The stories are unified by mythological chronology, by the relationships among the characters and their strange transformations, and especially by Ovid's technique of suggesting human motivation, conflict, and suffering through mythical figures. Though Ovid makes no pretense of believing in the gods he writes of and his tone is sometimes playful, the stories he tells are not simply fantastic and amusing. Ovid charms the reader with the wit and grace of his style and his disarmingly light tone as he tells a tale half seriously which often reveals human conflict, weakness, or courage.

After an invocation asking the gods for their aid as he relates the story of eternal change, Ovid describes the imposition of order on chaos, the creation of man, and the various ages—gold, silver, bronze, and iron. Because of the corruption of man, Jupiter caused a great flood to envelop the world. Only the virtuous husband and wife, Deucalion and Pyrrha, survived. From the oracle of Themis they learned they must throw stones over their heads; from these came the race of man. From the earth came animals and strange creatures, one of which was the dreadful dragon, the Python, which Apollo killed at Delphi. Here the god organized the Pythian Games in memory of his victory. Since no laurel yet existed, the victor at the games was awarded a garland of oak. Ovid uses this bit of legend as a transition to his story of the transformation into a laurel of Daphne, the nymph who fled as Apollo pursued her. Skillfully Ovid continues from one myth to another, linking them as though they were parts of one great story. Some of the most moving tales are those of Phaethon, whose daring brought about his downfall; Narcissus, the beautiful youth doomed by his inability to love anyone but himself; Actaeon, who, transformed into a stag, was torn to bits by his own dogs; and Pentheus, killed by his own mother.

One of Ovid's greatest skills is his capacity to reveal the human passions and conflicts of his heroines. He depicts Medea as a woman violent in love and in hate, torn between her desire for Jason and her loyalty to her father; then, when Jason forsakes her, entirely dominated by her hatred. Another woman who chooses to deceive her father for the sake of her beloved is Scylla, the heroine of the *Ciris*. Ovid's Scylla is at once a more realistic and less complicated character than the tormented heroine of the *Ciris*. The Scylla of the *Metamorphoses* is simply a young girl who, enchanted by the handsome Minos, manages to convince herself that she must betray her land and her father to win his love. Her pathetic rationalizations and her panic when Minos rejects her are touching, for she does not understand either herself or her beloved. Like many of the figures whose metamorphoses Ovid describes, she is impelled and destroyed by emotions she hardly comprehends. Ovid deals with her transformation briefly and lightly, returning to the story of Minos.

In telling of the sad fate of Orpheus, who twice lost his beloved Eurydice, Ovid's approach is half serious. Orpheus' tone is light as he explains to Pluto and Proserpina that the god of love was stronger than his own power to overcome his suffering at the loss of Eurydice, and he slyly suggests that this god must surely be known in Hades. Ovid's Orpheus looking back at Eurydice does not have the tragic stature of the traditional mythical figure; instead he seems pathetic and even a bit foolish.

Ovid often seems to be mocking the heroic or tragic implications of the myths he tells. He employs his narrative skill, his insight into human psychology, and his urbane wit to accomplish his own transformations—of the heroic figures of myth into rather ordinary human beings whose adventures and metamorphoses symbolize the conflicts and sufferings of daily life. Ovid understands the pain of human conflict, but he cannot ignore its absurdity and its humor.

Meter. GREEK. Ancient Greek meter was essentially quantitative; the metrical pattern was determined by the length of time needed for each syllable. Syllables were either long (—) or short (◡), and a short syllable was considered to take half the time of a long syllable. Groups of long and short syllables were organized in various types of feet as follows:

Dactyl: — ◡ ◡   Choriamb: — ◡ ◡ —
Spondee: — —   Paeon: — ◡ ◡ ◡ or ◡ ◡ ◡ — or ◡ ◡ — ◡
Iamb: ◡ —   Dochmius: ◡ — — ◡ —
Trochee: — ◡   Epitrite: — ◡ — —
Anapest: ◡ ◡ —   Dactylo-epitrite: a combination of
Tribrach: ◡ ◡ ◡   the dactyl and the epitrite
Cretic: — ◡ —   Logaoedic: a combination of the
Bacchius: ◡ — —   dactyl and the trochee

The patterns of these feet were not rigid: within certain restrictions many variations were made possible by the substitution of a long syllable for two short ones or two short syllables for a long one (resolution).

The chief meters resulting from the various combinations of the above feet are:

Dactylic hexameter, the oldest known Greek meter and the meter of epic poetry, is composed of six feet, primarily dactyls with spondees as variations. The last foot of the line is composed of two syllables, the second being either short or long. If the syllable is short, the time remaining offers the person reciting an opportunity to pause briefly. Another opportunity to pause is provided by the caesura occurring within the second, third, or fourth foot.

Elegiac couplet consists of a line of dactylic hexameter alternating with a line of dactylic pentameter, i.e., a line composed of "five" feet. In this line two full feet are followed by a half foot consisting of a single long syllable; this pattern is repeated in the second part of the line. Thus the four full and two half feet may be considered equivalent to five feet. Sometimes the second line of the couplet is described as dactylic hexameter, with half of the third and sixth feet silent. (See ELEGIAC POETRY):

$$— \overline{◡◡} — \overline{◡◡} — \overline{◡◡} — \overline{◡◡} — ◡◡ — \overline{◡}$$

$$— \overline{◡◡} — \overline{◡◡} — \ \| \ — ◡◡ — ◡◡\overline{◡}$$

Iambic trimeter consists of six iambs (two iambs, trochees, or anapests made up a single metrical unit):

$$\bar{\smile} - \smile - \mid \bar{\smile} - \smile - \mid \bar{\smile} - \smile -$$

Archilochus was the first writer known to have used this meter, which later became the meter of dialogue in Greek tragedy (see IAMBIC POETRY). Variation is possible in the first syllable of each metrical unit, and two short syllables may be substituted for other long ones under some conditions. Other variations are possible, especially in comedy.

The *choliamb* or *scazon*, a halting iambic meter, the invention of which was attributed to Hipponax, is iambic trimeter in which the last foot consists of either a trochee or a spondee.

Trochaic tetrameter consists of eight trochees; variation is possible in the last syllable of the first three metrical units:

$$- \smile - \bar{\smile} \mid - \smile - \bar{\smile} \parallel - \smile - \bar{\smile} \mid - \smile - (\smile)$$

Other variations such as tribrachs and anapests are also possible. Trochaic tetrameter occurs in Greek tragedy.

Anapestic dimeter consists of four anapests; variation occurs through the substitution of a long syllable for two short ones, thus creating spondaic feet:

$$\bar{\smile}\smile - \bar{\smile}\smile - \mid \bar{\smile}\smile - \bar{\smile}\smile -$$

This meter, which has a marching quality, occurs in entrance and exit songs of the chorus in Greek drama.

Lyric verse, both choral and monodic, employs many of the feet described above: the dactylic, the trochaic, the paeonic, the dochmiac, the dactylo-epitritic, and logaoedic. Sometimes several types of feet are combined in a stanzaic pattern. The choruses of Greek tragedy employ dactyls, trochees, paeons, and other feet.

Some of the principal forms of lyric verse are:

Sapphic:

three lines of: $- \smile \mid - \bar{\smile} \mid - \smile\smile \mid - \smile \mid - \bar{\smile}$

and a fourth line of: $- \smile\smile \mid - \bar{\smile}$

Alcaic:

two lines of: $\bar{\smile} \mid - \smile \mid - \bar{\smile} \mid - \smile\smile \mid - \smile \mid -$

followed by: $\bar{\smile} \mid - \smile \mid - \overset{\smile}{-} \mid - \smile \mid - \bar{\smile}$

$$- \smile\smile \mid - \smile\smile \mid - \smile \mid - \bar{\smile}$$

Phalaecean (sometimes called hendecasyllabic), a line of eleven syllables:

$$\overset{\smile}{-}\overset{\smile}{-} \mid - \smile \smile \mid - \smile \mid - \smile \mid - \overset{\smile}{-}$$

Glyconic:

$$\overset{\smile}{-}\overset{\smile}{-} - \smile \smile - \smile -$$

Asclepiadean meters of many types, for example:

$$\overset{\smile}{-}\overset{\smile}{-} \mid - \smile \smile \mid - \mid - \smile \smile \mid - \smile \mid \smile$$
$$\overset{\smile}{-}\overset{\smile}{-} - \smile \smile - - \smile \smile - - \smile \smile - \smile -$$

Anacreontic (used by Anacreon and postclassical writers):

$$\smile \smile - \smile - \smile - -$$

Pherecratic:

$$- - \mid - \smile \smile - \mid -$$

LATIN. The development of Roman meter took place in three main stages: (1) the period of Saturnian verse, (2) the verse of the Republic, and (3) the verse of the Empire.

1. *Versus Faunius* or *Saturnius* (Saturnian verse) is very irregular. It is accented, alliterative verse with a heavy pause within the line, resembling Old English verse. The Roman poets Livius Andronicus and Naevius used Saturnian verse.

2. The verse of early drama, however, is essentially a quantitative verse, imitative of the Greek. Plautus employs trochees, cretics, and bacchiacs in the *cantica* (portions sung) and iambic senarius (six iambs) and trochaic and iambic septanarius (seven trochees and seven iambs) for dialogue. Later Latin drama employs iambic trimeter, but varies it with spondees and anapests, a technique learned from the earlier dramatists. Latin epic was written in dactylic hexameter. Lyric poets also used many of the Greek meters described above, adapting them to the Latin language.

3. During the last fifty years of the Republic there was a new emphasis on regularity and precision in meter, and fairly close imitation of Greek metrical patterns, which the poets of the Augustan and later periods continued.

Metis. In Greek mythology, the first wife of Zeus. When Metis conceived Athene, Zeus, fearing that she would bear him a son more powerful than he, swallowed her. Athene emerged from the head of Zeus.

Mezentius. See AENEID VII-X.

Middle Comedy. See under COMEDY.

Miles Gloriosus. See THE BRAGGART WARRIOR.

Mimnermus (Mimnermos). A Greek poet born at Colophon in Ionia who flourished during the second half of the seventh century B.C. Most of those fragments of his work that remain are elegiac love poems or reflections on the brevity of youthfulness and pleasure. He was the first poet to employ elegiacs in love poems, one of which was about "Nanno," a flute player.

Minerva. Originally an Italian goddess of arts and trades. Minerva was later identified with the Greek goddess Athene and became a goddess of war and wisdom, as well as crafts; she is sometimes regarded as the inventor of musical instruments.

Minos. A mythical king of Crete. Because the name Minos occurs in a great many Greek myths about Crete, it is thought to have been either a title or the name of a number of Cretan monarchs. Minos, Rhadamanthus, and Aeacus, who were known as virtuous and just kings, became judges of the dead in Hades (see *Aeneid* vi). The best-known Greek myths that deal with Minos depict him as a son of Zeus and EUROPA and tyrant of Crete. He married Pasiphae, who bore him two sons and two daughters, Phaedra and Ariadne. When Minos broke his promise to sacrifice to Poseidon a magnificent white bull given him by the god, Poseidon made Pasiphae fall in love with the bull. Pasiphae asked Daedalus to construct a cow's form in which she could receive the animal as her lover. Ovid writes of this strange love affair in *Metamorphoses* viii and of the child of this union, the Minotaur, who was part bull and part man. Deeply ashamed, Minos had Daedalus construct a huge labyrinth in which he concealed the Minotaur, to whom he fed seven Athenian young men and women every year until Theseus finally killed the Minotaur. For Minos' attack on the city of Megara and his deception of Scylla see CIRIS.

Minotaur (Minotaurus). See MINOS and THESEUS.

Mnemosyne. In Greek mythology, the personification of memory and the mother of the Muses.

Moirai. See FATES.

Momus (Momos). A son of Night. Momus became the personification of censure and criticism.

monody. See LYRIC POETRY.

Moralia. See PLUTARCH.

Moretum (Salad). A Latin poem in dactylic hexameter, very doubtfully attributed to VERGIL. The poem describes Simylus, a farmer, preparing his breakfast on a cold winter morning, aided by his servant, Scybale. After he has eaten, the farmer goes off to work in the fields.

Morpheus. The Greek god of dreams.

Moschus (Moschos). A Greek poet, born in Syracuse during the second century B.C. His remaining works consist of a few brief pastorals, *The Runaway Love*, a poem on Aphrodite's search for Eros, and an epyllion called *Europa*, which tells of how Zeus in the form of a bull carried Europa away to Crete where she became his bride. Though the *Lament for Bion* is attributed by some authorities to Moschus, others believe it was written by a student emulating Bion's lament for Adonis.

Mostellaria. See THE HAUNTED HOUSE.

Mother-in-Law, The (Hecyra). A comedy by TERENCE adapted from a play by Apollodorus, probably influenced by Menander's *The Arbitration.* The Prologue of *The Mother-in-Law* reveals that in two previous productions (one in 165 B.C. and one earlier in the year of the present production, 160 B.C.) the play was unsuccessful. Terence asks the audience at least to listen in silence.

Pamphilus, a young Athenian, unwillingly left his mistress, the courtesan Bacchis, and obeyed his father's order that he marry Philumena. Since at first Pamphilus longed only for Bacchis, he did not consummate his marriage. Soon he grew to love his wife, but at this point his father sent him to Imbros on business, and his wife remained at her mother-in-law's house. Philumena stayed there for only a few days and then went home to her parents.

When Pamphilus returns he discovers that Philumena is about to bear a child. Her mother explains to the disillusioned husband that shortly before Philumena married Pamphilus, she was ravished by a man she did not know. Pamphilus, who now loves his wife, still feels that he cannot take her home. Sostrata, his mother, and Laches, his father, beg him to relent and bring his wife home, but he refuses.

Finally Philumena's mother recognizes a ring that Bacchis is wearing as one that Philumena once owned. Pamphilus had taken this ring from a girl he ravished. This girl, of course, is Philumena; thus the father of her baby is her own husband. Pamphilus is grateful to his former mistress for restoring his faith in his wife, to whom he is now reconciled.

Musaeus (Mousaios). (I). A legendary Greek poet thought to have lived before Homer. Orphic poems (see ORPHISM) and oracles were believed to be written by Musaeus.

Musaeus (Mousaios). (II). A Greek poet of the fourth century A.D. or later who wrote a poem on Hero and Leander.

Muses (Mousai). In Greek mythology, the nine daughters of memory, goddesses of the arts. They were worshiped at Pieria and on Mount Helicon. Postclassical writers assigned particular arts to the Muses: Calliope, epic poetry; Clio, history; Euterpe, the flute; Melpomene, tragedy; Terpsichore, dance; Erato, the lyre; Polyhymnia, sacred song; Urania, astronomy; Thalia, comedy. Hesiod tells of their birth in THEOGONY. See also THAMYRIS.

Mycenae (Mykenai). A great and powerful ancient Greek city situated at the northeastern end of the plain of Argos, twelve miles inland from the gulf of Argos. Like all ancient cities, Mycenae had a citadel and a great palace built on a hill. The city is also famous for its "beehive" tombs (*tholoi*), which are very large and shaped like beehives. The acropolis of Mycenae was surrounded by high walls built of limestone blocks of various sizes, a style of architecture known as "Cyclopean," because the legendary founder of Mycenae, Perseus, is said to have arranged for the Cyclopes to build these walls (Pausanias, *Description of Hellas,* II, 16, 3–6). The *Bibliotheca* indicates how the rule of the city of Mycenae passed from Perseus' line to that of Pelops (III, 4,

4–6). Perseus had five sons and a daughter. One of the sons, Sthenelos, married Nikippe, the daughter of Pelops. Her brothers, Atreus and Thyestes, after quarreling with their father, went to their sister at Mycenae. When Eurystheus, the son of Sthenelos, was killed, the people of Mycenae chose Atreus as their ruler. It is his son Agamemnon who is king of Mycenae in the ILIAD. On returning from Troy, Agamemnon was killed by his wife Clytemnestra and her lover Aegisthus (see the ODYSSEY and Aeschylus' ORESTEIA). Clytemnestra and Aegisthus ruled Mycenae until they in turn were killed by Orestes, the son of Agamemnon and Clytemnestra. Orestes became king of Mycenae and was succeeded by his son, Tisamenus. During the period of his reign Mycenae fell to the Dorian invasion.

Actually the city of Mycenae probably dates from a time before the coming of the Greeks, and may originally have been founded by Cretan settlers. Certainly Mycenaean civilization resulted from a combination of the cultures of the pre-Greek or Pelasgian people with that of the Greek invaders and the strong influence of Minoan (Cretan) customs on both. Mycenaean civilization reached its height from 1400 to 1100 B.C., when Mycenae was the richest and most powerful city in the Aegean area (see ACHAEANS). In the *Iliad*, Agamemnon is king not only of Mycenae but of Corinth, Cleonae, and many other cities, including Argos. He seems to be lord of the entire northeastern Peloponnesus, which the city of Mycenae probably dominated. Moreover, Mycenaean settlements outside of Greece existed throughout the Mediterranean area in Cyprus and Syria and even in Asia Minor.

In Aeschylus' *Agamemnon*, Agamemnon is king of Argos rather than of Mycenae. Actually the two cities can be regarded as one state. Probably Mycenae held the central power from 1400 to 1100 B.C., though there are authorities who believe that Argos always dominated the area. Certainly Argos was the leading center of the entire Argolid during the historical period. Shortly after the defeat of Troy by the Greeks, around 1100 B.C., the Dorian invasion destroyed Mycenae. From then on the great civilization of Mycenae was significant only in literature.

The first excavations at Mycenae were made by Heinrich Schliemann in 1874. In 1876 he made significant discoveries at the entrance to the Acropolis near the well-known Lion Gate, so called because of the two lionesses face to face sculptured upon it. Schliemann uncovered the famous Grave Circle and explored five royal graves, which contained precious jewelry, beautiful gold death masks, and other objects of art and remains of human bodies. Schliemann's account of his excavations and discoveries are contained in his book *Mycenae*, 2nd ed., rev. (Scribner's, 1880). In 1877 M. Stamatakes, an associate of Schliemann, discovered a sixth grave. These excavations and succeeding ones by Chrestos Tsountas, and more recently by A. J. B. Wace, John Papadimitriou, George E. Mylonas, and others have turned up much material related to the Homeric poems. Explorations have substantiated the

Homeric epithets for Mycenae, "the well-built city," city of "the wide streets," and "rich in gold." The palaces found at Mycenae, as well as at Tiryns, an ancient city nine miles away, and at Troy are similar to the palaces described by Homer. Also the weapons and shields of Homeric warriors are similar to those depicted on Mycenaean vases and jewelry. A golden cup with two doves sculptured on its handles found in a tomb at Mycenae is like the one which Homer describes as the cup of Nestor.

Myrrha. See ADONIS.

N

Naevius, Gnaeus. A Roman poet, born around 270 B.C. He fought in the First Punic War and was imprisoned for offending the Metelli, an important family, who, declared Naevius, "were made consuls of Rome by Fate." The reply of the consul Metellus in Saturnian verse (see METER) has become famous: *"Dabunt malum Metelli Naevio Poetae"* ("The Metelli will give the poet Naevius cause to regret it"). Naevius was ultimately banished from Rome and died in Utica in 201 B.C. In the epitaph he wrote for himself Naevius proudly declares that after his death the Romans no longer knew how to speak the Latin language.

Naevius invented the FABULA PRAETEXTA; it is known that he wrote at least two such plays on Roman subjects, *Romulus* and *Clastidium*. He also wrote tragedies based on Greek ones; of these only sixty lines remain. In drama Naevius was mainly known for his comedies; thirty-four titles and one hundred thirty lines of his *fabulae palliatae* remain. He is best known for his *Bellum Punicum*, an epic poem in Saturnian verse on the First Punic War, in which, after tracing the legendary origins of Rome and Carthage, he tells of Rome's heroic victory in the war. Only fragments of this work remain.

Narcissus (Narkissos). In Greek mythology, an extremely beautiful boy, the son of the river-god Cephisus and the nymph Leiriope. Though the nymph Echo loved Narcissus, he cared only for himself and paid no attention to her. In *Metamorphoses* III, Ovid tells how Narcissus fell in love with his own image reflected in the water of a well and finally died of anguish because he could not reach this beloved whom he worshiped.

Natural History (Naturalis Historia). An encyclopedia in thirty-seven books (first century A.D.) by PLINY THE ELDER. The work contains about twenty thousand entries on the natural sciences, the arts, customs, religion, and other subjects, as well as digressions in which the author expresses his philosophical and moral views. The entire first book is taken up with a table of contents and a list of hundreds of authorities both Roman and foreign whom Pliny claims to have consulted for this work. Some scholars doubt that Pliny actually consulted all the sources he lists. Book II deals with physics and mathematics; Books III–VI, with geography and ethnology; Book VII, with anthropology and the physiology of man; Books VIII–XI, with animals, fish, birds, and insects; Books XII–XIX, with botany; Books XX–XXVII, with medical attributes of plants; Books XXVIII–XXXII, with the medicines derived from animals; and Books XXXIII–XXXVII, with mineralogy and the use of minerals in medicine and art.

Pliny's vast work is a strange combination of important factual material about the arts, sciences, and customs of his time and obvious errors that he sets down as facts. Some of the most interesting parts are the descriptions of "wonders," which, though they clearly have no basis in fact, are fascinating in their imaginative appeal. Thus Pliny describes "odd people," such as giants and dwarfs, people of remarkable strength or vision, unusual births and other "wonders." His remedies for illnesses are bizarre: he suggests swallowing earthworms in wine to cure asthma, or eating the dung of ringdoves with beans to cure urinary problems, or kissing a mule's nostrils to cure catarrh. Despite Pliny's preoccupation with the curious, his work does contain a wealth of factual information about Roman life of the period, especially details about social customs and daily experience. Also his discussions of painting and sculpture reveal a great deal about the history of ancient art. As a moralist Pliny constantly inveighs against the weakness of man, the only creature who must be taught all that he knows, who is guilty of excesses and cares only for luxury, and who battles with his own kind. Man brings his misfortunes on himself. A great admirer of nature, Pliny recommends a simple, natural way of life.

Nausicaa (Nausikaa). In Greek mythology, the daughter of Alcinous, king of the Phaeacians. One of the most delightful characters in the ODYSSEY (VI–VIII), Nausicaa is also the heroine of Robert Graves' novel *Homer's Daughter*.

Nemesis. An offspring of Night. In Greek literature, Nemesis personifies the wrath of the gods at man's *hubris*.

Neoptolemus (Neoptolemos; also called Pyrrhus [red-haired]). The son of Achilles and Deidamia. After the death of Achilles he came to Troy to take part in the Trojan War. His character is developed with great variety by the many authors who use him in their works. For example, in Sophocles' PHILOCTETES, Neoptolemus is a gentle and wise young man, who at first reluctantly gives in to Odysseus' persuasions and deceives Philoctetes, but soon regrets his error, befriends and protects Philoctetes, and finally has an important dramatic role in persuading him to return to Troy. In Vergil's AENEID (II) and Seneca's *The Trojan Women* he is a brutal figure. See also Euripides' ANDROMACHE.

Nephelai. See THE CLOUDS.

Nepos, Cornelius. A Roman historian and biographer whose praenomen is not known, born around 100 B.C. in northern Italy. Most of his life was spent at Rome, where his friends included Catullus, who dedicated his poems to Nepos; Cicero; and Titus Pomponius Atticus. Nepos did not engage in politics and apparently devoted himself entirely to writing. He wrote a history of the world, *Chronica;* a collection of incidents, anecdotes, and facts called *Exempla;*

biography; and poetry. His only surviving work is the fragmentary *De Viris Illustribus* (*On Illustrious Men*), originally in at least sixteen books, of which twenty-four lives remain. Most of these are of Greek leaders, though one deals with a Persian and two with Carthaginians. The most interesting life is of Atticus, whom Nepos eulogizes. The date of Nepos' death is unknown; it occurred sometime after 32 B.C., when Atticus died.

Neptune (Neptunus). Originally an Italian god, who was identified by the Romans with the Greek god Poseidon and acquired his attributes.

Nereus. In Greek mythology, a sea-god, the son of Pontus and Ge. He was married to Doris, who bore him the Nereids (sea nymphs). Nereus, like Proteus, was a prophet who could constantly change his shape.

Nero (Nero Claudius Caesar). The emperor of ROME from A.D. 54 to 68. His name originally was Lucius Domitius Ahenobarbus; after he was adopted by Claudius he assumed the name Nero. See Tacitus' ANNALS XII–XVI. Another contemporary source for his life is Suetonius' *Lives of the Caesars*. See also SENECA THE PHILOSOPHER, and the play OCTAVIA.

Nerva, Marcus Cocceius. The emperor of ROME from A.D. 96 to 98.

Nessus (Nessos). See THE WOMEN OF TRACHIS.

Nestor. See ILIAD, ODYSSEY III, and PYLOS.

New Comedy. See under COMEDY.

Nicias (Nikias). See THE PELOPONNESIAN WAR VI, VII.

Nicomachean Ethics. A prose treatise (later than 334 B.C.; probably between 333 and 323 B.C.) by ARISTOTLE in ten books. Translations: W. D. Ross, 1942; Martin Ostwald, 1962; John Warrington, 1963.

BACKGROUND. In Aristotle's opinion, because man is a political animal, a social creature, the most important science is political science. Happiness can result only from living a life of virtue in society. Thus the *Nicomachean Ethics* explores the *ethos* or character of man to determine the kind of life he requires to achieve happiness. The *Politics*, a sequel to the *Ethics*, considers the type of government and society that will make such a life possible.

SUMMARY. *Book I.* All the various activities, arts, and studies of man seek some good, which is their purpose, and some goods are more significant than others. For man politics is the true approach to the good. Because ethics is not an exact science, one cannot expect scientific proof when discussing this subject. Most people would agree that the greatest good for man is happiness, but there is no agreement on a definition of happiness. Most people believe that happiness results from pleasure, material possessions, or public esteem. The Platonic view is that there is an Idea of the good, which includes and surpasses all the various concepts. However, the method for discovering the good suggested here is an inductive one, which starts with the facts, with what is known. The popular conceptions of happiness—pleasure, material possessions, and honor—cannot be accepted as a true definition. Moreover, the good cannot be regarded as an Idea in the Platonic sense, which is common to all concepts of it. The good is the final goal of an activity. Happiness, the ultimate good, can be considered only in relation to the particular functions and virtues of man. Various questions are raised about the nature of happiness: Can it be learned? Does it come by chance? Was Solon correct in declaring [as the Chorus suggests at the end of *Oedipus the King*] that no man could be called happy until his life was over and thus could be judged as a whole? Happiness is beyond praise, but virtue can be praised. The two types of virtue, intellectual and moral, are discussed.

Book II. Moral virtue, which can be learned or acquired, is a condition of one's character. Moral virtue motivates a man to reject the extremes and to choose the mean. Virtue is the mean between excess and defect. Both the extremes and the mean are discussed. Virtue implies choice, and hence man's responsibility for his acts is assumed.

Book III. Various virtues and vices are defined and analyzed: courage and cowardliness, or rashness; restraint and indulgence. Self-indulgence is more voluntary and therefore more blameworthy than cowardice.

Book IV. Discussion of the vices and virtues is continued: generosity, stinginess, and wasteful extravagance; magnificence and vulgar prodigality; magnanimity or deserved pride and humility and vanity; ambition and lack of ambition; even temper and irascibility and inability to feel proper anger; kindness or friendliness and slavish submissiveness and churlishness; honesty and boastfulness and false modesty; humor and boorishness. Shame, which is a feeling rather than a virtue, is proper to the young; shamelessness of committing evil is characteristic of the corrupt man.

Book V. Justice is defined and analyzed.

Book VI. Intellectual virtue is analyzed, the intellect being divided into the part that is concerned with those things that are invariable and the part that considers the variable. The main intellectual virtues include scientific knowledge, artistry, practical knowledge, intuition, and wisdom. Philosophic wisdom produces happiness; practical wisdom directs a man toward virtuous action.

Book VII. Temperance and self-indulgence are analyzed, and pleasure is discussed in relation to both.

Book VIII. Friendship is an essential virtue for man, for one cannot live without friends. There are three kinds of friendships, two of which are imperfect; love of a friend because he is useful or because he gives pleasure. The third, ideal friendship, exists between good men who are equal in virtue and have each other's best interests at heart. Equality and inequality among friends is discussed. In the highest type of friendship, loving is more significant than being loved. Where friendship exists, justice is also present. If possible there should be an equal exchange of benefits among friends; in unequal friendships, however, a man should do whatever he can for his friend, even when he cannot make an equal return—for example, in the case of a son and his father, who may be considered unequal friends, since the father can never be literally repaid.

Book IX. Reasons for breaking friendships are discussed. A man must like himself in order to be a friend to another. Goodwill, though related to friendship, lacks its intensity; agreement on principles and action is also related to friendship. The satisfactions of generosity and the nature of self-love are explored. The good man loves himself and enjoys the very fact that he exists. Various questions about friendship are raised and discussed: Does a happy man need friends? Should one make as many friends as he can? Does one need friends more when he is unfortunate than when he is fortunate? Friendship essentially means living together and sharing experiences.

Book X. The next topic, pleasure, is an important one because pleasure and pain are basic responses of human beings and are employed in teaching the young. There are two main schools of thought on the subject of pleasure, one of which regards it as good and the other as evil. The philosopher Eudoxus regarded pleasure as good because he felt it was the object of all experience. Actually pleasures differ; there are good and evil pleasures. The pleasures proper to man are those of the good and happy man.

The ultimate aim of human life is happiness; thus happiness must be defined. Happiness exists for its own sake and is thus self-sufficient. It is a virtuous activity and involves the noblest qualities of man; since man's noblest activity is thought, happiness is the act of contemplation. The divine in man is reason; living on his noblest level in contemplative activity, man reaches toward immortality. Men must be trained to lead virtuous lives in accordance with reason. To accomplish this end, legislation is required that will demand that men fulfill the best of their potentialities.

Niobe. In Greek mythology, the daughter of Tantalus. She had seven sons and seven daughters. In her pride Niobe claimed that she was superior to Leto, the mother of only two children, Apollo and Artemis. Niobe was punished by Apollo and Artemis, who killed all her children, and Niobe herself wept until she was transformed into a stone, from which her tears continued to fall.

Nisus (i). See AENEID IX.

Nisus (ii). King of Megara and father of Scylla. See CIRIS.

Nomoi. See LAWS.

Numa Pompilius. According to Roman legend, the successor of Romulus and the second king of Rome. Numa was loved by the goddess Egeria, who would come to him in a grove near Rome. He was honored by the Romans for his wisdom and goodness. His period was sometimes considered a golden age, and he supposedly introduced many religious rites and customs into Rome.

O

Oceanus (Okeanos). In Greek mythology, regarded as a god of the water surrounding the earth. Oceanus is also represented as a Titan, the husband of Tethys, and the father of the river-gods and water nymphs. In the *Iliad*, Oceanus is considered the father of the gods. He appears in Aeschylus' PROMETHEUS BOUND.

Octavia. A tragedy sometimes attributed to SENECA, but probably written by an unknown dramatist. The play is the only complete *fabula praetexta* (play on a Roman subject) that remains. Nero's wife Octavia, whom he despises, expresses her grief and jealousy of his mistress Poppaea. When Nero threatens to kill Octavia, Seneca persuades him to be more moderate in his behavior. Nero divorces Octavia and marries Poppaea. The Roman people rally around Octavia and rebel against Nero, but the rebellion is suppressed, and Nero sentences Octavia to death.

Octavian (Gaius Octavius). The grandnephew of Julius Caesar, born in 63 B.C. After his adoption by Caesar his name was Gaius Julius Caesar Octavianus. As the first Roman emperor he was called Imperator Caesar Augustus. For his career as a triumvir and as emperor of Rome see ROME and ANTONY.

Odes (Carmina). Lyrics (23 B.C.), by HORACE, mainly in alcaic strophe, sapphic, various asclepiadean, alcmanic, and various archilochian meters. Translations: in verse, J. Conington, 1870; in verse, Theodore Martin, 1888; in prose, C. E. Bennett, 1914; in verse, Hugh Macnaghten, 1927; in verse by various translators, ed. H. E. Butler, 1929; in verse, Joseph P. Clancy, 1960; in verse, Helen Rowe Henze, 1961; in verse, James Michie, 1963.

S U M M A R Y . Horace's four books of odes contain 103 poems on a great variety of subjects: political and patriotic poems, drinking songs, serious statements about the exalted role of the poet, the voyages of friends and their returns, the brevity of life and the necessity of "seizing the moment" of joy, the value of moderation, the "golden mean," the satisfactions of a simple and peaceful way of life. A few poems, deal with love, but lightly and rather superficially. Horace's ladies have lovely names, such as Chloe and Lalage, and they are described as graceful, pretty creatures, but they never seem to be real women. The poems on love, like the drinking songs, are mainly light in tone and spirit; though not intended to be sung, they have the lyrical grace and delicacy of songs.

The most moving of Horace's odes deal with the inevitability of death and the possibility of achieving immortality through poetry. The poems on death tell of the swiftness with which the "years glide by" and through a series of graphic details suggest the approach of death (ɪ, xxviii; ɪɪ, iii, xiv). Knowing that all too soon death must claim him, man should "seize the day" (*carpe diem*), enjoying the present with an intense awareness that its pleasures are passing (ɪ, xi; ɪɪ, iii). The poet, however, is assured of immortality for he has "built a monument more durable than bronze" and "shall not entirely die" (ɪɪɪ, xxx). In ɪɪ, xx Horace imagines himself transformed into a swan after death, and he predicts that his works will continue to live throughout the world. Not only the poet gains immortality through his verse, but the great heroes of the past. "Many great men lived before Agamemnon," says Horace, "but unknown, unwept, they are surrounded forever by darkness because they lacked a sacred poet" (ɪv, ix).

Some of the odes deal with themes similar to those of the *Satires:* the value of a simple life and the "golden mean." In ɪɪ, xvi, Horace declares that all men pray for peace, which can be achieved only by a simple way of life and a mind free of fear and greed. He himself is content with his small farm and his gift of song. The same idea is treated in ɪɪ, xviii, in which Horace says he does not envy the rich; indeed, they court him. Content with his simple life on the Sabine Farm, he desires no more. In ɪɪ, x, Horace praises *auream mediocritatem* ("the golden mean"), suggesting that those who value moderation avoid the dangers and difficulties of any extreme. The golden mean should not be regarded as mediocrity; it is rather a precious standard that one can attain only by proper evaluation of the extremes. As Horace points out, "The huge pine is more often shaken by the wind, great towers crash, and lightning strikes the tops of mountains."

The first six odes of Book ɪɪɪ, known as the Roman Odes, are exalted in tone and patriotic in content. Horace speaks of himself as *Musarum sacerdos* ("the priest of the Muses"), and in these odes he recommends a code of conduct suitable to the patriotic Roman. In ɪɪɪ, i, he speaks of simplicity; in ii, of the glory of dying for one's country; in iii, of tenacity of purpose and a sense of justice; in iv, of wisdom; in v, of courage in war; and in vi, of piety.

Odysseus. The son of Laertes and Anticlea. He is one of the best-known figures of ancient Greek myth and literature. For some comments on his names, Odysseus and Ulysses, see the ODYSSEY, *Mythical Background.* Both in the ILIAD and the *Odyssey*, Homer depicts Odysseus as a resourceful, courageous, wise, and extremely vital figure. Though he is sometimes childishly boastful and deceitful, he is essentially an extremely appealing character. The very ambivalence of Odysseus' traits, especially his cleverness and his resourcefulness, made it possible for writers to characterize him in a variety of ways. In Sophocles'

PHILOCTETES, Odysseus' resourcefulness, an admirable quality in the hero of the *Odyssey*, becomes an interest in mere expediency without regard for other human beings. In Sophocles' AJAX Odysseus reveals a sense of justice; in Euripides' HECUBA he is a brutal man. RHESUS again presents him as the shrewd warrior. The Latin writers, Horace in *Satire* II, 5, Vergil in the *Aeneid*, and Seneca in *The Trojan Women* all depict him as a cold, treacherous figure.

Odyssey, The (Odysseia). Epic by HOMER, in 24 books of dactylic hexameters. Most authorities agree that the *Odyssey* dates from the ninth century B.C. Translations: in verse, George Chapman, 1614; in prose, Samuel Butler, 1900; in verse, H. B. Cotterill, 1911; in prose, T. E. Shaw (Lawrence of Arabia), 1932; in prose, E. V. Rieu, 1950; in verse, Ennis Rees, 1960; in verse, Robert Fitzgerald, 1961.

(For historical, religious, and social backgrounds of the *Odyssey* see ILIAD.)

MYTHICAL BACKGROUND. Odysseus, known to Roman authors as Ulixes (Ulysses), existed as a historical-mythical character before his appearance in the Homeric poems. W. B. Stanford points out that the twelve Greek variations on his name—among them Odysseus and Oulixes—indicate the possibility that the character in the *Iliad* and the *Odyssey* results from the merging of two separate figures before the time of Homer. Stanford suggests that the "primeval Ulysses may have been a historical person, a prince of Ithaca, . . . an Egyptian trader, or a captain in some Minoan fleet. Or else, as some scholars suggest, he may have been a pre-Greek sea-god (whence the enmity of his Olympian successor, Poseidon), or a solar divinity, or a year-daimon" (*The Ulysses Theme* [Blackwell, 1954], p. 9). Though Odysseus no doubt existed as a historical or mythical figure before Homer's time, unfortunately there is no evidence of him earlier than the *Iliad* and the *Odyssey*.

In the *Odyssey* numerous folk tales, or *Weltmärchen,* are combined and adapted to suit the character and personality of Odysseus. Thus he is at once the traditional returning hero who avenges the crimes against his wife and his homeland, the giant-slayer, the prince who comes from afar to woo a beautiful princess, the stranger who strings the bow when all others have failed, and many other traditional mythical figures; at the same time, he asserts his own remarkable identity. In fact, his personality transforms the myths that are adapted to his saga.

Odysseus displayed his usual courage and cunning during the ten years that he fought in the Trojan War. According to some accounts he was the one who proposed the idea of the wooden horse, in which the Greek warriors who finally took Troy were hidden. The *Odyssey* begins in the tenth year after the fall of Troy and tells of Odysseus' ten years of adventure before reaching his homeland, Ithaca. He is the victim of the wrath of three deities: Athene, who is angry at the Greeks because Ajax, son of Oïleus, violated Cassandra in the temple of Athene on the night that Troy was captured; Poseidon, because Odysseus blinded the god's son, Polyphemus; and Helios, because Odysseus' men consumed his oxen. One wrath replaces the other as Odysseus progresses in his adventures. Athene's wrath accounts for his initial wanderings; when Athene, somewhat inconsistently, has ceased to be angry at Odysseus and comes to his aid, the wrath of Poseidon still pursues him; and it is Helios who, with Zeus' help, kills Odysseus' men and leaves him alone to face the rest of his difficulties. Furthermore, Poseidon raises a storm that almost destroys Odysseus after Athene has persuaded Zeus himself to aid him. The anger of these three gods helps to account for Odysseus' difficulties and thus is fitted into the various folk tales that make up his adventures. In the *Odyssey* powerful Greek deities and the subtle figure of Odysseus enter into the traditional motifs of *Weltmärchen* and, by their presence, change and enrich the meanings of these tales.

SUMMARY. *Book I.* The *Odyssey* begins with an invocation to the Muse, as the poet asks for help in telling the story of Odysseus, the man of many resources, who, after destroying the citadel of Troy, roamed all over the world. Early in the poem, the theme of Odysseus' experience, his great capacity for learning and enduring, is emphasized. Homer says that his hero saw the cities of many men, and he learned their customs. He endured much suffering in his attempts to save himself and his comrades, but his comrades' folly in eating the oxen of Helios, the Sun-god, brought about their deaths.

After this brief summary, we are told that all the survivors of the Trojan War except Odysseus have already returned to their homes. Odysseus remains in Ogygia, the home of the nymph Calypso (The Secreter), who delays Odysseus in the hope that he will remain with her. Except for Poseidon, all the gods pity Odysseus; but Poseidon, who hates Odysseus for blinding his son Polyphemus, pursues Odysseus with rage until the very day of his return to Ithaca. Since Poseidon has now gone to visit the Ethiopians, half of whom live where the sun goes down and half where the sun rises, the rest of the gods assemble in the palace of Zeus on Olympus to discuss the fate of Odysseus. Zeus has been thinking of Aegisthus, the lover of Clytemnestra, whom Agamemnon's son Orestes has killed. This is the first of many references to Orestes' vengeance against his mother and her lover for their murder of his father, Agamemnon. Orestes is constantly used as an example of moral conduct in the *Odyssey*. Pondering on Aegisthus' punishment, Zeus concludes that though men blame the gods for their troubles, it is actually their own evil that causes them suffering greater than that allotted to them by fate. (Thus Zeus explicitly states an idea significant in much of Greek literature—that man is essentially responsible for his acts and their consequences.)

Athene replies to Zeus that Aegisthus has received a punishment he deserved, but her sympathies are with Odysseus. Throughout the poem she defends and helps Odysseus, for she is clearly the goddess closest to the man of many resources. In their craftiness, their wit, their pleasure in themselves, their agile minds, adept at solving a difficult problem and inventing an effective and imaginative tale, Athene and Odysseus are much like. Athene goes on to tell Zeus that Odysseus remains in deep despair on the island of Ogygia, longing for death, because he can envision no way of returning to Ithaca. She asks Zeus why his heart is unmoved by Odysseus' fate. Zeus replies that he has not forgotten the great Odysseus, wisest of men and most generous in his offerings to the gods. It is Poseidon who cannot forgive Odysseus for blinding the Cyclops. Concluding that Poseidon cannot withstand all the other gods, Zeus resolves to help Odysseus. Athene suggests sending Hermes, the divine messenger, to Ogygia to tell Calypso that she must allow Odysseus to leave. Meanwhile, Athene herself will go to Ithaca to inspire Telemachus, Odysseus' son, with more spirit, so that he will call an assembly of the Ithacans and reproach the crowd of Suitors, who, like parasites, consume his wealth while they court his mother, Penelope. Athene will then send Telemachus to Sparta to seek news of his father.

Arriving at Ithaca, Athene assumes the form of Mentes, a Taphian chieftain. She sees the Suitors amusing themselves while their squires and pages prepare food and wine for them. At first no one but Telemachus notices the goddess. Telemachus has been sitting and dreaming of the day when his father will return and drive away the Suitors. The young man greets Athene as Mentes and offers her his hospitality. He leads her into a large hall to a carved chair with a stool for her feet. A maid brings a golden jug so that they may wash their hands and a table for their meal. They eat well and drink out of golden cups. The Suitors enter, and they too feast. Phemius, the minstrel, has begun to sing a song accompanying himself on the lyre when Telemachus tells Athene his woes, his hatred of the Suitors, and his fears that his father is dead. He then asks Athene who she is, where she comes from, and whether she has visited Ithaca before. She tells him her name is Mentes and invents a tale to supply Mentes' background. She pretends that she came to Ithaca because she thought Odysseus was already home, and she insists that he is still alive. She remarks on the resemblance between Telemachus and his father and recalls Odysseus' bravery. She then advises Telemachus to call an assembly at which he must tell the Suitors to depart. If Penelope wishes to remarry, Telemachus must send her to her father, who will provide a marriage feast. Telemachus himself must seek news of his father, first from Nestor at Pylos and then from Menelaus at Sparta. Most significantly, she reminds him that he is no longer a child and must give up his childish ideas. Thus wisdom both literally and figuratively inspires Telemachus to take on the courage and strength of manhood as Athene reminds him of the valor of Orestes.

When Athene leaves Telemachus, disappearing like a bird through an opening in the roof, he has her spirit within him, and he feels the change. He is more manly and courageous in his treatment of his mother and the Suitors. Penelope is amazed when Telemachus orders her to her quarters, and the Suitors are shocked when he announces that in the morning he will call an assembly so that he can formally order them to leave his palace. Eurymachus, one of the Suitors, inquires about Telemachus' guest and whether he has brought news of Odysseus. Telemachus replies that it is certain that his father will never return, but he does not reveal his visitor's identity. He then retires to his room, where all night long he plans the journey Athene has suggested.

Book II. At dawn Telemachus orders the criers to summon his fellow countrymen to the assembly. Wise old Aegyptius blesses the man, as yet unknown to him, who has called the assembly, for there has been none for twenty years, since Odysseus' departure. Telemachus announces that it was he who summoned the Ithacans and publicly asks the Suitors to leave his home; they are parasites, he says, who are consuming his wealth. Antinous replies in anger. He says it is Penelope who is guilty, for she kept the Suitors on tenterhooks for three years, giving them some reason to hope that she would marry one of them, but asking them to restrain their ardor until she could finish weaving a shroud for Laertes, the aged father of Odysseus. She wove by day, and by night she undid her work. At last a maid gave her secret away. Antinous insists that Telemachus order his mother to marry the man her father will choose for her. He goes on to praise Penelope's skill in weaving, her intelligence, and her capacity to achieve whatever she wishes. However, he declares, her cleverness in avoiding the choice of a new husband will only result in the Suitors' remaining at the palace of Odysseus. Telemachus replies that he cannot cast out his mother, nor does he wish to repay her dowry to her father, Icarius. Once again, he begs the Suitors to depart and goes on to say that he will pray to the gods for a day of reckoning when he can destroy the Suitors.

Zeus sends an omen as a comment on these words. Two eagles fly from a mountaintop. When they are above the meeting hall, they flap their wings and look down at the crowd with glances that prophesy death. They then strike each other with their talons, tearing at each other as they fly eastward over the town. Haliserthes, a soothsayer, interprets this omen to mean that Odysseus will soon return to destroy the Suitors, but Eurymachus in his pride mocks the soothsayer, saying that the Suitors do not fear Telemachus or anyone. He demands that Telemachus arrange for his mother's marriage. Telemachus says he will no longer entreat them to leave, but will go to Sparta and Pylos to seek news of his father. Mentor, an old friend of Odysseus', then says that he does not blame the Suitors so much as he does those who accept their crimes apathetically.

When the assembly is dismissed Telemachus prays to Athene, who comes to him disguised in the form of Mentor. She praises him for his manliness, comparing him with his father, and advises him to prepare for his journey. Returning to the palace, Telemachus finds the Suitors feasting. When Antinous asks him to join them Telemachus tells them he is now old enough to feel his strength. He goes to his father's storeroom to prepare for his journey. Athene, disguised as Telemachus, chooses twenty men to accompany him. She then lulls the Suitors to sleep and, once more taking the form of Mentor, joins Telemachus and his crew as they set sail for Pylos.

Book III. Telemachus and his companions arrive at Pylos, where they find the people on the seashore, sacrificing black bulls to Poseidon. Athene urges Telemachus not to be shy and to approach Nestor immediately to obtain information about Odysseus. Nestor and his sons welcome Telemachus and ask him and his company to join their feast in honor of Poseidon. After Athene and Telemachus pray to Poseidon and feast with the others, Telemachus identifies himself and questions Nestor about Odysseus. Nestor first speaks of the Trojan War and the great suffering the Greeks endured. He goes on to praise Odysseus, who surpassed all in intelligence. He then tells of how, after the Greeks had destroyed Troy, Zeus and Athene caused them great distress when they set out for home. Athene, angry at the Greeks because Ajax, son of Oïleus, had violated Cassandra in the temple of Athene on the night that Troy was captured, caused Agamemnon and Menelaus to quarrel. Menelaus thought that the Greeks should leave at once for their homes, but Agamemnon wanted them to remain and make offerings to Athene in an effort to appease her. Some of the Greeks did remain at Troy for a while, making offerings to Athene, and others, including Nestor, set sail for their homes. Though Odysseus and his followers were among these, they changed their minds after reaching Tenedos and returned to give their allegiance to Agamemnon. Nestor continued on his journey until he reached Pylos, but he returned without knowledge of the men left behind. However, news reached him at Pylos that Neoptolemus, the son of Achilles, and Philoctetes had arrived at their homes with their followers. Idomeneus also was safely home. Agamemnon was killed by Aegisthus soon after his return. Nestor then says that he has heard of the problems Telemachus has had with the Suitors and wishes that Athene may come to help Telemachus as she has helped Odysseus. When Telemachus pessimistically replies that he cannot hope for such good luck, Athene in the form of Mentor scolds him, saying that a friendly god can bring a man home, no matter how far he has strayed. She says she would rather endure great hardship before returning home than come home to die as Agamemnon did. But, of course, all must die in the end; even the gods cannot shield someone they love from the common fate of death.

Telemachus asks Mentor to end this sad conversation. He still doubts that his father will return. He wishes to learn how Agamemnon met his death and why Menelaus did not attempt to prevent it. Nestor then informs him that Aegisthus, remaining in Argos during the Trojan War, seduced Clytemnestra and persuaded her to accept his plan to murder her husband. Menelaus, unfortunately, could not return home immediately after the war. On his way home part of his fleet was destroyed in a storm and with his five remaining ships he was driven to Egypt at the time when Aegisthus murdered Agamemnon. Aegisthus ruled Mycenae for seven years. In the eighth year of his rule Orestes returned from Athens and killed Aegisthus. Nestor warns Telemachus not to stay away from his home for too long. However, he does urge him to pay Menelaus a visit.

Telemachus spends the night in the palace of Nestor, and in the morning, accompanied by Nestor's son Peisistratus, he leaves Pylos for Sparta in a chariot that Nestor has provided.

Book IV. When Telemachus and Peisistratus arrive at Sparta they are impressed by the luxury and beauty of Menelaus' palace. The hall seems to reflect the splendor of the sun's and the moon's light. After they have bathed, dressed, and eaten, Telemachus tells Peisistratus that he believes the court of Zeus on Olympus must resemble the magnificent palace of Menelaus. The comment reveals his youth and lack of experience. Menelaus, overhearing it, says, "No man may vie with Zeus. His palace and all that he owns are immortal." Menelaus acknowledges, however, that few men can equal him in the wealth he has accumulated in seven years of wandering through Cyprus, Phoenicia, Egypt, Libya, and other places. He has had little joy in his wealth, though, for he returned to find his brother Agamemnon dead. Moreover, he misses his beloved comrades who died fighting at Troy, and he laments for Odysseus, who labored hardest at Troy and now is lost. When Telemachus hears his father's name, he weeps, and Menelaus is deeply embarrassed. At this point Helen appears with her women. Beautiful and tactful, she approaches Telemachus and Menelaus and immediately recognizes the resemblance between Telemachus and Odysseus. When she points out the likeness, Menelaus also remarks on it and expresses his joy at welcoming the son of his friend. When Menelaus speaks of his love for Odysseus, the whole company weeps until Peisistratus begs them to cease. While they feast, Helen puts an Egyptian drug into their wine that banishes their sorrowful memories. She then suggests that they entertain each other by telling stories. She begins by telling of how, during the Trojan War, the ingenious Odysseus disguised himself as a beggar and entered the Trojans' city. She was the only one who recognized him, but she did not disclose his identity. Menelaus says that Odysseus' courage and strength saved the Greeks hidden in the Trojan Horse.

After this story the company decides to retire for the night. In the morning Telemachus asks Menelaus for news of his father, and Menelaus replies that when he was in Egypt he had news of Odysseus from the sea-god Proteus, the Old Man of the Sea. Seeking a means to escape from Pharos, an island in the sea off the mouth of the Nile, Menelaus appealed to Eidothea, the daughter of Proteus. She told him how to trap the ever-elusive and ever-changing Proteus, who could give him excellent directions for his journey home. When Menelaus seized Proteus, Proteus gave him the advice he required. He then said that Ajax, son of Oïleus, was drowned on his way home from Troy, that Agamemnon was killed, and that Odysseus was held captive on the island of Ogygia, the home of the nymph Calypso. Proteus then prophesied that Menelaus would not die in Argos, but would go to the Elysian plain at the end of the world in the land without snow or strong winds. Menelaus followed the advice of Proteus and returned home. After giving this account of his adventures, Menelaus invites Telemachus and Peisistratus to remain with him for twelve days, but Telemachus says that he must return to Pylos. He refuses Menelaus' gift of three horses because Ithaca has pasture lands for goats rather than for horses. Menelaus then says that he will give him a mixing bowl of silver and gold made by Hephaestus.

Meanwhile, the Suitors at Odysseus' palace plan to wait for Telemachus' ship in the straits between Ithaca and Samos and kill the young prince. Medon, the herald, tells Penelope of this plot, and she weeps in despair. Eurycleia, the nurse, suggests that she pray to Athene for help. Athene sends a phantom of Penelope's sister Iphthime to the bedside of Penelope to comfort her.

Book V. The scene shifts to Olympus, where Athene once more asks Zeus to help Odysseus. Zeus sends Hermes to Calypso to tell her that she must release Odysseus. He declares that Odysseus must now set off for Ithaca, but his journey will be a difficult one. After twenty days he will reach Scherie, the land of the Phaeacians, who will take him home in their ship, laden with valuable presents.

When Hermes arrives at Ogygia, he looks around at the exotic beauty of the island and then finds Calypso in her delightful cavern. While Hermes is with Calypso, Odysseus is sitting on the shore, weeping and longing for home, the victim of his own apathy and despair. When Calypso hears Zeus' command she urges Odysseus to get to work and build a boat. Though at first Odysseus distrusts Calypso, imagining that she plots mischief against him, he finally takes her advice and, despite his fears about the dangerous voyage ahead, is willing to set sail. He says he is accustomed to suffering and trusts in his powers of endurance. He spends four days building his boat and on the fifth bids farewell to Calypso and sets sail for home. For seventeen days he follows the course Calypso has suggested, but on the eighteenth Poseidon, returning from his visit to the Ethiopians, catches sight of him and sends a great storm, which upsets Odysseus' boat and hurls him into the sea. Exhausted and frightened, he struggles to save his life. Finally regaining his boat, he sits helpless as the winds toss it over the waves. At last the sea-goddess Leucothea pities him and comes to his aid. She advises him to remove his clothes and swim to the shore of Scherie. She gives him a veil to put around his waist, which will protect him with its divine powers. When he reaches shore he must throw the veil back into the sea. Odysseus decides to cling to the ship as long as he can, but soon Poseidon sends another huge wave, and Odysseus is forced to plunge into the sea. Athene sends a strong breeze from the north to help Odysseus, who swims for two days and two nights. Finally, on the third dawn he spots land. He soon discovers, however, that it is a rocky coast without a harbor. With great difficulty he swims to the mouth of a river and prays to its god for help. His prayers are answered; the river restrains its waves, and at last Odysseus makes the shore at the mouth of the river. He lies down to sleep in a thicket under the branches of two intertwining trees, covering himself with leaves, preserving his life as a man does a glowing bit of wood under ashes. The image suggests Odysseus' powers of endurance, his marvelous vitality as he encounters the great difficulties of life.

Book VI. While Odysseus sleeps, Athene helps him by appearing to Nausicaa, the beautiful young daughter of Alcinous, king of the Phaeacians. Athene, disguised as a friend of Nausicaa, suggests that the young woman ought to be preparing for marriage. She must go to the washing pools the next day and clean her clothes to prepare for marriage. Nausicaa is too shy to reveal her true motive for the project to her father, so she says that she wishes to wash her brother's clothes. Alcinous, guessing her real reason, gives her permission and provisions for the day. Nausicaa and her companions wash the clothes and then bathe. After they eat they play with a ball as they wait for the clothes to dry. When their ball falls into the sea, the maidens cry out and awaken Odysseus, who has been sleeping nearby. Though Odysseus is worried about the kind of reception he will meet among this strange people, he realizes he must face whatever awaits him. As he courageously goes forth, he is compared with a mountain lion in his power and need. When the maidens see him, all except Nausicaa run away in fear. Nausicaa, however, meets him with dignity and courage. [Like the traditional princess of folklore, of which she is a charming and individualized adaptation, she is awaiting a prince from abroad who must prove his powers in order to win her. In her dignity and innocence she is the prototype of the young woman on the threshold of adulthood, but she is also a subtle and interesting individual character. Her naïveté and her flirtatiousness, her quick wit, and her kindness, charm us. Furthermore, we are moved by the way in which she responds to a more complicated hero than ever appeared in the traditional folk tale from which she springs.] When Odysseus confronts her he immediately exhibits his cunning and resourcefulness. He begins by flattering her, asking whether she is a goddess or a mortal. If she is a mortal, he says, her parents are indeed fortunate to have such an offspring, but most fortunate of all will be the man who wins her as his wife. He then goes on to imply that he is a man of experience who has endured many hardships, and he ends by asking her to pity him. Nausicaa's reply is a charming mixture of moralizing and gentle assurance. She tells Odysseus that because his ordeals were sent by Zeus, he could no nothing but endure them. Then she offers to help him. She orders the maidens to feed and bathe Odysseus, but Odysseus chooses to bathe himself. When Athene makes Odysseus appear more attractive than before, Nausicaa confesses to her companions that he is the type of man she could desire for a husband. With her unique charm she lets Odysseus know her feelings by suggesting that he go to the palace of her parents alone after she and her maidens have left, for if he accompanied them, the young men of the town whom she has spurned would think Odysseus is her future husband. She gives him directions for finding the palace of Alcinous and suggests that he speak first to her mother, Arete. Odysseus prays to Athene that the Phaeacians may treat him kindly.

Book VII. Nausicaa arrives at the palace and retires to her room. Odysseus follows, covered by a mist with which Athene protects him. The goddess then disguises herself as a young girl and meets Odysseus on the way to lead him to the palace of Alcinous. As Odysseus walks through the town, he observes and marvels at its harbors with their fine ships, the assembly hall, and the lofty walls. Though he is tired and hungry, he does not miss the opportunity to observe and enjoy the world around him. When Athene and Odysseus reach the palace, Athene tells him to go first to Queen Arete and ask her help. The goddess then leaves him. Odysseus hesitates before entering the palace. Once again, in spite of his misgivings, he pauses to enjoy the beauty of the bronze walls, the golden doors, and the other beautiful features of the palace. Finally he enters, enveloped in a mist that covers him until he reaches Queen Arete and King Alcinous. The mist disappears as he clasps Arete's knees and begs her to help him return to his home. Echeneus, one of the Phaeacian elders, encourages Alcinous to offer this suppliant his hospitality and the king raises Odysseus and seats him on a polished throne. He is then offered food and drink. Alcinous suggests that the Phaeacian captains and counselors go home for the night and that on the next day they entertain their guest and discuss his passage home. When Alcinous remarks that Odysseus may be a god in disguise, Odysseus replies that he certainly is no god, that indeed he will match his sorrow with those who have borne the heaviest burden of woes. He hopes only to return to his home. He is so convincing that the Phaeacians applaud him and agree to arrange for his journey home.

After the captains and counselors have left, Arete asks Odysseus who he is and where he comes from. Odysseus, ever guarded and cautious, tells her only about his experiences on the island of Ogygia, the seven years with Calypso and how he finally left her only to meet with the wrath of Poseidon in the storm that almost killed him. He then tells of his meeting with Nausicaa, praising the girl for her good sense and kindness. He goes so far as to distort the facts in his effort to please her parents; when Alcinous criticizes Nausicaa for not bringing Odysseus home with her, Odysseus says that Nausicaa asked him to follow along with her servants, when actually she had instructed him to come alone later on. Alcinous says that if Odysseus wishes to remain in Scherie, he may marry Nausicaa, but if he wishes to leave, Alcinous will not keep him from doing so. Odysseus prays to Zeus that Alcinous may do all he has promised. Then he retires for the night.

Book VIII. At dawn Alcinous leads Odysseus to the place of assembly. Athene has spread the news of the stranger's arrival among the Phaeacians, who gather at the meeting place to see Odysseus. The king addresses his people, telling them that they must make arrangements at once to send the stranger home. They must launch their ship and choose fifty-two oarsmen of proven ability for her crew. He then invites them to his palace, where they will entertain their guest. He also summons the bard Demodocus.

After the ship is launched the Phaeacians gather at the palace, where the bard Demodocus sings a lay about the quarrel of Odysseus and Achilles. Odysseus weeps when he hears this song, and Alcinous, observing his guest's despair, tactfully invites the company to engage in new activities: boxing, wrestling, jumping, and running contests. After various contests have taken place, Laodamas, Alcinous' son, suggests that the Phaeacians ask Odysseus what sport he excels in, but Odysseus responds sadly that he is too weary and sorrowful to care about games. However, when Euryalus, one of the Phaeacians, challenges his ability as an athlete and remarks that he is merely a merchant who sails about seeking profits, Odysseus angrily decides to show his ability. He seizes the largest disk and hurls it farther than any of the others. Athene, disguised as one of the men, points up his triumph, and Odysseus, encouraged, boasts of his skill in boxing, wrestling, running, and archery. He challenges any Phaeacian except his host, Laodamas, to a contest.

Alcinous answers him, saying he understands Odysseus' anger at Euryalus' insult. He goes on to say that the Phaeacians are not perfect as boxers or wrestlers. They can run fast and are excellent seamen, but the activities they really take pleasure in are feasting, the music of the lyre, dancing, clean linen, hot baths, and their beds. He then calls forth dancers, who perform for Odysseus, and Demodocus recites a charming lay about the love of Ares, the war-god, and Aphrodite. The song tells of how Hephaestus, the skilled craftsman of the gods, traps his wife, the beautiful but faithless Aphrodite, in the arms of her lover Ares by means of a marvelous net that Hephaestus has created with great artistry. When the lovers are caught in each other's arms, Hephaestus calls the other gods to witness the sad and comic event. Sadly he observes that Aphrodite despises him because he is lame and that she admires the handsome butcher Ares. Despite the pathos of his situation, the gods laugh at the sight of Ares and Aphrodite trapped in the net.

After this song, there is dancing, and then Odysseus is given many gifts. A little later Nausicaa comes to say good-bye to Odysseus in a touching scene. Unlike the typical princess of folklore, she must accept the departure of the prince. This she does with dignity, expressing the wish that Odysseus will remember her when he returns to his own land. Odysseus tells her that he will worship her for the rest of his life.

After Odysseus feasts with Alcinous and other Phaeacians, Demodocus sings a lay about the construction of the wooden horse of Troy. When Odysseus hears this song, he again begins to weep. Noticing his guest's distress, Alcinous orders the bard to stop playing. He then turns to Odysseus and asks him his name and the land from which he comes. He wishes also to know about Odysseus' wanderings and the people and places he visited.

Book IX. Odysseus tells Alcinous who he is and begins the story of his adventures. After leaving Troy he and his men went first to Ismarus, the home of the Cicones, which they sacked, killing the men and taking their wives and their treasures. Odysseus wished to leave Ismarus as soon as possible, but his men delayed until the Cicones obtained help, and a battle followed in which six warriors from each of Odysseus' ships were killed.

They set sail and were driven by a current and the north wind to the country of the Lotus-eaters. When some of Odysseus' men explored the land, the natives gave them lotus to taste. This food banished all thought of returning home: they wished to remain forever among the Lotus-eaters. Odysseus forced them to return to the ships, and once more they set sail.

Their next stop was the land of the Cyclopes, wild, uncivilized giants, whose name means Round-Eye and refers to their one eye in the center of their foreheads. [The story of the Cyclops is a traditional folk tale which occurs in many different versions in different cultures. In Homer's version the traditional story of the one-eyed giant who is blinded by the hero is enhanced with details taken from other traditional folk tales (see Denys Page, *The Homeric Odyssey* [Oxford University Press, 1955], pp. 3-20). Moreover, Homer changes and adapts the traditional story to express the personality of his hero and to further the development of his theme.] The Cyclopes are one of the uncivilized peoples whose violent, lawless ways astonish Odysseus and whom he manages to escape through his ingenuity. The Cyclopes do not plant or till the soil; their crops come up unsown. They do not have assemblies or laws or accepted customs. Each man is the lawmaker of his family, and no one cares about his neighbor.

When Odysseus and his men first landed, they explored the land of the Cyclopes with pleasure. They hunted, enjoyed their meals, and then slept on the seashore. The next day Odysseus and twelve of his best men took some wine and food with them and set off for the cave of the Cyclops. Not finding him at home, they entered and looked around. They discovered baskets full of cheeses and pens of lambs and kids. Lighting a fire, they made offerings to the gods and ate some cheese as they awaited the arrival of Polyphemus. When the Cyclops finally entered the cave, he closed the entrance with a huge stone. After milking his ewes, he lighted a fire and saw the strangers. Odysseus reminded him of his religious duty to be hospitable, but the Cyclops jumped up, seized two of Odysseus' men and dashed their heads on the ground till their brains burst out and were spattered on the earth. Then he devoured them limb by limb, eating like a mountain lion. After this feast he went to sleep. In the morning he consumed two more men, then left to take his flocks to pasture, again closing the entrance. While Polyphemus was gone, Odysseus and his men sharpened the giant's huge wooden staff to a point, hardened it in the fire, and hid it. On his return the Cyclops consumed two more men. Odysseus then gave him a great deal of wine in order to confuse him. When the Cyclops asked Odysseus his name, he replied that his name was Nobody. Polyphemus declared that he would eat Nobody last. Finally, overcome by the wine, he fell into a drunken sleep and vomited forth wine mixed with remains of the men he ate. Odysseus and his men then blinded the Cyclops with the staff. When Polyphemus cried out for help, saying that Nobody was destroying him, his friends did not come to his rescue.

Odysseus now conceived of a plan of escape. He tied the Cyclops' rams together in groups of three. Each middle ram carried one of the men tied under its breast. When the Cyclops felt the backs of the animals on their way out of the cave, he did not discover the presence of the men. The prize ram of the flock carried Odysseus. When this animal left the cave carrying Odysseus, the Cyclops stopped to speak to it. In a touching scene that evokes the reader's pity for the loneliness of even so hideous a monster as the Cyclops, Polyphemus asked the ram why it lingered behind the others of the flock. He imagined that it was grieving because its master had been blinded.

When Odysseus and his men at last set sail from the land of the Cyclopes, Odysseus could not resist taunting Polyphemus. Even after the giant hurled a huge rock at them and Odysseus' men scolded him for his rashness, he continued to gloat over the Cyclops. Finally, in his pride, he revealed to Polyphemus that it was Odysseus who blinded him. Odysseus paid for his arrogance, for the Cyclops prayed to his father, Poseidon, to bring many difficulties to Odysseus before he reached home and great trouble at home when he did arrive there.

Book X. Odysseus' next stop was the island of Aeolia, the home of Aeolus, to whom Zeus had given power over the winds. Odysseus stayed with Aeolus for a month, and, when he left, Aeolus gave him a leather bag that contained the winds. Aeolus placed this tightly closed bag in the hold of Odysseus' ship and summoned a western breeze to send the fleet across the sea. For ten days Odysseus and his men sailed on. They were already within sight of Ithaca when, unfortunately, Odysseus fell asleep, and the crew, suspecting that the bag contained gold and silver, opened it, allowing the winds to rush out in a storm. The fleet was driven back to Aeolia, but this time Aeolus refused to help Odysseus and dismissed him angrily. They sailed for six days and on the seventh reached Telepylus, the land of the Laestrygones, gigantic cannibals. Odysseus anchored his ship outside the harbor while the rest of the fleet sought the shelter of the cove. Antiphates, the chief of the Laestrygones, roused his fellow countrymen, who destroyed all the ships except Odysseus' own and killed and ate their crews. Only Odysseus and his crew escaped with their ship. They journeyed on in despair, grieving for their lost friends. Soon they came to the island of Aeaea, the home of the beautiful goddess Circe, who struck half the crew with her magic wand and turned them into swine. Odysseus, however, was given a powerful drug by Hermes that made him immune to Circe's magic power. Circe was amazed at Odysseus' resistance and asked him to be her lover. She also agreed to free his men. Odysseus remained with Circe for a year and then asked her to send him home, but the goddess told him that he must first descend into Hades in order to consult the shade of Tiresias, the blind Theban prophet. Though Odysseus wept over this new challenge, he agreed to go. Circe then gave him directions for reaching Hades and advice about what to do when he arrived.

Book XI. [In this book Odysseus makes his well-known descent into the world of the dead, another traditional motif, which has become a significant element in epic since Homer's time and has also been used metaphorically in much other poetry and fiction. The eleventh book of the Odyssey is thought originally to have been a separate poem about Odysseus' descent into the Underworld, which was incorporated into the Odyssey (see Denys Page, The Homeric Odyssey, pp. 21–51) and adapted to its theme. Though Odysseus is reluctant to undertake so hazardous an experience, with his usual courage and curiosity he takes advantage of this unique opportunity; the journey provides him with knowledge denied most men: insight not only into the experience of the dead but into his own living self.]

Circe provided a favorable breeze, and Odysseus' ship sailed across the River of Ocean to the land of the Cimmerians, who live in a city of perpetual darkness at the edge of the world. The men left their ship and made their way along the banks of the River of Ocean to Hades. Odysseus made the proper sacrifices, and the souls of the dead came swarming around him. He promised to cremate the body of his dead comrade Elpenor and to raise a barrow for him. He then spoke to the prophet Tiresias, who warned him not to touch the cattle of the sun-god. Tiresias also told Odysseus of the Suitors, who were consuming his food and attempting to win his wife Penelope, and he prophesied that Odysseus would kill them. After this victory, Tiresias said, Odysseus must again set forth on his travels. He must take an oar with him and travel until he comes to a people who know nothing about the sea and do not even use salt. When he finds another traveler who says that Odysseus is carrying a winnowing fan on his shoulder, he must plant his oar in the ground, make a sacrifice to Poseidon, return home, and make offerings to all the gods. Death, the prophet said, would come to Odysseus gently from the sea when he is an old man.

After learning about his future from Tiresias, Odysseus spoke to the soul of his mother, Anticleia, who told him that she had died of longing for him. She spoke to him about his son and about his father's sorrow because he had not returned to Ithaca. When Odysseus tried to embrace his mother, she slipped through his arms. Anticleia explained that after death the body is gone and only the soul remains: such is the law of human nature. She advised her son to remember what he had learned in Hades, so that he might tell his wife about it.

Odysseus saw and spoke to many other souls, among them that of Agamemnon, who warned him to learn from his own sad experience not to trust too much in his wife. Encountering the spirit of Achilles, Odysseus said that he envied him, for he was fortunate and honored in life as in death. But Achilles declared that he would rather be a serf bound to a poor man who had no land than be a king among the dead. The only soul that remained apart from Odysseus was that of Ajax, son of Telamon, who had not forgiven Odysseus for having won the arms of Achilles, for which they contended. Ajax had killed himself in his fury at being denied the arms. Odysseus now regretted winning these accursed arms that brought Ajax to his death.

Odysseus then saw many souls in torture, Tityus, Tantalus, and Sisyphus. He met the soul of Heracles, who spoke of the many labors he had to perform when he was alive. Odysseus wished to meet more dead heroes, but when many thousands of dead spirits came crowding around him, he retreated in panic and ran quickly to his ship. He and his men were carried by the current down the River of Ocean.

Book XII. Odysseus and his men returned to Aeaea to burn the corpse of Elpenor. Circe greeted them, remarking on Odysseus' courage and on the extent of his knowledge. "For most men," she said, "one death is sufficient, but you will have met death twice." Odysseus rested for a day with Circe, who advised him on how to behave in his encounters with the Sirens, who entice men with their music and then destroy them; with Scylla, a monstrous creature with twelve feet and six heads, each of which has three rows of teeth; and with Charybdis, a huge whirlpool. Circe then told him that his next stop would be Thrinacia, where the sun-god's cattle and sheep were pastured. These animals, she warned him, must not be touched.

When the ship approached the island of the Sirens, Odysseus, following the advice of Circe, stopped the ears of his men with wax so that they could not hear the tempting and destructive song of the Sirens. He himself, once again seeking knowledge, no matter how painful the acquisition, but aware of his human limitations, ordered his men to bind him to a mast of the ship. In this way he could hear the song of the Sirens, yet avoid death. The Sirens urged him to draw near, tempting him with knowledge of the past and the future, and Odysseus begged his men to set him free. Forewarned, they only tightened his bonds and rowed away.

They managed to pass Charybdis safely, but Scylla snatched up and devoured six of Odysseus' men. Soon they reached Thrinacia, the island of the sun. Odysseus, remembering the warnings of Tiresias and Circe, preferred not to land, but was swayed by the entreaties of his weary men, who promised not to touch the cattle of Helios. They were delayed on the island by storms, and, when their food was gone, in Odysseus' absence the men were persuaded by Eurylochus to eat the sun-god's cattle. When Odysseus heard what they had done, he cried out in despair. Soon after they set sail, Zeus sent a storm at

Helios' request and destroyed the ship with a thunderbolt. The men were thrown overboard and killed. Odysseus managed to survive, though he was thrown back to Charybdis. He drifted for nine days, and on the tenth reached the island of Ogygia, the home of Calypso. After staying with her for seven years, he came to the island of Scherie, where he now concludes the tale of his adventures.

Book XIII. The Phaeacians give Odysseus many valuable presents and send him home in one of their ships, escorted by young nobles. Throughout the voyage Odysseus sleeps. When they reach Ithaca the Phaeacians lift Odysseus, still asleep, and place him on the sand of Ithaca. They pile the gifts beside him and depart for Scherie. To punish the Phaeacians for aiding Odysseus, Poseidon turns their ship into a rock as it is approaching home.

When Odysseus awakes he does not recognize his own country. As he weeps bitterly in disappointment, Athene appears in the guise of a young shepherd and tells Odysseus that he is in Ithaca. Instead of revealing himself, Odysseus invents a complicated story about himself and his adventures. He says that he heard of Ithaca in Crete, where he killed Idomeneus' son Orsilochus for trying to take away the spoils Odysseus had won at Troy. [The story, like most of those that Odysseus invents to hide his identity, reveals his rich imagination, his love of a good "lying tale," and his pride in his own courage and powers of endurance, even when he pretends to be someone else.] Athene smiles with pleasure at Odysseus' tale, enjoying his cunning, then transforms herself into a tall, beautiful woman. She calls Odysseus the great deceiver, who dearly loves his own lies. She then tells him that he must no longer attempt to deceive her, for they are both capable of great cunning and eloquence. When she teases him for not recognizing her, though she is with him in all his adventures, Odysseus replies that it is hard for a mortal to recognize a goddess who is always assuming a new disguise. Moreover, he reminds her, she did not help him in all his wanderings and sufferings before he reached Scherie. Once again, he asks her if he is really back in Ithaca. The goddess says it is just like him to be so cautious and describes the qualities of Odysseus that she admires: he is civilized, clever, self-controlled. Another man in similar circumstances would have immediately rushed home to his family. Odysseus, however, takes his time, first making sure of his wife's loyalty. Athene assures him that Penelope has been faithful. She then helps him to hide his treasures in a cave, and they make plans for the destruction of the Suitors. Athene will disguise Odysseus as an old vagabond, and he will go first to his loyal swineherd Eumaeus, who will give him information about affairs in Ithaca. Meanwhile, she will go to Sparta to bring Telemachus home. Athene touches Odysseus with her wand, and he turns into a dirty, old vagabond.

Book XIV. Odysseus finds Eumaeus in his farmyard, cutting leather for sandals. The swineherd does not recognize him, but welcomes the stranger and offers him food and drink. Odysseus asks Eumaeus who his master is, adding that he may have met him in his travels. Eumaeus answers sadly that it is easy enough to invent tales about his master Odysseus, but he is certain that he is dead. Odysseus, no doubt enjoying the irony, assures Eumaeus that Odysseus is alive and that he will return to Ithaca that very year. Eumaeus will not be reassured. When the swineherd asks Odysseus who he is and where he comes from, Odysseus plunges into one of his stories with great pleasure. He says that he is a native of Crete, the son of a wealthy man and his concubine, and goes on to tell a long, complicated tale in which he depicts himself as a heroic and adventurous man, who, like Odysseus, fought courageously at Troy and encountered many exciting experiences in the years following. Finally, he tells of hearing about Odysseus in the land of Thesprotia. He exclaims over the treasures that Odysseus is said to have collected, and he declares once again that Odysseus will soon return to Ithaca. When he finishes his long tale of adventures and hardships, Eumaeus expresses his sympathy, but he cannot accept the story about his master. Odysseus then decides to test Eumaeus' hospitality by indirectly suggesting that the swineherd lend him a cloak to cover himself with during the cold night. He tells another story of how Odysseus, Menelaus, and he led an attack against Troy. As they lay watching before the city walls, the night grew cold, and having no cloak, he turned to Odysseus with his problem. Odysseus, he points out, was gifted at scheming as well as at fighting, and he sent one of the men who accompanied them to Agamemnon with a message, knowing that the man would leave his cloak behind. Eumaeus understands the hint and provides Odysseus with a bed and warm coverings.

Book XV. Athene goes to Sparta to advise Telemachus to return to Ithaca. She warns him that the Suitors are lying in ambush in the straits between Ithaca and Samos, so he must take a different route. When he lands in Ithaca, he must first go to the swineherd Eumaeus. The next morning Telemachus and his companion, Peisistratus, bid farewell to Menelaus, who gives Telemachus many precious gifts. When they reach Pylos, Peisistratus leaves Menelaus at his ship. Before embarking Telemachus sacrifices and prays to Athene. He is approached by a prophet, Theoclymenus, who appeals to him for shelter. Theoclymenus has fled from Argos after killing a man. Telemachus invites him to accompany him to Ithaca, and they set sail.

Meanwhile, in Ithaca, Eumaeus urges Odysseus to remain with him until Telemachus returns. He answers Odysseus' questions about his father, Laertes, and his mother, Anticleia. Laertes, he says, grieves for his son and his dead wife. The old man leads a wretched life, praying only for death to release him from his suffering. Eumaeus then tells his own story, that he was born the son of King Ctesius on the island of Syrie and was kidnapped by a slave girl, who gave him to Phoenician traders. Eventually they sold him to Laertes. When Odysseus and Eumaeus go to bed at last, it is almost dawn. That same dawn Telemachus lands at Ithaca and sets off for the home of Eumaeus.

Book XVI. When Eumaeus sees Telemachus he jumps up and embraces him as if the young man were his own son. Telemachus enters the house and sees

Odysseus but, of course, does not recognize him. He is upset because his difficulties at home with the Suitors prevent his offering hospitality to the stranger, but he promises to give him a cloak and tunic, a sword and sandals, and says he will help him to go wherever he wishes. Odysseus expresses his wrath at the Suitors and says he wishes he were young enough to deal with them, or that he were Odysseus' son, or that Odysseus himself had returned. Eumaeus then proposes to send a message to Laertes about Telemachus' return. When Eumaeus leaves, Athene comes to Odysseus and tells him it is now time to let his son know who he is so that they may together plan the destruction of the Suitors. She promises to help them in the battle. She then restores Odysseus to his true form.

When Telemachus returns to the hut, he is amazed at the transformation and guesses that Odysseus is a god. Odysseus tells the young man that he is his father, but Telemachus at first refuses to believe him, for he fears the gods are playing a trick on him. When Odysseus convinces Telemachus that he really is his father, the young man throws his arms about Odysseus' neck, and father and son weep together. They then discuss plans for overcoming the Suitors. Telemachus reveals his maturity and sound judgment as he questions certain of his father's ideas and suggests plans of his own. Odysseus decides to resume the form of the old vagabond and warns Telemachus not to reveal to anyone that his father has returned.

While Odysseus and Telemachus are making their plans, the Suitors, in despair over Telemachus' return, hold a meeting to discuss their failure to kill him. Penelope approaches them and denounces Antinous for the plot against her son. Eurymachus, another Suitor, tries to comfort her with lies.

Book XVII. At dawn Telemachus leaves for the palace to see his mother. He tells Eumaeus to take Odysseus to the city, where Odysseus must beg for his meals. He pretends that he has too many problems to cope with the needs of the vagabond. Eurycleia and Penelope greet Telemachus warmly. The Suitors try to speak to him, but he turns away from them and joins his friends, Mentor, Antiphus, and Haliserthes. Soon Theoclymenus appears at the palace, and Telemachus welcomes him, offering him food and drink. Telemachus then tells Penelope what he has learned from Menelaus about his father. Theoclymenus, the seer, swears that Odysseus is now in Ithaca, planning his revenge on the Suitors.

Meanwhile Odysseus and Eumaeus set out for the town on foot. Soon they meet Melanthius, the goatherd, driving some goats to be slaughtered for the Suitors. Assuming that Odysseus is the beggar he appears to be, Melanthius insults and kicks him. Odysseus controls his rage and does not return the blow, but Eumaeus cannot restrain himself. He prays that Odysseus may return to punish Melanthius for his evil ways. Melanthius retorts with the wish that he could be as certain that Telemachus would be overcome that day by the Suitors as he is that Odysseus will never return. When Odysseus and

Eumaeus reach the palace, Odysseus' old dog Argus recognizes his master and then dies. In the palace Odysseus begs the Suitors for food. Antinous insults him and hurls a stool at him, which strikes him on the right shoulder. Once again Odysseus is forced to restrain himself. Telemachus, though extremely upset by this humiliation to his father, holds back his tears and plans his revenge. His manliness is expressed as much in his restraint under extreme pressure as in his courage in action. Penelope asks Eumaeus to bring the stranger to her rooms. When Eumaeus delivers her message, Odysseus says he will come at sunset to avoid the anger of the Suitors. Eumaeus returns to his hut, leaving Odysseus in the palace.

Book XVIII. A beggar named Irus comes to the palace and challenges Odysseus to fight. Odysseus tries to avoid fighting with him, but Antinous urges them on. Though Odysseus decides to give Irus only a gentle blow in order to avoid revealing himself, he smashes the bones in Irus' jaw. He then removes Irus from the palace, and is given food and drink by the Suitors. When Amphinomus, one of the Suitors, drinks to the health of the vagabond, Odysseus tries to warn him that the Suitors will soon be punished by Odysseus. Though Amphinomus is disturbed by these words, he does nothing to save himself from his doom.

Wishing to inflame the desire of the Suitors for Penelope and thus increase her value to Odysseus, Athene visits her and makes her exceedingly beautiful. When she appears before the Suitors, they respond warmly and give her precious gifts. After Penelope leaves, Eurymachus taunts Odysseus by suggesting that Odysseus work for him on his farm. Odysseus answers seriously, saying he wishes that Eurymachus and he could compete as laborers or soldiers. He could then show this braggart who is the better man. He ends his remarks with the wish that Odysseus would come home. This answer angers Eurymachus, who hurls a stool at Odysseus. Telemachus scolds the Suitors and suggests that they go home.

Book XIX. When Odysseus and Telemachus are left alone, they prepare for the battle with the Suitors. Odysseus decides that the helmets, shields, and spears should be removed from the hall to the storeroom. Athene lights their way, and Telemachus recognizes the light as a good omen. After Telemachus has gone to bed, Penelope comes to see Odysseus. She asks him who he is and where he comes from. Instead of answering her questions, Odysseus begins by praising Penelope and asking her not to try to find out his background, for recalling the past brings him only sorrow. Penelope speaks of her own sadness, her longing for her husband, and the unwelcome attentions of the Suitors. She asks Odysseus again who he is, and he, with great pleasure, invents a long tale about the person he pretends to be and about Odysseus himself, whom he manages to praise with obvious relish. As in former tales, he says he was born in Crete. This time he claims to be Aethon, a son of Deucalion and the brother of Idomeneus. He welcomed Odysseus to Crete when a storm drove his ship there on his way to Troy. He remarks on Odysseus' popularity, how all the women admired him. His tale is so effective that Penelope weeps when she hears it. Odysseus comforts her, assuring her that Odysseus is alive and near, in the land of Thesprotia, and that he will soon return to Ithaca.

Penelope then orders Eurycleia to wash Odysseus' feet. In doing so Eurycleia notices a scar on Odysseus' thigh, the result of a wound from the tusk of a boar that had attacked Odysseus on a hunt with his grandfather Autolycus. Eurycleia recognizes the scar and knows at once that her master has returned. She is about to exclaim with joy when Odysseus warns her to be silent, and she promises to keep his secret.

Penelope again speaks to Odysseus of her suffering and her indecision about whether to remain at Odysseus' palace or to choose one of the Suitors as a husband. She tells him a dream she has had about an eagle that killed twenty geese. The eagle explained to her that he was really her husband who had symbolically killed all the Suitors. Odysseus promises her that her dream will come true. She then tells him that she intends to hold a contest among the Suitors to see whether one of them can string Odysseus' bow and shoot an arrow through twelve axes standing in a row, a difficult feat which Odysseus was able to perform. She will marry the man who is skillful enough to succeed in this contest. Odysseus encourages her to hold the contest soon, assuring her that Odysseus will return before any of the Suitors has been able to string the bow and shoot an arrow. Penelope leaves him and retires to her room.

Book XX. Odysseus is lying sleepless, planning his attack on the Suitors, when he hears a group of servants of the palace, who are the Suitors' mistresses, laughing as they leave the palace. Angered at their licentiousness, he wants to kill them all, but he controls his rage, reminding himself of all he has endured that prepared him for his present difficulty. He remembers that it was cunning rather than force that saved him when he was caught in the cave of the Cyclops. Athene comes to him as he lies tossing and puts him to sleep. In the meantime, Penelope awakes and prays to Artemis for death to end her suffering. Odysseus is disturbed by the sound of her anguish; he awakens and prays to Zeus for a good omen, and Zeus answers with thunder.

The next morning Eumaeus comes to the palace and greets Odysseus. Melanthius the goatherd appears and again taunts Odysseus. Then Philoetius, the cattleman, arrives. He speaks warmly to Odysseus, sympathizing with his poverty-stricken appearance. He remarks that the beggar reminds him of his master Odysseus, who may be in such sad condition now. Struck by Philoetius' loyalty, Odysseus assures him that Odysseus will return to kill the Suitors.

The Suitors gather to enjoy a feast. One of them, Ctesippus, throws a cow's hoof at Odysseus. Telemachus exclaims angrily that it is lucky for Ctesippus that the bone missed Odysseus. Telemachus says openly that he is no longer a child and that he will have no more of this behavior in his palace. The Suitors feast and laugh, but suddenly they see blood on the food and grow frightened.

Theoclymenus interprets this as an omen of disaster for them, but they laugh at him, then taunt Telemachus and Odysseus.

Book XXI. Athene encourages Penelope to challenge the Suitors with the bow and the axes. Penelope announces that the man who can string the bow and shoot an arrow through the twelve axes will win her as his wife. Telemachus is the first to try. In his fourth attempt he is about to string the bow when he is stopped by a sign from Odysseus, who shakes his head, indicating that his son must not succeed. This display of Telemachus' strength and skill signifies that he has reached manhood and that he is now competing with his great father rather than merely relying on him to defeat the Suitors. Telemachus now pretends that he is too weak to string the bow. Some of the Suitors attempt it and fail.

Meanwhile, Odysseus, Eumaeus, and Philoetius meet outside the palace, and Odysseus reveals himself to his two faithful servants. He then tells them how they can assist him in defeating the Suitors. They are to follow him inside, where he will ask for the bow, which the Suitors will refuse to give him. Eumaeus must bring it to him. The women must be told to lock the doors leading to their quarters and to stay in their rooms despite any sounds they may hear from the men's quarters. Philoetius must lock and tie the gates of the courtyard.

Odysseus returns to the palace, and Eurymachus admits that he cannot string the bow. Odysseus says that he would like to try his strength, but as he has predicted, the Suitors refuse to give him the bow. Penelope urges them to allow him to try, but Telemachus, who wants her to be safely in her quarters when the fighting begins, tells her that the bow is his concern and that she must go to her room and attend to her own work. Eumaeus brings the bow to Odysseus, who strings it and shoots an arrow through the twelve axes. Telemachus puts on his sword, takes a spear, and stands beside his father.

Book XXII. Odysseus takes off his rags and leaps upon the threshold of the great hall, holding his bow. Declaring he will now aim for a target no man has hit before, he shoots and kills Antinous. When the Suitors see their comrade fall, they cry out and rush about the room seeking arms, but these have been removed. They threaten to kill Odysseus, but, when he reveals who he is, they grow pale and frightened. Eurymachus begs him to spare them, blaming Antinous, their leader, for their crimes. In answer Odysseus offers them the choice of fighting with him or fleeing in the foolish hope of saving their lives. Eurymachus urges them to fight. He draws his sword and leaps at Odysseus, but Odysseus kills him with an arrow. Telemachus kills Amphinomus and then goes off to bring weapons and armor from the storeroom. He also gives arms to Eumaeus and Philoetius, the faithful servants. Melanthius, the goatherd, has discovered that the arms are hidden in the storeroom, and he arms twelve of the Suitors. Seeing these Suitors armed, Odysseus guesses that Melanthius has entered the storeroom. Telemachus sends Eumaeus and Philoetius to investigate and discovering Melanthius there, they overcome him, bind him, and leave him in the storeroom.

Athene comes in the form of Mentor to help Odysseus, who recognizes her despite her disguise. With Athene's help Odysseus, Telemachus, Eumaeus, and Philoetius kill all the Suitors. The minstrel Phemius and the herald Medon are spared. When Eurycleia sees all the dead Suitors, she begins to cry out in triumph, but Odysseus stops her, reminding her that it is wrong to gloat over the dead. He then orders the maids who have been the Suitors' mistresses to remove their bodies and clean the hall. After they have performed this work they are hanged. Melanthius is tortured and mutilated. Odysseus fumigates the hall. Eurycleia then summons the women of the palace, who welcome Odysseus.

Book XXIII. Eurycleia tells Penelope that the stranger whom the Suitors mocked is really Odysseus and that he has slain them all, but Penelope cannot believe that her husband has returned. She goes down to the hall and sits opposite Odysseus, but says nothing to him. Telemachus reproaches his mother for her silence, but Odysseus understands her hesitation. Odysseus tells Telemachus that they must pretend that a wedding feast is taking place in the palace, so that the news of the Suitors' deaths will not spread before Odysseus and Telemachus can leave for their farm. Odysseus orders the women to dress and the minstrel to play his lyre. Odysseus bathes and dresses; with Athene's help he appears handsomer than ever, but Penelope still seems unmoved. Like the returning hero of folklore, Odysseus must prove himself to her. Penelope tests him by suggesting that Eurycleia remove Odysseus' bed from his bedroom and place it outside. At once Odysseus explains that the bed cannot be moved, for he himself constructed it according to a secret plan from an olive tree that grew within the walls of the palace, using the trunk as his bedpost. When Penelope hears these words, she is convinced that the stranger is indeed her husband, and runs to embrace him. Odysseus and Penelope retire and tell each other all they have endured during their long separation. Athene prolongs the night so that they may enjoy their love. In the morning Odysseus leaves Penelope and, accompanied by Telemachus, Eumaeus, and Philoetius, goes to visit his father, Laertes.

Book XXIV. Hermes gathers the souls of the dead Suitors and leads them to Hades, where they meet the souls of Achilles, Patroclus, Antilochus, Ajax, and Agamemnon. The soul of Achilles has been expressing pity for Agamemnon, who then comments on the death of Achilles, magnificent even in defeat. Agamemnon speaks of the mourning for Achilles and says that the nine Muses sang a dirge for him. The mourning lasted for seventeen days and nights, and on the eighteenth day the body of Achilles was buried. Agamemnon contrasts Achilles' glorious death with his own ignoble one. This talk is interrupted by the arrival of the Suitors. Agamemnon questions one of them, Amphimedon, asking what has happened that so many young men should come to Hades at the same time. When Amphimedon reports the recent downfall of the Suitors, Agamemnon expresses his envy of Odysseus, who returned to find a faithful wife.

Meanwhile, Odysseus and his companions reach the farm of his father, Laertes. Odysseus sends the others into the house, and he finds his father, alone, shabby, and wretched. At first Odysseus does not identify himself but instead invents one of his tales. He pretends to have met Odysseus more than four years before his arrival at Ithaca. Laertes weeps and groans. Odysseus, pitying the old man, embraces him and tells him that he is his son. Laertes demands proof, and Odysseus shows him his scar and tells him how he acquired it. He also names all the trees his father gave him when he was a child. Laertes now believes him and is overcome with joy, but he is also fearful of the reaction of the Ithacans to the news of the death of the Suitors. Odysseus comforts him and together they go to the house.

Hearing of the death of the Suitors, the Ithacans gather in an Assembly. Eupeithes, the father of Antinous, urges the Ithacans to avenge the deaths of the Suitors. Medon and Halitherses try to persuade them to take no action, but most of the Ithacans follow Eupeithes to battle. Athene joins Odysseus and his party and helps them to overcome these opponents. Laertes observes proudly that his son and his grandson are competing for glory. Inspired by Athene, even old Laertes fights bravely and kills Eupeithes. Finally, Zeus sends a thunderbolt, Athene orders Odysseus to stop the battle, and in the form of Mentor, Athene brings peace.

COMMENTARY. Aristotle, discussing the questions of structure and theme in Homer's epics, says that the *Iliad* is "simple and tragic," the *Odyssey* "complicated and ethical" (*Poetics*, XXIV, 2). This ethical or moral tone of the *Odyssey* is perhaps its most striking characteristic. The whole story of the poem clearly leads up to the destruction of the evil Suitors and the rewards won by Penelope for her patience and devotion, by Odysseus' faithful servants for their loyalty, by Telemachus for his newly acquired boldness and virility, and by Odysseus for his courage, his intelligence, his resourcefulness, and his endurance. Moreover, throughout the poem reward and punishment are constantly mentioned. Odysseus' men are punished for eating the oxen of Helios; Odysseus himself pays heavily for taunting the Cyclops; the Suitors' mistresses die as a result of their licentiousness. The *Odyssey* contains many explicit didactic statements about the correct way to treat a guest, the proper gifts to present, moderation, and self-restraint.

On a deeper level the ethical nature of the poem is related to its basic theme, the value of experience or knowledge of the world and of man. Practically everybody in the *Odyssey* learns something from his experience, but the most significant learning experiences are those of Telemachus and Odysseus.

When we first meet Telemachus he is a sorrowful boy, brooding over his difficulties with the Suitors and dreaming of the day his ideal father will come and drive them away. Athene's visit to him is a clear sign that he is beginning to grow up and become a man; she inspires him to give up his dreams and his despair for action. He learns something of the world outside Ithaca in his journeys to Pylos and Sparta. He overcomes his shyness and questions the heroes, Nestor and Menelaus, learning not only about his father but about the great events of his time—the Trojan War and the experience of the great men involved in it. When Odysseus does return, Telemachus courageously and wisely assists him in plotting the destruction of the Suitors, and is finally his father's equal as a leader and warrior.

The learning experience of Odysseus is an even richer one. At the very beginning of the *Odyssey* we are told that in his travels he saw many peoples and learned their customs. His travels take him to lawless savage people, such as the Cyclopes and the Laestrygones, and to the civilized, kind, and peace-loving Phaeacians. He experiences strange adventures with monsters and deities; he gains knowledge forbidden most men from the Sirens and from the souls in Hades, where he learns not only about the past and the future, but about his own nature and about death itself. Odysseus is a rich, ambivalent character—resourceful and cunning, magnanimous and childishly boastful, sometimes cruel and deceitful, but always courageous and marvelously vital. He exhausts the possibilities of experience and grows in vitality as in wisdom. Odysseus' broad experience suggests the possibilities of life itself; his trials and victories over hardship and despair convey man's capacity to endure.

The structure of the *Odyssey* is complicated, not only because of the complexity of its central figure, but because the poem actually has three main stories, into which are woven many smaller tales. The major sections are: Books I–IV, which deal with the difficulties of Telemachus with the Suitors at Ithaca and his experiences traveling to Pylos and Sparta; Books V–XIII, which contain Odysseus' wanderings until he reaches Ithaca, including the retrospective narrative of his adventures; and Books XIV–XXIV, which tell of Odysseus' return to Ithaca, his meeting with Telemachus, and the defeat of the Suitors. The three plots are skillfully united in the last section.

The structure, characters, and plot of the *Odyssey* have served as models for many writers of poetry and prose. The figure of Odysseus recurs in widely differing contexts and interpretations; he reappears as Tennyson's symbol of the endless seeker of experience in his poem "Ulysses"; as James Joyce's wandering Jew, Leopold Bloom, in his novel *Ulysses*; as Nikos Kazantzakis' sensuous and gentle adventurer, Zorba, in his novel *Zorba, the Greek*; and as the more philosophical, deeply experienced, wise hero of Kazantzakis' *The Odyssey, A Modern Sequel*. W. B. Stanford, in a fascinating study *The Ulysses Theme* (Blackwell, 1954) traces Odysseus' presence in drama, poetry, fiction, and other works.

Not only the character of Odysseus but the brilliant plot structure and distinctive atmosphere of the poem have been widely imitated. Writers since Homer's time have employed the voyage as a quest for knowledge. Vergil adapts the long, retrospective narrative to the requirements of his own story. His hero, Aeneas, differs greatly from Odysseus in character and purpose, yet he tells a tale of wandering and adventure similar to that of the hero of the *Odyssey*. The very atmosphere of the *Odyssey* is evoked as Aeneas tells of his experiences with Scylla and Charybdis and the Cyclops. In our own time, Joyce and Kazantzakis have best succeeded in re-creating the atmosphere of the *Odyssey*, in which magic and wonder pervade the everyday world of practical reality.

Oeconomicus (Oikonomikos). See XENOPHON.

Oedipus (Oidipous). The son of Laius and Jocasta and king of Thebes. He is one of the best known and most interesting of the Greek mythical heroes. For his character and his tragic story see Sophocles' OEDIPUS THE KING and OEDIPUS AT COLONUS, Euripides' THE PHOENICIAN WOMEN, Seneca's OEDIPUS and his *Phoenician Women*, and Statius' THEBAID.

Oedipus. A tragedy by SENECA, based on Sophocles' OEDIPUS THE KING. Seneca's *Oedipus* is a poor play in itself and can hardly be taken seriously when compared with Sophocles' *Oedipus*, which Aristotle used as his model for tragedy in the *Poetics* and has always been considered to be one of the greatest tragedies. Seneca's play introduces the character Manto, daughter of the prophet Tiresias. In interpreting omens that emerge from a sacrifice, she predicts the tragic experiences that Oedipus and his family will endure. Seneca's main interest in this play seems to be rites of necromancy, which are described in great detail. Creon reports that the ghost of Oedipus' father Laius is brought forth through such rites and describes how Laius revealed his son's guilt. Jocasta, after calling Oedipus a parricide, and suggesting that he complete his work by killing her, stabs herself and falls dead on stage.

Oedipus at Colonus (Oidipous epi Kolonoi). A tragedy (c. 409 B.C.) by SOPHOCLES. Translations: in verse, Thomas Francklin, 1759; in prose, R. C. Jebb, 1904; in verse, F. Storr, 1912; in verse, Theodore Howard Banks, 1953; in verse, Robert Fitzgerald, 1956 (revised); in verse, Paul Roche, 1958.

MYTHICAL BACKGROUND. When the parricide and incest of Oedipus were disclosed, Oedipus blinded himself and begged Creon, the brother of Oedipus' wife and mother, Jocasta, to send him into exile, but Creon said that he must first consult the oracle to see what Apollo commanded. Oedipus remained at Thebes for some years, until Creon and other Thebans decided that his presence polluted the land and that he must leave the city. By this time Oedipus wished to spend his last years at Thebes, but his sons, Polyneices and Eteocles, did nothing to help him remain. As Oedipus says in the *Oedipus at Colonus*, they allowed him to wander, a beggar, banished from his home, while his two daughters, Ismene and Antigone, were the only ones who cared for him. Antigone accompanied Oedipus in his wanderings. At first Polyneices and Eteocles, attempting to avoid the curse that plagued their family, allowed Creon to rule Thebes; but soon each wanted the throne of

Thebes for himself, and Eteocles, with the help of Creon, banished Polyneices, who fled to Argos. There he married Argeia and persuaded her father Adrastus to wage war on Thebes. Meanwhile, Oedipus and Antigone have come to the grove of the Eumenides, the Kindly Goddesses, at Colonus, a village near Athens.

S C E N E . Colonus before the grove of the Eumenides.

S U M M A R Y . Oedipus, old and blind, enters led by his daughter Antigone. They have arrived at the grove of the Eumenides, the Kindly Ones, at Colonus, about a mile northwest of Athens. A Stranger enters and tells Oedipus he must not sit on the holy rock of the Eumenides. Oedipus then realizes that he has arrived at the place where he is destined to die. When the Stranger tells Oedipus that Colonus is ruled by Theseus, king of Athens, Oedipus asks the Stranger to summon Theseus, for he wishes to tell the king that the land where he is buried will be blessed. After the Stranger leaves Oedipus tells Antigone of a prophecy he received from Apollo which informed him that he will be a blessing to the land where he is buried and a curse to the land that banished him.

The Chorus of Citizens of Colonus enters. When Oedipus tells these men who he is, they recoil and demand that he leave Colonus. Antigone pleads eloquently for her father, evoking the pity of the men; nonetheless they fear his presence. Oedipus then defends himself, saying he committed his crimes in ignorance. The Chorus is moved by his argument and decides that the king must determine whether Oedipus may stay.

Ismene enters and informs Oedipus and Antigone that Polyneices and his allies are about to attack Thebes, and that Creon now wants Oedipus near Thebes because the oracles declare that the presence of Oedipus can save the city. When Oedipus dies Creon wishes to bury him on the boundaries of Thebes, thus preventing his body from polluting the soil of the city, yet gaining the opportunity to offer religious rites at his burial place. Oedipus asks whether his sons have heard of these prophecies, and, when Ismene says that they have, Oedipus complains that their desire for the throne was stronger than any wish for their father's return. He hopes that the gods will allow neither of them to rule Thebes and remembers that they did nothing to prevent his banishment. He says he will not return to Thebes.

The Chorus then advises Oedipus to perform rites of atonement to the Eumenides, because he trespassed in their sacred grove, and Ismene goes to perform these. Oedipus returns to his defense of himself to the Chorus. Once more with deep feeling he pleads earnestly; he killed his father, who would have killed him, and he did so in ignorance.

Theseus enters; he treats Oedipus with great kindness and welcomes him as a citizen of Athens. After Theseus leaves, the Chorus sings an ode that tells Oedipus of the beauty and tranquility of the place to which he has come. Creon enters to destroy the pleasant mood that the ode suggests. He tries to persuade Oedipus to return with him, but Oedipus angrily refuses, saying that Creon will not take him to his old home, but will merely let him remain on the borders of Thebes. Creon then tells Oedipus that his men have taken Ismene prisoner and now his attendants seize Antigone and carry her off. However, Theseus returns and, on hearing what has happened, pursues Creon's men. He soon comes back to Oedipus with Ismene and Antigone.

Theseus then tells Oedipus that a kinsman of Oedipus is begging for an opportunity to speak with him. Oedipus soon guesses that it is his son, Polyneices, and declares that he hates the sound of his voice. Antigone pleads with her father to allow her brother to come to him. She reminds Oedipus of all the suffering his own parents caused him and warns him that bad feelings breed evil. Oedipus consents and Polyneices enters. He tells Oedipus that he was banished from Thebes by Eteocles and that he has organized seven squadrons to fight for the kingdom. Because the oracles declare that whichever side has Oedipus as an ally will win the war, he beseeches his father to aid him. Oedipus is violently angry at this request. He reminds Polyneices that he thrust him out of Thebes and says that he does not regard him as his son. He orders him to leave, laying on him the curse that he may die by the hand of his kin and kill the man who banished him. Polyneices, in despair at his father's hatred and his curse, begs Antigone to give him burial and proper funeral rites. She tries to persuade Polyneices not to fight and make the prophecies of their father come true, but Polyneices cannot turn back from his purpose. He says a final farewell to his sister and leaves to meet his doom.

The Chorus sings of how evil follows evil, destroying those in power, and then remarks on the sound of thunder. Oedipus asks that Theseus be summoned, for the thunder is a sign that his predestined death is approaching. When Theseus comes, Oedipus takes him to a secret place, which Theseus must never reveal and where Oedipus will meet his death. The place is to be a sacred defense for Athens. The Chorus prays to the gods of the Underworld that Oedipus may find peace in death. A messenger then enters, announcing that Oedipus has died. Only Theseus was allowed to know how and where he died. Oedipus' end was gentle; he passed mysteriously from life to death. Antigone and Ismene enter weeping, and the Chorus comforts them. When they ask Theseus if they may see their father's tomb, he tells them that no mortal may approach this sacred and hidden place. The sisters then decide to return to Thebes.

Oedipus the King (Oidipous Tyrannos; Oedipus Rex). A tragedy (probably c. 430 B.C.) by SOPHOCLES. Translations: in verse, Thomas Francklin, 1759; in prose, R. C. Jebb, 1904; in verse, F. Storr, 1912; in verse, David Grene, 1942; in verse, Theodore Howard Banks, 1956; in verse, Albert Cook, 1957; in verse, Paul Roche, 1958; in verse, H. D. F. Kitto, 1962.

MYTHICAL BACKGROUND. Laius, king of Thebes, the father of Oedipus, abducted Chrysippus, a son of Pelops. The oracle of Delphi informed him that his punishment for this crime would be to be killed by his own son. In an attempt to avoid this fate, Laius pierced the feet of his three-day-old son and had him exposed on Mount Cithaeron. The shepherd who was ordered to leave the child to die pitied it and gave it to a shepherd from Corinth. Oedipus (which means "swollen foot") was then taken to King Polybus of Corinth, who brought him up as his own son. As a young man Oedipus was told by the oracle of Delphi that he would kill his father and marry his mother. Like his real father, Laius, Oedipus attempted to avoid this fate. He left Corinth. On his way to Thebes he encountered his father, whom he did not recognize, and killed him in a quarrel. He arrived at Thebes at a time when the city was being threatened by the Sphinx, a monstrous creature with the head and breast of a woman and the body of a winged lion, who had come to live on a rock near the city. She challenged every passer-by with the riddle "What walks on four legs in the morning, on two at noon, and on three in the evening?" Those who could not solve this riddle were thrown from the rock to their death. Oedipus was wise enough to know that the answer was "man" in the three stages of his life: the infant, the fully grown man, and the old man, leaning on a staff. Defeated, the Sphinx committed suicide by throwing herself from the rock, and Oedipus was hailed as a hero by the Thebans, who accepted him as their king. He married Laius' widow Jocasta, who, unknown to Oedipus, was his own mother; she bore him two sons, Polyneices and Eteocles, and two daughters, Antigone and Ismene.

SCENE. Thebes, before the palace of Oedipus.

SUMMARY. As the play opens, Oedipus, king of Thebes, addresses a group of suppliants, headed by a Priest of Zeus, who have come to ask for his assistance in conquering a plague that is destroying Thebes. The Priest tells Oedipus that because of the plague the land, the herds, and the women of Thebes have become barren. Oedipus replies with compassion, expressing his grief not only for himself and for the suppliants before him, but for the state as a whole. He tells them he has sent his kinsman Creon to consult the oracle of Apollo at Delphi as to the cause of the plague. When Creon returns he informs Oedipus that the city of Thebes is polluted by the presence of the murderer of Laius, the former king. In order to cleanse the city of the plague, the murderer of Laius must be found and punished. When Oedipus asks Creon what prevented the Thebans from searching thoroughly for the killer of Laius at the time of his murder many years ago, Creon tells him that the Sphinx was causing them so much trouble with the riddle she presented that they could not deal with the riddle of Laius' death. Oedipus then declares that he will once more make hidden things known, referring to his past victory over the Sphinx and confidently assuming that he will solve this present problem as satisfactorily as he solved the riddle posed by the Sphinx.

The Chorus of Theban Elders enters, singing of its fears of the plague and of its suffering. The old men pray to the gods for help. Oedipus then addresses them and the other Thebans, saying that anyone who knows anything about the murderer must reveal it at once. If the killer admits his crime, he will not be harmed, but will merely be banished. Oedipus curses the killer and anyone who helps or shelters him.

The blind prophet, Tiresias, for whom Oedipus has sent, enters, led by a boy. Tiresias attempts to avoid the question of who the murderer of Laius is, but when Oedipus accuses the prophet of withholding information in order to destroy Thebes, Tiresias declares that Oedipus is himself the killer he seeks. Oedipus refuses to believe the prophet's words, which convince him that Tiresias and Creon are plotting against his throne. When Tiresias adds that Oedipus is living in shame with his own kin, Oedipus takes this as a meaningless insult. Deriding the prophet, he reminds him that when Thebes was plagued by the riddle of the Sphinx, it was he, Oedipus, not the prophet, who solved her riddle. Tiresias continues to warn Oedipus, saying that this day will reveal his birth and bring about his destruction, but Oedipus regards these remarks as "riddles." As he leaves, Tiresias comments ironically on Oedipus' great skill in comprehending riddles.

The Elders comment on the prophet's utterances, which make them fearful, yet they are loyal to Oedipus. Creon enters and Oedipus immediately accuses him of plotting against Oedipus' throne and life. Though Creon defends himself reasonably, Oedipus wrathfully says that he wants Creon killed. Hearing the angry words, Jocasta enters and tries to soothe her husband and her brother. When Creon leaves, Jocasta questions Oedipus about his anger at her brother. He says that Creon has used Tiresias as his spokesman to accuse Oedipus of killing Laius. Jocasta replies that mortals can know nothing about prophecies. Her first husband, Laius, was told by a priest of Apollo that it was his fate to be killed by his own child. Attempting to prevent such a disaster, Laius tied his infant son's ankles together and ordered that he be exposed on a mountain. Laius was later killed by robbers at a spot where three roads meet. Clearly, then, it is folly to be concerned about prophets' words. Though Jocasta's intention is to reassure Oedipus, her words only disturb him. Her statement that Laius' death occurred at a place in Phocis where three roads meet, shortly before Oedipus' arrival at Thebes, makes Oedipus fear that he was indeed the slayer of Laius. Jocasta goes on to report that the one surviving member of Laius' party was a servant. On finding Oedipus ruling in place of Laius, he asked to be allowed to work as a shepherd far from the city. Oedipus is now deeply disturbed. When Jocasta asks what troubles him, he explains: his father was Polybus, king of Corinth, his mother, Merope. At a banquet someone accused Oedipus of not being the real child of his parents. Disturbed by this taunt, Oedipus went to the oracle of Delphi to find out who his true parents were, but the oracle only told him that he was fated to kill his father and to marry his mother. Oedipus decided to avoid this fate by leaving Corinth forever. On his way to Thebes he encountered a stranger in a carriage at a place where three roads meet. When the stranger and his companions attempted to thrust Oedipus from the path, Oedipus killed the stranger. Now he fears it was Laius. Oedipus clings to one hope: Jocasta has said that Laius was slain by many robbers. He asks her to send for the surviving servant in the hope that the man will repeat this version of the episode and not claim that Laius was killed by one man.

Oedipus and Jocasta enter the palace, and the Chorus sings an ode on the general subject of how *hybris* (insolence) breeds the tyrant. Thus they implicitly express their fears that Oedipus may be revealed as the tyrant who slew Laius and replaced him. This fear threatens their confidence in their king and in the religious rites that govern the kingdom and their lives. Jocasta enters and is praying to Apollo when a Messenger from Corinth comes in and reports that Polybus, king of Corinth, is dead and that the people of Corinth want Oedipus to return as their king. When Oedipus enters and hears the news, both he and Jocasta rejoice: they no longer need fear the oracular prophecy that he will kill his father. Oedipus, however, still fears that he will violate the bed of his mother. The Messenger from Corinth attempts to reassure Oedipus by telling him that he is not really the child of Polybus and Merope. He himself found Oedipus as a baby on Mount Cithaeron and gave the baby to the childless King Polybus, who brought him up as his own child. By now Jocasta has guessed the truth, that Oedipus is the child she bore to Laius and that Laius exposed on Mount Cithaeron in the fear that his son would one day kill him. Jocasta begs Oedipus to seek no further knowledge of himself, but he attributes her warning to her fear that he will discover he is of low origin. Jocasta rushes into the palace, and Oedipus proudly assumes that he is the offspring of Fortune. The Chorus echoes his feelings, suggesting that he may be the child of Apollo or some other god.

The shepherd who worked for Laius is brought in and unwillingly reveals that Oedipus is the son of Laius. The Shepherd admits that he was told to expose the child of Laius and Jocasta, but out of pity gave it to the shepherd who has now come as a messenger from Corinth bearing the news of Polybus' death. Oedipus now realizes that he is the son of Laius and Jocasta and that he has murdered his father and married his mother. He cries out in agony and rushes into the palace. The Chorus sings a sorrowful ode, which contrasts with its previous joyous and hopeful one, saying that the fate of Oedipus is a warning and lamenting his suffering. A Messenger from the palace reports that Jocasta has committed suicide and that Oedipus has blinded himself. As he struck at his own eyeballs with a golden brooch torn from the clothing of the dead Jocasta, Oedipus cried out against his own eyes, which had failed to see the truths that could have saved him from disaster.

Oedipus comes out of the palace, his face still bloody. The Chorus and Oedipus sing alternately of his sorrows and suffering (*kommos*). Creon enters, and Oedipus asks to be sent away as an exile. Creon says that he must first learn the will of Apollo. Oedipus' daughters, Antigone and Ismene, are brought in by an Attendant. Oedipus embraces and weeps over his daughters and asks that they be allowed to go with him into exile, but Creon will not consent. The play ends as the Chorus utters a familiar Greek maxim: "Judge no man happy until his whole life has been lived."

COMMENTARY. Sophocles' *Oedipus Tyrannus* is the best-known of the ancient Greek tragedies. In the *Poetics* Aristotle expresses his admiration for the play and refers to it frequently as an example of excellent dramatic technique. It was adapted and imitated by many writers: by Corneille in 1659, Dryden and Lee in 1679, Voltaire in 1718, Yeats (whose translations are really adaptations) in 1912 and 1927, and Cocteau in his *The Infernal Machine* in 1934.

Critical interpretations of the play are as varied as are the dramatic adaptations. Though contemporary critics seem to be divided mainly on the question of responsibility, i.e., is Oedipus the victim of fate or of his human weakness, most commentators would agree that although Oedipus must bear some degree of responsibility for his action, he can hardly be considered guilty of the crimes he unknowingly commits. Indeed, despite all the instances one can find in the play to show that Oedipus turns away from knowledge of himself, he is more heroic than most men in his struggle to attain it. In his search for self-knowledge Oedipus discovers resources of which he was previously unaware: a capacity for intellectual honesty that overcomes the pride that prohibits it and a power of endurance that exalts him and those who, as chorus or audience, are involved in his destiny.

Oenomaus (Oinomaos). In Greek mythology, a king of Elis. See Pindar's CHORAL LYRICS, *Olympian* I.

Oenone (Oinone). See PARIS and Ovid's HEROIDES V, in which Oenone writes to Paris, who has deserted her. Tennyson deals with this theme in his poem "Oenone."

Ogygia. The island of Calypso in the ODYSSEY (I, V).

Old Comedy. See under COMEDY.

Olympus (Olympos). A mountain between Macedonia and Thessaly, regarded in Greek mythology as the home of the gods.

On Oratory (De Oratore). Prose dialogue (55 B.C.) in three books by CICERO. Translations: E. W. Sutton and H. Rackham, 1942.

SUMMARY. Cicero imagines a discussion on oratory that took place in 91 B.C. at the villa of the orator Lucius Licinius Crassus at Tusculum. He and Marcus Antonius, a great orator and the grandfather of Mark Antony, are the principal speakers. Also present are the lawyer Quintus Mucius Scaevola, Gaius Aurelius Cotta, who was to become a well-known political figure, and Publius Sulpicius Rufus, a young politician later proscribed by Sulla. In Book II these men are joined by Quintus Lutatius Catulus, a follower of Marius who was later proscribed by him, and Catulus' half brother Gaius Julius Caesar

Strabo Vopiscus, a lawyer and politician who was also proscribed by Marius. Cicero's use of the dialogue form differs from Plato's; in Plato the minor characters serve mainly as foils for Socrates, whereas in the *De Oratore* they have a much more important function. Despite the fact that Crassus is the most significant character and Cicero's spokesman, the views of the others, especially Antonius, in opposing his, expose the other side of each question. The truth then lies not in Crassus' answers, but somewhere between his views and those of Antonius, or, perhaps more justly, the truth includes both points of view.

Book I. Before beginning the dialogue, Cicero addresses his brother Quintus, who has asked him to write a more polished and mature work on rhetoric than his early *De Inventione*. Great orators, says Cicero, are rare because oratory demands great artistry and learning. Early in the *De Oratore* Cicero makes a distinction between "mere verbiage" and sound oratory. He wishes the reader to grasp the magnitude and difficulty of a study of this art, for without vast knowledge and skill the orator will produce only "empty rhetoric." The orator must have cultivation, charm, and urbanity; he must know precedent and law, and, indeed, the entire history of the past.

The dialogue begins with Crassus' remarks on the important function of oratory in the state. Oratory, he says, always flourishes in a free society. Crassus eloquently describes the great virtues and powers of oratory. This art, which reveals man's noblest attribute, his power to speak reasonably, has been responsible for the formation of civilized communities and a lawful way of life. Scaevola then remarks that Crassus exaggerates both the ability and the power of the orator, an objection that leads to Crassus' development of his ideas on the skill and function of the orator. He compares the ability of the orator to that of the poet. The orator should have inborn talent and careful training. Crassus next speaks at length about the three types of orations, the five traditional divisions of rhetoric, and the proper organization of an oration. Antonius objects to some of Crassus' ideas.

Book II. After the arrival of Catulus and Caesar, Antonius continues to present his point of view: oratory, he says, is not a science, but certain principles can be derived from experience. Catulus agrees that theoretical training without experience is of little value. After a discussion of methods of obtaining the sympathy of the audience, Caesar speaks of various types of wit. Antonius then continues to present his own views as opposed to those of Crassus.

Book III. After making the point that style and content cannot be separated, that it is impossible to achieve an elegant style without first having ideas, and that at the same time no idea can have distinction without clarity of style, Crassus discusses diction, adornment, word order, rhythm, figurative language, and various other stylistic matters.

On Style. The treatise *On Style*, formerly attributed to Demetrius (Demetrios) of Phalerum (Phaleron), who lived during the third century B.C., is now thought to be the work of Demetrius of Tarsus. Though most contemporary scholars agree that the treatise was written as late as the first century A.D., some, including G. M. A. Grube, the author of an excellent translation (1961), think that the traditional date—the third century B.C.—is the correct one. Actually there is no certainty about either the author or the date.

On Style is a handbook dealing with the correct writing of prose. Demetrius was obviously influenced by Aristotle and Theophrastus, to whom he refers. The treatise is divided into five parts; the first introduces the subject and discusses sentence structure, and the others deal with the four kinds of style: the stately or grand, the plain, the elegant, and the forceful. Each of these styles is analyzed, and the student is warned against their misuse. Thus a perversion of the stately style results in frigidity, and each of the other styles has a fault corresponding to its quality. Demetrius gives many illustrations from the poets to make his points. Whereas *On Style* lacks the depth and insight of the work of Aristotle or "Longinus," it is an interesting and practical treatise that reveals its author's broad knowledge and good taste.

On the Civil War (De Bello Civili). An unfinished epic poem (often erroneously called *Pharsalia*) by LUCAN. The poem, written in the first century A.D., is in ten books and deals with the civil war between Caesar and Pompey. Lucan's epic is written in the traditional heroic meter, dactylic hexameter, but he omits other epic conventions, such as the intervention of deities. He does, however, employ much supernatural machinery, such as oracular pronouncements, witches, and omens. Lucan obviously supports the Republicans; his heroes are Cato, Pompey, and the Senatorial party. Though Caesar is the villain of the poem, Lucan cannot help revealing his grudging admiration for Caesar's courage and military talents.

Though Lucan's emphasis on the horrible details of battle and death are offensive in their obvious sensationalism, and he indulges too often in rhetorical flourishes and Stoic moralizing, *De Bello Civili* offers an interesting interpretation of some of the leading historical figures of the first century B.C. Pompey, especially, is portrayed vividly and sympathetically. His dream and his thoughts before the battle of Pharsalus, his defeat, his flight to Lesbos and to Egypt, and his death are presented with deep feeling and great artistry in the most moving parts of the poem.

On the Nature of Things (De Rerum Natura). A didactic, philosophical poem in dactylic hexameter (first part of the first century B.C.) by LUCRETIUS. Translations: parts of Books I, II, III, and V, in verse, John Dryden, 1692; in prose, C. Bailey, 1910; in prose, H. A. J. Munro, 1914; in verse, William Ellery Leonard, 1921; in prose, W. H. D. Rouse, 1924; in prose, Ronald Latham, 1951; in verse, L. L. Johnson, 1963.

SUMMARY. *Book I.* In an invocation to Venus, Lucretius asks the goddess of creation and productivity to be his associate as he explains the nature of the universe in order to dispel men's irrational fears through a revelation of the scientific laws of natural and human life. In describing Venus' nurturing influence on all of creation, Lucretius expresses his own passionate response to the natural world—the heavens, the productive earth, the seas, the herds of animals, and all living creatures. After addressing his friend Gaius Memmius, Lucretius asks Venus to put Mars, the spirit of destruction, to sleep so that the world may have peace. In this way Lucretius introduces his symbols of creation and destruction, continuity and change, the principles that he regards as basic to all life.

Lucretius then begins his attempt to relieve man of care by explaining the Epicurean atomic theory of matter, which contradicts the religious conception of life (see EPICURUS). Epicurus, says Lucretius, first relieved man of the burden of religion, which crushed his very life, for it was Epicurus who set the laws of nature against the myths about the gods and thus struck a blow against religion. Lucretius insists that scientific thought is not impious; indeed, he says, it is religion that has caused and committed acts of impiety: for example, the sacrifice of Iphigenia (dramatized by Euripides in *Iphigenia at Aulis*), which Lucretius describes with compassion for the young girl and hatred of the religion that compelled her father to murder his child.

One of the main reasons men heed the superstitious teachings of religion is their fear of the afterlife. They do not understand the nature of the soul and are afraid of punishment after death. This fear and darkness of spirit will be overcome by the light of knowledge (the opposition of darkness and light pervades the *De Rerum Natura*), by studying *"naturae species ratioque,"* the external view and the basic laws of nature, a phrase Lucretius repeats several times in the poem. Natural law will reveal that all life springs from atoms.

The first principle of the Epicurean atomic theory is that nothing can be created from or reduced to nothingness. Nature is a process of change and continuity. Rain disappears into the earth, but it promotes the growth of trees, fruit, and grain. All matter, though ever-changing, remains part of life in some form. Life or nature is essentially composed of two elements: atoms, which are invisible, indivisible, and indestructible; and void or emptiness. Atoms are the smallest particles; they are solid and contain no void, and all things are composed of them. Lucretius refutes some of the theories of earlier scientific thinkers, such as Heraclitus, Empedocles, and Anaxagoras, and then returns to his discussion of matter, declaring that matter and the universe itself are infinite.

Book II. The second book begins with Lucretius' well-known tribute to philosophy, which can provide man with a sanctuary to protect him from needless suffering and conflict. In their blindness to reality most men have false values, desiring power and wealth instead of knowledge, the only source of peace.

Lucretius then returns to his discussion of atoms, which, he says, are continually moving at a greater speed than that of light. They move in a downward direction, propelled either by their own weight or by other atoms, and as they move they sometimes swerve. Because of this swerve (*clinamen*) they collide with other atoms and join with them to form living things. Matter never increases or decreases. Despite the static appearance of objects, all things are ever in motion. Atoms of various sizes and shapes are responsible for the endless variety of nature. Smooth atoms give pleasure to the senses; hooked atoms are responsible for bitter tastes and rough textures. The same applies to other sensations. Atoms have a limited number of shapes and sizes, but atoms of each shape are infinite in number.

There is everlasting warfare in nature between creation and destruction. Daily the sound of a funeral dirge and the cry of a newborn child are mingled. All things are composed of a variety of atoms. The earth consists of the largest variety of atoms and thus is rightfully called the Mother of the gods, beasts, and men. Earth should not be worshiped as a goddess in elaborate ceremonies. The gods, who are immortal and entirely removed from man, cannot be touched by his devotion or prayers. It is not improper to use such symbolic names as Neptune for the sea, Ceres for corn, Bacchus for wine, and Mother of the gods for the earth, but one must not treat these phenomena with superstitious fear or awe, for the earth is without sensation; it is composed of atoms that create all its qualities.

The laws that govern the union of atoms determine the various types of living beings and inorganic matter. Atoms are without color, but color results from the combination, position, and movement of atoms. Atoms do not have heat or cold, sound or smell, feeling or any temporary qualities, for atoms are immortal. Certain combinations of atoms result in life and feeling. When a being dies, his atoms are not destroyed but are dispersed and then form other combinations. Since there is infinite space and an infinite number of atoms, other worlds must exist. Once again Lucretius insists that the gods are entirely removed from the affairs of men. As all things change and decay, so one day the earth will be destroyed. Even now it is in a state of decay.

Book III. The book begins with an invocation to Epicurus, who brought light to man, teaching him the truth that destroys fear. Lucretius then turns to the nature of the soul in order to help man overcome his fear of death, which drives him to seek power and riches before all else, for these, man believes, extend his life. Man's spirit and mind are material, a part of his body, like his hands, feet, or eyes. The mind is located in the middle of the breast and the spirit, which is found throughout the body, is directed by the mind, which governs the spirit and the rest of the body. When the mind is deeply affected, the whole body responds. Both mind and spirit (or soul) are made up of very small, round atoms; evidence of this composition is the extremely rapid activity of the mind. Mind and spirit are born with the body, and like the body, they are mortal. Lucretius next offers twenty-eight proofs of the mortality of mind and soul, which he now treats as one.

Because the soul is mortal, we will experience nothing after death. Therefore death should not matter to us, and certainly should not be feared. Lucretius then presents the arguments of an imaginary "adversary" who reminds him of all the pleasures of life of which death will rob him, surely enough reason to fear death. Lucretius reasonably answers this argument with the assertion that man will not miss the experiences of life when he is dead. He asks, "If you have had contentment in life, why not withdraw like a well-fed guest from a banquet?" Man must accept the law of nature: without change there is no continuity. No one goes to Tartarus; the matter of his body is essential for further creation.

A brilliant passage follows, in which Lucretius denounces the myths of suffering in the afterworld, declaring that they are merely symbolic representations of daily life on earth. Tantalus, Tityus, Sisyphus, and the other mythical characters depicted as enduring torture in Hades are actually the victims of their own greed, ambition, and other irrational desires here on earth. The life of a fool is indeed hell on earth. Great men of the past have died, even the great and good King Ancus. Why, then, should you, foolish and wicked men, fear death? [The passage reminds one of Achilles' words to Lycaon in ILIAD XXI.] Men waste their time and energy trying to avoid the fears that oppress them, actually trying to flee from themselves. Only a knowledge of the nature of the universe and the laws of life can help them.

Book IV. Lucretius speaks of his vast undertaking in this poem, in which he attempts to teach by pleasing. After a lengthy explanation of sense perception he asserts that all knowledge and reason depend on this perception by the senses. He then analyzes the workings of the mind and describes the mechanism of fantasy. He warns the reader not to assume that the human body was made for a particular purpose; on the contrary, human beings discovered uses for the various parts of their bodies. Next he discusses the need for food and sleep. Dreams reflect our daily activities, our interests, fears, and desires. The next topic is the physical causes of sexual desire. Lucretius advises the reader to avoid the anguish of immoderate passion, which deprives a man of judgment and reason. The lover is too often deceived and ensnared by a woman, so that he regards her flaws as virtues and loses his dignity and reason in his ridiculous infatuation. Though women are often false, some women can love sincerely and with deep feeling. Lucretius then considers the causes of the inheritance of family characteristics, which may even be those of a great-grandfather, and of sterility.

Book V. Epicurus has accomplished more than any of the gods, for he has freed man from the darkness of delusion. Without a free mind and spirit the good life is impossible. Thus Epicurus is more truly divine than many who are so regarded. The next subject is the mortality of the universe, which Lucretius establishes by tracing the origin and development of the world and of living creatures. The gods, who live outside the world of men, did not create the world and therefore are not to be celebrated. The world resulted from various combinations and movements of atoms. Because the elements that make up the world—earth, water, air, and fire—are mortal, the world itself must be mortal. In the constant war among the elements, one will eventually conquer the others and bring an end to the world.

The creation of the world through the accidental combinations of atoms is then described; first the earth, then the ether, the sky, the sun, the moon, and the seas came into being. After explaining the nature and movments of the heavenly bodies, Lucretius describes the development of the earth and the evolution of animals and men. He speaks of the struggle of the creatures to survive, how some failed because of their weaknesses and others succeeded through strength or cunning. He denies that the monsters of fable ever existed. Next he traces the development of man from early cave dweller to the citizen in society. He describes the growth of language, the discovery of fire, the organization of cities, and the development of law. As Lucretius considers the growing power and wealth of man, he takes the opportunity to declare that only a simple way of life and a contented mind can bring happiness. Those who struggle for power and position are not fulfilling their true desires and needs; their values are false, and they will never achieve wisdom or contentment. After tracing the origins of religion, which he attributes to ignorance and fear, Lucretius deals with the development of various tools, crafts, and arts.

Book VI. The book begins with another tribute to Epicurus, Athens' noblest gift to man. Lucretius then turns to a scientific explanation of thunder, lightning, winds, clouds, storms, hurricanes, the rainbow, snow, and other natural occurrences. Next he speaks of the causes of disease and, imitating Thucydides, he gives an account of the plague at Athens in 430–429 B.C.

COMMENTARY. Henri Patin, writing about Lucretius in *Etudes sur la poésie latine* (Paris, 1883), speaks of *"l'anti-Lucrèce chez Lucrèce,"* that which is opposed to Lucretius within Lucretius. The phrase suggests one of the main reasons that a scientific explanation of the universe is also a great poem. Patin refers to the conflict within Lucretius that is both reflected and resolved in the *De Rerum Natura*. The poet who says that the chief goal of man should be a tranquil spirit is himself passionately engaged in controversy, and the materialist who declares that death is nothing loves the world whose mortality he accepts with his own. The *De Rerum Natura* reveals Lucretius' absorption in the material universe, his responses to the rhythms of mutation and continuity, his delight in the eternal laws of nature as they reveal themselves beneath her changing surface. Lucretius' materialism does not merely explain the physical nature of reality; it discloses the marvelous variety of nature and her secret laws. Thus his explanation of what he considered to be scientific principles has the effect of revelation. His passionate devotion to his subject and his emotional response to the wonders of the material universe make the *De Rerum Natura* an intensely moving poem. Furthermore, Lucretius' conception of death as "nothing," as outside man's experience and therefore meaningless, is not facile optimism. Actually he is speaking about life rather than about death, for life can be satisfactory only on the condition that man accept death for what it is. The strong arguments of the "adversary" and the intensity with which Lucretius accumulates his mass of evidence indicate that the poet knows that such an acceptance is not easy, but he is convinced that it is ultimately man's only, if difficult, choice. As Camus says in *The Rebel*, "Lucretius' hero . . . opens the first attack on divinity in the name of human suffering" (trans. Anthony Bower [Alfred A. Knopf, 1956], p. 31).

On the Peace. See ISOCRATES.

On the Sublime. See LONGINUS ON THE SUBLIME.

Orator. Rhetorical work (46 B.C.) by CICERO, addressed to M. Junius Brutus. Earlier in 46 B.C. Cicero criticized the Atticists in his *Brutus*. In a reply, Brutus apparently asked Cicero to depict the perfect orator. Cicero says he is drawing a portrait of a person who has never actually existed; he is attempting to capture in words the ideal qualities that sometimes appear while an orator is speaking, but are seldom, perhaps never, apparent at all times, even in the best of orators. The ideal orator must be proficient in the three styles of oration: the grand, the plain, and the median. Cicero again attacks the Atticists, suggesting that if the men of that school are seeking an "Attic" example, they model themselves on the greatest of orators, Demosthenes. After discussing the three types of speeches, the deliberative (to the legislature), the forensic (to judicial audiences), and the epideictic, the last of which Cicero treats condescendingly, he deals with the technical requisites of a good oration. In his long discussion on style he emphasizes rhythm, declaring that he has written more extensively on the rhythms of prose than anyone before him.

Oresteia. A trilogy (458 B.C.) by AESCHYLUS, three tragedies: *Agamemnon*, *The Libation Bearers* (*Choephoroi*), and *The Eumenides*. Translations: in prose, H. Weir Smyth, 1922; in verse, Gilbert Murray, 1920–25; in verse, Richmond Lattimore, 1953; in verse, Philip Vellacott, 1959; in verse, Paul Roche, 1963; in verse, Peter Arnott, 1964; in verse, Robert Fagles, 1975.

MYTHICAL BACKGROUND. Pelops, the son of Tantalus, had two sons, Atreus and Thyestes. When Atreus became king of Argos, Thyestes challenged his rule and seduced Atreus' wife, Aerope. Atreus expelled Thyestes, but later allowed him to return to Mycenae, pretending to forgive him. At a feast Atreus served his brother the bodies of two of Thyestes' own children. When Thyestes discovered what he had eaten, he cursed the house of Atreus and took flight from Argos, accompanied by the one son who remained to him, Aegisthus.

Atreus' son, Agamemnon, became king of Argos. He married Clytemnestra and had four children, Iphigenia, Orestes, Electra, and Chrysothemis. Agamemnon's brother Menelaus married Helen, the most beautiful woman in the world, and became king of Sparta. When Helen was abducted by Paris, son of King Priam of Troy, Agamemnon and Menelaus led the Greek forces against Troy in the Trojan War. When the brothers set out for Troy, their ships were delayed at Aulis by poor weather. Calchas, the prophet, told Agamemnon that if they wished to leave Aulis, Agamemnon must fulfill the desire of the goddess Artemis by sacrificing his daughter Iphigenia to her. Agamemnon sacrificed his daughter, and the ships set sail for Troy. While Agamemnon was fighting in Troy, his wife, Clytemnestra, took Aegisthus as her lover and planned the murder of her husband when he returned. Clytemnestra sent her son Orestes out of the city to prevent his interference in her plans. After ten years of fighting, the Greeks conquered Troy, and Agamemnon set sail for home, bringing with him Cassandra, a daughter of King Priam and a prophetess, whom he had taken as a captive and made his mistress.

AGAMEMNON. S U M M A R Y . On the roof of the palace of Agamemnon at Argos, a watchman is spending the night looking for a signal fire that will announce the fall of Troy. While he is expressing his forebodings of trouble for the House of Atreus, he sees a beacon light in the sky, a signal that Troy has fallen and the war is over. After the watchman leaves, the Chorus of Argive Elders enters and sings of the ten years of pain and destruction endured by the Greeks during the Trojan War. They themselves were too old to fight, but many young men were killed in what seems to the Chorus an unjust war. As the elders sing, Clytemnestra enters and burns incense on the altars to the gods. The old men ask her for what she is giving thanks, then continue to sing of the Trojan War, going back to the sacrifice of Iphigenia, which they interpret as a sign of Agamemnon's evil desire for bloodshed and war. Artemis demanded that he sacrifice his daughter if he wished to set sail for Troy, and Agamemnon, eager for battle, was willing to kill his own child, a symbol of the young lives to be destroyed in battle. The old men also sing of Clytemnestra's bitter anger at this sacrifice of her child, her hatred of her husband, and her desire for vengeance. They call upon Zeus to indicate the way to knowledge. For man the price of wisdom is suffering. The choral ode thus relates the events of the past to the present action and introduces the main themes of the play—the problem of justice in both personal and civic affairs and the agonizing cost that human beings pay to achieve knowledge of themselves and other men.

Clytemnestra then tells the Chorus of the signal fires and their message of the Greek victory. She speaks with sympathy of the sufferings endured by the conquered Trojans and says that the conquerors must revere the gods of Troy and must not destroy her shrines. The Chorus then gives thanks to Zeus for the victory of the Greeks. Zeus, the god of hospitality, has punished the Trojans for Paris' criminal violation of the hospitality of Menelaus, whose wife Paris abducted. Nonetheless, the Chorus' attitude toward the war is critical: so many slain, they say, for the sake of a disloyal woman. There is anger against the sons of Atreus because of the ten long years of suffering. Their own hope, say the Elders of Argos, is to be neither conqueror nor victim in war.

Now a Herald enters, announcing that Agamemnon will soon arrive at Argos.

He expresses joy at the victory over the Trojans, but cannot help dwelling on the agonies both the Greeks and the Trojans endured during the ten bitter years of war. Clytemnestra then enters and speaks of her loyalty and love for Agamemnon and her joy at his return. The Leader of the Chorus hints at the hypocrisy of her words.

The Chorus returns to the subject of the Trojan War and of Helen, the beautiful woman who bred death. The love of Paris and Helen is depicted in images of war and death. The Chorus here explicitly states one of the themes of all Greek tragedy: corruption breeds corruption; sorrow springs from wrong-doing. Behind present suffering lies past corruption.

At this point Agamemnon enters, followed by the captive Cassandra. In its greeting to Agamemnon the Chorus speaks ambiguously. Though the Elders welcome their king, they suggest that they were critical of his decision to fight for the sake of Helen. The Chorus here again dwells on a theme significant throughout Greek tragedy: man falls victim to his own blindness, his own unwillingness to see the truth. A wise king, the Chorus implies, can see beneath the surface of ceremony and flattery. But Agamemnon only speaks proudly of his victory. Totally involved in his own glory, he does not see the dangers he is facing in his own home. Clytemnestra enters with attendants carrying purple cloths. In a hypocritical speech she tells of her love for Agamemnon and her joy in his safe return; she urges him to walk into the palace on the purple cloths that the attendants have spread for him. Though Agamemnon makes a show of refusing, for he knows that walking on the purple cloth will be regarded as an act of *hybris* (pride), he is easily persuaded by Clytemnestra, who appeals to his egotism and his arrogance. He tells Clytemnestra to treat Cassandra gently and walks proudly into the palace. Clytemnestra follows Agamemnon into the palace, leaving Cassandra behind. After the Chorus sings of its fears, which, like dreams, are hard to interpret, for they are merely forebodings of danger, Clytemnestra comes out again and scornfully commands Cassandra to enter the palace. Cassandra neither moves nor speaks, but, after Clytemnestra returns to the palace Cassandra cries out in pain, addressing Mother Earth and Apollo, the god who inspires her with prophecy that will never be believed because she spurned his love. Cassandra foresees her own death. She speaks also of the doomed House of Atreus, recalling the horrors of its past, the feast of Thyestes, and predicting the murder of Agamemnon and the vengeance of Orestes. As she enters the palace, knowing that she is going to her death, Cassandra with great nobility relates her fate to that of all men, limited by their mortality.

As the Chorus comments on the limitations of man, Agamemnon is heard within, crying out that he is being murdered. The Chorus expresses its fear and anxiety by speaking not as a unit but individually, one Elder suggesting that they call for help, another that they bring help themselves. The palace doors are opened and Clytemnestra comes out. The bodies of Agamemnon and

Cassandra are revealed. Clytemnestra speaks of how she murdered her husband and Cassandra, expressing great satisfaction in her vengeance. The death of Agamemnon gave her new life, she declares. When the Chorus reproaches her, Clytemnestra justifies her deeds by reminding the Elders of Agamemnon's sacrifice of her child, Iphigenia. Clytemnestra then speaks of her jealousy of Agamemnon's mistresses at Troy and of Cassandra. Regarding herself as Justice, Clytemnestra insists she has only inflicted the proper punishment on Agamemnon. The Chorus, however, regards her deeds as evil and predicts that she herself will be punished.

Clytemnestra's lover Aegisthus then enters, hailing the day as one on which proper vengeance has been done. He explains that he helped plan the murder in order to avenge Atreus' crimes against his father Thyestes. Aegisthus exults in his power as ruler of Argos. The Chorus places its last hope for justice in a prediction that Orestes will return and punish the murderers. As the play ends Clytemnestra and Aegisthus speak contemptuously to the Chorus, an indication that the pair will rule Argos tyrannically.

THE LIBATION BEARERS (Choephoroi). S U M M A R Y . Years after the murder of Agamemnon, his son Orestes, now a young man, returns from Phocis to Argos to avenge the death of his father. Accompanying Orestes is his friend Pylades, son of Strophius, king of Phocis. The two young men approach the tomb of Agamemnon, where Orestes leaves a lock of his hair. He then notices a group of Slave Women (the Chorus) and with them his sister Electra. The Chorus has been commanded by Clytemnestra to appease the soul of Agamemnon with offerings at his tomb, for the Queen is troubled by frightening dreams. The Chorus speaks of Clytemnestra's guilt and the terror it brings her and of how evil is inevitably punished. Electra turns to the Slave Women for advice, asking them what she is to say as she pours libations to her father. Surely she cannot say that these offerings come from an adoring wife, her mother. The Slave Women advise her to pray for all those who hate Aegisthus and for the return of her brother Orestes. When the Chorus tells her to pray for someone to make Clytemnestra and Aegisthus pay with their lives for the life of Agamemnon, Electra questions this code of simple vengeance; she asks if it is right to pray for murderous vengeance. She prays to the soul of her father for the return of Orestes and for herself a heart more understanding than her mother's and a purer hand. Electra then notices the lock of hair on Agamemnon's tomb; observing that it is very like her own hair, she suspects that Orestes has returned. When she sees footprints that resemble hers, she is even more certain. Orestes comes out of hiding and gives her a final piece of evidence that he is her brother: he shows her a cloak she once made for him.

After the brother and sister express their joy at being together again, Orestes reveals that the oracle of Apollo commanded him to avenge his father's murder by killing Clytemnestra and Aegisthus. If he fails to do so, he will suffer greatly, tortured by guilt in the form of the Furies sent by his dead father; he will be an outcast, without honor in his land. Yet Orestes hesitates to kill his mother. Like Electra, he recoils from the old code of blood vengeance. The Chorus urges him on, reminding him of the merciless killing of his father. In a long, lyrical interchange between Orestes, Electra, and the Chorus, Orestes is persuaded by the emotional intensity of the Chorus and Electra's reminders of how unjustly their father and they were treated, and he agrees to murder his mother and Aegisthus. After lamentations and prayers to Agamemnon, the Chorus tells Orestes of Clytemnestra's dream that she gave birth to a serpent, which she nursed as if it were her child and which bit her breast and drew blood. Orestes takes the dream as prophetic and plans his vengeance.

Electra and the Chorus must keep Orestes' plans secret. He and Pylades will disguise themselves as travelers from Phocis and thus gain entrance to the palace. After Orestes, Pylades, and Electra leave, the Chorus sings of the dreadful crimes committed by various women because of their violent passions.

Orestes and Pylades enter and knock at the gate of the palace. When Clytemnestra asks them what they want, Orestes tells her that he has come from Phocis bringing news of the death of Orestes and an urn containing his ashes. Though Clytemnestra is relieved to hear this news, she pretends to be stricken with grief. She offers Orestes the hospitality of the palace, and all but the Chorus leave the stage.

The women pray that Orestes may accomplish his purpose; they then greet Cilissa, Orestes' old nurse, who tells them that Clytemnestra has ordered her to summon Aegisthus to meet the strangers and hear further details of the information they have brought. Cilissa sees through the hypocrisy of Clytemnestra; the old nurse speaks of her own sorrow at the news of Orestes' death, but to Clytemnestra, she says, the news is actually pleasing. The Chorus suggests to Cilissa that she tell Aegisthus to come to the palace without his armed attendants. When the nurse leaves, the Chorus returns to its prayer for Orestes, asking Zeus to help him slay the murderers.

Aegisthus comes in, saying that he is eager to question the travelers. He then enters the palace. Soon a cry is heard within, and an attendant of Aegisthus comes out to announce that Aegisthus has been slain. When Clytemnestra hears of his death, she calls for an ax with which to defend herself. Orestes and Pylades enter with their swords drawn. Clytemnestra mourns over Aegisthus and begs her son to spare her life. She reminds Orestes of how she nursed him when he was a baby. Moved by her words, Orestes hesitates and turns to Pylades for advice. Pylades reminds him of the command of Apollo, and despite his misgivings, Orestes takes his mother into the palace and kills her.

The Chorus sings of its pity for Clytemnestra and Aegisthus in their downfall, but declares that justice demanded their deaths. The doors of the palace are opened, revealing Orestes standing by the bodies of Aegisthus and Clytemnestra. Attendants stand by, holding the robe in which Agamemnon was murdered. Orestes attempts to justify and even to take pride in his act of vengeance, but he must admit that despite his victory he feels grief and pain. He says he will leave the land, an outcast. The Chorus tries to comfort him, insisting that the murders were justified, but Orestes sees the Furies (Erinyes), the winged goddesses with bloody eyes and snakes in their hair, who pursue the guilty. Orestes says that the Furies have been sent by Clytemnestra, and, driven by the madness of guilt, he flees Argos.

EUMENIDES. SUMMARY. Before the temple of Apollo at Delphi the Pythian Priestess prays to the many gods of the oracular shrine, the Mother Earth, Themis, Artemis, and especially Apollo, Athene, and Zeus. The scene is a peaceful one, but the pleasant mood is shattered when the Priestess enters the temple and finds Orestes, stained with blood, at the central altar and before him, on the steps of the altar, the hideous Furies, asleep. After describing this scene the Priestess leaves, and the doors of the temple open, revealing Orestes at the altar, the sleeping Furies, and Apollo and Hermes. Apollo assures Orestes that he will never abandon him. The God of Light despises the dark Furies. He tells Orestes to go to Athens, where Athene will help him to find deliverance from his guilt and suffering. In Athens Orestes will find justice. Hermes guides Orestes as they leave. The Ghost of Clytemnestra then approaches the Furies and scolds them for allowing the tortured Orestes to escape. As the Furies wake they mutter and cry, expressing their anger at Orestes' flight. They inveigh against the young god of light, Apollo, and promise that Orestes will not escape their torture. Apollo returns and orders the Furies to leave his temple. The Furies, the principle of dark and primitive vengeance, argue with Apollo, the god of light. They say that Apollo is protecting a man guilty of his mother's murder, but Apollo replies that Orestes was obliged to kill Clytemnestra, who slew her husband. The marriage relationship, Apollo says, is more sacred than even a blood relationship.

The scene shifts to Athens, where Orestes holds fast to a statue of Athene before her temple on the Acropolis. He prays that Athene will free him of the tortures of the avenging Furies. The Furies enter, seeking Orestes. When they see him with his arms around the statue of Athene, they vow that they will consume the very nerves of his body with the tortures of guilt. Orestes then prays to Athene, describing his long penance, his wanderings from shrine to shrine seeking release from his guilt. But the Chorus of Furies insists that justice is its province: born of Night, the Furies were commanded to pursue those guilty of murder. Their code is that blood atones for blood; their conception of law is vengeance. They resent the power of Apollo, a young god, who threatens their frightful power. They declare that their rule is based on fear and no one shall replace them.

Athene enters and is told by the Furies of Orestes' matricide. Athene says that she must also hear Orestes' version of his deed. When Orestes tells Athene that he was ordered by Apollo to slay his mother and that he has paid heavily for his crime and has sought to expiate it, Athene says that Orestes' case must be tried before a jury of Athenian citizens. After a choral ode in which the Furies once again express their conception of justice as simple vengeance, Athene enters with a jury of twelve Athenians, followed by a crowd of people. Athene will judge the case, and Apollo will defend Orestes against the accusations of the Furies. Apollo's defense is based on the fact that he himself followed the command of Zeus in urging Orestes to kill Clytemnestra. Moreover, he says, the true parent is not the mother, who merely carries the child, but the father whose seed the mother receives. The vote of the jury is a tie, and Orestes is acquitted by Athene's deciding vote. Given the right to return to his homeland, Orestes thanks Athene and leaves. Apollo also goes out, and the Furies appeal to justice to hear their case. They feel dishonored by the younger gods and threaten to destroy Athens, which has scorned them. Athene then pleads with them gently and reasonably, urging them not to turn their wrath against men. She offers them a place of honor in Athens and a share in the dignity of the city. Despite the protests of the Furies, Athene continues to plead with them. Her reasonableness, her dignity, her calm, her offers of peace and beauty in exchange for violence and vengeance finally persuade the Furies to give up their old bloodthirsty form and to accept their new role as Eumenides (Kindly Ones) and their new home in Athens. As Athene leads the Chorus to its cave, the play ends with a song of joy. Reason has conquered violence and fury; Orestes' madness and the blood that stained the House of Atreus are the price man in his limitations has paid for a new concept of justice, which replaces the old law of vengeance. The conflict between these two principles reaches its culmination in the matricide of Orestes and his consequent guilt and madness. It is resolved by the patience and reasonableness of Athene, goddess of wisdom, who transforms dark fury into beneficence and productivity.

COMMENTARY. Among the modern plays clearly influenced by the *Oresteia* are Robinson Jeffers' play in verse *The Tower Beyond Tragedy* (1924), Eugene O'Neill's *Mourning Becomes Electra* (1931), and T. S. Eliot's *The Family Reunion* (1939). Eliot, Tate, and other contemporary poets allude to the myth frequently in image and symbol.

Orestes. In Greek mythology, the son of Agamemnon and Clytemnestra. Pindar deals with Orestes in *Pythian* XI. His story is told in the following dramas: Aeschylus' ORESTEIA, Sophocles' ELECTRA, Euripides' *Iphigenia in Aulis*, IPHIGENIA IN TAURIS, ELECTRA, ORESTES, and ANDROMACHE, and Seneca's *Agamemnon*. He is mentioned frequently in the ODYSSEY.

Orestes. A tragedy (408 B.C.) by EURIPIDES. Translations: in prose, E. P. Coleridge, 1891; in verse, Gilbert Murray, 1911; in verse, A. S. Way, 1912; in verse, William Arrowsmith, 1958.

MYTHICAL BACKGROUND. Orestes killed his mother, Clytemnestra, and her lover Aegisthus to avenge their murder of his father, Agamemnon (see Aeschylus' ORESTEIA, Sophocles' ELECTRA, and Euripides' ELECTRA). Because he had murdered his mother, Orestes was tortured and driven mad by the Furies, goddesses of vengeance.

SCENE. Argos, before the royal palace.

SUMMARY. While Orestes sleeps, Electra, who has been caring for him in his insanity, speaks of the past and present crimes and sufferings of the House of Atreus. Orestes' present anguish is thus related to the continuous conflict and pain of his family. Electra blames Apollo for ordering Orestes to slay his mother and says that she shares her brother's guilt. She describes the disease of madness that is consuming her brother, his frenzy and his few lucid moments. To add to their sorrows, the Argives have decreed that Orestes and Electra are polluted by matricide; no one may shelter them or even speak to them. Today the Argives will determine their sentence, which probably will be death. Only one possibility of escape from this sentence exists: Menelaus, Agamemnon's brother, has just returned from his wanderings after the Trojan War and will soon arrive at Argos. His wife Helen and their daughter Hermione were sent ahead and are already at the royal palace. Electra hopes that Menelaus will assist her brother and her.

Helen comes out of the palace and expresses sympathy for Electra and grief for her dead sister Clytemnestra. She wishes to make an offering at the tomb of Clytemnestra, but fears the wrath of the Argives against her, for it was her love affair with Paris that caused the Trojan War. Finally she sends her daughter Hermione to make the offering and returns to the palace. Electra speaks with contempt of the vain, egotistical Helen, who was the cause of suffering for her and all of Greece.

When the Chorus of Argive Women enters, Electra asks them to be quiet so that they will not awake Orestes. Electra tells the women that it was the oracle of Apollo that forced her brother and her to commit the crime. She weeps for her dead mother and father. When Orestes awakes, Electra comforts him, telling him that Menelaus will soon arrive. Orestes' madness returns, and he is tortured by the Furies. When this fit passes, Orestes blames Apollo for his matricide and his suffering.

When Menelaus arrives, he is horrified by Orestes' appearance and asks what sickness consumes him. Orestes replies that his sickness is of the soul, and, after decribing his suffering to Menelaus, asks his help. Tyndareus, Clytemnestra's father, arrives; violently angry at Orestes, he condemns the whole idea of blood vengeance, saying that Orestes might have brought a legal charge against his mother instead of killing her. He tells Menelaus not to help Orestes, but to allow the Argives to kill him by stoning. Despite Orestes' attempt to justify his act, Tyndareus says he will go to the Argive council to persuade the citizens to kill Orestes and Electra. Orestes then turns to Menelaus, pleading for his help and reminding him that Agamemnon, his father, helped Menelaus when Helen went off to Troy with Paris. Menelaus tries to evade his responsibility by saying he is weak and can hardly fight the Argives. He promises to try to persuade them to act more temperately.

When Menelaus leaves, Orestes feels he is entirely deserted. However, his friend Pylades soon arrives and offers to help him. They will attempt to justify Orestes' matricide to the Argive council.

After a choral ode recounting the past crimes and the present sorrows of the House of Atreus, Electra comes out of the palace and hears from a messenger that Orestes has vainly attempted to defend himself before the council. The citizens of Argos have decided that he and Electra must die. If they agree to commit suicide, they can escape stoning. Electra weeps for herself and her family.

Orestes and Pylades enter. Orestes, impatient with Electra's lamentations, embraces and says farewell to her. Pylades says he is determined to die with Orestes and Electra, but since they must all die, they ought to plan some misfortune for Menelaus, who deserted Orestes. He suggests that they kill Helen. Electra then proposes that they seize Hermione as she is returning from Clytemnestra's grave and hold the girl as a hostage, so that after killing Helen they may demand help from Menelaus. Orestes and Pylades go into the palace, and Electra waits for Hermione. As Electra speaks to the Chorus, Helen is heard within, crying that she is being murdered. When Hermione returns, Electra persuades her to enter the palace, where Orestes captures her.

As the Chorus remarks that Helen has been punished for the suffering she brought on the Greeks, the Phrygian Eunuch comes out of the palace and describes the death of Helen. Orestes appears and cruelly taunts the Eunuch, then returns to the palace. As the Chorus observes Menelaus approaching, Orestes and Pylades are seen on the roof of the palace, where they are holding Hermione. Orestes shouts to Menelaus that the doors of the palace are locked, and he may not enter. He threatens to murder Hermione and set fire to the palace unless Menelaus persuades the Argives to allow Orestes, Electra, and Pylades to live and Orestes to rule Argos. Orestes, with the help of his friends, is about to set fire to the palace when Apollo appears with Helen. The god explains that he rescued Helen when Orestes was about to kill her; Helen is now a goddess, who, with her brothers Castor and Polydeuces, will offer help to mariners. Menelaus must choose a new wife. Orestes is to leave Argos and go to Athens, where he will face a trial for the murder of his mother. He will win his case and marry Hermione. Electra is to marry Pylades. Apollo will make peace between Orestes and the Argives, and Orestes will rule Argos. Orestes is now convinced that Apollo is a true prophet. Menelaus agrees to give Hermione to Orestes, and the play ends happily.

Orion. In Greek mythology, a giant and a great hunter. Orion fell in love with Aero (sometimes called Merope), the daughter of Oenopion, king of Chios, who agreed to their marriage, but constantly postponed it. When Orion in a drunken state spoke harshly to his beloved, Oenopion asked Dionysus to punish him. The god made Orion sleep and allowed Oenopion to blind him. Orion regained his sight in Lemnos and then attempted to find Oenopion to punish him for his cruelty, but Oenopion had fled from Chios. Orion became a hunter of Artemis in Crete, but he was killed by the goddess, in one version of the myth, because she was jealous of Eos' love for him. In another version Orion pursued the Pleiades, the seven daughters of Atlas, and both he and they were transformed into constellations.

Ornithes. See THE BIRDS.

Orpheus. In Greek mythology, a pre-Homeric poet and musician who originated in Thrace. As the greatest of musicians, Orpheus is connected with the god Apollo. Orpheus played the lyre with such artistry that his music moved rocks and trees and calmed wild animals. When he accompanied the Argonauts on their journey, his music helped his companions to resist the Sirens. For the well-known story of Orpheus' love for Eurydice, her flight from the advances of Aristaeus, which resulted in her death, and Orpheus' fruitless attempt to recover her from Hades, see Vergil's GEORGIC IV. Ovid also deals with Orpheus' descent into Hades in *Metamorphoses* X, and with his dismemberment by a band of Thracian Maenads, incensed by his apathy to women after the death of Eurydice, in *Metamorphoses* XI. (Another explanation for their violence was that Orpheus interrupted their orgiastic rites.) The birds, beasts, stones, and trees all wept for the great musician Orpheus. His head and his lyre were carried down the stream Hebrus, and as they floated his lips sang and his lyre played mournful strains. In Ovid's version of the myth Orpheus and Eurydice were united in Elysium. The dismemberment of Orpheus is similar to that of Pentheus in *The Bacchae* and was probably related to a Dionysian rite.

Orphism. One of the mystery religions of ancient Greece, based upon Orphic writings, a number of books attributed to Orpheus in antiquity. The religious movement reached its height during the sixth century B.C. "The specific belief of Orphism was that the soul of man was a fallen god or demon impatient of its imprisonment in an alien body, and due for a cycle of perpetual reembodiment on earth" (Michael Grant, *Myths of the Greeks and Romans* [Weidenfeld and Nicolson, 1962], p. 312). The Orphics believed that a man's soul was immortal and that he had to perform a frequent rite of purification in order to preserve the immortal spirit within him. Emphasizing guilt and retribution, the Orphics regarded Hades as a hell in which sinners were punished. It is thought that Orphic rites included the tearing and devouring of an animal that symbolized a god.

Osiris. See ISIS.

Otho, Marcus Salvius. The emperor of ROME in A.D. 69. See Tacitus' HISTORIES. Biographical sources include Suetonius' *Lives of the Caesars* and Plutarch's life of Otho.

Otus (Otos) and Ephialtes. In Greek mythology, giants, the sons of either

Aloeus or Poseidon, The brothers, Otus and Ephialtes, often called the Aleoids or Aloidae, threatened to wage war on the gods and tried to pile the mountain Ossa on Olympus and Pelion on Ossa, so that they could reach the dwelling of the gods in heaven, but Zeus killed them.

Ouranos. See URANUS.

Ovid (Publius Ovidius Naso). A Roman poet, born in 43 B.C. at Sulmo (Sulmona), ninety miles east of Rome. In TRISTIA IV, 10 he says that his family was of equestrian rank and that he had a brother a year older than he. He received a traditional education in rhetoric at Rome and Athens. From early childhood, Ovid says, he loved to write poetry, and, though his father attempted to persuade him to prepare for a career in public life, his talents and instincts determined that he would be a poet. Whatever he wrote became a poem. Although he did hold some minor public positions, his only real interest was poetry. His literary friends included Tibullus, whose death Ovid mourns in AMORES III, 9, Propertius, Gallus, and Aemelius Macer. Ovid married three times and had one daughter, Perilla, by his third wife.

Ovid's AMORES, HEROIDES, *Ars Amatoria* (ART OF LOVE), REMEDIA AMORIS, MEDICINA FACIEI and a tragedy, *Medea,* only two lines of which have survived, were published before A.D. 8; by that date he had completed but not yet revised the METAMORPHOSES. In A.D. 8 Ovid's whole way of life was changed when Augustus sentenced him to banishment at Tomis (Constanza, on the west coast of the Black Sea) and banned his poems from public libraries. The exact cause of this punishment is still not known; the "error" Ovid speaks of in *Tristia* IV, 10 may refer to his involvement with Augustus' licentious granddaughter Julia. Possibly the *Amores* and the *Ars Amatoria* offended Augustus, who was attempting to reform the morals of Rome. Banishment was extremely painful to Ovid, an urbane man who loved Rome; he says that in his despair he burned many of his poems. Though he constantly yearned for Rome and kept hoping for permission to return home, he continued to write at Tomis. There he probably finished the FASTI and composed the *Tristia* (Poems of Sorrow), the EPISTULAE EX PONTO, the HALIEUTICA (a work on fishing in the Black Sea), and the IBIS (a bird regarded as sacred by the Egyptians), an imitation of a lost poem by Callimachus. Ovid died at Tomis in A.D. 18.

Ovid's poetry reveals a rare union of great narrative skill and brilliant lyrical technique. Though he is a painstaking craftsman, his high spirits and wit suggest spontaneity. In his love poetry he deals lightly and humorously with passion and disappointment, and in the *Metamorphoses* and the *Heroides* he reduces heroic figures to ordinary people; nevertheless, Ovid's insight into human psychology is profound. He probes deeply into human nature with wit and compassion. Although his advice in the *Ars Amatoria* is humorous and playful, it conveys Ovid's broad observation and understanding of human experience. His wit is never cruel; one always feels beneath it an acceptance of and pleasure in the people and experiences he describes.

Ovid is capable of expressing deep feelings of pain over the death of Tibullus or over his own sad lot in exile (*Tristia*), and sincere dedication to his craft as a poet, which he believed would bring him immortality. In *Amores* I, 15 and III, 9 and in the Epilogue to the *Metamorphoses*, Ovid declares that so long as poetry exists he will continue to live.

His prediction has certainly come true. His influence has been vast and powerful. During the Middle Ages, Ovid was a popular poet, quoted and alluded to extensively by Chaucer and Gower. No Latin poet had greater importance in the English Renaissance. The works of Spenser, Marlowe, Ben Jonson, and especially Shakespeare reveal how significant Ovid's influence was. During the neoclassical period Dryden and Pope translated him and emulated his wit and his metrical and verbal skill. In the twentieth century the allusions to Ovid of Yeats, Joyce, Pound, Eliot, and other major poets suggest that his influence is still an important one.

P

Pacuvius, Marcus. Roman playwright and painter, a nephew of Ennius, born at Brundisium (Brindisi) around 220 B.C. He went to Rome, where he became well known as a painter and tragedian. In his old age he retired to Tarentum and died there around 130 B.C., at the age of ninety. The names of twelve tragedies of Pacuvius are known, among them a *fabula praetexta* called *Paulus*. Only fragments consisting of about four hundred lines of these plays survive. Cicero regarded Pacuvius as the best of the Roman tragedians.

paean (paian). A Greek choral ode, originally written to celebrate the god Apollo and later other gods. Only fragments of Pindar's paeans survive.

Palamedes. A hero of the post-Homeric stories of the Trojan War. Because Palamedes exposed Odysseus' pretense of madness when he was attempting to avoid fighting at Troy, Odysseus wrote a letter supposedly from Priam to Palamedes, offering him money if he were willing to be a traitor to his allies. The letter was found in Palamedes' tent, and he was stoned to death.

Palatine Anthology. See GREEK ANTHOLOGY.

Palinurus. See AENEID V, VI.

Pallas. See AENEID VIII, X.

Pallas. An epithet for Athene, perhaps originally the name of another goddess with whom Athene was identified. The meaning of Pallas is unknown, though often interpreted as "maiden."

Pan. The Greek god of herds and shepherds, who originated in Arcadia and was mainly worshiped there. Pan, regarded as the son of Hermes, Zeus, or some other god, is credited with the invention of the shepherd's flute. The Roman god Faunus is associated with him.

Panaetius (Panaitios). See STOICS.

Pandarus (Pandaros). A Trojan hero in the ILIAD (IV, V).

Pandora. In Greek mythology, a woman created by Hephaestus out of clay at the command of Zeus, who wanted vengeance on Prometheus. All the gods contributed to Pandora's beauty and charm (her name means "all gifts"), but they gave her a box that contained many evils and warned her never to open it. They then sent her to Epimetheus ("afterthought"), the brother of Prometheus ("forethought"). Epimetheus had been told by Prometheus never to accept a present from Zeus, but, when he saw the lovely Pandora, he ignored his brother's advice. Pandora, unable to overcome her curiosity about the contents of the box, opened it, and out came all the evils and sorrows that human beings have endured since her time. However, the box also contained hope, which has provided solace for man. Pandora's story is told in Hesiod's *Theogony*.

Panegyricus (Pangyrikos). See ISOCRATES.

Parallel Lives. See PLUTARCH.

Parcae. See FATES.

Paris. In Greek mythology, a son of King Priam of Troy and Hecuba. Before Paris was born Hecuba dreamed that she had given birth to a firebrand that would burn the whole city. Hoping to avoid the fulfillment of this prophetic dream, Priam exposed his infant son on Mount Ida. A shepherd reared him and gave him the name Paris. When he grew up Paris gained a reputation as a defender of shepherds and their flocks, and thus was called Alexander (defender of men). He married Oenone, the daughter of the river-god Cebren, but left her when Aphrodite offered him the most beautiful woman in the world. Paris went to Troy at a time when Priam was honoring his memory with funeral games. He was recognized by his sister Cassandra and welcomed by his parents. Paris then made a voyage to Sparta, where he fell in love with the beautiful Helen, the wife of King Menelaus. See Ovid's HEROIDES V for Oenone's expression of her grief. For the "judgment of Paris," the abduction of Helen, and its disastrous consequences see the ILIAD and HEROIDES XVI and XVII. Paris also appears in *Rhesus*.

Parmenides. A Greek philosopher, born at Elea (Latin Velia, modern Castellammare della Brucca) in southern Italy (c. 540 B.C.). According to Plato, Parmenides spoke with Socrates, and he is one of the principal speakers in Plato's dialogue PARMENIDES. In a poem in hexameter verse addressed to his pupil Zeno, Parmenides expresses his philosophical ideas in three divisions: "The Prologue," "The Way of Truth," and "The Way of Opinion." Only fragments of this work remain. According to Parmenides reality is indivisible, immutable, and whole. Change is only illusion. The only true perception of reality is that which indicates an unchanging Being; man is deceived by his senses, which do not lead him to an understanding of true being but only to the erroneous notion that change and destruction are involved in the function of the universe. Parmenides established the Eleatic school of philosophy.

Parmenides. A dialogue by PLATO named for the philosopher who founded the Eleatic school. The philosophical system of Parmenides regards the objective and unchanging world of being as reality; all that changes is mere illusion. In the dialogue Parmenides and his disciple Zeno speak with Socrates and others. The Eleatic method of considering opposites is used, and a theory of ideas is discussed.

Parnassus (Parnassos). A mountain in central Greece, thought to be a dwelling place of Apollo and the Muses. Parnassus was also sacred to Dionysus.

partheneion (maiden song). An ancient Greek choral lyric ode, sung by a group of young girls. Like most ancient odes, it contained a myth, a didactic or moral statement that follows from the myth, and references to those involved in the festival for which it was written. The *partheneion* is lighter in spirit than are most choral odes. Alcman, Simonides, Bacchylides, and Pindar wrote *partheneia*, but only fragments of these remain; one fragment of a PARTHENEION of Alcman consists of about half the original poem.

Partheneion (Maiden Song). A choral lyric by ALCMAN (second half of the seventh century B.C.). Translations: in prose, J. M. Edmonds, 1922; in verse, Gilbert Highet, in *The Oxford Book of English Verse in Translation*, ed. T. F. Higham and C. M. Bowra, 1938; in verse, Willis Barnstone, 1962.

SUMMARY. The fragment of Alcman's *Partheneion* that was found in Egypt in 1855 is the earliest example of choral poetry of any length that we possess. The ode was intended to be sung by a chorus of young girls to celebrate the Spartan goddess Orthia. The chorus of eleven is led by Hagesichora (which means "leader of the chorus" and may not be the actual name of the young woman). After recounting the myth of how Heracles avenged the death of his friend Oeonus, who was slain by the sons of Hippocoon, by waging war on them and killing several of them, the poet states a moral maxim, a conventional part of the choral ode. Then the members of the chorus engage in a lighthearted contest, one group praising the beauty of Hagesichora and the other that of Agido. Though the fragment consists of only about half the original poem, it suggests the nature of the maiden song.

Pasiphae. See MINOS.

pastoral poetry. The literary pastoral combines the stylized and artful with the spontaneous and natural. In pastoral poems shepherds and cowherds sing of love and friendship, often in subtle language and complicated meters. They sometimes represent poets, and their language reflects a knowledge of both the country and the literary world of the town. The form, which was created by Theocritus, who flourished around 270 B.C., has sources in earlier literature as well as in the natural world of country life. It has been shown that the choruses of Aristophanes' *The Acharnians* and *Peace,* which emphasize the fertility and productivity of nature as opposed to the destructiveness of war, contain suggestions of the pastoral atmosphere and spirit (J. S. Phillimore, *Pastoral and Allegory* [Oxford University Press, 1925]). Moreover, the shepherds of ancient Greece did sing as they tended their flocks. It is therefore not strange that Theocritus, who knew and loved the country, should associate the poets of his time with the shepherds to whom song was a natural expression of thoughts and feelings.

The pastorals of Theocritus reflect the poet's response to external nature, but they are essentially the sophisticated and artful work of a skilled craftsman, whose shepherds and cowherds represent the poet and his friends. The *Harvest Home* (*Idyl* VII), for example, hardly suggests the thoughts, the feelings, or even the setting of the actual countrymen. The artificiality of the pastoral is an essential quality of the form, and as the pastoral develops it becomes more prominent, as do references to contemporary affairs.

In Vergil's *Eclogues* the country is a stylized setting for his graceful shepherds; here plums are "waxen," streams are "crystal," and grass is "softer than sleep itself." The chief evils are Boreas (the north wind) and the hot sun. But a good fire protects the shepherd against the wind, and shade is provided by the arbutus and the vines of Bacchus, or among "sacred springs." Vergil consciously created in the *Eclogues* a golden world in which plants and animals have the grace and charm which only human attributes could give them. The humanized animals he creates gracefully respond to the feelings of their masters. Vergil's pastoral world is a mythical society of sophisticated animals and simple men. The stylized language he employs and his frequent use of circumlocution help to suggest the beauty, the grace, and especially the artificial, conventional qualities of the pastoral setting. Yet even in Vergil one can sometimes experience the real country—the fertility of the earth and the actual labor of man and animal—breaking through the elegant confines of the pastoral conventions.

The pastoral has been one of the most popular of the genres that the modern world has inherited from the ancient one. Throughout the Renaissance and the seventeenth and eighteenth centuries, English and Continental poets imitated and translated the pastorals of Theocritus and Vergil. Dryden and Pope revitalized the form in Augustan England, adapting it to their own times and gifts. Perhaps the greatest poem that emerges from this tradition is Milton's *Lycidas*, in which the very conventional elements are employed to intensify the sense of loss and grief.

Patroclus (Patroklos). A son of Menoetius and the dearest friend of Achilles. See the ILIAD.

Pausanias. Greek travel writer (c. second century A.D.). He was the author of *Hellados Periegesis* (*Description of Greece*), a guide in ten books to the various cities, monuments, and works of art of Greece. He includes myths and legends, historical facts, local customs, and various other information. *Description of Greece* is valuable to the student of Greek history and religion.

Peace (Eirene). An Old Comedy (421 B.C.) by ARISTOPHANES. Translations: in verse, Benjamin B. Rogers, 1924; in verse, Arthur S. Way, 1934.

BACKGROUND. By 422 B.C., in both Athens and Sparta, there were strong movements for ending the Peloponnesian War. Both Cleon, the Athenian demagogue, and Brasidas, the brave Spartan leader, were dead. The Athenians had suffered serious defeats since their victory at Pylos (425 B.C.), and the Spartans had long tried to end the war. Early in 421 B.C. a peace treaty was signed. Unfortunately this peace was temporary, and hostilities began soon again. In *Peace*, produced at the time when Athens and Sparta were negotiating a treaty to end hostilities, Aristophanes argues for peace and suggests the delights of a peaceful way of life for Athens.

SCENE. On the right, the farmhouse of Trygaeus; on the left, the palace of Zeus; in the center, a cave.

SUMMARY. Before the farmhouse of Trygaeus (Vineman) one of his slaves makes cakes of dung and another tosses them into the stable where a dung beetle consumes them. The slaves express their distaste for their disagreeable task and for the creature they are feeding. Their master, says one slave, is a madman who constantly speaks to Zeus. Soon Trygaeus is seen astride the huge dung beetle that he hopes will take him to Zeus so that he can ask the god to bring peace to Greece and thus save his people.

Trygaeus on the beetle is lifted by means of the machine, and finally he comes to Zeus' palace. He dismounts and knocks at the door, and is immediately insulted by Hermes, who calls him a scoundrel and tells him that Zeus and the other gods have moved to the very end of heaven because of their anger at the Greeks. The gods have given the Greeks many opportunities for peace, all of which have been rejected, and now the gods have left their former home to War, who will replace them in ruling the Greeks. Hermes goes on to inform Trygaeus that War has placed Peace in a pit and has heaped stones on her so that she cannot get out. War is now planning to collect all the cities of Greece in a great mortar and pound them. At this point War comes in with his mortar, crying out against mortals. He throws leeks, garlic, cheese, and honey into the mortar to represent cities of Greece, and then asks his slave Tumult to bring him a pestle. As Trygaeus expresses his fears that War will pound the Greek cities to pieces, Tumult returns to announce that he can find no pestle because Athens' pestle, Cleon, and Sparta's pestle, Brasidas, are dead. War decides to construct his own pestle and leaves, followed by Tumult.

Trygaeus addresses the Greeks, saying this is the moment to remove Peace from her pit, and he begs laborers, merchants, artists, and others to join in the work. The Chorus of Farmers and Laborers from all parts of Greece enters, eager to help restore Peace, the best of goddesses. The men shout and dance in their joy at the prospect of laying down arms. Just as they begin to plan their work Hermes enters and tries to stop them, but they bribe him with promises of rich offerings. After much labor Trygaeus and the Chorus liberate Peace, Opora (goddess of the harvest), and Theoria (Festival) from the pit. Trygaeus and the Chorus hail these deities and praise their beauty. Then Hermes points out that the folly and corruption of Greek leaders, especially the demagogues, caused the loss of Peace for so long. Peace reveals to Hermes that she tried many times to come to the Greeks after the battle of Pylos, but was rejected by them. Hermes then tells Trygaeus that he may take Opora with him as his wife, and he may lead Theoria to the Senate, her old home. Trygaeus cannot find his dung beetle, and is told that the creature is now harnessed to Zeus' chariot. With Opora and Theoria, Trygaeus returns to earth.

In the parabasis the Chorus praises Aristophanes for his courage in criticizing the illustrious men of Athens and for his comic art. Trygaeus asks his slaves to prepare Opora for marriage while he takes Theoria to the Senate. After his return he and his slave are roasting meat for a feast when the prophet Hierocles approaches. He predicts that the peace will be broken and then asks for food and drink. Trygaeus beats him and he runs away.

After a choral ode praising the comforts and joys of peace, a Sickle Maker, grateful to Trygaeus, who has restored his business, comes in to present him with wedding gifts of sickles and casks. Then various business men who made a profit on war—an armorer, a crest maker, a manufacturer of breastplates, and others—arrive, complaining that Trygaeus has ruined them, and are soon sent away. Two young boys, the sons of the Athenian general Lamachus and the cowardly Cleonymus, recite passages from the Greek poets that suggest the deeds of their fathers. As the feast begins Opora appears, and Trygaeus and the Chorus evoke Hymen in a marriage song.

Pegasus (Pegasos). In Greek mythology, a winged horse created from the blood of Medusa when Perseus cut off her head. Pegasus helped Bellerophon kill the Chimaera.

Pelasgians. The name (meaning "sea people") usually given to the inhabitants of Greece before the coming of the Achaeans.

Peleus. In Greek mythology, a son of Aeacus and father of Achilles. Banished from Aegina for murdering his brother, Peleus went to Phthia, where King Acastus purged him of this murder. Hippolyte, the wife of Acastus, became infatuated with Peleus, and, when he did not respond to her, accused him of adultery. Acastus left Peleus to die on Mount Pelion, but he managed to survive, and there he married the nymph Thetis, who bore him Achilles. Catullus tells of the marriage of Peleus and Thetis in an epyllion (64). Peleus, as an old man, plays an important role in Euripides' ANDROMACHE.

Pelias. See JASON and Euripides' MEDEA.

Peloponnesian War, The. A prose history (c. 400 B.C.) by THUCYDIDES. Translations: Benjamin Jowett, 1881; E. C. Marchant, 1900; C. F. Smith, 1919; Rex Warner, 1954; John H. Finley, Jr., 1963.

SUMMARY. *Book I.* The Peloponnesian War is the most significant war in history up to the present and the most important historical event. This conclusion is substantiated by an examination of Greek history prior to this war. After a brief discussion of the Trojan and Persian Wars and the background of the present war—the Spartan League and the Athenian Empire—Thucydides writes of his method as an historian. In reporting speeches, he cannot give the exact words of the speaker but will be as accurate as possible. In general his aim is to be exact and to suggest historical principles through an account and an analysis of contemporary events, so that his work will provide a clue to future events.

The main cause of the Peloponnesian War was Sparta's fear of the enormous power of Athens. One of the immediate causes was the intervention of Athens in the war between Corinth and Corcyra. The second cause was Sparta's aid to Potidaea in its revolt against Athens. Thucydides then describes a meeting of the Peloponnesian League at Corinth and analyzes the chief differences between the Athenian and Spartan temperaments. Then he tells of how an Athenian embassy at Sparta tried and failed to prevent the Spartans from declaring war. He goes back to the fifty years following the Persian Wars and describes the growing power and imperialism of Athens during this period. When the Spartans realized that the Athenians were threatening them, they consulted the oracle of Delphi, who encouraged them to hope for victory in war with Athens. Spurred on by her allies, Sparta prepared for war. Meanwhile, Sparta attempted to cause internal strife in Athens and to turn the Athenians against their leader Pericles. At an Athenian Assembly, Pericles encouraged his people, speaking of the great power of the Athenian navy. He accepted the fact that the Spartans would invade Attica; the Athenians would control the sea. Though Athens did not desire war, Pericles was certain that war was near, and he urged the Athenians to prepare.

Book II. War started in the spring of 431 B.C. The Thebans attacked Plataea, an ally of Athens, to whose aid Athens came. In the conflict between Athens and Sparta, most of the Greek states supported Sparta, regarding her as their liberator from Athenian domination and imperialism. The rather restrained and cautious speech of King Archidamus to the Spartans makes the speech of Pericles to the Athenians seem vigorous and assured, even as he suggested to the country people of Attica that they move inside the city walls. The Spartans attacked Attica, and the Athenians began their naval assault on the Peloponnesus.

A public funeral was held at Athens the next winter for those who died in the first campaign of the war, and Thucydides gives an account of Pericles' funeral address, which has become a well-known statement of the Athenians' conception of their democracy. Pericles spoke of the political, social, and cultural achievements of Athens, extolling its respect for freedom and individuality and its reverence for beauty. In speaking of the great dignity and beauty of Athens, Pericles declared, he was also praising the dead, for their courage and virtue made Athens the noblest of cities. In attempting to comfort the parents and relatives of the dead warriors, Pericles reminded them of the traditional heroic code of conduct: the courage and patriotism of the dead heroes would live forever in their fame.

Next Thucydides deals with the plague that overwhelmed Athens in 430–429 B.C., killing many and demoralizing the Greeks.

The Athenians, discouraged, criticized the policies of Pericles, who regained their confidence, but soon after in 429 B.C. died of the plague.

Book III. Thucydides describes the rebellion of Lesbos against Athens and its defeat by the Athenian forces. The demagogue Cleon proposed to destroy the people of Mitylene in Lesbos, but the Athenians voted to rescind his edict in time to save the Mityleneans. The people of Plataea, however, who were defeated by the Spartans, were not so fortunate. The Spartans destroyed the city and killed all its inhabitants.

Corcyra was torn by internal struggle between the oligarchic and the democratic parties, the Spartans aiding the oligarchs and the Athenians the democrats. Such struggles between opposing factions, siding with the Athenians and the Spartans, took place in many of the Greek city-states.

The rest of the book deals with the campaigns of the sixth year of the war.

Book IV. When the Athenians defeated the Spartans at Sphacteria, an island near Pylos, in 425 B.C., the Spartans sought peace, but they soon realized that the Athenians' demands would be immoderate. Despite additional Athenian conquests, the successes of the great Spartan general, Brasidas, forced the Athenians to agree to a truce with the Spartans for one year (423–422 B.C.) and to return their prisoners.

Book V. In 422 B.C. fighting began again. Both Brasidas and Cleon were killed at Amphipolis. In the tenth year of the war (421 B.C.) Athens and Sparta agreed to make peace and to form a fifty years' alliance. For about seven years neither state invaded the other, but the allies of Sparta objected to the treaty, and in reality there never was peace, because both sides engaged in hostile acts. In both Athens and Sparta the war parties demanded that the war be resumed. The war party that now ruled Athens was ruthless in its imperialistic policy. When an Athenian expedition demanded the submission of the neutral state of Melos and the Melians refused to give in, the Athenians barbarously killed all the men of Melos and sold the women and children as slaves. Thucydides suggests the ruthlessness of the Athenians and the tragic dignity of the doomed Melians in the discussion between the Athenian envoys and the Melian commissioners. (See also Euripides' THE TROJAN WOMEN.)

Book VI. Alcibiades, a handsome and brilliant but arrogant disciple of Socrates, supported the invasion of Sicily by the Athenians. Despite the objections of Nicias, one of the leaders of the peace party, the Athenians voted for the invasion under the leadership of Nicias, Alcibiades, and Lamachus. Just as the Greek forces were about to set sail, many herms, busts of the god Hermes with a phallus set on a pillar, a symbol of fertility, were destroyed throughout Athens. Although Alcibiades was suspected of involvement in this sacrilege, which demoralized the people of Athens, he set forth on the expedition to conquer Sicily. After the Athenians had taken Catania as a base, Alcibiades was summoned to Athens to face trial, but managed to escape to Sparta. When the people of Syracuse appealed to Sparta for aid, Alcibiades persuaded the Spartans to agree. Alcibiades also advised the Spartans to employ Decelia, near Athens, as a fortress. The Athenian general Lamachus was killed in battle, and Nicias, sick and confused, did not prevent the landing of Gylippus, the Spartan leader who came with his forces to aid the people of Syracuse.

Book VII. Nicias wrote to Athens, asking that either the expedition be recalled or new forces be sent. He also asked to be allowed to give up his command because of his illness. The Athenians responded by electing two new generals, Demosthenes and Eurymedon, and sending them with reinforcements to Sicily. After the Athenians were defeated in an attack by night, Demosthenes suggested that the Athenian forces retreat to Greece, but at this point Nicias would not agree. After another Athenian defeat the forces of Syracuse closed up the Great Harbor with ships, thus preventing the Athenians from escaping. When the Athenians decided to try to escape despite this blockade, they were defeated. In desperation they attempted to escape by land, but this last hope was also defeated. After an agonizing struggle Demosthenes and Nicias were captured and executed, and the Athenians that survived were taken prisoner. Most of these died, and a few were sold into slavery.

Book VIII. After the terrible defeat of the Athenian forces in Sicily, the oligarchs seized power and set up the tyrannical Council of Four Hundred, which desired peace with Sparta. This Council was then deposed, and Athens was ruled by five thousand of the richest and most powerful citizens. Alcibiades was allowed to return to Athens. Thucydides' account breaks off in 411 B.C.

Pelops. In Greek mythology, the son of Tantalus. His father cut him up and served him to the gods at a banquet. Only Demeter ate a bit of the shoulder, for the other gods soon realized what Tantalus had done. They restored Pelops and gave him an ivory shoulder to replace the one eaten by Demeter. For an objection to this myth, and for the story of Pelops' victory over Oenomaus, king of Elis, see Pindar's CHORAL LYRICS, *Olympian* I. For the story of how the rule of Mycenae passed from Perseus' line to that of Pelops see MYCENAE. Pelops' murder of Myrtilus, the driver of Oenomaus' chariot, is usually regarded as the origin of the curse on his descendants, Atreus and Thyestes and the family of Atreus' son Agamemnon. According to Cedric Whitman (*Homer and the Heroic Tradition* [Harvard University Press, 1958], p. 36), "Pelops himself is rather a complex figure, combining elements of heroic legend with the myth of death and resurrection."

Penelope (Penelopeia). In the ODYSSEY, the daughter of Icarius and the faithful wife of Odysseus. See HEROIDES I.

Pentheus. In Greek mythology, a king of Thebes. See Euripides' THE BACCHAE. His story is also told in Theocritus' *Idyl* XXVI.

Pericles (Perikles). An Athenian statesman, born around 500 B.C. He came from a distinguished family, and was a cultivated man who was nicknamed the "Olympian" because of the dignity of his presence and speech. Pericles became the political leader of Athens around 461 B.C. and retained this position until his death in 429 B.C. This period is known as the Age of Pericles. According to Thucydides, Pericles wished to make Athens the "educator" of Greece; certainly he envisioned Athens as an ideal democracy and cultural center. Though he made some effort to unify the Greek states, his ambitions for Athens were to some extent responsible for Athens' imperialist policy, which brought her into conflict with the other states and ultimately led to her destruction.

Athens was at war during a large portion of the period of Pericles' leadership. Between 459 and 446 B.C. she waged war against Sparta, Corinth, Aegina, and Boeotia; in 440 B.C. Athens put down the rebellion of the island of Samos; and in 431 B.C. she entered the Peloponnesian War against Sparta and her allies. Pericles died two years after this war had begun. Thucydides' account of Pericles' funeral address in honor of those who had died in the first campaign of the war is generally regarded as a statement of Pericles' idealized conception of Athenian political and cultural life (see THE PELOPONNESIAN WAR I, II).

Despite the constant demands of warfare, Pericles devoted much attention to the cultural life of Athens. The Parthenon and the Propylaea were constructed during the period of his leadership. Plutarch's life of Pericles is interesting for its discussion of his character and his relationship with the learned *hetaera* (courtesan) Aspasia, though Plutarch exaggerates her influence on Pericles, suggesting that it was to please her that Pericles entered the war against the Samians. An interesting novel *Pericles, the Athenian* by Rex Warner appeared in 1963, in which Pericles' life is told by his friend the philosopher ANAXAGORAS.

Peri Hupsous. See LONGINUS ON THE SUBLIME.

Perikeiromene (The Shearing of Glycera, The Girl Who Gets Her Hair Cut Short, The Rape of the Locks, She Who Was Shorn). A New Comedy (possibly c. 302 B.C.) by MENANDER. Translations: in prose, L. A. Post, 1929; in prose and verse, Francis G. Allinson, 1930; in verse, Gilbert Murray, 1942; in prose, Lionel Casson, 1960.

BACKGROUND. The extant fragment of *Perikeiromene* contains less than half the play. At the beginning of the play Polemon comes home from war to find his mistress, Glycera, in the arms of Moschion, her rich young neighbor. Glycera knows that Moschion is mistaken in assuming that Myrrhine, the wealthy woman he lives with, is his mother, for Glycera is aware that Moschion, like her a foundling, is her own twin brother. Neither Moschion nor Polemon knows these facts, however. Polemon, in a jealous rage at the sight of Moschion embracing Glycera, cuts off his mistress' hair.

SCENE. Corinth, before the houses of Polemon and Pataecus.

SUMMARY. The goddess Misapprehension appears and tells of how Glycera and her twin brother, Moschion, exposed as infants, were found by a woman who reared the girl herself and gave the boy to the wealthy woman Myrrhine. When Glycera grew to young womanhood, the woman who reared her, having become very poor, entrusted her to the care of Polemon. Before the woman died she told Glycera the story of how she was found and how her twin brother was given to Myrrhine. Glycera kept the secret, because she did not want to threaten the excellent position of Moschion. When Polemon bought the house next door to Myrrhine's, Moschion was attracted by the beauty of Glycera, and the evening before when he saw her at her door he embraced her. Her lover, returning at that moment, was overcome by jealousy and cut off her hair.

Polemon, who is staying in the country, sends his servant Sosias to bring him a cloak. Sosias is aware that Polemon's real purpose in sending him home is to get some information about Glycera. Glycera, upset by the violent behavior of her lover, has decided to send her slave, Doris, to Myrrhine to ask for her help. There is a passage missing here, in which Myrrhine probably agrees to let Glycera come to stay with her. When Davus, Moschion's slave, learns that Glycera will be living with Myrrhine, he rushes off to tell his master the good news, pretending that he persuaded the girl to come there so that Moschion would have an opportunity to court her. When Moschion sends Davus into the house to find out if Glycera is ready to receive him, Myrrhine tells him to go away. Nonetheless, Moschion and Davus go inside. In the meantime, Sosias has come back to find out more about Glycera, and, discovering that she is living next door, concludes that she has gone to her lover, Moschion.

Polemon comes in with many friends, among them an elderly man, Pataecus, who has agreed to help Polemon regain Glycera, whom Polemon regards as his wife. As they go into Polemon's house, Moschion, greatly disturbed, leaves his house. Here again a long passage is missing, which probably deals with Moschion's discovery that Glycera does not desire a love affair with him. Possibly he hears something about his real relationship to her. Glycera and Pataecus come out of the house as she explains to the old man that she has no interest in Moschion as a lover. She is very angry at Polemon, who has treated her so badly, and says she will not return to him. Proudly she declares that she is of free birth and sends Doris to bring a casket which contains some embroidered linens that were found with her when she was an infant. As Pataecus looks at the embroidery, he realizes that it belonged to his wife and that Glycera is his daughter. Moschion, who has heard this conversation, now realizes that he is Glycera's brother. Pataecus then tells Glycera that her mother died in bearing the twins, and because he had just lost all his money, he exposed his children.

In another missing passage Moschion probably is reunited with his father and sister. Polemon now deeply regrets his mistreatment of Glycera, for he fears she will never return to him. She forgives him, however, and Pataecus gives her to Polemon as his wife. Pataecus also decides to arrange a marriage for Moschion.

Persa. See THE GIRL FROM PERSIA.

Persai. See THE PERSIANS.

Persephone. In Greek mythology, the daughter of Zeus and Demeter. She was also called *Kore* (the Maiden). One day when Persephone, accompanied by the daughters of Oceanus, was picking flowers in Enna in Sicily, the earth opened and the god Hades appeared in a chariot of gold. He abducted Persephone and took her to the lower world. She became his wife and the queen of the Underworld. The story of the abduction of Persephone is told in HOMERIC HYMN II and in Ovid's *Metamorphoses* v. Demeter, seeking her daughter all over the earth, heard Persephone's cries from the Underworld. Finally Demeter learned that Hades had seized her child. When Demeter, in her wrath over the loss of her daughter, made the earth barren, Zeus ordered Hermes to lead Persephone back to her mother. Hades, however, had tricked Persephone into eating pomegranate seeds, sacred to the lower world; thus she was obliged to return to him for one third of every year. Demeter, generally known as an earth goddess, is considered by some scholars as essentially a corn goddess, and the disappearance of Persephone is regarded as either a symbol of the planting of seeds in the earth or the storage of corn underground after the harvest; her reappearance would then represent the flourishing corn crops. Persephone was sometimes associated with Artemis. The double roles of Demeter and Persephone as earth or agricultural goddesses and as goddesses associated with immortality is discussed under ELEUSINIAN MYSTERIES.

Perseus. In Greek mythology, the son of Zeus and Danaë. For Perseus' birth see ACRISIUS. Ovid tells of his heroic accomplishments in *Metamorphoses* IV and v. One of Perseus' greatest feats was killing Medusa, one of the Gorgons, and gaining possession of her head, which had the power of turning to stone anyone who looked directly at it. In performing this heroic deed Perseus was aided by the gods.

After he had captured Medusa's head, it became his most powerful weapon. With its aid he turned Atlas into a mountain and saved the maiden Andromeda by transforming a sea monster into a rock. After turning Phineus, another of her suitors, into stone, he married Andromeda. Perseus rescued his mother from the tyrant Polydectes of Seriphos and petrified him. Accidentally Perseus slew his grandfather Acrisius. According to one version of his story the remorseful Perseus refused to accept the kingship of Argos and spent his last days in Asia, where his son Perses became king of the Persians. Another view is that Perseus exchanged the kingship of Argos for that of Tiryns and founded MYCENAE, which passed, according to the *Bibliotheca*, from Perseus' line to that of Pelops.

Persian, The. See THE GIRL FROM PERSIA.

Persians, The (Persai). A tragedy (472 B.C.) by AESCHYLUS. Translations: in verse, Robert Potter, 1777; in verse, E. D. A. Morshead, 1908; in prose, Walter and C. E. S. Headlam, 1909; in prose, H. Weir Smyth, 1922; in verse, G. M. Cookson, 1922; in verse, S. G. Benardete, 1956; in verse, Philip Vellacott, 1961.

BACKGROUND. *The Persians* is the only surviving Greek tragedy based upon historical material, the war of the Greeks and the Persians (492–479 B.C.). This play deals with the Greek victory at Salamis (480 B.C.), when Xerxes, the son of Darius, was defeated by the Greek forces.

SCENE. Susa, the capital of the Persian Empire, before the council hall of the Persian kings. The tomb of Darius is in the background.

SUMMARY. The Persian Elders, who have remained at home to guard the kingdom while the young men have gone off to war against the Greeks, are tortured by fears that the Persians will be defeated. The Elders describe the magnificent Persian warriors who, led by Xerxes, left their homeland in the hope of conquering the Greeks. The Persians have never been surpassed in warfare, yet the gods may be plotting disaster for these heroes, while their wives and mothers wait fearfully for their return. As Atossa, the mother of Xerxes, enters with her retinue, the Chorus greets her humbly. Atossa tells the Elders she has had a frightening dream, which seems to prophesy the defeat of Xerxes. When she arose in the morning, she went to make offerings to the gods to prevent disaster, but then she saw an omen, an eagle attacked by a hawk, which again terrified her. The Elders try to comfort Atossa. They ask her to pray to the shade of Darius for help. Atossa questions the Chorus about Athens—where it is and what sort of nation it is. The Chorus informs her of Athens' great strength and its democratic institutions.

A Messenger enters and announces that in a naval battle at Salamis the Persian forces have been defeated by the Athenians. The Chorus cries out in despair as the Messenger describes the Persian heroes dead on the shores of Salamis. Atossa questions the Messenger, who tells her that Xerxes is still alive, though many great heroes have been killed. When the Messenger remarks that the Greeks won despite the superior forces of the Persians, which greatly outnumbered those of the Greeks, Atossa says the gods take care of the city of Athene. In answer to Atossa's questions the Messenger recounts the dreadful details of the battle which was so disastrous to the Persians. Even many of those who managed to escape in flight from the Athenians died of hunger and thirst on their way home. When Atossa hears this painful account, she remembers her prophetic dream. In the hope of learning about the future she goes to pray to the gods and to the dead.

The Chorus sings to Zeus, who has brought so much sorrow upon its nation. The Elders describe the weeping and suffering of the women of Susa, whose men have been killed in war. The proud land of Persia has been humbled. Atossa returns and asks the Chorus to help her to call forth the shade of Darius from his tomb. As the Chorus chants, invoking the shade of their former king, Atossa pours libations to the gods of the Underworld. The Ghost of Darius comes from the tomb and asks the Elders what misfortune afflicts the state. When Atossa tells him of the defeat of the Persians by the Athenians, the Ghost of Darius realizes that the prophecy of the oracle that Zeus would punish the proud Xerxes has been fulfilled all too quickly. Xerxes has been the victim of his own rashness. When man is arrogant and rash, says the Ghost, the gods intensify his folly and aid in his destruction. Xerxes, in the pride and folly of youth, has hastened the fulfillment of the oracle. Atossa tries to defend her son, saying he was influenced by men who spoke of the great deeds of his father, Darius. The Ghost of Darius recounts the noble accomplishments of past kings of Persia; now Xerxes has destroyed the glorious state. The Ghost warns the Elders that the Persians must never again attack Greece. He goes on to explain that because the Persian warriors impiously profaned the statues, shrines, and temples of the Greek gods, they will be punished and very few of them will return home. Moreover, the Persians will again be defeated by the Greeks at Plataea (in 479 B.C.). The graves of the Persian dead will warn posterity that pride destroys man. The Ghost then tells Atossa to greet and comfort their son Xerxes. After bidding farewell to the Elders the Ghost of Darius disappears into the tomb. Atossa goes out as the Chorus begins to sing of the fall of Darius' mighty empire.

Xerxes in torn clothing enters with a few followers. He inveighs against Fortune, which has brought destruction to the Persian race and wishes he had died with the many heroes who fell in battle. The Chorus and Xerxes lament for the dead heroes, the youthful promise of the land. Xerxes blames himself for the ruin of his nation as he describes the deaths of the Persian leaders. He has rent his clothing in his grief, and he tells the Elders to weep as he weeps, to respond to his sorrow by beating their breasts, groaning, and tearing their clothing as they lead him to his palace.

COMMENTARY. On one level *The Persians* exalts the democratic institutions and the great power of Athens, which defeated a mighty nation attempting to enslave it. On a second level the play reveals the pain of a defeated people, the Persians, who might be any nation that has been conquered. Perhaps the play's most significant suggestion of the dignity of the Athenian citizen is Aeschylus' compassionate portrayal of the enemy of his people. He does not gloat over the defeated Persians; he suggests that they are the sad victims of their own arrogance, a flaw to which all human beings are subject.

Persian Wars, The. A history (second half of the fifth century B.C.) by HERODOTUS. Translations: George Rawlinson, 1858; A. D. Godley, 1920–24; Aubrey de Selincourt, 1962; Harry Carter (revised), 1962.

SUMMARY. *Book I.* Herodotus begins by stating his purpose: to keep alive the story of the great deeds of the past and more specifically the causes and heroic actions of the wars between the Greeks and the Persians. According to the accounts given by informed Persians, the beginnings of hostility between Greeks and Asians can be traced to the abduction of women, the first being the abduction by the Phoenicians of a group of Greek women, among them Io, daughter of Inachus, king of Argos. Retaliation by the Greeks finally resulted in the Trojan War, which was regarded by Easterners as an attack on all the East.

In recent history the first to commit hostile acts against the Greeks was Croesus, king of Lydia (560–546 B.C.), who conquered Greek cities of Asia

Minor. This conquest by Croesus marked the first loss of freedom by the Greeks. Herodotus then digresses to tell of how the family of Croesus, beginning with his ancestor Gyges, became the rulers of Lydia and how Croesus' father Alyattes extended the Lydian Empire. When Croesus became king of Lydia, he conquered the Greek cities of Asia Minor. Many great men came to visit Croesus, among them Solon, the Athenian poet and legislator [impossible because of chronology]. Having decided to make war on the growing Persian Empire, Croesus consulted the oracles and put his faith in the pronouncement from Delphi, which declared ambiguously that if Croesus attacked Persia, he would bring about the destruction of a mighty empire. In preparing for war Croesus sought the allegiance of the Greek states. There is now a digression, giving the origins and history of Athens and Sparta and a discussion of the tyranny of Pisistratus of Athens, who managed through shrewdness and deceit to return as tyrant after having twice lost his sovereignty.

Herodotus returns to Croesus' attack on the Persians, who were led by Cyrus. After crossing the Halys River, Croesus attacked Pteria, but Cyrus soon arrived with an army, and in the ensuing battle many were slain on both sides, and neither side was victorious. Cyrus then laid siege to Sardis, Croesus' capital city. He conquered the city and captured Croesus, who was saved from being burned to death by the intervention of Apollo. When Croesus scolded the oracle for misleading him, the oracle replied that he was paying for the misdeeds of his ancestor Gyges. Furthermore, Croesus' own responsibility was clear since he misinterpreted the oracular prophecy, which said that he would bring about the destruction of an empire.

Another digression follows on the mores of the Lydians. Herodotus then writes of the Medes and tells of Cyrus, who defeated his own grandfather Astyages, king of Media, and brought the Medes under the control of the Persians. Herodotus describes various social, political, and religious customs of the Persians and tells of the development of the Persian Empire. He describes Cyrus' defeat of Assyria and speaks of its capital, Babylon, which Cyrus took. Finally, when Cyrus attacked the Massagetae, he was overcome and killed by their queen Tomyris.

Book II. After the death of Cyrus his son Cambyses became king of Persia. Herodotus tells of Cambyses' attack on Egypt and then speaks of Egyptian geography, history, and social, political, and religious customs.

Book III. Herodotus recounts Cambyses' other expeditions and describes his madness and his death (522 B.C.). Darius through trickery became the king of Persia. Darius' empire is described, and the wealth of his vast possessions is recounted. During Darius' reign the Babylonians revolted; Zopyrus, a Persian of noble rank, cut off his nose and ears in order to deceive the Babylonians and help the Persians to retake the city.

Book IV. Darius led an attack on Scythia (512 B.C.). The geography and the religious, social, and military customs of Scythia are described. Darius led another attack against Cyrene and Libya, and the geography and customs of these places are discussed.

Book V. The Persian defeat of Thrace is described. The Persians then negotiated with Macedonia. The Ionians rebelled against Persian rule (499 B.C.). There is another digression on Athens and Sparta at this point. The Athenians and the Eretrians helped the Ionians in their rebellion, and assisted them in burning Sardis, but Persia managed to put down the rebellion.

Book VI. The rebellion of the Ionians is concluded with the destruction of their city, Miletus (494 B.C.). There is a digression telling of how Miltiades, the Elder, ruled the Chersonese. The younger Miltiades returned to Athens when the Persian army was victorious in Ionia. In 492 B.C. Mardonius, the son-in-law of Darius, set out to invade Eretria and Athens because they had helped the rebellious Ionians. Mardonius succeeded in conquering Thasos and Macedonia, but his entire fleet was then destroyed in a storm, and he had to give up his expedition. When Darius required that the Greek cities give him earth and water, symbols of submission, many cities complied, despite objections from Athens and Sparta. A digression follows on Spartan history and political and social customs. The war of Athens against Aegina is described.

The Persian army took Naxos, the Cyclades Islands, Carystus, and Eretria, but it was defeated at Marathon by the Athenians and the Plataeans (490 B.C.). Though the Athenians were aided by the Plataeans at Marathon, their forces were much smaller than those of the Persians. Miltiades persuaded them to fight, and under his leadership they conquered the Persians, who returned to Asia. The two thousand Spartans who arrived too late to aid their allies returned home. The great hero of Marathon, Miltiades, was unsuccessful in his attack on Paros. He was fined and soon died of wounds he received in battle.

Book VII. While he was preparing for further campaigns against the Greeks, Darius died (486 B.C.), and his son Xerxes came to the throne. Before taking up the attack on the Greeks, Xerxes had to put down a rebellion in Egypt. He then met with his advisors to discuss a new campaign against the Greeks. His cousin Mardonius, who longed for glory, urged Xerxes to fight, but his uncle Artabanus, fearing the destruction of the Persians, warned Xerxes not to take this advice. Angrily Xerxes called his uncle a coward and, encouraged by a dream which both he and Artabanus had, decided to resume the war on the Greeks.

Extensive preparations for the war were made; the Persians built a bridge over the Hellespont and dug a canal through Mount Athos; Xerxes had the greatest army ever assembled. Finally they set out for Greece. Though some of the Greek cities sent symbols of surrender, many realized that the Persian invasion was aimed at all of Greece. It was Athens who led the Greek states in defending their freedom. The Athenian leader Themistocles advised the Athenians to build up their navy and defend themselves at sea. In 481 B.C.

there was an alliance of those Greek states that were determined to resist the Persian attack. Their embassies seeking unity with other Greek states were unsuccessful. The Persians conquered Thessaly, and later on in the war the Thessalians willingly aided their conquerors.

The Greeks then decided to guard the Pass of Thermopylae and to place their fleet off Artemisium, which was nearby; thus the army and the fleet would be able to communicate. The attacking Persian army greatly outnumbered the few thousand Greeks who, led by King Leonidas of Sparta, defended the pass. When the onslaught of the Persians became most severe, many of the allies managed to escape to their homes, but the Thespians and the Thebans stayed with the Spartans at Thermopylae, and all were killed by the Persians (480 B.C.). Their great courage was celebrated in various inscriptions on monuments. Among these was the famous epitaph that Simonides wrote for the Spartans: "Go, stranger, and tell them in Lacedaemon that we lie here obedient to their orders." When Xerxes discovered the corpse of Leonidas, he commanded that the head be cut off and the trunk nailed to a cross.

Book VIII. At Artemisium the Greek fleet decided to retreat toward the south, and the Persian fleet followed. The Greek fleet was stationed in the Bay of Salamis. Meanwhile the Persians destroyed Attica, occupied Athens and left the Acropolis in ruins. The Persian fleet, stationed at Phalerum, prepared for battle with the Athenian fleet. At the Battle of Salamis (480 B.C.) the Greeks, led by the Athenians and the Aeginetans, defeated the Persians. Those that remained retreated to Sardis. The Greeks offered thanksgiving for their victory at Salamis and celebrated the glory of Themistocles, who led them.

A Persian general, Artabazus, seized Olynthus, but was defeated in his attack on Potidaea in the Chalcidice. Mardonius attempted to persuade the Athenians to ally themselves with the Persians and sent Alexander of Macedon as his spokesman to Athens, but the Athenians would not consider his suggestion.

Book IX. Mardonius then led his army from Thessaly to Attica. When Athens received help from Sparta, however, Mardonius drew back to Boeotia. The Greek and Persian armies fought at Plataea, where the Greeks won a great victory (479 B.C.). The Greek fleet was also victorious against the Persians at Mycale (479 B.C.), and at the close of that year the Athenians attacked and conquered Sestus, the strongest fortress in the whole region of the Chersonese.

Persius (Aulus Persius Flaccus). A Roman satirist, born at Volaterrae (Volterra) in Etruria in A.D. 34. His family was prominent and wealthy, and he received an excellent education both at Volaterrae and later at Rome, where he studied with the well-known rhetorician Verginius. Flavus. At sixteen Persius entered the school of the Stoic philosopher L. Annaeus Cornutus, who became his lifelong friend and exerted a strong influence on him. The poet Lucan was his fellow student. Persius expresses his admiration and affection for his teacher in the fifth of his SATIRES. Most of Persius' brief life was devoted to study and writing. He was deeply attached to his mother and sister and had many friends among the Stoics. When he died in A.D. 62 he left behind only some poems written in his youth and his six extant satires. Cornutus, to whom Persius left his library and his literary remains, destroyed the early poems and asked Persius' friend, the poet Caesius Bassus, to edit the satires.

As a satirist Persius has neither the charm of Horace nor the passion of Juvenal. A scholarly poet, he speaks not to the men of the Forum or the world beyond it, but to a few private persons who are sympathetic to his tastes and his rather limited view of life, which is based on strict Stoic morality. His allusions are literary, his subjects mainly philosophical. Even in his first satire, which begins, as Juvenal's does, with an attack on current literature, Persius expresses disapproval indirectly, alluding to Horace, Lucilius, and Vergil. Though he mentions the connection, so significant in Juvenal, between the decadence in literature and the corruption in society, he hardly develops the idea. Furthermore, he severely attacks the most harmless creatures, the grandmother or aunt uttering foolish prayers over a baby or the farmer praying that he may discover a treasure (*Satire* II). Even when his criticisms seem justifiable, Persius' language and tone give his satires the quality of literary exercises; they lack the excitement and intensity of feeling that make Juvenal's criticisms of man and society great poems. Although Persius uses dialogue, the language of his poetry seldom gives the effect of speech. His obscure allusions and rather stilted phrasing make his style difficult and at times harsh. Despite these shortcomings, however, Persius is not an uninteresting poet. He is often witty and clever, and in a brief space he gives a good picture of the decadence of literature in a society that placed a higher value on ostentation and trickery than on sincerity and honest workmanship. See also SATIRE.

Pervigilium Veneris (The Vigil of Venus). A Latin poem in trochaic tetrameter, the author and date of which are unknown. Judging by its style, most authorities consider the *Pervigilium Veneris* a work of the third or fourth century A.D. The poem, which was written for a spring festival in honor of Venus Genetrix, gracefully and vividly suggests the reawakening of nature and the experience of love. An excellent translation has been made by the poet Allen Tate.

Petronius Arbiter, Gaius. A Roman statesman and writer, lived during the first century A.D. He was a consul during the reign of Nero and for a time a favorite of the Emperor, who regarded him as his *arbiter elegantiae* (judge of good taste). Tacitus' description of Petronius in *Annals* XVI is of an elegant man of exquisite taste, somewhat overrefined and jaded, but not without talent or a sense of decorum. Tacitus also tells how the lies of the schemer Tigellinus made Nero suspect Petronius of intrigue. When in A.D. 65 Petronius received the Emperor's order that he remain at Cumae, a sign that he must expect a death sentence, he decided to take his own life by opening his veins. Petronius is usually regarded as the author of the fragmentary Latin novel THE SATYRICON, though there is no conclusive evidence to establish his authorship.

Phaeacians (Phaiakes). See ODYSSEY VI–VIII, XIII.

Phaedo (Phaidon). A dialogue by PLATO.

S C E N E . The account is given in Phlius in the Peloponnesus; the events take place in the prison of Socrates.

S U M M A R Y . Socrates discusses death with Phaedo, the narrator, and other friends who have gathered in his prison on the day he is to die. According to Socrates, the philosopher is willing to face death, but he will not commit suicide, for it is unlawful. Men belong to the gods and therefore must wait for death until the gods summon them. For the true philosopher death represents a release from the body; therefore the philosopher pursues death all of his life. Death frees the soul from the body and allows it to devote itself entirely to the pursuit of absolute wisdom and truth.

Since all that Socrates has said presupposes the immortality of the soul, Cebes, a disciple, asks him to prove that the soul continues to live after the death of the body. Socrates then offers a series of proofs of the immortality of the soul. One of these is based on the ancient theory of reincarnation, which assumes that the soul lives after death. Because all things are generated out of their opposites, the living must spring from the dead, and the soul must continue to live after the body dies. Another proof is based on the assumption that knowledge results from recollection; such recollection would not be possible unless the soul had an existence previous to the one in the body. In its previous existence the soul had knowledge of absolute qualities (Theory of Ideas) or essences; hence man realizes that the objects he sees are mere approximations of perfect forms. This realization is another indication of the soul's previous existence independent of the body.

Another proof rests on the very nature of the soul itself. The soul, which is invisible, returns to the realm of absolute ideas and, like them, becomes immortal and immutable. Some souls have been corrupted by their association with the concerns of the body, and have difficulty leaving the visible world after the body dies. If a man has lived the virtuous life of a philosopher, however, his soul will readily leave the body and join the gods.

After answering various objections to his proofs Socrates returns to the Theory of Ideas, which he explains in some detail as evidence of the immortality of the soul. He concludes by showing that because the idea of death and the idea of the soul exclude each other, the intrinsic nature of the soul excludes the possibility that it will die. As the odd number cannot participate in the nature of the even one, the immortal soul cannot partake of death.

Cebes is now convinced by Socrates' proofs, but Simmias, another disciple, points out that Socrates' whole argument depends on an acceptance of the Theory of Ideas. Socrates then goes on to speak of the life after death and insists that man's chief concern while alive should be the pursuit of wisdom and virtue, so that when he dies his soul will join the gods.

After this speech Socrates bathes and prepares for death. He says farewell to the members of his family and calmly drinks the poison. When his friends weep, Socrates scolds them. His last words are to his friend Crito, asking him to pay a debt to the god Asclepius.

Phaedra (Phaidra). See Euripides' HIPPOLYTUS, Ovid's HEROIDES IV, and Seneca's PHAEDRA.

Phaedra. A tragedy by SENECA probably based on a lost first version of Euripides' HIPPOLYTUS, as well as on the extant play. Seneca's *Phaedra* differs from Euripides' *Hippolytus* in many respects: in Seneca's play Phaedra herself tells Hippolytus of her love for him; she falsely declares to Theseus that Hippolytus has tried to ravish her and admits her crime only after the dead body of Hippolytus is brought in. Seneca's most important character is the passionate and tortured Phaedra.

Phaedrus (Phaidros). A dialogue by PLATO. Socrates and Phaedrus sit under a plane tree by the Ilissus and discuss rhetoric. Through a series of speeches on love, Socrates points out the differences between the usual rhetoric, the aim of which is to deceive, and true rhetoric, founded on truth and logic. In this dialogue Socrates speaks of the two kinds of madness: the one which is mere insanity and therefore an evil and the other, which is a divine gift, the madness of prophets and poets. Only he who is inspired with the divine madness of the Muses can be truly regarded as a poet. Moreover, the madness of love is a gift of the gods. Then, turning to a discussion of the soul, Socrates uses the famous simile of the soul as the charioteer driving two horses, one of which is ignoble (sensual) and the other noble (spiritual). The soul, held back by the ignoble steed, longs to reach heaven, where pure essences exist. The Theory of Ideas is then elaborated. Divine madness allows a man to comprehend absolute being, pure essence.

Phaethon. In Greek mythology, the son of Helios and Clymene. In *Metamorphoses* I and II, Ovid tells of how Phaethon, in order to prove that he was descended from Helios, went to see his father, who promised to give him any gift he desired. When Phaethon asked for the right to drive the chariot of the sun for one day, Helios reluctantly kept his promise, but Phaethon was unable to control the horses of Helios. They broke from their course, and the earth began to blaze with fire. Zeus sent a bolt of lightning to destroy Phaethon, who fell into the River Eridanus. Phaethon's sisters mourned him as though their only function in life was to weep, and finally they were transformed into poplars and their tears became amber.

Phalaris. A tyrant of Acragas (Latin Agrigentum, modern Agrigento) in Sicily (sixth century B.C.) notorious for his inhuman cruelty. *Epistles* attributed to Phalaris were revealed by the scholar Richard Bentley to be spurious (*Dissertation Upon the Epistles of Phalaris*, 1699).

Pharsalia. See ON THE CIVIL WAR.

Pheres. The father of Admetus. See Euripides' ALCESTIS.

Philebus (Philebos). A dialogue by PLATO that considers the nature of the good and its connection with pleasure and wisdom.

Philip of Macedon. A king of Macedon and father of Alexander the Great. Philip II, the younger son of Amyntas, king of Macedon (390–369 B.C.), was born in 382 B.C. When his older brother died in 359 B.C., Philip became regent for his young nephew Amyntas, but in a short time he took the title King of Macedon. Determined to conquer the Greek city-states on the coast of Macedon, Philip reorganized and improved the Macedonian army. He soon conquered the cities of Amphipolis, Pydna, Potidaea, Methone, and Olynthus. DEMOSTHENES warned the Athenians against the danger they faced from Philip's advances in his conquest of Greece. See ATHENS.

Philoctetes (Philoktetes). Greek warrior, the son of Poias. He is mentioned by Homer as left on the island of Lemnos nursing his terrible wound. He is the hero of Sophocles' PHILOCTETES, and he appears in Seneca's *Hercules Oetaeus*, where he lights the pyre of Heracles and is given Heracles' great bow and the arrows that never miss their mark.

Philoctetes (Philoktetes). A tragedy (409 B.C.) by SOPHOCLES. Translations: in verse, Thomas Francklin, 1759; in prose, R. C. Jebb, 1904; in verse, F. Storr, 1912; in verse, David Grene, 1957.

MYTHICAL BACKGROUND. Philoctetes obeyed Heracles' command that he light the pyre on Mount Oeta, on which Heracles was burned alive. As a reward Philoctetes received Heracles' fabulous bow and his arrows, tipped with poison, which never missed their mark. Philoctetes joined the Greek leaders who set sail to fight against Troy. On their way they stopped at an island near Lemnos, where Philoctetes was bitten by a serpent sacred to the goddess Chryse. The wound which resulted would not heal. When the Greeks were disturbed by the smell of Philoctetes' suppurating wound and his cries of anguish, Odysseus advised them to abandon him in Lemnos, an uninhabited island. There he remained, alone except for an occasional brief encounter with a passing voyager, for ten years. In the last year of the Trojan War, the Greeks received a prophecy that Troy could not be taken without the aid of Philoctetes and the famous bow and arrows of Heracles. Odysseus, accompanied by Neoptolemus, the young son of the dead Achilles, set out for Lemnos to use any means to bring Philoctetes and the bow to Troy.

SCENE. The desert island of Lemnos.

SUMMARY. As Odysseus and Neoptolemus approach the cave that is Philoctetes' home on the island of Lemnos, Odysseus speaks of the day, ten years ago, when he left the wounded hero there. Philoctetes is not in his cave. Neoptolemus, who has looked inside, describes the leaves heaped up on the floor for a bed and the rough cup made of wood. Then he sees rags stained with the discharge of Philoctetes' wound spread out to dry in the sun. Odysseus tells Neoptolemus he must trick Philoctetes into coming to Troy, because Philoctetes hates the Greeks who abandoned him and would never go with them willingly. Neoptolemus must pretend that he has quarreled with the Greek leaders, who have given Achilles' arms to Odysseus rather than to him, and that he is on his way home to Scyros. If he does not pretend to hate Odysseus, he will never gain the confidence of Philoctetes. Like his father, Achilles, Neoptolemus detests deceit; he suggests to Odysseus that they enlist the aid of Philoctetes by persuasion rather than by trickery. Odysseus, however, cares only for success, whatever the means, and he finally persuades the reluctant Neoptolemus to accept his plan.

In a lyrical dialogue the Chorus of Sailors and Neoptolemus speak of the means they will use to capture Philoctetes. The Sailors pity Philoctetes as they imagine his painful and lonely existence. Soon they hear a labored footstep and a cry of distress, the sounds of Philoctetes approaching. As soon as Philoctetes sees Neoptolemus and the Sailors, he guesses that they are Greeks and begs them not to avoid him because of his disgusting appearance. Neoptolemus introduces himself as the son of Achilles and pretends that he knows nothing about Philoctetes, not even his name. Shocked to hear that his plight and his suffering are unknown to the Greeks, Philoctetes tells his tragic story of pain and abandonment and of the long years of loneliness. Bitterly he says he owes his wretched condition to Agamemnon, Menelaus, and Odysseus, and begs the gods to avenge the crimes against him. Neoptolemus expresses his sympathy for Philoctetes, pretending that he too has been badly treated by the Greek leaders, who, he says, gave his father's arms to Odysseus. When Neoptolemus says that he plans to sail home to Scyros, Philoctetes asks the young man to take him back to Greece, either to Scyros or to Euboea, which is not far from his home on Oeta. Neoptolemus and the Chorus agree to do as he asks. Now that Philoctetes thinks he is about to be released from his wretched life, he speaks proudly of his powers of endurance during the past ten years.

Two Sailors sent by Odysseus enter, one in the disguise of a merchant, who pretends his purpose is to warn Neoptolemus that some of the Greek leaders are coming to force Neoptolemus and Philoctetes to accompany them to Troy. The Sailor tells of the prophecy uttered by the captured Trojan seer, Helenus, that Troy cannot be taken unless Philoctetes is persuaded to rejoin the Greek forces. Odysseus hopes that Philoctetes will come to Troy willingly but, if he refuses, he will take him by force. Philoctetes declares he will never willingly go to Troy. He urges Neoptolemus to prepare to sail for Greece. As they discuss their preparations for departure, Neoptolemus asks Philoctetes to let him hold and examine the miraculous bow. Philoctetes gives it to him, and the two enter the cave.

The Chorus speaks of the suffering of Philoctetes, describes the dreadful pain he endures when he experiences one of the periodic attacks caused by his festering wound, and hopes he will finally find peace when he returns to his home. Just at this point Philoctetes cries out in agonizing pain. One of his attacks is coming on. The pain is so intense that he begs Neoptolemus to cut off his foot. Finally, after a second attack, the pain subsides and Philoctetes, who now must sleep for a while, asks Neoptolemus to guard his bow while he rests. The Chorus considers this a good time for Neoptolemus to leave Philoctetes and escape with the bow, but the young man refuses to do so. Soon Philoctetes awakes, happy to see that Neoptolemus has not deserted him. Neoptolemus begins to express his conflicting feelings, hidden by his attempt at deception. He realizes that in employing lies and trickery he has been untrue to his own nature, and he reveals to Philoctetes the plot to take him to Troy. Philoctetes, violently angry at the young man he has trusted, begs him to return his bow, without which he cannot live. Neoptolemus does not know what to do; he pities Philoctetes, yet he feels obliged to keep his word to the Greek leaders. At this point Odysseus enters and demands that Neoptolemus give him the bow. He says he will force Philoctetes to come to Troy if he cannot persuade him to fight as a free warrior. Philoctetes, who cannot forgive the wrongs of the Greeks, declares he will kill himself rather than aid those who deserted him. Odysseus scornfully tells Philoctetes he may remain in Lemnos forever, and declares that he will employ Philoctetes' bow to win glory. As Philoctetes pleads with Neoptolemus for help, Odysseus and Neoptolemus leave him, taking the bow.

In despair Philoctetes addresses his cave, the place associated with his pain and his loneliness, saying he will now remain there till he dies. The Chorus wisely tells him that he must not blame the gods or fate for his present suffering; he has made his own choice, preferring pain and loneliness to a new opportunity for heroic fulfillment among the Greeks. Soon Neoptolemus returns with Odysseus following him and demanding to know why the young man has come back to Philoctetes. Neoptolemus has returned to atone for his deceit and to restore the bow to Philoctetes. Odysseus leaves, threatening to return with armed men. As Neoptolemus is returning the bow to Philoctetes, Odysseus reappears. Philoctetes is about to kill him, but is prevented by Neoptolemus, and Odysseus is allowed to leave.

Neoptolemus patiently tries to persuade Philoctetes that it is in his own self-interest to accompany the Greeks to Troy, where his wound will be healed and he will accomplish heroic deeds. Gently and wisely Neoptolemus points out that a man must endure the sufferings the gods send him, but Philoctetes clings to his pain, torturing himself. He is unwilling to accept the promise of a cure and of great fame as a warrior. When Neoptolemus sees that Philoctetes cannot be persuaded, he agrees to take him to his home. As they are about to leave Lemnos, Heracles appears. No doubt representing the heroic nature of Philoctetes, he orders him to go to Troy. There with his mighty bow, Philoctetes will kill Paris and help to bring about the destruction of the city. Philoctetes responds happily, saying this is the voice he has longed to hear, and he promises to obey Heracles' command. He takes a last look at Lemnos and bids farewell tenderly to the place where he endured so much suffering, for he is saying good-bye to a part of himself.

COMMENTARY. Most critics of Sophocles' *Philoctetes* regard the central problem of the play as a conflict between the individual and the demands of society. Edmund Wilson in a well-known essay "The Wound and the Bow" (in *The Wound and the Bow: Seven Studies in Literature* [Oxford University Press, 1947], pp. 272–295) interprets the two chief symbols of the play as the artist's frailty and his power, in order to develop the thesis that society is obliged to accept the artist's disability if it desires his talent. The essay, while inspired by the *Philoctetes* and extremely interesting in itself, is actually not an interpretation of the play. Philoctetes' conflict is as much an inner one as an external one. Before he can make peace with his society, the Greeks fighting against Troy, Philoctetes must make peace with himself. He must resolve the conflict between his longing to retreat into the desert island of loneliness and despair, which Lemnos symbolizes, and his need to escape from this preoccupation with himself and reenter the world, despite the fact that it contains and sometimes even approves of the cruelty of an Odysseus or the Atridae. In agreeing to be healed of his wound and to use the bow to achieve glory, Philoctetes at once fulfills the demands of Heracles, actually those of his own heroic nature, and the requirements of his society.

Philomela. In Greek mythology, a daughter of Pandion, a king of Athens, and the sister of Procne. Procne's husband Tereus, the king of Thrace, became infatuated with Philomela. He raped the young girl and cut out her tongue so that she could not report his crime. Philomela wove a tapestry telling her story and showed it to her sister, who avenged Tereus' crime by murdering her own son Itys and serving him in a meal to her husband. When Tereus tried to kill Philomela and Procne, he was transformed into a hoopoe, Philomela into a nightingale (or a swallow), and Procne into a swallow (or a nightingale). Ovid tells this story in *Metamorphoses* VI.

Phineus (I). In Greek mythology, a king of Salmydessus. Phineus was blinded by Zeus, according to one legend, because he allowed his second wife to persuade him to blind the children of his first wife, Cleopatra, daughter of Boreas. Helios ordered the Harpies to seize Phineus' food. Phineus was helped by the Argonauts.

Phineus (II). See PERSEUS.

Phlegethon. A river in Hades.

Phocylides (Phokylides). A Greek poet, born at Miletus who flourished during the middle of the sixth century B.C. He wrote elegiacs and hexameters, mainly didactic. Very little of his work survives.

Phoebe (Phoibe). A Titan, later regarded as the moon and identified with Artemis.

Phoenician Women, The (Phoinissai). A tragedy (c. 409 B.C.) by EURIPIDES.

Translations: in prose, E. P. Coleridge, 1891; in verse, Arthur S. Way, 1912; in verse, Elizabeth Wyckoff, 1958. *Won 2nd place.*

MYTHICAL BACKGROUND. Employing the myth of the House of Oedipus, Euripides changes and adapts it to his own purpose. Whereas in Sophocles' *Oedipus the King* Jocasta kills herself as soon as she discovers she has married and borne children to her son, in *The Phoenician Women* she is alive some time after this discovery. Oedipus, who traditionally dies before the battle between his sons, is alive during this event. Another change in the myth is the addition of the story of Menoeceus, a son of Creon. Euripides manages to include in this play traditional material employed by Sophocles in *Oedipus the King, Oedipus at Colonus,* and *Antigone* and by Aeschylus in *The Seven Against Thebes.* In her opening speech Jocasta summarizes the necessary background.

SCENE. Thebes, before the royal palace.

SUMMARY. Jocasta traces the ancestry of Oedipus back to Cadmus, the founder of the family. From Cadmus and his wife Harmonia sprang Polydorus, the father of Labdacus. Labdacus was the father of Laius, whom Jocasta married. Despite the warning of Apollo to Laius that if he bore a son he would be killed by this offspring, Laius and Jocasta had a child, Oedipus. Mindful of the god's prophecy, Laius exposed his son, but the infant was found by a servant and was reared by Polybus and Merope, the king and queen of Corinth. When he grew up Oedipus suspected that they were not his real parents. On his way to the shrine of Apollo to ask the god who his parents were, he met Laius at a place where three roads meet (in Sophocles' *Oedipus the King* he meets Laius after leaving the shrine of Apollo). There father and son, not knowing each other, quarreled, and Oedipus slew Laius. Oedipus then went to Thebes, solved the riddle of the Sphinx, and unknowingly married his mother, Jocasta. They had two sons, Eteocles and Polyneices, and two daughters, Antigone and Ismene. When Oedipus discovered that he had married his own mother, he blinded himself. His sons kept him hidden inside the palace, hoping that his dreadful past might be forgotten. Oedipus cursed his sons, saying they would divide their heritage with swords. Attempting to escape the curse, Eteocles and Polyneices agreed that they would take turns ruling Thebes, each for a year at a time. For the first year Polyneices went into exile, allowing his brother Eteocles to reign, but when he returned to claim his term on the throne, Eteocles refused to relinquish it and banished his brother. Polyneices went to Argos, married the daughter of King Adrastus and, with the king's help, raised an army, the Seven against Thebes, in order to seize the throne of Thebes by force. Polyneices and his forces are now at the seven gates of Thebes, but Jocasta has persuaded her sons to call a truce and to meet in an attempt to settle their dispute peacefully.

Jocasta ends her speech with a plea to Zeus that her sons be reconciled, and goes into the palace. Antigone and her Old Servant appear on the roof of the palace, from which they can see the Argive army. The Servant points out the seven Argive leaders; Antigone can barely make out the form of her brother Polyneices in the distance. After Antigone and the Servant descend from the roof, the Chorus of Phoenician Women enters, singing of its dedication to Apollo. The women salute Thebes and sing of the impending conflict between the two brother kings.

Polyneices comes in, fearful of what awaits him. He is soon joined by Jocasta, who expresses her love for her sons and her sorrow over the sufferings of her family. Polyneices speaks of his exile and his marriage to the daughter of Adrastus. Then he expresses his desire for the great power that wealth brings. When Eteocles joins Polyneices and Jocasta, she tries to reconcile her sons, but neither of the brothers will give up his ambition for the kingdom and power. Jocasta realizes that ambition is destroying her sons, but neither will listen to her entreaties. Instead they reveal their hatred for each other, threatening each other with death. Eteocles cries out that Polyneices (much strife) is well named and orders him to go. The brothers return to their armies.

After a choral ode dealing with the city of Thebes, its legendary past, and its present conflict, Eteocles returns, soon followed by Creon. Together they plan the defense of the city. Seven champions will defend its seven gates. Eteocles prays that he may meet his brother in combat. If he should be killed, says Eteocles, Creon must marry Antigone to Creon's son, Haemon, and care for Jocasta. He then says he will go to see Tiresias because the seer may be able to prophesy the outcome of the conflict. His last command to Creon is to leave the body of Polyneices unburied if the Argives are defeated.

After Eteocles goes out, the Chorus relates the present hatred and strife between the brothers to the old curse on the family of Oedipus. Tiresias is then led in by his daughter. They are accompanied by Menoeceus, another son of Creon. Tiresias declares that Thebes has long been infected with the shame of the incest of Oedipus, whose sons tried to hide their father's deed, but now are the victims of the family curse. The seer predicts great slaughter in warfare and then warns that Thebes will be ruined unless all members of Oedipus' family depart from the city. Moreover, Menoeceus must be killed as a sacrifice to Thebes. Creon must choose between his love for his city and his son. Tiresias leaves Creon in despair, but, determined to save his son, Creon tells Menoeceus to flee from the land before Tiresias has a chance to make his prophecy known to the Theban leaders. Menoeceus says he will obey his father, but when Creon leaves he reveals to the Chorus his plan to sacrifice himself for Thebes and goes out. The Chorus sadly sings his praises.

A Messenger enters, calling for Jocasta. He bids her to cease lamenting, for, after Menoeceus sacrificed himself, Thebes defended itself nobly against the first attack of the Argives. Polyneices and Eteocles are still living. However, the brothers now plan to meet in a single contest. Jocasta calls Antigone, and together they rush off to try to prevent the brothers from fighting. Creon comes in with attendants carrying the body of Menoeceus. Weeping over his son, Creon says he has come for Jocasta, who must prepare Menoeceus' body for burial. A second Messenger arrives and announces that before Jocasta could stop the combat between her sons, they killed each other. As Polyneices lay dying, he expressed his pity and love for the brother he slew. His last wish was to be buried in Thebes. Overwhelmed with grief, Jocasta took the sword of one of her dead sons and killed herself. She now lies dead, embracing her sons. The battle between the Argives and the Thebans continued until the Thebans defeated the aggressors.

Soon Antigone comes in with attendants carrying the bodies of Jocasta, Polyneices, and Eteocles. Antigone bewails the sorrows of the House of Oedipus and calls to her blind father to come forth. Learning of these newest tragedies, Oedipus laments for his wife and his sons. Then Creon, who has inherited the throne of Thebes from Eteocles, informs Oedipus that he must leave the city. Oedipus declares that fate doomed him even before his birth to a life of pain beyond that endured by any other man. He wonders who will care for him, an old, blind man in exile. Creon insists he cannot allow Oedipus, the polluter of the land, to remain in Thebes. Creon also decrees that Polyneices is not to be buried. Death is the penalty for anyone who attempts to give him the rites of burial.

Antigone insists she will bury Polyneices despite the decree of Creon. She says she will not marry Haemon, but instead will share the exile of Oedipus. Antigone guides her father to the corpses of Jocasta, Polyneices, and Eteocles, and he touches them tenderly. Oedipus then reveals to Antigone a prophecy that he will finally find a haven in Colonus, where he will die. As Oedipus speaks of how he fell from a position of dignity and grandeur as a king esteemed for wisdom and power to his present wretched state, he and Antigone leave Thebes.

Phoenician Women, The (Phoenissae). An incomplete tragedy by SENECA, based on Euripides' THE PHOENICIAN WOMEN. Seneca's play consists of two fragments, which may have been parts of two plays or of a single unfinished play. *Gorboduc*, the first English tragedy, written by Sackville and Norton, was based on this fragmentary work.

Phoenix (Phoinix). See ILIAD IX.

Phormio. A comedy (161 B.C.) by TERENCE. Translations: in prose, John Sargeaunt, 1912; in verse, W. Ritchie, 1927; in verse, F. Perry, 1929; in prose, Barrett H. Clark, with omitted passages added, in George Duckworth, ed., *The Complete Roman Drama*, 1942; in prose, Frank O. Copley, 1958; in prose, Lionel Casson, 1960; in prose, Samuel Lieberman, 1964.

SCENE. Athens, before the houses of Demipho, Chremes, and Dorio.

SUMMARY. *Phormio* is an adaptation of Apollodorus' comedy *The Claimant*. Phaedria, the son of Chremes, fell in love with Pamphila, a music girl, but could not afford to buy her. Phaedria's cousin Antipho, the son of Demipho, met Phanium, a sad young girl whose mother had recently died, and fell in love with her. He longed to marry her, but because she had no dowry, he knew his father, then in Cilicia, would object to the marriage. Phormio, the delightful and ingenious parasite, came to the rescue. He told Antipho of an Athenian law requiring orphans to marry their nearest relatives and promised to take an oath in court swearing that Antipho was the nearest relative of Phanium. In this way Antipho and Phanium were able to marry.

When Demipho comes back to Athens, Antipho runs away. Chremes, who has been in Lemnos, has also returned home. Demipho learns of his son's marriage and decides to break it up. Once again Phormio intervenes. He offers to marry Phanium himself if Demipho will give him thirty *minae*. The angry Demipho refuses to do so, but Chremes agrees to give the parasite the money. When Chremes sees Sophrona, Phanium's nurse, he realizes that Phanium is his own daughter, the child of a mistress he had in Lemnos. Meanwhile, Phormio, having obtained the thirty *minae*, gives the money to Phaedria so he can buy his music girl.

Demipho and Chremes now accept the marriage of Antipho and Phanium, but Chremes, who does not know what has happened to the money he gave Phormio, insists that the parasite return it to him. Phormio pretends that he spent the money, but Demipho and Chremes are unsatisfied with his explanation. When they threaten to punish the parasite, he tells Chremes' wife Nausistrata of her husband's love affair in Lemnos. Nausistrata asks Chremes how he can disapprove of his son's having a mistress when he himself has had two wives, and she invites the resourceful Phormio to dinner.

Phrynichus (Phrynichos). One of the earliest Athenian tragedians, sixth century B.C. He is said to have won his first prize in the dramatic contests in 512 B.C. He is regarded as the first dramatist to introduce female parts (though the roles were taken by male actors). Some of the names of his plays are known: *Alcestis, Antaeus, The Capture of Miletus, Egyptians, The Daughters of Danaus, The Phoenician Women, The Women of Pleuron, Tantalus, Troilus,* but only fragments of them are extant. Phrynichus was admired in his own time and by the generations that followed him.

Picus. An Italian agricultural deity. He was also considered to be the first king of Italy.

Pindar (Pindaros). Born either in 522 or 518 B.C. at Cynoscephalae, a village about half a mile west of Thebes. In his youth he went to Athens, where he studied the technique of the lyric with Agathocles and Apollodorus. (See CORINNA.) At Athens he probably met the playwright Aeschylus.

Pindar was proud of his Theban birth and claimed that he was descended from the Theban aristocrats, the Aegeidae. Certainly his sympathies were with the aristocracy, and much of his poetry was commissioned by noble families of Greece. When Pindar was about twenty years old the aristocratic Thessalian family of the Aleuadae commissioned him to write his first victory ode (*Pythian* x), and thereafter he was successful in his aim: to associate with and praise the high-born and the victorious (*Olympian* i, *Pythian* ii). During the Persian Wars, when the oligarchs of Thebes collaborated with the Persians, Pindar was probably troubled by conflicting feelings of loyalty to Thebes and sympathy and admiration for Athens (*Isthmian* viii).

In 476 B.C. Hiero i, tyrant of Syracuse, invited Pindar to visit Sicily, where he remained for two years. Pindar died either in 442 or 438 B.C., at the age of eighty, in Argos. His work (see CHORAL LYRICS) was much admired both during his lifetime and after his death by Greek, Roman, and English poets and critics.

Pindar used the Dorian dialect as a literary language. Bold and extravagant imagery combined with a grave and exalted tone create the powerful music that since his time has been regarded as "Pindaric." About one fourth of Pindar's work survives, mainly *epinicia*. The other poems, which are fragmentary, include all the major forms of choral lyrics: hymns, paeans, dithyrambs, prosodia (processional songs), maiden songs, dance songs, encomia, and dirges. See BACCHYLIDES and EPINICION.

Pisistratus (Peisistratos). See ATHENS.

Plato (Platon). Born either at Athens or Aegina in 428 B.C. His family was aristocratic, and his uncles Critias and Charmides were leaders of the oligarchs who established the rule of the Thirty, the tyrannical group that ruled Athens in 404–403 B.C. Critias was the leader of the Thirty and was responsible for many of the extreme and tyrannical acts of the oligarchs that aroused the hatred of the Athenians and finally were instrumental in bringing about civil war. Though Plato condemned the extreme repression and cruelty of the Thirty, he was sympathetic to the aristocratic, antidemocratic faction and admired the Spartan form of government.

Plato probably became acquainted with Socrates in 407 B.C., and was his disciple until Socrates was put to death in 399 B.C. In Plato's dialogues Socrates is the spokesman for Plato's point of view. After the death of Socrates, Plato left Athens for Megara, then traveled widely before returning to Athens. By 387 B.C. he had established his school, the ACADEMY, where he taught philosophy. In 368 B.C. Dion, brother-in-law of Dionysius i, ruler of Syracuse, invited Plato, whom he had met when Plato visited Syracuse on his travels, to return in order to train Dionysius ii, who had just succeeded to the throne. The project had to be abandoned when it was interpreted as a means by which Dion could seize power, and Plato left Syracuse and was back at Athens in 366 B.C. A later visit in 362 B.C., for the purpose of teaching Dionysius ii philosophy, was also unfruitful. From this time on Plato remained in Athens, where he died in 347 B.C.

It is thought that all of Plato's written works remain. He wrote mainly in the dialogue form, regarding his writings as a popular expression of his philosophical ideas. Though there is still some question about the dates of Plato's works, agreement as to their order has been reached by scholars on the basis of style, and they have been arranged in three groups. In the first group, the

"Socratic," Socrates is the most important person, dramatically and convincingly exposing the errors of his opponents. The works that belong to this group are APOLOGY (Socrates' speech at his trial, not in dialogue form), CRITO, CHARMIDES, LACHES, EUTHYPHRO, HIPPIAS MINOR, HIPPIAS MAJOR, ION, and LYSIS. In the second group Socrates is also the major speaker, and in these works he is the exponent for some of his own or Plato's basic doctrines, such as the Theory of Ideas. The works included in this group are ALCIBIADES, EUTHYDEMUS, CRATYLUS, GORGIAS, MENO, MENEXENUS, PARMENIDES, PHAEDO, PHAEDRUS, PROTAGORAS, REPUBLIC, SYMPOSIUM, and THEAETETUS. In the third group, the products of Plato's later life, Socrates has a position of lesser importance or does not appear at all. To this group belong CRITIAS, SOPHIST, POLITICUS, TIMAEUS, PHILEBUS, and the LAWS. In antiquity thirteen *Epistles* were attributed to Plato, but modern scholars regard only three, the third, the seventh, and the eighth, as certainly Plato's. These "letters," which were written for publication, have to do with Plato's involvement with the rulers of Syracuse.

The moral doctrines of Plato's philosophy are related to and spring from his idealistic conception of reality. The Theory of Ideas, perhaps his best-known concept, is, simply stated, a belief that the reality perceived by man through his senses is merely a copy or an approximation of an essential *form* of reality, which is not limited by time or space or mutability. The idea or form of reality actually exists, though for most people it can only correspond to an abstraction. Plato's dualism pervades all of life; the forms or ideas of things are the essential reality for him. In order to achieve knowledge of these ideas or forms one must be capable of "pure intellect" or "pure reason," for, as Plato says in the seventh book of the *Republic*, "As being is to becoming, so is pure intellect to opinion." Only through the method of dialectic can pure reason operate, for dialectic is a science that deals with first principles. The fundamental "idea" is the conception of the good. Until a man is capable of understanding the idea of the good, he is not able to apprehend reality. He lives in a world of shadows, perceived only by the senses. Thus comprehension of the good, or virtue, is the means to all knowledge. Morality and metaphysics become one through the Theory of Ideas.

The figure of Socrates, questioning all clichés and stock responses, leads the reader to Plato's conception of reality. One of Plato's greatest achievements is his depiction of this prototype of the philosopher, at once the wisest and humblest of men, whose declaration that "an unexamined life is not worth living for man" expresses the intellectual curiosity and excitement that characterize him. The exactness and purity of Plato's language and his use of the techniques of drama, dialogue, scene, and suspense help to establish the nobility and wisdom of Socrates. Moreover, Plato's brilliant style and his powerful use of myth suggest the poet rather than the philosopher. In his dialogues he often creates a society of men struggling against their own limitations for a glimpse of truth.

The influence of Plato has been so great that any brief discussion of it must be superficial. Platonic thought pervades Christianity and has influenced philosophy and literature for two thousand years. Without understanding the philosophy of Plato it is impossible to read Spenser, Wordsworth, or Shelley. The Neoplatonists and the Cambridge Platonists built on his foundation. Plato has become the chief source of philosophical idealism for Western civilization.

Plautus, Titus Maccus (or **Maccius**). A Roman comic playwright, born about 255 B.C. in Sarsina, a town on the border of Umbria. A child of a poor family, he came to Rome at an early age and worked, possibly as a carpenter, in the theater. He may also have been an actor, and it is said that he worked in a flour mill. Eventually Plautus became known as a playwright and was able to devote himself entirely to his writing. He died in 184 B.C.

Of the one hundred thirty plays attributed to Plautus, some may have been written by imitators. Twenty extant plays and a fragment are generally regarded as the work of Plautus: AMPHITRYON, THE COMEDY OF ASSES (*Asinaria*), THE POT OF GOLD (*Aulularia*), THE TWO BACCHIDES (*Bacchides*), THE CAPTIVES (*Captivi*), CASINA, THE CASKET (*Cistellaria*), CURCULIO, EPIDICUS, THE TWIN MENAECHMI (*Menaechmi*), THE MERCHANT (*Mercator*), THE BRAGGART WARRIOR (*Miles Gloriosus*), THE HAUNTED HOUSE (*Mostellaria*), THE GIRL FROM PERSIA (*Persa*), THE CARTHAGINIAN (*Poenulus*), PSEUDOLUS, ROPE (*Rudens*), STICHUS, THE THREE-PENNY DAY (*Trinummus*), TRUCULENTUS, and the fragmentary VIDULARIA. Very few of these plays can be dated with any certainty.

Plautus' comedies are *palliatae*, that is, adaptations of Greek New Comedy of the fourth and third centuries B.C. Some of Plautus' sources were the works of the Greek playwrights Demophilus, Diphilus, Menander, and Philemon. Most of Plautus' comedies deal with the romantic problems of wealthy young men of Athens. Recognition of lost relatives and discovery of unknown identities are the principal motifs. Despite their stereotyped plots, however, there is great variety of tone and structure in Plautus' plays. Though Plautus retains the characters of Greek comedy, often mocking Greek customs and attitudes, both his interest in the Roman society in which he lived and his unique comic genius assert themselves in his plays. His powers of observation and his understanding of human motivation make it possible for him to invest even his comic type characters with the qualities of real people. In his less interesting plays Plautus is unable to go beyond the mere conventions of New Comedy, and the endless complications of his contrived plots are mechanical and dull. Usually, however, he exploits the humorous possibilities of the complicated plots he adapts, and the absurdity of the events results in exuberant comedy. Furthermore, Plautus uses ridiculous situations to suggest the pathos of human weakness: the silly fantasies of his braggart soldiers and his lecherous old men and the complicated schemes they contrive or in which they are caught can be touching as well as amusing. Large sections of Plautus' plays are written in lyric meters; these passages may have been sung.

The influence of Plautus on English comedy of the Renaissance and the seventeenth century is evident in such plays as the earliest known English comedy *Ralph Roister Doister* by Nicholas Udall, Shakespeare's *Comedy of Errors* and, less obviously, his *The Taming of the Shrew*, Ben Jonson's *The Case Is Altered*, *The Alchemist*, and *Every Man in His Humor*, Thomas Heywood's *The Captives* and *The English Traveller*, and John Dryden's *Amphitryon*. One of Plautus' most delightful plays, *Amphitryon*, has been imitated by Molière, by Rotrou, and, more recently, by Jean Giraudoux in *Amphitryon 38*.

Pleiades. See ORION.

Pliny the Elder (Gaius Plinius Secundus). A Roman writer, born in A.D. 23 at Comum (Como). His family was wealthy and influential, and early in his life Pliny went to Rome, where he studied with Pomponius Secundus, a Roman statesman, an account of whose life Pliny later wrote. After serving in the army for ten years he practiced law at Rome. When Vespasian became emperor of Rome (A.D. 70), Pliny was appointed procurator (agent of the emperor in the provinces) in Gaul, Africa, and Spain. In A.D. 79 Pliny was in charge of a fleet at Misenum when Vesuvius erupted. A man of enormous intellectual curiosity, he went to investigate the cause of the smoke coming from the mountain and was killed by the fumes. The episode was described in a letter from Pliny's nephew Pliny the Younger to Tacitus (VI, 16). Another letter from Pliny the Younger (III, 5) tells of his uncle's continual devotion to his studies and his great love of knowledge, his feeling that no book was so bad that something could not be gained from reading it. The letter also lists his many books: a treatise on the use of a javelin when on horseback; the life of Pomponius Secundus; a history of the wars in Germany in twenty books; *The Students*, a work on oratory in six volumes; a study of linguistics in eight books; a continuation of a history by Aufidius Bassus; and finally the NATURAL HISTORY, in thirty-seven books, Pliny's only surviving work.

The *Natural History*, an encyclopedia finished in A.D. 77, shows its author's enormous range of knowledge of ancient authorities and of the arts and sciences of his own time, but it also reveals his curious inclination to accept wonders as facts. The work is of great interest to the student of ancient society because of what it tells about customs, attitudes, and beliefs of the period. During the Middle Ages and later Pliny was regarded as a scientific authority and was an important influence on European literature of the Renaissance.

Pliny the Younger (Gaius Plinius Caecilius Secundus). The heir and nephew of PLINY THE ELDER, born at Comum (Como) in A.D. 61 or 62. Pliny belonged to a wealthy family and received an excellent education, partly at Rome, where he studied with Quintilian. At eighteen Pliny began to practice law; he was extremely successful in his profession and became one of the outstanding speakers of his time. After holding a number of political posts he was nominated for a consulship by the Emperor Trajan in A.D. 100, and in A.D. 103 he became augur. About A.D. 111 Pliny became governor of Bithynia. Though the exact date of his death is unknown, it is certain that he died before A.D. 114.

Only one of Pliny's orations is extant, the *Panegyricus* to Trajan, delivered when he became consul. Pliny is known for his ten books of *Letters*, which were clearly composed with the expectation that they would be published. The *Letters* were published in groups, possibly arranged by Pliny himself: Books I–II between A.D. 97 and 98, Books III–VI at a later date not known, Books VII–IX between A.D. 108 and 109, and Book x (consisting of Pliny's official correspondence with Trajan) sometime after Pliny's death.

Though Pliny's letters are important for what they reveal of his society, his character, and his interests, they are not personal in quality. Pliny addresses not the particular recipient but the general reader. Even letters to his wife have the quality of public utterances. Among the best known of the *Letters* is one describing the eruption of Vesuvius in which his uncle Pliny the Elder was killed (VI, 16), one to Tacitus telling of Pliny's adventures hunting boar (I, 6), and another to Tacitus dealing with Pliny's plan to found a school at his native Comum so that children would not have to leave home for their education (IV, 13). Other subjects Pliny deals with are his life on his Tuscan estate, his love of nature, public affairs, literature, and personal experiences. The letters of the tenth book written to Trajan from Bithynia contain interesting historical material, especially about Pliny's problems as governor. He writes about legal matters, practical needs, problems relating to the treatment of Christians, and financial questions.

Plotinus (Plotinos). A Greek philosopher, born in Egypt (c. A.D. 205), Plotinus was the founder of the Neoplatonic school of philosophy. From about A.D. 244 he lived and taught in Rome. His writings, the *Enneads* in six books, were edited by Porphyry, one of his disciples.

Plutarch (Ploutarchos). A Greek biographer, born at Chaeronea in Boeotia around A.D. 46. Little is known about his life. He lived in Rome for a while and visited Athens and possibly Alexandria, but returned to Chaeronea, where he was a priest of Delphi. Here he wrote most of his biographies and philosophical works. Plutarch was an extremely learned man, and his broad knowledge of literature and philosophy is reflected in his work. In the later years of his life he held various public positions in Chaeronea. He died around A.D. 120.

Plutarch's extant works consist of the fifty *Parallel Lives*, twenty-three pairs, in which a Roman and a Greek are contrasted, and four single lives; and the *Moralia*, seventy-seven essays, some in the form of dialogues, others in the form of letters or exposition, on many different subjects. Most of Plutarch's biographies deal with political and military leaders. His intention in telling and contrasting the lives of famous men is frankly didactic. However, in analyzing the moral qualities of such figures as Lycurgus, Solon, Pericles, Cicero, Alcibiades, Alexander, Marius, Sulla, Antony, Caesar, Brutus, and Pompey, Plutarch seems to enjoy relating fascinating anecdotes not always relevant to his main theme. Although he is not always accurate in the factual material he presents, Plutarch's analyses of character reveal an understanding of human feeling and motivation. Moreover, he recounts incidents and invents dialogue with the skill of a novelist. In re-creating historical events, such as battles or important trials, Plutarch describes the motives and emotions of the participants. His brief description of Cicero encountering his murderers and his detailed narration of the downfall and death of Antony and Cleopatra are vivid and extremely moving. *Parallel Lives*, in the translation made by Thomas North in 1579 from the French version of Amyot, was extremely popular during the Renaissance; Shakespeare employed North's translation in writing *Julius Caesar, Coriolanus,* and *Antony and Cleopatra.*

Some of the titles of the essays that make up Plutarch's *Moralia* will suggest the great variety of subjects on which he wrote. Many of the essays are didactic: the *Education of Children, How to Study Poetry, How to Know a Flatterer from a Friend, Advice to Married Couples, Concerning Garrulity, On Restraining Anger,* and *How to Profit from Enemies.* Others deal with religious questions, the best-known being *On Superstition; On the E at Delphi,* in which Plutarch explains the letter *E* on the temple of Apollo; *The Oracles at Delphi;* and *On the Cessation of Oracles.* Other essays are *On the Face That Appears in the Moon, On the Origin of Gold,* and *On the Reasoning of Animals.*

Pluto (Plouton). See HADES.

Plutus (Ploutos). In Greek mythology, the son of Demeter and Iasion and the god of wealth.

Plutus (Ploutos). A Middle Comedy (388 B.C.) by ARISTOPHANES. Translations: in verse, Benjamin B. Rogers, 1924; in verse, Arthur S. Way, 1934.

SCENE. Athens, a public square; in the background is the house of Chremylus.

SUMMARY. A blind old man enters, followed by Chremylus and his slave, Cario, who complains of being enslaved to a fool. He wonders why his master insists on following a blind man, and finally Chremylus explains that when he consulted Apollo as to whether his only son must give up his principles in order to succeed, the oracle replied that he must follow the first man he encountered after leaving the temple and persuade this man to come home with him. The blind man was the first person he saw. Attempting to interpret the oracular command, Chremylus and Cario approach the blind man, and after some persuasion he tells them he is Plutus, god of riches. Because as a young man Plutus declared he would visit only the virtuous, Zeus, jealous of man, blinded the god of wealth so that he could not know the good from the evil. If ever he recovers his sight, Plutus declares, he will go only to the good— but unfortunately, as soon as people obtain wealth they become wicked.

Chremylus hopes to restore Plutus' sight. Since the god of riches is responsible for all the good and evil in the world, when Plutus has regained his sight, he can use his great power to solve the problems of man. Plutus goes home with Chremylus and Cario goes off to summon the farmers, friends of Chremylus, who are working in the fields, so that they may partake of the gifts of Plutus.

Cario returns with the Chorus of Rustics, who dance in delight when they discover the presence of Plutus. Soon Blepsidemus, a friend of Chremylus, approaches, curious about Chremylus' sudden wealth and amazed to discover that despite his riches he has not abandoned his friends. Blepsidemus agrees to aid Chremylus in restoring the eyesight of Plutus. They are about to lead him to the Temple of Asclepius, the god of healing, when a squalid and ugly woman, the goddess of Poverty, tries to stop them. When the men discover who she is, they become frightened, but Chremylus regains his courage and threatens to expel her from Greece. Poverty and Chremylus then argue about the value of riches, Chremylus declaring that once Plutus has his sight again, he will find the just men and reward them; as a result all men will try to be good. Poverty replies that if all men were rich, no one would be willing to work. Poverty, she says, motivates men to produce. Chremylus lists all the horrors of poverty: hunger, disease, ugliness, and dirt. Finally he defeats Poverty and sends her off to jail, as he, Cario, and Blepsidemus lead Plutus to Asclepius.

Soon Cario returns and happily announces to the Wife of Chremylus that Asclepius has restored Plutus' eyesight. Plutus enters, greeting the sun and the city of Athens. Now he will give wealth only to the good. A Just Man comes in to thank Plutus for restoring his fortune; he is followed by an informer, furious at the god of riches, who has taken away his occupation. Another complaint is made by an Old Woman whose lover no longer needs her. The gods are also angry. Hermes appears and announces that mortals are no longer making offerings to the gods. Hermes, the god of fraud, thievery, and tricks, has no more followers; famished, he gives up his allegiance to Zeus to preside over gymnastic contests for Plutus. A priest of Zeus also renounces Zeus and accepts Plutus as his god. Plutus then promises the Old Woman that her lover will visit her that evening. Then the god of riches marches off the stage in a procession to the Acropolis, where he will be given a place of high honor.

Poenulus. See THE CARTHAGINIAN.

Poetics (Peri Poietikes). A fragmentary prose treatise (probably about 330 B.C.) by ARISTOTLE. Translations: Thomas Twining, 1789; S. H. Butcher, 1902; Ingram Bywater, 1909; W. H. Fyfe, 1926; L. J. Potts, 1953; G. M. A. Grube, 1958.

SUMMARY. *Chapter I.* All the arts—poetry, drama, music, painting—are based on the principle of imitation (*mimesis*); the arts differ from each other in the media they use and in their objects and methods of imitation. The media of poetry, drama, and music are rhythm, language, and harmony, used individually or together.

Chapter II. The objects of imitation are the actions of people, who must be represented as either better or worse than they actually are or as they are in life. Homer and the tragedians depict men as nobler than they are in life; the comic dramatists as worse than they usually are.

Chapter III. The manner or method of imitation may be narrative, in which the author speaks either as himself or as another person (e.g., Homer), or dramatic, in which all the characters act and speak for themselves. Drama is the name given to poetry that depicts action.

Chapter IV. Poetry derives from and fulfills two basic human needs: (1) it is instinctive in man to imitate and to learn by imitation; man derives pleasure from imitations of reality, even imitations of objects that in themselves are ugly or displeasing, and (2) man instinctively responds to rhythm and harmony. As poetry developed from crude improvisation into an art, it took two main paths, the heroic and the comic, both of which can be found in Homer. The further development of these types lies in tragedy and comedy. Tragedy grew out of the dithyramb (a choral hymn sung in honor of Dionysus) and comedy out of phallic songs. Tragedy, having developed slowly, has reached its perfect form. Aeschylus was the first dramatist to add a second actor; moreover, he placed greater importance on the dialogue than on the chorus. Sophocles then added a third actor and introduced scene painting. Trochaic tetrameter, the original meter associated with the satyr play and with dancing, was replaced by iambics, which are more appropriate to dialogue.

Chapter V. Comedy is an imitation of the ludicrous or ugly and the defective but not the painful. The first steps in the development of comedy are unknown. Comic fables originated in Sicily. Epic and tragedy are alike in their imitation in verse of the actions of noble characters. There are, however, many differences between the two genres. Epic is narrative and is written in only one meter. Epic is unrestricted in time, whereas the action of tragedy is usually confined to a day.

Chapter VI. Tragedy is an imitation of an action that is significant, complete, and of a proper magnitude, enhanced by language that is artistically and appropriately varied. Tragedy is dramatic rather than narrative. Through pity and fear tragedy brings about a purgation (*catharsis*) of such feelings. There are six elements in tragedy: spectacle, song, language, plot, character, and thought. Plot, the imitation of the action, is the most important element of tragedy, for tragedy is an imitation not of people but of the actions of life. Character is revealed through action. Moreover, the most moving parts of tragedy are the *peripeteia* (reversal) and the *anagnorisis* (discovery or recognition), and these are implicit in the plot. Next in importance is character, and third is *dianoia* (the thought or intention behind a character's words). After these come language, song, and spectacle.

Chapter VII. A plot must be complete; it must have a beginning, a middle, and an end. The length of the plot must be such that it can easily be remem-

POETICS

bered and can contain the events that convincingly lead to a change from good fortune to bad or bad fortune to good.

Chapter VIII. Unity of plot depends not on the unity of the hero but on unity of action. Any incident that is not essential destroys the unity.

Chapter IX. The poet does not record what has occurred; he depicts what may happen, indeed, what probably will happen in accordance with the laws that govern human life. The historian, for example, Herodotus, records the events that have taken place; the poet reveals what will probably take place. Thus poetry is more philosophical and more significant than history. History deals with the particular, poetry with the general and universal. The poet is concerned with the essential and the probable. When a poet employs an historical subject, he must impose unity upon it. The worst kind of plot is the episodic one, in which events follow each other without any apparent relationship or cause. The most effective plot evokes pity and fear by combining the unexpected with the necessary or unavoidable.

Chapter X. Plots can be either simple or complex, as are the events of life. A simple plot is one in which there is a change of fortune without reversal or recognition. A complex plot contains either reversal or recognition or both these elements, which develop from the nature of the plot itself.

Chapter XI. Reversal is a change in an action, when the outcome is the opposite of what was expected, yet the change is logical and in accordance with the laws of necessity. Recognition is a change from ignorance or lack of knowledge to knowledge or insight. The most effective tragic experience is created when reversal of situation and recognition of persons come together, because this combination evokes pity and fear. A third part of the plot is suffering (*pathos*), pain or death.

Chapter XII. The divisions of tragedy are prologue (the part before the chorus enters), episode (action between choral odes), exode (action following the last choral ode), parados (entrance song and dance of the chorus), and stasimon (choral ode). The kommos (*commus*) is a lyrical dialogue between the chorus and characters.

Chapter XIII. An ideal tragedy should have a complex plot, which evokes pity and fear. In order to inspire these emotions the action must involve a change of fortune. This cannot, however, be the story of an entirely virtuous man thrust from a high and enviable position to a low one, because such a change produces shock rather than pity and fear. Nor can the action depict an evil man moving from a low position to a prosperous state. The downfall or destruction of a thoroughly corrupt man is an equally unsatisfying action. "Poetic justice" does not arouse pity and fear; it is moralistic rather than tragic. The action that inspires pity and fear is one in which a man who is not entirely virtuous nor thoroughly corrupt, but, like most people, somewhere between these two extremes, experiences great misfortune as a result not of evil but of *hamartia,* an error in judgment. Pity is aroused because his suffering is undeserved, fear because the fallen hero is so like those in the audience observing him. The hero must be a well-known and apparently fortunate and prosperous man, like Oedipus or Thyestes. The most effective ending of a tragedy is an unhappy one. Although audiences like plays in which the good are rewarded and the bad punished ("poetic justice"), these are actually more like comedies than like tragedies.

Chapter XIV. Pity and fear should be produced not by external and spectacular effects but rather by the plot itself. The plot that will most effectively arouse pity and fear deals with a tragic incident involving people who are dear to each other: for example, the slaying of a brother by a brother or a father or mother by a son. Such an act may be performed consciously or without conscious knowledge. Another possibility is that a character may consciously plan to kill someone dear to him and then stop himself from doing so, and a fourth type, in Aristotle's opinion the best, is one in which a character plans to kill someone dear to him whom he does not recognize and learns the identity of the person before he commits the act.

Chapter XV. There are four qualities that make for satisfactory characters: they must be essentially good or ethical; their traits must be appropriate to their natures (propriety); they must be true to life; and they must be consistent. In portraying character as in developing plot, the poet must be constantly aware of the law of the probable or necessary. The *deus ex machina* should not be employed as a part of the essential plot structure; it may be used only to explain events that are outside the drama itself, past or future incidents that are related to the plot but not essential to it.

Chapter XVI. Recognition may occur in many ways: the first and least effective method is by external signs, birthmarks, scars, tokens; the second and also an ineffective method is some external incident arranged by the poet—for example, Orestes' revelation of his identity in Euripides' *Iphigenia in Tauris;* the third type occurs when a character suddenly remembers something from the past; the fourth is through reasoning logically; the fifth is through false reasoning which nonetheless leads to revelation; the sixth and best type of recognition comes naturally and inevitably from the plot itself.

Chapter XVII. When a dramatist is writing a play, he should try to visualize the events and to experience vicariously the emotions of his characters. The poet often has a type of inspired madness.

Chapter XVIII. A tragedy has two essential parts: complication and denouement. The complication consists of all action preceding the climax, the point at which the great change in the hero's fortune takes place; the denouement consists of all action from the change in fortune to the end of the play. There are four types of tragedy: (1) the complex, which contains reversal and recognition, (2) the pathetic, which depends upon feeling or suffering, (3) the moral, and (4) the simple. The poet must be aware of the differences between epic and tragedy. Tragedy can never contain the many incidents of an epic.

The chorus of a tragedy should have an essential role in the play and can be considered one of the actors.

Chapter XIX. Thought (*dianoia*) is expressed through the rhetorical techniques used in the speeches of the characters.

Chapter XX. This chapter is a brief summary of the various parts of speech and their use.

Chapter XXI. Words are either current, foreign, metaphorical, decorative, invented, extended, contracted, or changed. Various types of metaphor and invented words are discussed.

Chapter XXII. Excellent style is clear but not low; it combines the common with the unusual. Metaphor must be used with propriety.

Chapter XXIII. Like tragedy, epic poetry must have unity of action. This is achieved by a single, complete action with a beginning, a middle, and an end. In this respect epic, like tragedy, differs from history. Homer, for example, does not attempt to tell the whole story of the Trojan War. Instead, he takes a small part of the war and brings in episodes related to it.

Chapter XXIV. Epic also resembles tragedy in its types: simple, complex, pathetic, and moral. Though epic has no music or scenery, like tragedy, it has reversal, recognition, thought, and diction. There are, however, many differences between tragedy and epic. Epic is longer and, because it is narrative rather than dramatic, can have a more complicated structure than tragedy. The meter of epic is always dactylic hexameter; this is the most suitable because of its heroic, majestic quality. The epic poet does enter into his poem in his own voice. The epic produces the effect of wonder far more than does tragedy. The wonderful or the marvelous is created through the irrational.

Chapter XXV. One cannot apply the same critical standards to the poet and the politician, for their aims are different. Inaccuracy in the details of a description is unimportant in poetry, but failure to imitate properly creates a serious error. The poet may use what is factually impossible to create truth or to suggest an ideal. We must judge the dramatist's thoughts and language in relation to the character speaking, for a fault may be a character's, not the playwright's. In art, probability is far more important than possibility. What is probable though impossible is preferable to what is possible but improbable. The irrational is not always in opposition to reason.

Chapter XXVI. Tragedy, which is superior to epic, is the noblest of the literary arts.

COMMENTARY. Aristotle's *Poetics*, a fragmentary work which is probably a collection of his lecture notes, raises many problems in interpretation. Hundreds of commentaries on the *Poetics* discuss the meanings of such terms as *catharsis*, *mimesis*, and *hamartia*. *Hamartia*, for example, has been translated "tragic flaw," "error of frailty," or, as in the summary above, "error in judgment." Each of these translations actually presents a critical interpretation of the term and consequently suggests its own view of Aristotle's ideas. One of the most useful commentaries is *Aristotle's Theory of Poetry and Fine Art* by S. H. Butcher, which first appeared in 1894 and subsequently was re-edited three times. Butcher's views are interesting and often brilliant and can be very effectively contrasted with those of a contemporary scholar Gerald Else, whose *Aristotle's Poetics: The Argument* (Harvard University Press, 1957) is an exciting, original, and challenging interpretation.

Politeia. See REPUBLIC.

Politicus (Politikos). A dialogue by PLATO on the subject of the good ruler or statesman.

Pollux. See DIOSCURI.

Polybius (Polybios). Greek historian, born at Megalopolis about 202 B.C. His father Lycortas, was an important member of the Achaean League, and succeeded his friend Philopoemen as general of the League (a confederation of Achaean cities which united in an effort to avoid domination by Macedon from 281 to 146 B.C.). Polybius was engaged in the diplomatic and military affairs of the Achaean League. Because the League took a neutral position in the war between Macedon and Rome, when the Romans defeated the Macedonians in the battle of Pydna (168 B.C.), the decisive battle of the third Macedonian War, the Romans demanded a thousand Achaeans in important positions as hostages, and among them was Polybius. As a hostage in Italy, Polybius became the tutor of the sons of Aemilius Paullus, the victorious leader of the Romans in the war against Macedon. The younger son, Publius Scipio Aemilianus, became Polybius' lifelong friend. Though Polybius was permitted to return to Greece in 150 B.C., he left home once more to accompany Scipio to Carthage during the Third Punic War, and he was at Carthage when it was finally destroyed by Scipio in 146 B.C. Polybius also witnessed the fall of Corinth in the same year. During the last years of his life he traveled and wrote. His *History*, the work for which he is known, originally consisted of forty books, of which the first five survive complete; there are also extant sections from Books Six to Sixteen and Book Eighteen, as well as some other fragments. Polybius also wrote a life of Philopoemen and a work called *Commentaries on Tactics*, but neither work has survived. He died in 120 B.C. as the result of a fall from a horse.

Polybius' *History*, which in its complete form dealt with the history of Rome from 262 B.C. to 120 B.C., reveals his knowledge of warfare and geography, as well as his personal involvement in many of the events he relates. With accurate documentation, sound scholarship, and historical insight Polybius describes the rise of Rome to her position of dominance in the Mediterranean area. He analyzes the constitution of Rome, which he feels is largely responsible for her remarkable achievement. Polybius' style is simple and direct, and he is often didactic. Though his *History* is not remarkable as a piece of literature, it is an impressive and accurate record of the growth of Roman power during his lifetime.

Polydeuces (Polydeukes). See DIOSCURI.

Polydorus (Polydoros). The youngest son of Priam and Hecuba. For the story of Polydorus' murder by Polymestor see Euripides' HECUBA and Vergil's *Aeneid* III.

Polymestor. See Euripides' HECUBA.

Polyneices (Polyneikes). A son of Oedipus. For his contest with his brother Eteocles over the throne of Thebes and the problem of the burial of Polyneices see Aeschylus' SEVEN AGAINST THEBES, Sophocles' OEDIPUS AT COLONUS and ANTIGONE, Euripides' THE PHOENICIAN WOMEN, Seneca's *The Phoenician Women*, and Statius' THEBAID.

Polyphemus (Polyphemos). A Cyclops, son of Poseidon. For his encounter with Odysseus see the ODYSSEY IX and Euripides' THE CYCLOPS. For his love of Galatea see Theocritus' IDYLS VI, XI and ACIS. He also appears in the AENEID III.

Polyxena (Polyxene). A daughter of Priam and Hecuba. See Euripides' HECUBA and Seneca's THE TROJAN WOMEN.

Pompey (Gnaeus Pompeius Magnus). A Roman general, born in 106 B.C. He was named "the Great" by Sulla, the leader of the aristocratic party, whom Pompey supported in his youth. After great military successes in Spain, Pompey was recalled by the Roman Senate to help suppress the rebellion of slaves led by Spartacus. Pompey arrived when Crassus had already led a successful campaign against Spartacus. Though Pompey and Crassus never trusted each other, they joined forces and, supported by their armies, demanded that the Senate accept them as consuls in 70 B.C. During their consulship Pompey and Crassus attempted to undo the reforms of Sulla and succeeded in reducing the power of the Senate. In 67 B.C. Pompey was successful in eliminating piracy in the Mediterranean, a victory that resulted in his increased power and prestige. In 66 B.C. the Senate gave him absolute command over the huge Roman army at war with King Mithridates of Pontus. Pompey defeated Mithridates, and added Bithynia, Pontus, and Syria to Rome's provinces. Returning home in 62 B.C. with great wealth taken by the Roman soldiers from the conquered people of Asia Minor, Pompey rewarded his soldiers and contributed to the treasury of Rome. For his relationship with Caesar, his role in the first triumvirate, his renewed allegiance with the Senate, and his death in 48 B.C. see CAESAR and Lucan's ON THE CIVIL WAR.

Pontus (Pontos). In Greek mythology, the Sea.

Poseidon. In Greek mythology, a son of Cronus and Rhea and a brother of Zeus. After Cronus was forced to vomit up Poseidon and his brothers and sisters and they overcame their father, Zeus, Poseidon, and Hades cast lots to determine which part of the world they would rule. Poseidon became god of the sea. He is also the earthshaker and the god of horses. With Apollo Poseidon built the walls of Troy. For his hatred of Odysseus see the ODYSSEY. Poseidon's symbol of authority is the trident.

Posidonius (Poseidonios). See STOICS.

Pot of Gold, The (Aulularia). A comedy by PLAUTUS, based on a lost Greek play of unknown authorship. In the Prologue the Household God of Euclio, an old Athenian miser, announces that he intends to disclose to Euclio a pot of gold buried in the house by his grandfather. The Household God will reveal the treasure for the sake of Euclio's daughter Phaedria, whom Lyconides, a young Athenian, has seduced. The god will also help Phaedria to win Lyconides as her husband.

When Euclio discovers the pot of gold, he is so afraid it will be stolen from him that he conceals it and pretends he is still poor. Fearing that his secret will be discovered, he is suspicious of everyone. Meanwhile, Eunomia, the mother of Lyconides, persuades her bachelor brother Megadorus to marry. He decides to ask Euclio for his daughter, despite the fact that she has no dowry. Though suspicious of Megadorus' motives, Euclio agrees to hold the wedding that day.

Preparations for the wedding are made. Euclio conceals his treasure in the Temple of Faith, but, on seeing Strobilus, the slave of Lyconides, enter the temple, he returns, berates Strobilus, and leaves to hide the treasure in a grove outside the city walls. He is unaware that Strobilus is following him.

Lyconides tells his mother that he has seduced Phaedria and urges her to prevent the marriage. Soon Phaedria is heard crying out in pain; she is giving birth to Lyconides' child.

Euclio comes in terribly upset, declaring that he is ruined. His treasure has been stolen by Strobilus. Lyconides mistakes Euclio's rage over the loss of his money for anger at the seducer of his daughter. He confesses that he seduced Phaedria at a feast of Ceres and promises to marry her. He goes on to tell Euclio that Phaedria has just had a child and that Megadorus has agreed to break his engagement for the sake of his nephew. Strobilus now enters and admits to Lyconides that he has stolen Euclio's pot of gold. The rest of the play is missing; probably Lyconides returned Euclio's treasure and married his daughter, and no doubt the old miser then gave the pot of gold as a wedding present to his daughter and son-in-law.

Pratinas. One of the earliest Greek tragedians and the inventor of the SATYR PLAY, from Phlius in the northern Peloponnesus. Evidence exists that he competed in one of the dramatic contests with Aeschylus and Choerilus. It is thought that he wrote fifty dramas, of which thirty-two were satyr plays, but very few fragments of these are extant.

Priam (Priamos). In Greek myth, son of Laomedon and the last king of TROY. Priam had fifty sons and fifty daughters by several wives. Hecuba, the best-known of these wives, bore him nineteen sons. The children of Priam most often referred to in Greek and Latin literature are Paris, Hector, Deiphobus, Troilus, Cassandra, and Polyxena. Priam appears in the ILIAD and the AENEID (II).

Priapea. Eighty poems to Priapus, three of which have been attributed to VERGIL by some scholars. In each of these Priapus speaks: in the first, of his hatred of the cold; in the second and third, of his attributes and powers as a god of fertility who protects herds, vineyards, and gardens.

Priapus (Priapos). See PRIAPEA.

Procne (Prokne). See PHILOMELA.

Procrustes (Prokrustes). A legendary bandit who seized travelers in the neighborhood of Eleusis and tied them to an iron bed. He would make his victims fit the size of the bed by either stretching them if they were too short or cutting off their legs if they were too tall. Theseus killed Procrustes.

Prodicus (Prodikos). See SOPHISTS.

Prometheus (Forethought). In Greek mythology, a son of the Titan Iapetus and Clymene or Themis. According to Hesiod, Hyginus, Pausanias, Ovid, and other writers, Prometheus created men out of clay, and the goddess Athene gave them life. In the *Theogony*, Hesiod tells how Prometheus aided men when they faced the problem of sharing a sacrificial victim with the gods. By concealing the best parts of a slain ox in its hide and wrapping the bones in fat, Prometheus tricked Zeus into choosing the least desirable parts of the animal. Though Hesiod apparently feels obliged to say that the omniscient god knew what he was doing when he chose the fat and bones, Zeus' subsequent anger at Prometheus indicates that he was duped by the Titan. The episode explains why men sacrificed to the gods the least desirable parts of an animal. Angry at Prometheus, Zeus ordered Hephaestus to create PANDORA to plague Prometheus and all men. Zeus also withheld fire from man. Again Prometheus came to man's aid: he stole fire, in one version, from heaven, in another, from Hephaestus, and carried it to earth in a fennel stalk. For Zeus' punishment of Prometheus see Aeschylus' PROMETHEUS BOUND.

Zeus was troubled by a prophecy that he was in danger of begetting a son who would overthrow him. Prometheus knew that this prophecy applied to the child of Thetis, who was destined to bear a son stronger than his father. Only Prometheus could prevent Zeus' marriage to Thetis, whom the god loved. Prometheus refused to disclose the secret. According to one legend Prometheus was released from his tortures by Heracles; according to another he finally revealed the secret of the prophecy regarding the child of Thetis and thus obtained his release.

It is generally believed that Prometheus was originally a fire-god who was replaced by Hephaestus. The heroic figure of Prometheus has come to symbolize enlightenment and rebellion against tyranny. Shelley's *Prometheus Unbound*, which was influenced by Aeschylus' *Prometheus Bound*, is perhaps the best-known modern work based on the myth. See also Robert Bridges' poem "Prometheus, the Firegiver" and interesting studies of the myth by Louis Séchan, *Le mythe de Prométhée* (Paris, Presses Universitaires de France, 1951), and C. Kerényi, *Prometheus, Archetypal Image of Human Existence* (London, Thames and Hudson, 1963).

Prometheus Bound (Prometheus Desmotes). A tragedy (date uncertain, possibly c. 478 B.C.) by AESCHYLUS. *Prometheus Bound* is the first play of a trilogy; the second and third plays, *Prometheus Unbound* (*Prometheus Luomenos*) and *Prometheus the Fire-bearer* (*Prometheus Pyrphoros*), have not survived. Translations: in verse, J. Case, 1905; in verse, R. Whitelaw, 1907; in verse, E. D. A. Morshead, 1908; in prose, Walter and C. E. S. Headlam, 1909; in verse, Clarence W. Mendell, 1926; in verse, Robert C. Trevelyan, 1939; in prose and verse, David Grene, 1942; in verse, Philip Vellacott, 1961; in verse, Paul Roche, 1964.

MYTHICAL BACKGROUND. In the war between the Titans, led by Cronus, and the gods, led by Cronus' son Zeus, Prometheus (Forethought) aided Zeus, who finally overcame Cronus and became king of the gods. Zeus was a harsh and proud ruler, who decided to destroy the race of man. Prometheus, a noble Titan, felt deep compassion for men; he stole from heaven the most valuable gift of fire and gave it to them. For this disobedience Zeus ordered his ministers, Power and Force, and the god Hephaestus to chain Prometheus to a barren cliff, where he would endure endless torture.

SCENE. A barren cliff in Scythia.

SUMMARY. Power and Force with their prisoner Prometheus and the god Hephaestus come to Scythia, a barren land at the end of the world. Zeus has commanded his ministers and Hephaestus to bind Prometheus to a cliff and leave him here. Hephaestus pities Prometheus and unwillingly obeys Zeus' orders. As Power urges him on, Hephaestus places shackles on Prometheus' limbs and nails him to the rock. After Hephaestus and Force leave, Power scornfully remarks to Prometheus that the gods mistakenly named him "Forethinker," for he seems to need someone to advise him. Then Power also leaves. Alone, Prometheus calls on the air of heaven, the winds, the waters, the earth, and the sun to look upon the tortures he must endure. He cannot help speaking, though speech itself is painful. He declares that he stole fire, the source of arts and knowledge, to give it to mortals—and thus must undergo torture for loving mankind.

The Chorus of Ocean Nymphs enters in a winged chariot. The Nymphs pity Prometheus and comment on the cruelty of Zeus. Prometheus then tells them of how he, a Titan, helped Zeus in his war against the Titans, suggesting that Zeus imprison them in Tartarus. When Zeus triumphed he decided to destroy the race of man and create a new race. Prometheus alone felt pity for man and is now suffering for his generosity. Zeus, the tyrant, has turned against the one who aided him.

The next to enter is Oceanus, who comes on a winged beast. Offering Prometheus his sympathy, he pleads with him to be silent and stop defying Zeus. Oceanus says he will ask Zeus to release Prometheus, but Prometheus urges him not to displease Zeus.

After Oceanus leaves, the Nymphs weep for Prometheus. They say that all mankind will sympathize with him. Prometheus answers by telling of his love for mankind, to whom he gave the power of speech and intellect. He taught men the laws of the universe, numbers, and language. He showed them how to cure disease. He led men who lived in the blindness of ignorance to light. Prometheus then goes on to say that the day will come when he will be released from his bonds. When the Chorus asks Prometheus whether Zeus must submit to the laws of fate, Prometheus says even Zeus must accept these laws. The Nymphs question Prometheus about the future of Zeus, but he will not reveal this secret.

The maiden Io, in the form of a heifer and tormented by a gadfly, enters and calls on Zeus to end her painful wanderings. She asks Prometheus if he knows what will happen to her, and he says he will tell her if she insists. First the Chorus wishes to know her story. Io then tells of how Zeus fell in love with her and changed her into a heifer. Hera sent Argus, who had a hundred eyes, to watch her. A gadfly constantly pursued her. Even after Argus was killed, Io was tortured, wandering from land to land. When she finishes her story Prometheus begins to tell her of her future wanderings. She interrupts to cry out in agony, praying for death. Prometheus tells her to imagine his woes, for he cannot die, but must suffer until Zeus is overthrown. When Io asks Prometheus whether Zeus, the tyrant, will ever be deposed and who will do the deed, Prometheus tells her that Zeus will make a marriage that will bring about his downfall, for the son of this marriage will be stronger than the father. No one but Prometheus can prevent this disaster to Zeus, and he will do so only if freed from his bonds. Io asks who can free Prometheus against Zeus' will, and Prometheus predicts that a descendant of Io's will release him. Prometheus then continues to predict the wanderings of Io and her arrival in the city of Canopus, where Zeus will restore her to her former shape, and she will bear him a son Epaphos. A descendant of this son will found a royal line in Argos, from which will come a powerful bowman (Heracles) who will free Prometheus.

After hearing this prophecy Io is once more tortured by the gadfly and resumes her wanderings. Prometheus speaks to the Chorus of the marriage that will destroy Zeus if he is not warned—and no god can warn him but Prometheus. Hermes then enters and tries to persuade Prometheus to reveal what marriage will overthrow Zeus, but Prometheus refuses to tell him. Prometheus says he has no fear of Zeus, and even when Hermes tries to frighten him with threats that Zeus will break the cliff in two with lightning and thunder and hurl him into Hades, Prometheus remains steadfast. The Chorus refuses to leave him, and as the play ends, Zeus sends lightning and thunder and an earthquake which swallows Prometheus and the Chorus.

Propertius, Sextus. A Roman poet, born in Assisium (Assisi) in Umbria between 50 and 48 B.C. He came from an equestrian family. His parents died when he was a boy, and some of his property was confiscated for the veterans of Octavian's army in 40 B.C. Though Propertius studied law, he devoted himself to poetry. There is some evidence to suggest that as a young man he had a brief and trivial affair with a girl named Lycinna and that the only deep passion he felt was for a woman possibly named Hostia, whom he calls Cynthia in his poems. She may have been a courtesan; if so it was illegal for Propertius to marry her. Apparently Propertius was devoted to Cynthia for some time, though they quarreled frequently. His ELEGIES cannot be taken as autobiographical records, but they do reveal intense feelings and the pain of an unhappy love relationship. Propertius also tells of ending this love affair, and, though the poems dealing with its conclusion are bitter ones, later poems about a quarrel with Cynthia and her death are tender. Maecenas, the patron of Vergil and Horace, befriended and encouraged Propertius, and among his literary friends was the poet Ovid. The date of Propertius' death is unknown, but there is evidence that he died before A.D. 2.

Propertius' elegies appeared in four books: Book I around 28 B.C., Book II around 25 B.C., Book III around 22 B.C., and Book IV around 16 B.C. Most of the elegies deal with Propertius' love for Cynthia and the suffering he endures in this relationship. Like Catullus, he seems to be revealing intimate experiences and conflicts to the reader. How closely these poetic revelations parallel Propertius' actual experience is, of course, unknown. As Georg Luck points out, "The appeal of this love-poetry lies in its universality. Although his love for Cynthia is in the foreground, Propertius is not trying to picture—autobiographically, as it were—one person's passion, but the typical lover's love. Reality is transformed to suit a more general theme" (*The Latin Love Elegy,* Barnes & Noble, 1960, p. 136). Ezra Pound's adaptation of some of the elegies in his *Homage to Sextus Propertius* reflects little of the subtlety of Propertius in his self-revelations, but it does transmit some of his vitality and intensity.

Proserpina. The Roman name for PERSEPHONE.

Protagoras. A Greek philosopher of the fifth century B.C. Protagoras was the best-known of the SOPHISTS. He is the chief speaker in Plato's *Protagoras.*

Protagoras. A dialogue by PLATO named for the famous Sophist who lived during the fifth century B.C. In the dialogue Socrates speaks with Protagoras and two other famous Sophists, Hippias and Prodicus, about pleasure as a good. They conclude that all virtue is contained in knowledge.

Proteus. The "Old Man of the Sea." In ODYSSEY IV, Proteus is a seer who constantly changes his shape to avoid answering questions. He appears also in Vergil's GEORGIC IV.

Pseudolus. A comedy (191 B.C.) by PLAUTUS, based on an unknown Greek source, possibly more than one play. It is known that Cicero's friend Roscius played the role of Ballio, the procurer, and this may have been regarded as the leading part. The clever slave Pseudolus, however, is a more interesting character. The play deals with the love of Calidorus, a young Athenian, for the courtesan Phoenicium and his inability to raise the money to buy her. To add to his problems and the complications of the plot, an officer in the Macedonian army has paid fifteen of the twenty *minae* required for her purchase; he and the procurer have agreed that Phoenicium is to be given to the person who brings the remaining five *minae* and a token that the procurer gave the officer.

Pseudolus agrees to help Calidorus. When Simo, Calidorus' father, refuses to give him the money for the girl, Pseudolus declares he will manage to dupe the procurer. Simo agrees to give him the money if he succeeds. Impersonating a slave of the procurer, Pseudolus manages to prevent Harpax, the officer's slave, from taking the procurer the five *minae* and the token. Pseudolus also persuades Harpax to give him the token. Then Charinus, a friend of Calidorus', lends him the five *minae* and arranges for Simia, a slave of his father, to impersonate Harpax. The ruse works; the procurer gives up Phoenicium, and Simo gives the triumphant Pseudolus his money.

Psyche. The heroine of the story of Cupid and Psyche (Gr. soul) in *The Golden Ass* by Apuleius. Psyche was a young girl whose beauty made even Venus envious. When Venus sent her son Cupid to inspire Psyche with love for some ugly creature, Cupid could not help falling in love with her himself. He took her to a magnificent palace, but warned her that she must never try to see him. Psyche was frightened by the remarks of her jealous sisters, who said that her lover might be a serpent that would devour her. One night, she held a lamp over the sleeping Cupid and looked at him. Delighted at the sight of the god, Psyche trembled, and a drop of hot oil from her lamp fell on Cupid and awakened him. The god was angry at the faithless Psyche and immediately left her. Psyche then roamed the earth, seeking her beloved. Venus imposed many tasks on Psyche, the last of which was to bring back from Persephone a box containing beauty. When Psyche obtained the box, she could not control her curiosity. Opening it, she found it apparently empty, but its contents made her fall into a deathlike sleep. Finally Cupid awakened the sleeping Psyche and took her to Olympus, where Jupiter allowed the lovers to be married.

Punic Wars. See CARTHAGE and ROME.

Pygmalion. In Greek mythology, a king of Cyprus, who fell in love with the statue of a woman. In Ovid's version in *Metamorphoses* x, Pygmalion is a sculptor who falls in love with a statue he has made. Aphrodite imbues the beautiful statue with life, and Pygmalion marries her. The myth has been used many times in literature; the best-known works based on it are W. S. Gilbert's *Pygmalion and Galatea* and Bernard Shaw's *Pygmalion*.

Pylos. A Mycenaean city in the western Peloponnesus. According to Homer, Pylos was a kingdom ruled by Neleus and his more famous son Nestor, the garrulous old warrior of the ILIAD. In the ODYSSEY, Telemachus visits Nestor in the hope of obtaining information about his father Odysseus. Late in the 1930's Professor Carl Blegen conducted the excavation of what he believed to be the site of Nestor's Pylos in Messenia. There Blegen discovered the first tablets with the script Linear B (see CRETE) ever found on the mainland of

Greece. After World War II Blegen returned to the excavations at Pylos. He has found evidence that Neleus and Nestor were actual rulers of Pylos and that Nestor renovated a palace built (c. 1300 B.C.) by Neleus. Blegen has found indications of Pylos' commercial success, particularly as a center of trade. The palace and the city of Pylos were destroyed around 1200 B.C., most likely by invading Dorians.

Pylades. In Greek mythology, the friend of Orestes, who helps Orestes to avenge the murder of his father Agamemnon (see Aeschylus' *The Libation Bearers* under ORESTEIA, Sophocles' ELECTRA, Euripides' ELECTRA and ORESTES) and later goes with him to Tauris (see Euripides' IPHIGENIA IN TAURIS).

Pyramus (Pyramos). Hero of the tale of Pyramus and Thisbe. According to legend, Pyramus, a young Babylonian, fell in love with Thisbe, his neighbor. In *Metamorphoses* IV Ovid tells of the tragic events that resulted from their parents' refusal to allow them to marry. Through a crevice in the wall between their homes the lovers managed to speak to each other and arranged to meet by the tomb of Ninus, under a tall white mulberry tree. Thisbe arrived first, but, seeing a lion approaching, hid in a cave. As she ran away the girl dropped her white cloak, which the lion stained with blood. When Pyramus arrived and found the bloodstained cloak, he assumed that the lion had killed Thisbe and stabbed himself in grief. Thisbe soon discovered her dying lover; leaning upon his sword, she took her own life. The blood of the lovers made the fruit of the mulberry tree red.

Pyrrho (Pyrrhon) of Elis. See SKEPTICS.

Pyrrhus (Pyrrhos). See NEOPTOLEMUS.

Pythagoras. A Greek philosopher born (c. 580 B.C.) at Samos. Pythagoras believed in and taught the transmigration of souls and claimed prophetic powers. He founded a school at Crotona, in southern Italy, which was like a religious order with ascetic practices. He was a brilliant mathematician and astronomer. None of Pythagoras' works are extant.

Q

Quintilian (Marcus Fabius Quintilianus). A Roman rhetorician, born around A.D. 35 at Calagurris (Calahorra) in Spain. His father was a well-known rhetorician in Rome, and there Quintilian was taught by the famous grammarian Remmius Palaemon and the brilliant rhetorician Domitus Afer. Quintilian became a distinguished teacher in Rome, the first rhetorician to establish a public school and receive payment from the state. He also practiced law. Quintilian achieved great success as a pleader, a teacher, and a rhetorician, and he was honored by his contemporaries. His personal life, however, was a sad one: he married late and lived to mourn the deaths of his wife and his two sons. The exact date of Quintilian's death is not known, but it is certain that he died before A.D. 100.

In his INSTITUTIO ORATORIA, Quintilian mentions his treatise on the causes of the decadence of Roman oratory (*De Causis Corruptae Eloquentiae*), but the work has not survived. His only extant work is the *Institutio Oratoria*, a treatise in twelve books concerned not only with the training of an orator but with educational theory, literary criticism, and many technical aspects of style and rhetoric.

Like Cicero, whom he admired, Quintilian believed that oratory served a vital function in the state. An orator, he felt, must be a "good man." Throughout the *Institutio Oratoria* Quintilian expresses the idea that an orator must not study the rules of rhetoric for their own sake but for the purpose of serving the state through dignified and polished speech. The *Institutio Oratoria* was highly regarded in antiquity. Though practically unknown during the Middle Ages, it had a powerful influence on Renaissance and seventeenth-century prose style and literary criticism. Along with Cicero's rhetorical works, the *Institutio Oratoria* was studied in English schools, and Quintilian was regarded as an important guide by such writers as Sir Thomas Elyot, Ben Jonson, Thomas Wilson, and John Dryden. In the last century the study of rhetoric has gone out of fashion, but Quintilian's sensitive literary criticism, his intelligent approach to the education of children, and the appealing and dignified personality that emerges from his *Institutio Oratoria* are still admired. Edmund Wilson's affectionate mockery in his poem *Quintilian*, "Quintilian, in mild elation/ Pondered a peroration," expresses the modern impatience with rhetorical figures, but it also invokes the engaging rhetorician who delighted in the possibilities of language and in his own skill in exploring them.

R

Remedia Amoris (Remedies for Love). An elegiac poem by OVID. The poem teaches the reader how to free himself from an unhappy or inconvenient love affair. Like Ovid's other didactic poems on love, *Remedia Amoris* is witty and light in tone.

Remus. See ROME.

Republic (Politeia). A dialogue by PLATO. Translations: J. L. Davis and D. J. Vaughan, 1866; Benjamin Jowett, 1868; A. D. Lindsay, 1935; Paul Shorey, 1937; Francis M. Cornford, 1942.

SCENE. The home of Cephalus in the Piraeus, the seaport of Athens.

SUMMARY. *Book I.* Socrates and Glaucon have gone to the Piraeus to observe a festival. They meet Polemarchus, Adeimantus, Niceratus, and others, who invite them to the home of Cephalus, the father of Polemarchus. When Socrates and Polemarchus begin to discuss the question "What is justice?" Polemarchus proposes a definition by Simonides that justice means returning to everyone what is due or appropriate to him, being kind to friends and unkind to enemies, but Socrates reveals the flaws in this definition. Thrasymachus enters the argument and suggests that justice is the "interest of the more powerful," demonstrating his definition with the point that justice in the state is upheld by the government, which is more powerful than the citizens. When Socrates declares that governments often commit errors and that it is sometimes just to act against the interest of the more powerful, Thrasymachus replies that the government always acts in its own interest and thus cannot err. Socrates then shows that in government, as in every art, the interest lies not in the superior but in the subject. When Thrasymachus insists that a ruler uses his subject for his own advantage and therefore it follows that injustice is more profitable for a man than justice, Socrates refutes his argument by demonstrating that a good governor is always concerned with the governed; he is paid for the benefits gained by his subjects. Moreover, he convinces Thrasymachus that the unjust man tries to win the advantage over both the just and the unjust, whereas the just man tries to outdo only the unjust. Furthermore, anyone who is competent in a field or art and thus wise and good does not attempt to surpass those equally competent but only the incompetent; thus the wise and good do not attempt to surpass people like themselves but only people who are unlike them.

Socrates' conclusion is that the just are wise and good and the unjust without knowledge and evil. Injustice results in conflict and lack of unity, justice in harmony and unity. Injustice, because it does not allow for unity in man and the state, can be regarded as a weakness, not as a source of power. Socrates then points out that the essential virtue of man's soul is justice, without which neither the soul nor the man who possesses it can thrive. The just man is satisfied and happy, the unjust man unhappy. Therefore injustice cannot be more advantageous than justice. However, the problem that remains is the true nature of justice.

Book II. Glaucon and Adeimantus take up the argument, declaring that those who praise justice are concerned with its advantages rather than with its essential nature. They raise the question of whether a man would not be willing to act unjustly if he were unafraid of enduring the injustice of others. Justice, they suggest, may very well be a compromise demanded by life in society. If the gods do exist, what is their attitude toward the just and the unjust? An unjust man may expiate his acts by sacrifice; thus, is he not better off in this life than the just man, and as well off in the afterlife?

To answer these questions Socrates decides to study the nature of justice on a broader scale: in following the development of a state, he and his associates can trace the development of justice and injustice. Society and the state arose because of man's dependence on his fellows. One of the first steps in living together in a community is the division of labor, a process that becomes more complicated as the state develops. Then trade and the export and import of goods spurs on production, and new types of work develop. The demand for luxuries as well as necessities requires new skills and professions, and may even give rise to a need for more land, which may result in war. The state must then have an army or a class of Guardians. These men must be strong and courageous, they must have vitality and a capacity for gentleness, and they must be interested in philosophy. Their education must be planned from childhood. As children they must be told no stories that deny the dignity of the gods; they must not learn that the gods engage in warfare, that they violate treaties, that they mistreat man, that they present themselves in various forms on earth, or that they deceive mortals. Although much in Homer is to be praised, the passage (in *Iliad* II) in which Zeus sends Agamemnon the dream cannot be recommended. Neither poets nor teachers should be allowed to tell such stories about the gods.

Book III. To train a man to be brave one must make him unafraid of death. Whatever he is taught should inspire him to be honest, self-controlled, and courageous. Therefore he must not learn passages in Homer or other poets that deal with the horror of death or of life in Hades. Socrates considers the descriptions in the *Iliad* of the deaths of Patroclus and Hector and many other passages in Homer as unsuitable for inspiring future Guardians with courage. The poets who teach the Guardians must write in a simple, direct style, and they must train the young men to speak in this manner. These future Guardians must not be exposed to soft music or to complicated rhythms. Their education in literature and music should teach them restraint and harmony. They must also be taught gymnastics, which trains not only the body but the spirit as well. The intellectual and physical education they receive will give the Guardians a conception of beauty and harmony.

The rulers of the state will be chosen from this group of Guardians, because the rulers are the noblest of the state's protectors. The other Guardians will assist the rulers in protecting the state. The third class will consist of farmers and craftsmen. The rulers or Guardians and their auxiliaries or soldiers will live simply in a camp (like the leaders of Sparta).

Book IV. The rulers will not allow extreme wealth or poverty in the state; they will prohibit new ideas in education. Apollo of Delphi will decide on all questions of religion and ceremony.

Now that the good state has been planned, Socrates considers the question of justice in this state. Because this state is a good one, it must be wise, brave, temperate, and just. In analyzing the first three qualities, wisdom, courage, and temperance, Socrates indicates that wisdom is the quality of the rulers, courage of the soldiers or auxiliaries, and temperance of all classes in the state. He then goes on to show that justice teaches a man to be concerned only with his own affairs and not to interfere in the affairs of others. In a just state each of the three classes attends to its own duties and does not interfere with the rights and duties of the others. Thus justice allows the first three virtues to flourish in the state.

The same definition is then applied to the individual. Every man has the three elements of reason, spirit, and appetite, which are the chief characteristics of each of the three classes. As the harmony of the three classes produces a just state, so the harmony of these three elements in an individual produces a just man. A just man has a harmonious and healthy mind, an unjust man a disturbed and sick one. Socrates begins to analyze the chief types of human minds and political constitutions.

Book V. Socrates' friends then ask him to speak of the roles of women and children in the state, and reluctantly he agrees to do so. Women are to be educated as men are, trained according to their abilities for the various classes and married to men whose work they will share. Children will not be brought up by their parents but by those appointed by the state.

Next Socrates discusses the training of children for warfare and the proper methods of dealing with cowardly and courageous men. He objects to plundering the dead in battle, considering such acts cowardly and despicable.

When Adeimantus asks Socrates to prove that it is possible to organize the state he has described, Socrates says that he has been defining the ideal state; the demonstration of its possible existence is another consideration. The only fair request at this time is for him to indicate how the imperfect states that now exist can be made to approach the ideal state. The most important step in accomplishing this end is to make philosophers the rulers of the state.

The nature of the philosopher is then discussed. He loves all wisdom, and, unlike the pretender who cares only for beautiful objects, the true philosopher seeks the essence of beauty. The lover of wisdom is concerned with real existence (essential being), not with mere opinion.

Book VI. Since philosophers are able to understand the eternal and the essential, they should be the rulers of the state. The philosopher is characterized by: a love of knowledge which leads to the essence of being, a hatred of the false and deceitful and a love of truth, an indifference to physical pleasures and to money, generosity and nobility of spirit, gentleness, a sense of justice, quickness in learning and ability to remember, a harmonious mind and temperament.

When Adeimantus remarks that many who study philosophy are eccentric and evil, Socrates replies that the corrupt political conditions of the state cause this corruption in philosophers. The only remedy is for the state to control the study of philosophy. Socrates then returns to the subject of the philosopher as ruler of the state, once again considering the education of the rulers. The most significant of their studies will be the conception of the good. When he is asked to define the good, Socrates cannot answer directly but instead suggests its meaning by explaining the nature of Ideas or essences, which for him are the only reality (Theory of Ideas). He makes a distinction between the world perceived by the senses and the realm of abstract ideas, which can be reached only by pure reason or intelligence.

Book VII. In order to illustrate the meaning of a true education, Socrates introduces the well-known and much-quoted image of the cave. He asks his friends to imagine men living in a subterranean cave, where they are chained with their backs to its entrance. Behind these men a fire is burning. Between the chained men and the fire is a road. A wall built along the road hides the people who walk along it; however, the light of the fire casts a shadow of the objects they carry on their heads on the wall of the cave which the prisoners face. These shadows provide for the prisoners their only view of reality. If one of the prisoners were freed from his chains and allowed to experience daylight and external reality, his first reaction would be pain and shock. Slowly he would grow accustomed to this new "reality" and learn to appreciate it. In this new condition the freed man compared to the prisoners is like a philosopher compared to most ordinary men. Moreover, if the prisoner were to return to his cave, the others would laugh at his enlarged conception of reality. Nonetheless, even having returned to the cave, the man once freed can use his superior knowledge of reality to advantage. So the philosopher who has pursued essential reality can use his knowledge in worldly affairs. As the prisoner had to turn around in order to experience the real world, so in true education the soul is turned from darkness to light, so that reason, the vision of the soul, may perceive reality. The soul is turned toward reality by education, which leads the mind away from the material world to the unchanging and essential nature of being. To achieve this conception of reality one must study arithmetic, geometry, astronomy, harmony, and dialectics.

Book VIII. Socrates now returns to the subject of the different types of human beings and political constitutions or forms of government. As governments can be classified in five groups: aristocracy, timocracy, oligarchy, democracy, and tyranny, so men can be classified in the same way. The ideal state—the aristocracy—has already been described. Now the other four states and the individuals corresponding to them are analyzed. Plato's contempt for democracy is openly expressed in this analysis. Democracy, he feels, leads naturally to tyranny.

Book IX. The discussion of types of governments and individuals is concluded with a comparison of the best (the aristocratic) and the worst (the tyrannical) government and man.

As man's nature is composed of three elements—reason, spirit, and appetite—he seeks three kinds of pleasure. To the philosopher wisdom is the highest pleasure; to the high-spirited man, the lover of victory, honor; and to the appetitive man, gain or money. The noblest pleasure is wisdom; next is honor; and last is wealth. Only the philosopher is capable of true pleasure, for true pleasure is associated with reason and law. Thus Thrasymachus' argument that a man may gain from injustice is invalid. It is to everyone's advantage to live in a just state. Under ideal circumstances justice is inherent in men's souls, but if it is not, external law can provide for justice. The just man, like the ideal state, strives for perfect harmony.

Book X. Socrates returns to the subject of poetry and the question of imitation. He declares that the artist, in painting an object, produces only a copy of a copy, since his painting is a copy of a physical object, which itself is merely an approximation of the ideal or essence of the object. The poet, too, can produce only such limited representations of reality. The imitator knows little about the object he represents. Since the rational part of man does not respond to imitations, they appeal to an inferior part of his nature. Poetry can corrupt man by encouraging weakness. Thus no poetry except hymns to the gods and encomia of virtuous men will be allowed in the ideal state.

Socrates then discusses the immortality of the soul. He returns to the question of justice, declaring that the just man's reward is justice itself. His greatest reward comes in the afterlife. The story of the warrior Er, son of Armenius, is told to illustrate the just man's reward in the afterlife. Er, who was killed in battle, returned to life after twelve days and described his experience in the afterlife. He tells of how the souls are judged, rewarded, and punished. He describes the process of reincarnation, indicating that wisdom and justice guide a man in choosing a good future life.

Rhea (Rheia). Ancient Greek earth goddess, daughter of Ge and Uranus. She was the wife of Cronus, to whom she bore Demeter, Hestia, Zeus, Hera,

Hades, and Poseidon. For Rhea's involvement in the dethronement of Cronus see Hesiod's THEOGONY. Rhea was first worshiped in Crete. Later the Greeks identified her with Cybele, the Asiatic mother goddess, and worshiped her in orgiastic rites related to those in honor of Dionysus. Under many different names Rhea was worshiped throughout Asia and Greece and in Rome. In Asia, Rhea, like Cybele, was followed by a band of Corybantes, priests who engaged in wild dances and other orgiastic rites; in Greece by Curetes, Cretan demigods, who had protected the infant Zeus. Rhea is often represented as accompanied by a lion, her sacred animal. Among the Romans she was identified with Ops, a goddess of the harvest.

Rhesus (Rhesos). A king of Thrace and an ally of the Trojans in the Trojan War. See RHESUS and the ILIAD X.

Rhesus (Rhesos). A tragedy by an unknown author; believed by some authorities to be EURIPIDES and by others to be a dramatist of the fourth century B.C. Translations: in verse, Gilbert Murray, 1911; in verse, Arthur S. Way, 1912; in verse, Richmond Lattimore, 1958.

MYTHICAL BACKGROUND. *Rhesus* is based on the tenth book of the ILIAD, sometimes called the "Doloneia."

SCENE. Before the tent of Hector on the plain of Troy.

SUMMARY. The Chorus of Trojan Guards enters, calling for Hector, the leader of the Trojan forces. Having observed beacon fires burning in the Greek camp and the Greek army obviously planning some action, the Guards urge Hector to arm his people and their allies. Hector suggests that the Greeks may be planning to leave Troy that night. He regrets following the advice of the prophets who told him to wait for daybreak for his attack on the Greeks and gives orders that his men be awakened and told to arm themselves. Aeneas enters, asking what all the tumult is about. He disapproves of Hector's plan to attack the Greeks and suggests that he send a spy into the Greek camp to find out if they really intend to flee. Hector accepts this advice and, when Dolon offers to disguise himself and spy on the Greeks, Hector praises his courage. Dolon demands Achilles' immortal horses as his reward when the Greeks are conquered. Hector gives his word that they will be his. Dolon disguises himself as a wolf and boldly goes forth as the Chorus asks Apollo to guide him.

A Shepherd enters to tell Hector that King Rhesus of Thrace is arriving with his army to aid the Trojans. Hector, sure of victory at this point, bitterly remarks that when he least needs allies he seems to have many. Nonetheless he agrees to accept the help of Rhesus, whom the Chorus welcomes. Rhesus enters proudly, vowing that in one day he will destroy the Greeks' wall, burn their ships, and kill their leaders. He is eager to engage in combat with Achilles and his men, but Hector informs him that Achilles has withdrawn from battle and tells him of other great Greek heroes—Ajax, Diomedes, and Odysseus. Rhesus proudly announces that he will capture and slay Odysseus.

Hector advises Rhesus to get some sleep, and they go out with their attendants.

The Trojan Guards watch for a while and then leave to call replacements. Odysseus and Diomedes enter, carrying Dolon's disguise. They are following directions obviously given them by Dolon, whom they have captured and killed. Finding none of the Trojan leaders, they are about to turn back when Athene appears and advises them to kill Rhesus and capture his beautiful swift horses. Athene sees Paris approaching, but will not allow Diomedes to kill him. Odysseus and Diomedes go out.

Pretending to be Aphrodite, Athene soothes Paris, who, fearing the presence of spies, has been calling for Hector. Paris returns to his post. Odysseus and Diomedes have killed Rhesus and are pursued by the Guards. Pretending to be an ally, Odysseus gives the Trojan password *Phoebus,* which he has learned from Dolon, and he and Diomedes escape. Now the Guards begin to wonder whether they have allowed the cunning Odysseus to escape. Soon the Charioteer of Rhesus enters. He has been wounded and, moaning in pain, he tells of how Odysseus and Diomedes killed Rhesus. When Hector comes in he is furious with the Guards for allowing the Greeks to enter. The Thracian Charioteer suspects Hector of murdering his master for his horses. Hector defends himself and says that the deed was probably done by Odysseus. He comforts the wounded Charioteer and orders his men to take him to his house.

As the Chorus chants sorrowfully, the Muse of the Mountains appears above, holding the body of her dead son Rhesus in her arms. She mourns for him and curses Odysseus, Diomedes, and Helen, who have left her childless. Then she sadly tells how she had begged Rhesus not to fight at Troy, for she knew he would die. It was Athene who gave Odysseus and Diomedes the power to kill her son. The Muse then speaks of Thetis, the mother of Achilles, who soon will also mourn for her son, and of the sorrow of all mothers who lose their children. After the Muse vanishes, Hector points to the dawn and orders the Trojans and their allies to arm themselves for battle.

Rhetoric (Rhetorika). Treatise (c. 330 B.C.) in three books by ARISTOTLE. Translations: J. E. C. Welldon, 1886; R. C. Jebb, 1909; John Henry Freese, 1926.

SUMMARY. *Book I.* Rhetoric, which is similar to dialectic, since both have to do with general rather than specialized knowledge, is also an art, because rhetoric can be organized according to a theory or system. Earlier writers of manuals on rhetoric do not deal with enthymemes (proofs), but instead emphasize irrelevant subjects, such as ways to arouse emotions. Their aim seems to be to create prejudice rather than to bring about justice based upon logic.

The enthymeme, a type of syllogism, is the method by which proof can be demonstrated and is a way of arriving at truth. Rhetoric has the power to reveal truth in spite of the false reasoning of poor advocates; it makes it possible for a person to set forth his case in language all can understand rather than in specialized or scientific terms. Both rhetoric and dialectic deal with and can prove opposites, and can help a man to overcome unfair opposition. If the argument is raised that rhetoric may be misused, the same can be said of all valuable things and qualities, except virtue.

Rhetoric is the art of discovering all methods of persuasion about all subjects. To persuade, one uses proofs, such as laws, witnesses, oaths, and other technical means, or proofs based upon the character of the speaker, emotional appeals, and logical demonstration. Thus an orator must have a logical mind; he must comprehend human character and be able to evaluate it, and he must know the quality of emotion and what causes it. It follows that rhetoric is related not only to dialectic but to ethics and politics.

Whereas the enthymeme is deductive, the example, another method of proof, is inductive. All proofs are enthymemes or examples.

There are three kinds of rhetoric which are appropriate to three types of audiences, for every speech consists of three parts: the speaker, his subject, and his audience. The deliberative speech is concerned with events of the future; the forensic speech deals with the past, and the epideictic, or occasional, usually treats of the present, though it may refer to the past or future. The deliberative speech persuades or dissuades, the forensic accuses or defends, and the epideictic praises or blames.

Since the deliberative oration must deal with the nature of happiness and those things that produce or prevent this state, happiness must be defined. Happiness presupposes good fortune as well as *arete*, security, wealth, power; a happy man has noble birth, friends, wealth, children, health, honor, physical beauty. The deliberative oration must also consider the nature of the expedient and the good. Since the epideictic oration praises or blames, the orator must be aware of the nature of virtue and evil. The forensic orator must understand the motivation behind bad conduct, the psychological state of the man who commits a crime, and the typical victims of crimes.

Book II. The orator making either a deliberative or a forensic speech must convince his audience that he is intelligent, virtuous, and kind. A long analysis of the emotions follows in relation to achieving a reputation for kindness. Next, men are classified in accordance with their feelings, virtues, habits, practices, ages, birth, wealth, and general fortune.

The subjects common to all types of rhetoric are discussed: the possible and the impossible, whether or not an event has taken place or will take place, and largeness or smallness, magnification or extenuation. All types of rhetoric use examples and enthymemes. Examples can be events that have taken place or can be made up by the orator. Maxims, which are general statements, are the propositions or inferences of enthymemes when the steps of the syllogism are omitted. A real enthymeme includes the proposition, the syllogism, and the inferences or conclusions drawn from it. Various types of enthymemes are analyzed.

Book III. The next subject is style; the orator must know not only his subject but how to express himself. Prose style differs from poetic style, which has been discussed in the *Poetics.* Clarity and propriety are essential qualities of prose style. The orator should use metaphors and other means to achieve speech that is "distinctive" or unusual, that is, not commonplace, but at the same time with an appearance of naturalness; prose should be artful but not artificial.

Next, faults of style and their causes are discussed. A definition of the simile is followed by an analysis of the use of similes, particles, clauses, diction, gender, and number. Propriety is defined, and the rhythm of prose, periodic structure, and antithesis are discussed. A pleasant and instructive style employs metaphor, antithesis, and expressions which actually re-create reality. For each type of rhetoric there is an appropriate style, which is analyzed.

Every speech must have two sections: one in which the subject is stated and the other in which proof is given. Two more sections may be added: an exordium and an epilogue. The exordium is an introduction, like a prelude or a prologue. Various types of exordia are analyzed in relation to the purpose of the speaker. The next subject is methods of eliminating prejudice and suspicion from the audience. Narrative is then discussed as a technique in the three kinds of oratory. The analysis of proof is resumed at this point with reference to the kinds of proof appropriate to each of the three types of oration. Then questions and ridicule are considered as rhetorical techniques. The last subject is the epilogue, in which the speaker declares that he has accomplished what he promised his audience and shows that the position of his adversary is untenable.

Rome (Roma). A city on the Tiber, center of the Roman world. The legendary date of the founding of Rome is 753 B.C., when, according to Roman myth, Romulus, its first king, established Roma Quadrata (Square Rome), a fortified settlement on the Palatine Hill, near the Tiber River. The Romans regarded themselves as the descendants of the Trojans, who, after the fall of Troy in 1183 B.C., had followed their leader Aeneas to their new home in Italy (see AENEID). Aeneas' son Ascanius (Iulus) founded Alba Longa, a town in Latium about fifteen miles from Rome. He became the first of a line of Alban kings, the last of which was Amulius, who seized the throne from Numitor, the rightful king. To make certain that Numitor's daughter, Rhea Silvia, would not marry and bear offspring who might demand their hereditary right to the throne, Amulius made her a Vestal Virgin, sworn to chastity. When Rhea Silvia bore the twins Romulus and Remus, whose father she claimed was Mars, Amulius had her imprisoned and the twins put into a chest, which was thrown into the Tiber. (This story is one version of the universal folk tale of the exposure of the hero and his miraculous survival.) The chest was washed ashore near the Palatine Hill, where Romulus and Remus were suckled by a she-wolf, an animal sacred to Mars. They were found by Faustulus, a herdsman, who with his wife, Acca Larentia, reared them. When Romulus and Remus grew up, they deposed Amulius and restored Numitor as king of Alba Longa. They then planned to build a city in the place where they had been washed up on the shore. An omen determined that Romulus would be its king. As Romulus labored to establish his city, Remus expressed his scorn for his brother's work by leaping over the rising walls of the city, and Romulus killed him.

Since the new city had no women, Romulus devised the plan of extending an invitation to the Sabines, a neighboring tribe, to come with their wives and daughters to view games that were part of a festival. The Romans then seized the Sabine women and drove the men away. As a result of the "rape of the Sabines," a war broke out between the Romans and the Sabines, but the two peoples were finally reconciled and lived in peace. After a long reign, Romulus was taken to heaven and was thereafter worshiped as a god. Six more kings ruled Rome: Numa Pompilius, Tullus Hostilius, Ancus Marcius, Tarquinius Priscus, Servius Tullius, and Tarquinius Superbus. During their reigns Rome prospered; the city was enlarged and surrounded by a wall that took in the seven hills.

Though Rome's Trojan origin, the above account of the founding of the city, and many of the tales dealing with the reigns of the seven kings are legendary, Rome may have been established by settlers from Alba Longa and no doubt was ruled by kings in the beginning. The area of Rome was inhabited as early as the second millennium, but the actual city was probably not established until about 575 B.C. During the early years of Rome's existence the city was greatly influenced by the Greek colonies in south Italy and by the Etruscans, north of the Tiber. During the sixth century B.C. the Etruscans became the most powerful people in Italy. There is evidence that they conquered Rome, whose last three kings were probably Etruscan. In 510 B.C. the Romans, under the leadership of Lucius Junius Brutus (who may be a later invention), expelled the last king, Brutus' uncle Tarquinius Superbus, and Brutus became one of the first of the two praetors (later called consuls) of Rome. Brutus is said to have sacrificed his own sons who tried to restore the Tarquins. (See *Aeneid* VI, 817–823.)

From 509 to 27 B.C. Rome was a republic. Its unwritten constitution provided for two chief magistrates, known as consuls in classical times, a Senate, and a popular Assembly. At first the state was ruled by the aristocracy, who supplied the members of the Senate and all the executive offices. Only gradually and after bitter internal strife did the lower economic and social classes gain any real voice in the government.

During the early years of the Republic the Romans were threatened by other peoples who inhabited the plain of Latium, by various hill tribes, such as the Umbrians and the Samnites, and by their old enemies the Etruscans. After defeating the Latins in the battle of Lake Regillus in 496 B.C., the Romans offered them equality and support in their struggles with other tribes. The Romans and Latins became allies. Rome resisted the onslaughts of the hill tribes and made peace with the Etruscans. A disastrous defeat by the Gauls in 390 B.C. interrupted the growth of Roman power in the peninsula. After a number of setbacks Roman expansion resumed with the gradual conquest of the hill tribes (Samnite Wars) and the defeat of Pyrrhus, a Greek king who invaded Italy early in the third century B.C. By about 270 B.C. Rome's authority in Italy was no longer threatened.

Rome's supremacy in Italy was now established; ahead of her lay the struggle for world dominion. Her conquest of CARTHAGE (in the Punic Wars), Macedonia, Spain, Greece, North Africa, Gaul, Britain, Syria, and Asia Minor made her the greatest power of the ancient world. During the last century of the Republic, Rome was racked by internal conflict or actual civil war, caused by the clashing interests of the conservative aristocracy, the ambitious businessmen, and the disenfranchised masses. The professionalization of the army made it possible for ruthless leaders to engage in armed contests for power. The brothers Gracchi (Tiberius Sempronius Gracchus, d. 133 B.C. and Gaius Sempronius Gracchus, d. 121 B.C.) attempted to achieve economic and social reforms: the redistribution of land, the fixing of a fair price for corn, the extension of the Roman franchise to all Latins, but they were defeated. Early in the first century B.C. the struggles between Marius and SULLA racked the Roman state, as did later the conspiracy of CATILINE. Then Julius CAESAR's conquests of Gaul from 58 B.C. to 50 B.C. led to another period of civil war between the forces of Caesar and those of POMPEY (49–45 B.C.). (Lucan's epic poem *On the Civil War* deals with this period.)

The dictatorship of Julius Caesar ended with his assassination in 44 B.C. This was followed by the conflict between the triumvirate ANTONY, Octavian, and Lepidus and the leaders of the Senatorial party, Brutus and Cassius. With the defeat and death of Brutus and Cassius at Philippi in 42 B.C., whatever remained of the Roman republic also died. Conflict then arose between Antony and Octavian, concluding with the defeat of Antony in 31 B.C. at Actium and his death in 30 B.C.

Octavian now ruled the Roman Empire. In 27 B.C. the Senate gave him the title Augustus and, while insisting he was only *princeps* (leader), he actually became the first Roman emperor, with absolute power in political, military, and economic affairs. Under Augustus there was peace at home, and the Romans continued to make conquests abroad, expanding their territory in Europe, Egypt, central Asia Minor, and Numidia (in North Africa). Augustus reorganized the system of taxation in Rome and introduced financial reforms. He attempted to raise the moral and cultural standards of Rome. Augustus boasted that he had found the city brick and left it marble. Certainly he was responsible for the erection of many fine public buildings and for magnificent additions to the Forum. He encouraged the poets Horace and Vergil and the historian Livy, and it is their work that has established the Augustan Age as the greatest period of Rome's artistic productivity.

Tiberius (ruled A.D. 14–37), the successor of Augustus, followed his example in his attempts to retain republican elements within imperial government. Though he made an effort to increase the power of the Senate and requested the aid of this body, he never succeeded in obtaining its support. Contemporary scholars agree that the Roman historians Suetonius and Tacitus were unduly harsh in their treatment of Tiberius. Even Tacitus, who depicts him as a corrupt and ineffective ruler, admits that he was successful in establishing good provincial governments (see ANNALS I–VI).

The emperors who followed Tiberius varied a great deal in character and achievement. Caligula, who ruled briefly (A.D. 37–41), is generally regarded as a tyrant whose excesses reflected his unstable character. His successor Claudius (ruled A.D. 41–54), on the other hand, was essentially a humane and dedicated ruler, whose accomplishments included the extension of Roman provincial territory, the reform of public finance, the establishment of public works, and the improvement and extension of the Imperial Civil Service.

His successor Nero (ruled A.D. 54–68) is notorious for his vanity and cruelty. During the early years of his reign he was restrained by the influence and advice of the philosopher Seneca and the commander of the guard Afranius Burrus. They could not, however, prevent him from committing matricide, and, after the death of Burrus and the retirement of Seneca, the tyranny of Nero was unchecked. Opposition to him increased at Rome, and rebellions broke out among the Roman forces in Gaul and in Spain. When Nero realized that his power as emperor was gone and the Praetorian Guards had turned against him, he fled from Rome and went into hiding. Learning that the Senate had declared him a public enemy, he decided on suicide. (See ANNALS XII–XVI.)

Tacitus remarks that though at first the news of Nero's death was welcomed by the Romans, it later brought forth various responses, for the people realized "that an emperor could be made elsewhere than at Rome" (*Histories* I, 4). Galba (ruled A.D. 68–69) was declared emperor by his army in Spain; then he was accepted by the Roman Senate. As emperor he was unpopular with the Senate, the Army, and the Roman people and was finally assassinated when Otho (ruled A.D. 69) was proclaimed emperor by the Praetorians. After a few months Otho was overthrown by Vitellius (ruled A.D. 69), who was declared emperor by the German army. He in turn ruled only a few months before he was deposed by the army of Vespasian. (See HISTORIES.)

Vespasian (ruled A.D. 70–79) restored peace to the Roman world. He proclaimed himself censor, a position that allowed him to determine the composition of the Senate. He was an absolute but comparatively just ruler. His son Titus, who succeeded him (ruled A.D. 79–81), was an attractive and generous man, popular with the Roman people. The character of his successor Domitian (ruled A.D. 81–96) is more difficult to determine. In his life of

Domitian, Suetonius says that the emperor's need of money caused his greed and his terror of assassination his cruelty. Ancient writers, such as Pliny, Tacitus, and Juvenal, depict him as a harsh and cruel monarch, whose reign brought terror to the Roman citizen. Though contemporary scholars regard these accounts as exaggerated, there is little doubt that Domitian was an autocratic ruler, unpopular with the Senate and the Roman people. His assassination in A.D. 96 ended a time of harsh rule. The reigns of the next three emperors, Nerva (ruled A.D. 96–98), Trajan (ruled A.D. 98–117), and Hadrian (ruled A.D. 117–138), can be considered the close of the classical period. These were reasonable and wise rulers, who made valuable contributions to the political, social, and cultural life of the Empire. (Sources for Roman history include the works of LIVY, TACITUS, SALLUST, and SUETONIUS.)

Ancient Rome has become a symbol of dignity and splendor. For the poets and historians of the Empire, the period of the early Republic represented a simple, dignified way of life inspired by dedication and integrity. To the modern world Rome has become a pervading myth. The concept of *Romanitas,* as Tertullian calls it, the feeling that a Roman image gave gravity and significance to a work of art or a way of life, existed throughout English history almost until the present. The legend of England's Roman origin is to be found recorded not only in Geoffrey of Monmouth, Wace, and Layamon, but in practical details of state affairs. Paul Stapfer tells of how the Roman legend "made its way into the most secret transactions in diplomacy, politics, and in war" during the Middle Ages. In fact, Edward III attempted to prove in a letter to Pope Boniface that England, because of its Trojan origins, was superior to Scotland (P. Stapfer, *Shakespeare and Classical Antiquity,* trans. Emily J. Carey [C. K. Paul, 1880], p. 201).

To the Elizabethan, Rome was the land of heroes, faithful warriors at Troy, and exalted leaders of the Republic and the Empire. Renaissance England accepted and honored the myth of its Trojan origins. Shakespeare portrayed Roman civilization from several points of view. In *Coriolanus* he presented the old Rome of legend, when the tribunes won out against the pride of a man who, in spite of his flaw, exemplified the dignity of Roman *gravitas.* The Rome of the city-state struggling to keep the Republic alive is portrayed in *Julius Caesar.* Finally, in *Antony and Cleopatra,* Shakespeare suggests the splendor and corruption of the Empire. The English Augustans consciously attempted to impose upon their own time a myth of grandeur based upon Roman civilization. John Dryden, Joseph Addison, Alexander Pope, and Jonathan Swift all employ Roman allusions and images as examples of nobility, propriety, and wisdom.

Romulus. See ROME.

Rope (Rudens). A comedy (date unknown) by PLAUTUS. Translations: in prose, Paul Nixon, 1932; in verse, F. A. Wright and H. L. Rogers, 1924; in prose, Cleveland Clark, 1942; in prose, Frank O. Copley, 1956; in prose and verse, Lionel Casson, 1960; in prose, Samuel Lieberman, 1964.

SCENE. A seacoast near Cyrene in Africa.

SUMMARY. *Rope* is a romantic comedy based on a Greek play by Diphilus. In the Prologue, delivered by the constellation Arcturus, the audience is told about the sad life of Daemones, an old Athenian who now lives in Cyrene. He has lost all his property; his daughter Palaestra was kidnaped and sold to the procurer Labrax, who took her to Cyrene. Plesidippus, a young Athenian living in Cyrene, fell in love with Palaestra and gave Labrax some of the money needed to purchase her. Labrax agreed that Plesidippus could have the girl as soon as he paid the rest, but the procurer broke his promise when his friend Charmides urged him to take Palaestra and another girl, Ampelisca, to Sicily, where they would bring him a great deal of money. Labrax, Charmides, and the two girls set sail for Sicily, but Arcturus brought about a storm, and they were shipwrecked. Now the procurer and his friend are stranded on a rock while the two girls are brought to shore in a small boat.

When Palaestra and Ampelisca reach land, they go to pray at the altar of Venus. Soon the priestess Ptolemocratia asks them to enter the temple. When Trachalio, Plesidippus' slave, enters, seeking his master, he discovers Palaestra and Ampelisca. Soon Labrax and Charmides hurry in to find the girls. When Palaestra and Ampelisca resist them, the procurer and his friend try to force them to leave the temple. Trachalio summons Daemones, who comes with his slaves and defends the girls. Trachalio calls Plesidippus, and Labrax is overcome, bound, and taken off to jail.

Palaestra and Ampelisca go home with Daemones. When his slave Gripus retrieves Labrax's trunk from the sea, Palaestra finds in it a casket of tokens that identify her as the lost daughter of Daemones, who now arranges for her marriage to Plesidippus. Thus the lovers are reunited, Ampelisca and Gripus are freed, and even Labrax is forgiven his sins by Daemones and invited to dinner.

Rudens. See ROPE.

S

Sallust (Gaius Sallustius Crispus). A Roman historian, born in 86 B.C. at Amiternum (San Vittorino), fifty miles northeast of Rome. Though of a plebeian family, Sallust rose swiftly to a position of importance in Rome. In 59 B.C. he became quaestor and in 52 B.C. tribune of the people. Though in 50 B.C. he was accused of immorality and expelled from the Senate, he regained his political power when Caesar repaid him for his loyalty by appointing him quaestor in 49 B.C. and later governor of Numidia. After Caesar's assassination, Sallust, who had accumulated a great fortune, lived in splendid retirement on his magnificent estate, the *horti Sallustiani* (the gardens of Sallust), which later became the possession of Roman emperors. Sallust spent the years of his retirement writing history. His surviving works are a monograph, the *Bellum Catilinae* (*The Conspiracy of Catiline*), the *Bellum Jugurthinum* (*The Jugurthine War*), and fragments of the *Historiae*, a history of the years 78 to 67 B.C. Sallust died in 35 B.C.

In his *Bellum Catilinae*, Sallust says that he regards the Catilinarian conspiracy as an important episode in Roman history because Catiline's crime was so unusual and seriously threatened the state. Though Sallust denounces the conspirators, he is more concerned with defending Caesar than in praising Cicero, who exposed Catiline and his followers. In general Sallust's portrait of the *optimates* (aristocracy) is a critical one; he wonders what has happened to the traditional Roman ideals of dignity and integrity. Sallust's monograph on Catiline is most valuable for his characterization of Catiline himself and for his vivid presentation of events of his own period.

The Jugurthine War deals with events of the late second century B.C., when Rome defeated Jugurtha, the ambitious and cruel king of Numidia. Q. Caecilius Metellus led the Roman armies against him, but failed to destroy his power. It was Marius, the leader of the *plebs*, who finally defeated him and led him captive through the streets of Rome. Jugurtha was imprisoned and died in 104 B.C. Sallust's "Introduction" to *The Jugurthine War* is a moralistic lament on the degeneracy of the times in which he lives. As in the *Bellum Catilinae*, he sadly recalls ancient Roman virtue, which seems no longer to exist. Even men of humble birth, once known for virtue, now are dishonest in their pursuit of political power and prestige. *The Jugurthine War* contains many examples of the decadence of the Roman aristocracy, its base motives and intrigues. In depicting Marius, the leader of the *plebs,* Sallust suggests a man of energy, ambition, and even integrity, but he implies that a desire for power was to become Marius' main motivation.

Sallust, who emulated Thucydides, is regarded as the first "scientific" Roman historian; he attempted to be factual and scholarly. Like Thucydides, Sallust invented appropriate speeches for the principal historical figures, and his reports of events are sometimes distorted by his own point of view. Nonetheless, his depiction of historical figures is always interesting, his style is vivid the dramatic, and his indignation at the corruption he witnessed and describes with such power seems to stem from sincere concern and conviction.

Samia. See THE GIRL FROM SAMOS.

Sappho. Greek lyric poet, born c. 600 B.C. at Eresus in Lesbos. Like other citizens, including the poet Alcaeus, she left the island during the period when a series of tyrants were in control of the government. Sappho lived in Sicily for some years, returning to Lesbos when, as she says, her hair was white. It is known that Sappho had brothers, one of whom was Charaxus. Her husband was named Cerkylas and her daughter Cleis. In Lesbos, Sappho was the head of a school or cult of young girls devoted to the study of poetry and music and probably to the worship of Aphrodite, goddess of beauty and love. Many of Sappho's love poems were written to the young girls who made up this group. The date of Sappho's death is unknown.

The ancients greatly admired Sappho's poetry and regarded her as the Tenth Muse. Her poems (see LYRICS) were organized in seven books, but unfortunately most of her work is lost, and only one complete poem survives. Sappho wrote in the Aeolic dialect, mostly monody, but she also composed some charming epithalamia to be sung by a chorus. Only fragments of these survive.

Despite the tragic loss of most of Sappho's poetry, she has been studied, praised, and emulated from her own time to the present. Sappho's capacity to suggest an intensely personal experience in a phrase or a sentence accounts for the power of even the briefest of her fragments. Plato, Dionysius of Halicarnassus, and "Longinus" all admired her work. Catullus and Horace imitated her; one of Ovid's HEROIDES (XV) is a letter from Sappho to Phaon; Horace, Byron, Swinburne, Sara Teasdale, Edna St. Vincent Millay, H. D., and other ancient and modern poets imitate her work and speak of her with reverence.

Sarpedon. The son of Zeus and Laodamia (or Europa); a warrior on the side of the Trojans in the ILIAD.

satire. Quintilian calls satire "entirely ours" (Roman). *Satura* had a long history before it became an authentic literary genre. It probably originated in oral contests in extemporaneous verse held by rustics during religious festivals and other celebrations. Out of these there probably developed a crude drama containing music and comic dialogue, but no actual plot. The word *satura* (medley) described the mixed elements of these rough performances and was then applied to the literary genre, in which were combined witty and serious criticism, either in exposition or dialogue or both, of social customs and attitudes, personal values and behavior, and literary standards and performances.

The first Roman literary attempts at satire were by Ennius and Pacuvius. Of their works only a few fragments of Ennius' satires survive. Actually it was Lucilius who first established the form that later satire was to take. Lucilius' satires were written mainly in hexameter verse. Though Horace criticizes the roughness of Lucilius' style, he also acknowledges his debt to Lucilius, declaring it is his own delight to "shut up words in feet *Lucili ritu* [in the manner of Lucilius]" (*Satire* II, 1). HORACE, PERSIUS, and JUVENAL all imitated Lucilius in their social and literary criticism. All extant Roman satire is in dactylic hexameter.

Another Roman satirist, Varro, whose satires were written in a mixture of prose and verse, imitated the dialogues of Menippus, a Greek philosopher of the third century B.C. Unfortunately none of Menippus' work and only fragments of Varro's *Menippean Satires* have survived.

The most brilliant and moving ancient satires were written by Horace and Juvenal, whose work retained the mixed elements that the name *satura* and the origin of the form suggest: the expression of personal feeling, social and literary criticism, serious and comic elements, straightforward exposition and moralizing, witty, ironic, or angry attacks, and dialogue and other dramatic techniques. Both these writers greatly influenced the development of modern satire.

Satires (Sermones) of HORACE. Poems (35–30 B.C.) in dactylic hexameter. Translations: in verse, J. Conington, 1870; in verse, Sir Theodore Martin, 1888; in prose, H. Rushton Fairclough, 1926; in verse, Smith Palmer Bovie, 1959.

SUMMARY. In his essay on satire John Dryden makes a distinction between the raillery of Horace and the declamation of Juvenal. "Horace," he says, "laughs to shame all follies, and insinuates virtue rather by familiar examples than by the severity of precepts." As a satirist Horace takes the *persona* or role of the gentle, paternal critic of human folly. In the first satire of the first book he asks why one cannot tell the truth with laughter as a teacher gives children sweets to persuade them to learn to read. Again in *Satire* I, iii he says we must treat our friends as a father treats his child; we must not be disgusted by their blemishes. Though this method seems gentle enough, when Horace goes on to give a pathetic picture of the father deceiving himself by describing his deformed child euphemistically, the ironic nature of Horace's laughter becomes clear. In the disparity between the blemish and the "paternal" euphemism for it there is humor and pathos, but there is also awareness of the flaw. Horace's chief satirical techniques are euphemism and understatement, the manner of speech of a kindly reformer, who sets up as his norm the simple life of honest pleasure on the Sabine Farm. Against this standard of a plain and frugal life he measures the follies and affectations of most men.

Horace's *Satires* deal with many subjects: the behavior of man in society; poetry, especially his own work, which he defends; the superiority of the country to the city; and his own way of life on the Sabine Farm. The first satire of the first book deals with the false values that drive men to seek money and position, but prevent them from enjoying life. Horace concludes that true happiness is to be found only in moderation, the "golden mean." In the second satire of the first book he develops this theme, particularly in connection with sexual extremes. Obviously influenced by Lucilius, Horace draws a series of character sketches of types who illustrate his thesis: extremes of any kind are unnatural and destructive. They are avoided when man enjoys a simple life, which Horace describes in many of his satires, using his own peaceful way of life as an example. In I, vi, addressed to Maecenas, Horace declares he has no ambition to achieve political or social success; content with the approval of Maecenas, he is proud of his humble origins and of his father, who, though poor, gave his son a fine education and good values. Now, Horace says, he lives more comfortably than a senator. He then describes a typical day of simple pleasure: he strolls about shopping and listening to the fortunetellers; he eats simply, reads, writes, and enjoys his leisure without the torments of ambition. In II, ii, in which Horace deals with the same theme, the peasant Ofellus, Horace's neighbor, tells of the benefits a wise man can derive from plain living. In II, vi the fable of the country mouse and the city mouse illustrates Horace's point that life on his Sabine Farm is much to be preferred to the more luxurious life of Rome. Horace again deals with false values in III, iii, humorously describing the four "ruling passions" or madnesses of mankind: greed, ambition, extravagance, and superstition.

Horace's criticisms of the ambitions and values of his fellow men brought accusations of slander against him. In several satires he defends himself, setting forth his aims as a satirist. In I, iv he declares that he is not attacking individuals but general vices. His aim is to correct the faults of mankind as he has corrected his own, through the examples taught him by his father. The writers of Old Comedy were unrestrained in their attacks on the wicked, and the satirist Lucilius followed their example. However, Lucilius was a careless writer who never polished his work. In I, x Horace again speaks of Lucilius, who, despite his satiric power, has many faults as a poet because he never learned to revise his work. Had he lived in Horace's own time, he would no doubt have been a more conscious stylist. Horace declares that he is not disturbed by the criticisms of his work; he writes not for a popular audience but for great men, such as Vergil, Maecenas, and Aristius Fuscus. In II, i Horace writes his best defense of himself as a satirist. In a dialogue with Gaius Trebatius Testa, a well-known lawyer contemporary with Cicero, Horace wittily expresses his attitude toward his work. When Trebatius suggests that Horace give up writing altogether, Horace declares that for him the chief delight in life is to "shut up words in feet." No matter what the condition of his life, no matter what awaits him, no matter where he lives, he must write.

Other subjects of Horace's satires are a journey to Brundisium (I, v); Priapus, the god of gardens (I, viii); a bore whom Horace cannot avoid (I, ix); legacy hunting in Rome (II, v); the Stoic idea that only the wise man is free (II, vii); and a dinner party at which Maecenas was the guest of honor (II, viii).

Satires (Saturae) of JUVENAL. Poems (end of the first and beginning of the second century A.D.) in dactylic hexameter. Translations: Satires I, III, VI, X, XVI in verse, John Dryden, 1693; in verse, William Gifford, 1852; in prose, G. G. Ramsay, 1918; in verse, Rolfe Humphries, 1958; in verse, Hubert Creekmore, 1963; in verse, Jerome Mazzaro, 1965.

SUMMARY. *Satire I.* In the first satire Juvenal announces his aims as a satirist. Like Martial, he declares he will deal not with the conventional subjects of myth, which have become stale by now, but with the passions and vices of men. When he observes the corruption around him, it is "difficult not to write satire." One must have a "heart of iron" to endure the evils of Rome—the homosexuals marrying each other, the *nouveaux riches* and their extravagant affectations, the informers, thieves, extortionists, and murderers in power. It is a world in which "honesty is praised and then starves." "Indignation," Juvenal says, "creates verses." His subjects will be "whatever concerns men, their wishes, fears, wrath, pleasure, happiness, their comings and goings." Never was there more corruption. Money is regarded as a god by the Romans, and is used for the most disgusting and wasteful self-indulgence. Realizing that he does not have the freedom of his ancestors to express his indignation, Juvenal declares he will refer only to those whose ashes lie beneath the monuments along the great roads.

Satire II. The second satire attacks the hypocrisy of those who pretend to be guided by the strict morality of the Stoic philosophers but actually indulge in debauchery. Juvenal tells of how the emperor Domitian, having seduced his own niece Julia, revived the harshest moral laws. Juvenal's chief target is homosexuality. He describes the homosexual dressed in clothing of gauze or engaging in women's rites in honor of the Bona Dea, or using cosmetics and mirrors in the manner of the emperor Otho, who took a mirror along with him to the battlefield. Observing Gracchus, once a priest of Mars, dressed as a bride and participating in a homosexual "marriage" ceremony, Juvenal cries out in pain and rage to Mars, father of the city, asking how a descendant of a noble old family of Rome could have fallen so low. What would the great leaders of the Republic think of the degradation of their descendants and their nation?

Satire III. Juvenal's friend, Umbricius, has decided to leave Rome. While his possessions are being packed, he tells Juvenal why he can no longer bear to remain in Rome. An honest man, Umbricius declares, can no longer survive in that decadent city where only the hypocrite, the liar, the murderer, and the thief can flourish. Many Greeks and Orientals have settled in Rome, bringing with them their decadent manners and evil customs. At Rome only wealth is admired; only the rich are treated decently, while the poor are ridiculed and humiliated. Housing is poor and expensive in Rome, and there are many fires; the city is noisy, crowded, dirty, and dangerous. Bidding his friend farewell, Umbricius tells Juvenal that if he ever returns to his native Aquinum, he will gladly visit him and listen to his satires. (Samuel Johnson's poem "London" is an imitation of this satire.)

Satire IV. The satire begins with an account of how Crispinus, once a fish peddler and then a colonel in the bodyguard of the emperor Domitian, paid for a single mullet more than the fisherman himself or a whole estate would cost, then ate it all by himself.

This brief tale of the self-indulgence and extravagance of the parvenu Crispinus is followed by a mock-heroic account of the emperor Domitian's problem when a monstrous turbot was presented to him. Because the palace contained no vessel large enough to hold this fish, Domitian summoned his cabinet to help him solve the problem of how to cook the fish. The cabinet consists of men whom Domitian hates; "on their faces," says Juvenal, "had settled the pallor of their great and wretched friendship" with the emperor. A scathing description of the ministers follows. Then Domitian suggests the possibility of cutting up the fish, but Montanus protests that it must be spared such a disgrace. This minister advises that a special pot be made in which to cook the turbot, and the problem is solved.

Satire V. Juvenal gives a detailed and vivid account of the humiliations to which the Roman patron subjected his clients or dependents. The exactness of detail and the bitter tone of the satire suggest that Juvenal is drawing on his own experience as a client. After many months of serving his patron, the client is finally asked to dinner. He is given the least desirable place on the least important of the three couches which the diners occupy. The host Virro eats excellent food and drinks fine old wine, but his client is given dreadful food and drink. Even the servants scorn the client. If the client were suddenly to obtain a great deal of money, then Virro would treat him as a friend, for money is the "brother" of Virro. Do not assume, says Juvenal, that Virro provides such poor food and drink for his client because he is stingy; it is rather because he wishes to humiliate the poor fellow, hoping to see him weep with anger. The satire ends with the bitter suggestion that the role of the client is no better than that of the slave. (Martial frequently deals with this subject.)

Satire VI. This violent attack on women is addressed to Postumus, who is considering marriage. From Juvenal's point of view, he would be better off committing suicide. Chaste women no longer exist; all women are unfaithful to their husbands. They are attracted to actors and gladiators, but scorn serious and learned men. Women have courage only for mischief. In illustrating the sins of women, Juvenal describes the insatiable lust of the empress Messalina. After a detailed and disgusting picture of the empress' efforts to satisfy her desires by pretending to be a harlot in a brothel, Juvenal declares that lust is the least of women's sins. He warns Postumus against the pride of a woman with all the virtues. Then he speaks of women's affectations, cruelty, and deceitfulness. Women think a bed is the best place to quarrel with their husbands. Juvenal warns against the extravagant woman and the musical one. Worse than these is the knowledgeable type, who must know what is happening all over the world. But worst of all is the intellectual woman, the expert on poetry, grammar, rhetoric, law, and other subjects. Juvenal next deals with the shameful ways in which women adorn themselves, their gaudy jewelry and ugly cosmetics. He goes on to speak of their superstitions and then of their unwillingness to bear children and their frequent abortions. Women drive their husbands mad with magic charms and often kill their husbands and children. Juvenal asks if he is going beyond the bounds of satire and dealing with the material of tragedy. Answering his own question, he declares that every street has its Clytemnestra.

Satire VII. Juvenal looks forward to the encouragement of learned men by the new emperor (possibly Hadrian). Poets and other learned men have always been badly treated and have never been able to earn adequate money. A poet requires financial security to be able to write freely and happily. Horace and Vergil were fortunate, for they had no concerns except their poetry. Today rich men will do little to help poets. The only patronage of any value is that of a successful actor, who will reward poets as the great patrons of former days always did, with power and wealth. Historians, pleaders in the courts, rhetoricians, and teachers all starve. Parents require that a teacher know everything, but they are unwilling to pay for his work.

Satire VIII. Though Juvenal had great respect for the noble old families of Rome, viewing their degenerate descendants, he asks, "What good is a noble ancestral line," when you are a gambler, a homosexual, or a dealer in poison? "The only true nobility is virtue." No matter what his background, a virtuous man should be honored as a member of the nobility. Great and learned orators and the bravest soldiers have come from the lower classes, while the descendants of the noble families accomplish little. Addressing the highborn Ponticus, Juvenal says he must not be content to rest upon the reputation of his family. He must be a brave warrior, a fair judge, an honest and compassionate governor. If his associates and his wife are honest, he may trace his ancestry back to the mythical Latin king Picus. If, however, he is motivated by ambition and lust, then his noble ancestry will serve only as a "torch" to cast light on his corruption. After describing the infamy of many men descended from a noble line, including the emperor Nero and the conspirator Catiline, Juvenal declares that the great Cicero, who saved the state despite the machinations of Catiline and Cethegus, came from a humble family of Arpinum. Of course, says Juvenal in a powerful parenthetical statement, "it was a free Rome that called Cicero its parent and the father of his country." Another man from a poor family of Arpinum was Marius, who, in his youth, labored as a farmer but became a consul of Rome and overthrew the Teutones and the Cimbri, Germanic tribes that threatened Italy. The last of the good Roman kings was the child of a slave. It is better to be the child of Thersites (see ILIAD II) and have the courage of Achilles than to be the child of Achilles and be like Thersites.

Satire IX. In a conversation with Naevolus, a disgusting and pathetic man who has earned his living by selling his body, Juvenal reveals the sordidness of his way of life and the corruption of the society in which he functions. Naevolus is in despair, because many men have derived a substantial income from work such as his, but he has worked hard and has little to show for his labors, which include providing offspring for impotent men. Fortune, which rules men's lives, he declares, is unwilling to hear his prayers.

Satire X. The greatest of Juvenal's satires was imitated by Samuel Johnson in the poem "The Vanity of Human Wishes," a title which briefly states Juvenal's theme. In all the world, he says, there are only a few men who can remove themselves from the "fog of error" and who have enough insight to distinguish between the good and the harmful. "When," asks Juvenal, "does reason motivate what we fear or desire?" Very often the answer to a prayer brings only destruction. The very gift of eloquence has often brought death; men have been ruined by their own strength and by the money they carefully saved. Nero sent the wealthy lawyer Longinus into exile and ordered the wealthy Seneca to commit suicide. "Rarely will a soldier be sent into an attic." The most frequent of all prayers is for a great deal of money, but no one drinks poison out of an earthen vessel; one must fear only to drink from a cup set with jewels. Democritus, the laughing philosopher, was amused by the folly of his own time (fifth century B.C.); what would he say to the affectations, excesses, and corruption of the present?

The things for which we pray either do us no good or are extremely harmful. Power and the envy it evokes have destroyed many men. When Sejanus was the favorite of the emperor Tiberius, the people envied and admired him, but once he fell from power and was sentenced to death, he was scorned and denounced by the mob. The Roman people, who once elected their leaders and were involved in political and military affairs, now care only for bread and the circus games. Pride and the foolish desire for excessive wealth and power brought about the fall of Sejanus and other men who were once leaders or kings.

Every young boy prays that he will have the eloquence of Cicero or Demosthenes, yet their eloquence caused the death of both these great orators. Every general prays for the spoils of war, for these are the signs of what he considers to be glory. Yet this desire for honor has destroyed many a nation; moreover, the monuments bearing the names of the victorious generals will themselves perish. Hannibal, the mighty conqueror, finally poisoned himself in defeat. The whole world was too small for Alexander the Great; but in Babylon, where he died, a sarcophagus offered room enough. When people are ill, they pray for long life, but old age is full of anguish. The old are ugly and all alike in their trembling voices and limbs, their baldness, their toothless mouths, their inability to enjoy any of the pleasures of life, their susceptibility to disease, and the weakness of their intellects. Mothers pray that their children may be beautiful, but beauty is often destructive. No ugly young man was ever emasculated by a tyrant; Nero never took an unattractive young man as a favorite.

What then shall one pray for? Since the gods care more for man than man cares for himself, it is wise to allow them to provide what is best. However, if one must pray for something, pray for a "healthy mind in a healthy body," for a brave soul that does not fear death and can bear hard work of any kind, that does not know anger or desire, and prefers the labors of Hercules to the luxury of the glutton Sardanapalus. Only virtue can assure a peaceful life.

Satire XI. The first part of the poem deals with Rutilus and other impoverished and foolish gluttons who are heavily in debt because they will not deny themselves rare and expensive foods. Juvenal quotes the maxim "Know thyself," declaring that it descended from the heavens and "should be fixed in the heart and memory whether a man seeks a wife or wants a seat in the Senate." A man should know his own capacities in "things large and small"; even when he buys a fish, he must not desire a mullet when he can afford only a gudgeon.

In the second part of the satire Juvenal invites his friend Persicus to dinner at his Tiburtine farm. Persicus will discover that Juvenal lives according to the principles he advocates. They will enjoy fresh food supplied by the farm and will feast as did members of the Senate in the distant past when Romans lived with simple dignity. For entertainment they will read aloud from Homer and Vergil.

Satire XII. Juvenal's friend Catullus has escaped shipwreck, and Juvenal hails the day that brought this good fortune. He will offer sacrifices to Juno, Minerva, and Jupiter. He describes the terrible storm at sea that forced his friend to throw his cargo overboard. Finally the sea grew calm, and the ship was able to land at Ostia. As he offers his sacrifices in thanksgiving for his friend's safe return, Juvenal remarks that he has no ulterior motive, since Catullus has three heirs. He is not like those who will do anything to obtain the legacy of a rich man without offspring. Juvenal then speaks of the fantastic sacrifices such unscrupulous men will make to prove their devotion to a rich and childless man. If they have a daughter, they will offer her as a sacrifice, imitating Agamemnon, who sacrificed his child Iphigenia.

Satire XIII. Juvenal tells his friend Calvinus, who has been cheated out of a large sum of money by a dishonest acquaintance, that an evil deed torments the man who commits it, for his own conscience convicts him. Calvinus must not indulge in wrath inappropriate to his loss. Surely life has taught him to endure evil. What day exists that does not reveal theft, perfidy, fraud, and murder for the sake of money? There are very few honest men. The present age is worse than the age of iron; it is so corrupt that nature can discover no metal to use as its name. (For the ages of man see WORKS AND DAYS and Ovid's *Metamorphoses*.) Long ago in the age of Saturn men were honest and so well behaved that, if a young man did not rise in the presence of his elders, men thought he had committed a crime. Today if a friend returns money entrusted to him, he is regarded as a marvel. Calvinus must realize that the crime committed against him is only one among a great number committed every day, nor must he regret that the man who deceived him goes unpunished. What would Calvinus gain even if the man were killed, since his money would not be restored? Moreover, only foolish people can gain satisfaction from vengeance. Most important, the guilty man cannot escape the punishment inflicted by his own conscience, which constantly torments him. Such a man is never free to enjoy life; ever aware of his crime, he is punished by his incessant fear of punishment.

Satire XIV. Usually the poor example of parents is responsible for the sins of children. The gambler's son will gamble; the glutton's son will care only for rich foods; the cruel father will teach his son to obtain satisfaction from the suffering of others; and the licentious woman will train her daughter in corruption. Only a very unusual youth will fail to follow the example of an evil parent. Therefore, if for no other reason, one should refrain from evil for the sake of one's children. The only vice children will not willingly imitate is avarice, because it often disguises itself as the virtue of thrift. Thus fathers try very hard to instill this evil in their children, urging them to emulate the miser so that they may one day amass huge fortunes. The noble Romans of ancient times were content with two acres of land; today such a plot would be considered too small for a garden. The main cause of crime is the lust for money, which leads men even to murder. Fathers urge their sons to obtain money by any means. "The smell of money is good, no matter the source" is the maxim young people are taught. Men will take any risk for money, yet a huge fortune causes only anxiety. A millionaire must constantly guard his wealth. Alexander the Great envied the philosopher Diogenes, content in his tub, a home easily repaired or replaced. A man needs only enough money to satisfy his hunger and thirst, as much as Epicurus or Socrates required.

Satire XV. After speaking of the strange customs of the Egyptians, who worship animals, yet will eat human flesh, Juvenal tells of an incident that took place in Egypt in A.D. 127. For a long time there was a feud between the citizens of the neighboring towns of Ombi and Tentyra. During a battle between them one of the inhabitants of Tentyra was hurrying away in fear when he fell to the ground. He was immediately seized by the enemy, who cut up his body and ate it. Juvenal expresses his horror at this monstrous deed, for which no known punishment is sufficient. Nature provided man with tears as a sign of his capacity for tenderness and compassion, his noblest qualities. No virtuous man is untouched by any human sorrow. Man's capacity for compassion separates him from the animals; it is responsible for the arts and practices of civilized society.

Satire XVI. The sixteenth satire, which is fragmentary, tells of the great privileges that soldiers enjoy. In court a soldier receives far better treatment than a civilian, and soldiers are allowed to make wills while their fathers are alive, because the money a soldier earns is not controlled by his father.

Satires (Saturae) of PERSIUS. Poems (first century A.D.) in dactylic hexameter. Translations: in verse, John Dryden, 1693; in prose, J. Conington, 1893; in prose, G. G. Ramsay, 1918; in verse, J. Tate, 1930; in verse, W. S. Merwin, 1961.

SUMMARY. *Satire I.* In a dialogue between Persius and a friend, Persius deals with the theme that Rome's decline in morality is reflected in its literature. Persius declares that he cannot help laughing at the hypocrisy of the degenerate Romans he observes. The poetry he hears is licentious and pretentious, yet it is praised by most Romans. Men who cannot write a simple straightforward description attempt heroic verse. When his friend says that contemporary poetry is at least graceful, Persius quotes "Arma virum," the first two words of the *Aeneid,* to remind him of what real poetry is. Compared with Vergil's work, contemporary poetry is mere bombast. Since both Lucilius and Horace criticized their fellow men, why, asks Persius, may he not speak openly? (This poem owes much to Horace and no doubt influenced Juvenal's first satire.)

Satire II. It is the birthday of Persius' friend Macrinus and thus an occasion for prayers to the gods. Macrinus can pray aloud because he need not be ashamed of his requests, but most men, says Persius, pray in public for a good mind and a good reputation, but secretly they pray that their rich relatives may die so that they may inherit their money. Old grandmothers pray that their grandchildren may become rich and powerful. People pray for health but destroy their bodies with excessive food; they pray for wealth but waste what they have in sacrificing to the gods. They believe that the gods value gold as human beings do. One must not judge the gods by debased human standards. The gods will honor a man of pure and noble soul with simple offerings.

Satire III. Persius criticizes those who know what is right but do not act on their knowledge. He seems to be chiding himself for laziness and childish self-indulgence. He knows that he should be working hard and seriously. A man must know himself and what he is destined to do.

Satire IV. Alcibiades, overly proud of his ancestry, his handsome appearance, and his eloquence, thought he knew a great deal about the affairs of the state of Athens. Actually he had poor values and little knowledge. Most people know little about themselves, though they arrogantly claim to know all about their neighbors. Despite the praise of his acquaintances, a man must look at himself candidly and acknowledge his own limitations.

Satire V. After a loving tribute to his teacher and friend, the Stoic philosopher Lucius Annaeus Cornutus, who guided him and taught him true values, Persius turns to the subject of freedom. Men think they want freedom, but the Stoic says that one cannot be truly free unless he knows how to live. Without proper values a man, though apparently free, is actually enslaved by his own passions—by the desire for wealth, luxury, or power, by love, or by superstition.

Satire VI. In this satire, addressed to his friend Caesius Bassus, Persius speaks of his right to use his income to enjoy a comfortable way of life despite the objections of his heir, who is fearful that little will be left for him.

Saturae (of Juvenal and Persius). See SATIRES.

Saturn (Saturnus). Originally an agricultural deity of Italy, later identified with the Greek Cronus and thus the father of Jupiter, Juno, Neptune, and Pluto. Saturn, whose name means "the sower," was the husband of Ops, a goddess of the harvest and of wealth. As a legendary king of Rome, Saturn was celebrated for introducing agriculture and thus establishing Roman civilization. His reign was considered a golden age, in memory of which the Romans held the Saturnalia, a festival at the end of December. During this period presents were exchanged, and all people, even slaves, were freed from the customary restraints. The temple of Saturn was located at the foot of the Capitoline Hill.

Satyricon. A fragmentary Latin novel in prose and verse, generally attributed to PETRONIUS ARBITER. The main plot of the novel deals with the escapades of Encolpius and Ascyltus and their servant Giton, who travel about southern Italy. "Trimalchio's Dinner," the most famous episode in what remains of the *Satyricon,* is an extremely funny account of the vulgarity of the *nouveau riche* Trimalchio and his boorish and pretentious guests. As Trimalchio drinks a great deal, he becomes sorrowful, but he is delightfully amusing to the reader as he discusses his will and demands a rehearsal of his funeral. The narration of the banquet is interrupted by two stories, one about a werewolf and the other about how witches took a boy and left in his place a figure of straw. The *Satyricon* is witty, ribald, lively, and gay. The work contains bizarre incidents, brilliant conversation, and realistic details of daily life. A good translation has been done recently by William Arrowsmith (1959).

satyr play. Like tragedy, the satyr play probably grew out of the early Greek dithyramb (see TRAGEDY). It was regarded by Aristotle as an intermediate stage in the development of tragedy. Satyric drama is thought to have been invented by Pratinas. The language and structure of the satyr play resemble those of tragedy; however, the chorus is made up of satyrs, who are often obscene, and the satyr play in general deals with the grotesque and comic features of myth. Satyr plays were performed at the festivals following groups of three tragedies, probably to provide relief for the audience from the intense emotional experience of tragic drama. The only remaining examples are Sophocles' ICHNEUTAI and Euripides' THE CYCLOPS.

satyrs. In Greek mythology, followers of the god Dionysus. The satyrs were minor gods associated with the country and with the quality of fertility in nature and man. Their form was essentially that of men, but they had many of the characteristics of the goat or the horse—pointed ears, a tail, and sometimes goats' legs. They are represented in Greek literature as wild and licentious creatures who constantly engage in mischief. See DITHYRAMB, TRAGEDY, SATYR PLAY, SILENUS, Sophocles' ICHNEUTAI, and Euripides' THE CYCLOPS.

Scylla (Skylla) (I). In Greek legend, a monster with twelve feet and six heads, each of which had three rows of teeth. Scylla lived in a cave opposite the whirlpool Charybdis and snatched and killed passing seamen. See ODYSSEY XII.

Scylla (Skylla) (II). Daughter of Nisus, king of Megara. See CIRIS and Ovid's METAMORPHOSES.

Selene. See ENDYMION.

Self-Tormentor, The (Heauton Timorumenos). A comedy (163 B.C.) by TERENCE. Translations: in prose, John Sargeaunt, 1912; in verse, W. Ritchie, 1927; in verse, F. Perry, 1929; in prose, anonymous translator in George Duckworth, ed., *The Complete Roman Drama*, 1942.

S C E N E . A country road near Athens, before the houses of Menedemus and Chremes.

S U M M A R Y . *The Self-Tormentor* is adapted from a comedy of the same name by Menander. As Menedemus, an old man, is working hard on his land, he is approached by his neighbor Chremes, who cannot understand why Menedemus, a wealthy man over sixty, is driven constantly to labor. When Menedemus asks him why he is concerned about other people, Chremes replies in a verse that has become famous: *Homo sum: humani nil a me alienum puto* ("I am a human being; I consider nothing human alien to me"). Menedemus then reveals that he is a tormented man who seeks relief from his guilt in labor. He feels responsible for forcing his son Clinia to become a mercenary in a foreign army. When Clinia fell in love with Antiphila, a poor girl, Menedemus was scornful of his son's feelings. He spoke harshly to the young man, frequently contrasting Clinia's self-indulgence with his own youthful bravery and resourcefulness, constantly pointing out that he had joined the army as a young man and thus achieved success and wealth. Finally Clinia left home to join the army of the king of Persia.

Soon Chremes' son Clitipho tells his father that Clinia has just come back from Asia and is now staying at Chremes' house. Clinia still loves Antiphila. Clitipho is in love with a courtesan named Bacchis, but has no money to support her. The two friends arrange for Bacchis to stay at Chremes' house in the role of Clinia's extravagant mistress; Antiphila will also come, pretending to be the servant of Bacchis.

Chremes informs Menedemus that his son has returned and that his beloved has degenerated into an extravagant and demanding courtesan. After a long series of complications it is discovered that Antiphila is the lost daughter of Chremes. Menedemus and Clinia are reconciled. Chremes, discovering that Bacchis is actually the mistress of Clitipho and that he has been the dupe of his son and his slave Syrus, declares he will disinherit his son.

A marriage is arranged for Clinia and Antiphila. The repentant Clitipho is forgiven by his father and, determined to change his ways, reluctantly agrees to obey his father's command that he get married.

Semele. In Greek mythology, the mother of Dionysus by Zeus and no doubt originally an earth-goddess. For the myth of her love affair with Zeus and the birth of Dionysus see THE BACCHAE.

Semonides. A Greek poet born on the island of Samos, who flourished during the middle of the seventh century B.C. He was one of the colonizers of the island of Amorgos, which became his home. Very little of his work survives. One extant fragment is a satire on women, in iambics, in which he compares them with animals. Another fragment tells of the wretchedness of human life.

Seneca, Lucius Annaeus (known as the Philosopher). A Roman philosopher and playwright, a son of Seneca the Rhetorician, born around 4 B.C. at Corduba (Cordova) in Spain. A weak and sickly child, he was brought to Rome where he received his education. He began his career as a lawyer and acquired a great deal of wealth. Seneca became quaestor (financial officer) around A.D. 33 and a member of the Senate; he also achieved fame as an orator, a philosopher, and a writer. The emperor Caligula is said to have been so jealous of Seneca's abilities that he would have had him killed had he not been certain that Seneca, who always suffered from poor health, would soon die. When Claudius became emperor in A.D. 41, his wife Messalina had Seneca charged with immoral conduct with Caligula's sister Julia Livilla. As a result Seneca was sent into exile in Corsica. Agrippina, Claudius' second wife and the mother of Nero, desired Seneca as the tutor for her young son and persuaded Claudius to recall him in A.D. 49.

During the early years of Nero's reign, both Seneca and Afranius Burrus, commander of the guard, had a strong influence on him, but by A.D. 59 they were incapable of restraining Nero from violent and sadistic behavior. In fact, Seneca and Burrus had a part in Nero's successful plot to murder his mother Agrippina. After the death of Burrus in A.D. 62 Seneca, realizing the danger of his position at court, offered his great wealth to Nero and retired, devoting himself to his writing. In A.D. 65 he was accused of involvement in the conspiracy of Piso to assassinate Nero and was commanded to commit suicide. Tacitus (in *Annals* xv) describes Seneca's calm acceptance of the sentence. When his wife

Paulina declared that she wished to die with him, he cut the veins in both their arms with a single stroke. Nero, however, ordered that Paulina's suicide be prevented; her wounds were bandaged, and she survived.

Readers of Seneca's philosophy have been troubled by the disparity between the high ethical standards set forth in his philosophical writings and the many compromises of his life. As a Stoic, Seneca believed and argued that the good life is a simple one that follows the laws of nature, that only a wise man, without fear or desire, can truly be an emperor in spirit, though he live in poverty. Yet Seneca himself sometimes sacrificed his integrity; he was willing to stoop to flattery and even to involvement in murder.

Seneca was a prolific writer, but not all his works have survived. His speeches, some philosophical writings, and treatises on natural history and geography are lost. There is insufficient evidence to date with any certainty much of his surviving prose and drama. Among his extant works are twelve *Dialogi* (DIALOGUES), actually ten treatises on philosophical subjects in twelve books.

Other extant writings consist of *Apocolocyntosis* ("The Metamorphosis into a Pumpkin"), an amusing work in prose and verse, mocking the dead Claudius who, instead of being deified, is transformed into a pumpkin; two long treatises, the fragmentary *De Clementia* (*On Clemency*), originally in three books, and *De Beneficiis* (*On Benefits*) in seven books; *Naturales Quaestiones* (*Natural Questions*), a work on natural science from a Stoic point of view; 124 *Epistulae Morales*, letters to his friend Lucilius that are actually brief essays on both philosophical subjects and Seneca's own experiences; and nine or possibly ten tragedies: HERCULES FURENS, THE TROJAN WOMEN (*Troades*), THE PHOENICIAN WOMEN (*Phoenissae*), MEDEA, PHAEDRA, OEDIPUS, AGAMEMNON, THYESTES, and HERCULES OETAEUS. These nine tragedies are adaptations of Greek plays; OCTAVIA, which is probably not his, deals with Nero's divorce from his wife Octavia. Though Seneca's plays are modeled on those of the Greek tragedians, they differ from them in theme, characterization, and style. Probably they were written not for dramatic performance but for recitation before a sophisticated audience. Certainly the declamations, the epigrams, and the stichomythia, well-known characteristics of Seneca's technique, suggest that he appealed to a small group trained to appreciate the dexterity of the author. Seneca's interpretations and adaptations of the Greek characters and myths he employed reflect his limited view of life itself. For the most part his characters suffer the effects of excessive feeling, thus illustrating the Stoic disapproval of passion. Morover, their conflicts are simpler than those of the great figures of Greek tragedy. In Seneca the characters are not involved in a struggle with a destiny they strive to comprehend, nor are they really undergoing any inner conflict; they are the victims of excessive emotional intensity, which is externalized in violent and sensational behavior.

Seneca's tragedies have been criticized for their excessive display of violent passion, their sensationalism, their Stoic moralizing, and the artificiality of their style; this criticism is justifiable if one regards them as plays to be performed. If, however, the reader is able to experience them as dramatic readings, the stylistic tricks seem less offensive, and Seneca's psychological insight into destructive passion can often be moving. Certainly his plays reveal an understanding of human drives and suffering that the Stoic philosophy as exemplified in his philosophical writings lacks. In his treatises Seneca's analyses of human emotion, such as grief or anger, seem superficial, his traditional Stoic remedies impossibly rigid and inhuman.

Despite his many shortcomings as a philosopher and dramatist, Seneca exerted a powerful influence on the modern world. During the Middle Ages his moral writings were admired by the Christian church, and he himself was considered almost Christian. Seneca's tragedies, translated into English in 1581 (*Tenne Tragedies*, by "several hands") profoundly affected Elizabethan drama. One of the earliest English tragedies, *Gorboduc* by T. Norton and T. Sackville, was obviously modeled on Seneca's plays, and his influence is plain in the tragedies of George Gascoigne, Thomas Kyd, Ben Jonson, Christopher Marlowe, and Shakespeare.

Seneca, Lucius Annaeus (known as the Elder or the Rhetorician). A Roman rhetorician, born at Corduba (Cordova) in Spain in 55 B.C. As a child he was brought to Rome to be educated. Seneca married Helvia, by whom he had three sons, Lucius Annaeus Seneca (the Philosopher); Marcus Annaeus Novatus, who assumed the name Gallio on his adoption by Junius Gallio and became governor of Achaea (he is mentioned in the New Testament, Acts XVIII, 12–17); and Marcus Annaeus Mela, father of Lucan. In Rome, Seneca studied rhetoric and became acquainted with the famous orators and rhetoricians of the period. As an old man he still remembered passages from their declamations, which he assembled with commentaries of his own in his *Oratorum et Rhetorum Sententiae Divisiones Colores* (Pointed Phrases, Headings, and Interpretations of Orators and Rhetoricians), which is addressed to his sons and originally consisted of ten books of *Controversiae* (debates) and two of *Suasoriae* (arguments) on hypothetical subjects. Seneca died around A.D. 39.

Books I, II, VII, IX, and X of Seneca's *Controversiae* and one book of the *Suasoriae* are extant in fragmentary form. These arguments on historical and mythological subjects illustrate the training in rhetoric that was given in Seneca's time. The emphasis, particularly in the *Controversiae*, on stylistic tricks illustrates the decline in oratory that Tacitus was to lament in his *Dialogue on Orators*. Historically Seneca's work is significant for what it reveals of rhetorical training during the reigns of Augustus and Tiberius and for the interesting comments in some of the prefaces to the *Controversiae* on orators and rhetoricians of the period.

Sermones (of Horace). See SATIRES.

Seven Against Thebes, The (Hepta epi Thebas). A tragedy (467 B.C.) by

AESCHYLUS. It is the third play of a trilogy; the first two plays, *Laius* and *Oedipus*, have not survived. Translations: in verse, A. S. Way, 1906; in verse, E. D. A. Morshead, 1908; in verse, G. M. Cookson, 1922; in prose, H. Weir Smyth, 1922; in verse, David Grene, 1956; in verse, Philip Vellacott, 1961.

MYTHICAL BACKGROUND. When the parricide and incest of Oedipus were disclosed, Oedipus begged to be sent into exile, but Creon, the brother of Oedipus' wife, Jocasta, said that the oracle must be consulted before such a decision was made. Oedipus lived on in Thebes, for some years, until Creon and other Thebans decided that his presence polluted the land and that he must leave the city. By this time Oedipus wished to remain in Thebes, but, when his two sons, Eteocles and Polyneices, did not defend him, he was forced to leave with his daughter Antigone, who led him and took care of him. Before he died Oedipus prophesied that his sons would kill each other. The two brothers quarreled over the rule of Thebes. Eteocles exiled Polyneices, who then went to Argos, where he married Argeia, the daughter of Adrastus. Polyneices persuaded Adrastus to wage war on Thebes. Adrastus led the expedition; Polyneices and six other warriors joined forces to make up the Seven Against Thebes.

SCENE. Thebes, within the citadel.

SUMMARY. As the play opens, Eteocles, a brave and noble king, is addressing a crowd of citizens, urging them to endure the attack of the Argives with courage and to fight boldly. A Theban spy then enters and informs Eteocles that the seven leaders of the attacking armies have sworn to Ares that they will destroy Thebes or die. He left them casting lots to determine which of the seven gates of Thebes each of them should besiege. Eteocles prays to Zeus and the other gods to help defend his city. He then goes out with his attendants and most of the citizens.

The Chorus of Theban Women enters and sings of its terror at the attack of the Seven. Eteocles returns, scolds the women for their wild, uncontrolled fear, and tries to soothe them. After he leaves the stage, the women sing an ode in which they say that the words of Eteocles cannot overcome their sense that some terrible doom threatens their city.

Eteocles enters with six warriors, and the spy enters from the other side of the stage. In a long lyrical interchange between the spy, Eteocles, and the Chorus, the spy tells Eteocles which of the seven attackers will besiege each gate of Thebes, and Eteocles names one of the warriors with him as its defender. The seventh gate is to be attacked by Eteocles' brother, Polyneices, and to be defended by Eteocles. The Chorus, dreading bloodshed between brothers, begs Eteocles not to defend the seventh gate; but Eteocles, though mindful of his father's curse and foreseeing his own death in the terrible struggle, accepts his fate and goes forth to battle.

The Chorus then sings of the curse inherited from Laius, father of Oedipus, and passed down the generations; the theme of the ode is a recurrent one in Greek tragedy: the struggles and sorrows of the present are rooted in the past. The spy then comes in and announces that Thebes is safe, but Polyneices and Eteocles have killed each other. As the Chorus laments, Antigone and Ismene enter with a group of mourners carrying the bodies of Eteocles and Polyneices. The Herald announces that the counselors of Thebes have declared that Eteocles is to be buried with full honors, but Polyneices is to lie unburied, to be consumed by the dogs. Antigone refuses to accept this edict and says she will place a handful of earth on Polyneices' body, as a sign of burial.

COMMENTARY. Most scholars agree that the play as Aeschylus wrote it ends with the mourning of the Chorus over the bodies of the brothers. The final scene, probably added later, is perhaps derived from Sophocles' *Antigone*.

Sextus Empiricus. See SKEPTICS.

Sibyl. See AENEID VI.

Silenus (Seilenos). In Greek mythology, a satyr. He originated in Asia Minor as a water spirit who created springs and fountains; later he was associated with the watering of the vines and soon after with wine. In Greek mythology and literature Silenus is a satyr and an attendant of Dionysus. He is also the father of the satyrs, a wild creature with a broad nose, thick hair, and pointed ears. In Greek literature there are sometimes references to a number of Sileni, who are older than ordinary satyrs and always drunk. Silenus and the satyrs appear in Euripides' THE CYCLOPS and Sophocles' ICHNEUTAI.

Silvae. See STATIUS.

Silvanus. A Roman god of the woods.

Simonides. Greek poet, born at Ceos (c. 556 B.C.), and the first to earn his living by writing poetry. He traveled a great deal, spending time in Thessaly, in Athens at the court of the tyrants Hippias and Hipparchus, and in Sicily at the court of Hiero, tyrant of Syracuse, during the Persian Wars and in old age. He was the uncle of the poet Bacchylides and knew the leaders of the Greek world. After a long and successful career as a poet Simonides died in 467 B.C. either at Syracuse or at Acragas.

Simonides wrote both monodic and choral lyrics, iambics and elegiacs, especially a large group of elegiac epigrams. Though Simonides is said to have invented, or at least established, the form of the EPINICION, only brief fragments of his epinicia remain. He is best known for his brilliant and moving epigrams written in elegiacs, especially for those celebrating the dead heroes of the Persian Wars. His epitaph for the dead at Thermopylae is universally known (see THE PERSIAN WARS VII). Fragments of dirges, encomia, and poems on such subjects as *arete* and human accomplishment reveal his lyric artistry. Simonides was revered by ancient writers, who quote and praise him. Plato uses his definition of justice in the Republic as the starting point of his whole discussion; in the *Protagoras*, Socrates turns to Simonides' poem on human imperfection

397

in seeking to define virtue. Aristotle quotes him in his *Rhetoric,* and Quintilian praises his capacity to express feeling. The *Greek Anthology* includes epitaphs by Simonides.

Sinon. See AENEID II.

Sirens (Seirenes). See ODYSSEY XII.

Sisyphus (Sisyphos). A legendary king of Corinth who attempted to avoid dying by chaining Death. For this and various other offenses the cunning Sisyphus was punished in the Underworld by being forced to roll a huge stone up a hill, which, just as it reached the top, would roll down again. In his essay "The Myth of Sisyphus," Albert Camus has interpreted the myth brilliantly.

Skeptics. A school of philosophy founded by Pyrrho of Elis (c. 365–275 B.C.), who had been a member of Alexander's expedition to India. Pyrrho left no written works, but his philosophical doctrines were made known by his pupil Timon of Phlius, who went to live in Athens and remained there till his death around 230 B.C. Timon's poem *Silloi* ("squint-eyed" pieces) in three books, of which only brief fragments remain, mocks all philosophers except Pyrrho and other Skeptics. The Skeptics held the position that it is impossible to understand the nature of reality or to attain absolute knowledge. Therefore, man should not attempt to solve ethical problems, but should accept the world as he finds it. Two works written in Greek by the physician Sextus Empiricus, a Skeptic of a later period (late second century A.D.), contain the main doctrines of the school: *Pyrrhonean Outlines* sets forth the position of the Skeptics and *Against the Mathematicians* attacks grammarians, orators, astrologers, musicians, and philosophers, as well as mathematicians as dogmatists who can never arrive at truth.

Socrates (Sokrates). Perhaps the most famous of the Greek philosophers (b. 469 B.C.). Socrates left no writings and is chiefly known through the works of Plato and Xenophon. He was born at Alopeke near Athens, and married Xanthippe, who is traditionally regarded as a shrew. As a young man Socrates, like his father Sophroniscus, worked as a sculptor, but he soon turned to philosophy and spent his days walking about the city, attempting to enlighten the youth of Athens by talking with them. For Socrates' ideas, his defense against the accusations of the Athenians, and his death in 399 B.C., see PLATO and Plato's SYMPOSIUM, CRITO, PHAEDO, and APOLOGY. See also Aristophanes' THE CLOUDS, and XENOPHON.

Solon. Greek poet and statesman born at ATHENS C. 640 B.C. He came to maturity at a difficult period in Athenian history, when the people, weighed down by debts, political inequality, and economic and social deprivation, were ready to revolt against the aristocratic class, to which Solon belonged, and to accept the leadership of a tyrant. To prevent such a rebellion, in 594 B.C. Solon was appointed "sole archon" with power to reform the laws of Athens. This he did by canceling debts, doing away with the penalty of slavery for unpaid debts, reforming the organization of the Senate (*Boule*) and the popular Assembly (*Ecclesia*), to which he admitted every adult Athenian male, and setting up a popular court of appeal (*Heliaea*). As a result of these and other reforms Solon is known as the father of Athenian democracy. He is also Athens' first poet and was regarded as one of the Seven Sages.

Employing iambic and elegiac verse, Solon wrote on political and philosophical themes. In the two hundred fifty lines of his poetry which remain, he writes of the troubles of his beloved Athens, for which he blames the greed, arrogance, and injustice of her leaders and justifies the reforms he has made; he warns the Athenian people against accepting the rule of a tyrant; he addresses the Muses in a prayer for prosperity—but never at the cost of his ethical values; and he considers the role of Zeus and destiny in the lives of men. In one poem he speaks of the ten ages of man from childhood to old age, in another of the misery to which all human beings are subject. Despite the brevity of the fragments of Solon's work, there emerges from them the personality of a wise and humane leader, deeply concerned about the essential political, social, and philosophical problems of his time. Solon died about 558 B.C.; his biography appears in Plutarch's *Lives*.

Sophist (Sophistes). A dialogue by PLATO in which the discussion begun in *Theaetetus* is continued. The characteristics of the sophist and the nature of "not-being," which is related to a definition of knowledge, are considered.

Sophists. Scholars and teachers of the theory of knowledge and the art of rhetoric. This class of traveling lecturers and teachers flourished in Athens during the middle and end of the fifth century B.C. The best known of the Sophists were Protagoras of Abdera, Gorgias of Leontini, Hippias of Elis, and Prodicus of Ceos. The Sophists gave public lectures and taught classes on the theory of knowledge, political theory, and the techniques of rhetoric. They were the first teachers to charge a fee. Though they cannot be said to have had a systematic philosophy, their approach to philosophical questions was essentially skeptical. The statement, "Man is the measure of all things," attributed to Protagoras, suggests their point of view. Plato attacked the Sophists, whom he regarded as corrupters of those they professed to teach. He objected to Protagoras' theory of knowledge and to the Sophists' reliance on the art of persuasion, their contention that the disputant must make the "weaker" argument appear the "stronger" one.

Because of this emphasis on rhetorical techniques, the term *Sophist* came to mean one who attempts to deceive by clever argumentation and who overemphasizes minutiae. They are satirized by Aristophanes in THE CLOUDS, in which Socrates is erroneously identified with their school.

The revival of interest in declamation, the oratory of display, rhetorical flourishes and tricks of style in the second century A.D. is known as the "Second Sophistic."

Sophocles (Sophokles). Greek tragedian, born around 496 B.C. at Colonus, the scene of Oedipus' death ("Singer of sweet Colonus and its child," says Matthew Arnold). The son of Sophillus, a wealthy manufacturer of armor, Sophocles was given a traditional education in music, dancing, and gymnastics. When the Greeks defeated Xerxes in the battle of Salamis in 480 B.C., the young Sophocles led the chorus that celebrated the victory in song and dance. Throughout his life he was known for his handsome appearance, his grace, and his musical skill, as well as for his genius as a dramatist. His life was for the most part a tranquil and successful one. He held public positions of honor; he was elected a *strategus*, or general, twice and was appointed one of ten *probouloi*, or commissioners, who in 413 B.C. investigated the possibility of a revision of the constitution of Athens. It is said that when the god Asclepius came to cleanse Athens after a plague, Sophocles was chosen to welcome and house the god, whose priest he was. In his work he was prolific and successful, and at twenty-seven, when he first competed for the prize in tragedy, he defeated the great Aeschylus. Thereafter he was honored and rewarded for his plays and at his death was revered as a hero. Aristophanes says of him, "Content in life, he is content in death" (*Frogs*, l. 82). The great success and honor that Sophocles achieved suggest a fulfilled and happy man, but should not create the stereotype of the tranquil and blessed Sophocles, which has unfortunately come to exist. No writer has depicted human suffering and conflict with more understanding and truthfulness than Sophocles, and it is helpful to remember Edmund Wilson's contradiction of the cliché: "Somewhere even in the fortunate Sophocles there had been a sick and raving Philoctetes" (*The Wound and the Bow* [Oxford University Press, 1947], p. 293).

Sophocles was married twice and had two sons, Iophon, the child of his first wife Nicostrate, and Ariston, the child of his second wife, Theoris. Iophon became known as a tragic dramatist, and Ariston's son, Sophocles, wrote tragedies and produced those of his grandfather. There is an interesting though probably apocryphal story that Sophocles was brought to court by his son Iophon, who questioned his father's ability to conduct his affairs at the age of ninety. To demonstrate that his faculties were unimpaired Sophocles read the choral ode on Colonus from the *Oedipus at Colonus*, which he had just written —and won his case (Plutarch, *Moralia*). Shortly after writing this last play Sophocles died, in 406 B.C.

Of the 120 to 130 plays that Sophocles wrote only seven tragedies and a large fragment of a satyr play remain, although the titles of more than one hundred of his plays are known and some small fragments exist. The seven tragedies are AJAX (c. 447 B.C.), ANTIGONE (c. 442 B.C.), OEDIPUS THE KING (c. 430 B.C.), ELECTRA (c. 418–414 B.C.), THE WOMEN OF TRACHIS (c. 413 B.C.), PHILOCTETES (409 B.C.), OEDIPUS AT COLONUS (produced in 401 B.C. after Sophocles' death). The satyr play is ICHNEUTAI (c. 440 B.C.).

The innovations that Sophocles made in tragedy were the introduction of a third speaking actor, a more extensive use of scenery than Aeschylus, an increase in the number of the chorus from twelve to fifteen, and the development of the single play rather than the trilogy or tetralogy. More impressive than these, however, is his imposition of his genius upon the traditional material of Greek myth. Sophocles' characters are at once individuals and universal figures; his themes are deeply personal and broadly social. No artist has surpassed him in depicting the suffering and the dignity of man in his search for the truth about himself, which is both the terrible price and the reward of his contest with fate.

sophrosyne. An important term in Greek literature, meaning self-restraint, temperance, a sense of balance.

Sparta (Sparte; also called **Lacedaemon).** Capital of Laconia; the most important city of the Peloponnesus in historical times. Sparta was located on the right bank of the Eurotas, the chief river of the territory of Laconia. According to Greek mythology Sparta was established by Lacedaemon, a son of Zeus and Taygete. Lacedaemon married Sparta and named his city after her. During the period of the Trojan War, Menelaus, the husband of Helen and the brother of Agamemnon, was the king of Sparta. After the Dorian conquest, Sparta was ruled jointly by two kings, who represented a union of the two tribes. In the eighth and seventh centuries B.C. Sparta waged two wars against the neighboring state of Messenia and conquered it. During the seventh century B.C. Sparta, like most of the Greek states, was an oligarchy, though the dual monarchy existed with its powers reduced. At this time Sparta was not yet the highly conservative military dictatorship it was to become after the final conquest of Messenia. Poets and other artists were still welcome at Sparta; in fact, the choral lyric first flourished there (see ALCMAN and TYRTAEUS).

After the second war against Messenia, perhaps because the ruling class of Dorians feared an uprising on the part of the Helots, slaves who were mainly Messenians taken in war, Sparta became a dictatorship in which the lives of the citizens were entirely controlled by the state. Sickly children were exposed at birth, and healthy boys could remain with their families only until they were seven. From then on their education was mainly in warfare, and they were obliged to live in barracks until the age of thirty. Even girls had to take physical exercise. In every way possible the rulers of Sparta discouraged intellectual or artistic interests. Only physical prowess and military skill were valued.

Sparta would not cooperate with the Ionian Greeks in their resistance to Persian domination in 499 B.C. Later, faced with Persia's threat to all Greece, the Spartans united with the Athenians in the struggle against Persia (see THE PERSIAN WARS). The poet Simonides celebrated the heroism of Spartan warriors at Thermopylae; at Plataea and other battles they also revealed skill and courage. This cooperation between Athens and Sparta ended when Persia was defeated, and the two city-states became involved in conflicts that finally led to the Peloponnesian War (see ATHENS and THE PELOPONNESIAN WAR). Sparta's victory in this war in 404 B.C. made her the dominant state in Greece, but this position of power lasted only thirty years. She was defeated by Thebes at the battle of Leuctra in 371 B.C., and during the period when Philip of Macedon dominated the area of Greece, Sparta, though never actually conquered, lost both territory and her commanding position in the Greek world.

Sphekes. See THE WASPS.

Sphinx. A mythological monster. The name *Sphinx* is usually translated "Strangler" or "Throttler"; Michael Grant says it "more probably means 'tight-binder,' the demon of death" (*Myths of the Greeks and Romans* [Weidenfeld & Nicolson, 1962], p. 221). In Egypt, where they originated, Sphinxes were monsters with the lower body of a lion and the upper body and head of a man. In Greece the Sphinx had the body of a winged lion and the breast and head of a woman. The Sphinx has an important role in Sophocles' OEDIPUS THE KING.

Statius, Publius Papinius. A Roman poet, born at Naples about A.D. 40. His father, a teacher of literature, taught his son the craft of poetry. Statius expresses his gratitude to his "learned parent" in *Silvae* v, 3, as he mourns his death, and begs his father's spirit to continue to inspire him, for without his father's guidance he feels unable to write. Statius soon won recognition as a poet. He left Naples and went to Rome, where he remained until A.D. 94, writing and giving public recitations from his epic poem the THEBAID. Statius married but had no children; his wife had a daughter by a previous marriage, and Statius adopted a slave boy, whom he regarded as a son and whose death he mourns deeply in his last, unfinished poem (*Silvae* v, 5). In A.D. 94 Statius returned to Naples and died there around A.D. 96.

Among the works of Statius that have not survived are a libretto for *Agave,* a pantomime, and an epic poem on Domitian's wars in Germany. His surviving works are *Silvae,* five books of thirty-two poems that appeared from A.D. 92 until A.D. 96 or after; the *Thebaid,* an epic poem published around A.D. 92, on which Statius spent twelve years; and one book and part of a second of an epic poem the *Achilleid,* which he left unfinished. The *Thebaid,* which deals with the conflict between Oedipus' sons Polyneices and Eteocles, was much admired during the Middle Ages, and Statius himself was regarded as a Christian. Chaucer considered Statius the equal of Homer and Vergil, and Dante, who obviously admired Statius, depicts him in purgatory telling Vergil that reading his work has inspired Statius to become a Christian. The modern world has judged Statius more severely; most critics would agree that sensationalism, sentimentality, and excessively long descriptions mar his epic. Though Statius admired and tried to emulate Vergil's tone and style, he had neither the insight nor the skill to write a great epic. Still there are moving scenes and dramatic episodes in the *Thebaid,* and it is interesting to compare Statius' interpretations of the traditional figures of the Theban myth with those of the Greek tragedians. The fragment of Statius' *Achilleid* deals with Achilles' youth, when his mother Thetis disguised him as a girl and concealed him in Scyros. The thirty-two poems of *Silvae* are mainly rather artificial eulogies, descriptions, consolations, compliments, and other conventional types of verse. In a few, such as the well-known poem to Sleep (v, 4) and the laments for his father and his son, mentioned above, Statius is less mannered, and the feelings he expresses seem genuine.

Stesichorus (Stesichoros). Although only about fifty lines of the many works of Stesichorus remain, he is an important figure in the history of Greek poetry. His name means "setter or arranger of the chorus." It is thought that Stesichorus lived during the first half of the sixth century B.C., that he was born at Himera in Sicily, and that his real name was Teisias. According to legend he was punished with blindness for writing a poem criticizing Helen. To atone for, his crime he wrote his *Palinodia* (recantation), declaring that Helen was a chaste woman, that she never went to Troy with Paris, and that it was only a phantom of Helen who accompanied Paris. This is the version of the myth that Euripides uses in his *Helen.*

Stesichorus is known as the inventor of the HEROIC HYMN, and he wrote such hymns on the heroes of the Trojan War. He is also regarded as the inventor of the triadic structure of the choral lyric, which became the basic structure of Pindar's odes and of the choral odes of tragedy. He wrote twenty-six books of poetry, mainly choral heroic odes, which probably provided a great deal of the material used by the great tragedians. He is highly praised by Horace, Quintilian, and other ancient critics.

stichomythia. Dialogue in which the two speakers alternate in single lines of verse.

Stichus. A comedy, produced in 200 B.C., by PLAUTUS; based on Menander's *The Brothers.* Plautus' play has hardly any plot; it consists of a number of scenes involving tenuously related groups of characters. Stichus, the slave for whom the play is named, is significant only in the last episode. The first part of the play deals with the unsuccessful efforts of Antipho, an old Athenian, to persuade his daughters Panegyris and Pamphila, to divorce their impoverished husbands, who have been abroad for three years. The sisters, comparing themselves with the faithful Penelope of the *Odyssey,* refuse to give up their husbands. In the second part of the play Panegyris' husband Epignomus, who has made his fortune, returns to Athens. Antipho is now pleased with his daughter's husband. The parasite Gelasimus expects an invitation to a good dinner from the wealthy Epignomus, but is disappointed. The third episode deals with the return of Pamphila's husband Pamphilippus, who has also acquired great wealth, but poor Gelasimus cannot obtain a dinner from him either. The last part portrays the merry homecoming celebration of Stichus, the slave of Epignomus, and his friends.

Stoics. A school of philosophy established in Athens at the end of the fourth century B.C. by ZENO of Citium. The Stoics conceived of the universe as material but permeated or directed by a divine principle which they called Zeus, Fate, Providence, or Nature. The basic precept of Stoicism is that man, who is "self-sufficient," must live "in accordance with nature." His chief aim must be the attainment of perfect reason. Once he has attained this reason, man will no longer desire money, political power, or fame. Only the wise man is free and happy. Thus, the poor man may be equal or superior to the king, for wisdom and virtue are the only true values. The Stoic is "apathetic" because he does not value physical health, emotional satisfaction, or material possessions, and he accepts pain, grief, and even death as part of nature.

Stoicism had three main phases. The major philosophers of the Early Stoa (late fourth century–middle third century B.C.) were Zeno of Citium and his followers CLEANTHES, Chrysippus of Soli in Cilicia, Zeno of Tarsus, and Diogenes the Babylonian. The leaders of the Middle Stoa (second–first century B.C.) were Panaetius of Rhodes, whose lost treatise "On Duties" was the model for Cicero's *De Officiis,* and his disciple Posidonius, whose continuation of Polybius' *History* and other works have not survived, and Hecaton. The major figures of the Late Stoa, which was Roman (first century–second century A.D.), are SENECA THE PHILOSOPHER, EPICTETUS, and MARCUS AURELIUS.

Strabo (Strabon). A Roman historian (c. 64 B.C.–A.D. 19). Strabo was born in Amasia, in Pontus, and spent a good deal of his life in travel. His extant *Geographica,* written in Greek in seventeen books, deals with the history, geography, natural phenomena, and customs of the people of the Roman Empire of his period.

strophe. A stanza in a Greek choral ode. As the word, meaning "turn," implies, it is sung by the chorus as it turns one way, the antistrophe as it turns in the opposite direction.

Styx. In Greek mythology, the chief river of the Underworld.

Suetonius (Gaius Suetonius Tranquillus). A Roman historian, born around A.D. 70 into a family of equestrian rank. Little is known about his life. He was a good friend of Pliny the Younger, who used his influence with the emperor Trajan to obtain for Suetonius the rights of the *ius trium liberorum,* tax exemptions and various other privileges granted a father of three children, but given sometimes to other persons. Suetonius practiced law and worked as a secretary for Hadrian. Most of his time, however, was devoted to scholarship and writing. Suetonius died around A.D. 140.

Most of Suetonius' work is lost. Among his extant writings are parts of *De Viris Illustribus (On Famous Men),* which appeared between A.D. 106 and 113 and consisted of lives of famous literary figures of various types. Large portions of the sections "De Grammaticis" and "De Rhetoribus," on grammarians and rhetoricians, as well as lives of Horace, Lucan, and Terence, are extant. Biographies of Vergil, Tibullus, and Persius are also accepted by some scholars as the work of Suetonius. Suetonius' best-known work is his LIVES OF THE CAESARS (*De Vita Caesarum*), biographies of Julius Caesar and the Roman emperors from Augustus to Domitian. This work, which appeared about A.D. 121, contains some valuable historical information and a great deal of material about the personal lives and habits of the emperors.

Sulla, Lucius Cornelius. A leader of the aristocratic party at Rome, lived from 139–78 B.C. In 107 B.C. Sulla was sent by Marius, who had defeated the Numidian king Jugurtha, to demand his surrender. Marius' opponents then claimed that Sulla was actually responsible for the victory over Jugurtha, and from this time on there was great hostility between Marius and Sulla. In 81 B.C., after three years of civil war between the members of the popular party (*populares*) and those of the aristocratic party (*optimates*), in which Sulla's forces were victorious, Sulla became dictator of Rome. He reformed the constitution, greatly increasing the powers of the Senate. In 79 B.C. Sulla retired from public life. Sallust describes his character in the *Bellum Jugurthinum,* and Plutarch wrote a life of him.

Suppliants, The (Hiketides; The Suppliant Women). A tragedy (c. 460 B.C.) by AESCHYLUS. It is the first part of a trilogy; the second and third plays, which are not extant, were probably *The Egyptians* and *The Daughters of Danaus.* Translations: in verse, E. D. A. Morshead, 1908; in prose, Walter and C. E. S. Headlam, 1909; in prose, H. Weir Smyth, 1922; in verse, G. M. Cookson, 1922; in verse, S. G. Benardete, 1956; in verse, Philip Vellacott, 1961.

MYTHICAL BACKGROUND. Zeus fell in love with the maiden, Io, daughter of Inachus, the first king of Argos. The jealous Hera transformed Io into a heifer (in most other versions of the myth, Zeus transformed Io in order to disguise her) and tortured her with a gadfly which pursued the girl as she fled from country to country. Finally, in Egypt, Zeus restored Io to her original form, and she conceived the god's child, Epaphus, whose great-grandsons were Aegyptus and Danaus. Aegyptus, who became king of Egypt, had fifty sons, and Danaus had fifty daughters. When the fifty sons of Aegyptus proposed marriage to the fifty daughters of Danaus, their offers were rejected. Fearful of their violent suitors, the fifty maidens fled Egypt with their father and sought refuge at Argos, the land from which Io, their ancestor, had originally come.

SCENE. A sacred grove near the shore of Argos, where there is an altar and statues of the gods.

SUMMARY. The Chorus of the Fifty Daughters of Danaus prays to Zeus for aid in their exile. The maidens tell of how they fled Egypt to avoid marrying their kinsmen. At last they have arrived in Argos, from which Io, their famous ancestor, the beloved of Zeus, first came. They weep over their sad lot, remembering how they fled their home in terror. They pray that the strange, new land will have mercy on them and beg Artemis, the maiden goddess, to help them escape forced marriage. If the Olympian gods do not help them, they will strangle themselves and go to the gods of the Underworld.

Danaus advises his daughters to be cautious. He says he sees a group of armed men coming who may be the leaders of Argos, and he tells his daughters to cling to the altars as suppliants. As the maidens pray to Zeus, Apollo, Poseidon, and Hermes, Pelasgus, king of Argos, enters with his attendants and soldiers. Recognizing the maidens' clothing as foreign, Pelasgus asks them what land they come from. The Leader of the Chorus says that they are of Argive descent through Io and that they fled Egypt to escape forced marriage. Pelasgus fears that if he protects the suppliant women, he will face war with Egypt; yet he responds to the sacred rights of suppliants to protection. He decides to put their case to the Argive assembly. If the people agree to grant the maidens the protection of Argos, they may remain in the city. The Leader of the Chorus warns Pelasgus that if the maidens are not allowed to remain in Argos, they will hang themselves at the altars of the gods. The King realizes that such deaths would pollute the city, but he also fears war with the Egyptians if he agrees to protect the maidens. With great compassion he tells his attendants to lead Danaus to the city's shrines, so that he may ask the people of Argos to protect him and his daughters. After Danaus goes off with the attendants, Pelasgus promises the maidens that he will try to persuade the Argives to help them. Then he too leaves.

The maidens pray to Zeus for aid, reminding the king of the gods that they are descended from him and Io. They tell the story of Io's wanderings, her sufferings, her arrival in Egypt, and the birth of her son Epaphus. Danaus returns and tells his daughters that the Argives have voted unanimously to protect them. The maidens sing a song of thanks, praying that Argos, the land that shelters them, may be happy and fruitful. Danaus says they have prayed wisely, and then warns them that he has frightening news: he sees an Egyptian ship approaching Argos. The maidens are terrified, but their father comforts them, assuring them that the Argives will protect them. He advises them to remain at the shrine, while he goes to the Argives for aid. The maidens fearfully appeal once more to Zeus.

The Herald of Aegyptus enters with attendants and tries to force the maidens onto the ships, while they cry out in terror. Just as the maidens cry that all hope is lost, the King of Argos returns with his men and orders the Herald of Aegyptus to leave Argos. The maidens will remain in Argos. The Herald warns Pelasgus that the Egyptians will wage war against Argos, but Pelasgus is not frightened. After the Egyptian Herald and his followers leave, Pelasgus asks Danaus and his daughters to enter the city of Argos. The maidens thank Pelasgus for his kindness, and they bless the city of Argos. They pray to Zeus that they may never be obliged to marry their kinsmen; though they honor Aphrodite, they fear forced marriage with hated bridegrooms.

Suppliants, The (Hiketides; The Suppliant Women). A tragedy (420 B.C.) by EURIPIDES. Translations: in prose, E. P. Coleridge, 1891; in verse, Arthur S. Way, 1912; in verse, Frank Jones, 1958.

MYTHICAL BACKGROUND. After the armies of the Seven against Thebes were vanquished (see Aeschylus' SEVEN AGAINST THEBES and Euripides' THE PHOENICIAN WOMEN), the Thebans would not permit the Argive leaders to be buried. The mothers of the dead Argive chieftains have come to

Athens to ask King Theseus' aid in gaining burial for their sons, so that they may find peace in Hades.

S C E N E . Before the temple of Demeter at Eleusis, a deme of Athens.

S U M M A R Y . Aethra, on the steps of the altar before the temple of Demeter, prays to Demeter that Athens, her son Theseus, and she may prosper. She then speaks of the suppliant mothers, grouped around her, who hope to gain permission to bury their dead sons, and of King Adrastus of Argos, who mourns for the army he led against Thebes. Adrastus has asked Aethra to enlist the aid of Theseus in obtaining burial for the dead heroes, and she has sent for her son.

The Chorus of Argive Suppliants begs the help of Aethra. Weeping and tearing at their faces in grief, the women want only to embrace the dead bodies of their sons and then to bury them. Theseus enters, alarmed by the sight and sound of mourning. After Aethra tells him who the mourners are, Adrastus explains how Polyneices persuaded him to fight against Thebes, despite the warnings of the prophet Amphiaraus, who foresaw the defeat of the Argives. Adrastus regrets his rashness in disregarding the warning of the gods and begs Theseus to help him to obtain the bodies of his colleagues from the Thebans. Theseus replies by commenting on the various qualities of man, his capacity for reason and his pride, which all too often overcomes his reason and deludes him into regarding himself as wiser than the gods. Theseus is reluctant to involve Athens in bloodshed, which may result if he demands the bodies from the Thebans, and to hurt his own people because of the poor judgment of Adrastus. The Chorus pleads with Theseus for help, and Aethra weeps in sympathy. When she says that Athens' honor is at stake in the cause of the suppliants, Theseus finally agrees to ask the Athenian people to vote approval of his plan to try to persuade the Thebans to allow burial, and, if persuasion fails, to use force.

After a choral ode, in which the Suppliants express the hope that Athens will help them, Theseus returns with a Herald whom he plans to send to Creon, king of Thebes, with the message that Theseus requests the Argive warriors' bodies for burial. If Creon refuses to give them up, Athens will declare war. At this point a Theban Herald appears, demanding that Theseus drive Adrastus out of Athens and give up all thoughts of burying the warriors. If the Athenians do not obey this order, Thebes will declare war. Theseus replies that he is merely upholding the religious law of Hellas in insisting on giving burial to the dead, and he will fight for what he feels is just. When the Herald leaves angrily, Theseus gives orders for the gathering and organization of his troops for the attack on Thebes.

After Theseus goes out, the Chorus prays for Athenian victory, and soon a Messenger arrives to report Theseus' defeat of the Thebans. Theseus dealt mercifully and justly with his enemies, stopping the battle as soon as he could reclaim the bodies for the Argives. Adrastus admits his earlier folly and speaks of the dependence of man on the will of the gods. The folly of man produces war, which accomplishes nothing. The bodies of the seven Argive leaders are carried in, and, after the Chorus and Adrastus lament over them, they are taken out for burial. The funeral pyres are lighted as the Chorus sings of its sorrow. Evadne, the wife of Capaneus, one of the Argive leaders whose corpse was hallowed and buried apart from the others because his death resulted from a lightning bolt of Zeus, appears on a cliff over the pyre of Capaneus. She sings of her grief and her desire to join her husband in death. Despite the entreaties of her father, Iphis, she jumps into the pyre.

The Sons of the dead chiefs enter, carrying urns that hold the ashes of their fathers. The Chorus of Children and the Chorus of Mothers sing of their sorrow. Theseus charges the Sons of the chiefs to remember and pass on to their children what they have seen of Athens' justice and her generosity to Argos. Athene appears as the *deus ex machina* and asks Theseus to make Adrastus swear that the Argives will never make war on Athens. She then speaks to the Sons of the Argive leaders, prophesying that as grown men they will avenge the deaths of their fathers. As the play ends, Adrastus goes to take the sacred oath suggested by Athene.

Suppliant Women, The. See THE SUPPLIANTS.

Symposium (Symposion). A dialogue (between 384 and 369 B.C.) by Plato.

B A C K G R O U N D . Apollodorus tells of the discussion of love, which took place some years ago (in 416 B.C.) at a banquet at the home of Agathon. Apollodorus heard of the discussion from Aristodemus, who was present at the banquet.

S U M M A R Y . After dinner the guests agree to drink in moderation and to speak in praise of Eros, or love. Each of the guests gives his views on the subject. Phaedrus speaks first, honoring the god of love for his gifts, chief among which is the love of one man for another. Since lovers will sacrifice their lives for each other, love between men has a military value. An example of such love is that of Achilles for Patroclus (in the *Iliad*).

The next speaker is Pausanias, who distinguishes between "heavenly love" and "common love." Common love is actually mere physical lust, whereas heavenly love, which exists only between men and boys who have reached puberty, is permanent, spiritual, noble, and virtuous.

Eryximachus, unsatisfied with the conclusion of Pausanias' speech, continues to discuss the two kinds of love. Using scientific language, he explains that love affects all things. As a physician he knows that in the body as in all of nature there are healthy and diseased elements, which are in opposition to each other. Medicine reconciles these opposites through the process of love. Love, in human life as in nature, establishes harmony.

Aristophanes' speech, which follows, is distinguished by the fantastic humor and brilliant insights characteristic of his plays. He declares that men have never truly appreciated the power of love. To understand this power one must first know the true nature of man. Originally there were three sexes: male, female, and a combination of the two. Moreover, human beings were round in shape, and had two faces, four feet, four hands, and two of all other organs. When these powerful creatures attacked the gods, Zeus cut them in half to humble them. Apollo healed the wounds, and human beings appeared as they now do. As soon as human beings were thus divided, each half desired to be united with the other. This yearning for the half that was cut away is the origin of love, which can be defined as a desire for union with the other part of oneself to restore the original wholeness. Those who honor the god of love will find peace and wholeness in union with a beloved.

After Agathon has delivered a highly contrived tribute to the beauty of Eros, Socrates, by questioning Agathon, arrives at a definition of love: it is a desire for that which one does not possess, a desire to possess the good and the beautiful. Socrates then delivers his speech. He says that he learned about love from Diotima of Mantineia, a prophetess, who proved to him that love is not beautiful or good. Love is a *daimon,* a spirit that is "intermediate between the divine and the mortal." This spirit serves as an interpreter between gods and men. Love is the child of the god *Poros,* or Plenty, and *Penia,* or Poverty, and his parentage is reflected in his fortune. Love is poor and rough, but he is courageous and strong, wise and resourceful. Love desires beauty, wisdom, and virtue; he is a philosopher by nature. Sometimes he flourishes, and at other times he is unsatisfied. He is a mean between ignorance and wisdom. Love leads men to desire the beautiful and the good and to produce beauty through off-spring, either human or intellectual. Because they long for immortality people have children, but another and perhaps more certain form of immortality is to be achieved through the fame of a noble and virtuous deed or the creation of art that is wise and virtuous. The offspring of the union of two minds and souls is more certain of immortality than is the child resulting from physical union. A mature man who loves a youth with a noble and good soul will have a closer bond with him than does many a married man with his wife. Even more exalted than a spiritual love relationship is the highest stage of love. This is to be achieved by a series of steps: first one must love one beautiful form, then all beautiful forms; next he will learn to love the beauty of laws, sciences, and all beautiful pursuits, practices, and ideas. Finally he will arrive at the conception of absolute beauty. In loving absolute beauty, one reaches truth and approaches immortality.

After the audience has applauded the words of Socrates, Alcibiades, who is drunk, enters. He is asked to speak in praise of love, but he prefers to praise Socrates, whom he compares to Silenus. Soon a band of revelers enters, and everyone drinks a great deal of wine. Some of the guests depart. Aristodemus, who has fallen asleep, awakes at dawn to find Agathon, Aristophanes, and Socrates still talking. After a while Aristophanes can no longer stay awake;

then as the day dawns Agathon also falls asleep. Seeing his friends asleep, Socrates leaves for the Lyceum, where he bathes; then he spends the day in his usual fashion.

Symposium (Symposion). See XENOPHON.

Syracuse (Syrakousai). Principal city of Sicily and a Corinthian colony. Both Pindar and Bacchylides addressed choral odes to Hiero I (see CHORAL LYRICS), tyrant of Syracuse from 478 to 467 B.C.

T

Tacitus, Cornelius. Roman historian. Little is known about his early life. His name appears as Publius Cornelius Tacitus in one manuscript of his work; it appears in other manuscripts as Gaius Cornelius Tacitus. Neither the place nor the date of his birth is known. It is thought that he was born in the north of Italy around A.D. 55 and that he came from an aristocratic family. In A.D. 78 Tacitus married the daughter of Cn. Julius Agricola, whose biography he later wrote. Tacitus may have been a military tribune and held various public positions under the emperors Vespasian, Titus, and Domitian. When Tacitus was consul in A.D. 97 under the emperor Nerva, he delivered the funeral address for the famous and admirable general Verginius Rufus. Tacitus was governor of Asia around A.D. 112, during the reign of Trajan. The exact date of Tacitus' death is unknown; he probably died around A.D. 117.

The DIALOGUE ON ORATORS (*Dialogus de Oratoribus*) is the earliest work (c. A.D. 81) attributed to Tacitus, but its authorship has been questioned. It deals with the decline of oratory in his time. Both his biography of his father-in-law, AGRICOLA, and the GERMANIA, a study of the German people and their country, appeared around A.D. 98. Tacitus' greatest works are his HISTORIES (*Historiae*), which originally covered the period from January 1, A.D. 69 to the year A.D. 96 and appeared between A.D. 104 and 109, and the ANNALS (*Annales*), also a history, which originally dealt with the period from the death of Augustus in A.D. 14 to the death of Nero in A.D. 68, and was probably written between A.D. 115 and 117. Both these works are now fragmentary.

One of the most gifted of the ancient historians, Tacitus reveals remarkable insight into human character and political events. Though Tacitus is not as objective as he claims to be in the *Annals* (*sine ira et studio*, "without wrath or partiality"), his bias cannot really be regarded as a flaw. Without being moralistic, Tacitus is a moralist who assumes that history teaches values: respect for honesty and dignity and scorn for cruelty and tyranny. The reader is always aware of Tacitus' admiration for the Republic and the freedom it offered the Roman citizen and of his hatred for the tyranny of the emperors. He expresses his sorrow and anger at their corruption and cruelty, not through declamation but through brilliant analyses of their motivations. With the skill of a novelist or a dramatist Tacitus describes and analyzes historical figures and re-creates the world in which they lived. His style is intense, epigrammatic, and concise; it is a formal, highly polished style which conveys something of the dignity and integrity of Tacitus' own personality as it emerges from his description and interpretation of his time.

Tantalus (Tantalos). In Greek mythology, the father of Niobe and PELOPS. There are several versions of Tantalus' crime against the gods: either he cut up the body of Pelops and fed him to the gods, or he stole nectar, or he told the gods' secrets. Tantalus was punished in Hades by being placed in water, which he longed for but could never reach, or near fruit, which he could never taste, or below a huge stone that continually threatened him.

Tartarus (Tartaros). In Greek mythology, the part of the Underworld where guilty souls are punished. See AENEID VI.

Tecmessa (Tekmessa). See Sophocles' AJAX.

Telamon. In Greek mythology, the king of Salamis and father of the great warrior Ajax and of Teucer.

Telemachus (Telemachos). The son of Odysseus and Penelope. For his character and story see the ODYSSEY.

Telephus (Telephos). In Greek mythology, a son of Heracles who became king of the Mysians. Wounded by Achilles, Telephus was told by the Delphic oracle that he could be healed only by his wounder. Telephus discovered that the oracle meant not Achilles himself but the rust from Achilles' spear. Telephus was the hero and title of a lost tragedy by Euripides, which Aristophanes satirizes in *The Acharnians*.

Terence (Publius Terentius Afer). A Roman comic playwright, born around 195 B.C. in Carthage. He was a slave whose owner Terentius Lucanus, a senator, took him to Rome, educated, and freed him. As a freedman Terence took his benefactor's name. He became a friend of Scipio Aemilianus, the well-known general, consul, and literary patron. After writing six plays (all of which are extant) Terence went on a journey to Greece. He died in 159 B.C.

The titles of his plays and the dates of their production are: THE WOMAN OF ANDROS (*Andria*), 166 B.C.; THE MOTHER-IN-LAW (*Hecyra*), 166 and 165 B.C.; THE SELF-TORMENTOR (*Heauton Timorumenos*), 163 B.C.; THE EUNUCH (*Eunuchus*), 161 B.C.; PHORMIO, 161 B.C.; and THE BROTHERS (*Adelphi*), 160 B.C. Like Plautus, Terence imitated the Greek writers of New Comedy, and all of his plays are adaptations of Greek originals. In fact Terence stayed closer to his sources than did Plautus; in the prologue to *The Eunuch* he defends himself against the accusation of plagiarism. He was also charged with practicing *contaminatio* (combining two Greek sources into one Latin comedy); in the prologue to *Andria* he argues that this technique was employed also by Naevius, Plautus, and Ennius. Though Terence's comedies resemble those of Plautus in the general nature of their plots, their stock characters—the courtesan, the young man in love, the disapproving father—and in their use of mistaken identity and eventual discovery, their quality is essentially quite different. Terence employs double plots, which he fuses with great skill. His tone is quieter than that of Plautus, his comedy more gentle. He avoids the farcical humor so common in Plautus, and his characters are more subtle and more realistic. Terence is more interested in the admirable qualities of human beings; even his courtesans are generally appealing and honest women. He is a more careful stylist than Plautus, employing few Roman allusions and achieving greater consistency of tone and structure.

The influence of Terence on English comedy is clearly indicated in such plays as John Marston's *The Parisitaster*, Beaumont and Fletcher's *The Scornful Lady*, Thomas Shadwell's *The Squire of Alsatia*, William Wycherley's *The Country Wife*, Charles Sedley's *Bellamira*, Thomas Otway's *The Cheats of Scapin*, Richard Steele's *The Tender Husband*, Henry Fielding's *The Fathers*, and Robert Bridges' *The Feast of Bacchus*. Thornton Wilder draws on Terence's *Andria* in his novel *The Woman of Andros*.

Tereus. See PHILOMELA.

Terpander (Terpandros). A Greek poet, born at Antissa in Lesbos, who flourished during the first part of the seventh century B.C. He spent most of his life in Sparta. Although only a few lines of his poetry remain, he is known for his development of the *nomos*, an ancient monodic hymn sung in honor of a god to the music of the lyre and the flute. Terpander is also celebrated for having established music and lyric poetry in Sparta.

Tethys. One of the Titans, the wife of Oceanus.

Teucer (Teukros) (I). In Greek mythology, a son of Telamon and half brother of Ajax. Teucer fought on the side of the Greeks in the Trojan War and was considered the best archer. He appears in the ILIAD, Sophocles' AJAX, and Euripides' HELEN.

Teucer (Teukros) (II). According to legend the first king of TROY.

Thales. A Greek philosopher (c. 624–546 B.C.). Thales, who established the first Greek philosophical school, was born in Miletus. He traveled to Egypt, where it is said he determined the height of the pyramids by measuring the length of their shadows. He also predicted an eclipse of the sun on May 28, 585 B.C. His best-known idea is that all things originate from water, the essential element of all matter. Thales left no written works.

Thamyris. In Greek mythology, a poet and musician who dared to challenge the Muses. For his pride the Muses maimed (perhaps blinded) him and deprived him of his great skill as a musician. He is mentioned in *Iliad* II.

Theaetetus (Theaitetos). A dialogue by PLATO named for an Athenian mathematician. The subject of the dialogue is knowledge, but no satisfactory definition is found. The discussion is continued in *Sophist*.

Theagenes and Chariclea. See AETHIOPICA.

Thebaid (Thebais). Epic poem in twelve books (c. A.D. 92) by STATIUS. The subject is the conflict of Oedipus' sons Eteocles and Polyneices for the throne of Thebes (see also Aeschylus' *Seven Against Thebes*, Sophocles' *Oedipus the King, Oedipus at Colonus*, and *Antigone*, and Euripides' *Phoenician Women*).

Imitating earlier epics, especially the *Aeneid,* Statius writes in hexameter verse and employs the usual conventions of the epic—the intervention of the gods in human affairs, long speeches, funeral games, and others. The gods of Statius are, for the most part, mere conventions; he says that ultimate power resides in both Jupiter and Nature.

After an invocation to the emperor Domitian, Statius describes the blind Oedipus doomed to guilt and darkness. Dwelling on the hideous details of Oedipus' appearance and his deeds, he creates an atmosphere of horror that pervades the entire poem. Oedipus is a sensational figure in the *Thebaid;* his suffering and the conflicts of his children become the material of melodrama. Both his curse on his sons in Book I and his laments over them in Book XI, when he says his affection has come too late, dramatize the horror of the story of Oedipus, but they do not suggest either his tragic conflict or his final insight. Statius obviously enjoys the gory details of Oedipus' self-mutilation: after his sons have murdered each other, Oedipus wishes his eyes were restored to him so that he could destroy them again. A large part of the poem deals with events leading up to the war against Thebes. Eteocles is inspired by the ghost of Laius to break his agreement with Polyneices that each of them would rule for a year. The marriages of Polyneices and Tydeus to the daughters of Adrastus are described. There is a long catalogue of the forces from Argos and later a list of the Theban forces.

The actual war begins in Book VII and continues through Book X. Among the many episodes described is the death of the seer Amphiaraus, who is swallowed with his chariot in an opening of the earth and descends into the Underworld. Finally, in Book XI, Polyneices and Eteocles come together in single combat and both are killed. In this book Statius also tells of Creon's unwillingness to bury Polyneices, the suicide of Jocasta, and the banishment of Oedipus. In Book XII Antigone and Polyneices' wife Argeia bury him; Theseus comes to demand the bodies of the Argive warriors and kills Creon.

Thebes (Thebai). An ancient city in Boeotia. According to Greek mythology, Thebes was founded by Cadmus, son of Agenor. Cadmus was seeking his sister Europa, who had been carried off by Zeus, when the Delphic oracle told him to give up his search, follow a cow until it lay down, and there establish a city. The cow finally stopped in southern Boeotia. Deciding to sacrifice the cow to Athene, he sent some of his men to a nearby spring for water, which he needed for the rites. Cadmus' men were slain by a dragon that guarded the spring. Cadmus then killed the dragon and, obeying the orders of Athene, sowed its teeth. Armed men arose, who began to fight with each other when Cadmus threw a stone among them. The five survivors helped Cadmus to erect the Cadmea, which was to become the citadel of Thebes, and became the founders of Thebes and the ancestors of its aristocracy.

Thebes is famous in Greek literature as the kingdom of Oedipus, a descendant of Cadmus, and as the scene of the dreadful warfare between Oedipus' sons, Polyneices and Eteocles. Their stories are told in Sophocles' *Oedipus the King*, Seneca's *Oedipus*, Aeschylus' *Seven Against Thebes*, Euripides' *The Phoenician Women* and *The Suppliants*, Seneca's *The Phoenician Women*, and Statius' *Thebaid*. An entire Theban epic cycle, which transmitted the myths of the family of Oedipus, is lost. The names of two of the most important epics of the cycle are the *Thebais* and the *Oedipodia*, both of which are thought to have been composed during the eighth century B.C.

In historical times Thebes was a powerful enemy of ATHENS. Thebes supported Persia during the Persian War and was instrumental in starting the Peloponnesian War (see THE PELOPONNESIAN WAR II). When Athens was defeated in this war, Thebes demanded that the city be destroyed. The poet PINDAR was proud of his Theban birth.

Themis. A Titan and goddess of order. Themis, which means "institution," represents the quality of justice. In the *Iliad* she summons the gods and men to assemblies.

Themistocles (Themistokles). Athenian statesman and general, born near the end of the sixth century B.C. He became archon in 493 B.C., and during the Second Persian War was appointed *strategus* (commander) of the Athenian fleet. Many historians regard Themistocles as the greatest statesman of his period. Mainly through his efforts Athens became a great sea power. His brilliant leadership was responsible for Athens' victory in the Battle of Salamis. At this time, says Herodotus (*The Persian Wars* VIII, 124), Themistocles was regarded by all as the wisest of the Greeks, and for some years after, he shared the political leadership of Athens with Aristides and Xanthippus. By 472 B.C., however, the period of his power and influence was over. He was ostracized by the Athenians and went into exile in Argos. When Pausanias, the Spartan commander at Plataea, was accused of intrigue with Persia, Themistocles was implicated in the crime. No doubt unjustly, he was accused of treason. When Athenian and Spartan officials came to arrest him, he fled from Argos to Corcyra, then to Epirus, and finally found refuge with Admetus, king of the Molossians, who helped him escape to Macedonia and finally to Asia Minor. Until the death of Xerxes he remained in hiding on the coast of Asia Minor. When Artaxerxes became king of Persia, Themistocles decided to seek protection at his court. Thucydides gives the contents of Themistocles' letter to Artaxerxes, appealing for his aid (I, 136). Artaxerxes welcomed Themistocles and made him governor of the district of Magnesia, where he died in 459 B.C. He won high honor among the Persians, who erected a monument to him in the market place of Magnesia. Plutarch and Nepos wrote lives of Themistocles.

Theoclymenus (Theoklymenos) (I). A prophet in the ODYSSEY (XV, XVII, XX).

Theoclymenus (Theoklymenos) (II). See Euripides' HELEN.

Theocritus (Theokritos). Greek poet; flourished first half of the third century B.C. He was probably born in Syracuse, on the southeast coast of Sicily. He spent some time at Cos, an island near Halicarnassus, and also some time at Alexandria, when Ptolemy II, Philadelphus, was king of Egypt. Evidence suggests that he studied medicine at Samos with the well-known physician Erasistratus. A fellow student was his friend Nicias, mentioned in the IDYLS.

At Cos, Theocritus admired and emulated the poet and critic Philitas. *Harvest-Home* no doubt contains references to people he knew during this part of his life. After living for a while at the court of Ptolemy in Alexandria, Theocritus returned to Sicily and may have spent the rest of his life there. His extant works include the *Idyls* and *Epigrams* (Inscriptions). Theocritus' greatest achievement is his invention of the pastoral, which has been imitated and emulated since his time (see PASTORAL POETRY).

Theognis. A Greek elegiac poet. Born in Megara (between Athens and Corinth), he probably flourished in the second half of the sixth century B.C. He was an aristocrat who apparently lost his wealth and property during one of the many conflicts between the aristocracy and the lower classes that are characteristic of this period in the Greek states. Embittered by these losses and convinced that all virtue resides in aristocracy, Theognis expressed in a number of elegiac poems his hatred for the plebeians and his nostalgia for the past when the power of the aristocracy was unquestioned. These poems are really moral precepts addressed to a young man called Cyrnus, son of Polypaus. The 1400 lines remaining from the collection of Theognis' poems contain the work of other poets as well as that of Theognis. Possibly other poets writing on similar themes added their verses to his, or these were put in the same collection, which became a "songbook"—a group of poems to be performed to the music of the flute. The parts addressed to Cyrnus can probably be attributed to Theognis.

Theogony (Theogonia). Genealogy in dactylic hexameter. Most scholars attribute it to Hesiod (c. eighth century B.C.), some to an imitator. Translations: in verse, C. A. Elton, 1812; in prose, A. W. Mair, 1910; in prose, H. G. Evelyn-White, 1920; in prose, Norman O. Brown, 1953; in verse, Richmond Lattimore, 1959.

SUMMARY. The poet addresses the Muses of Helicon who, he says, came to Hesiod as he was tending his flocks and told him that they know how to speak of false events as though they were true, but they also know how to speak the truth. The Muses then gave Hesiod an olive shoot and inspired him to sing of the race of the gods.

After praising the nine Muses and their sweet songs, the poet tells of their birth from Mnemosyne (Memory) and Zeus. The man whom the Muses love is blessed. They relieve man of troubles and sorrows through song. The Muses are then asked to tell the poet how the earth and the gods came to exist and to describe the creation of the sea, the stars, and all things.

The poem records in chronological order the births of the gods and the generations that sprang from them. Beginning with Chaos, which existed first, the poet traces the origins of Earth, which came next, and Eros, which conquers the souls of men and gods. Chaos brought forth Erebus (primeval darkness) and Night, and they in turn bore Aether (the upper air) and Day. Earth brought forth Heaven, and from their union came the Titans (the most fearful of which was Cronus), the Cyclopes, and the giants with a hundred arms and fifty heads.

The poet describes the rebellion against the Father, Heaven, by the Titans led by Cronus and helped by the Mother, Earth. After the victory of the Titans, Heaven and Earth were separated. The births of many other gods and goddesses are recounted. Cronus, now the ruler, feared the children his wife Rhea bore him and swallowed them when they were born. Rhea concealed Zeus to prevent Cronus from consuming him, and finally Zeus overcame his father Cronus and became ruler of the gods. Cronus was forced to expel the children he had swallowed, and Zeus divided the universe with them. Zeus' war with the Titans and his cruel treatment of Prometheus are described. An account is given of Zeus' defeat of the monster Typhoeus, the son of Tartarus and Ge. Then the poet recounts the offspring of Zeus from his unions with goddesses and mortals.

Theophrastus (Theophrastos). It is said that his name was Tyrtamus, but he was called Theophrastus ("godlike speaker") by his teacher, Aristotle. He was born around 370 B.C. at Eresus in Lesbos, the birthplace of Sappho. He left his homeland for Athens, where he studied first with Plato and then with Aristotle. After Aristotle's retirement as head of the Peripatetic School, Theophrastus took his place. He was much admired by his many pupils, among them the playwright Menander. Theophrastus died in 287 B.C., when he was about eighty-five years old.

Theophrastus' range of interests was wide, and he wrote on a variety of subjects—philosophical, scientific, and literary. Unfortunately much of his work is fragmentary, and a great deal has been entirely lost. His extant writings include a *Natural History of Plants* and the *Growth of Plants*, a brief treatise on *Metaphysics*, and his best-known work, CHARACTERS, which may originally have been part of a larger work. *Characters* is a study of thirty types or characteristics of people, which shows remarkable insight into human failings and weaknesses. With wit and gentle satire Theophrastus reveals characteristic human absurdities.

Many critics have noticed the resemblance of Theophrastus' characters to the types of Menander's comedies, which were written during the same general period. Theophrastus' *Characters* was admired and imitated by seventeenth-century French and English writers, among them La Bruyère in France and Joseph Hall, Thomas Overbury, John Earle, and Samuel Butler in England. Characters like those of Theophrastus' were an important part of much satirical poetry of the period.

Theseus. In Greek mythology, the son of Aethra and of the mortal Aegeus, king of Athens, or the god Poseidon. For the story of Theseus' birth see AEGEUS;

417

for his first meeting with Aegeus see Bacchylides' CHORAL LYRIC XVIII. In *Metamorphoses* VII, Ovid also tells of Theseus' arrival in Athens and of Medea's unsuccessful attempt to poison him. Theseus then proved his courage to the Athenians by killing a huge bull, which Heracles had brought from Crete. When Theseus learned that seven Athenian girls and seven boys were sacrificed annually to the Cretan Minotaur, he set out for Crete to kill the monstrous creature. Bacchylides describes Theseus' voyage to Crete in CHORAL LYRIC XVII. In *Metamorphoses* VIII, Ovid briefly tells how Ariadne, a daughter of Minos, fell in love with Theseus and gave him a ball of thread to guide him through the Labyrinth in which Minos had concealed the Minotaur, and of how Theseus took Ariadne with him when he left Crete, only to desert her on the island of Dia (Naxos). For the story of Theseus' triumphant return to Athens and Aegeus' suicide see AEGEUS.

After Theseus became king of Athens and helped to unify Attica, he overcame the Amazons and fell in love with their queen Hippolyta (in some versions Antiope), who bore him a son, Hippolytus. When the Thebans would not permit the burial of those who followed the Seven against Thebes, Theseus waged war on Thebes to uphold the religious laws of Hellas (see Euripides' THE SUPPLIANTS). Theseus also aided the outcast Oedipus (see Sophocles' OEDIPUS AT COLONUS) and the grief-stricken Heracles, who, in a fit of madness, had killed his wife Megara and children (see Euripides' THE MADNESS OF HERACLES). Theseus was a friend of Pirithous, with whom he descended into Hades in an attempt to kidnap Persephone. For the tragic story of Theseus' marriage to Phaedra and his responsibility for the death of his son Hippolytus see Euripides' HIPPOLYTUS. Plutarch wrote a life of Theseus. Mary Renault has told Theseus' story in two brilliant novels, *The King Must Die* (1958) and *The Bull from the Sea* (1962).

Thesmophoriazusae Thesmophoriazousai; Women Celebrating the Thesmophoria; Ladies' Day. An Old Comedy (411 B.C.) by ARISTOPHANES. Translations: in verse, Arthur S. Way, 1934; in prose and verse, Dudley Fitts, 1959; in prose and verse, David Barrett, 1964.

BACKGROUND. The Thesmophoria was a three-day festival held annually in November in honor of Demeter and her daughter Persephone. The festival was sacred to women, and no man was allowed to attend the rites. In the *Thesmophoriazusae* Euripides employs the festival as a background for his theme: a criticism of the plays of Agathon and Euripides. He mocks the style, language, and stage techniques of both writers and especially Euripides' concern with and treatment of women. Aristophanes' THE ACHARNIANS criticizes Euripides' treatment of heroes and his THE FROGS gives more extensive criticism of Euripides' style and ethical position.

SUMMARY. Euripides and his father-in-law, Mnesilochus, are outside the home of the tragic poet Agathon. They are planning to ask Agathon to go to the Thesmophorion disguised as a woman and defend Euripides against the women who are planning to kill him because he has been so critical of females in his plays. Agathon is rolled out on his bed. An obvious homosexual, he lies there dressed in a saffron tunic, with many articles of female apparel about him. He sings part of one of his tragedies, taking the parts of leader of the chorus and then of the chorus. Despite Euripides' pleas, Agathon refuses to go to the Thesmophorion, and finally Mnesilochus offers to go instead. Euripides and he borrow female clothing from Agathon, and shaved and disguised, Mnesilochus leaves for the festival.

The scene is now the Thesmophorion. Women (the Chorus) are gathered around an altar at the center. Behind the altar is a platform. Mnesilochus enters and, trying to imitate the voice and movements of a woman, speaks to an imaginary slave girl. He sits down among the women as the woman Herald begins the prayers for the festival. Soon the women express their grievances against Euripides and agree that he should be put to death for his revelations of their deceptions and vices. Mnesilochus attempts to defend Euripides by mentioning many vices of women that Euripides has not revealed. Hearing this new criticism of themselves and the defense of Euripides, the women become very angry and begin to strike the disguised Mnesilochus, when a well-known homosexual, Clisthenes, comes in and informs them that there is an old man among them whom Euripides has sent to hear their plans. The women soon suspect and prove that Mnesilochus is the culprit. As Clisthenes rushes out to report Mnesilochus' crime to the magistrates, the Leader of the Chorus suggests that they burn Mnesilochus to death. Attempting to find a means of escaping their anger, Mnesilochus decides he must reach Euripides in some way. The best plan he can think of is to imitate one of Euripides' own characters in the *Palamedes*, who wrote a message on oars. Since Mnesilochus can find no oars, he writes his message on wooden statues and throws them all around. While Mnesilochus sits and waits for Euripides to arrive, the Leader of the Chorus speaks to the audience about the inferiority of men to women.

Impatient for Euripides' arrival, Mnesilochus decides to attract him by imitating the character of Helen in Euripides' play of the same name, because this is his latest and perhaps favorite work. As Mnesilochus begins to recite the role of Helen, Euripides enters and takes the role of Menelaus in the play. However, when a Magistrate and a Scythian Policeman approach, Euripides quickly leaves. Mnesilochus is taken prisoner and tied to a post. He then takes the role of Euripides' Andromeda. Euripides, off stage, takes the role of Echo, repeating the last few words of everything said by Mnesilochus and the Policeman. Finally Euripides appears as Perseus to rescue Andromeda, but he cannot outwit the Scythian Policeman. Again Euripides leaves, but he soon returns, disguised as an old procurer, accompanied by a dancing girl and a girl playing the flute. He is reconciled with the Thesmophoriazusae, who accept his vow never again to criticize women. The Chorus then agrees to help him to free Mnesilochus. Euripides attracts the attention of the Scythian Policeman to the young girls he has brought with him. The Policeman is soon infatuated with the dancing girl, and when he goes off to make love to her, Euripides frees Mnesilochus, and both quickly leave. When the Policeman returns, looking for his prisoner and the old procurer, he is dismayed to find them gone. He asks the Chorus where they have gone, but the women give him the wrong directions, thus indicating that they have made peace with Euripides.

Thespis. Possibly a legendary figure; usually considered to be the father of Greek tragedy. It is thought that Thespis flourished around 535 B.C. and that he introduced impersonation into the performances of the dithyrambic chorus, thus creating the first actor. He probably provided a speaking part for this actor, but no written work by Thespis exists. In the *Ars Poetica*, Horace says that Thespis invented tragedy, that he carried his plays about in wagons, and that they were acted by people whose faces were smeared with wine lees (ll. 275–277).

Thessaly (Thessalia). Section of N. Greece known for its horses. It was believed that witchcraft and magic flourished in Thessaly. The Centaurs lived there, and the Argonauts set forth on their journey from Iolcos in Thessaly.

Thetis. A sea-goddess and the mother of ACHILLES. See PELEUS, the ILIAD, and Euripides' ANDROMACHE.

Thisbe. See PYRAMUS.

Thrasymachus (Thrasymachos). A Greek rhetorician who lived during the last half of the fifth century B.C. He appears in Plato's REPUBLIC and is mentioned in his *Phaedrus*. His contribution to Attic prose was in the development of the "middle" style, between the ornate style of Gorgias and the prose of ordinary speech.

Three-Penny Day, The (Trinummus). A comedy (not earlier than 194 B.C.) by PLAUTUS, based on *The Treasure* by Philemon. While Charmides has been abroad, his wasteful son Lesbonicus has spent his father's money and has even sold his house to Charmides' friend Callicles. Callicles has found a treasure hidden in the house, but has kept his discovery secret. He intends either to return it to Charmides when he comes home or to draw on it when Charmides' daughter requires a dowry, because her extravagant and self-indulgent brother has wasted so much money that he is unable to provide one for her. Though Lesbonicus' friend Lysiteles offers to marry the girl without a dowry, Lesbonicus, aware that such a marriage would humiliate him and his family, decides he must find some way to marry his sister off properly. Callicles and his friend Megaronides, determined to use part of the treasure for the girl's dowry without letting Lesbonicus know the source of the money, hire a rogue for three pennies who is to pretend that he has brought the money from Charmides. Their plan does not work out, however, for the rogue meets Charmides, returning from abroad, and tells him that he must deliver letters from Charmides to Lesbonicus and Callicles. Charmides soon learns of all that has happened in his absence. He promises to give Lysiteles his daughter and a large dowry, and even agrees to forgive Lesbonicus, who will be married to the daughter of Callicles.

threnos. Greek choral lyric expressing the grief of mourning. A chorus sang this dirge to the music of the flute at a funeral or at a feast in honor of the dead.

Thucydides (Thoukydides). Greek historian, born about 460 B.C. at Athens, of a family that may have had Thracian origins. During the eighth year of the Peloponnesian War between Athens and Sparta he was elected general and sent to Thrace, where he fought against the great Spartan general Brasidas. When Brasidas captured Amphipolis, Thucydides was forced to go into exile, which lasted for twenty years. He returned to Athens in 404 B.C. and died soon after in about 400 B.C. His history of the Peloponnesian War was left unfinished.

Near the beginning of THE PELOPONNESIAN WAR, Thucydides says that he is writing with exactness and objectivity about events he has witnessed; he regards his history not as an ephemeral work but as one that will last forever, for his purpose is to suggest historical principles through an account and an analysis of contemporary events. Thucydides' accuracy, his effort to suggest a clue to the future through a history of the present, and his method of employing speeches, incidents, documents, and records of oracular prophecies make his history both a fascinating account of events in ancient Greece and a commentary on the behavior of men.

Thyestes. A tragedy by SENECA for which there is no extant model. It is known that Greek and other Roman dramatists employed the myth of Thyestes, but only fragments of some of their plays survive, and these do not seem related to Seneca's tragedy. Seneca's *Thyestes* was his most popular and influential play during the English Renaissance. The subject is the revenge of Atreus on his brother Thyestes, who seduced Aerope, the wife of Atreus, and stole from him a magic ram with a golden fleece, the owner of which was assured the right to the throne of Mycenae. The scene of the play is before and within the palace of Atreus at Mycenae.

As the play begins, the ghost of Tantalus predicts that his descendants will commit horrors besides which his own crimes will seem innocuous. Then the Fury speaks of all the dreadful acts and suffering of the family of Tantalus. The Chorus of Mycenaean Men continues the terrible tale. Next Atreus enters, furious at his brother Thyestes and obsessed by a desire for revenge. He contrives a hideous plan: he will ask Thyestes to return to his home and offer to share the throne with him; then he will kill the sons of Thyestes and serve them to their father at a banquet.

Ironically, when Thyestes arrives, he rejoices at being home. He takes a Stoic position, desiring no wealth or power; it is his sons who persuade him to have faith in Atreus and to help them regain their hereditary rights. The most sensational and horrible scenes of the play follow. First a messenger reports on how Atreus has sacrificed the sons of Thyestes and used their dismembered bodies to prepare a meal for their father. Even more dreadful is the scene in which Thyestes, alone at a banquet table and unaware that he has just consumed his own sons, tries to celebrate his return to his land, but is troubled by forebodings of sorrow. Soon Atreus, gloating over his revenge, reveals the heads of Thyestes' sons and tells their father he has feasted on their bodies. Thyestes cries out to the seas, the lands, and the Underworld and predicts that the gods will avenge Atreus' inhuman crime.

Tiberius Claudius Nero Caesar. The emperor of ROME from A.D. 14 to 37. See Tacitus' ANNALS I–VI. Suetonius and Plutarch also wrote about the life of Tiberius.

Tibullus, Albius. A Roman elegiac poet, born around 48 B.C. Little is known about his life. He came from a family of equestrian rank and was one of the poets who belonged to the circle of the orator and writer M. Valerius Messalla, an aristocrat who supported the republican party at the battle of Philippi. Though Messalla was loyal to Augustus when he became emperor, he remained a republican in principle. Like his contemporary Maecenas, he was a well-known patron of poets. He may have given Tibullus his country estate at Pedum, between Praeneste and Tibur. Tibullus' friend Horace addresses him in *Epistle* I, 4, and Ovid mourns Tibullus' early death (19 B.C.) in *Amores* III, 9.

Two books of Tibullus' ELEGIES appeared during his lifetime: the first, *Delia*, in 26 B.C. and the second, *Nemesis*, in 19 B.C., just before his death. Both books are named for women whom Tibullus addresses as his beloved. According to Apuleius (in the *Apologia*), Delia's real name was Plania. A third book, a collection of poems by members of Messalla's circle that may contain some of Tibullus' poems, was divided into two books during the Renaissance, but is now considered one by most scholars. It contains six elegies by Lygdamus, expressing affection for Neaera; a poor poem called "Panegyricus Messallae," the author of which is unknown but almost certainly not Tibullus; six brief poems by a woman called Sulpicia, possibly the niece of Messalla; five poems on Sulpicia's love for Cerinthus, which may be by Tibullus; and two other poems of unknown authorship.

Tibullus is chiefly known as a love elegist; his graceful poems convey genuine tenderness for the women he calls Delia and Nemesis. The personality of the poet that emerges from his elegies is gentle and sometimes melancholy. Though Tibullus expresses the pain as well as the delights of love, and some of his poems reveal bitter suffering, he does not seem to be tortured by love that partakes of hate, as do Catullus and Propertius. Other subjects of Tibullus' poems are a boy he likes, a ritual he has observed in the country, the victories of Messalla, and the glory of Rome.

Timaeus (Timaios). A dialogue by PLATO, named for a Pythagorean philosopher, and dealing with the creation of the universe and the laws that govern it. Critias tells a story of the imaginary island Atlantis, once conquered by the Athenians, now sunk in the Atlantic. The story is continued in Plato's *Critias*.

Timon of Phlius. See SKEPTICS.

Tiresias (Teiresias). In Greek mythology, a blind Theban prophet, the son of Eueres and Chariclo. Many tales exist about the cause of his blindness. One account is that when Tiresias was seven years old the gods blinded him because he disclosed to men things the gods did not wish them to know. According to another legend he was struck blind because he looked at Athene while she was bathing. According to another, because Tiresias had killed a female snake, he had been transformed into a woman for a period of his life. He was asked by Zeus and Hera to settle their dispute as to whether man or woman enjoys love-making more; when Tiresias declared that Zeus' point of view was correct Hera blinded him. To compensate for the loss of his sight Zeus gave Tiresias the gift of prophecy.

The blind prophet Tiresias has an important role in ancient literature. He appears in the Underworld in ODYSSEY XI. One of the most dramatic and ironic scenes in Sophocles' OEDIPUS THE KING is that in which Oedipus taunts the blind Tiresias, who knows all that Oedipus is yet to discover about himself. In Euripides' THE BACCHAE, Tiresias warns Pentheus not to reject Dionysus; Ovid re-creates this scene in *Metamorphoses* III, where Tiresias declares that, in his blindness, he perceives life all too well. Tiresias also appears in Euripides' THE PHOENICIAN WOMEN, Sophocles' ANTIGONE, and Seneca's OEDIPUS, where he is accompanied by his daughter Manto.

Tiryns. An ancient city in Argolis that Proteus, the brother of Acrisius, was believed to have built. He was helped by the Cyclopes, who erected its Cyclopean walls (see MYCENAE). Heracles was reared in Tiryns. The city was first excavated by Schliemann and Dörpfeld in 1884–85, and the work was continued under the supervision of Dörpfeld and others.

Titans (Titanes). Pre-Olympian gods of Greece. Oceanus, Coeus, Crius, Iapetus, Hyperion, Cronus, Rhea, Theia, Themis, Mnemosyne, Phoebe, and Tethys were the children of Ge (Earth) and Uranus (Sky). The Titans, who were overcome by Zeus, were probably gods worshiped before the Olympians. Their defeat may indicate that the worship of the Olympians has replaced the earlier religion. See Hesiod's THEOGONY and Ovid's *Metamorphoses*.

Tithonus (Tithonos). In Greek mythology, a son of Laomedon. Tithonus was beloved of Eos, who asked Zeus to make Tithonus immortal, but she failed to ask that he be granted eternal youth. Tithonus grew very old and so frail that he could hardly move; he could only make pathetic sounds as he prayed for death. According to one version of the myth, Eos, pitying the shrunken old man, transformed him into a grasshopper. Tennyson wrote a poem called "Tithonus."

Titus Flavius Sabinus Vespasianus. The emperor of ROME from A.D. 79 to 81. A contemporary source for his life is Suetonius' *Lives of the Caesars.*

Tityus (Tityos). In Greek mythology, a giant whom Apollo and Artemis killed. In Hades, Tityus was tied while vultures consumed his liver.

Tomis or Tomi. A city (the modern Constanta in Roumania) on the west coast of the Black Sea, to which OVID was banished in A.D. 8 by an edict of Augustus.

Trachiniai. See THE WOMEN OF TRACHIS.

Tragedy. According to Aristotle in the POETICS, tragedy, the noblest form of Greek art, originated in the dithyramb, the choral ode sung in honor of the god Dionysus. In a famous essay, "An Excursus on the Ritual Forms Preserved in Greek Tragedy" (pp. 341–363 in Jane Harrison's *Themis*, 2nd ed. rev. [Cambridge University Press, 1927]), Gilbert Murray develops the thesis that there is a basic relationship between tragedy and early worship of Dionysus. Murray contends that ancient tragedy grew out of a *Sacer Ludus*, a ritual dance, or sacred play, in honor of the god Dionysus, who, in this role, was a vegetation deity or Year Daimon, representing the "cyclic death and rebirth of the Earth and the World, i.e., for practical purposes, of the tribe's own lands and the tribe itself." Though Murray acknowledges that "Tragedy, as we possess it, contains many non-Dionysiac elements," he finds in extant Greek tragedy the basic pattern of the Year Daimon's cycle. There has been opposition to this theory (see especially A. W. Pickard-Cambridge, *Dithyramb, Tragedy, and Comedy*, rev. T. B. L. Webster [Oxford University Press, 1962]), but most scholars would agree that tragedy arose from the performances of the dithyrambic chorus, which sang and danced every spring to honor Dionysus, a god of fertility and of the vine. Dressed like satyrs, this chorus of fifty probably enacted in a ritual dance stories from the life of the god. (See also THE BACCHAE.)

It is thought that ARION was the first to insert dialogue between the dithyrambic chorus and its leader into the performance, thus introducing the first real dramatic element. THESPIS, generally regarded as the father of ancient Greek tragedy, is thought to have introduced impersonation into these bits of dialogue. At first poets may have employed myths dealing with Dionysus and then turned to other mythical subjects. It is probably from these beginnings, of which there are no remains, that early tragedy, which was mainly lyrical, emerged.

The first known tragedian is Choerilus, who was followed by Pratinas and PHRYNICHUS, the latter apparently a gifted dramatist, of whose plays only fragments remain. During the fifth century B.C. the great Athenian tragedians AESCHYLUS, SOPHOCLES, and EURIPIDES emerged. Except for *The Persians* of Aeschylus, all their extant plays are based on traditional myths. Employing well-known plots and characters, these dramatists interpreted them to express their individual conceptions of man involved in a struggle to understand himself, his fate, and his place in human society and the universe.

In Athens some tragedy was performed at the Lenaea, a festival of the wine-press, held annually during January–February. The more important occasion for the performance of tragedy, however, was the festival of the Great or City Dionysia, held annually in March–April in honor of Dionysus. For three consecutive days three dramatists competed in the great contests held at this time, each offering three tragedies and a satyr play. A jury of Athenians awarded prizes to the authors of the best plays and to their sponsors. Wealthy citizens were obliged by the state to bear the costs of dramatic performances. The playwrights themselves often directed their plays, and may even have acted in them.

Generally Greek tragedy is constructed according to the following basic pattern: the play opens with a *prologue,* a brief scene or monologue that provides necessary background; then there is a *parodos,* the entrance song and dance of the chorus. This is followed by the first *episode,* a scene of the play, usually with dialogue. After this there is a *stasimon,* a choral ode that the chorus delivers "in its place" in the orchestra of the theater. There follow a series of episodes and choral odes, and occasionally a *commus (kommos),* a lyric interchange between actors and chorus. Finally the *exodos* or last scene of the play takes place, and the chorus leaves the stage.

All the parts in Greek tragedy were taken by men. Usually three actors and a chorus managed all the roles. The stylized and symbolic nature of the characters was heightened by the masks worn by the actors and by the *cothurnus (kothornos),* the high-soled boot that was part of their costume.

In Rome, LIVIUS ANDRONICUS was the first to adapt Greek tragedy to the Roman stage. Other Roman dramatists, such as Ennius, Pacuvius, and Accius adapted Greek tragedies and composed FABULAE PRAETEXTAE. Though tragedy was written during the Augustan period, none remains. The only remaining examples of Roman tragedy, the plays of SENECA, were probably not intended for dramatic performance.

Trajan (Marcus Ulpius Trajanus). The emperor of ROME from A.D. 98 to 117.

Trinummus. See THE THREE-PENNY DAY.

Tristia (Poems of Sorrow). Elegiac epistles by OVID. Book I was written between A.D. 8 and 9; Book II in A.D. 9; Book III between A.D. 9 and 10; Book IV between A.D. 10 and 11; Book V between A.D. 11 and 12. Translations: in prose, H. T. Riley, 1869; in prose, Arthur L. Wheeler, 1924.

S U M M A R Y . *Tristia* is a collection of epistles which Ovid began to write on his journey into exile in Tomis; he continued to add to the collection until A.D. 12. Except for the letters sent to Augustus and members of his household, one to Perilla (III, 7), and those to Ovid's wife, the recipients are not named, as they are, for the most part, in the *Epistulae Ex Ponto,* composed between A.D. 12 and 16. *Tristia* expresses Ovid's despair over his exile and his hope that he may be allowed to return to Rome.

In I, 1 Ovid addresses his book, telling it to go to the city, though he is forbidden to accompany it. The book must go without adornment for it is the work of an exile. Ovid apologizes for the imperfections of his poems, which were written in sadness. Though in this poem and in several others he hints at the causes of his exile, he never states them directly or specifically. In I, 1 Ovid speaks of Augustus' anger at him. Now, says Ovid, he no longer wishes for fame; it is sufficient that he does not detest poetry, for his very talent and popularity brought about his banishment. In I, 3, writing about the last night he spent in Rome before he left for exile in Tomis, and the anguish of the members of his household, Ovid insists that he committed an "error" but no "crime." In II, which is one long poem addressed to Augustus, Ovid again deals with the causes of his exile. Lines 103–106 give the impression that Ovid "saw" something forbidden; he compares himself to Actaeon, who was destroyed because he saw Diana naked. The passage suggests the possibility that Ovid observed some licentious adventure of Augustus' granddaughter, Julia, but there is no conclusive evidence on the matter. Since in II Ovid also claims, as in I, 1, that his own talents destroyed him, referring bitterly to Augustus' ban on the *Ars Amatoria,* and then in II, line 207 speaks of two causes for his banishment, a "song" and an "error," it seems likely that his sentence resulted both from Augustus' displeasure at the licentious wit of the *Ars Amatoria* and from some incident involving Julia. *Tristia* II is a long plea for mercy. Though the poem is essentially a defense of the *Ars Amatoria* and of Ovid's own innocence, and is an argument intended to sway Augustus, it is a moving poem, especially in its expression of sorrow and loneliness.

Perhaps the best known of the *Tristia* poems is IV, 10, in which Ovid tells the story of his life. He speaks of himself as the poet of "tender love," tells of his family and of how, early in life, though he tried to accept his father's advice that he choose a "practical" profession, he could not prevent himself from writing poetry. He thought of poets as "gods." Then Ovid speaks of his literary friends: Propertius reading his poems to him; Ponticus, the epic poet; Bassus, skilled in iambics. Ovid saw Vergil, but did not know him. In a beautiful passage Ovid declares that "greedy fate" denied him the friendship of Tibullus, who died in 19 B.C. Tibullus, says Ovid, was the successor of Gallus as an elegiac poet, and Propertius was the successor of Tibullus. Ovid himself is fourth in the line. He goes on to speak of his popularity as a poet, his personal life, and his three marriages. He then writes of the sorrow of exile and of his unconquerable will to survive and to write despite the wretched conditions of his life in Tomis. His muse has made life endurable; poetry is his guide and companion, and it will assure his immortality.

Triton. In Greek mythology, a son of Poseidon and Amphitrite. Triton was a merman, who is sometimes described as living with his parents in the sea. His attribute was a great sea shell, on which he blew to control the waves. The story of Triton's drowning of Misenus, who proudly summoned the gods to vie with him in blowing on the shell, is told in *Aeneid* VI. In some myths a number of mermen called Tritons occur.

Troades. See THE TROJAN WOMEN.

Troilus (Troilos). A son of Priam whom Achilles killed in the Trojan War.

Trojan Women, The (Troades). A tragedy (415 B.C.) by EURIPIDES. Translations: in verse, Gilbert Murray, 1911; in verse, Edith Hamilton, 1937; in verse, Richmond Lattimore, 1947; in prose, I. K. and A. E. Raubitschek, assisted by Anne L. McCabe, 1954; in prose and verse, Philip Vellacott, 1954.

MYTHICAL BACKGROUND. The Greeks have just captured Troy and the Trojan women are now captives of the Greek leaders.

SCENE. A battlefield at Troy. At the back, the walls of Troy; in front, huts in which the captured women are kept.

SUMMARY. As Hecuba lies asleep on the ground, Poseidon enters and speaks of his love for Troy and his despair over her fall. He tells of how the Wooden Horse helped to bring about the destruction of the city, the walls of which he and Apollo had built. Poseidon speaks of the captive women about to become the slaves of the Greek leaders. He looks sadly at Hecuba, who has lost so many children and her husband in war. Now her daughter Cassandra has become the slave of Agamemnon. Athene enters and offers to aid Poseidon in bringing trouble to the Greeks. Athene is angry because Ajax, son of Oïleus, ravished Cassandra in Athene's temple, and the Greeks have allowed him to go unpunished. Poseidon says he will raise a storm that will kill many of the Greeks on their way home.

As the day dawns Hecuba awakes. She laments the fall of Troy but encourages herself to endure in the face of calamity. Yet she cannot help weeping for her dead children and her fallen land. She calls to the other Trojan women in the huts, and they come forth to join her. Hecuba and the Chorus then lament the fate of Troy and their own unhappy future, when they will be slaves of the Greek leaders. One woman wonders who her master will be, while another weeps for her dead child. Soon the Greek herald Talthybius appears and announces that the women's fates have been determined by lot: Cassandra will go to Agamemnon; Polyxena, another of Hecuba's daughters, is to be sacrificed at the tomb of Achilles; Andromache is to go to Pyrrhus (Neoptolemus), the son of Achilles; and Hecuba will be the slave of Odysseus, king of Ithaca. Hecuba sadly remarks that the man who is now her master is a deceitful, pitiless person.

Talthybius sends his men to find Cassandra, who soon comes out of a hut, dressed in the white robes and wreath of a priestess and carrying a torch in her hand. Lost in her prophetic vision, she sings to Hymen, the god of marriage, then prophesies the death of her captor, Agamemnon. Cassandra attempts to

427

comfort Hecuba by telling her that the Greeks have suffered as much in warfare as the Trojans. Though Talthybius tries to stop her, Cassandra goes on to predict the future woes of Odysseus and Agamemnon. Finally she says farewell to her mother, her city, her dead father and brothers, and leaves with Talthybius and the soldiers. Hecuba recounts the painful tale of her own fall from wealth and power to wretchedness. She weeps over the loss of her husband and children and imagines herself, the mother of the noble Hector, in the role of a slave. The Chorus sings a tragic ode about how the Trojans welcomed the Wooden Horse, unaware that it contained the Greek warriors who were to destroy their city.

The Leader of the Chorus sees a chariot approaching, and on it Andromache with her child Astyanax in her arms. Andromache and Hecuba express their sorrow over the fallen Troy and their dead husbands. Andromache cries out, condemning Paris, who sacrificed Troy for his evil love of Helen. Andromache tells Hecuba that Polyxena has been slain at the tomb of Achilles. When Hecuba weeps for her daughter, Andromache says she envies Polyxena, whose death is sweeter than her own life. Hecuba heroically answers that life always offers hope. Talthybius enters with a group of soldiers and reluctantly announces that the Greeks have decided to kill Astyanax in order to prevent his growing up to avenge the destruction of Troy. The child will be thrown from the walls of Troy. Andromache says a last, tragic farewell to her child. As Talthybius takes the child from Andromache's arms, he wishes a less sensitive man than he were given the painful task.

The Chorus then sings of an earlier defeat of the Trojans: Heracles and Telamon of Salamis waged war against King Laomedon and destroyed his city. The gods once loved the Trojans—Ganymedes and Tithonus were their favorites —but now they feel no love for the Trojan race.

Menelaus enters with a band of soldiers. Delighted that Helen is among the captured Trojan women, he tells his soldiers to drag her before him. When they bring her out of the hut, she stands before her husband and calmly asks if her death has been decreed. Menelaus tells her that all the Greeks agreed that he was to kill her. Helen asks to be allowed to speak and reveal her innocence. Menelaus angrily says that he wants to kill her, not listen to her; but Hecuba, who wishes to see Helen die, begs Menelaus to allow Helen to defend herself so that Hecuba can answer her, for even Menelaus does not know the real corruption of Helen. Helen then blames her crime on Paris and the goddess Aphrodite. She claims that she tried to escape from Troy, but was kept prisoner. Skillfully she takes the role of a wronged woman begging her husband's pity. Hecuba insists that Helen is lying; she scoffs at Helen's attempts to blame the gods and Paris, saying that Helen followed Paris because she was infatuated with him and remained in Troy quite willingly. Justice, says Hecuba, demands that Helen be slain. Menelaus knows that Hecuba speaks the truth, yet he cannot help being influenced by Helen's power. As

Helen kneels before him, clasping his knees, he insists that she means nothing to him; yet he does not kill her. He declares that he will punish her when they return to Argos, but Hecuba, the Chorus, and the audience know that she will win him over by her beauty. As Menelaus, Helen, and the soldiers go out, the Chorus asks Zeus why the sacrifices and prayers of the Trojans meant nothing to him.

Talthybius enters with the corpse of Astyanax. He tells Hecuba that Andromache has left Troy and that Hecuba must bury Astyanax. Hecuba holds the child's body in her arms and asks how brave warriors could fear this baby. With the help of the Chorus she prepares to bury her grandchild. Then she symbolically heals the child's wounds and buries him on Hector's shield, which Andromache had begged Pyrrhus to leave for this purpose. Observing the flames of her fallen city, Hecuba is about to spring into the fire, but she is restrained by the soldiers who have returned with Talthybius to lead the remaining women to the Greek ships. As the walls of Troy fall in flames, the women go to the ships.

COMMENTARY. *The Trojan Women* emphasizes the effects of war on the women and children of the defeated Trojans, yet it depicts the sufferings and the empty victory of the Greeks as well. The play reveals the wounds that war inflicts on both the conquered and the victors. Talthybius is debased by his part in the murder of Astyanax, and Menelaus' reward is regaining a faithless wife, to whom he is still enslaved. The play was written shortly after the Athenians had conquered and destroyed the island of Melos because its people wished to remain neutral in the Peloponnesian War (see THE PELO-PONNESIAN WAR V). In *The Trojan Women* Euripides uses a traditional myth to suggest the brutality to which even the noble Athenians could descend in warfare. The story of fallen Troy could be that of Melos or of any people who fall victim to the hostility of their fellow men. The tragic irony of the play is that Hecuba and the other Trojan women retain a courage and a dignity which their Greek conquerors have lost. The soldiers in this play are not inspired by the heroic code of the Homeric warrior (see ILIAD); the only heroism that Euripides deals with is that of the widows and mothers of the defeated Trojans.

Trojan Women, The (Troades). A tragedy by SENECA based on Euripides' play of the same name and on his depiction of the sacrifice of Polyxena in *Hecuba*. Seneca's play is centered around the sacrifice of Polyxena to the ghost of Achilles and the murder of Hector's son Astyanax. As Pyrrhus and Agamemnon argue about the sacrifice of Polyxena, Agamemnon reveals his sympathy for the Trojans, whose land has been destroyed, and tries to prevent further bloodshed. Pyrrhus is brutal. Ulysses, like his model in Euripides' *Hecuba*, is detached and cold as he demands that Andromache give up her son. As in both plays by Euripides, the captive women are heroic and dignified in their sorrow. Whereas the bitterness of Euripides' captive women implies a tragic protest against their destiny, Seneca's women, especially the Chorus, seem to accept their dreadful plight stoically. Nonetheless, they are effective and moving figures.

Tros. See TROY.

Troy. In ancient times many cities called Troy (Troia) or Ilium (Ilion) existed successively on the hill now called Hissarlik, which is situated in northwest Asia Minor at the entrance to the Hellespont (the Dardanelles). The legendary founder of Troy is Teucer, son of the River Scamander in Crete and the nymph Idaea. Thus the Trojan people are sometimes called Teucrians. Dardanus, a son of Zeus, migrated to the kingdom of Teucer and there, at the foot of Mount Ida, founded the city of Dardania. Dardanus married the daughter of Teucer, Batia. One of Dardanus' sons was Erichthonius, whose son, Tros, gave the name Trojans to the people of Ilium and the name Troy to the city. Ilus, a son of Tros, founded the city of Ilion. This city was joined with Troy and Dardania to form the great city of Ilium or Troy. From Ilus were descended two Trojans famous in literature, Priam, son of LAOMEDON, and Aeneas, son of Anchises.

The city of Troy ruled by Priam and, according to epic tradition, attacked by the Greek forces led by Agamemnon, is now called by archeologists Troy VIIa. Six earlier settlements on the site of Troy had been destroyed, some by enemy invaders and Troy VI by an earthquake. Priam's Troy, built on the ruins of former settlements, existed from around 1300 B.C. to around 1183 B.C., when it was once more destroyed, this time, it is thought, by the Greeks. The Trojans were probably of the same race as the Achaeans and spoke the same language. Their weapons were similar to those of the Greeks, and they worshiped the same gods. Troy's citadel (called Pergamon) stood on a hill and was surrounded by huge walls of brick. Troy ruled not only the people who lived on the Trojan plain, but also the Dardanians, who inhabited the valley of the Scamander. Troy was able to control trade going through the Hellespont and could demand a toll from all ships. The city profited not only from this but from the sale of fresh water to sailors detained by unfavorable winds. Thus Troy grew rich and powerful as a trade route and possibly as a market place for traders from many areas.

Excavations at Troy were first begun by Heinrich Schliemann in 1870, and during the next twenty years he organized and led seven major excavations at the site of Hissarlik. Schliemann wrote many books on his explorations, among them *Troy and Its Remains* (London, 1874) and *Ilios, the City and the Country of the Trojans* (London, 1880). Although Schliemann thought he had unearthed the remains of Priam's city, it was later discovered by his successor, Wilhelm Dörpfeld, that Schliemann had found earlier remains, those of the first and second cities rather than of Priam's. Dörpfeld's excavations, carried out in 1893–94 and described in his *Troja und Ilion* (Athens, 1902), turned up remains of Troy VI, which he and other scholars thought was Priam's Troy. More recent excavations by Carl W. Blegen and other members of the

University of Cincinnati team have shown that Troy vi was overwhelmed by an earthquake about 1350 B.C. and that the reconstruction which took place afterward created many physical changes, but did not prevent a continuity of culture from Troy vi to Troy viia. Moreover, Troy viia has been established as the city ruled by Priam. According to Blegen the Trojan War took place around 1240 B.C., over fifty years earlier than the traditional date. (See Blegen's *Troy and the Trojans* [Praeger, 1963].) Troy viia had a brief life; though scholars cannot determine its actual length, some believe it lasted only as long as one generation of men and others that it remained for a century.

Excavation has yielded evidence of the Troy Homer describes: its walls, fortress, terraces around the walls, and a great many remains of horses' bones which suggest the accuracy of Homer's epithet "horse-taming Trojans." There is also archeological evidence that Troy viia was destroyed by warfare during the period generally accepted as that of the Trojan War. However, the hot and cold springs that Homer depicts no longer exist, and the two rivers, the Scamander and the Simois, follow courses different from those Homer describes. (See the ILIAD.)

Truculentus. A serious comedy by PLAUTUS, based on an unknown Greek play. The play, which has practically no plot, is mainly a representation of human weakness. The action is centered around the schemes of the courtesan Phronesium, who will employ any deceit to obtain all she can from her three lovers: Stratophanes, a braggart soldier; Diniarchus, a young Athenian; and Strabax, a young man from the country. She even pretends she has borne the soldier's child. The baby Phronesium pretended was hers turns out to be the child of Diniarchus and a girl he has seduced. Diniarchus promises to marry the girl and asks Phronesium to give him his baby, but when the courtesan pleads with him to let her use the child to deceive the soldier for three more days, he agrees. Diniarchus goes off, promising to return occasionally, and Stratophanes and Strabax are left competing for Phronesium. They argue violently until she agrees to allow both of them to remain her lovers. The play is named for Strabax' slave Truculentus.

Turnus. The king of the Rutuli in the AENEID.

Twin Menaechmi, The (Menaechmi). A comedy by PLAUTUS. Translations: in verse, B. B. Rogers, 1908; in prose, Paul Nixon, 1917; in verse and prose, Edward C. Weist and Richard W. Hyde, 1942; in prose, Frank O. Copley, 1949; in verse, Lionel Casson, 1963; in prose, Samuel Lieberman, 1964.

S C E N E . Epidamnus, a seaport on the western coast of Greece.

S U M M A R Y . *The Twin Menaechmi*, one of Plautus' most successful comedies, is based on an unknown Greek play. The Prologue informs the audience that a merchant from Syracuse had twin sons, Menaechmus and Sosicles. When Menaechmus was seven years old he was taken from his father by a merchant from Epidamnus. The grieving father died, and the grandfather of the twins changed Sosicles' name to Menaechmus to commemorate the lost boy. Menaechmus I, who was adopted by the merchant who had kidnaped him and inherited the old man's fortune when he died, now lives in Epidamnus with his wife. The other twin, Menaechmus II, has been seeking his brother for six years and has now arrived in Epidamnus, unaware that Menaechmus I lives there.

As the play begins Peniculus (Sponge), a parasite, enters, planning to beg a meal from Menaechmus I. At this point Menaechmus I leaves his house with one of his wife's dresses under his cloak. He has been quarreling with his wife, who constantly scolds him and spies on him. Now he is off to see his mistress Erotium, who lives next door and to whom he will give his wife's dress. Menaechmus I invites Peniculus to dinner at Erotium's house; while the meal is being prepared, they go off to town.

Meanwhile, Menaechmus II has arrived in Epidamnus with his slave Messenio, who warns him that Epidamnus is full of swindlers, rogues, and immoral women. Soon Menaechmus II is mistaken for his twin brother by Cylindrus, Erotium's cook. This is the first in a long series of such errors, which create the confusion and humor of the play. Next, Erotium, assuming Menaechmus II is the Menaechmus she knows, tells him that dinner is ready and she is awaiting her beloved. Though shocked at the familiarity of a woman he has never seen before, he agrees to go into her house.

Menaechmus II has had a fine time at Erotium's house. He has promised to have the dress given her by Menaechmus I adorned by an embroiderer, and, as he leaves the house with the dress, he meets Peniculus, indignant because he has missed his dinner. Menaechmus II cannot understand Peniculus' threats that he will reveal all he knows to Menaechmus' wife. Erotium's slave comes out to ask Menaechmus II to have a bracelet repaired for her mistress. Soon the wife of Menaechmus I, encouraged by the parasite, scolds her husband, just back from town, for giving her clothing to his mistress. When Menaechmus I asks Erotium to return the dress, he is confused by her insistence that she gave him the dress as well as a bracelet. Certain that her lover is trying to deceive her, Erotium goes into her house and will not return.

Menaechmus II is then scolded by the wife of Menaechmus I, who asks for her dress, and, when Menaechmus II speaks to her insultingly, she declares she will divorce him and sends for her father. The old man decides that Menaechmus II is insane. Attempting to scare the old man away, Menaechmus II intentionally behaves like a madman until the old man calls a doctor. By the time the doctor appears, Menaechmus II has left. Soon Menaechmus I returns; the doctor begins to question him and quickly concludes that he is insane and needs treatment at the doctor's own home. When four slaves attempt to take Menaechmus I there, Messenio, mistaking him for his master, comes to his aid and sets him free. Messenio then goes off on an errand and encounters Menaechmus II. Soon the two of them meet Menaechmus I. Messenio is shocked at seeing "the mirror" of his master, and the twin Menaechmi finally recognize each other. Menaechmus II frees Messenio, and Menaechmus I decides to sell his property in Epidamnus—including his wife—at auction and return to Syracuse with his brother.

Two Bacchides, The (Bacchides). A comedy (possibly 189 B.C.) by PLAUTUS, probably an adaptation of a lost play by Menander called *The Double Deceiver.* The beginning of *The Two Bacchides* is lost. Mnesilochus has written from Ephesus to his friend Pistoclerus in Athens, asking him to find his beloved Bacchis, a courtesan from Samos who was taken to Athens by a Captain Cleomachus. Mnesilochus asks Pistoclerus to have the girl released from Cleomachus, to whom she is bound for a year. Bacchis' sister, who has the same name and is also a courtesan, lives in Athens. She informs Pistoclerus that her sister has arrived, and he soon realizes he has found the sweetheart of Mnesilochus. When it is apparent that Pistoclerus has fallen in love with Bacchis of Athens, Lydus, his father's slave and his tutor, strongly disapproves of his choice.

Soon Chrysalus, the slave of Mnesilochus, arrives at Athens and is told by Pistoclerus that Bacchis of Samos wishes to buy her freedom from Cleomachus, but has no money. Chrysalus is sympathetic to the young lovers, and plans to use the money of Mnesilochus' father Nicobulus, which he has with him, to free Bacchis. The complications increase: Mnesilochus arrives at Athens and, hearing of Pistoclerus' love for a girl called Bacchis, assumes that his friend has betrayed him. Finally he learns that the twin girls are both called Bacchis. Because in his despair Mnesilochus had returned Nicobulus' money to him, the scheming Chrysalus finds another way to deceive the old man and again obtain money from him. When Nicobulus discovers he has been deceived by the slave, he is very angry. He and Philoxenus, the father of Pistoclerus, are worried about their sons, and together they go to the house of Bacchis of Athens. The twins charm Nicobulus and Philoxenus; Nicobulus forgives his son, and the two old men enter the house where they, their sons, and the twin Bacchides will spend the evening.

Tyndareus (Tyndareos). A king of Sparta, the husband of LEDA. He appears in Euripides' ORESTES.

Typhoeus or Typhon. The monstrous son of Tartarus and Ge. His head was made of one hundred serpents, and his voice was terrifying. Zeus overcame him with a thunderbolt and threw him into Tartarus.

Tyrrhenians. See ETRUSCANS.

Tyrtaeus (Tyrtaios). A Greek poet who went to Sparta around the middle of the seventh century B.C., during the second Messenian War. According to legend, when the Spartans were in need of help in their struggle with the Messenians, they asked the Athenians to send them a general. Instead, the Athenians sent the lame poet Tyrtaeus, who inspired the Spartans to heroic conduct with his songs. Actually it is not certain where Tyrtaeus was born. He wrote mainly war songs in elegiacs, encouraging the young men of Sparta to fight bravely and reminding them of the heroic code of conduct which demands courage and loyalty. A passage in one of his poems describing the disgraceful scene of an old man with white hair and beard lying dead in war is reminiscent of a passage in the *Iliad* in which Priam begs Hector to remain and guard him lest he, an old man, be slain by the Greeks. It is no disgrace, he says, when a young man dies fighting heroically, but an old man killed in war is a shameful sight (XXII, 59–76). Tyrtaeus was probably aware of the Homeric passage, which he adapts as a warning to young warriors, lest they ignore their obligation to fight courageously. Only fragments of Tyrtaeus' poem survive.

U

Ulysses (Ulixes). See ODYSSEUS.

Uranus (Ouranos). In Greek mythology, the heavens. In Hesiod's *Theogony*, Uranus is regarded as the son of Ge (Earth), as well as her husband.

V

Valerius Flaccus, Gaius. A Roman poet who lived during the first century A.D. Practically nothing is known of his life. His unfinished epic poem ARGONAUTICA, of which he wrote eight books, was dedicated to the emperor Vespasian. Valerius Flaccus died around A.D. 90.

The *Argonautica* of Valerius Flaccus was influenced by both the *Argonautica* of Apollonius Rhodius and Vergil's *Aeneid*. Though the contents of the first four books of Valerius Flaccus' epic are fairly similar to those of Apollonius' *Argonautica*, the Latin poem is longer, less episodic, and more serious in tone. Valerius Flaccus introduces the story of King Aeëtes' conflict with his exiled brother Perses, who tries to seize the throne of Colchis, and the defeat of Perses. Medea is the most interesting figure in both versions of the *Argonautica*. Because Valerius Flaccus is obviously more interested in human motivation and conflict than is Apollonius, his depiction of Medea's suffering as she must choose between her overwhelming love for Jason and her loyalty and duty to her father is even more effective than Apollonius' version.

Valerius Maximus. Roman writer (first century A.D.). He is the author of *Facta et Dicta Memorabilia*, nine books of anecdotes intended for orators' use.

Varro, Marcus Terentius. A Roman writer, born in 116 B.C. in Reate (Rieti), a town in the Sabine country. He was regarded by Quintilian as "the most learned of Romans." He was born into a family of the equestrian rank, and studied at Rome under Lucius Aelius Stilo, the philologist, and at Athens under Antiochus of Ascalon, a philosopher of the Academic school. A follower of Pompey, Varro held the positions of tribune, curule aedile, and praetor. The members of the First Triumvirate put him in charge of awarding grants of land to veterans in Campania. As a lieutenant under Pompey, Varro aided in the conquest of pirates in the Mediterranean and supported Pompey in his war with Caesar. After Pompey's death Varro was pardoned by Caesar and returned to Rome, where Caesar put him in charge of organizing a public library of Greek and Latin literature. After Caesar's assassination Mark Antony had Varro proscribed and his property confiscated, but Octavian saved him from death. Varro lived in retirement, reading and writing, until his death in 27 B.C.

It is thought that Varro wrote seventy-four works, which altogether made up 620 books. Many of his writings were destroyed when his library was seized, along with his other possessions, by the Second Triumvirate; other works were lost later. It is known that he wrote in many genres and on a wide variety of subjects, among them literature, history, science, antiquities, and biography. Only fragments remain of his 150 books of *Menippean Satires* (see SATIRE). He also wrote *Hebdomades vel de Imaginibus,* fifteen books of biographies of important figures of Greece and Rome, with a portrait and an epigram for each, and forty-one books of *Antiquitates Rerum Humanarum et Divinarum* (*Antiquities of Things Human and Divine*). Fragments remain of essays on literary history, among which is a list of plays by Plautus regarded as genuine. Varro also wrote on philosophy, history, geography, and law. A lost work, *Disciplines,* in nine books, treated music, medicine, grammar, and rhetoric.

Except for fragments, the only remains of Varro's writings are Books v–x of his *De Lingua Latina* (*On the Latin Language*), in poor condition, and his *Res Rusticae,* a work in three books on farming, addressed to his wife. *Res Rusticae,* a difficult, technical work in dialogue form, was used by Vergil in his *Georgics* and by Pliny in his *Natural History.*

Venus. The Roman goddess of love. Originally a goddess of spring, who protected vines and gardens, she was later identified with the Greek goddess Aphrodite. As Venus Genetrix, she is the mother of the Romans, who traced their ancestry back to Aeneas, the son of Venus and Anchises. See AENEID.

Vergil or **Virgil (Publius Vergilius Maro).** Roman poet, born in 70 B.C. at Andes, near Mantua. His father, who was either a farmer or a potter, gave his son a good education at Cremona and Milan. Later, Vergil completed his education at Rome, where he studied with Epidius, the rhetorician, and Siro, the Epicurean philosopher. He then went back to Mantua, where it is thought he began to write the ECLOGUES in 43 B.C. After the victory of Antony and Octavian over Brutus and Cassius at Philippi in 42 B.C. (see ROME), the confiscation of land in Mantua and Cremona resulted in Vergil's loss of his farm. It was later restored through the help of friends who had influence with Octavian (see ECLOGUES I and IX). Either Pollio, the governor of Cisalpine Gaul, or Maecenas, a wealthy patron of the arts, introduced Vergil to Octavian.

In 37 B.C., the year the *Eclogues* were published, Vergil and his friend the poet Horace went on a trip to Brundisium, which Horace describes in *Satire* I, v. Vergil spent seven years on the composition of the GEORGICS, which appeared in

29 B.C. For the rest of his life he worked on his great epic, the AENEID. In 19 B.C. Vergil began a journey to Greece and Asia, where he hoped to spend three years revising the *Aeneid*, but in Athens he was persuaded by Augustus to accompany him back to Rome. On this journey Vergil died of fever at Brundisium and was buried at Naples. Before his death Vergil asked his friends Varius and Tucca to burn the manuscript of the *Aeneid* because he felt it was not ready for publication. Fortunately, however, Augustus ordered Varius and Tucca to edit the *Aeneid*, deleting what they felt was unnecessary but adding nothing; then, at the command of Augustus, the poem was published. A probable example of these deletions is the four lines that, in some editions of the *Aeneid*, precede the traditional opening and announce that the author of the *Eclogues* and the *Georgics* now takes up the subject of war.

A number of poems grouped together under the title *Appendix Vergiliana* has been attributed to Vergil by some scholars, though most doubt that he is their author. The *Appendix Vergiliana* includes poems on a gnat (CULEX), on the transformation of Scylla into a seabird (CIRIS), on the preparation of a farmer's breakfast (MORETUM), and on the hostess of an inn (COPA). Other titles are DIRAE (or Curses), CATALEPTON (or Trifles), LYDIA, PRIAPEA, EPIGRAMMATA, and AETNA.

Vergil has generally been regarded as the greatest of the Latin poets. Employing traditional myths and genres of the Greek literature that was his inheritance, he transformed them through his own insight and his own majestic voice. Even the *Eclogues*, which are closest to Greek models, contain passages that suggest the depth and nobility that are later to mark his work. The *Georgics*, on one level a standard didactic poem on farming, is actually one of the great nature poems, for Vergil discloses the variety and beauty of the natural world and the dignity of the man who understands the earth through his labor.

In his greatest poem, the *Aeneid*, Vergil tells the story of the founding of the Roman Empire, but this is only a part of his theme, for, in depicting Aeneas' struggle to achieve this heroic mission, Vergil reveals man's essential struggle with his fate. The *Aeneid* deals not only with achievement and success, but with the inevitable price in waste and suffering that man pays for any heroic accomplishment. Aeneas fulfills his mission only after he has learned of the essential tragedy of all human experience and has accepted the paradox that great hopes are weighed down with painful responsibilities and great achievements qualified by the inescapability of human limitation. With depth and compassion Vergil explores the inextricable union of the heroic and the tragic in human destiny.

More than any other ancient work, the *Aeneid* became for modern civilization its own *publica materies*. No other ancient poem inspired such varied allusions, interpretations, and adaptations. Moreover, during the Middle Ages, Vergil himself was regarded as a magician and a prophet who foresaw the coming of the Messiah. For Dante, Vergil is a teacher and a guide. Chaucer summarizes parts of the *Aeneid* in "The House of Fame," and in "The Knight's Tale" he echoes Boccaccio's allusion to the temple of Juno (*Aeneid* 1). For Fulgentius, the *Aeneid* was a moral allegory. Mapheus Vegius added a thirteenth book to the *Aeneid,* in which Aeneas ascends to the heavens. During the Renaissance and the neoclassical period in England, Vergil became the ideal image of the poet. Milton alludes to and imitates him frequently; his very vocabulary and rhythms are often Vergilian. Seventeenth-century translators of *Paradise Lost* into Latin use phrases from the *Aeneid* that sometimes transmit Milton's meaning fairly well. Throughout John Dryden's career as a poet he emulated Vergil, and the aim of serious poets of the seventeenth century was to write a great epic like the *Aeneid*. Though in the nineteenth century Vergil was not the dominant source and model that he was in earlier periods, his influence is felt in the work of such major poets as Tennyson and Wordsworth. In our own time, Allen Tate, Delmore Schwartz, W. H. Auden, and other poets evoke the *Aeneid* in image and symbol.

Vespasian (Titus Flavius Sabinus Vespasianus). The emperor of ROME from A.D. 70 to 79. See Tacitus' HISTORIES and Suetonius' *Lives of the Caesars.*

Vesta. The Roman goddess of the hearth.

victory ode. See EPINICION.

Vidularia (The Chest). A fragmentary comedy by PLAUTUS, the plot of which is not unlike that of *Rope* (*Rudens*). In *Vidularia* a young man is identified by tokens found by fishermen in a chest.

Virbius. See DIANA.

Virgil. See VERGIL.

Vitellius, Aulus. Emperor of ROME in A.D. 69. See Tacitus' HISTORIES.

Vulcan (Volcanus). The Roman god of fire. He was associated with Hephaestus and acquired his attributes.

W

Wasps, The (Sphekes). An Old Comedy (422 B.C.) by ARISTOPHANES. Translations: in verse, Benjamin B. Rogers, 1924; in verse, Arthur S. Way, 1934; in verse, Douglass Parker, 1962.

BACKGROUND. *The Wasps* reveals the Athenians' delight in litigation, and the corruption of the law courts by the demagogues, particularly Cleon, who exerted his influence on the Athenians' jurors by increasing their pay.

SCENE. Athens, before the house of Philocleon. The house is surrounded by a large net.

SUMMARY. Obeying the order of Bdelycleon (Hater of Cleon), Sosias and Xanthias, two slaves of his father Philocleon (Lover of Cleon), have been keeping watch all night so that Philocleon cannot leave the house to serve as a juror. Bdelycleon has been watching from the roof. He will use any means to prevent his father from satisfying his inordinate passion for jury duty. Bdelycleon has tried to persuade his father to give up this mania, but since all other means have failed, he has prevented the old man from going out by putting nets all around the courtyard and having the house constantly guarded.

Bdelycleon calls down to the slaves to inform them that his father is trying desperately to find some means of escape. Hearing a noise in the chimney, the young man asks who is there. Philocleon emerges, crying, "I am the smoke." When this trick fails, he declares that he wants to sell his ass. Bdelycleon, sensing another trick, goes in to get the ass himself, only to find Philocleon clinging to its belly, an obvious parody of Odysseus' escape from the Cyclops. Finally Bdelycleon locks his father in the house, but in a little while he sees the old man climbing under the tiles of the roof, preparing to fly like a bird.

The Chorus of Old Jurymen disguised as wasps enters, seeking Philocleon. He appears at a window, begging them to release him, so he can join them in court. He decides to gnaw through the net while his son is asleep, and has almost managed to escape when Bdelycleon awakens. With the help of Xanthias and Sosias, Bdelycleon manages to restrain Philocleon and to drive back the "wasps," who have been helping him. Then Philocleon and Bdelycleon argue about the role of the juror. Philocleon mentions the dignity and power of the juror, who is feared and flattered by the most illustrious men in Athens. He goes on to speak proudly of the unlawful methods used to gain acquittal and the dishonesty and faithlessness of jurymen. Moreover, he insists that the

439

jurors are the favorites of the demagogues. Cleon protects and flatters them. As a juror Philocleon earns money that inspires the respect of his wife and daughter. Bdelycleon's answer to this praise of the juryman is the statement that comedy cannot adequately deal with a "disease" so long established. He indicates to his father how he is used and cheated by the demagogues, given a small amount of money to act as their lackey. It is actually the demagogues who gain wealth and power at the expense of the Athenian people. Bdelycleon promises to provide for his father if only he will no longer allow himself to be used as a tool of the demagogues.

The Chorus and Philocleon cannot deny the truth of Bdelycleon's words. When Bdelycleon promises to permit his father to hold trials at home, the old man agrees to give up his position as a juror. The first case Philocleon tries is that of the dog Labes, who is accused of stealing cheese. The trial of the dog is, of course, a parody of the entire legal process, and it is also a means of again attacking Cleon as a thief and as a leader who will not leave the safety of Athens to engage in battle. Philocleon is so much influenced by the arguments of his son, who is the attorney for the defense, that he acquits the dog. Then, realizing he has been fooled into giving a favorable verdict, he faints in shame. His son comforts him, and they go into the house.

The Chorus delivers the parabasis, telling the audience that Aristophanes has a complaint: the Athenians have not appreciated all the benefits the dramatist has conferred upon them. He has exposed vice and revealed the truth, but the Athenians do not understand his work. They did not appreciate *The Clouds* when it was presented the previous year. The old men then explain their disguise as wasps, who represent the true Attic character—brave, relentless, gregarious, resourceful.

Bdelycleon consoles his father for his foolish acquittal of Labes by taking him to a banquet. The son tries to teach his father how to behave properly, but Philocleon resists him. After a brief choral ode, in which the old men attack Cleon and other illustrious Athenians, Xanthias comes in and describes the boorish behavior of Philocleon, who drank more than all the other guests at the banquet, shouted, and insulted everyone there. Soon Philocleon enters, drunkenly laughing and singing, and accompanied by a flute girl. Guests whom he has offended follow him angrily. Bdelycleon takes the girl into the house. Then, after Philocleon is accused by several people of destroying their property and assaulting them, he is led into the house by his son. The Chorus sings of the filial love and kindness of Bdelycleon. Soon Philocleon returns, and, dressed as Polyphemus in Euripides' *Cyclops*, he dances wildly with the Chorus.

Woman of Andros, The (Andria). A comedy (166 B.C.) by TERENCE. Translations: in prose, John Sargeaunt, 1912; in verse, W. Ritchie, 1927; in verse, F. Perry, 1929; in prose, anonymous translator in George Duckworth, ed., *The Complete Roman Drama*, 1942; in prose, Samuel Lieberman, 1964.

S C E N E . Athens, before the houses of Simo and Glycerium.

S U M M A R Y . *The Woman of Andros* is based on Menander's comedies *The Lady of Andros* and *The Lady of Perinthos*. In his Prologue, Terence defends his technique of combining the plots of two plays (*contaminatio*) against the criticisms of Luscius Lanuvinus, a rival playwright, and other detractors.

Pamphilus, a young Athenian, is in love with Glycerium, a woman from Andros. When Glycerium becomes pregnant, Pamphilus promises to marry her. He is distressed, however, because his father Simo has arranged for him to marry Philumena, the daughter of Chremes. Pamphilus does not know that Chremes, disapproving of Pamphilus' obvious affection for Glycerium, who, he believes, is the sister of a courtesan, has decided not to allow his daughter to marry him. In an effort to understand the real reason for Pamphilus' reluctance to marry Philumena, Simo does not tell him of Chremes' decision and warns his slave Davus not to aid Pamphilus in preventing the marriage. In a long soliloquy Davus expresses his fear of being punished by Simo and his desire to help his young master Pamphilus.

Pamphilus is wretched over his father's command that he marry that day; he respects his father, who has always been generous to him, but he loves Glycerium and wishes to make her happy. Hearing that Glycerium is about to give birth to their child, he is still more disturbed. Meanwhile, Pamphilus' friend Charinus is unhappy because he has heard that Philumena, whom he loves, is to be married to Pamphilus. When Pamphilus reveals to Charinus that he has no desire to marry Philumena and Davus discloses the fact that Chremes has called off the marriage, Charinus is delighted. His joy is brief, however, for soon Simo, hearing of the birth of Glycerium's child, persuades the hesitant Chremes to allow Pamphilus to marry Philumena. Pamphilus, Davus, Charinus, and Glycerium are all deeply distressed at this news. Davus comes to the rescue by placing Glycerium's baby at Simo's door and suggesting to Chremes that this is Pamphilus' child and that the baby's mother, Glycerium, is really an Athenian citizen; thus Pamphilus is obliged to marry her. Chremes, of course, again decides that Pamphilus may not marry his daughter. Simo has Davus put in chains to punish him for interfering.

Despite these apparently insoluble difficulties, all turns out well in the end. Crito, an old man from Andros, appears in Athens and reveals that Glycerium is actually an Athenian citizen and the lost daughter of Chremes. Simo now permits Pamphilus to marry Glycerium, and Chremes agrees to the marriage of Charinus and Philumena. Davus, freed from his chains, rejoices in his master's good fortune.

Women of Trachis, The (Trachiniai). A tragedy (possibly c. 413 B.C.) by Sophocles. Translations: in prose, R. C. Jebb, 1904; in verse, L. Campbell, 1906; in verse, F. Storr, 1912; in verse, Esther S. Barlow, 1938; in verse, Michael Jameson, 1957.

MYTHICAL BACKGROUND. After Heracles had defeated the river-god Achelous, who was a suitor of Deianira, and Heracles and Deianira were married, they left the city of Pleuron, where Deianira had lived with her father, Oeneus. On their journey they came to the River Euenus, which was flooded. Nessus, a centaur, was paid to carry Deianira across the river, and in so doing attempted to violate her. Heracles shot Nessus with a poisoned arrow from his famous bow. In the last moments of his life Nessus advised Deianira to save some of his blood, which would be useful as a means of regaining the love of Heracles if she should ever lose it. Heracles was forced to perform many labors for Eurystheus. Because he slew Iphitus, he was sent into exile with his family, and they settled in Trachis. He was also forced to be a slave to Queen Omphale of Lydia. It is now fifteen months since Heracles left his family for Lydia.

SCENE. Before the home of Heracles at Trachis.

SUMMARY. Deianira enters with her nurse, to whom she gives a long account of her many past and present sorrows. She speaks of her youth, when, before marrying Heracles, she was courted by the river-god Achelous, who frightened her with the various forms he took. After Heracles rescued her from this monstrous suitor and married her, her troubles continued, for Heracles was constantly involved in laboring for some master. Then he killed Iphitus, the son of his host, King Eurytus, and Deianira and her children were forced into exile. Fifteen months before, Heracles left his family, and Deianira has had no word from him. The nurse advises her to send her son, Hyllus, in quest of his father. Hyllus comes in and tells his mother that he has heard a rumor that for a year Heracles was the slave of the Lydian queen Omphale, but his servitude to her is now ended. At present he is getting ready to wage war on King Eurytus of Oechalia, in Euboea. Deianira informs Hyllus that before Heracles left he revealed to her an oracular prophecy that either he would meet death in Euboea, or after this last labor he would finally enjoy a peaceful life. Hyllus goes off to find out more about his father.

The Chorus of Women of Trachis comes in and asks where Heracles can be. The women speak of the sadness of Deianira and of her fears for her husband. They try to cheer her; it is true, they say, that no human being escapes pain, but joy comes also to mortals, for Zeus cares for man. Deianira confides her fears and troubles to the Chorus. When Heracles went away, he left a tablet inscribed with his will because in fifteen months he would either die or at last be allowed to live peacefully. This day marks the end of the fifteen months, and she is terrified lest the first part of the prophecy be fulfilled.

A Messenger enters and announces that Heracles has conquered his enemies and will soon return home. Deianira and the Chorus, delighted at the news, express their joy, and the Chorus sings its thanks to Apollo and Artemis. Lichas, the herald of Heracles, comes in with a group of women whom Heracles has captured in battle. He tells Deianira that Heracles is alive and well and that he is still in Euboea, fulfilling a vow to dedicate altars and land to Zeus. The herald tells of how Zeus punished Heracles by allowing him to be sold as a slave to Queen Omphale by King Eurytus and how Heracles vowed to enslave Eurytus in vengeance. Eurytus, who had once been Heracles' host, had taunted Heracles and incensed him to the point where he killed Eurytus' son, Iphitus. Zeus, angry at this crime, had Heracles sold as a slave. Now Eurytus has been killed, and Heracles, free and victorious, will soon return home. Despite her joy at this good news, Deianira is upset at the sight of the unhappy captive women. She is especially drawn to Iole, a young girl whom she questions about her parents. Iole does not answer, nor does Lichas reveal that Iole is the daughter of Eurytus and the beloved of Heracles.

After Lichas and the women go into the house, the Messenger reveals to Deianira that Heracles really waged war on Eurytus because he refused to give Heracles his daughter, Iole, whom Heracles desired as his mistress. In distress Deianira asks what she should do. The Messenger advises her to question Lichas. When Lichas returns, Deianira and the Messenger press him to tell what he knows about Iole. Deianira says she does not censure her husband's flirtation; in fact she feels compassion for the innocent Iole. Finally Lichas confesses that Heracles does love Iole and that he did attack Oechalia for her sake. Heracles did not tell Lichas to conceal his love for Iole from Deianira; Lichas himself wished to spare her. He asks her to be kind to Iole, and Deianira agrees to do as Lichas suggests. She then asks Lichas to take a gift from her to Heracles.

The Chorus sings of love, which conquers even the gods, and of the contest between the river-god Achelous and Heracles for the hand of Deianira. Soon Deianira comes out and confesses to the women that she cannot endure sharing her husband with a young mistress. However, she has a solution to her problem: she will send Heracles a robe smeared with the blood of Nessus. This will act as a love potion to bring him back to her. She gives the robe to Lichas, who will deliver it to Heracles. Lichas and Deianira go out, and the Chorus prays that Heracles, the conqueror, will be reconciled to his wife by the magic love potion. Deianira returns in terror, for the piece of wool with which she smeared the robe with Nessus' blood has shriveled into dust. She now fears that Nessus has tricked her into poisoning her husband. If Heracles dies, she cries out, she must kill herself.

As the Chorus tries to comfort Deianira, Hyllus enters. He declares that he wishes his mother were dead, for she has slain his father. He then tells of how Lichas gave the robe to Heracles as he was offering sacrifices to Zeus for his victory over Eurytus. When Heracles put on the robe, it clung to him, and he began to feel agonizing pain. As the poison entered his body, racked with pain, he killed Lichas, who was innocent of any crime, and cursed his marriage and

his wife. Hyllus has brought the dying Heracles back to Trachis. Once more
Hyllus curses his mother, praying that Deianira may be pursued by the Furies
for killing Heracles, noblest of men.

Deianira silently goes into the house. After a choral ode that expresses
sympathy for Deianira, who did not realize what she was doing when she
unwittingly caused her husband's death, the Nurse comes out and announces
that Deianira has stabbed herself to death with a sword. When Hyllus realized
that his mother was innocent, he reproached himself for causing her death. As
the Chorus laments for Heracles and Deianira, Hyllus, an Old Man, and attendants enter, carrying Heracles on a litter. Hyllus cries out in sorrow as
Heracles in agonizing pain pleads with his son to kill him. Heracles says he has
never endured such agony. When Heracles expresses a wish to kill Deianira,
Hyllus tells him that she has killed herself. He defends his mother, explaining
that she was innocent of any intent to kill Heracles, but was deceived by the
trick of Nessus. Heracles then realizes that the prophecy has been fulfilled that
he would never be killed by a living being but by one who dwells in the world
of the dead. The prophecy that he would be released from his labors has
also come true, since in death one cannot toil. Heracles orders Hyllus to
carry him to the peak of Mount Oeta, where there is a shrine to Zeus. There
Hyllus must place his father, still living, on a funeral pyre and without weeping
cremate him. Hyllus hesitates to obey, calling the deed patricide, but he agrees
to follow his father's order if he can avoid lighting the torch himself. He also
agrees to marry Iole, though he does so only to please his dying father. As the
attendants carry Heracles to Mount Oeta, Hyllus sadly declares that the gods
are without pity; unmoved, they look down upon the suffering of men.

Works and Days (Erga kai Hemerai). A didactic epic (possibly eighth
century B.C.) in dactylic hexameter by HESIOD. Translations: in verse, George
Chapman, 1618; in verse, C. A. Elton, 1812; in prose, A. W. Mair, 1910; in
prose, H. G. Evelyn-White, 1920; in verse, Richmond Lattimore, 1959.

SUMMARY. Hesiod asks the Muses to speak of their father, Zeus, who
determines the lives of men. Zeus can give men strength and make them power-
less; he hurls the proud man down from his heights and lifts the humble man
to prosperity. After this introduction Hesiod turns to his subject; though he
does not state his theme explicitly, his aim is to teach his readers how to
get along in a life that is full of problems and uncertainties. Thus he explains
to his brother Perses, to whom the poem is addressed, that there are two kinds
of strife: one is pure hostility, which ultimately leads to war and other evils;
the other, which inspires man to compete with his neighbors in accomplishment,
is helpful to man. Hesiod then tells the myth of Pandora, who released all the
evils man endures and brought about suffering and toil. He traces the history
of man's life, depicting the Five Ages: the first, a Golden Age, when men lived
a godlike existence, free from care and suffering; the second, a Silver Age, not
so noble or so pleasant as the first, for during the second age evil and sorrow
came into the world; the third, a Bronze Age, a time of war and violence; the

fourth, a Heroic Age, better and nobler than the third, immediately preceded Hesiod's own time, and was an age of heroes and demigods such as the Seven against Thebes and the warriors who fought at Troy; the fifth age is Hesiod's own, and he wishes he were not of this brutal Iron Age, in which men work and suffer continually. He predicts that the evil of his race will increase until finally Zeus destroys it.

After demonstrating that happiness and prosperity result from goodness, and that only suffering can come from evil, Hesiod says that a man who hurts others actually harms himself more than any other victim. He then gives Perses advice on how to live an upright life and reap the rewards of toil and honesty. He goes on to show that hard work as a farmer or trader allows a man to avoid poverty and care. In a series of maxims that take up half the poem Hesiod discusses the morality of daily life and recommends what he considers proper behavior. Many of these maxims are mere superstitions. The poem concludes with advice on the best days of the month and the appropriate seasons for harvesting, plowing, navigation, and other work.

X

Xanthus and Balius (Xanthos and Balios). In Greek mythology, the immortal horses of Achilles. See ILIAD XIX.

Xenophanes. A Greek poet (sixth century B.C.). Xenophanes was born at Colophon in Ionia and traveled through much of the ancient world. Only fragments remain of his poem on nature, written in hexameters, and of his elegies. Xenophanes objected to the current polytheism of the Greeks and believed in a single deity.

Xenophon. Greek writer, born c. 430 B.C. at Athens. As a youth he admired Socrates and became one of his disciples. Following the advice of his friend Proxenus, a Boeotian, Xenophon went to Sardis to become a member of the forces of Cyrus the Younger, second son of King Darius II of Persia. Only after he had joined the Expedition of the Ten Thousand did Xenophon learn it intended to drive Cyrus' brother Artaxerxes from the throne of Persia. In the battle against the army of Artaxerxes at Cunaxa in Babylonia (401 B.C.) Cyrus was killed, but his Greek followers were determined to find their way home rather than submit to being taken by the Persians. When the Persians managed to seize and kill the Greek generals of the Ten Thousand and the troops were left in despair, Xenophon was elected one of the new generals. Despite enormous difficulties he successfully led the troops from Cunaxa through Armenia to the Black Sea and finally to Byzantium. Xenophon then joined the forces of the Spartan king Agesilaus, who was fighting against Artaxerxes (396 B.C.). Xenophon remained with Agesilaus when the Spartans fought and defeated the Athenians and the Thebans at the battle of Coronea (394 B.C.). Thus Xenophon was declared an exile by the Athenians, and his property was confiscated. The Spartans rewarded him with an estate at Scillus, in Elis, and he remained there for the next twenty years. In 370 B.C. he was forced to leave Scillus by the Eleans, who seized it after the battle of Leuctra. Xenophon then went to Corinth, where he remained despite Athens' repeal of his exile. He died around 355 B.C. Both of his sons fought for Athens in the battle of Mantinea (362 B.C.), one of them, Gryllus, dying in combat.

Xenophon's writings reflect his experiences in the affairs of his time. His *Anabasis*, the best-known of his works, is an account of his adventures with the Expedition of the Ten Thousand. In seven books of prose Xenophon tells of

Cyrus' quarrel with his brother Artaxerxes, his preparations for warfare against him, his organization of the army of Greek recruits, and the march of the Ten Thousand from Sardis to Babylonia. He then goes on to describe the battle of Cunaxa, in which Cyrus was killed, and the difficult retreat of the Ten Thousand. Xenophon's *Memorabilia, Apology,* and *Symposium* give a portrait of Socrates as Xenophon saw him, a less interesting figure than the great Socrates of the Platonic dialogues. Xenophon's interpretation of Socrates as a thinker no doubt reveals more about the limitations of Xenophon than about the capacities of Socrates. In *Oeconomicus,* Xenophon deals with household affairs, as his title suggests; in a dialogue between Socrates and Ischomachus, such subjects as the management of an estate, orderliness, and the proper training of a wife are discussed. *Cyropaedia (The Education of Cyrus)* is a moralistic narrative about the life of Cyrus the Great. Both Cyrus and the Persian Empire are idealized and set up as examples before the reader. *Hellenica* represents Xenophon's attempt to imitate the method of Thucydides. Xenophon writes of Greek history from 411 B.C., the point where Thucydides stops, to 362 B.C. Xenophon's lack of objectivity, his obvious prejudice in favor of the Spartans, and his rather superficial approach to history make his work far inferior to that of Thucydides. *Agesilaus* praises the Spartan king who was Xenophon's friend, glorifying both his noble needs and his virtuous character. Other works by Xenophon are *Hiero,* a dialogue in which Hiero I, tyrant of Syracuse, and Simonides consider the lives of the tyrant and of the ordinary man; *Revenues,* which is concerned with ways of increasing the income of Athens; and the *Constitution of the Lacedaemonians,* which describes the Spartan way of life and customs, which Xenophon greatly admires.

Though Xenophon lacks both the historical insight and the literary skill of Herodotus and Thucydides, his work is interesting because of the factual information it contains about Xenophon's times and because it suggests the author's vitality and his involvement in the history he records.

Xerxes. A king of Persia who appears in Aeschylus' THE PERSIANS. See also THE PERSIAN WARS VII.

Z

Zeno (Zenon) (i). Greek philosopher of Elea (Latin Velia, mod. Castellammare della Brucca) in southern Italy (fl. middle of the fifth century B.C.). Zeno was one of the most important followers of PARMENIDES. In a book called *Epicheiremata (Attacks)* Zeno defended the philosophy of Parmenides by showing that his opponents' views were essentially paradoxical. Only fragments of this work survive.

Zeno (Zenon) (ii). Greek philosopher, who flourished about 300 B.C. He was born at Citium (Kition) in Cyprus and is thought to have been of Phoenician origin. Zeno lived in Athens, where he studied philosophy and established a school in the *Stoa Poikile* (the "Painted Porch," so called because it was decorated with the work of famous artists, among them Polygnotus), from which the name STOIC is derived. As the founder of Stoicism, Zeno believed that in order to live a good life man must follow nature and live in harmony with its laws, that only virtue can bring happiness, and that only the wise are free. Diogenes Laertius' life of Zeno summarizes his main philosophical principles.

Zethus (Zethos). See ANTIOPE (i).

Zeus. The chief god of the Greeks. His name, which means "bright," or "shining," is a Greek version of the weather or sky-god worshiped by all Indo-Europeans. His attribute is the thunderbolt; and his home, the sky. He is the son of Cronus and Rhea; his birth in Crete and his contest with and victory over Cronus are described by Hesiod in the THEOGONY (see also CURETES). Hesiod also tells of Zeus' war with the Titans and of his cruelty to PROMETHEUS (see Aeschylus' PROMETHEUS BOUND). The stories of Zeus' origin suggest that, though he displays the features of an Indo-European weather god, primitive Mediterranean rituals of killing and consuming a deity in order to absorb his powers are also part of his heritage.

Hundreds of myths tell of Zeus' powers and his adventures. In Greek literature he is at times a symbol of divine justice and goodness, and at others, a licentious Achaean warlord, glorying in his powers; sometimes he is both at once. Zeus, the king of the gods, provided good and evil for men. He could foresee future events, which he occasionally permitted men to know through dreams and oracles. Zeus was the god of hospitality and defended the hearth. In literature the myths of his amorous adventures are sometimes humorous, but these myths may derive from fertility rites to ensure the fruitfulness of the land, or they may have originated in the claims of nobles that they were descended from Zeus. See the ILIAD, *Religious Background.*